DATE DUE

Demco, Inc. 38-293

The PSI Handbook of Virtual Environments for Training and Education

The PSI Handbook of Virtual Environments for Training and Education

DEVELOPMENTS FOR THE MILITARY AND BEYOND

Volume 2
VE Components and Training Technologies

Edited by Denise Nicholson,
Dylan Schmorrow, and Joseph Cohn

Technology, Psychology, and Health

PRAEGER SECURITY INTERNATIONAL
Westport, Connecticut · London

Library of Congress Cataloging-in-Publication Data

The PSI handbook of virtual environments for training and education : developments for the
military and beyond.
    p. cm. – (Technology, psychology, and health, ISSN 1942–7573 ; v. 1-3)
    Includes bibliographical references and index.
    ISBN 978–0–313–35165–5 (set : alk. paper) – ISBN 978–0–313–35167–9 (v. 1 : alk. paper) –
    ISBN 978–0–313–35169–3 (v. 2 : alk. paper) – ISBN 978–0–313–35171–6 (v. 3 : alk. paper)
1. Military education–United States. 2. Human-computer interaction. 3. Computer-assisted instruction. 4. Virtual reality. I. Schmorrow, Dylan, 1967- II. Cohn, Joseph, 1969- III. Nicholson, Denise,
1967- IV. Praeger Security International. V. Title: Handbook of virtual environments for training
and education. VI. Title: Praeger Security International handbook of virtual environments for training and education.
U408.3.P75 2009
355.0078'5–dc22   2008027367

British Library Cataloguing in Publication Data is available.

Library of Congress Catalog Card Number: 2008027367
ISBN-13: 978–0–313–35165–5 (set)
        978–0–313–35167–9 (vol. 1)
        978–0–313–35169–3 (vol. 2)
        978–0–313–35171–6 (vol. 3)
ISSN: 1942–7573

First published in 2009

Praeger Security International, 88 Post Road West, Westport, CT 06881
An imprint of Greenwood Publishing Group, Inc.
www.praeger.com

Printed in the United States of America

The paper used in this book complies with the
Permanent Paper Standard issued by the National
Information Standards Organization (Z39.48–1984).

10 9 8 7 6 5 4 3 2 1

To our families, and to the men and women who have dedicated their lives to educate, train, and defend to keep them safe

CONTENTS

SERIES FOREWORD

LAUNCHING THE TECHNOLOGY, PSYCHOLOGY, AND HEALTH DEVELOPMENT SERIES

The escalating complexity and operational tempo of the twenty-first century requires that people in all walks of life acquire ever-increasing knowledge, skills, and abilities. Training and education strategies are dynamically changing toward delivery of more effective instruction and practice, wherever and whenever needed. In the last decade, the Department of Defense has made significant investments to advance the science and technology of virtual environments to meet this need. Throughout this time we have been privileged to collaborate with some of the brightest minds in science and technology. The intention of this three-volume handbook is to provide comprehensive coverage of the emerging theories, technologies, and integrated demonstrations of the state-of-the-art in virtual environments for training and education.

As Dr. G. Vincent Amico states in the Preface, an important lesson to draw from the history of modeling and simulation is the importance of *process*. The human systems engineering process requires highly multidisciplinary teams to integrate diverse disciplines from psychology, education, engineering, and computer science (see Nicholson and Lackey, Volume 3, Section 1, Chapter 1). This process drives the organization of the handbook. While other texts on virtual environments (VEs) focus heavily on technology, we have dedicated the first volume to a thorough investigation of learning theories, requirements definition, and performance measurement. The second volume provides the latest information on a range of virtual environment component technologies and a distinctive section on training support technologies. In the third volume, an extensive collection of integrated systems is discussed as virtual environment use-cases along with a section of training effectiveness evaluation methods and results. Volume 3, Section 3 highlights future applications of this evolving technology that span cognitive rehabilitation to the next generation of museum exhibitions. Finally, a glimpse into the potential future of VEs is provided as an original short story entitled "Into the Uncanny Valley" from Judith Singer and Hollywood director Alex Singer.

Through our research we have experienced rapid technological and scientific advancements, coinciding with a dramatic convergence of research achievements representing contributions from numerous fields, including neuroscience, cognitive psychology and engineering, biomedical engineering, computer science, and systems engineering. Historically, psychology and technology development were independent research areas practiced by scientists and engineers primarily trained in one of these disciplines. In recent years, however, individuals in these disciplines, such as the close to 200 authors of this handbook, have found themselves increasingly working within a unified framework that completely blurs the lines of these discrete research areas, creating an almost "metadisciplinary" (as opposed to multidisciplinary) form of science and technology. The strength of the confluence of these two disciplines lies in the complementary research and development approaches being employed and the interdependence that is required to achieve useful technological applications. Consequently, with this handbook we begin a new Praeger Security International Book Series entitled *Technology, Psychology, and Health* intended to capture the remarkable advances that will be achieved through the continued seamless integration of these disciplines, where unified and simultaneously executed approaches of psychology, engineering, and practice will result in more effective science and technology applications. Therefore, the esteemed contributors to the *Technology, Psychology, and Health Development Series* strive to capture such advancements and effectively convey both the practical and theoretical elements of the technological innovations they describe.

The *Technology, Psychology, and Health Development Series* will continue to address the general themes of requisite foundational knowledge, emergent scientific discoveries, and practical lessons learned, as well as cross-discipline standards, methodologies, metrics, techniques, practices, and visionary perspectives and developments. The series plans to showcase substantial advances in research and development methods and their resulting technologies and applications. Cross-disciplinary teams will provide detailed reports of their experiences applying technologies in diverse areas—from basic academic research to industrial and military fielded operational and training systems to everyday computing and entertainment devices.

A thorough and comprehensive consolidation and dissemination of psychology and technology development efforts is no longer a noble academic goal—it is a twenty-first century necessity dictated by the desire to ensure that our global economy and society realize their full scientific and technological potentials. Accordingly, this ongoing book series is intended to be an essential resource for a large international audience of professionals in industry, government, and academia.

We encourage future authors to contact us for more information or to submit a prospectus idea.

Dylan Schmorrow and Denise Nicholson
Technology, Psychology, and Health Development Series Editors
TPHSeries@ist.ucf.edu

PREFACE

G. Vincent Amico

It is indeed an honor and pleasure to write the preface to this valuable collection of articles on simulation for education and training. The fields of modeling and simulation are playing an increasingly important role in society.

You will note that the collection is titled virtual environments for *training and education*. I believe it is important to recognize the distinction between those two terms. Education is oriented to providing fundamental scientific and technical skills; these skills lay the groundwork for training. Simulations for training are designed to help operators of systems effectively learn how to operate those systems under a variety of conditions, both normal and emergency situations. Cognitive, psychomotor, and affective behaviors must all be addressed. Hence, psychologists play a dominant role within multidisciplinary teams of engineers and computer scientists for determining the effective use of simulation for training. Of course, the U.S. Department of Defense's Human Systems Research Agencies, that is, Office of the Secretary of Defense, Office of Naval Research, Air Force Research Lab, Army Research Laboratory, and Army Research Institute, also play a primary role—their budgets support many of the research activities in this important field.

Volume 1, Section 1 in this set addresses many of the foundational learning issues associated with the use of simulation for education and training. These chapters will certainly interest psychologists, but are also written so that technologists and other practitioners can glean some insight into the important science surrounding learning. Throughout the set, training technologies are explored in more detail. In particular, Volume 2, Sections 1 and 2 include several diverse chapters demonstrating how learning theory can be effectively applied to simulation for training.

The use of simulation for training goes back to the beginning of time. As early as 2500 B.C., ancient Egyptians used figurines to simulate warring factions. The precursors of modern robotic simulations can be traced back to ancient China, from which we have documented reports (circa 200 B.C.) of artisans constructing mechanical automata, elaborate mechanical simulations of people or animals. These ancient "robots" included life-size mechanical humanoids, reportedly capable of movement and speech (Kurzweil, 1990; Needham, 1986). In those early days, these mechanical devices were used to train soldiers in various phases of combat, and military tacticians used war games to develop strategies. Simulation technology as we know it today became viable only in the early twentieth century.

Probably the most significant event was Ed Link's development of the Link Trainer (aka the "Blue Box") for pilot training. He applied for its patent in 1929. Yet, simulation did not play a major role in training until the start of World War II (in 1941), when Navy captain Luis de Florez established the Special Devices Desk at the Bureau of Aeronautics. His organization expanded significantly in the next few years as the value of simulation for training became recognized. Captain de Florez is also credited with the development of the first flight simulation that was driven by an analog computer. Developed in 1943, his simulator, called the operational flight trainer, modeled the PBM-3 aircraft. In the period after World War II, simulators and simulation science grew exponentially based upon the very successful programs initiated during the war.

There are two fundamental components of any modern simulation system. One is a sound mathematical understanding of the object to be simulated. The other is the real time implementation of those models in computational systems. In the late 1940s the primary computational systems were analog. Digital computers were very expensive, very slow, and could not solve equations in real time. It was not until the late 1950s and early 1960s that digital computation became viable. For instance, the first navy simulator to use a commercial digital computer was the Attack Center Trainer at the FBM Facility (New London, Connecticut) in 1959. Thus, it has been only for the past 50 years that simulation has made major advancements.

Even today, it is typical that user requirements for capability exceed the ability of available technology. There are many areas where this is particularly true, including rapid creation of visual simulation from actual terrain environment databases and human behavior representations spanning cognition to social networks. The dramatic increases in digital computer speed and capacity have significantly closed the gap. But there are still requirements that cannot be met; these gaps define the next generation of science and technology research questions.

In the past decade or so, a number of major simulation initiatives have developed, including distributed interactive simulation, advanced medical simulation, and augmented cognition supported simulation. Distributed simulation enables many different units to participate in a joint exercise, regardless of where the units are located. The requirements for individual simulations to engage in such exercises are mandated by Department of Defense standards, that is, high level architecture and distributed interactive simulation. An excellent example of the capabilities that have resulted are the unprecedented number of virtual environment simulations that have transitioned from the Office of Naval Research's Virtual Technologies and Environments (VIRTE) Program to actual military training applications discussed throughout this handbook. The second area of major growth is the field of medical simulation. The development of the human patient simulator clearly heralded this next phase of medical simulation based training, and the field of medical simulation will certainly expand during the next decade. Finally, the other exciting development in recent years is the exploration of augmented cognition, which may eventually enable system users to completely forgo standard computer interfaces and work seamlessly with their equipment through the utilization of neurophysiological sensing.

Now let us address some of the issues that occur during the development process of a simulator. The need for simulation usually begins when a customer experiences problems training operators in the use of certain equipment or procedures; this is particularly true in the military. The need must then be formalized into a requirements document, and naturally, the search for associated funding and development of a budget ensues. The requirements document must then be converted into a specification or a work statement. That then leads to an acquisition process, resulting in a contract. The contractor must then convert that specification into a hardware and software design. This process takes time and is subject to numerous changes in interpretation and direction. The proof of the pudding comes when the final product is evaluated to determine if the simulation meets the customer's needs.

One of the most critical aspects of any modeling and simulation project is to determine its effectiveness and whether it meets the original objectives. This may appear to be a rather straightforward task, but it is actually very complex. First, it is extremely important that checks are conducted at various stages of the development process. During the conceptual stages of a project, formal reviews are normally conducted to ensure that the requirements are properly stated; those same reviews are also conducted at the completion of the work statement or specification. During the actual development process, periodic reviews should be conducted at key stages. When the project is completed, tests should be conducted to determine if the simulation meets the design objectives and stated requirements. The final phase of testing is validation. The purpose of validation is to determine if the simulation meets the customer's needs. Why is this process of testing so important? The entire development process is lengthy, and during that process there is a very high probability that changes will be induced. The only way to manage the overall process is by performing careful inspections at each major phase of the project.

As the organization and content of this handbook make evident, this process has been the fundamental framework for conducting most of today's leading research and development initiatives. Following section to section, the reader is guided through the requirements, development, and evaluation cycle. The reader is then challenged to imagine the state of the possible in the final, Future Directions, section.

In summary, one can see that the future of simulation to support education and training is beyond our comprehension. That does not mean that care must not be taken in the development process. The key issues that must be addressed were cited earlier. There is one fact that one must keep in mind: No simulation is perfect. But through care, keeping the simulation objectives in line with the capabilities of modeling and implementation, success can be achieved. This is demonstrated by the number of simulations that are being used today in innovative settings to improve training for a wide range of applications.

REFERENCES

Kurzweil, R. (1990). *The age of intelligent machines.* Cambridge, MA: MIT Press.
Needham, J. (1986). *Science and civilization in China: Volume 2.* Cambridge, United Kingdom: Cambridge University Press.

ACKNOWLEDGMENTS

These volumes are the product of many contributors working together. Leading the coordination activities were a few key individuals whose efforts made this project a reality:

Associate Editor
Julie Drexler

Technical Writer
Kathleen Bartlett

Editing Assistants
Kimberly Sprouse and Sherry Ogreten

We would also like to thank our Editorial Board and Review Board members, as follows:

Editorial Board

John Anderson, Carnegie Mellon University; Kathleen Bartlett, Florida Institute of Technology; Clint Bowers, University of Central Florida, Institute for Simulation and Training; Gwendolyn Campbell, Naval Air Warfare Center, Training Systems Division; Janis Cannon-Bowers, University of Central Florida, Institute for Simulation and Training; Rudolph Darken, Naval Postgraduate School, The MOVES Institute; Julie Drexler, University of Central Florida, Institute for Simulation and Training; Neal Finkelstein, U.S. Army Research Development & Engineering Command; Bowen Loftin, Texas A&M University at Galveston; Eric Muth, Clemson University, Department of Psychology; Sherry Ogreten, University of Central Florida, Institute for Simulation and Training; Eduardo Salas, University of Central Florida, Institute for Simulation and Training and Department of Psychology; Kimberly Sprouse, University of Central Florida, Institute for Simulation and Training; Kay Stanney, Design Interactive, Inc.; Mary Whitton, University of North Carolina at Chapel Hill, Department of Computer Science

Review Board (by affiliation)

Advanced Brain Monitoring, Inc.: Chris Berka; Alion Science and Tech.: Jeffery Moss; Arizona State University: Nancy Cooke; AuSIM, Inc.: William Chapin; Carlow International, Inc.: Tomas Malone; CHI Systems, Inc.: Wayne Zachary; Clemson University: Pat Raymark, Patrick Rosopa, Fred Switzer, Mary Anne Taylor; Creative Labs, Inc.: Edward Stein; Deakin University: Lemai Nguyen; Defense Acquisition University: Alicia Sanchez; Design Interactive, Inc.: David Jones; Embry-Riddle Aeronautical University: Elizabeth Blickensderfer, Jason Kring; Human Performance Architects: Richard Arnold; Iowa State University: Chris Harding; Lockheed Martin: Raegan Hoeft; Max Planck Institute: Betty Mohler; Michigan State University: J. Kevin Ford; NASA Langley Research Center: Danette Allen; Naval Air Warfare Center, Training Systems Division: Maureen Bergondy-Wilhelm, Curtis Conkey, Joan Johnston, Phillip Mangos, Carol Paris, James Pharmer, Ronald Wolff; Naval Postgraduate School: Barry Peterson, Perry McDowell, William Becker, Curtis Blais, Anthony Ciavarelli, Amela Sadagic, Mathias Kolsch; Occidental College: Brian Kim; Office of Naval Research: Harold Hawkins, Roy Stripling; Old Dominion University: James Bliss; Pearson Knowledge Tech.: Peter Foltz; PhaseSpace, Inc.: Tracy McSherry; Potomac Institute for Policy Studies: Paul Chatelier; Renee Stout, Inc.: Renee Stout; SA Technologies, Inc.: Haydee Cuevas, Jennifer Riley; Sensics, Inc.: Yuval Boger; Texas A&M University: Claudia McDonald; The Boeing Company: Elizabeth Biddle; The University of Iowa: Kenneth Brown; U.S. Air Force Academy: David Wells; U.S. Air Force Research Laboratory: Dee Andrews; U.S. Army Program Executive Office for Simulation, Training, & Instrumentation: Roger Smith; U.S. Army Research Development & Engineering Command: Neal Finkelstein, Timothy Roberts, Robert Sottilare; U.S. Army Research Institute: Steve Goldberg; U.S. Army Research Laboratory: Laurel Allender, Michael Barnes, Troy Kelley; U.S. Army TRADOC Analysis Center–Monterey: Michael Martin; U.S. MARCORSYSCOM Program Manager for Training Systems: Sherrie Jones, William W. Yates; University of Alabama in Huntsville: Mikel Petty; University of Central Florida: Glenda Gunter, Robert Kenny, Rudy McDaniel, Tim Kotnour, Barbara Fritzsche, Florian Jentsch, Kimberly Smith-Jentsch, Aldrin Sweeney, Karol Ross, Daniel Barber, Shawn Burke, Cali Fidopiastis, Brian Goldiez, Glenn Martin, Lee Sciarini, Peter Smith, Jennifer Vogel-Walcutt, Steve Fiore, Charles Hughes; University of Illinois: Tomas Coffin; University of North Carolina: Sharif Razzaque, Andrei State, Jason Coposky, Ray Idaszak; Virginia Tech.: Joseph Gabbard; Xavier University: Morrie Mullins

SECTION 1

VIRTUAL ENVIRONMENT COMPONENT TECHNOLOGIES

SECTION PERSPECTIVE
Mary Whitton and R. Bowen Loftin

Anyone desiring to build an effective virtual environment based training system must make knowledgeable selections of hardware and software for the system that delivers the training content and allows the trainee to interact with that content. The goal of this section is to introduce the hardware and software—the *component technologies*—that make up the virtual environment (VE) system so that readers can make informed decisions when trade-offs are necessary during system design. The component technologies are as disparate as a laser system that displays images directly on the retina, software that controls semi-autonomous agents, and intersimulator data communication standards. The chapters in this section provide some tutorial information; they are intended to update, rather than duplicate, information available in Stanney's (2002) *Handbook of Virtual Environments*.

Figure SP1.1 shows how VE systems are related to other parts of this book. System and fidelity requirements are inputs to the VE system design process. The application requirements drive component selection, as well as provide such ancillary constraint data as cost targets and portability goals.

When VE systems are in use, they can receive session specific data from and send data to training support technologies, systems that track trainee progress and define training sequences. Any data needed for after action review, to evaluate trainees, or to document training effectiveness is output from the VE training system, typically in the form of logs of events from the individual VE stations and logs of network traffic. Volume 3, Section 1 (not called out in Figure SP1.1) includes descriptions of several training systems.

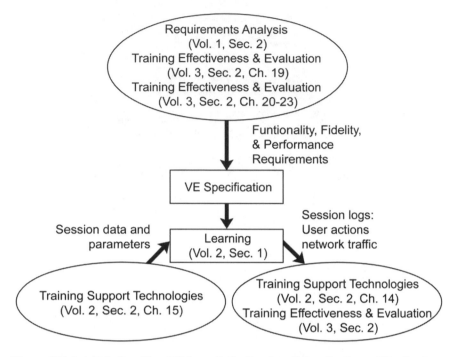

Figure SP1.1.   Relationship of Volume 2, Section 1 to Other Sections of the Book

The authors of the chapters were given almost total freedom to present their topics as they chose. This was so that they could emphasize what, from their own experiences, they know to be the important considerations when using the technology in an integrated system. The consequence of this freedom is that the chapters do not share a common structure, and a subtopic area covered in one chapter may not appear in another. So be it.

INTRODUCTION TO VE COMPONENT TECHNOLOGIES

In popular use, the term *virtual environment* has been applied to systems as dissimilar as a fully immersive simulator for a multiengine airliner and an interactive game played on a smart phone.[1] Despite the differences in the complexity and cost, the components of the two systems have much the same functionality: both accept user input, both use that input in an application program, and both provide feedback to the user.

---

[1]VE researchers do not agree on a definition of a VE (or whether to use the term virtual environment or virtual reality), and they define the difference between a VE application and an interactive three-dimensional computer graphics application in a variety of ways based on factors such as field of view of the display, whether the scene changes when the user moves his or her head, and the level of the user's engagement with the activity in the virtual scene.

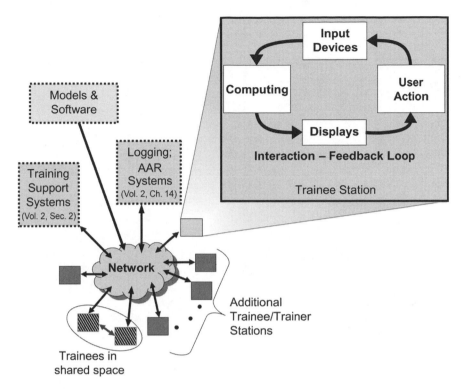

Figure SP1.2.   VE System Components. The exploded block shows the functional components of a system for a single trainee. Such stations are replicated and connected by the network for team training. Also connected via the network are training support systems, logging/after action review systems, and storage for models and programs. See Table SP1.1 for additional detail. Figure courtesy of Computer Science, UNC–Chapel Hill.

The block on the right in Figure SP1.2 is a high level functional and data-flow diagram of a stand-alone VE system. The four elements in that diagram form a continuous *interaction-feedback* loop: the user performs some action, devices or sensors translate user action into input data, computing elements determine a response to the input, and display devices provide feedback to the user of changes caused by the input. Table SP1.1 expands on Figure SP1.2 with a list of components of virtual environment systems and includes pointers to chapters in which the topics are discussed in more detail.

Immersion and Interactivity

Virtual environments have two characteristics that, along with the content, are the three major factors determining the quality of the user's VE experience. Virtual environments are *immersive,* that is, they substitute synthetically generated

Table SP1.1. Examples of component technologies in virtual environment systems are listed. More information is available in the chapters enclosed in parentheses.

Hardware	Software	Content/Data
Input – Trackers (Welch and Davis, Volume 2, Section 1, Chapter 1) – Microphones (Sadek, Volume 2, Section 1, Chapter 4) – Wands, Gamepads, and so forth – Physiological monitors	**Operating System (McDowell, Guerrero, McCue, and Hollister, Volume 2, Section 1, Chapter 8)**	**Models (Whitton and Loftin, Volume 2, Section 1, Section Perspective)** – Shape – Appearance – Behavior (Whitton and Loftin, Volume 2, Section 1, Section Perspective; Petty, Volume 2, Section 1, Chapter 9)
Computing (McDowell, Guerrero, McCue, and Hollister, Volume 2, Section 1, Chapter 8) – CPU, Memory – Graphics – Networking	**Networking (McDowell, Guerrero, McCue, and Hollister, Volume 2, Section 1, Chapter 8)** – Communication standards	**Scenarios (Shadrick and Lussier, Volume 2, Section 2, Chapter 18)**
Output – Visual Display (Bolas and McDowall, Volume 2, Section 1, Chapter 2; Towles, Johnson, and Fuchs, Volume 2, Section 1, Chapter 3) – Headphones and speakers (Sadek, Volume 2, Section 1, Chapter 4) – Other senses (Başdoğan and Loftin, Volume 2, Section 1, Chapter 5)	**Application Simulators (McDowell, Guerrero, McCue, and Hollister, Volume 2, Section 1, Chapter 8)** – Entity behaviors (Petty, Volume 2, Section 1, Chapter 9)	**Model Creation Tools (Whitton and Loftin, Volume 2, Section 1, Section Perspective)** – Shape – Appearance

Rendering
- Visual (Whitton and Loftin, Volume 2, Section 1, Section Perspective; McDowell, Guerrero, McCue, and Hollister, Volume 2, Section 1, Chapter 8)
- Audio (Sadek, Volume 2, Section 1, Chapter 4)
- Other senses (Başdoğan and Loftin, Volume 2, Section 1, Chapter 5)

Speech (Whitton and Loftin, Volume 2, Section 1, Section Perspective)
- Voice recognition
- Speech understanding
- Speech synthesis

SW Tools (McDowell, Guerrero, McCue, and Hollister, Volume 2, Section 1, Chapter 8; McDowell, Volume 2, Section 1, Chapter 10)
- Middleware
- Game engines
- Physics engines

Systems & System Issues
Augmented & Mixed Reality (Henderson and Feiner, Volume 2, Section 1, Chapter 6)
Dismounted Infantry (Templeman, Sibert, Page, and Denbrook, Volume 2, Section 1, Chapter 7)
Simulation sickness (Drexler, Kennedy, and Malone, Volume 2, Section 1, Chapter 11)
Evaluation (Whitton and Brooks, Volume 2, Section 1, Chapter 12)

sensory input for sensory data from the real world, and virtual environments are *interactive,* that is, when a user does something that generates an input to the system, the results of that input are almost immediately apparent. According to some strict definitions of a virtual environment system, minimally a VE system must immerse the user in synthetic visual imagery and must change that imagery at interactive rates when the user turns his or her head.

Immersion

Users depend on data they gather with their senses to understand the situation in which they are placed and to inform their decisions and actions. VE system designers must know if it is possible for the system to generate the sensory cues the user needs for accurate decision making and action.

Users are *immersed* in synthetic sensory input by various displays, most often visual and audio. More rarely VE users are presented with haptic, vestibular, olfactory, or taste stimuli. The quality of the *immersion* is determined by the quality of the models used for objects, sounds, and so forth, the quality of the software used to simulate or *render* the synthetic stimuli, and the characteristics of the devices that deliver the stimuli.

Good immersion requires that the system have good models—sufficient object detail, sufficiently subtle behaviors of entities, and so forth. Rendering, particularly for visual and audio stimuli, requires highly accurate simulation of the physics of light and sound waves. After the data are rendered, they must be displayed or delivered to the user in a manner such that the user can perceive them. For instance, it may not be possible to hear subtle noises if the system uses cheap speakers. Likewise, if the critical visual cue for detecting a threat occupies only a single pixel on a handheld device's 320×240 pixel screen, then that combination of object size and display resolution is inappropriate for training that particular threat-detection task.

The quality of the entire virtual experience depends on the quality of both the immersion and the content. The content and the sensory stimuli together can cause changes in the user's psychological and physiological state: the user may feel as if he or she is *present* in the virtual scene (and not in a laboratory), may feel emotions, and may exhibit changes in his or her physiological state, such as a rise in heart rate if encountering a stressful situation. (The use of the word *immersion* to refer exclusively to the synthetic stimuli delivered to the user, and the use of the word *presence* to refer to a component of the user's psychological state, have been, and remain, controversial among VE researchers. Witmer and Singer (1998) and Slater (1999, 2003) offer differing opinions.

Interactivity

Both moving around and making things happen in a virtual environment are examples of *interactions* between the user and the environment. Ideally, the user sees the effect of his or her input almost immediately after making an action. If the user senses no delay between input and feedback, the system is called *interactive.* For example, if a user pushes a joystick to indicate forward motion, and he or she moves though the scene in no more time than it would take to make a real step forward, the system is interactive.

The time between user action/input and a change in the display is the *end-to-end latency* of the system; this latency is the time it takes data to travel around the interaction-feedback loop in Figure SP1.2. It is generally accepted that an application is interactive if this latency is around 50 milliseconds (about 3 frames at a 60 frame per second frame update rate). System latency as low as 40 milliseconds has been shown to decrease task performance in visual search tasks (Wickens, 1986).

Components of VE Systems

Input Devices and User Interfaces

The target application dictates the choice of *input devices* for a particular VE system. For instance, a helicopter simulator will have devices that function like the helicopter control stick, pedals, and collective and provide input to the vehicle dynamics simulator. As another example, an infantry member might hold a rifle-like device on which a tracker is mounted. The tracker readings control where the rifle appears in the visual scene, and, when the rifle is fired, the readings are used by the simulation to determine what the round hit. Input devices for training systems range from the familiar controllers for computer games (keyboards, mice, buttons, joysticks, dials, sliders, pedals, steering wheels, the Wii remote, and so forth) to sophisticated reproductions of the actual control panels of aircraft, ships, and tanks.

Trackers are a special category of input device that measure and report the position and/or orientation (together called *pose*) of objects in the scene. Other sensors that might be in the (real) training environment include microphones for voice input, video cameras recording trainee behavior, and physiological monitors worn by the trainee to record such data as heart rate.

Good usability engineering practice for user interfaces is to build, test, revise, test again, and so on. Many factors affect how successful a device and interface will be. Questions that should be asked during development include the following: Is the interface natural and intuitive? Is using it fatiguing? How well does it reproduce or approximate the way the target user does the task in the real world? How hard is it to learn the interface? After someone has learned the interface, is there any residual cognitive effort required to use it, and does that effort detract from a user's ability to focus on and perform his or her main task? Does the interface interfere with another interface in the system?

Computing and Networking

Today the computing components of VE systems are almost always standard, off-the-shelf computers. When configured with high performance graphics boards or chips, high end laptops and office PCs have sufficient CPU and graphics processing power to generate scenes with the level of realism adequate for many training tasks. Custom-configured clusters of computers may be required to drive multiscreen displays or perform calculations for complex physical simulations.

At run time, the computer is loaded with model data and with application software, including rendering software. Models of objects and entire virtual scenes can be specific not only to a single training application, but also to a particular training scenario.

In addition to the main application control program, the software may include programs for graphics, physics simulation, simulators for specific vehicles, and programs to control semi-automated forces. Once the session begins, the main application program manages input from the user, the model data, and the various software components in order to generate displays for the user.

Networking VEs for Team Training

While a user can learn individual level skills on a stand-alone VE system and may be able to learn the rudiments of a team task on a stand-alone system, teams need to train as teams. The left side of Figure SP1.2 shows multiple VE systems networked together for team training. Trainee specific portions of the training application are executed on each system.

In order for each user's application software to maintain a correct view of the state of the entire scenario, local state data have to be distributed across the network to the other trainees' stations. The more trainees and the more moving objects, such as vehicles, that are in a scenario, the more state data have to move across the network, and the higher the potential for network delays. Network delays can adversely affect system interactivity, which may reduce trainees' abilities to perform their tasks, which, in turn, may reduce the efficacy of the system for training. The standard reference on networked virtual environments is Singhal and Zyda (1999) now supplemented by those authors' book on networked games (Singhal & Zyda, 2008).

Outputs: Displays and Logs

Display devices and data logs are the primary outputs of virtual environment systems. Displays provide instantaneous and ephemeral feedback to the users; logs are a permanent record of what occurred.

Display is the generic term used for the presentation of any type of sensory data to the user. Visual displays are essential; audio is common; and touch (haptics), smell, and taste are more difficult to implement and are used only where cues from those senses are essential for task performance or to increase the realism of a virtual setting to a very high level.

In a training context, *logs* may include user inputs (keystrokes, button pushes, or pose data from trackers), the state of all the simulators and entities in the session, and voice communications. The data can be collected at each time step of the simulation or at predetermined milestones in the training episode. *Logs* are the inputs to systems that can replay training sessions. Used as part of an after action review, a replay can enhance the value of training sessions by enabling the trainers and trainees to discuss the actual sequence of events that occurred.

Some existing training systems log only data that are passed between stations over the network. While a useful level of after action review can be performed with these data, because the logs contain no data about individual behavior, there is little or no ability to evaluate an individual's performance and diagnose his or her weaknesses.

INTRODUCTION TO THE CHAPTERS IN THIS SECTION

This section is organized with chapters on individual component technologies coming before chapters on topics concerning the whole VE system. Two chapters, inserted where they seem to make the best sense, illustrate the additional issues that arise when components are integrated in a system to meet specific user needs.

Trackers and Visual Displays

Many practitioners differentiate VEs from other interactive three-dimensional graphics applications by requiring that, to be a VE system, the user's view of the scene must change when the user turns his or her head. To accomplish change in the view, the user's head pose must be measured and reported to the application. Trackers (Welch and Davis, Chapter 1) are input devices that constantly, and at a minimum of 60 times per second, report the position and/or orientation of the object to which they are attached. In the case of a head tracker, the tracker data are used by the computing components to determine the point of view from which the virtual scene is rendered.

Both head-mounted displays (Bolas and McDowall, Chapter 2) and projection displays (Towles, Johnson, and Fuchs, Chapter 3) more fully immerse the user in a virtual scene than do desktop LCD flat-panel displays or the small screens of handheld devices. The user experience and the level of infrastructure required by head-mounted displays and projectors differ radically and these two chapters will help the reader understand the benefits and drawbacks of each.

"Mixed and Augmented Reality for Training" (Henderson and Feiner, Chapter 6) overlay synthetically generated information on a view of the real world, or combine real and virtual elements into a single scene. The chapter discusses the special benefits of augmented reality (AR) and mixed reality for a number of specific training applications and expands on the previously presented information on head-mounted displays and tracking to address the peculiar requirements of AR and mixed reality systems. The authors of this chapter use the logically more appropriate term *head-worn displays* rather than the term head-mounted displays.

Displays for the Other Senses

In VE systems designed to provide high quality immersion, providing high quality audio (Sadek, Chapter 4) (that is, spatial audio of high fidelity) is arguably second in importance only to supplying high quality visual stimuli. The audio stimuli may even be more important than the quality of the visuals in some specific training or rehabilitation applications. This chapter comprehensively covers the subject—the fundamental science, the computations required, how to select between headphones and speakers, and how to prevent damage to users' hearing.

Displays for the other senses are discussed in multimodal display systems: haptic, olfactory, gustatory, and vestibular (Başdoğan and Loftin, Chapter 5). These four senses—also known as touch, smell, taste, and orientation/acceleration—are much less frequently stimulated in VE systems than the visual and audition systems, and this chapter explains why by pointing out the difficulties of doing so. The lack of *something to feel,* the lack of haptic stimulation, is considered by many to be the most frequent cause of breaks in the VE user's illusion of being present in the synthetic scene.

User Input: Meeting Complex User Needs

"Designing User Interfaces for Training Dismounted Infantry" (Templeman, Sibert, Page, and Denbrook, Chapter 7) illustrates both how important it is that the system designer has a complete understanding of the interaction needs of the customer and how complex it can be to integrate multiple input devices to meet those needs. A locomotion interface becomes complex when it has to support the ability to look and aim a weapon in one direction while moving in another direction (including backwards and sideways), at any speed.

Computing: Behavior Models, Computing Requirements, and Game Engines

Populating a large battlefield with a real human operator for each vehicle is prohibitively expensive. A solution to that problem is an important class of software that generates *semi-automated forces* with the characteristic that one human (or an artificially intelligent system) can control many synthetic entities (individuals or collectives). "Behavior Generation in Semi-Automated Forces" (Petty, Chapter 9) describes how behaviors are programmed for these entities.

The chapter on computing requirements (McDowell, Guerrero, McCue, and Hollister, Chapter 8) looks in detail not only at hardware and software requirements driven by the visual displays, but also at the computing requirements of physics simulators (collision detection and response), rendering for senses other than visual, supporting sensor networks that may be in the (real) training environment, and supporting communications.

Computer games have many of the same characteristics as training systems, and games are increasingly used for training. "Games and Gaming Technology for Training" (McDowell, Chapter 10) discusses how games and *game engines* can be used as training tools. The author concludes with a thoughtful analysis of what it will take for game technology to be better accepted in the training community.

Evaluating the VE System and Components

The final chapter of the section is devoted to evaluation of component technologies (Whitton and Brooks, Chapter 12). Using a format of short case studies and lessons learned, the chapter looks at methods and metrics for evaluating both individual component technologies and entire systems. The chapter concludes with a short discussion of the role of usability engineering in the development of VE components and systems.

LOOKING TO THE FUTURE

VE Components Become Commodity Products

This section of this volume examines VE component technologies as they relate to the design, development, and deployment of VE systems intended for training. If one looks into the intermediate future (say, 5 to 10 years), can one envision these components moving from specialized, laboratory artifacts to commodity products?

Within the VE component technologies described in this section only computing has been "commoditized" to the point that a sophisticated VE system can be built around a computing platform that is readily available for $10,000 or less. Contrast this to VE development in the early 1990s when the necessary computing platforms could cost $250,000 to $1,000,000. Sadly, such a reduction in cost (or increase in capability) has not occurred in most other VE component technologies. Nonetheless, there is hope.

The recent success of the Wii from Nintendo, for example, demonstrates that an input device, if manufactured in quantities of 100,000 or more can be both capable and relatively inexpensive. It is a virtual certainty that at least some other VE component technologies will follow suit, especially if they become part of a popular game system (like the Wii). On the display side, stereo-ready, consumer-grade, large-screen, real-projection televisions based on Texas Instruments' DLP technology are now available from two manufacturers (http://www.dlp.com/hdtv/).

We can expect that technologies such as tracking, spatial audio, and head-worn displays will be commoditized and, thus, provide a significant impetus to the development and deployment of VE systems for training.

Moving toward the Holodeck

Star Trek's holodeck, eerily like the ultimate display described by Sutherland (1965), is often cited as a model of the ideal virtual environment system. One way to define a research and development agenda is to compare the capabilities of current VE technologies to the capabilities of the holodeck. Defining characteristics of the holodeck make it a good model for a team training environment: the (real) people participating are together in a shared space, there are perfect instances of real objects (vehicles, weapons, control panels, tools, and so forth) available, and the virtual people are indistinguishable from the real. Where is our technology inadequate today? Table SP1.2 is partial list of areas in need of improvements.

Major questions that remain are whether we will be able to make virtual training as realistic as live training and thus provide safe and possibly more readily accessible ways to start trainees up the learning curve, increasing their confidence and the probability that they will perform successfully, and whether we have to

Table SP1.2.   A Partial List of Improvements Needed in VE Component Technologies

Category	Need
Visual Displays	• Displays that offer proper stereo views for multiple trainees working in the same space. • Computing and graphics hardware to support such displays. • High resolution, bright, wireless head-worn displays.
Haptic Displays	• New methods of delivering tactile and haptic feedback. What can we do to approximate the ability to sit on virtual chairs? This is perhaps the most challenging of all the technologies of the holodeck. Sutherland (1965) described it thusly, "The computer can control the existence of matter."

Sensors	• Unencumbering, fast, accurate full-body tracking without encumbrances.
	  ○ Tracking data to control movement of avatars (virtual bodies of self and other humans) and autonomous virtual humans.
	  ○ Data accurate enough that movement of vitual humans looks natural and movement of avatars of real people contains the idiosyncratic movement patterns of each individual.
	  ○ Tracking data accurate enough to control models of fingers so that participants/trainees have full use of their hands for interacting with the VE.

Speech	• Speech recognition and understanding systems sufficiently fast to allow a natural flow of verbal interaction.
Mixed Reality	• Systems of displays, trackers, and sensors to support augmented and mixed reality systems so that real objects can be used while participating in a scenario.

Tools	• Content development tools easy and fast enough that a user can train tonight against a tactic first seen in battle today.
	  ○ Model builders: real things and places; behaviors; sound.
	  ○ Scenario builders including automated narrative/storyline generation.
	  ○ Automatic generation of scenario variants.
	• Evaluation and error diagnosis tools that accept event logs as input.

have full realism to train all skills. Fully immersive systems, today's approximations of the holodeck, require considerable supporting infrastructure in terms of
trackers, computers, and displays. The low infrastructure solution has always
been envisioned as nothing more encumbering than a pair of sunglasses.

Beyond the Holodeck: Radically Different Technology

Looking into the future more than 25 years, one can speculate about the *ultimate virtual environment*. First, let go of Sutherland's idea of a *room* with
computer-controlled matter and focus on what the human experience with the
ultimate display should be—an experience just as real as being there. People have
such experiences now—dreams. Dreams can be vivid, multisensory experiences
that are identical in fidelity to the real world. Dreams provide evidence that the
human brain has all the processing power needed for the ultimate VE.

The ultimate VE system would use a biological computer (the human brain) at
least for graphical and other sensory display production. The system would rely
on direct coupling to the human nervous system for both input and output. The
challenge is discovering how to stimulate the brain, especially the channels associated with the sense organs, so that external sensory stimulation is not required
and so that the content of the VE dream can be controlled. Already, devices delivering direct stimulation to the vestibular system are available, though still crude
(see Başdoğan and Loftin, Chapter 5).

Obviously there are major barriers to overcome—both of a technical and of a
cultural nature—before this VE system based on direct coupling of a computer
to the user's brain and nervous system can be realized. Yet the potential is clearly
there, if content can be created, implanted, and experienced safely, efficiently,
and effectively.

ACKNOWLEDGMENTS

The authors would like to thank Jeremy D. Wendt and Chris VanderKnyff for
their help in the preparation of Appendix A and Ramy Sadek for providing
Appendix B. Preparation of this chapter was supported in part by funding from
the Office of Naval Research.

REFERENCES

Cassell, J., Sullivan, J., Prevost, S., & Churchill, E. (Eds.) (2000). *Embodied conversa-
tional agents*. Cambridge, MA: The MIT Press.
Johnsen, K., Dickerson, R., Raij, A., Harrison, C., Lok, B., Stevens, A., & Lind, D. (2006).
Evolving an immersive medical communication skills trainer. *Journal on Presence:
Teleoperators and Virtual Environments, 15*(1), 33–46.
Jurafsky, D., & Martin, J. H. (2008). *Speech and language processing* (2nd ed.). Upper
Saddle River, NJ: Prentice Hall.
Luebke, D., Reddy, M., Cohen, J., Varshney, A., Watson, B., & Huebner, R. (2002). *Level
of Detail for 3D Graphics*. San Francisco: Morgan Kaufmann.

Moller, T., & Haines, E. (2002). *Real time rendering.* Natick, MA: A. K. Peters.

Mori, M. (2005). Bukimi no tani [The uncanny valley] (K. F. MacDorman & T. Minato, Trans.). (Originally published in 1970; *Energy, 7*(4), 33–35.) Retrieved April 22, 2008, from http://graphics.cs.ucdavis.edu/~staadt/ECS280/Mori1970OTU.pdf

Pharr, M., & Humphreys, G. (2004). *Physically based rendering: From theory to implementation.* San Francisco: Morgan Kaufmann.

Shirley, P, Ashikhmin, M., Gleicher, M., Marschner, S., Reinhard, E., Sung, K., et al. (2005). *Fundamentals of computer graphics.* Wellesley, MA: A. K. Peters.

Singhal, S., & Zyda, M. (1999). *Networked virtual environments: Design and implementation.* Reading, MA: Addison-Wesley.

Singhal, S., & Zyda, M. (2008). *Networked games: Design and implementation.* Reading, MA: Addison-Wesley.

Slater, M. (1999). Measuring presence: A response to the Witmer and Singer questionnaire. *Presence: Teleoperators and Virtual Environments, 8*(5), 560–566.

Slater, M. (2003). A note on presence terminology. *Presence-Connect, 3*(1). Retrieved April 21, 2008, from http://www.presence-connect.com

Stanney, K. (Ed.). (2002). *Handbook of virtual environments: Design, implementation, and applications.* Mahwah, NJ: Erlbaum Associates.

Sutherland, I., (1965). The ultimate display. *Information Processing 1965: Proceedings of IFIP Congress, 65*(2), 506–508.

Traum, D., Swartout, W., Gratch, J., Marsella, S., Kenny, P., Hovy, E., et al. (2005). Dealing with doctors: A virtual human for non-team interaction. *Proceedings of the 6th SIGdial Workshop on Discourse and Dialogue* (pp. 232–236). East Stroudsburg, PA: Association for Computational Linguistics.

Wickens, C. D. (1986). The effects of control dynamics on performance. In K. R. Boff, L. Kaufman, & J. P. Thomas (Eds.), *Handbook of perception and human performance* (pp. 39-1–39-60). New York: Wiley.

Witmer, B., & Singer, M., (1998). Measuring presence in virtual environments: A presence questionnaire. *Presence: Teleoperators and Virtual Environments, 7*(3), 225–240.

APPENDIX A: MODELING AND RENDERING

Mary Whitton and Jeremy Wendt

This appendix is a basic introduction to two of the fundamental elements of computer graphics: *three-dimensional (3-D) modeling* and *rendering*. Given its length, the appendix is little more than a framework, some definitions, a few targeted references, and *keywords* for searching the World Wide Web, digital libraries, or library catalogs. For those who want to learn more about computer graphics, a good basic textbook is *Fundamentals of Computer Graphics* by Shirley and colleagues (2005).

Rendering programs start with models and generate images. Inputs to rendering programs are object shape, object appearance, and scene-lighting models; models of dynamics define how objects move and change from one rendered frame to the next. Pharr and Humphreys (2004) and Moller and Haines (2002) are texts on the general topic of rendering and *real-time rendering,* respectively. The large number of popular press books on topics such as *computer graphics, 3-D modeling, rendering,* and *animation* speaks to the wide use of these techniques today.

Art meets technology. Modeling for computer graphics is a combination of art and technology: the art is in defining the shape and appearance; the technology is in the programs and hardware that render the objects and scenes. For the art and technology to serve the application well, the artists and the technologists must collaborate among themselves and, for training applications, with training experts and subject matter experts. The team goal is to produce a set of models that instantiates the training experience that the trainers imagined.

Developing high-quality *art assets*—the models of objects in the scenes, the artwork used to color them, and the lighting of the scene—can require many months of work by many artists and programmers. Although highly trained and experienced professionals produce better-looking models than amateurs or less highly trained professionals, the level of artistic quality available in top-of-the-line computer games requires more resources (time, money, and people) than most training projects can afford. *Digital media* and *computer animation* services are available from small businesses and independent contractors, as well as from large production houses.

MODELING OBJECTS—SHAPE AND SURFACE APPEARANCE

Object Shape

In most VE and graphics systems, object shape is defined by a *triangle mesh* that approximates the shape of the object's outer surface. Triangles are used because they are the most efficient data format for modern graphics processors. Models can be created in *geometric modeling* programs, by software procedures (*procedural modeling*), or from *3-D-range images*. Collections of ready-to-use *3-D models* are available for purchase. Reference books on *shape modeling* are almost all specific to particular software packages; research references are generally specific to a method of modeling and its associated mathematics.

Geometric Modeling

Geometric modeling software is available with a wide variety of capabilities and costs. Some packages, for example, Google SketchUp, are free and easy to learn, but have limited features. Autodesk's professional products 3ds Max and Maya integrate tools for sophisticated modeling, animation, and rendering, but the learning curve is steep. There are well over two dozen *3-D modeling software* packages; many of them are available at no cost.

Procedural Modeling

Procedural modeling techniques generate objects by following a set of rules. Procedural methods can be used to create enough buildings for a city or enough trees for a forest. *L-systems* are rules that generate plants, and *fractal* procedures produce realistic-looking synthetic terrain, clouds, mountains, and coastlines. Procedural modeling programs are available for purchase, as are ready-to-use models of plants.

Terrain

Models of the earth's surface are called *terrain models* or *digital elevation models,* and they are often available at no cost.

Range Data—Modeling Real Places

LIDAR (light detection and ranging) and *scanning-laser range finder* technologies measure the distance from the scanner to the surface of objects in the space being scanned. The 3-D points located by the scanner are converted into a triangle mesh model of the space. Some systems achieve very high realism by using color photographs of the scene as texture maps.

Object Surface Appearance

As of this writing, *texture mapping* is the most widely used method of adding appearance detail to objects. Textures are images that are applied like decals to the surface of objects during *rendering*. Texture maps add such visual detail as color, patterns, dirt, and rust. Photographs and other 2-D media can be used as textures, as can the output of 2-D painting programs (*paint programs*). As hardware and software support has increased, the use of variants of texture mapping such as *bump mapping, normal mapping,* and *displacement mapping* has grown. These maps modify the rendering calculations in ways that increase visual realism with minimal increase in rendering time.

Issues and Considerations

Object Numbers and Complexity

The more objects and the more detail in each object (that is, the more triangles in the overall model), the higher the computational load and the more likely that latency will increase and reduce interactivity. Luebke and his colleagues (2002) describe techniques that reduce the computational load of large datasets.

Dynamic Shape Model Modification

Some applications modify object models during program execution in order to provide visual feedback of shape changes caused by the collision of objects, for example, human tissue deforming when pushed by a surgical tool. Both the physical simulation and the model modification require significant computational resources.

SCENE LIGHTING

Lighting effects can be used to create cinematic effects ranging from joy to terror, as well as to generate such familiar effects as shadows and reflections. Lighting, like texture mapping, is part of the process of *rendering* a virtual scene. The rendering process simulates the physics of the interaction of lights with surfaces and computes the final color of each pixel.

Fixed Function and Programmable Lighting Pipelines

OpenGL (open graphics library) and Direct3D are application programming interfaces (APIs) for writing both 2-D and 3-D graphics applications. The packages support a fixed set of lighting effects, including both the diffuse and specular components of direct lighting—light that comes from light sources defined by their position, color, and shape. Both OpenGL and Direct 3D support application-specific lighting effects through programmable shaders. *Shaders* are programs that run on graphics processing units (GPUs). NVIDIA and ATI, major suppliers of GPUs, both provide extensive resources for developers. See Chapter 8—McDowell, Guerrero, McCue, and Hollister—for a further discussion of shaders.

Global Illumination

Real objects are lit not only by light coming directly from a light source, but also by light reflected from other objects in the scene. *Global illumination* rendering techniques include light from interreflections when calculating the color of a surface. *Radiosity* and *ray tracing,* the two best-known global illumination techniques, are computationally expensive and are not used in interactive applications. Radiosity can be precomputed for static (nonmoving) scene configurations and the lighting stored in special textures called *light maps* that are applied to objects during rendering.

Issues and Considerations

Build versus Buy

Most application developers choose to buy rendering software because it is not cost-effective to have a dedicated in-house rendering software team. There are many *2-D and 3-D graphics API* and graphics *middleware* and *game engine* products available. They range in price from free and very low cost with minimal features to high cost with concomitant capability. Middleware and game engine software offer functionality at a higher level than APIs, but at a sufficiently general level that they can be used in a wide variety of applications.

Lighting Simulation Quality and Interactivity

Many applications strive to render a new frame about every 16 milliseconds. (The 16 milliseconds figure is related to the *refresh rate* specification of displays. See Chapter 3—Towles, Johnson, and Fuchs.) Many applications set the fidelity of their lighting simulation at a level that uses all of the computing resources available for the time left after other essential per-frame operations (for example, managing user interface devices and computing collisions and collision responses) are completed.

MODELING OBJECT MOVEMENT DYNAMICS

Besides looking right, objects must behave correctly when they interact with other objects or entities in the scene. Simulators define the motion of virtual objects and entities that can move under their own power. Unpowered objects move (and possibly change shape) in response to external forces (for example, as a result of colliding with another object or entity).

Simulators

Vehicle Simulators

Vehicle simulators are programs that compute an approximation of the behaviors and state of a real vehicle. The behavior is based on internal state (for example, remaining fuel), user input to the vehicle's control system (for example, braking, or turning), and physical constraints of the environment (for example, slope of the road, or collisions). Data from the simulator are used to compute feedback for the user. For instance, if the oil overheats, the virtual oil gauge light would come on.

Semiautomated Forces

Semiautomated forces are the topic of Chapter 9—Petty. Often the purpose of semiautomated forces is to have large numbers of entities in a training scenario without large numbers of actual participants. Semiautomated forces respond in preprogrammed ways to high-level commands issued by a human in response to changing conditions.

Virtual Humans

A convincing virtual human must look real and move realistically and must, without human input, respond appropriately to its environment and situation. *Motion capture* or *mocap* is one way to define the movements of virtual humans. (See Chapter 1—Welch and Davis for more on motion capture.) If the virtual human is performing a predefined movement, the desired movement can be performed by an actor and recorded using the motion capture system. To generate unscripted movements, models of common movements (for example, start, stop, run, walk, or jump) can be recorded individually and then linked in various sequences to form new movements.

Models of body positions characteristic of various emotional states can be recorded and used to control virtual humans so that the virtual humans are able to communicate emotions through *body language*. Advances in *facial animation* are resulting in more believable motion of the mouth and the surrounding facial tissue when virtual humans speak.

The Uncanny Valley

Human judgment of the realism of virtual humans is not monotonic with model quality. When model quality gets high, humans surprisingly become more intolerant of small flaws in appearance and behavior that they would have accepted in a lower-quality model. Only when the model is close to perfect do ratings of realism again rise. Mori (1970) observed this phenomenon with respect to the realism of robot faces, and it has since been observed with respect to the appearance and motion of virtual humans.

Collision Detection and Response

The two fundamental operations associated with collisions are *collision detection* and *collision response*. Detecting collisions is a matter of testing whether two models touch or overlap in virtual space and determining the moment of collision. Collision response algorithms determine the correct response to a collision (changes in object models, changes of direction, and so forth) by simulating the physics of the collision event—the velocity of the objects, their material properties, friction, and so forth.

Collisions between *rigid bodies* can be detected and responses computed at interactive rates; collisions involving one or more *deformable bodies* such as the medical instrument-human tissue example used earlier, are much more computationally expensive and rarely interactive. *Physics engines* are software packages that simulate collision response based on Newtonian physics. Physics engines vary in computational precision, speed, and price.

Simulations of any kind are expensive. They require considerable programmer time to develop and considerable computer speed to execute. Even when using commercial packages, developers must be careful not to overload the system so that the latency grows to the point that interactivity is compromised and the system becomes unusable.

APPENDIX B: SPEECH AND LANGUAGE SYSTEMS: RECOGNITION, UNDERSTANDING, AND SYNTHESIS

Ramy Sadek

In many, if not most, domains, human interactions occur via speech. Thus, speech recognition and understanding, together with speech generation, may be essential components of a VE based (or, for that matter, any) training system. This appendix provides a brief introduction to speech and language systems that could be used in a VE developed for training.

Speech and language systems are much sought after in VEs and are a highly active area of research. Broadly, there are four components to a complete language system: *speech recognition, understanding, reasoning,* and *speech synthesis*. Of these components, understanding and reasoning are the least accessible to VEs. These two areas mark cutting-edge research, so developer and end-user packages do not yet exist. The few groups working in these areas rely on in-house software built for the specific needs of their research. Therefore projects seeking this functionality will need to collaborate with a specialized research group.

Speech recognition and synthesis are more accessible technologies. Commercial, academic, and open-source recognition packages are available and include the Hidden Markov Model Tookit (http://htk.eng.cam.ac.uk/), Institute for Signal and Information Processing Toolkit (www.ece.msstate.edu/research/isip/projects/speech/), Dragon NaturallySpeaking (www.dragontalk.com), and ViaVoice (www.nuance.com/). The recognition problem is a complex one, and to date no drop-in solutions allow the addition of speech recognition to a VE system. Integrating any of these packages with simulation software generally requires a dedicated engineer. The packages were designed with different aims. For example, one package may provide moderate accuracy for a large range of speakers, while another package offers high accuracy for a specific speaker for whom the system is tuned or "trained." Still other packages may aim to offer domain-specific recognition, for example, recognizing specific technical terms at the expense of recognizing a more general vocabulary. The best product choice is dependent on the specific needs and goals of each VE, and, fortunately, most of these packages offer clear descriptions of their functionality and features.

Speech synthesis or text-to-speech systems are somewhat easier to integrate since, at the most basic level, they take as input a piece of text. Some recognition packages (for example, ViaVoice) also offer text-to-speech capabilities. While text-to-speech capability is an open area of research, some packages offer drop-in solutions that require little custom programming effort. VEs requiring nuanced or emotional speech responses may require an engineer to fine-tune a commercial system, annotating and massaging the data to achieve life-like speech.

USING SPEECH RECOGNITION, UNDERSTANDING, AND SYNTHESIS SYSTEMS

For basic input-response interaction, some VE projects have matched verbal inputs to a set of predetermined responses to skirt the language understanding problem. This technique can work well if dialogue is restricted to a small domain. Examples of this include the *Virtual Patient* simulator that helps train (real) medical students how to interact with (real) patients by having them practice interviewing virtual patients (Johnsen et al., 2006).

A system using more sophisticated speech understanding techniques has been developed at the Institute for Creative Technology at the University of Southern California. Traum and his colleagues at the institute developed a speech system that is part of an immersive virtual reality system used to train military personnel in interactions with local, noncombatant populations. The training scenario described in Traum et al. (2005) requires the trainee, a real officer, to negotiate with a local computer-generated doctor with the goal of getting the doctor to relocate his clinic out of a danger zone. The trainee interacts verbally with the doctor and the computer-generated visuals convey, via the doctor's posture and gestures, additional cues to the doctor's state of mind during the exchange.

MORE INFORMATION

The first application for future commercial speech understanding products is likely to be in intelligent virtual agents. Advances can be tracked in the proceedings of the Intelligent Virtual Agents conference. Another source of information is proceedings of meetings of the Association for Computational Linguistics (ACL) and its special interest group on discourse and dialogue (SIGdial) and its special interest group SIGDAT for linguistic data and corpus based approaches to natural language processing. Two recommended references are Jurafsky and Martin (2008) and Cassell, Sullivan, Prevost, and Churchill (2000).

REFERENCES

Cassell, J., Sullivan, J., Prevost, S., & Churchill, E. (Eds.) (2000). *Embodied conversational agents*. Cambridge, MA: The MIT Press.

Jurafsky, D., & Martin, J. H. (2008). *Speech and language processing* (2nd ed.). Upper Saddle River, NJ: Prentice Hall.

Part I: Subsystem Components

Chapter 1

TRACKING FOR TRAINING IN VIRTUAL ENVIRONMENTS: ESTIMATING THE POSE OF PEOPLE AND DEVICES FOR SIMULATION AND ASSESSMENT

Greg Welch and Larry Davis

Estimating or *tracking* human and device motion over time is a central requirement for most virtual environment (VE) based training systems. In some cases it is sufficient to know a trainee's head or torso location [two-dimensional (2-D) or 3-D position only] within the training environment. Other cases require the full body *pose*—the position *and* orientation. Still other cases require complete body *posture*—the positions, orientations, and/or configurations of the trainee's arms, hands, legs, feet, as well as handheld devices (for example, surgical instruments or weapons). Sometimes this information must be known with precision and accuracy to better than a millimeter; sometimes less spatial and temporal resolution is needed.

Primary uses for motion tracking for *training* include real time and online simulation associated with a "live" training activity, and on- or offline assessment of performance or behavior. Live training is most often associated with VE tracking where, for example, a military trainee performing a room-clearing exercise might wear a head-mounted display (HMD) while moving around a virtual room looking for virtual enemies. In this case, at a minimum the trainees' heads would need to be tracked for the purpose of rendering the proper HMD imagery as they are moving around. Most likely their weapons would also need to be tracked to render it in the HMD imagery, and additionally perhaps their hands or other limbs would be tracked, so that they, too, could be properly rendered in the HMD imagery. Given the room-clearing scenario, one might want to know how efficiently the trainees moved during the exercise, where they were looking, where their weapons were pointing, and so forth.

In this chapter we look at tracking scenarios, technologies, and issues related to training in VE training systems. We explore the fundamental aspects of tracking only to the degree it is useful for considering, choosing, and using tracking systems for training. For further information about the fundamental technologies and methods used in tracking systems, we encourage the reader to refer to the many excellent existing survey articles (Ferrin, 1991; Meyer, Applewhite, & Biocca, 1992; Durlach & Mavor, 1994; Bhatnagar, 1993; Allen, Bishop, & Welch, 2001; Welch & Foxlin, 2002). In addition, Foxlin's (2002) chapter in Kay M. Stanney's *Handbook of Virtual Environments* is an excellent source of information about the requirements for tracking and the underlying fundamental technologies (Stanney, 2002, pp. 163–210). Beyond discussing the fundamental technologies, Allen et al. (2001, pp. 52–56) discuss the most common source/ sensor configurations, and both Allen et al.'s and Foxlin's chapters discuss the most common approaches and algorithms for estimating pose from the source/ sensor measurements.

The remainder of this chapter is organized as follows. In the first section we describe the tracking considerations relevant to the most common scenarios related to training. While we do not intend to provide a complete tracking survey in this chapter, in the second section we describe some of the tracking technologies available today for training. In the third section we discuss what we feel are the most important fundamental issues that one should consider when purchasing, installing, and using commercial tracking systems. Finally, in the fourth section we speculate just a little about where research and development are heading.

Note that portions of the third section "Fundamental Usage Issues" were reproduced or adapted (with ACM copyright permission) from the course notes for the ACM SIGGRAPH 2001 course "Tracking: Beyond 15 Minutes of Thought" (Allen et al., 2001).

TRACKING SCENARIOS

When choosing or using a motion tracking system for training purposes, one needs to consider many factors. Here we explore three particular issues: *what, where, and when to track.* Considering these issues in advance of choosing a tracking system should narrow the choices. It should also help to calibrate expectations for what might be possible in terms of precision, accuracy, robustness, and overall suitability, while also allowing the developers to focus on the relevant issues described in the fourth section "Looking Ahead."

What to Track

The primary consideration is *what* needs to be tracked, and for what purpose. While this might at first seem obvious, one tracking solution will rarely fit all circumstances. Review of the tracking scenario can reveal unrealistic expectations (practical limitations) or liberating opportunities to determine degrees of freedom, accuracy, and precision to accommodate the practical limitations of the available tracking technology.

In his excellent *Taxonomy of Usability Characteristics in Virtual Environments,* Gabbard distinguishes between "VE User Interface Input Mechanisms" and "Tracking User Location and Orientation" (Gabbard & Hix, 1997, pp. 24–25).

Although user interface mechanisms could potentially be included in a training application, here we will concentrate primarily on trainee pose and posture.

In VE, one needs to consider weight and bulk of tracking components placed on a user. However, for training, these potential distractions and biases are even more of a concern, as ideally the desired response is evoked in exactly the same situation as the real event. If the training environment relies on user-worn components that the trainees have to contend with, it might affect their performances and hence their training. The impact depends on how noticeable the component is and/or how it forces them to adjust their behavior. For example, for a marine doing live-fire training exercises, a full Lycra bodysuit instrumented with retroreflective spheres or inertial sensors could provide a wealth of information about the marine's dynamic posture, but the marine is likely to be very conscious of the suit, even if it is somehow integrated into his or her normal camouflage clothing. A global positioning system (GPS) and other devices can add weight, which corresponds to unusual forces on the body, which might be noticed. How noticeable a body-worn component is depends on the *relative* forces—something that is very noticeable on the hand might be less so on the back/torso.

Knowing what parts of the body need to be tracked will help determine the necessary degrees of freedom, accuracy, resolution, and so forth. For example, head tracking for head-mounted, display based virtual reality (VR) can be very demanding in particular in terms of delay-induced error ("Temporal Issues" in the third section). Because our heads are relatively heavy, and attached to the mass of the torso, people cannot translate their heads very fast. However, as pointed out by Ron T. Azuma, "At a moderate head or object rotation rate of 50° per second, 100 milliseconds (ms) of latency causes 5° of angular error. At a rapid rate of 300° per second, keeping angular errors below 0.5° requires a combined latency of under 2 ms!" (Azuma, 1993, p. 50). A more typical 50 milliseconds of delay corresponds to about 15° of error for such rotation. However, if one intends to use a room-mounted display system (projected imagery or flat panels), concerns about latency-induced rotational error are typically reduced dramatically. This is because such head rotation typically causes relatively small eye translation with respect to the fixed displays.

People can rotate their wrists at angular rates that are roughly comparable to head rotations, but they can translate their hands much faster than their heads, by rotating rapidly about the wrist or elbow. (Hands have much less mass than heads!) Typical arm and wrist motion can occur in as little as ½ second, with typical "fast" wrist tangential motion occurring at three meters per second (Atkeson & Hollerbach, 1985). Such motion corresponds to approximately 1 to 10 centimeters of translation throughout the sequence of 100 measurements used for a single estimate. For systems that attempt submillimeter accuracies, even slow motion occurring during a sequence of sequential measurements impacts the accuracy of the estimates. For example, in a multiple-measurement system with 30 millisecond total measurement time, motion of only three centimeters per second corresponds to approximately one millimeter of target translation throughout the sequence of sensor measurements acquired for one estimate.

Finally, it is critical to consider *how many* individuals one needs to track simultaneously for real time graphics or training/behavioral analysis. The primary concern is one of the *sociability* of the tracking system, as defined in Meyer et al. (1992). That is, how well does the approach/system support multiple simultaneous users? For example, an optical system could be more prone to occlusions from other trainees than magnetic or inertial systems. Even if the medium itself is relatively unaffected by multiple nearby users, as is the case, for example, with inertial sensors, one has to look at how one gets the data off the devices and processed simultaneously in real time. It is often hard enough to do this with one user, much less two or more. Sociability is something to investigate if you intend to track multiple trainees.

Where to Track

Beyond what one is tracking ("What to Track") one needs to consider *where* the tracking needs to be done. Some applications might require only small-scale tracking where the user does not walk around. For example, if one is looking at training a task involving manual dexterity of the hand or fingers, such as surgical suturing, one does not need wide-area tracking, but instead might get by with a couple of "glove" devices. If the pose of the hand (back or palm) is of interest over a small area, one might be able to use conventional single-sensor magnetic systems, such as those made by Ascension Technology Corporation or Polhemus, or inertial hybrids, such as those made by InterSense Inc.

For 6 DOF head tracking, the training task might involve only what some call "fish tank" VR, whereby the user stands or sits in front of a cathode ray tube monitor or flat panel display, viewing some imagery that requires head-motion parallax, and so forth. In such cases concerns about optical or acoustic occlusions are likely to be lessened, allowing consideration of vision (camera) based tracking, and so forth. If the allowable volume of motion is restricted, one might be able to use mechanical tracking such as the Shooting Star Technology ADL-1.

If one needs 6 DOF head tracking over a room or lab-sized space, one needs to be looking at such wide-area systems as the HiBall by 3rdTech, the IS-900 by InterSense, or a cellular magnetic system, such as the Ascension Flock of Birds. With an increase in working volume comes a likely increase in number of trainees. If multiple trainees need to be supported in a large space, one needs to consider the sociability of the candidate systems as mentioned in "What to Track."

Perhaps the most difficult tracking challenges are related to unusually large spaces, in particular, outdoors. Outdoor environments can present exceptional challenges in terms of the sheer scale of the working volume (and corresponding difficulties with sensor signals); difficulties in dealing with such uncontrollable environmental factors as too little or too much light, sound, and so forth; and even something as seemingly mundane as getting signals off the body-worn sensors of the individual trainees. The problem becomes one not of just signal strength and data bandwidth if the trainees will be distributed over a large outdoor area, but potentially one of *timing*—latency, synchronization, and so on. Over very large areas, for example, a live-fire desert training environment, certain technologies become impractical or impossible. For example, an active magnetic system could not be made to work over several kilometers. In such cases *self-tracking* approaches, such as those that make use of inertial devices, become more attractive as their accuracy and sensitivity do not necessarily depend on external infrastructure. On the other hand, there is no inertial tracking system that can function with reasonable bounded error in an unaided fashion over a large area (see "Inertial" in the second section for more detail). As such the approach would need to combine the inertial sensing with other approaches, such as GPS (which itself is limited to meters of accuracy), or even vision/camera based approaches.

When to Track

Finally, beyond what (or why) and where to track, one needs to consider *when* to track. By "when" we really mean when will the sensor data (whatever they are) be processed to generate pose or posture estimates. For example, if one needs to create computer-generated imagery for the trainee(s), one will need some form of *online* (active during the training) and *real time* (fast enough to keep up) estimations. In such cases, temporal issues such as latency (see "Temporal Issues" in the third section) might be of primary concern. If one is interested only in post-exercise pose or posture analysis, then as long as the sensor data can be collected in real time, and accurately timestamped if synchronization is needed, then the sensor data can be processed offline after the exercise to estimate the pose/posture that is then analyzed.

While the latter case (post-training analysis) might sound easier, in fact, waiting to process sensor data until later in time (offline) can mean that one needs to transmit and/or store tremendous amounts of data during the exercise. The pose/posture estimation from the raw sensor data, in effect, provides a form of compression of the sensor data, as many readings are (typically) combined into single estimates at a reduced rate.

On the other hand, analyzing sensor data in an offline fashion (after the exercise) means that one can effectively "look into the future" when filtering the data. The benefits of such noncausal filtering can be tremendous if, for example, the data have structured errors in them, gaps, and so on. Systems that operate in an online fashion cannot (by definition) look ahead in time and, therefore, can generate pose/posture estimates based only on past measurements. This can make such systems susceptible to data dropout, as well as unexpected changes in target (trainee) dynamics, such as transitions from still to rapid motion.

Note that it should be possible to take a hybrid approach, where some processing is done online, in real time (perhaps to both compress the sensor data and provide some online feedback or analysis to the trainers) and further pose/posture refinement and behavioral analysis (for example) are done later, offline.

TODAY'S TECHNOLOGIES

Once one has determined what is to be tracked and the reasons for tracking it, the remaining decision is the type of tracking technology to use. There are many factors to influence this decision, including the operating principle of the tracker, the required performance, and the cost.

In this section, we provide guidance in selecting commercial off-the-shelf (COTS) tracking systems. We first discuss the types of trackers, categorized by principle of operation, and give examples of COTS systems within each category. We then provide a list of tracker characteristics to consider when deciding upon a particular tracking system. Finally, we discuss choices that must be made when considering how one plans to interface with the desired tracking system.

The tracking system taxonomy found in Welch and Foxlin (2002) is used to classify the systems according to different operating principles. In addition, the specific tracking systems highlighted are limited to systems available for retail purchase at the time of writing. Some of the more popular trackers that have been discontinued by their manufacturers, such as the Boom (Binocular Omni-Orientation Monitor) 3C from Fakespace Labs or the ADL-1 from Shooting Star Technology, are often available through online auction sites. For more detailed discussion regarding operating principles and tracking in general, the reader may refer to Welch and Foxlin (2002) and Foxlin (2002).

Mechanical

Mechanical tracking systems use physical links to determine the pose of a tracked object. Mechanical tracking systems have the advantages of high update rates (number of pose reports per second) and high accuracy. However, the object being tracked is tethered to the tracker, limiting the range of motion.

Mechanical tracking technology is used for digitizers, as well as tracking hand motion and motion capture/pose determination. The MicroScribe G2LX from Immersion Corporation and the FaroArm from FARO Technologies are examples of digitizers, which are tracking systems used to create digital representations of real objects. The CyberGlove, also from Immersion, is a popular device for measuring hand movements. It uses changes in electrical resistance to indicate the amount of bending of the fingers. Another popular option is the X-IST DataGlove from noDNA that includes conductive bend sensors and piezoelectric pressure sensors. Two mechanical tracking systems used for motion capture are the Gypsy-6 from Animazoo (a mechanical system that uses inertial sensors) and the ShapeTape and ShapeWrapIII systems from Measurand that use fiber optic bend sensing.

Inertial

Inertial trackers use the earth's gravitational field to determine the pose of tracked objects. Inertial trackers can be very small, have low latency, and consume small amounts of power. Their drawback is that they suffer from drift (a gradual loss of measurement accuracy). The errors in accuracy accumulate because of the numerical integrations performed to convert accelerations and velocities into positions or angles. The tendency to drift is often mitigated by using inertial systems as part of hybrid tracking systems (see "Hybrid" in the second section).

A popular inertial tracker is the InertiaCube series from InterSense. The InertiaCube3 combines prediction algorithms with accelerometers and gyros to provide 360° of rotational measurement. Other examples of inertial tracking systems include the 3D-Bird from Ascension (180° in elevation and 360° in azimuth and attitude) and the MTx from Xsens (360° in all directions).

Acoustic

Acoustic trackers use ultrasonic sound (near 40 kilohertz) to determine the pose of objects. The time-of-flight differences from multiple sources are measured and position is determined based upon the characteristics of sound traveling in the air. However, multipath reflection of the emitted sound can severely degrade tracking performance, as can occlusions between the emitter and receiver. Acoustic tracking tends to suffer in outdoor conditions, as well as near walls, where air currents and noise can cause interference. Acoustic tracking is also used as part of hybrid tracking systems. Resolutions tend to be several millimeters, and accuracies can be difficult to maintain if conditions cannot be very controlled.

An example of acoustic trackers is the Hexamite HX11. The HX11 tracks the location of pulsed, ultrasonic emitters with chains of ultrasonic receivers. In theory, the system has no limit to the tracking coverage area.

Magnetic

Magnetic tracking systems use electromagnetic field differences to determine position and orientation. They offer good update rates and rugged performance. Two categories of magnetic tracking systems are systems that produce magnetic fields using alternating current (AC) and direct current (DC). An AC tracker is generally more accurate than a DC tracker. However, AC trackers produce eddy currents in surrounding metals that in turn produce small magnetic fields that degrade performance. In addition, the performance of both types of magnetic systems is degraded by the presence of external magnetic fields and ferroelectric materials.

Two classic VE tracking systems are the Polhemus Fastrak and the Ascension Flock of Birds. The Fastrak uses AC magnetic fields to determine position and orientation, while the Flock of Birds uses a pulsed, DC magnetic field. Recent demonstrations of the Polhemus PATRIOT wireless tracking system have shown considerable improvement regarding robustness to metallic interference. The PATRIOT is expandable and can track up to four objects simultaneously.

Optical

Optical tracking systems use the properties of light to determine the pose of tracked objects. Markers that emit light (active trackers) or reflect light (passive trackers) are used to determine pose. The arrangement of the light sources and sensors provide a subclassification for optical trackers. If the sensors are mounted on the object to be tracked, the approach is sometimes called "inside out." If the sensors are fixed, and the markers are attached to the object to be tracked, the approach is sometimes called "outside in." Optical trackers provide the highest accuracy of any tracking type typically being submillimeter, and they provide data in the 120 to over 1,000 frames per second reducing motion-blur artifacts. They suffer from line-of-sight issues, meaning the sensors or emitters can be blocked. Optical trackers that use infrared light often have difficulties in bright lights or direct sunlight. An important feature of an optical tracker is its field of view, meaning the angle through which its sensors can detect targets.

The HiBall tracking system from 3rdTech is an inside-out tracker capable of unlimited tracking coverage in theory. Another inside-out tracker is the Laser-BIRD from Ascension that has an infrared light source that sweeps through the tracked area.

Outside-in optical trackers include the DynaSight from Origin Instruments and the Certus from Northern Digital Inc. Both of these systems use active infrared emitters to determine the pose of tracked objects. The DMAS (Digital Motion Analysis Suite) from Motion Imaging Corporation is another outside-in system, but it is a markerless tracking system, tracking objects through analysis of video frames.

Many optical tracking sytems are used for motion capture in addition to pose tracking. Many are passive trackers that detect reflections from special markers in the tracked area. Examples of these systems include the OptiTrack from NaturalPoint, the PPT from WorldViz, the MX from Vicon, the Impulse from PhaseSpace Inc., the Eagle from Motion Analysis Corporation, and the ProReflex from Qualisys.

Radio Frequency and Ultrawide Band

Radio frequency trackers use differences in radio signals to determine position in an environment in meter or submeter resolutions. These differences include signal strength, signal content, and time of flight. Ultrawide band (UWB) communications use similar principles, but operate over a broader frequency range (for example, 2 GHz–7.5 GHz [gigahertz]).

The Ubisense system uses a pulsed UWB signal to determine the 3-D location of tags within the tracked area. Up to 1,000 tags can be located simultaneously by the system and simultaneous radio frequency (RF) communication occurs to dynamically change update rates. In this area, there have also been recent announcements from Thales on an indoor/outdoor RF tracking system and from

AeroScout regarding a Wi-Fi based active radio-frequency-identification tracking system.

Hybrid

As the name suggests, hybrid trackers combine multiple types of operating principles to provide increased robustness of pose measurements. Two examples of hybrid systems from InterSense are the IS-900 and the IS-1200. The IS-900 combines acoustic and inertial measurements, and the IS-1200 combines optical and inertial measurements. Another hybrid system is the Hy-BIRD from Ascension. It combines inertial and optical tracking methods for use in cockpit applications.

Factors to Consider when Evaluating Tracking Systems

After considering the factors intrinsic to the technology used by the tracker, a tracking system should be evaluated based upon its performance characteristics. These characteristics include the following:

1. Degrees of Freedom: three (orientation or position tracking only) or six (position and orientation tracking).
2. Accuracy: The absolute difference between the real position of the tracked object and the position reported by the tracker.
3. Resolution: The minimum change in the position of the tracked object that can be detected by the tracker.
4. Jitter: The instantaneous change in position from frame to frame, as reported by the tracker when the tracked object is stationary.
5. Drift: The gradual change in position (or bias) reported by the tracker over time.
6. Latency: The amount of delay between when the tracked object moves and when the data corresponding to the movement is transmitted.
7. Update Rate: The number of measurements that the tracker makes each second. This number may decrease as additional objects are tracked.
8. Range: In principle, the maximum distance that a single object can be tracked. To increase the range, additional sensors may be required.
9. Maximum Tracked Objects: The maximum number of objects that can be tracked simultaneously.
10. Operating Principle: Does the application environment enable the choice of tracking technology? For example, a magnetic tracker should not be used near a generator.
11. Untethered Operation: Can the tracked objects move freely or are they constrained by a wire, connector, and so forth?
12. Price.

In Figure 1.1, a table comparing many of these factors for the preceding tracking systems is presented. While this table is a starting point for investigations or discussions in choosing a tracking system, the reader is cautioned to

	Producer	DOF*	Accuracy (cm)*	Resolution (cm)*	Latency (ms)	Update Rate (Hz)	Range (m²)**	Expandable Range **	Max Tracked Objects ***	Operating Principle ****	Untethered Operation *****	Price ******
Microscribe G2LX	Immersion	3(pos)	0.03				2.2	No	1	Me	No	$7,990.00
Fusion FaroArm (8ft)	Faro Technologies	3(pos)	0.006				18	No	1	Me	No	$40,000.00
Shapetape (96 cm)	Measureand	6		0.03			4.7	No	1	Me	No	$6,505.00
Cyberglove (22 sensors)	Immersion	3(rot)	0.5 deg			110	263	No	1	Me	Yes	$16,700.00
X-IST DataGlove HR Wireless (21 Sensors)	No DNA	3(rot)				150	60	No	1	Me	Yes	$4,935.00
Gypsy 6	Animazoo	3(rot)	0.12 deg			120	31000	No	1	Me	Yes	$27,000.00
Shapewrap III Plus	Measureand	6				90	7835	No	1	Me	Yes	$32,605.00
Inertia Cube 3 Wireless	Intersense	3(rot)	0.25 deg	0.03 deg		180	2827	No	1	I	Yes	$3,495.00
3D Bird	Ascension	3(rot)	2.5 deg		6	160	64	No	1	I	No	$1,495.00
MTx	Xsens	3(rot)	0.5 deg	0.05 deg	15	512	79	No	1	I	Yes	$2,935.00
HX-11	Hexamite	3(pos)	2			40	20	Yes	30	A	No	$2,500.00
Fastrak	Polhemus	6	0.07	0.0005	4	120	7	Yes	4	Ma	Yes	$8,510.00
Patriot Wireless (2 Receptors)	Polhemus	6	0.76	0.038	20	50	167	Yes	4	Ma	Yes	$8,495.00
Flock of Birds	Ascension	6	0.18	0.05	10	144	29	Yes	4	Ma	No	$53,000.00
HiBall 3100	3rd Tech	6	0.04	0.02	1	2000	37	Yes	4	O	Yes	$197,330.00
MX (8 Cameras)	Vicon	6	0.1	0.04		240		Yes		O	Yes	
DynaSight	Origin Instruments	6	0.8		28	65		No		O	Yes	
ProReflex MCU 1200	Qualisys	6		0.005		1000	4900	Yes		O	Yes	$5,000.00
Eagle	Motion Analysis	6				500		Yes		O	Yes	$29,950.00
OptiTrack Foundation Package	NaturalPoint	6	0.05		10	100	144	Yes		O	Yes	$80,000.00
Impulse	PhaseSpace	6			10	480		Yes		O	Yes	$19,745.00
Certus	Northern Digital	6	0.015	0.001	11.3	4622	15	Yes		O	Yes	$34,000.00
LaserBird	Ascension	6	0.07	0.01		240	17	No		O	No	$19,000.00
PPT H (8 cameras)	WorldViz	6	0.25	0.025	20	175	2500	Yes	32	O	Yes	
PPT X (8 cameras)	WorldViz	6	0.5	0.1	18	60	100	Yes	8	O	Yes	
DMAS-6	Motion Imaging Corp	6			8.33	120		No	1	O	Yes	
Ubisense	Ubisense	3(pos)	15			39	400	Yes	1000	RF	Yes	$34,535.00
IS-900 VET	Intersense	6	0.3	0.075	4	180	140	Yes	4	H	Yes	$46,900.00
IS-1200	Intersense	6	0.5			180	15000	Yes	1	H	Yes	$10,000.00
HyBird	Ascension	6	0.07	0.01	8	75	28	No	1	H	No	$21,995.00

Figure 1.1. Comparison of Commercial Off-the-Shelf Tracking Systems

consider the issues presented in the "Fundamental Usage Issues" section of this chapter.

Interfacing with the Tracker

A final aspect to consider is the challenge of interfacing hardware and software for communication with the tracking system. Many tracking systems ship with DB-9 or DB-25 connectors for RS-232 serial data communications. The advantages of serial communication are fewer wires, longer cables, and a well-known standard. The main disadvantage is that all data must be converted into a serial format, transmitted, and then converted back from the serial format (which may differ between operating systems).

If the tracker uses a serial connection, fewer interface issues will arise if it is connected to a computer with a serial port on the motherboard. If a computer with a serial port is unavailable (as is the case with most laptops), a serial port expansion card can be added or a USB-to-serial converter can be used (USB = universal serial bus). USB-to-serial converters are inexpensive and do not require the addition of internal electronics, but they may pose problems communicating with the tracker.

The environment where the tracker will be used must also be considered when choosing the software interface. A sample application is included with the tracking system to allow measurement out of the box, but integration with existing applications requires more consideration. Typically, tracking systems ship with a C/C++ application programming interface for customized software integration. In addition, many tracking products also have software interfaces available in virtual world-building applications and in preexisting device interface libraries. Vizard, from WorldViz LLC (http://www.worldviz.com/), is a commercially available world-building application that is easy to learn. VR Juggler (http://www.vrjuggler.org/) is an open source software platform for virtual environment application development. At a more basic level, the Virtual Reality Peripheral Network (http://www.cs.unc.edu/Research/vrpn/) is a public domain set of libraries for distributed tracking/interface device connections that can be easily incorporated in custom applications. All three software packages contain ready-to-use interfaces for many of the tracking systems mentioned in this section and the capability to customize interfaces to accommodate other types of trackers.

FUNDAMENTAL USAGE ISSUES

For VE displays, one's overall goal is perfect, continuous registration and/or rigidity. For motion capture, one's overall goal is accuracy that is sufficient enough to do training-related behavioral analysis. In either case, tracking is hardly perfect. But it can often be made "good enough" if one chooses carefully to try and address the fundamental sources of error as much as possible.

There are several sources of error in estimates from tracking and motion capture systems. Whether looking at head tracking or hand tracking, the basic principles are the same. There are, of course, many causes of visual error in interactive computer graphics systems. There are many people who would argue that various errors originating in the tracking system dominate all other sources. In his 1995 Ph.D. dissertation analyzing the sources of error in an augmented reality (AR) system for computer-aided surgery, Rich Holloway stated,

> Clearly, the head tracker is the major cause of registration error in AR systems. The errors come as a result of errors in aligning the tracker origin with respect to the World CS [coordinate system] (which may be avoidable), measurement errors in both calibrated and multibranched trackers, and delay in propagating the information reported by the tracker through the system in a timely fashion.
>
> (Holloway, 1995, p. 135)

Holloway's dissertation offers a very thorough look at the sources of error in the entire VR pipeline, including the stages associated with tracking. It is a valuable resource for those interested in a rigorous mathematical analysis. Chapter 8 of the dissertation discusses some methods for combating the problems introduced by tracker error, in particular, delay.

For a person designing, calibrating, or using a tracking or motion capture system, it is useful to have some insight into where errors come from. As Michael Deering notes in his 1992 SIGGRAPH paper, "The visual effect of many of the errors is frustratingly similar" (Deering, 1992). This is especially true for tracking errors. We have seen people build VR applications with obvious head tracker transformation errors, and yet people had great difficulty figuring out what part of the long sequence of transforms was wrong—if it was a static calibration error, or a simple sign error.

Yet even when all of the transforms are of the correct form, the units of translation and orientation match, and all the signs are correct, there are still unavoidable errors in motion tracking, errors that confound even the most experienced of practitioners of interactive computer graphics. No matter what the approach, the process of pose estimation can be thought of as a sequence of events and operations. The sequence begins with the user motion and typically ends with a pose estimate arriving at the host computer, ready to be consumed by the application. Clearly by the time a pose estimate arrives at the host computer, it is already "late"—and you still have to render an image and wait for it to be displayed! "Motion Prediction" in the third section offers some hope for addressing the long delays and in some sense "catching up" with the user motion, but that does not mean that we do not want to minimize the delay and to understand how all of the various errors affect the outcome.

The sources of error in tracking and motion capture can generally be divided into two primary classes: *spatial* and *temporal* errors. We refer to issues and errors that arise when estimating the pose of an immobile target as *spatial issues*. (Note that spatial issues include measurement noise, which is generally a function of time, but statistically stationary.) We refer to issues and errors that arise when tracking a moving object as *temporal issues*. These issues include errors that arise from the inevitable sources of delay in the tracking pipeline (delay-induced error).

Spatial Issues

For an immobile sensor (static motion), we can further divide the measurement errors into two types: *repeatable* and *nonrepeatable*. Some trackers (for example, magnetic ones) have systematic, repeatable distortions of their measurement volume, which cause them to give erroneous data; we will call this effect static field distortion. The fact that these measurement errors are repeatable means that they can be measured and corrected as long as they remain unchanged between this calibration procedure and run time. See Livingston and State (1997) for an example of how this can be done.

One also needs to consider the *nonrepeatable* errors made by the tracker for an immobile sensor. Some amount of noise in the sensor inputs is inevitable with any measurement system, and this measurement noise typically leads to random noise or jitter in the pose estimates. By our definition, this type of error is not repeatable and therefore not correctable a priori via calibration. Moreover, jitter in the tracker's outputs limits the degree to which the tracker can be calibrated. The amount of jitter is often proportional to the distance between the sensor(s) and the source(s) and may become relatively large near the edge of the tracker's working volume.

While these effects are true for many source/sensor combinations, let us consider the effects related to image-forming digital cameras. There are two reasons we choose to look at cameras. For one, camera geometry should be relatively easy for most readers to understand. In addition, cameras are increasingly being used in tracking and motion capture systems, probably partly because of decreasing costs, increasing resolutions, and increasing image processing capabilities in computers in general (device and central processing unit bandwidth, and computation power).

Cameras effectively measure the number of photons arriving at each photo cell, over the period that the shutter is open. Those photons might have originated from an active tracking source such as a light-emitting diode, or they might originate from an ambient light source and be reflected by a passive tracking target or marker. In either case, there are two related issues that are useful to consider: the size, or cross section, of the target in the camera (the resolution of the target) and the amount of light reaching the camera (the brightness and/or contrast).

Most readers will be familiar with the notion that as a target being imaged by a camera gets farther away, its image gets smaller in the camera. Specifically, as shown in Figure 1.2, as the distance d to a target increases, the angle θ that the object spans in the camera's field of view decreases proportionally. The effect is twofold. First, the smaller the angle θ, the fewer camera pixels cover the target. Correspondingly, as the distance at which one is attempting to image a target

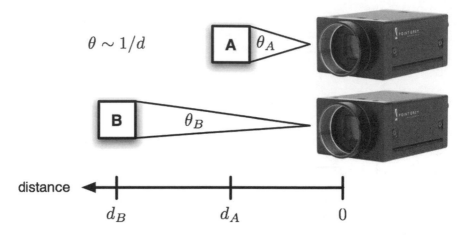

$$\theta \sim 1/d$$

distance

d_B d_A 0

Figure 1.2.   Relationship between Distance and Size of a Target as Imaged in the Camera

increases, so increases the projection or size of each pixel at that distance. In other words, as distance increases, one's ability to resolve fixed size objects in the world decreases.

While the purely geometric relationship between distance and size (or resolution) is important, in the case of cameras (and similarly for magnetic devices) one also needs to consider the decrease in light that reaches the camera with increasing distance. This affects the brightness of any light emanating from or reflected by the target, as measured by the camera. As with a camera, as the distance d to a target increases, the angle θ that the object spans in the camera's field of view decreases proportionally. However, as indicated in Figure 1.3, the brightness decreases at a rate proportional to the *square* of the distance.

This quadratic reduction is because the photons propagate away from the light source (or reflective patch) in a particular direction, covering some solid angle. For the sake of illustration, consider an omnidirectional light source, where the light propagates equally in all directions in a spherical manner. In this case, because the area of the surface of the wave front increases proportionally to the square of the distance, the density of photons on the surface of the wave front (density per surface area) decrease proportionally to the square of the distance. For a fixed size reflective patch on a tracking target for example, this means that the number of photons hitting the target decreases proportionally to the square of the distance.

Beyond distance to the target, it is usually the case that the angle between the normal direction (for example, the surface normal) of the target and the camera and/or light source plays a role in the number of photons reaching the surface or camera. Figure 1.4 provides a simple illustration of this. In some cases, for example, the brightness is proportional to cos α. In that case, if the surface is seen "straight on," then there is no attenuation of the light because cos(0) = 1. At the other extreme, if the camera is seeing the surface from an extreme angle, for

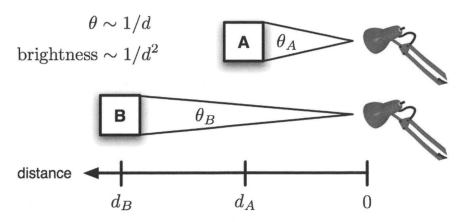

Figure 1.3. **Relationship between Distance and the Amount of Light (Brightness) Reaching a Target**

example, 90°, then there would be extreme attenuation of the light because $\cos(90°) = 0$.

Finally, one needs to consider that in a passive system, for example, vision based tracking systems with passive markers, the photons have to travel from the light source to the target as in Figure 1.3 and then from the target back to the camera (each photo cell) as in Figure 1.2. The effect is that the density of photons can, in some cases, decrease proportionally to the *square of the square* of the distance. In other words, the brightness is proportional to $1/d^4$.

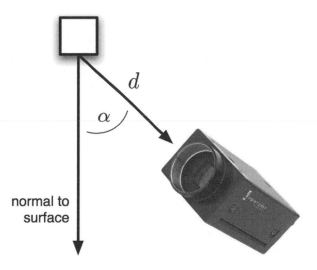

Figure 1.4. **Relationship between the Normal-Camera Angle and the Amount of Light (Brightness) Reaching a Target**

For image based systems, any reduction in brightness corresponds to a reduction in contrast (the ratio of brightest to darkest signal in the image), which corresponds to a reduction in the *effective* resolution at that distance. This effect can be illustrated or measured by the *modulation transfer function.* The shape of the modulation transfer function indicates the magnitudes of various spatial frequencies measured, compared to the spatial frequencies inherent in the scene. In general, the less light there is, the more difficult it is to resolve something. Thus the amount of light impacts the resolution of the system.

In some cases, one can precisely control the light; in others, one cannot. For example, some optical motion capture systems attempt to address modulation transfer function issues by using infrared lights that are located very near the cameras—oftentimes in a ring around each camera. If the timing of the lighting can be controlled precisely, one can "pump" a lot of photons into the scene just when the camera shutter is open, thus increasing the signal without unduly flooding the scene with infrared light.

With optical and other systems, one might also use differential signaling to improve the contrast and hence the signal-noise ratio. The idea is to take one image with the lights on (bright) and one with the lights off (dim). When one subtracts the two, the reflective objects should dominate the result, while other bright sources should be eliminated (subtracted out). There are practical limits on how much one can achieve with this approach, and there are temporal concerns as one must capture *two* sequential images to do the differencing. (The target might well be moving during the capture time!)

Temporal Issues

Beyond the spatial concerns covered in the previous section, there are several temporal concerns related to tracking. The problems include the rate at which discrete measurements are made of a moving target (any medium), the duration of each low level sample of a device (for example, how long a camera shutter is open), and the delay or latency from the time the measurement is made to the time the effect is "seen" by the remainder of the system (graphics subsystem, display, and so forth).

Delay-Induced Error

Any measurement of a nonrepeating, time-varying phenomenon is valid (at best) at the instant the sample occurs—or over the brief interval it occurs, and then becomes "stale" with the passage of time until the next measurement. The age of the data is thus one factor in its accuracy. Any delay between the time the measurement is made and the time that measurement is manifested by the system in a pose estimate contributes to the age and therefore the inaccuracy of that measurement. The older the tracker data are, the more likely that the displayed image will be misaligned with the real world.

We feel that concerns related to *dynamic error* (including *dynamic tracker error* and *delay-induced error* from above) deserve distinct discussion. This class of error is often less obvious when it occurs, and when one does recognize it, it is difficult to know where to look to minimize the effects. Further, it is literally impossible to reduce the delay to zero. One typically has to contend with overall system delays on the order of 10–100 milliseconds. See Meehan, Razzaque, Whitton, and Brooks (2003) for one example of the effects such delays can have.

First-Order Dynamic Error

Probably the most significant effect here is the overall *dynamic error* caused by continued user motion after a tracker cycle (sample, estimate, and produce) has started. If the user's head is rotating with an angular velocity of $d\,\theta/dt$ and translating with a linear velocity of dx/dt, then simple first-order models for the delay-induced orientation and translation error are given by

$$\varepsilon_{\mathrm{dyn},\theta} = \dot{\theta}\Delta t, \tag{1}$$

$$\varepsilon_{\mathrm{dyn},x} = \dot{x}\Delta t, \tag{2}$$

where Δt is the sum of the total motion delay Δt_m for the tracking system as described below, as well as Δt_g, the delay through the remainder of the graphics pipeline—including rendering and image generation, video synchronization delay, frame synchronization delay, and internal display delay. The *video synchronization delay* is the amount of time spent waiting for a frame buffer to swap—on average ½ the frame time. (*Synchronization delay* in general is described more later in the chapter.) The *internal display delay* is any delay added by the display device beyond the normal frame delay. For example, some liquid crystal display and digital light projector devices buffer images internally in a nonintuitive manner as they convert adjustable display resolution from the input to a fixed pattern of pixels on the screen, sometimes introducing several video frames of latency. The delay must be measured on a per-device basis if it is important.

Motion-Induced Measurement Noise

Clearly the placement of sources and sensors can affect the signal quality as described earlier. But there are often other *internal* (aka *intrinsic*) parameters that need to be specified. For example, for cameras one needs to specify the focus and aperture settings, gains, frame rates, and shutter/exposure times. In particular, here we want to point out the potential for motion-induced noise during a camera exposure, a magnetic current measurement, an acoustic phase measurement, and so forth. In a nutshell, just as the target motion is an issue for multiple measurements, it is often an issue for even a *single* measurement.

Without loss of generality, let us assume a regular camera update rate of $1/dt$. Each cycle can be divided into sampling (exposure) time τ_s, processing time τ_p, and idle time τ_i. The three times sum to the overall update period, that is,

$dt = \tau_s + \tau_p + \tau_i$. Because cameras integrate light over the nonzero shutter time τ_s, estimating camera motion or dynamic scene structure using feature or color matching always involves a trade-off between maximizing the *signal* and minimizing any motion-induced *noise*. If the shutter time is too short, the dynamic range or contrast in the image will be too low, reducing the *effective* resolution, increasing the measurement uncertainty, and negatively impacting the final motion or structure estimates. Conversely, if the shutter time is too long, the measurements will be corrupted by scene or camera motion (blur), again reducing the effective resolution, increasing the measurement uncertainty, and negatively impacting the final estimates. See, for example, Figure 1.5, which illustrates the amount of motion in the image planes of various cameras, under a changing scene. This issue is discussed more in Welch, Allen, Ilie, and Bishop (2007).

Sensor Sample Rate

Per Shannon's sampling theorem (Jacobs, 1993) the measurement or sampling rate r_{ss} should be at least twice the true target motion bandwidth, or an estimator may track an alias of the true motion. Given that common arm and head motion bandwidth specifications range from 2 to 20 Hz (hertz) (Fischer, Daniel, & Siva, 1990; Foxlin, 1993; Neilson, 1972), the sampling rate should ideally be greater than 40 Hz. Furthermore, the estimation rate r_e should be as high as possible so that slight (expected and acceptable) estimation error can be discriminated

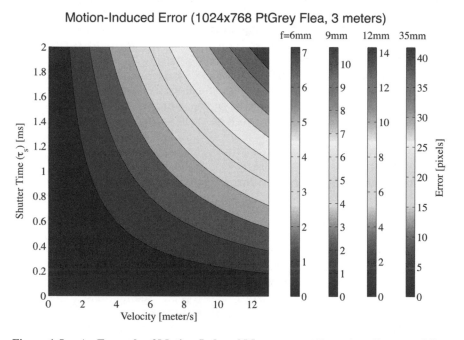

Figure 1.5.   An Example of Motion-Induced Measurement Error in a Camera while Imaging a Dynamic Environment (Moving Target or Camera)

from the unusual error that might be observed during times of significant target dynamics.

Synchronization Delay

While other latencies certainly do exist in the typical VE system (Mine, 1993; Durlach & Mavor, 1994; Wloka, 1995), tracker latency is unique in that it determines how much time elapses before the first possible opportunity to respond to user motion. When the user moves, we want to know as soon as possible. Within the tracking system pipeline of events (and throughout the rendering pipeline) there are both fixed latencies associated with well-defined tasks, such as executing functions to compute the pose, and variable latencies associated with the synchronization between well-defined asynchronous tasks. The latter is often called *synchronization delay,* although sometimes also *phase delay* or *rendezvous delay.* See, for example, Figure 1.6.

In the example of Figure 1.6, measurements and pose estimates occur at regular but *different* rates. Inevitably, any measurement will sit for some time before being used to compute a pose estimate. At best, the measurement will be read immediately *after* it is made. At worst the measurement will be read just *before* it is replaced with a newer measurement. On average, the delay would be ½ the measurement rate.

Figure 1.7 presents a more involved example, a sequence of intertracker events and the corresponding delays. Consider an instantaneous step-like user motion as depicted in Figure 1.7. The sequence of events begins at t_m, the instant the user begins to move. In this example the sensors are sampled at a regular rate $r_{ss} = 1/\tau_{ss}$, such as would typically be the case with video or a high speed analog to digital conversion. On average, there will be $\Delta\tau_{ss} = \tau_{ss}/2$ seconds of sample synchronization delay before any sample is used for pose estimation. Because the pose estimate computations are repeated asynchronously at the regular rate of $r_e = 1/\tau_e$, there will be an average of $\Delta\tau_e = \tau_e/2$ seconds of estimation synchronization delay, after which time the estimation will take τ_e seconds. Assuming a client-server architecture, such as Taylor (2006), the final estimate will be written

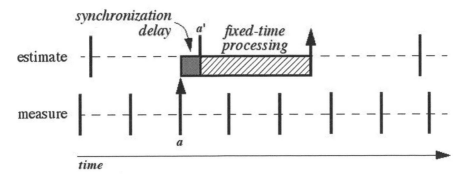

Figure 1.6. When a measurement is taken at time *a*, but not used to estimate the pose until time, the intervening time is called *synchronization delay.*

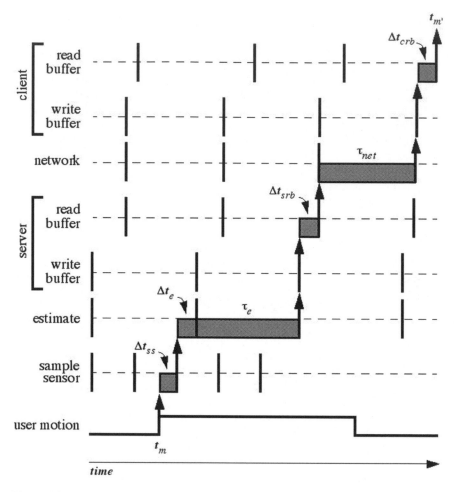

Figure 1.7.   An Example Sequence of Total Tracker-Related Events and Delays

to a server communications buffer where it is being read at a rate of $r_{srb} = 1/\tau_{srb}$ and will therefore wait an average of $\Delta\tau_{srb} = \tau_{srb}/2$ seconds before being read and transmitted over the network to the client. The network transmission itself will take τ_{net}, and the final client read-buffer synchronization delay will take $\Delta\tau_{crb} = \tau_{crb}/2$ seconds, where $\tau_{crb} = 1/r_{crb}$ (the client read-buffer rate). The total (average) motion delay in this example is then

$$
\begin{aligned}
\Delta t_m &= t_{m'} - t_m \\
&= \Delta t_{ss} + \Delta t_e + \tau_e + \Delta t_{srb} + \tau_{net} + \Delta t_{crb} \\
&= \frac{1}{2r_{ss}} + \frac{1}{2r_e} + \tau_e + \frac{1}{2r_{srb}} + \tau_{net} + \frac{1}{2r_{crb}},
\end{aligned}
\tag{3}
$$

where r_{ss} is the sensor sample rate, r_e is the estimate rate, $\tau_e = 1/r_e$, r_{srb} is the server read-buffer rate, τ_{net} is the network transmission time, and r_{crb} is the client read-buffer rate.

Note that this bound does not include any latency inherently added by pose estimate computations that also implement some form of filtering.

Total Tracker Error

Summing the *static measurement error* and the dynamic error, we get a total error of

$$\varepsilon_\theta \;\approx\; \varepsilon_{\text{stat},\theta} + \varepsilon_{\text{sa},\theta} + \dot{\theta}(\Delta t_m + \Delta t_g), \tag{4}$$

$$\varepsilon_x \;\approx\; \varepsilon_{\text{stat},x} + \varepsilon_{\text{sa},x} + \dot{x}(\Delta t_m + \Delta t_g), \tag{5}$$

where Δt_m is from Equation (3) and includes the remainder of the graphics pipeline delay as described in "First-Order Dynamic Error" in the third section. Clearly the final rotation and translation error is sensitive to both the user motion velocity and the total delay of the tracker and graphics pipeline.

Motion Prediction

When trackers are used to implement VE or AR systems, end-to-end delays of the total system will result in a perceived "swimming" of the virtual world whenever the user's head moves. The delay causes the virtual objects to appear to follow the user's head motion with a velocity-dependent error. The sequence of events in a head-mounted display system goes something like that shown in Figure 1.8.

The interval from t_0 to t_5 is on the order of 30 milliseconds in the fastest systems and upward to 200 milliseconds in the slowest. If the user is moving during this interval the image finally displayed at t_5 will not be appropriate for the user's new position. We are displaying images appropriate for where the user *was* rather than for where he or she *is*.

Time	Event
t_0	tracker measures user's pose
t_1	tracker reports the pose
t_2	application receives the reported pose
t_3	updated image is ready in the hidden buffer of a double-buffered display
t_4	buffer swap happens at vertical interval
t_5	image is scanned out to the display

Figure 1.8.   Time Series of Events in a Head-Mounted Display System

The most important step in combating this swimming is to reduce the end-to-end delay. This process can be taken only so far though. Each of the steps takes *some* time, and this time is not likely to be reduced to a negligible amount simply by accelerating the hardware.

After the avoidable delays have been eliminated, one can attempt to mitigate the effect of the unavoidable delays by using *motion prediction*. The goal is to extrapolate the user's past motion to predict where he or she will be looking at the time the new image is ready. As Azuma and Bishop (1995) point out, this is akin to driving a car by looking only at the rearview mirror. To keep the car on the road, the driver must predict where the road will go based solely on the view of the past and knowledge of roads in general. The difficulty of this task depends on how fast the car is going and on the shape of the road. If the road is straight and remains so, then the task is easy. If the road twists and turns unpredictably, the task will be impossible.

Motion predictors attempt to extract information from past measurements to predict future measurements. Most methods, at their core, attempt to estimate the local derivatives so that a Taylor series can be evaluated to estimate the future value. Several available commercial systems offer or support motion prediction. The differences among methods are mostly in the type and amount of smoothing applied to the data in estimating the derivatives.

The simplest approach simply extends a line through the previous two measurements to the time of the prediction. This approach will be very sensitive to noise in the measurements. More sophisticated approaches will take weighted combinations of several previous measurements. This will reduce sensitivity to noise, but will incur a delay in responding to rapid changes. All methods based solely on past measurements of position and orientation will face a trade-off between noise and responsiveness.

Performance of the predictor can be improved considerably if direct measurements of the derivatives of motion are available from inertial sensors. As described earlier, linear accelerometers and rate gyros provide estimates of the derivatives of motion with high bandwidth and good accuracy. Direct measurements are superior to differentiating the position and orientation estimates because they are less noisy and are not delayed.

Azuma and Bishop demonstrated prediction using inertial sensors that reduced swimming in an augmented reality system by a factor of 5 to 10 with end-to-end delay of 80 ms (Azuma & Bishop, 1994). Further, Azuma and Bishop (1995) show that error in predictions based on derivatives and simple models of motion are related to the square of the product of the prediction interval and the bandwidth of the motion sequence. *Doubling* the prediction interval for the same sort in input will *quadruple* the error.

LOOKING AHEAD

Given the rapid pace of technology advances, and active work in the fields, we expect that by the time this book is in print, some of the information will be outdated. This aging process will continue, as is the case with almost any technology-related book. This is one reason we have attempted to wrap discussion of today's technologies in the context of the fundamental circumstances and issues that are likely to continue to be relevant for the foreseeable future.

Any attempt to look ahead into the future faces even more difficult challenges. And yet we want to attempt to share with the reader what appears to be some emerging trends and potential opportunities. Our hope is that the combination of the previous material and this brief speculation will combine to help make the reader a better consumer of the available technologies, and perhaps a better tracking systems engineer when needed.

We would claim that many of the fundamental challenges related to head and hand tracking *indoors* for one or two users have been addressed to a point where very interesting VR work is being done without major issues related to tracking. It is arguably not the dominant problem it once was for circumstances involving only a *few* people. The dominant research challenges are largely related to the competing desires for increased performance and reduced infrastructure. These challenges continue to be tackled in corporate and university labs.

However, there remains the significant challenge of real time, online head, hand, and full-body tracking for *teams* of individuals, as might arise in team training applications. The major issue is that of the sociability of the current approaches, as defined in Meyer et al. (1992). As far as we know, all current commercial and research systems will begin to run into problems with more than a few colocated collaborating trainees. The issues include source or sensor bandwidth (cannot flash or image fast enough), processing speeds, signal synchronization, and signal interference between/by nearby users. In fact, we think there exists an interesting conflict between team training desires and the sociability shortcomings of today's centralized tracking systems: as trainees get closer to each other, the tracking information will likely become more critical, and yet that is precisely when the likelihood of interference from each other increases. It seems that to accommodate teams of colocated collaborating trainees researchers might have to rethink the entire single-user centralized approach.

Perhaps the most exciting (to us) area of ongoing research related to tracking for training in virtual environments is related to tracking *outdoors,* as would be needed for military training exercises, for example. The excitement in this area comes in two forms. First is the growing crossover between the computer graphics and computer vision communities. Some examples include work by Tobias Höllerer et al. at the University of California at Santa Barbara, Ulrich Neumann et al. at the University of Southern California, and Didier Stricker et al. at Fraunhofer-Gesellschaft. With simultaneous ongoing advances in computer vision algorithms and cameras, this synergy promises to provide some exciting capabilities in the not-so-distant future.

On the topic of cameras, the second form of excitement related to tracking outdoors is in the continually improving technologies that can be used outdoors. This includes rapid improvements to cameras, shrinking and more stable inertial sensors, and improved GPS, including differential signaling and pseudolites.

Happily, these improvements continue to be spurred on by other commercial demands.

On a final note, we think that perhaps acoustic/audio sensors are currently undervalued and might find new favor in addressing both team-training needs and outdoor tracking. (The InterSense acoustic hybrids are one shining counter-example.) With respect to team training, small acoustic devices could provide a complementary absolute reference for inertial sensors in a body-relative tracking scheme. The work by Vlasic et al. (2007) is a good example of this. With respect to tracking outdoors, we find it interesting that blind people use internalized models of environmental noise as an absolute reference for estimating their location. This includes sounds from traffic indicating the road and sounds from air conditioning units indicating a building. Just as researchers have realized that the human combination of vision and inertial (vestibular) sensing is valuable, we might also recognize the added value of environmental sounds as yet another source of absolute geospatial references.

REFERENCES

Allen, B. D., Bishop, G., & Welch, G. (2001). Tracking: Beyond 15 minutes of thought [SIGGRAPH 2001 Course 11]. In *Computer Graphics, Annual Conference on Computer Graphics & Interactive Techniques* (SIGGRAPH 2001 course pack edition). Los Angeles: ACM Press.

Atkeson, C. G., & Hollerbach, J. M. (1985). Kinematic features of unrestrained vertical arm movements. *Journal of Neuroscience, 5*(9), 2318–2330.

Azuma, R. T. (1993). Tracking requirements for augmented reality. *Communications of the ACM, 36*(7), 50–51.

Azuma, R. T., & Bishop, G. (1994). Improving static and dynamic registration in an optical see-through hmd. In *Computer Graphics, Annual Conference on Computer Graphics & Interactive Techniques* (pp. 197–204). Los Angeles: ACM Press.

Azuma, R. T., & Bishop, G. (1995). A frequency-domain analysis of head-motion prediction. In *Computer Graphics, Annual Conference on Computer Graphics & Interactive Techniques* (pp. 401–408). Los Angeles: ACM Press.

Bhatnagar, D. K. (1993). *Position trackers for head mounted display systems: A survey* (Tech. Rep. No. TR93-010). Chapel Hill: University of North Carolina at Chapel Hill.

Deering, M. (1992). High resolution virtual reality. In *SIGGRAPH '92: Proceedings of the 19th Annual Conference on Computer Graphics and Interactive Techniques* (pp. 195–202). New York: ACM.

Durlach, N. I., & Mavor, A. S. (Eds.). (1994). *National research council report on virtual reality: Scientific and technological challenges.* Washington, DC: National Academy Press.

Ferrin, F. J. (1991). Survey of helmet tracking technologies. *Proceedings of SPIE, 1456,* 86–94.

Fischer, P., Daniel, R., & Siva, K. (1990). Specification and design of input devices for teleoperation. *Proceedings of the IEEE Conference on Robotics and Automation* (pp. 540–545). Cincinnati, OH: IEEE Computer Society Press.

Foxlin, E. (1993). *Inertial head-tracking.* Unpublished master's thesis, Massachusetts Institute of Technology, Cambridge.

Foxlin, E. (2002). Motion tracking requirements and technologies. In K. Stanney, (Ed.), *Handbook of virtual environments: Design, implementation, and application* (pp. 163–210). Mahwah, NJ: Lawrence Erlbaum.

Gabbard, J. L., & Hix, D. (1997). *A taxonomy of usability characteristics in virtual environments* (Office of Naval Research Tech. Rep. Grant No. N00014-96-1-0385). Blacksburg: Virginia Polytechnic Institute and State University. Retrieved April 22, 2008, from http://people.cs.vt.edu/~jgabbard/publications/index.html

Holloway, R. L. (1995). *Registration errors in augmented reality systems.* Unpublished doctoral dissertation, University of North Carolina at Chapel Hill.

Jacobs, O. (1993). *Introduction to control theory* (2nd ed.). Oxford, England: Oxford University Press.

Livingston, M. A., & State, A. (1997). Magnetic tracker calibration for improved augmented reality registration. *Presence: Teleoperators and Virtual Environments, 6*(5), 532–546.

Meehan, M., Razzaque, S., Whitton, M. C., & Brooks, F. P. (2003). Effect of latency on presence in stressful virtual environments. *Proceedings of the IEEE Virtual Reality* (p. 141). Washington, DC: IEEE Computer Society.

Meyer, K., Applewhite, H., & Biocca, F. (1992). A survey of position trackers. *Presence, A publication of the Center for Research in Journalism and Mass Communication, 1* (2), 173–200.

Mine, M. R. (1993). *Characterization of end-to-end delays in head-mounted display systems* (Tech. Rep. No. TR93-001). Chapel Hill: University of North Carolina at Chapel Hill.

Neilson, P. (1972). Speed of response or bandwidth of voluntary system controlling elbow position in intact man. *Medical and Biological Engineering, 10*(4), 450–459.

Stanney, K. M., editor (2002). *Handbook of virtual environments: Design, implementation, and applications.* Mahwah, NJ: Lawrence Erlbaum.

Taylor, R. (2006). *Virtual reality peripheral network.* Retrieved April 22, 2008, from http://www.cs.unc.edu/Research/vrpn

Vlasic, D., Adelsberger, R., Vannucci, G., Barnwell, J., Gross, M., Matusik, W., & Popović, J. (2007). Practical motion capture in everyday surroundings. In *SIGGRAPH '07: ACM SIGGRAPH 2007* (p. 35). New York: ACM.

Welch, G. (1995). A survey of power management techniques in mobile computing operating systems. *ACM Operating Systems Review (SIGOPS-OSR), 29*(4), 47–56.

Welch, G. (1996). *SCAAT: Incremental tracking with incomplete information.* Unpublished master's thesis, University of North Carolina at Chapel Hill.

Welch, G., Allen, B. D., Ilie, A., & Bishop, G. (2007). Measurement sample time optimization for human motion tracking/capture systems. In G. Zachmann, (Ed.), *Proceedings of the IEEE VR 2007 Workshop on Trends and Issues in Tracking for Virtual Environments.* Aachen, Germany: Shaker Verlag.

Welch, G., & Foxlin, E. (2002). Motion tracking: No silver bullet, but a respectable arsenal. *IEEE Computer Graphics Applications, 22*(6), 24–38.

Wloka, M. M. (1995). Lag in multiprocessor virtual-reality. *Presence: Teleoperators and Virtual Environments, 4*(1), 50–63.

Chapter 2

VISUAL DISPLAYS: HEAD-MOUNTED DISPLAYS

Mark Bolas and Ian McDowall

Head-mounted displays (HMDs) came from the future—devices to envelop our eyes and ears and cloister us from the real world while immersing us in computer-generated fantasies limited only by our ability to algorithmically create them.

Looking back 40 years to Ivan Sutherland's (1963) "Sketchpad," it is easy to see that HMDs quickly progressed from science fiction to delivering grounded results. Systems are now used to visualize the placement of instruments in automobile interiors, to decide where to sink the next oil well, and to train personnel in virtual scenarios too dangerous for actual practice.

It is sometimes difficult, however, to separate the promise of these devices from the reality of their performance—especially when considering training applications that must accurately represent specific and well-defined environments. What makes this particularly vexing is that, while technical specifications can easily be compiled, it is difficult to understand the usefulness of these specifications with respect to a training system's effectiveness. Some specifications just do not matter, while others create artifacts that, while hard to predict, can make or break a system.

This chapter attempts to increase the decision maker's understanding by interpreting the user's experience of HMD technologies. It gives an overview of the physical, cognitive, and perceptual ramifications of common HMD choices and describes current design and technology examples. Readers interested in more detailed information are encouraged to look at *Head Mounted Displays: Designing for the User* by James E. Melzer and Kirk Moffitt (1997).

WHY CHOOSE AN HMD?

When creating display systems for immersive training applications, it is useful to think of an HMD as mapping pixels from its microdisplays out into a hypothetical three-dimensional virtual environment. For example, if the goal is to train a user how to fix an engine, then the pixels would best be placed in a manner representing an engine—a few feet away from a user and concentrated in a small area. If, however, the goal is to familiarize a user with a dense urban area, then the pixels would need to panoramically span a virtual area the size of a few city blocks. For a screen based display, the engine application might use a single large stereoscopic screen placed in front of the user, while the city would require a large multiscreen panoramic configuration.

This model of mapping pixels to a virtual environment's objects can be used to consider characteristics unique to HMDs when evaluating display systems for the following specific training tasks:

Flexible—As the above two examples highlight, the physical topology and required distribution of mapped pixels in a virtual space can vary greatly between different applications. HMDs can easily accommodate a range of training scenarios because they are available with a wide range of resolutions and fields of view. These choices allow the designer to tailor the display for the application at hand and to modify such choices to follow the demands of evolving system requirements.

Efficient—Because HMDs use head tracking to display imagery from the user's current point of view, they make the most out of every pixel they are fed. In contrast, a screen based system must render and display pixels everywhere, even if the user is not looking in that direction. Since the displays travel with the user's head, HMDs carry pixels to where they are needed, effectively multiplying resolution. For example, a single $1,280 \times 1,024$ HMD with a 60 degree field of view will fill a 360 degree virtual sphere six times over, thus effectively providing $7,680 \times 6,144$ accessible pixels over the sphere. Not only does this make efficient use of the displays, but it allows a single rendered viewpoint to provide imagery that normally would require six viewpoints.

Deployable—By decreasing the rendering requirements, HMDs can often be driven by a single laptop computer. This means an HMD, rendering computer, and head tracking system can fit in a single briefcase. In addition to simplifying maintenance and spares, many HMDs are designed to operate with no need for alignment and calibration—they can be easily carried to a location, turned on, and made ready to go.

Potent—By occluding the user from the real world and substituting a virtual world, HMDs exhibit a type of "perceptual potency" that is hard to duplicate with any other technology. In many virtual environment configurations, users can see their own body, physical details of the display system, and portions of the surrounding environment. While useful for some applications, such real world cues can detract from fully transporting a user to a virtual world. HMDs are often configured to completely cloister a user—to algorithmically control everything the user sees and hears.

This potency comes with a corresponding demand—the complete system must accurately portray the virtual environment and keep pace with a user's motion and expectations. For example, poor tracking and slow update rates cannot be tolerated as they degrade cues important for maintaining a sense of balance.

Such potency can be useful in scenarios developed to elicit strong responses. A classic example is found in experiments incorporating a virtual "pit room" that appears to the user as a ledge above a 20 foot virtual drop to a room below. Most users experience a strong sense of physical danger when observing the virtual pit from their apparently precarious standpoint on the ledge (Meehan, Insko, Whitton, & Brooks, 2002).

Accurate—User-specific imagery needs to be generated for every head position in a virtual environment because each user must see the scene rendered exactly from his or her perspective or the synthetic images will not match the user's movements. Such a mismatch can result in inaccurate and possibly misleading imagery. Screen based displays can easily accommodate a single head-tracked user, but multiple users pose problems due to the fact that participants in these systems are all looking at the same physical screens (Agrawala et al., 1997). HMDs have the luxury of providing each user with a personal display, each tracked to account for an individual's head position and orientation. As such, HMDs allow all participants in a training environment to be surrounded by accurate, perspective-correct imagery.

Observable—Because HMDs are tracked, they can easily be used to observe where the user is facing in an environment. For example, DaimlerChrysler Motors Company LLC employed a mechanically tracked HMD to enable ergonomic studies of proposed designs for automotive interiors. By being able to observe the view as seen by different-sized drivers, engineers were able to determine optimal sight lines and component placement (Brooks, 1999). This is particularly interesting in training applications that require a correlation between trainees' actions, their orientation, and what they actually see.

Available—The rising demand for consumer-grade digital entertainment technologies has led to the development of components that HMD based training systems have used to move beyond fiction into useful tools. Graphics technologies for video games have led to easier and lower cost modeling and rendering of synthetic worlds. The digital production of movies has led to the development of high performance motion-capture and tracking systems. The home-theater display market has created high resolution microdisplays that can be repurposed for HMDs. As such, tracking, rendering, and displays have reached a critical price-performance ratio that now enables HMDs to be cost-effectively applied to a number of new applications (Brooks, 1999).

HMD DESIGN CHARACTERISTICS

When matching HMDs to specific training tasks, it is instructive to recognize that HMDs are intimate interface devices—almost like pieces of clothing—and that there is a wide variety of design choices affecting function and comfort that can best be judged by simply trying the HMD on and looking around. Just as soldiers should "train as they fight," HMDs should be evaluated "as they will train." If this firsthand experimentation is done in a perceptually engaged and critical manner, decision makers can avoid prejudgments. It is easy to allow data sheets and specifications to cloud one's judgment and accept defects that are the result of poor design trade-offs or a limited range of adjustment. It cannot be overstated that while there are some stunningly good HMDs available, there are also stunningly bad ones as well. Toward this end, it is useful to consider the interplay between design choices and their optical, physical, and cognitive effects.

Overview of Visual Issues and Terms

Functionally, HMDs are similar to looking at a small display with a magnifying glass and then holding the display and magnifier up to the eye. The magnifier enables the user to focus on the display as it is brought closer to the eye. The closer to the eye it gets, the larger the image appears because it replaces more of the real world with the image from the display.

As such, the optical goal of an HMD is to make a small display appear large (*optical magnification*) and to subtend a large portion of a user's view (*field of view*). This is typically accomplished by either employing optics similar to a magnifying glass (*simple magnifier*) or a microscope (*compound optics*).

A quick feeling for the visual issues associated with HMDs can be had by considering a pair of binoculars. Binoculars must be held a certain distance away from the user's eyes (*eye relief*) and adjusted to align with the distance between the eyes (*interpupillary distance or IPD*). This alignment places the user's pupils within the small region in front of the lens, which provides a clear view of the magnified image (*eye box or exit pupil*). The lenses are then focused to place the magnified image at a virtual distance in front of the user (*focal plane*) that both eyes can focus upon (*accommodate*) and allow the eyes to triangulate (*converge*) on objects to form a stereoscopic view. Some binoculars, especially lower cost ones, will exhibit visual artifacts or *optical aberrations*. In HMDs, these artifacts include a rainbow effect (*chromatic aberration*), many types of blur (*spherical aberration, coma, astigmatism,* and *field curvature*), and warped appearance (*geometric distortion*). Readers interested in a classic text on optics design are encouraged to look at Warren J. Smith's (2000) *Modern Optical Engineering*. An excellent overview of HMD designs is presented in *Head-Worn Displays: A Review* by Cakmakci and Rolland (2006).

Exit Pupil (Eye Box)

Compound optics form a relatively small region called the exit pupil, which can be thought of as a small hole that is located slightly in front of the eyepiece. When the eye's pupil is aligned with the exit pupil, a clear image is seen. If the eye's pupil moves out of this region, light from the display becomes occluded: a portion of the image goes dark and often exhibits a characteristic kidney bean shape. The size of the exit pupil is constrained by the physics of the optical system. Small exit pupils generally allow for more aggressive optical designs, but are undesirable as they require careful alignment of the HMD with respect to a user's eyes.

Alternatively, simple magnifying optics are classified as nonpupil forming and deliver a comparatively large region where the eye will see a sharp magnified image from the display—similar to looking through a magnifying glass. Although simple magnifier designs have an ideal position for the user's eye (it lies along the optical axis of the eyepiece), the less ideal positions result in a slight blurring of the image that does not go dark and tends to degrade more gracefully than those of pupil-forming systems. Simple magnifiers, however, often require the use of larger optical components and displays.

On some HMDs with small exit pupils, the user will see a good image while looking forward, but a glance to the side will make the image go dark. The eye's pupil is located toward the surface of the eyeball, so a rotation of the eye causes the pupil to translate away from the exit pupil of the optics because the eye's center of rotation is located behind the pupil. It is important to pay attention to this on wide field of view (FOV) HMDs that claim a field of view that is mathematically correct but impossible to achieve by some users when they actually look toward the edges of a scene.

Interpupillary Distance Adjustment

Narrow exit pupils often require the left and right display optics to be closely aligned with the user's left and right eyes. Such an adjustment feature is often desired for compound optical systems. Typically, the IPD range for HMDs is specified as the total IPD, and HMDs may either adjust each display or the total IPD. IPDs vary across the population and generally range from 53 millimeter (mm) to 73 mm with an average of 63 mm (Kalawsky, 1993).

Should IPD adjustment be possible, care must be taken to reset it for each participant; otherwise the situation can be made worse due to the wide range of IPDs. A test pattern displayed on the HMD can be used to set the IPD; however, some users find it confusing so it may be advantageous to numerically set the IPD before the user puts on the HMD. In this case, an interpupilometer (a common piece of ophthalmic equipment) may be used to accurately measure the user's IPD without requiring the user's judgment. Most software used to render virtual imagery assumes an average IPD of 65 mm; ideally, however, it should incorporate specific users' IPDs as well. Simple magnifier systems can be designed to enable a wide range of IPDs with minimal image degradation, and some can be used without the need for IPD adjustments.

Accommodation and Convergence

When the eyes fixate on an object, a number of physiological actions occur. The two primary actions are the physical focusing of the eyes' lenses to accommodate the object and the action of differentially rotating each eye to converge on the object. The rendering of the virtual environment considers the slight viewpoint differences between a user's two eyes and draws near-field imagery with an offset between the left and right eyes. When viewing this pair of images, the user's eyes must rotate by different amounts based on how close each virtual object is—an object at infinity requires no convergence, while an extremely close object requires "crossed eyes." The stereoscopic nature of an HMD is derived from this effect.

HMDs magnify a microdisplay, thus fixing the focal depth of the pixels. As such, the distance at which the user's eyes accommodate when looking at a virtual object cannot be adjusted by the computer to correspond to its virtual distance. This creates a mismatch between the convergence cues that are rendered correctly and the accommodation (focus) cues that are fixed by the HMD optics.

This is a current limitation of commercially available HMDs and an area of active research (Akeley, Watt, Girshick, & Banks, 2004; Rolland, Krueger, & Goon, 2000). Screen based displays share this characteristic—the user accommodates on the surface of the screen, while trying to converge at the distance of the virtual objects. Some HMDs may be focused at different fixed depths and thereby be optimized for near-field or far-field training tasks.

Field of View

A user's natural FOV is constrained by the shape of the skull and the eye socket, with the nose blocking the central portion. This can be seen by closing one eye and looking around the periphery. For most people, the FOV of each eye is 120° vertical and 150° horizontal. The combined field from both eyes is 200° with a 100° *binocular overlap* region that provides stereoscopic cues (Velger, 1998). These metrics vary significantly based on face geometry, age, and eye characteristics.

For a given lens diameter, the closer the lens is to the eye, the larger the potential field of view. This can be observed by moving one's palm nearer to and away from the face. Assuming one could focus on the palm, it is clear that it needs to be touching the face to come close to subtending the full field of view of one's eye. Very wide FOV HMDs are constrained practically by the diameter of the optics and how close a user's eyes can be to the eyepiece.

The left and right eye images of many narrow FOV displays present to exactly the same region of a user's FOV. This arrangement is said to be 100 percent overlapped, and, except for differences due to stereo parallax, the images for each eye appear to be superimposed on each other. One approach to achieving a larger total field of view is to not fully overlap the images. This provides a central region with stereoscopic imagery, and peripheral regions without stereoscopic imagery. Wide FOV designs tend toward this arrangement, which is appropriate given its match with the human visual system and facial geometry.

Wide Fields of View

Narrow FOVs appear to force unnatural head and body movements while also limiting the natural motion of the eye. This need to move the head and body to explore a scene can be demonstrated by curling the fingers and touching the index and ring fingers to the thumb on both hands to create two cylinders. Holding the hands up to the face like a pair of virtual binoculars creates a resulting FOV approximating 45° per eye.

Tasks such as walking are possible with narrow displays, however, performance is greatly improved with a wider field of view display (Arthur, 2000). Melzer and Moffitt (1997) present a summary of papers that generally indicates that wider FOVs result in better performance for tasks requiring ego orientation, locomotion, and reaching, including orientation and navigation within an environment. A wide FOV also appears to be instrumental in establishing situational awareness. Melzer and Moffitt found that it helps "the user to establish visual position constancy and to understand events that occur over a panoramic visual field" (p. 224, per Wallach and Bacon, 1976).

Optical Artifacts

The art of optical design involves balancing such issues as cost and exit-pupil size with such visual artifacts as aberration and distortion. The question is not whether such artifacts are present, but whether the magnitude is great enough to detract from the goals of the training application. It is often the case that slight yet noticeable optical artifacts are unimportant, while features such as a light system weight or a wide FOV are mandatory.

Chromatic aberrations are caused by the dispersion of light through optical materials. They are particularly noticeable with thick or plastic lenses and are usually seen as a rainbow effect around the edges of the image. While these could be reduced with software techniques, they are not of primary concern with most modern HMDs. Geometric distortions are a warping of the image and can take many forms, including an outward warp called pincushion distortion or an inward warp called barrel distortion. These can be reduced through computation (Robinett & Rolland, 1992). Such correction is now being integrated directly into some HMD electronics or may be implemented as part of the software application. It is not easy to correct for the many types of optical blur that are inherently linked with the quality of an optical system's design. It is a multidimensional issue that can take many forms and is difficult to understand intuitively. As such it is best qualified through personal observation rather than solely through numerical specification.

Of particular concern are artifacts that cause visual discomfort. Most important among these are artifacts that cause incorrect imagery in the region of binocular overlap. These cause the eyes to strain as they attempt to correlate imagery seen by the left and right eyes. While such effects can be the result of poor optics, they are often caused by a physical misalignment that occurs over time and must be monitored by the system operator. Additionally, rendering software must be tested for accuracy in this regard. Misaligned imagery—including swapping eyes—is a common source of discomfort that lies with the software and complete system, not the HMD.

Resolution

Although the resolution of HMDs is most often described like a standard computer monitor (total number of horizontal and vertical pixels), the resolution of an HMD is best considered by the angle subtended by a given pixel, typically measured in minutes of arc and called the *angular resolution*. Values below three or four arc minutes per pixel begin to appear relatively crisp with human vision capable of better than one arc minute (National Research Council, 1997).

For a given display resolution, a narrow FOV HMD will create better angular resolution as it concentrates pixels in a smaller angle. In this way, a wide FOV will degrade the angular resolution. This can be mitigated with optical designs that create variable angular resolution across the field of view—the central region having better resolution than the periphery.

Optical artifacts, such as blur, can decrease the effective resolution. As such, a single-number specification for resolution should be but one of the metrics used when considering HMDs.

Weight

Specifying weight is similar to resolution: while lighter is obviously better, it is only one measure of how useful an HMD will be in practice. It must be balanced against the often competing physical characteristics of balance, rotational inertia, fit, and form.

Balance affects the downward rotational force placed on the neck. A 500 gram HMD with all the weight in the front will be more uncomfortable than a well-balanced 1,000 gram design. There are many approaches to counterbalancing an HMD that range from simply adding weight at the rear to complex optical configurations that fold the optical path around the head to locate mass away from the face, moving it backward and toward the sides of the head. Unfortunately, moving weight in this manner can increase rotational inertia—the amount of force a user will need to exert when quickly looking around. This is an important consideration for training applications that require rapid head motions approaching 1,000° per second squared (Bolas & Fisher, 1990).

Form

As discussed, some optical designs require that the HMD optics be well positioned relative to the wearer's eyes to within millimeters. The HMD needs to accurately hold electronics, optics, and displays, and it must adjust to fit a wide range of human heads with a firm grip that does not allow the system to slip during rapid head motions. There is a variety of mounting techniques that can best be judged by having a variety of users wear the system.

The physical form of the display needs to be considered with the target application in mind. For example, driving simulation and rifle training applications often use physical props that must be held close to the user's head. As such, the

HMD cannot extend far away from the user's face or it will interfere with a real steering wheel or gun sight.

Additional form considerations include the time it takes to fit and don an HMD, and making sure the HMD is compatible with required gear such as helmets and jackets and that it will not snag on cables or cloth. Ventilation, heat, and compatibility with the user's eyewear are additional concerns.

EXAMPLES

Optical Approaches

Wide Field of View

In 1985, NASA (National Aeronautics and Space Administration) Ames Research Center created a wide FOV HMD by integrating optics for viewing film based stereoscopic pairs (originally for the large expanse extra perspective [LEEP] wide-angle camera system) with liquid crystal display (LCD) panels that were roughly of the same size. This configuration was commercialized in the VPL Research, Inc. EyePhone, Fakespace Labs BOOM, and Howlett LEEP Video System I. Consumer-priced narrow FOV displays in the late 1990s (for example, the Sony Glasstron) turned attention away from immersive wide FOV displays toward narrow FOV designs more suitable as monitor replacements. This led to wide FOV HMD designs remaining largely static until the mid-2000s.

The recently introduced Fakespace Labs Wide5 provides a FOV exceeding 150°. A large pupil is created by incorporating modern LCD panel technologies and a single lens design. It originally was designed to provide a robust and portable virtual training system that could easily be deployed in the field for close-quarters battle training applications as part of the U.S. Navy's virtual training and environments program. To meet those requirements, it can be mounted to helmets with a standard night vision mount and incorporates a custom interface deriving stereoscopic pairs from a single digital visual interface signal available from a laptop. To increase the perceived resolution, the Wide5 has higher pixel density toward the central region.

Tiled Designs

Wide FOV HMDs can be created by tiling a number of smaller displays in a concave form in front of each eye. Tiles are composed of a display module and eyepiece optics that butt together and cover a portion of the perceived field of view. These displays generally require precise adjustment when the HMD is placed on the head to reduce visual tiling artifacts—the eyes must be aligned with each microdisplay and lens. Each microdisplay typically requires a video source, thus six displays per eye require 12 rendered viewpoints, making computing demands a significant system consideration, but also increasing resolution.

Kaiser Electro-Optics (now part of Rockwell Collins) created a display under contract to the Defense Advanced Research Projects Agency Electronic Technology Office in the 1990s incorporating a three by two matrix of displays for each eye. This display used small LCD displays driven by 12 separate graphics inputs. The resulting field of view was over 153° horizontal by 48° vertical (Arthur, 2000). Sensics Inc. has created a tiled display that uses a matrix of displays to create a wide FOV virtual image. Organic light-emitting displays (OLEDs) are used in a modular approach so the display may be configured in a variety of different ways, including a seven by three per eye arrangement of displays to provide a total of 4,200 × 2,400 pixels. In this tiled configuration, all 21 optical and display assemblies have to align with each of the user's eyes. This family of HMDs can be configured with fields of view ranging from 72° to 179° horizontal by 30° to 60° vertically.

High Resolution Inserts

The human eye has superior visual acuity in a small region known as the fovea. A few HMDs have been created that employ a wide field of view display coupled with a second display tracked to the fovea. This results in a wide FOV immersive experience, enhanced with the precision and clarity typical of narrow FOV displays. The implementation of this is complex as it requires tracking of the eye. There have been very few systems fielded using this approach. CAE created such a system used for helicopter simulation in 1981 (Velger, 1998).

Medium Field of View Displays

One of the earliest examples of an HMD used for virtual environment visualization was built in 1968 as part of Ivan Sutherland's groundbreaking work. This system used half-inch monochrome cathode ray tube (CRT) displays that provided a 40 degree field of view per eye. The image was reflected from partially silvered mirrors creating an augmented reality display system.

The Virtual Research V8 design and the NVIS, Inc. SX display are both popular displays in this range of FOV. The NVIS SX offers a horizontal field of view of 48.5° and vertical of 39.6° and uses 1,280 × 1,024 field sequential color ferroelectric liquid crystal on silicon (FLCOS) panels. The V8 uses lower resolution transmissive LCDs and has a horizontal field of view of 49° and vertical of 33°. Both weigh over two pounds. Typically, adjustment of the IPD is needed to achieve the best quality image and to reduce artifacts as the eye moves.

Rockwell Collins makes several HMDs in this FOV range. Its SIM EYE product employs a see-through optical design with the displays located to the sides of the head, and relay optics deliver the images to semitransparent eyepieces. Independent IPD adjustment is provided for each eye.

Narrow Fields of View—Personal Display Monitors

HMD with fields of view of around 25° are available at a fairly low cost. Most employ OLED or small LCD displays coupled with magnifying optics. Examples include OLED displays by eMagin Corporation and LCD based Vuzix (Icuiti) designs. Daeyang and IODisplays use liquid crystal on silicon (LCoS) displays and reflective magnifying designs. While many of these come bundled with head-tracking technologies, they are of limited utility for fully immersive training applications due to the restricted field of view. By way of example, a 25 degree FOV is equivalent to viewing a 21 inch monitor at 4 feet.

Alternative Optical Approaches

An HMD that incorporates a head-mounted projector uses a very different optical path. The projector directs an image from the user toward a retroreflective material that reflects the image back toward the user's eyes. This approach has shown promise for cockpit displays and other applications in which a type of virtual overlay can be implemented with cut sheets of retroreflective material (Fergason, 1997).

Displays that provide the user with multiple planes of focus are not yet practically deployed, but encouraging research by Akeley et al. (2004) shows that a subset of planes can be used to create a display that could alleviate some of the issues associated with the accommodation and convergence issues discussed previously.

HMDs that mix real world and virtual imagery provide many unique advantages. These are described in Henderson and Feiner, Volume 2, Section 1, Chapter 6—"Mixed and Augmented Reality for Training."

Display Technologies

The display requirements for HMDs are demanding because, ideally, they would be light and exhibit very high resolution, color depth, brightness, and contrast while using little power and creating few temporal artifacts. Naturally, achieving all these requirements simultaneously is challenging, and designers resort to the best solutions available at the time in the context of their overall system goals.

Field Sequential Liquid Crystal on Silicon Color Displays (FLCOS)

FLCOS displays reflect light, and the polarization of pixels controls brightness. These displays employ front illumination with a separate field sequential color light source. Such field sequential displays as FLCOS show a sequence of primaries for each pixel and the eye's persistence of vision integrates the sequential presentation of the colors and perceives the image in full color. Visual artifacts from field sequential color displays are generally not objectionable in narrow field of view conditions. In wide FOV HMDs, color flicker is an issue for some users as peripheral vision is more sensitive to motion and flicker.

Active-Matrix Liquid Crystal Displays (AMLCDs)

These displays are like those used in laptop screens and are typically thin-film transistor transmissive displays illuminated by a backlight. Pixels are composed of three subpixels (red, green, and blue). AMLCD displays are made by a variety of companies; Kopin Corporation makes very high resolution displays suitable for HMDs. A fast response time is needed to reduce the smearing of moving objects.

Organic Light-Emitting Displays (OLEDs)

OLEDs emit light from their surfaces, which enables both truer blacks and more compact optical designs because there is no backlight assembly. eMagin Corporation is currently the primary source for small form factor pixel-type displays. These displays are new, and improvements in lifetime, resolution, and size are expected.

Alternative Display Technologies

Several companies have made use of fiber-optic image pipes that decouple the display from the HMD. Laser based systems that project directly onto the retina will no doubt be part of the future HMD landscape. Microvision, Inc. continues to innovate with such laser based projectors. HMD designs have largely moved away from cathode ray tubes.

Mounting Approaches

Generally, a person can comfortably carry an additional 10 percent of his or her head weight for indefinite periods. As the typical head weighs approximately 10 kg, it is desirable to have an HMD that weighs less than 1 kg (kilogram). A brief overview of the numerous techniques that have been developed to mount HMDs follows.

On-Head Mounts

Spectacles—These designs are suitable for narrow field of view displays where the weight is minimal and the narrow field of view is achieved with small plastic lenses. FOV is under 30° and the weight is typically under a few ounces. The Vuzix (Icuiti) products are good examples.

Forehead Rest—HMDs like those from IODisplays and eMagin weigh around six to eight ounces and use more complex optics. The displays have a pad resting on the frontal bone and a strap around the back of the head and sometimes one over the crown of the head. The strap needs to be tight to create friction on the forehead mount, but provides purchase for the HMD.

Scuba Mask—Older systems, such as that from VPL, used heavier displays held on the face by a large contact area and a tight head strap grabbing the back of the head. This design adds a minimal amount of additional weight; however, the strap-type adjustment is inconvenient and has to be tight to hold the HMD in place. They often provide poor ventilation and can become humid.

Helmet Based—Kaiser Electro-Optics SIM EYE and L3 advanced helmet mounted displays (Sisodia et al., 2007) mount directly to a training or flight helmet; these designs permit the use of the pilot's own helmet. Typically there would be several sizes and helmet designs that need to be supported.

Head Strap—Fakespace Labs Wide5 and Virtual Research V8 incorporate a ratchet-style head strap that can be tightened to hold the HMD on securely to fit most people. This strap design does not grab the occipital so these work best with a counterweight. This design is relatively easy for the person wearing the HMD to adjust.

Exoskeletal—Disney, Kaiser Electro-Optics ProView, and other designs have employed a ridged exterior and a supple interior strap. The advantage is that the rigid exterior frame helps transfer the load of the HMD to the head strap and head in multiple places.

Webbing—SEOS Limited and others hang the HMD around the head and aim to balance the straps holding on the HMD. These designs get heavy rather quickly, are cumbersome to put on and remove, and are hard to keep accurately aligned with the eyes.

Over the Head with Rigid Frame—Sensics and Keio University Shonan Fujisawa Campus use designs that capture the occipital and leave the area near the ears unencumbered. These and other systems that are not counterweighted need to be tight in the back, and, consequently, are most easily adjusted by another person.

Counterbalanced Approaches

A number of display environments (for example, those designed for a seated user) do not require free movement while the user wears the HMD. In these situations, there may be advantages to counterbalancing the mass of the HMD with an external mechanical structure. This reduces the weight of the HMD on the user and may also afford precise tracking. Examples include the Fakespace BOOM and Disney's Aladdin ride, which used a cable system to counterbalance the displays.

CONCLUSION

To select an appropriate HMD, the decision maker will find it informative to physically try the display to fully gain an appreciation of its functionality and to spend time in the HMD, looking all around the image and questioning the effects. As discussed in this chapter, many of these effects and artifacts are quite subtle and require an engaged and observant test of the display as described here.

Step One: Don the HMD and move in a manner similar to the training application, paying attention to the effect of rapid or unusual exploratory motions. In addition to feeling for any uncomfortable physical sensations, such as looseness or offset center of mass, pay particular attention to the virtual images, looking for a bright and sharp environment across the entire field of view. An important step is to refit the helmet as often as required to optimize the experience.

Step Two: Now with the HMD properly fit, close and relax the eyes for 20 seconds, then look straight ahead for 10 seconds and roll the eyes around to explore the edges of the environment. Rotate the head and explore the environment in a manner consistent with the training application. Pay attention to optical artifacts that cause visual discomfort or that create a misleading virtual environment. It is often useful to alternate closing the left and then the right eye to look for differences, both while fixating on specific objects and while independently exploring the field of view for each eye.

When properly selected and integrated, HMDs leverage emerging technologies to create efficient and flexible training applications that are easily deployed. With the ability to completely cloister a user in a synthetic environment, HMDs can enable the development of virtual training scenarios that are impractical to duplicate in the real world.

REFERENCES

Agrawala, M., Beers, A. C., Fröhlich, B., Hanrahan, P., McDowall, I., & Bolas, M. T. (1997). The two-user responsive workbench: support for collaboration through individual views of a shared space. In *SIGGRAPH '97: Proceedings of the 24th Annual Conference on Computer Graphics and Interactive Techniques* (pp. 19–26). New York: ACM Press/Addison-Wesley.

Akeley, K., Watt, S. J., Girshick, A. R., & Banks, M. S. (2004). A stereo display prototype with multiple focal distances. In *SIGGRAPH '04: Proceedings of the 31st Annual Conference on Computer Graphics and Interactive Techniques* (pp. 804–813). New York: ACM Press.

Arthur, K. (2000). *Effects of field of view on performance with head-mounted displays.* Unpublished doctoral dissertation, University of North Carolina, Chapel Hill.

Bolas, M. T., & Fisher, S. S. (1990). Head-coupled remote stereoscopic camera system for telepresence applications. In S. S. Fisher & J. Merrit (Eds.), *SPIE: Stereoscopic displays and applications* (Vol. 1256, pp. 113–123). Bellingham, WA: SPIE.

Brooks, F. P., Jr. (1999). What's real about virtual reality? *IEEE Computer Graphics and Applications, 19*(6), 16–27.

Cakmakci, O., & Rolland, J. (2006). Head-worn displays: A review. *IEEE/OSA Journal of Display Technology, 2*(3), 199–216.

Fergason, J. L. (1997). *Retro-reflector based private viewing system.* U.S. patent number 5629806.

Kalawsky, R. (1993). *The science of virtual reality and virtual environments.* Wokingham, England: Addison-Wesley.

Meehan, M., Insko, B., Whitton, M., & Brooks, F. P., Jr. (2002). Physiological measures of presence in stressful virtual environments. In *SIGGRAPH '02: Proceedings of the 29th Annual Conference on Computer Graphics and Interactive Techniques* (pp. 645–652). New York: ACM Press.

Melzer, J. E., & Moffitt, K. (1997). *Head-mounted displays: Designing for the user.* New York: McGraw-Hill.

National Research Council. (1997). *Tactical display for soldiers: Human factors considerations.* Washington, DC: National Academy Press.

Robinett, W., & Rolland, J. P. (1992). A computational model for the stereoscopic optic of a head-mounted display. *Presence: Teleoperators and Virtual Environments, 1*(1), 45–62.

Rolland, J. P., Krueger, M., & Goon, A. (2000). Multi-focal planes in head-mounted displays. *Applied Optics, 39*(19), 3209–3215.

Sisodia, A., Bayer, M., Townley-Smith, P., Nash, B., Little, J., Cassarly, W., & Gupta, A. (2007). Advanced helmet mounted display (AHMD). In R. W. Brown, C. E. Reese, P. L. Marasco, & T. H. Harding (Eds.), *SPIE: Head and helmet-mounted displays XII: Design and applications* (Vol. 6557, p. 65570N). Bellingham, WA: SPIE.

Smith, W. J. (2000). *Modern optical engineering: the design of optical systems* (3rd ed.). New York: SPIE Press/McGraw-Hill.

Sutherland, I. E. (1963). Sketchpad: A man-machine graphical communication system. In *AFIPS Spring Joint Computer Conference* (pp. 329–346). Montvale, NJ: AFIPS Press.

Velger, M. (1998). *Helmet mounted displays and sights.* Norwood, MA: Artech House Inc.

Wallach, H., & Bacon, J. (1976). The constancy of the orientation of the visual field. *Perception and Psychophysics, 19,* 492–498.

Chapter 3

PROJECTOR BASED DISPLAYS

Herman Towles, Tyler Johnson, and Henry Fuchs

Many in the computer graphics community refer to the 1990s as the decade of virtual reality (VR), but the stage was set by the research and technologies developed during the 1980s. By the mid-1980s, Silicon Graphics Inc. had introduced its second-generation three-dimensional (3-D) workstation, the DataGlove was available from VPL Research, Inc., and Polhemus and later Ascension were delivering trackers. When it came to display, LEEP Optical was co-developing a head-mounted display (HMD) with NASA (National Aeronautics and Space Administration) Ames Research Center, and cathode ray tube (CRT) projectors were being marketed by Electrohome, Barco, Sony, and others. While projectors have been used in large-format, vehicle based simulation display since the 1970s (CAORF, 1975), by the early 1990s many VR researchers were focused on mobile VR, where HMDs proved to be the most cost-effective stereoscopic display solution.

But at SIGGRAPH 1993, the world also experienced a new vision for *projective* virtual environments with two landmark demonstrations: the *CAVE,* created by Carolina Cruz-Neira, Daniel J. Sandin, and Thomas A. DeFanti of the Electronic Visualization Lab–University of Illinois at Chicago, and the *Virtual Portal,* created by Michael F. Deering of Sun Microsystems Computer Corporation. These environments provided an almost unlimited field of view, reduced rotational mismatches between vestibular and visual cues, and provided the ability to walk around and observe everything and everyone in the shared space.

Since that introduction in 1992, the advantages of a projective virtual environment have not changed, but the expense and the complexity of rendering pixels everywhere have. Over the last decade the cost of rendering per projective display channel has dropped precipitously, from $50K 3-D workstations and $100K projectors to $5K personal computers (PCs) with superior graphics and $5K digital projectors that are smaller and more stable. Today graphic processing units (GPUs) have enough computational power and programmability to execute advanced warping and blending algorithms in real time, eliminating the need for special purpose hardware. Camera based calibration techniques, first demonstrated by Raskar et al. (1998) and Surati (1999), are being adopted into new products and are turning the arduous task of display setup and maintenance into the mundane. Projective research over the last decade has accelerated tremendously with new and better calibration methods and rendering techniques being introduced at technical conferences annually. Researchers are now rendering onto ordinary walls, eliminating the need for expensive, space-consuming screens. New passive stereoscopic solutions such as Infitec now exist that require no special display surface. In addition, software frameworks, including VR Juggler and Chromium, are evolving to greatly simplify the complexity of building applications that run on distributed rendering clusters. These developments collectively forecast a bright future for projective virtual environments.

Figures 3.1 through 3.6 are illustrative of the many *projective* virtual displays being utilized today. The remainder of this chapter discusses many issues to be considered in buying or building a projective display system, while highlighting recent research advances that will impact future products.

DESIGNING A CUSTOM PROJECTIVE VIRTUAL ENVIRONMENT

The design or purchase of any multiprojector display environment should begin with consideration of the application requirements and such fundamental questions as, What visual field of view (FOV) and acuity are required? Is stereoscopic display needed? Will the users be stationary or mobile? Should rear projection be used to avoid shadowing? What requirements, if any, should

Figure 3.1.   Six-projector spherical display with a 220° by 60° field of view that shows the tripod-mounted calibration camera in the foreground. Image courtesy of Dr. Chris Jaynes, Mersive Technologies.

Figure 3.2. A thirteen-projector, joint terminal attack controller (JTAC), virtual dome trainer with visuals by MetaVR, Inc., and display calibration by Mersive Technologies. Image courtesy of Air Force Research Lab (AFRL), Mesa, Arizona.

be placed on the display surface? The answers will vary greatly depending on the application. For example, if the application is scientific visualization, the design may focus on resolution and giving the viewer the ability to move to get a closer or different view of the data. In this situation, a display wall built with a rectilinear array of rear-mounted projectors may be ideal. If the application is a flight simulator, then the users are generally stationary and shadowing is not an issue, so a front-projection, forward hemispherical display may fulfill the out-the-window view requirements. Depending on the mission, high display resolution may be needed so the user can accurately identify ground detail or spot incoming aircraft. If the display is to be used for a variety of full-immersion virtual experiences, then a front-projection, hemispherical dome theater or a six-wall, rear-projected, user-tracked, stereoscopic CAVE may be excellent choices.

Defining the underlying display requirements of a virtual environment application begins to narrow the design choices, but in practice this is just the beginning of the system trade-offs that must be made. The following sections will highlight practical design issues that must be considered to build and calibrate the display system, but will also provide some understanding of the software architecture and rendering issues in developing applications.

A very useful reference that can be considered a companion to this chapter is the textbook by Majumder and Brown (2007). The book touches on many of the topics discussed below, in many cases in more detail. The goal of this chapter

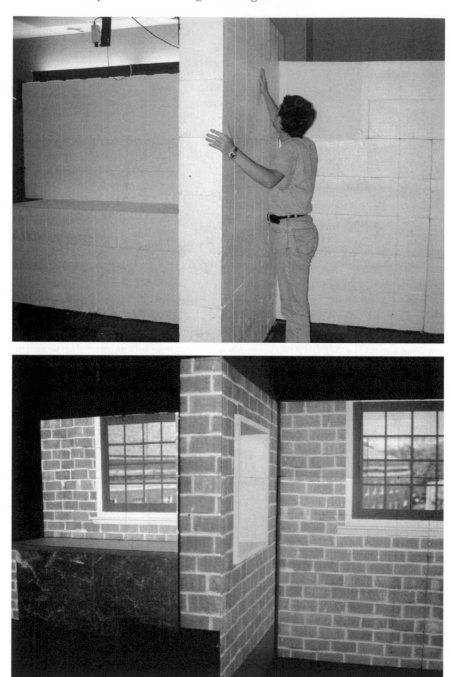

Figure 3.3.   Re-creation of a virtual space with spatial and visual realism by (top) using polystyrene blocks assembled to approximate real world models and (bottom) texturing the surfaces with six projectors. *Being There* **project at The University of North Carolina at Chapel Hill.**

Figure 3.4. Two digital flats simulating plaster walls used in conjunction with window and door props create a virtual room. A *FlatWorld* user is seen viewing a rear-projected stereoscopic virtual world through a physical door. Image courtesy of the University of Southern California Institute for Creative Technologies.

Figure 3.5. A classroom of second graders immersed inside of a 24 foot Elumenati GeoDome displaying *The Molecularium: Riding Snowflakes* using a single, wide field of view OmniFocus projector.

Figure 3.6.   An example of seamless warp-and-blend rendering with two projectors displaying onto three room walls with two corner columns. Department of Computer Science at the University of North Carolina at Chapel Hill.

is to complement that work—highlighting additional issues to consider in building projective virtual environments and reemphasizing others based on the experience of the authors.

Display Configuration

The most fundamental display configuration decision is to use front projection or rear projection. Rear projection has several advantages, including no viewer shadowing and nearly constant pixel density with orthogonal projection, but is largely limited to display onto planar screens. The biggest advantage of front projection is space saving—no additional room space behind the screen is needed. Another advantage of front projection is the ease of display onto smoothly curved surfaces, thus avoiding the difficult challenge of making display into corners photometrically seamless. For front surface this comes at a price, as the ideal location of the projectors is in the space of the users. Moving the projectors sufficiently out of the user space usually creates severe keystoning, which may be compensated by the projector's lens-shift adjustments. If not, any remaining geometric distortion must be addressed in the rendering process, which will be addressed in the section "Seamless Rendering." Some of the placement difficulties in both front and rear projection can also be solved using mirrors to fold the projector's optical path.

Determining the number of projectors and their locations for a given display surface shape can therefore be a complex task. For simple configurations (planar or cylindrical display shapes involving only a few projectors with nearly orthogonal projection), one can do a simple geometric analysis and reasonably expect to compute approximate pixel density, lens requirements, and location of the projectors. For more complex designs involving a large number of projectors and more complex display surface shapes, a computer-aided design (CAD) tool is useful.

Manufacturers and researchers actively engaged in the development of projective display systems have developed CAD tools to aid in the display design process. State, Welch, and Ilie (2006) describe a tool for interactive camera placement and visibility analysis that has also been utilized for the dual task of display system layout. 3D-Perception sells *CompactDesigner,* a sophisticated theater-design tool that provides 2-D/3-D view analysis, display-coverage diagrams, and resolution (pixel density) plots. This tool also warns of impossible positioning of projectors (for example, physical conflicts with other projectors), unwanted screen shadows, and projected regions that are outside a projector's depth of field (focus).

Focus Issues

To maximize the output light efficiency, projectors are designed with a large lens aperture, which can equate to a rather shallow depth of field. Furthermore, the lenses in commodity projectors are often optimized to focus on a planar screen parallel to the lens/imager plane. Therefore, the issue of focus cannot be summarily ignored in nonorthogonal display configurations.

The focus issue is moot with laser projectors, as lasers have small apertures and effectively infinite depth of focus. Unfortunately, their cost remains prohibitively high for most applications. With standard optical designs, keep in mind that increasing the distance of the projector to the screen will improve the depth of field, as will selecting a projector with a shorter focal length lens. For example, the fisheye lens used in the wide FOV OmniFocus projection system from The Elumenati has such a short focal length that the depth of field is nearly infinite.

In addition, Bimber, Wetzstein, Emmerling, and Nitschke (2005) have demonstrated the use of multiple overlapping projectors to improve overall display focus, and Brown, Song, and Cham (2006) developed an algorithm to precondition the imagery (adaptive sharpening) before projection to help ameliorate image defocus due to projector depth-of-field limitations.

Shadowing Issues

In front-projection theaters, shadowing caused by the viewer can be a design issue that may be mitigated with careful projector placement, but the use of shear projection geometries to minimize shadowing has practical limits set by depth-of-field and pixel-sampling considerations. While typically used to position an image and eliminate keystone distortions, projectors with lens shift can also be helpful in creating larger shadow-free viewing zones. The emergence of *lensless* projectors that use aspheric mirrors to create large-screen projection with an ultrashort throw distance can also be effectively used to minimize shadowing issues as demonstrated in Figure 3.7.

Several researchers have also demonstrated solutions for shadow elimination that use cameras to actively sense occlusions and dynamically modify the blending attenuation masks of two or more projectors that are illuminating the same surface region (Cham, Sukthankar, Rehg, & Sukthankar, 2003; Sukthankar, Cham, & Sukthankar, 2001; Jaynes, Webb, Steele, Brown, & Seales, 2001; Rehg, Flagg, Cham, Sukthankar, & Sukthankar, 2002).

Abutted versus Overlapped Display

For the purpose of keeping the rendering task as simple as possible, it is tempting to consider projector and screen layouts based on geometrically (horizontal and/or vertical) tiled images that only abut and have no optical overlap. Many rear-projected visualization walls and piecewise-cylindrical designs have been created this way. However, the practical difficulties of controlling lens (pincushion and barrel) distortion and setting up a tiled array with perfectly matched edges have fostered a great deal of research and some commercial solutions that

Figure 3.7.   A *Social Computing Room* utilizing 12 lensless, short-throw projectors that allow users to walk up within one foot of the front projected image without casting a shadow. Image courtesy of the Renaissance Computing Institute (RENCI) at the University of North Carolina at Chapel Hill.

achieve seamless display based on casually overlapped imagery and the use of more sophisticated camera based setup and rendering techniques. Until these advanced techniques are more universally supported, it may be wise to weigh the effectiveness versus cost of the two approaches.

Hardware Considerations

Projector Selection

A useful resource in selecting projectors is the Web site www .projectorcentral.com, but just comparing specifications is often inadequate. It is important to evaluate units firsthand and not to assume that a new model from a company will exhibit quality and features similar to those of previous models from the same vendor.

Projection Technologies

Nearly all projectors today are built with digital imaging devices, which enable lower cost and more stable solutions than CRT based projectors. Three digital imaging technologies are commonly used in today's projectors: LCD (liquid crystal display), LCoS (liquid crystal on silicon), and DMD (digital micromirror device). The first DMD projector was developed by Texas Instruments and is marketed with the DLP (digital light processing) label. LCoS, like DMD, is a reflective imager, while LCD is a transmissive imager. Sony's SXRD (Silicon X-tal Reflective Display) and JVC's D-ILA technologies are LCoS devices.

LCD and LCoS projectors use three-imager designs with complex optics for color separation and recombination. Three-chip DMD systems are available, but the time-modulated characteristic of DLP technology makes possible a single-chip design that utilizes a spinning optical-filter wheel to colorize the white-light source and sequentially present red, green, and blue (RGB) images. Today's DLP designs, especially those sold for the presentation market, often include a fourth *clear* filter segment that improves the contrast in gray-scale imagery at the expense of slightly desaturating color imagery and raising the black level.

A clear color filter complicates the blending of overlapping images in projector overlap regions (Stone, 2001). Therefore, developers may wish to select a DLP projector with only RGB filters or an operational mode that disables the use of the clear filter segment. Manufacturers marketing to the visualization and simulation markets are aware of this photometric issue.

Projector Specifications

The three parameters most commonly used to compare projectors are brightness, resolution, and contrast (ratio). Brightness of 2,000 to 4,000 lumens and native resolutions of one to two megapixels are commonplace, with up to eight megapixels of resolution in some LCoS units. Contrast is arguably the most critical display parameter, but the industry practice of specifying full-screen on-off ratios does not adequately characterize intraframe contrast, which is much lower due to internal reflections in the optical system.

Brightness and the lens system largely drive the size and weight of projectors. In 2008, the median weight of 2,000 lumen projectors is approximately 5.7 pounds, increasing to 13.1 pounds for 4,000 lumens, and 31.8 pounds for 6,000 lumens (data courtesy of www.projectorcentral.com).

A projector's horizontal FOV is commonly disguised in a specification known as throw ratio (*D/W*), which is defined as the ratio of the distance (*D*), measured from the lens to the screen, divided by the width (*W*) of the planar projected image. Many projectors provide a zoom lens for modifying the image size, and some high end projectors may offer interchangeable lens options. Zoom lenses typically exhibit radial distortion on each end of the zoom (*pincushion* at wide FOV and *barrel* at narrow FOV) that may need to be modeled in order to achieve seamless geometry in multiprojector displays.

Optical vignetting or the gradual darkening of the image toward the image periphery caused by shadowing in large aperture, multielement lens designs can create photometric challenges in multiprojector displays. Few vendors quote specifications for flat-field luminance variation, but it is not uncommon to find luminance in image corners to be 80 to 90 percent of that in the central optical field. Projectors with more than a 20 percent luminance variation should be avoided.

Sources of system latency or lag are always a concern in creating virtual environments. CRT based projectors typically have zero lag, but today's digital projectors may exhibit some image-processing latency. Few vendors quote a latency specification, but the authors have not seen specifications or measured delays exceeding one frame time.

Operating noise level of projectors is also unspecified by most vendors, but should be duly considered, especially in front-projection designs. While overall environment acoustics can be complex, it may be necessary to add additional baffling for projectors with more than 30 dBA (decibels) of operating noise. (Note: to avoid mirage-like optical distortion, it is also important to make sure the hot exhaust air from one projector does not vent into the optical path of a neighboring projector.)

The final two projector features to consider in selecting a projector are a serial control interface and a digital video interface (DVI). As the number of projectors in the display system increases, a serial interface can be critical for projector initialization and turning devices on and off. DVI provides an absolute pixel mapping from the graphics card to the projector's imager to avoid the clock phasing and jitter issues common to analog (video graphics array) video. It is also important to drive the projector at the native resolution to avoid resampling issues.

Stereoscopy Options

The stereoscopic presentation challenge is to deliver a unique image to each eye. While the solution for HMDs is to include a separate imager for each eye, in a projective environment it is necessary to display both left- and right-eye images onto the same screen and require the user to wear either *active* or *passive* stereoscopic glasses to discriminate between the two images.

Active stereoscopy is based on liquid-crystal shutter glasses that alternately open and close synchronized to the time-sequential presentation of the left- and right-eye images. Projector-shutter glass synchronization is achieved with an infrared emitter that is connected to the image generator or the projector. The time-sequential nature of active stereoscopy requires a high display-refresh rate (>100 hertz) to avoid perceived flicker. A single CRT projector can easily achieve this, but this image update rate is difficult to achieve with all but a few digital projectors (InFocus DepthQ and some three-chip DMD models). Two-projector (100 percent overlap) active stereoscopic solutions also exist.

In passive stereoscopy, the viewer's glasses use passive filters to discriminate between the left- and right-eye images that are simultaneously displayed by two projectors. Passive glasses are less expensive than active glasses and for that reason are popular for large-group stereoscopic theaters. Two types of stereoscopic image encoding are typically used—*polarization* and *anaglyphic.*

Both *linear* (vertical and horizontal) and *circular* (clockwise and counterclockwise) polarization are used to encode the two stereoscopic image pair. Linear polarization is very susceptible to left-right image cross talk with even a small amount of head tilt, while stereoscopic separation based on circular polarization is invariant to head tilt. At the same time, the quality of image separation with circular polarization has a wavelength dependency (for example, the separation of green imagery may be better than red and blue). As a result, linear polarization can provide better image separation than circular polarization, but because of the invariance to head tilt, most users consider circularly polarized stereoscopy superior to linear polarized stereoscopy.

Two additional factors must be considered with polarization based stereoscopy. First, the display surface (or screen in the case of rear projection) must be polarization preserving. Finally, converting a pair of DMD projectors into a linear- or circular-polarized stereoscopic system through the addition of external optical filters is straightforward as the output light is not inherently prepolarized. However, the light from LCD and LCoS projectors is, by nature of the device, linearly polarized, but for optical design reasons the polarization of the green image is commonly rotated 90° relative to the red and blue images. This means one cannot add a simple quarter-lambda retarding filter and create light that is circularly polarized with the same orientation (clockwise or counterclockwise) for the RGB images. More sophisticated frequency-selective retarders are required, or one can cleverly swap which projector displays the left- and right-eye green images.

In *anaglyphic* stereoscopy, the image encoding is based on wavelength-dependent multiplexing. Simple red-blue anaglyphic stereoscopy is useful for demonstration of basic stereoscopic principles, but multiplexing the two images into just two colors does not produce a practical full-spectrum solution for virtual environments. Another anaglyphic option, developed by DaimlerChrysler, is Infi-tec—an *interference filter technology* that divides the visible spectrum into two parts with eye-interleaved, three-band notch filters. Infitec is head-rotation invariant and does not require a polarization preserving screen or surface, but because of the spectral selectivity the two eyes can perceive different colors for the same displayed RGB value.

Screen Considerations

A full discussion of screen issues is outside the expertise of the authors, but we would be remiss if we did not at least stress the importance of screen materials and surface shape as these issues are important in creating a photometrically seamless and high contrast display environment.

Developers should actively research or seek out the advice of experts in the projection screen field to answer questions related to screen gain, view position dependencies, interreflection issues, ambient lighting and impact on contrast, polarization preserving surfaces for stereoscopy, and new high contrast screen options. Such companies as Da-Lite, Draper Inc., and Stewart Filmscreen Corporation can be a valuable source of information on screen and surface options.

An alternative trend to the use of screens is to project onto existing room surfaces and compensate for the geometric and photometric irregularities using camera based, closed-loop calibration. This approach promises rapid setup of multiprojector display systems in new locations.

Image Generators

The most fundamental issue facing display system developers is whether the display and application are designed to run on a single PC with multiple display outputs or a multiple-PC rendering cluster. If the number of projectors exceeds what can be configured on a single PC, or the performance of a single PC cannot deliver the desired application frame rate, then a cluster is the only choice.

Both NVIDIA and ATI Technologies have GPUs with two output channels, and high end workstations are available with sufficient cooling and power to support two to four GPUs. If more output channels are needed, one can consider an external expansion chassis, such as NVIDIA's Quadro Plex that supports up to eight output channels or a graphic expansion module (for example, Matrox Graphics Inc.'s TripleHead2Go) that can digitally split a single wide-screen channel into multiple nonoverlapping outputs.

To achieve temporally seamless display in a multiprojector system, one must synchronize the outputs of all graphic cards. If developing an *active* stereoscopic configuration, video synchronization is an absolute necessity. NVIDIA's Quadro G-Sync solution supports multicard *frame* lock (vertical interval synchronization), external genlock, and *swap* lock (synchronized buffer swaps). RPA Electronics Design, LLC also markets a synchronization kit for some NVIDIA cards. Software based synchronization solutions have been demonstrated on Linux and Windows systems by Allard, Gouranton, Lamarque, Melin, and Raffin (2003) and Waschbuesch, Cotting, Duller, and Gross (2006), respectively.

Tracking Requirements

Rendering a geometrically accurate scene for a user in a projective virtual environment requires knowledge of the user's eye position in the display space. Changes in desired display surface color caused by a view perspective change are, of course, defined by the rays between the eye and the virtual objects and how the intersection of those rays with the display surface move as the viewer moves.

In many geometric situations, the displayed scene may look reasonable and acceptable when viewed from a point other than the rendered viewpoint. This is particularly true when the display surface is second-order continuous as evidenced by our ability to accept perspective distortions on flat- or curved-screen presentations from a large variety of locations in a theater. Display surface discontinuities, such as the corners in a four-wall display environment, will produce more detectable geometric breaks in visual presence when the rendered and actual user viewpoints differ.

The need for tracking must be analyzed on a display-geometry and an application-specific basis. If needed, only the position of the user's eye is utilized in the rendering so it may be acceptable to approximate the eye position from a tracked position near the eyes without concern for tracker orientation.

It is very important for tracking latency in HMD based VR systems to be small in order to minimize the sensed mismatch between vestibular and visual cues that can occur when displayed imagery lags actual head rotation. In projective virtual environments, the virtual scene is rendered everywhere so the mismatch between these rotational cues is largely nonexistent. As a result, the authors theorize that the need for very low latency tracking in projective virtual environments is greatly diminished compared to operation with HMDs.

Seamless Rendering

When multiple projectors are combined to form a single display, the fundamental goal is to create a geometrically and photometrically *seamless* visual for the users. Geometrically, this means that overlapping images of projectors are properly coregistered with no perceptible position or slope discontinuities, and there are no apparent perspective distortions due to off-axis projection or projection onto nonplanar display surfaces. Photometrically, the areas where projectors overlap should be undetectable (not brighter or darker), and there should be no perceptible brightness or color differences that make the number of individual projectors discernible. Ideally, photometric correction should not compromise display contrast and should be independent of scene content.

These rendering challenges can seem daunting, and it is therefore understandable why the earliest projective virtual environments were designed to utilize the 3-D graphics pipeline unchanged—render a 3-D perspective scene based on the standard pinhole-camera model and a flat-image plane and then design the projector-screen configuration to match this model in an attempt to avoid any distortion. Geometric coregistration is then achieved by physically positioning the projectors as exacting as possible to tile the projective images while also avoiding any photometric overlap.

Beginning in the late 1990s and coinciding with the introduction of more affordable projectors, researchers began developing camera based calibration techniques and new rendering methods that would both relax the requirement for such a precise system setup and allow for more flexible display configurations. The key to these advancements was the realization that a projector is simply the dual of a camera and that is was possible to apply computer vision methods and projected structured light to calibrate projectors while also reconstructing the shape of the display surface. Given this information and the modern 3-D graphics processor, it was a relatively simple task to render predistorted images for an array of casually aligned projectors and produce a geometrically seamless visual. Parallel research in photometrics was simultaneously yielding new mathematical models and camera based calibration techniques for improved photonic uniformity.

The next two sections provide insights into these new geometric- and photometric-rendering advances and the camera based calibration techniques utilized.

Geometric Rendering

Remapping (Warping) Basics
An understanding of the geometric distortion created when projecting onto an arbitrarily shaped surface is the key to a successful rendering strategy. That understanding begins by considering the question: If standing at this location in the display space, what color should each (projector) pixel on the screen be to create a perspectively correct visual of the virtual scene?

Figure 3.8 illustrates this geometric problem and includes five objects from a virtual scene, a complex-shaped display surface, a projector pose, and viewer position. In determining the color of a given projector pixel (circled), we consider the location on the display surface where the projector pixel falls (point *A*) and determine what color in the virtual scene the viewer should observe at this point. In the case of the projector pixel illuminating point *A*, the viewer should observe point *B* in the virtual scene. Similarly, for a projector pixel located at point *C* on the display surface, the viewer should observe point *D* in the scene. Points *A* and *C* are determined by the geometry of the display surface and the location, orientation, and optical properties of the projector—all of which can be obtained by a calibration process. Points *B* and *D* in the virtual scene are obtained by forming a ray between points *A* and *C* and the known viewer location and intersecting these rays with the objects in the virtual scene.

This ray-tracing formulation of the problem effectively defines a mapping of 2-D points in the viewer's image to 2-D points in the projector's image. Figure 3.9 is illustrative of these two images. The amount of *warping* or predistortion in the projected image is a function of the display surface shape, the user viewpoint, and the calibration (position and orientation) of the projector.

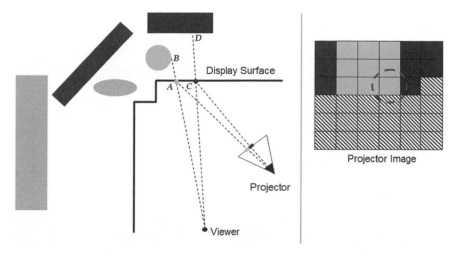

Figure 3.8.   Ray-Tracing Model Illustrating the Remapping from View Image Space to Projector Image Space

If this remapping is accurately established for each projector, there will be geometric continuity of the virtual scene between projectors.

Rendering for Planar Surfaces

In the special case where the projection is onto a planar surface, the remapping from viewer image to projector image can be represented with a single 3×3 matrix. This mapping between two images is called a *planar homography* and is completely determined by four pixel correspondences between the two images. In practice, the use of additional points provides greater accuracy.

Many developers (for example, Raskar, 2000; Chen, Sukthankar, Wallace, & Li, 2002; Raij, Gill, Majumder, Towles, & Fuchs, 2003; Ashdown, Flagg, Sukthankar, & Rehg, 2004) and others have calibrated large-tiled visualization walls based on computing two homographies—one representing the common mapping from the display wall to a *camera* image and a second homography from the camera image to each projector image. Concatenation of these two homographies defines a linear transform remapping the display wall to the projector image that, when preconcatenated with the application's projection matrix, allows the standard graphics pipeline to directly compute the corrected projector image at zero additional computation expense.

Rendering for Arbitrary 3-D Surfaces

Planar homographies cannot be used to perform the remapping from the viewer image to the projected image when the display surface is more complex than a single plane. To address this limitation, Raskar et al. (1998) describe a generic two-pass rendering method that is also able to compute the remapping for arbitrary surfaces using the GPU. The algorithm works as follows. In the first

Figure 3.9.   FlightGear simulation showing both (top) the undistorted viewer's image and (bottom) the projector's image with the predistortion required to compensate for a complex room corner.

pass, the ideal image to be observed by the viewer is rendered into texture memory. Then, in the second pass, the ideal image is warped in a way that compensates for the geometry of the display surface when displayed by the projector. The remapping is accomplished using projective texturing, in which the polygonal model representing the display surface is textured with the ideal image using texture coordinates computed by projecting the vertices of the model into the first-pass image. The textured polygonal model of the display surface is then rendered from the projector's perspective to obtain the image to be projected. Since the algorithm recomputes the ideal view and remapping on every frame, it can easily accommodate a tracked viewer.

If the display geometry and viewer position are static, then the pixel-to-pixel remapping (warping) operation is fixed. Another rendering strategy is to precompute the per-pixel remapping coordinates between the viewer and the projector images and then, at run time, look up the mapping (stored on the GPU as a 2-D floating point texture) and use it to index the ideal viewer image for each pixel in the output projector image. This technique for performing geometric correction was first proposed by Bimber et al. (2005).

A major advantage of using the per-pixel mapping approach is that both linear and nonlinear effects, such as projector lens distortion (Kannala & Brandt, 2006), can be combined into a single remapping lookup table. In the two-pass projective texturing approach, any lens distortion must be modeled independently of the perspective remapping operation. Johnson, Gyarfas, Skarbez, Towles, and Fuchs (2007) describe such a solution. Otherwise, the two representations are identical, as either can be used to generate the other.

Camera Based Calibration

Cameras are typically modeled by a 3×4 *camera matrix* that describes the mapping of 3-D world points to 2-D pixels in the camera's image space. The projection matrix is defined up to scale with 11 degrees of freedom, which includes six extrinsic parameters describing the 3-D position and orientation of the device, and five parameters describing intrinsic properties including focal length in x and y, the 2-D location of the principal point in the image, and a pixel skew factor. Given six or more 3-D world points and corresponding 2-D camera image points, it is possible to solve for the camera matrix (Hartley & Zisserman, 2000). Bouguet (2008) provides a set of MATLAB tools for calibrating cameras using a checkerboard pattern calibration object.

Given a calibrated camera pair, feature points *projected* onto the display surface can then be reconstructed in 3-D. Given this set of 3-D points and the corresponding 2-D points in projector image space, each projector can be calibrated using the same solution methods for cameras.

In addition to a model describing all projectors, an estimate of the display surface geometry is required for the second-pass rendering (warping) step. This surface representation may be explicit, as in the case of a surface mesh defined by the 3-D points used to calibrate the projectors, or implicit in the case that it is represented as a mapping that describes how pixels in one projector map to pixels in another projector. Such a mapping is equivalent to knowing the 3-D position of each projector pixel on the display surface (Brown, Majumder, & Yang, 2005; Quirk et al., 2006).

Display calibration is normally done as part of the system setup, but researchers have also demonstrated camera based calibration methods that run concurrently with the application to continuously refine the geometric and photometric calibration (Yang & Welch, 2001; Cotting, Naef, Gross, & Fuchs, 2004; Johnson & Fuchs, 2007; Zollmann & Bimber, 2007).

Photometric Correction

In a multiprojector display environment, geometric correction alone is not enough to give the user the impression of a single uniform display. There may be a number of photometric inconsistencies between projectors and also within individual projectors themselves. The goal of photometric correction is to eliminate these photometric differences.

Blending Basics

In regions of the display surface where the imagery of multiple projectors overlaps without compensation, a higher photometric intensity will be observed. For example, if the images of two identical projectors overlap, the luminance in the overlap region will be approximately twofold brighter than the neighboring nonoverlapped region. Two *blending* techniques are commonly used to compensate for this luminance gain—electronic attenuation of the input signal or the placement of a physical aperture mask in the optical path.

The naive approach to electronic compensation is to reduce the intensity of each projector's imagery equally at all points in the overlap region by an amount proportional to the number of overlapping projectors. There are two issues with this solution. First, the amount of attenuation needed cannot be correctly computed without knowledge of the projector's transfer response function (luminance output intensity as a function of the input value) or "gamma." In practice, most projectors have an S-shaped response function similar to Figure 3.10. This means the attenuation required to reduce the luminance on the screen by a desired percentage is a nonlinear function of the input intensity.

Second, slight geometric registration errors or even small lamp differences in the projectors will likely still leave an observable boundary if all overlapping pixels are attenuated equally. The human eye is very sensitive to intensity steps and slope discontinuities (Mach bands), so a better approach is to weight the contributions of the projectors with a function that smoothly transitions or blends between projectors in the overlap region. Raskar et al. (1999) describe such a method for generating attenuation masks for each projector that also takes into account the projector's response. In practice, a slope-continuous parametric function, such as a cosine curve, rather than a linear ramp, should be used in this computation.

Physical aperture masks placed in the optical path (external to the projector as shown in Figure 3.11) can also be used to blend the projected imagery in overlap

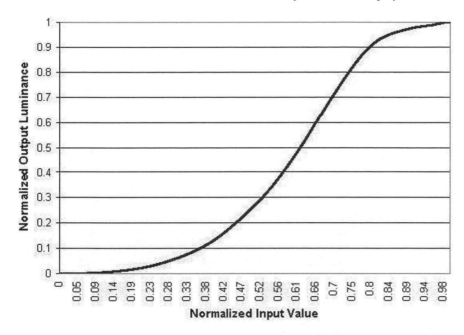

Figure 3.10. Typical Nonlinear Luminance Response of Projectors as a Function of Input

regions, but their application can also be very complex. Since these external masks are not in the focal plane of the projector, the resulting shadow has penumbra and umbra regions. The challenge is physically aligning the aperture masks so the penumbra regions of neighboring projectors overlap precisely within the projector overlap region, while also achieving a combined unity optical gain. Changing the width of the penumbra can be accomplished by moving the mask relative to the projector's optical axis. Achieving unity gain may require developing a mask that optically varies from transparent to opaque in a prescribed manner. These complex optical design considerations and physical placement challenges are easier to overcome in simple projector and screen configurations, such as planar visualization walls or cylindrical arrays, but vendors routinely create masks with curved edges that are optically nonlinear for application in multiprojector dome displays. In summary, while electronic compensation is by far a more flexible, reconfigurable blending solution, aperture masks can provide an absolute black in overlapping regions that electronic attenuation cannot. As black levels are reduced in future generation projectors, electronic attenuation should dominate.

Black Is Not Black

One major advantage of CRT based projectors over today's digital-imager technologies is the ability to adjust black to just human-discernible levels. Unfortunately, that is not the case with today's digital-imaging projectors. Black,

Figure 3.11.   Behind-the-screen view showing the aperture masks placed in the optical path for edge blending of the 24 projector Scalable Display Wall, November 2000. Image courtesy of Dr. Kai Li, Princeton University.

in regions of multiple projector overlap, is brighter than the black in nonoverlapping regions of display.

Blending using electronic input attenuation cannot solve this black-overlap problem, but physical aperture masks by their very nature can provide 100 percent optical attenuation.

To achieve absolute black uniformity electronically, Majumder and Stevens (2005) and others have computed a black-offset mask, which is applied in combination with an alpha-blending mask, to raise the level of blacks in nonoverlapped regions to match the black level in projector overlap regions. This can result in effective black blending, but at the expense of reduced display contrast. Many users or applications may find this reduction in contrast an unacceptable trade-off.

With today's commodity projectors, the best blacks are produced by LCoS projectors, followed by DMD and LCD designs. The good news is better black response is a commonly held design goal, and it is improving with each generation of imaging device, so this issue may fade away. For example, future high-dynamic-range projectors, built with two image modulators in series promise drastic contrast and black improvements, and affordable laser projectors will simply make the black issue disappear.

Advanced Photometrics

In addition to projector overlap, additional sources of luminance variation in multiprojector design are optical vignetting in each projector, lamp brightness differences from projector to projector, and inverse-square-law luminance variations created by the distance relationships between projectors and the screen surface.

To address all these issues, Majumder (2003) developed a unifying color model and new algorithms for computing more sophisticated alpha blending and black-offset masks based on achieving *perceptual* display uniformity rather than global intensity uniformity. Ashdown, Okabe, Sato, and Sato (2006) present a content-dependent framework for creating photometric compensation, which, like Majumder's research, balances strict compensation against dynamic range.

Color gamut is another property of projectors that may vary across makes and models. A display with color inconsistencies across its extent can be undesirable for the user. It is possible to partially correct for color inconsistencies across projectors by remapping the input values provided to each projector in such a way that the response of the projector to the new input matches as closely as possible the desired color (Wallace, Chen, & Li, 2003). Kresse, Reiners, and Knöpfle (2003) detail a color calibration method and algorithm that corrects color gamut differences between multiple projectors while also addressing the left-right eye color differences using Infitec stereoscopy.

Wetzstein and Bimber (2007) have also developed a generalized framework that utilizes a full-light transport model to perform image based radiometric compensation of many advanced photometric issues, including interreflections, refraction, and light scattering. Using a clever approximation for the inverse-light transport matrix, real time results have been demonstrated running on a GPU (shader program) for a single-projector configuration.

Warp-and-Blend Hardware

The warp-and-blend rendering techniques discussed in this section can all be implemented on GPUs from NVIDIA and ATI to support OpenGL and DirectX applications. Many of these advanced algorithms are implemented as custom pixel-shader programs on the GPU. The rendering cost of these operations is negligible compared to the cost of scene rendering in most applications, and therefore no additional latency is incurred.

Several external warp-and-blend solutions exist, including products from 3D Perception and SEOS Ltd., that are installed in the video stream between the GPU and the projectors. In addition, high end projectors from Barco, Christie Digital Systems, Digital Projection, Inc., 3D Perception, and others have built-in warp-and-blend engines.

The setup of external warp-and-blend engines has traditionally been done using screen overlays and a human in the loop making visual decisions on the quality of geometric and photometric continuity. The new trend by display systems vendors is automatic alignment algorithms that utilize one or more cameras for visual feedback. Barco, Mersive Technologies, SEOS, Scalable Display Technologies, and others are currently marketing such systems.

Sampling and Latency

Any image resampling operation is prone to sampling artifacts, so output quality differences can be a significant differentiator between warping engines. Warping done on the GPU typically utilizes the texturing hardware to do bilinear interpolation between four input pixels for each output pixel, but even more sophisticated reconstruction filters are possible.

Minimizing overall system latency can be an important goal in many high performance simulation environments. One source of additional latency can be in the geometric warp stage. Warping done on the GPU with a shader program should add minimum additional rendering cost or delay, but external warp-and-blend hardware inserted between the GPU and the projector can add processing latencies up to one display frame time depending on geometric remapping. For example, if the first output pixel from the warp engine is remapped from the 15th line of the input image, there is a small, additional display latency of 15 lines compared to the direct image generator output.

Application Development

Cluster Rendering Support

There are significant architectural differences in a simulation designed to run on a single PC versus a rendering cluster. New strategies for data (model data and run-time user input) distribution, as well as frame synchronization must be considered.

If developing a new application for cluster rendering, VR Juggler is an open source suite of application programming interfaces designed for VR application development with embedded support for distributed cluster rendering.

For existing single-PC, OpenGL applications, one should consider Chromium for multinode projective display support, as it requires no modification of the application code. Chromium is an OpenGL implementation that does not render the OpenGL stream to a frame buffer, but transparently forwards the commands (and data) to render PCs. These render nodes can be customized to do warp-and-blend rendering on the GPU or with external engines. Majumder and Brown (2007) provide a good overview of Chromium for multiprojector display. Other interesting architectures for distributed display include the SAGE (Jeong et al., 2005) and VIRPI (Germans, Spoelder, Renambot, & Bal, 2001) projects.

Warp-and-Blend Software Support

Using an external warp-and-blend engine has the advantage of not requiring any application code changes, but adds extra expense, incurs some small increase in system latency, and cannot handle view position changes in real time. Warp and blend implemented on the GPU has none of these disadvantages, but does require an initial investment to develop the warp-and-blend software (no open source implementations yet exist). Warp-and-blend functionality can be distilled

Figure 3.12. Futuristic virtual team training environment. (Top) The room with a few real objects and two trainees in standby mode and (bottom) then in operation. Sketches by Andrei State, University of North Carolina at Chapel Hill.

into two basic functions—a preDraw method that initializes rendering to GPU (texture) memory and a postDraw method that calls the warp-and-blend operator. With this strategy, the application code changes required to add warp and blend are rather simple.

CONCLUSIONS AND FUTURE OPPORTUNITIES

Great strides have been made since 2000 in reducing the cost and complexity of building large-scale projective environments. Projector size and costs continue to shrink, and LED light sources will soon replace all hot-filament light sources. New imaging technologies, such as the grating light value laser projector, hold great promise. Camera based automatic setup and calibration methods demonstrated in the research community are beginning to be incorporated into real world products. Warp-and-blend functionality is becoming more sophisticated as it migrates from external black boxes to programmable pixel-shader algorithms running on GPUs, and application software developers are exploring new frameworks, such as VR Juggler and Chromium, for distributed cluster rendering.

However, technology challenges still exist. Projectors with more resolution, better blacks and contrast, and a wider color gamut are needed. Prototype solutions for multiprojector shadow removal or improved depth of field must be taken to the next level of practice, and the search for multiuser stereoscopic solutions will continue.

Now imagine a large environment designed for immersive team training that combines some real objects with mostly virtual objects as shown in Figure 3.12. Autostereoscopic display, full-body tracking, real time physical simulation, spatialized audio, and tools for generating training scenarios are a few of the technologies that must be developed and integrated. Can such a projective environment be our next reality?

REFERENCES

Allard, J., Gouranton, V., Lamarque, G., Melin, E., & Raffin, B. (2003). SoftGenLock: Active stereo and genlock for PC cluster. *Proceedings of the Workshop on Virtual environments 2003—EGVE '03* (pp. 255–260). New York: ACM.

Ashdown, M., Flagg, M., Sukthankar, R., & Rehg, J. (2004). A flexible projector-camera system for multi-planar display. *Proceedings of the IEEE Conference on Computer Vision and Pattern Recognition—CVPR '04* (Vol. 2, pp. 165–172). Washington, DC: IEEE Computer Society.

Ashdown, M., Okabe, T., Sato, I., & Sato, Y. (2006, June). *Robust content-dependent photometric projector compensation.* Paper presented at the Third International Workshop on Projector-Camera Systems—PROCAMS '06, New York, NY.

Bimber, O., Wetzstein, G., Emmerling, A., & Nitschke, C. (2005). Enabling view-dependent stereoscopic projection in real environments. *Proceedings of the 4th IEEE/ACM International Symposium on Mixed and Augmented Reality—ISMAR '05* (pp. 14–23). Washington, DC: IEEE Computer Society.

Bouguet, J. Y. (2008). *Camera calibration toolbox for Matlab.* Retrieved April 18, 2008, from http://www.vision.caltech.edu/bouguetj/calib_doc/index.html

Brown, M. S., Majumder, A., & Yang, R. (2005). Camera-based calibration techniques for seamless multi-projector displays. *IEEE Transactions on Visualization and Computer Graphics* (Vol. 11, pp. 193–206). Piscataway, NJ: IEEE Educational Activities Department.

Brown, M. S., Song, P., & Cham, T. J. (2006). Image pre-conditioning for out-of-focus projector blur. *Proceedings of the 2006 IEEE Computer Society Conference on Computer Vision and Pattern Recognition—CVPR '06* (pp. 1956–1963). Washington, DC: IEEE Computer Society.

CAORF. (1975). Simulation at U.S. Merchant Marine Academy. Retrieved April 18, 2008, from http://www.usmma.edu/admin/it/simulator.htm

Cham, T. J., Sukthankar, R., Rehg, J. M., & Sukthankar, G. (2003). Shadow elimination and occluder light suppression for multi-projector display. *Proceedings of the International Conference on Computer Vision and Pattern Recognition—CVPR '03* (Vol. 2, pp. 513–520). Washington, DC: IEEE Computer Society.

Chen, H., Sukthankar, R., Wallace, G., & Li, K. (2002, October). *Scalable alignment of large-format multi-projector displays using camera homography trees.* Paper presented at the Thirteenth IEEE Conference on Visualization—VIS '02, Boston, MA.

Cotting, D., Naef, M., Gross, M., & Fuchs, H. (2004, November). Embedding imperceptible patterns into projected imagery for simultaneous acquisition and display. *Proceedings of the Third International Symposium on Mixed and Augmented Reality—ISMAR '04* (pp. 100–109). Washington, DC: IEEE Computer Society.

Cruz-Neira, C., Sandin, D. J., & DeFanti, T. A. (1993). Surround-screen projection-based virtual reality: The design and implementation of the CAVE. *Proceedings of the 20th Annual Conference on Computer Graphics and Interactive Techniques, SIGGRAPH 1993,* 135–142.

Germans, D., Spoelder, H., Renambot, L., & Bal, H. (2001, May). *VIRPI: A high-level toolkit for interactive scientific visualization in virtual reality.* Paper presented at Immersive Projection Technology/Eurographics Virtual Environments Workshop, Stuttgart, Germany.

Hartley, R., & Zisserman, A. (2000). *Multiple view geometry in computer vision.* Cambridge, United Kingdom: Cambridge University Press.

Jaynes, C., Webb, S., Steele, R. M., Brown, M., & Seales, W. B. (2001). Dynamic shadow removal from front projection displays. *Proceedings of the conference on Visualization—VIS '01* (pp. 175–182). Washington, DC: IEEE Computer Society.

Jeong, B., Jagodic, R., Renambot, L., Singh, R., Johnson, A., & Leigh, J. (2005, October). *Scalable graphics architecture for high-resolution displays.* Paper presented at IEEE Information Visualization Workshop, Minneapolis, MN.

Johnson, T., Gyarfas, F., Skarbez, R., Towles, H., & Fuchs, H. (2007). A personal surround environment: Projective display with correction for display surface geometry and extreme lens distortion. *Proceedings of the Annual IEEE Conference on Virtual Reality—VR '07* (pp. 147–154). Washington, DC: IEEE Computer Society.

Johnson, T., & Fuchs, H. (2007, June). *Real-time projector tracking on complex geometry using ordinary imagery.* Paper presented at the IEEE International Workshop on Projector-Camera Systems—PROCAMS 2007, Minneapolis, MN.

Kannala, J., & Brandt, S. (2006). A generic camera model and calibration method for conventional, wide-angle, and fish-eye lenses. *IEEE Transactions on Pattern Analysis and Machine Intelligence, 28*(8), 1335–1340.

Kresse, W., Reiners, D., & Knöpfle, C. (2003). Color consistency for digital multi-projector stereo display systems: The HEyeWall and the digital CAVE. *Proceedings of the Workshop on Virtual Environments* (pp. 271–279). New York: ACM.

Majumder, A. (2003). *A practical framework to achieve perceptually seamless multi-projector displays.* Unpublished doctoral dissertation, University of North Carolina, Chapel Hill.

Majumder, A., & Brown, M. S. (2007). *Practical multi-projector display design.* Wellesley, MA: A. K. Peters.

Majumder, A., & Stevens, R. (2005). Perceptual photometric seamlessness in tiled projection-based displays. *ACM Transactions on Graphics, 24*(1), 118–139.

Quirk, P., Johnson, T., Skarbez, R., Towles, H., Gyarfas, F., & Fuchs, H. (2006, October). *RANSAC-assisted display model reconstruction for projective display.* Paper presented at the IEEE VR 2006 Workshop on Emerging Display Technologies, Nice, France.

Raij, A., Gill, G., Majumder, A., Towles, H., & Fuchs, H. (2003, October). *Pixelflex2: A comprehensive, automatic, casually-aligned multi-projector display.* Paper presented at the IEEE International Workshop on Projector-Camera Systems—PROCAMS '03, Nice, France.

Raskar, R. (2000, March). *Immersive planar displays using roughly aligned projectors.* Paper presented at the Annual IEEE International Conference on Virtual Reality—VR 2000, New Brunswick, NJ.

Raskar, R., Brown, M., Yang, R., Chen, W. C., Welch, G., Towles, H., et al. (1999). Multi-projector displays using camera-based registration. *Proceedings of the Conference on Visualization—VIS '99* (pp. 161–168). Washington, DC: IEEE Computer Society.

Raskar, R., Welch, G., Cutts, M., Lake, A., Stesin, L., & Fuchs, H. (1998). The office of the future: A unified approach to image-based modeling and spatially immersive displays. *Proceedings of the 25th Annual Conference on Computer Graphics and Interactive Techniques—SIGGRAPH '98* (pp. 179–188). New York: ACM.

Rehg, J., Flagg, M., Cham, T., Sukthankar, R., & Sukthankar, G. (2002). Projected light displays using visual feedback. *Proceedings of the International Conference on Control, Automation, Robotics, and Vision—ICARCV '02* (Vol. 2, pp. 926–932). Washington, DC: IEEE Computer Society.

State, A., Welch, G., & Ilie, A. (2006). An interactive camera placement and visibility simulator for image-based VR applications. *Proceedings of the Eighteenth Annual Symposium on Electronic Imaging Science and Technology—IS&T/SPIE '06* (pp. 640-651). Bellingham, WA: SPIE.

Stone, M. (2001). Color and brightness appearance issues in tiled displays. *IEEE Computer Graphics and Applications, 21*(5), 58–66.

Sukthankar, R., Cham, T. J., & Sukthankar, G. (2001). Dynamic shadow elimination for multi-projector displays. *Proceedings of the 2001 IEEE Computer Society Conference on Computer Vision and Pattern Recognition—CVPR '01* (Vol. 2, pp. 151–157). Washington, DC: IEEE Computer Society.

Surati, R. (1999). *Scalable self-calibrating display technology for seamless large-scale displays.* Unpublished doctoral dissertation, Massachusetts Institute of Technology, Boston, MA.

Wallace, G., Chen, H., & Li, K. (2003). Color gamut matching for tiled display walls. *Proceedings of the Workshop on Virtual Environments 2003—EGVE '03* (Vol. 39, pp. 293–302). New York: ACM.

Waschbuesch, M., Cotting, D., Duller, M., & Gross, M. (2006). WinSGL: Software genlocking for cost-effective display synchronization under microsoft windows. *Proceedings of the Sixth Eurographics Symposium on Parallel Graphics and Visualization—EGPGV '06* (pp. 111–118). Amsterdam, The Netherlands: Elsevier Science Publishers.

Wetzstein, G., & Bimber, O. (2007). Radiometric compensation through inverse light transport. *Proceedings of the 15th Pacific Conference on Computer Graphics and Applications—PG '07* (pp. 391–399). Washington, DC: IEEE Computer Society.

Yang, R., & Welch, G. (2001, February). *Automatic and continuous projector display surface calibration using every-day imager.* Paper presented at the 9th International Conference in Central Europe on Computer Graphics, Visualization, and Computer Vision—WSCG '01, Plzen, Czech Republic.

Zollmann, S., & Bimber, O. (2007). Imperceptible calibration for radiometric compensation. *Short Paper Proceedings of the Twenty-Eighth Annual Conference of the European Association for Computer Graphics* (pp. 61–64). Aire-la-Ville, Switzerland: Eurographics Association.

Chapter 4

AUDIO

Ramy Sadek

Sound is a deceptively simple yet fundamental experience in daily life. Listeners derive much information about their surroundings through hearing. Characteristics of a surrounding space, as well as the locations, velocities, and sizes of scene elements are a few examples of information gathered by listening. In this sense, the ears lead the eyes, telling them where to look.

Auditory stimuli—if reproduced correctly—form a powerful link between participants' virtual worlds and the physical space in which training occurs. Conversely, poor audio reproduction creates an incongruity between the two spaces that marks the virtual space as clearly unreal, shattering the illusion of the virtual environment. When virtual environment (VE) training does not get audio right, the "virtual" aspect may be meaningless.

The familiar nature of auditory experiences leads to an intuitive understanding of sound and its behavior, leading many to oversimplify the delivery of audio. However, there are many challenges in reproducing the complex interactions of sound in the environment and the human auditory system. This chapter provides a general introduction to a variety of topics. Most of these topics are complex, making a complete discussion beyond the scope of the present discussion. The compromise is to include the information relevant to practitioners setting up an audio system for use in a virtual environment while offering suggested reading for thorough detail and advanced topics. Discussion follows the "99 percent rule," meaning definitions and explanations are true in essence, avoiding rigorous detail in favor of clarity and practicality.

Beginning with fundamentals, the chapter covers the design issues, implementation details, and trade-offs involved in such a setup. The first two sections, "What Is Sound" and "Psychoacoustics," cover the physical properties of sound and basic psychoacoustics. The next two sections discuss basic signal processing ideas and considerations for virtual environments, such as visual displays and rendering techniques. Loudspeakers and headphones are discussed in detail, and basic safety procedures are outlined, which should be employed in all VEs. Finally, hardware and software, environmental effects, and the trade-offs between them are covered.

WHAT IS SOUND? PHYSICAL QUANTITIES, WAVES, AND DECIBELS

In order to understand the issues involved in the design and setup of an audio system, it is important to first understand sound. In broad terms, the word *sound* refers to vibrations in the air within the audible range. Specifically, these vibrations are air-pressure fluctuations varying with time and space called *pressure waves.*

There are two characteristic types of wave: *transverse* and *longitudinal.* Transverse wave propagation is perpendicular to the motion defining the wave. For example, fluffing a sheet when making a bed creates a *vertical* displacement that travels *horizontally* along the length of the sheet. So the motion of this transverse wave is perpendicular to its direction of travel.

Conversely, longitudinal waves propagate in the same direction as the wave motion. Consider a tube open at one end, with a plunger at the other end. Moving the plunger forward into the tube increases the air pressure near the plunger in the direction of the plunger's motion. The pressure moves along the length of the tube toward the opening. Longitudinal pressure waves are the type of waves that comprise sound.

Sinusoids are a simple way to examine waves since a complete description of a sinusoid requires only three parameters: *amplitude, frequency,* and *phase.* Each of these variables plays a key part in the setup of an audio system and so merits a brief review.

Amplitude refers to the vertical extent of the wave about its center line. Put another way, amplitude represents the magnitude of oscillation. For example, a sine wave centered about the origin that ranges between -1 and $+1$ has amplitude 1 since each oscillation has a displacement magnitude of 1.

Frequency, measured in hertz (Hz) refers to the rate of oscillation; 1 Hz equals one oscillation per second. It follows that fast oscillations have high frequency values yielding a high pitched tone, while slow oscillations are of low frequency, creating low pitches. Frequency and wave *period* are inversely related. Period refers to the *time* required for the wave shape to repeat itself, while wavelength refers to the *distance* required for repetition. Therefore, wavelength refers to spatial quantities only, and frequency refers to temporal quantities.

Phase refers to time displacement of the sinusoid. For example, a sine wave (with zero phase) equals zero at the origin. Moving the sine wave along the x direction until its value at the origin equals 1 yields a wave identical to a cosine. Recall from trigonometry that a sine wave shifted $90°$ is equal to cosine. So cosine equals a phase-shifted sine wave.

Intensity refers to the average energy per square meter at a given displacement from the source. Energy in this case grows proportionally to the squared amplitude of the wave. Since sound waves emanate radially from a source, they are spherical waves around the source that grow with distance. The surface area of a sphere grows proportionally to its radius squared; therefore, the ratio of energy per unit area decays with inverse distance squared. Intensity varies directly with squared amplitude and inversely with squared distance.

Often it is necessary to compare sound intensities. Because the range of audible intensities is very large, it is helpful to use logarithmic units to describe quantities such as intensity and amplitude. The *decibel* (dB) is defined to be $10 \cdot \log_{10}(I_1/I_2)$. That is, a decibel is 10 times the logarithm of the ratio of the two intensities. Since decibels are defined in terms of a ratio between two quantities, the measure is a relative one. Therefore, to measure a given quantity measured in dB requires an implicit comparison against a standard reference. The standard reference level for sound intensity, I_0 equals 10^{-12} Watts per squared meter, which is (roughly) the lowest sound intensity audible by humans.

Often other quantities, such as power and pressure, are measured as a ratio of squares, in which case the decibel is $20 \cdot \log_{10}(A_1/A_2)$ since $\log_b(x^y) = y \cdot \log_b(x)$. To avoid confusion when reading specifications in decibels, keep in mind whether measured quantities are direct ratios or ratios of squares. For additional detail on waves and physical quantities, see Haliday, Resnick, and Walker (2007).

PSYCHOACOUSTICS

Psychoacoustics: Loudness, Frequency, and Delay

Loudness is the impression of intensity as interpreted by the auditory system; however, loudness is not a function of intensity alone, nor does it vary proportionally to intensity. Rather, loudness is a function of several factors, frequency foremost among them. The humanly audible frequencies range between approximately 20f and 20,000 Hz (20 kHz [kilohertz]). See Figure 4.1.

Fletcher-Munson curves are contours relating perceived equal loudness to sound-pressure level (vertical axis), and frequency (horizontal axis). The contours denote the sound-pressure levels (SPLs) at which frequencies are perceived to be equally loud. Another way to read the graph in Figure 4.1 is as a map of sensitivity to frequencies. Humans are most sensitive to frequencies in the middle range, as indicated by the lowest parts of the equal loudness contours.

The vertical axis (in dB) is logarithmic. Thus values along the contours have a great range. Consider, for example, the bottom contour, roughly 8 dB above reference level for frequencies near 2 kHz. A 50 Hz tone of equal loudness would require approximately 50 dB of amplification to sound as loud as the 2 kHz tone: a factor of over 300 times in amplitude, or 100,000 in power! This places demanding requirements on an audio system that (ideally) should reproduce the entire frequency range smoothly, without audible noise in the softest sounds or distortion in the loudest sounds.

There is a complex relationship between loudness and delay as well. For example, different combinations of delay and intensity can yield the same perceived source location. Delay refers to the time separating instances of similar sounds, for example, an echo. In general, delays up to 50 ms sound as though they are a single sound rather than a sound and an echo. The exact time at which this separation occurs depends highly on the nature of the sound. For example, clicks and other sharp sounds separate even when the delay is comparatively brief, while other sounds may support longer delays without separation.

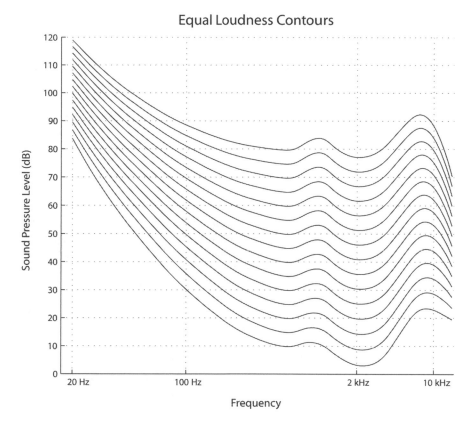

Equal Loudness Contours

Figure 4.1.   The human audible frequencies range between approximately 20 and 20,000 Hz (20 kHz [kilohertz]).

Delay is an important consideration of loudspeaker setup and calibration as it can greatly affect source localization, as will be described later.

Spatial Hearing

The auditory system localizes sound sources in several ways, each of which has important implications for audio setups in virtual environments. Two quantities are of primary importance: interaural intensity difference (IID) and interaural time difference (ITD). IID is the difference in acoustic energy received at the two ears, while ITD is the time delay between the two ears. Consider a source directly left of the listener. Sound waves from this source reach the left ear before the right ear (ITD); the right ear also receives less acoustic energy from the source (IID) due to the listener's *head shadow.*

IID and ITD are two components of a more general set of auditory cues described as a *head-related transfer function* (HRTF). HRTFs are based on anatomy: the shape of the ears (pinnae), head, chest, and shoulders define the

HRTF. Each anatomical interaction mutates sound waves differently, affecting the final waveform that reaches the eardrum. Resultant waveforms may differ greatly from the original source; hence the brain must decipher these differences to determine the spatial location of the source. The following sections discuss IID and ITD independently, but bear in mind that they are closely related components of an HRTF. Considering the HRTF as a function with phase, amplitude, and spectral components, IID is the amplitude component, ITD is the phase component, and reflections and absorptions by the body comprise the spectral component.

Multiple spatial positions can produce the same IID or ITD. Specifically a torus of points equidistant from both ears, called a torus of confusion, yields identical values. Because of this ambiguity, the IID and ITD components alone may not lead to accurate localization. Only the full HRTF, with phase, amplitude, and spectral components, provides enough information for accurate localization. Additionally, both IID and ITD localization are frequency dependent with ITD dominating localization up to around 700 Hz, and IID after roughly 1.5 kHz. For these reasons, localization of a good HRTF application ought to outperform that of an amplitude or delay panner alone.

Finally, note that the auditory system localizes frontal sources most accurately, while accuracy diminishes toward the sides and rear. Similarly, accuracy decays with vertical angle yielding relatively poor localization at moderate angles above and below the listener. See Blauert (1997) for details on spatial hearing.

Source Localization, IID, ITD, and Precedence

For a source directly in front of a listener (centered along the medial axis), ITD and IID equal zero because the paths from the source to each ear are the same length and have no head shadow. As the source moves to the left or right, ITD and IID vary accordingly. The converse holds as well; given two identical waveforms sent to each ear, the auditory system will perceive a single central source since ITD and IID equal zero. Adjusting loudness or delay of the waveforms to create a nonzero IID or ITD changes the angular displacement of the perceived source. The following subsections explain these phenomena in greater detail.

Amplitude: IID Localization

When there is no ITD, intensity plays a significant part in source localization. In this situation, the auditory system localizes based on loudness. For example, consider two loudspeakers in front of and facing a listener positioned between them. ITD equals zero. If the two loudspeakers emit the same signal, IID equals zero as well. The listener perceives a single source image centrally positioned between the loudspeakers. Increasing the amplitude of one loudspeaker signal moves the perceived source toward that loudspeaker. In a sense that loudspeaker has more weight in the localization.

Precedence: ITD Localization

The auditory system follows "the law of the first wavefront," interpreting source locations based on the direction from which acoustic energy first arrives.

This is commonly referred to as *precedence.* Whereas ITD measures the difference in arrival times of a *single* wavefront for a given incidence angle, the precedence effect refers to localization based on the ITD of the first wavefront of a sound arriving from multiple directions. For example, consider a set of loudspeakers and a listener who is close to a particular loudspeaker. If the loudspeakers emit identical sounds, a listener will localize based on the ITD from the direction of the nearest loudspeaker because its wavefront is the first arrival. This effect holds even when the nearest loudspeaker is significantly less loud than the farther loudspeakers.

Therefore, it is possible—within certain limits—to achieve the same perceived angle for a variety of intensity and delay combinations, which can be useful when calibrating an audio setup (see Rumsey, 2001)

BASIC DIGITAL SIGNAL CONCEPTS

Quantization

Digital signals are discrete representations of functions that are continuous in both scale and time; that is, they span an infinite number of values over an infinite number of points in time. Computers are able to process only discrete values, so continuous signals are discretized in both scale and time.

There is inherent error in discretization. The magnitude of the error is related to the size of the discrete steps used to represent the continuous signal. Greater precision in amplitude requires increased bit depth per sample. Similarly increased frequency requires a higher sampling rate. Both increase the amount of data required to represent the signal in digital format.

Nyquist Frequency

Representing a signal with maximum frequency F requires a sampling rate greater than $2F$ samples per second. Put another way, a digital signal generated by sampling at $2F$ samples per second can faithfully represent only frequencies below F Hz. This frequency, $2F$, is called the *Nyquist frequency,* after the physicist Harry Nyquist. The minimum sampling rate required to represent a given frequency is called the Nyquist rate.

This relationship requires that, for faithful reproduction, the input signal include no frequencies above F. This range—or band—of frequencies in the signal is limited, commonly expressed by the term *band limited.* Because the auditory system is unable to detect frequencies above 20 kHz, all humanly audible signal components are band limited. So a sampling rate at or above 40 kHz can reconstruct any humanly audible sound. Sampling rates below 40 kHz lose a portion of the audible range.

Certain assumptions of the mathematical model used to derive the Nyquist rate are physically unrealizable as circuits, so it is necessary to sample at a rate slightly faster than 40 kHz to allow reproduction of the entire audible frequency range when converting from digital signals to continuous (analog) signals (Watkinson, 2001).

CONSIDERATIONS FOR VIRTUAL ENVIRONMENTS

In a virtual environment, poor sound quality stands out. When audio fails to match visual cues in a film, audiences notice immediately, breaking their immersion. In virtual environments, a well designed audio system guides listeners to perceive audio cues as though emanating from the virtual world, aiding immersion and suspension of disbelief. Conversely, poor setups lead listeners to perceive sound as emanating from loudspeakers in specific locations, reinforcing the fact that the training experience is not "real." It is a common view that when audio is "done right," only experts can tell, but when "done wrong," all will notice. In other words, audio goes unnoticed unless it is malfunctioning. This view is misleading. A proper audio setup calls little attention to the system itself (for example, noise artifacts) and yields high sound quality appreciable by all audiences, not only experts. Experts listen actively for specific technical problems common to such systems, but the immersive, engaging effects of good sound are accessible to all listeners.

Implications for VE Design

Careful setup is crucial to achieve high quality audio. Decisions made during the design stage of the VE can greatly affect the audio quality. From the choice of visual display devices to the geometry of the room housing the VE setup, considering audio early in the design stages avoids difficult work-arounds, saving time and improving audio quality. Often the audio setup comes up late in the design process, reducing options and complicating design, which leads to a difficult implementation. Early focus on the audio setup during design saves time, money, and headaches.

Visual displays are common acoustic impediments, often interfering with placement of front loudspeakers. Unfortunately, there is no universal solution to this problem; all work-arounds are compromises with varying effectiveness. The visual display problem is one to tackle at the beginning of design to allow successful compromises.

Integration with Visual Displays

Currently, front projection display systems offer the best compromise, allowing high quality visual and audio performance. Recent advancements in screen manufacturing yield nearly acoustically transparent screens with excellent visual performance characteristics. These screens slightly attenuate high frequencies, but this is correctable with an equalizer. Some screen manufacturers offer equalizers pretuned to correct for their screens. Such an arrangement may save time and money; however, most virtual environment setups require significant equalization and calibration, eliminating the benefits of a preset device.

Front projection systems with acoustically transparent screens are the best choice because they allow high performance of both audio and video. From an audio perspective, front projection avoids many problems leading to an easier setup and better results than are possible with other visual displays.

When front projection is not feasible, the alternative options are hard to rank. When evaluating alternatives, there are a few things to consider. Loudspeakers must be unoccluded, pointing directly at the center of the listening space. Also, the auditory system is more sensitive to horizontal angles than vertical ones. Therefore, it is possible to place the front speakers above or below the display if the displacement is only a few degrees from planar. Large vertical displacement angles in front are ineffective, creating more problems than they solve, so it is unhelpful to raise or lower the loudspeaker more than a few degrees.

To the sides and rear, the human system is less sensitive to angular displacement, allowing vertical deviations less than 45°. Note that 45° is the extreme maximum, and certain material may sound objectionable with such large displacements. The greater the vertical angular of the rear loudspeakers, the more their spatial efficacy diminishes (Holman, 1999). In general, the main loudspeaker positions should be as planar as possible, with deviations the exception rather than the rule.

In some virtual environments, participants may view the virtual world from any direction (for example, head-mounted displays, curved screen enclosures, and so forth) so there is no sense of "front" and "rear" loudspeakers. These configurations require a larger number of loudspeakers for accurate localization.

Frontal imaging is most effective using three channels (right, left, and center) with a 30° angle between loudspeakers. The center channel stabilizes the audio image, which, in a two-channel configuration, is highly sensitive to precedence. This stability is very important in virtual environments as it helps to avoid the "snapping" effect wherein sound positions "snap" to the nearest loudspeaker when the participant moves or rotates his or her head. The 30° criterion demands 12 loudspeakers to cover 360° (for example, with an HMD setup), yet few commercial audio systems offer spatialization over 12 loudspeakers. Some systems do offer this capability, but have other trade-offs.

Room Acoustics

Room acoustics affect audio system performance greatly. The topic of room acoustics has been widely covered; however, most discussion has focused on sound in public spaces or in studio sound for post-production. While the same principles hold, the special needs of VEs emphasize and prioritize these factors differently.

In VEs, there are four primary concerns regarding room acoustics: ambient noise, standing waves, reverberance, and uneven room response. The goal of calibrating the audio system (see "Setup and Calibration") is to negate these effects.

Ambient noise must be reduced as much as possible since it severely detracts from the quality of reproduction. Some experts have drawn analogy to shining a light on a video screen or jittering the picture: these effects are irritating and destroy immersion. Similarly, white noise, hums, hisses, clicks, and so forth, detract immediately from the performance of the audio system. For example, it would be counterproductive to spend money and effort on a well designed and calibrated setup and then to leave noisy computers in the listening area.

When selecting a room for the VE setup, avoiding such loud building elements as large electrical transformers, elevators, or boiler rooms is essential since counteracting the sound of such massive objects is exceedingly difficult. When building a space specifically for a VE setup, use double walls and raised floors to isolate the room from outside noises. Ventilation ducts for heating and ventilation systems (even those designed for silence) should be fitted with acoustic vents. Consult an architect familiar with studio construction to ensure good design. Computers and other noisy equipment are best placed in a different room whenever possible, or at least in acoustic cabinets.

When room dimensions exactly match wavelength, a *standing wave* occurs. If the distance between two walls is an exact multiple of one period (half the wavelength), the room will have a standing wave of corresponding frequency. Standing waves also occur at all integer multiples of that frequency since their periods match room dimensions. They are called "standing" waves because they do not vary spatially. When plotted over time, they appear to stand in place, varying in amplitude but not phase/time. In particular, there are points, called *nodes,* that undergo zero displacement as the wave oscillates. So frequencies are lost completely at the node's position, yet elsewhere in the room they may be prominent.

These waves are detrimental to sound quality since they create large differences in frequency response throughout the listening space. It is a common misconception that nonparallel walls do not create standing waves. In fact, such a room will have standing waves at all wavelengths between the minimum and maximum separation distances. Rectangular rooms have the most predictable, controllable behavior, while exotic room shapes are often problematic.

Room modes, the resonant frequencies of a room's geometry, are closely related to standing waves. Room modes occur when sound waves of a particular frequency reflect between two or more walls at an integer multiple of the wave period. In other words, the reflected wave aligns perfectly with the source, creating resonances that overemphasize certain frequencies, coloring the sound. Careful selection of room dimensions and acoustic treatments are the best methods to minimize the effect of room modes. See Holman (1999) for details on selecting room dimensions.

Reverberance is due to the reflections of sound waves encountering surfaces. The character of the reverberance is a function of room dimensions, as well as the material properties of the reflecting surfaces. Because of this variability, each space has its own acoustic signature. Early reflections are the most significant component of this signature. In order to allow virtual environments to take on the acoustic signature of the virtual environment, the audio system must counteract the reverberance of the listening environment as much as possible. While complete elimination of room effects is generally not feasible, acoustic treatments and equalization can suppress the room signature sufficiently to allow a neutral listening environment and successful application of virtual reverberance (see "Environmental Effects").

Uneven room responses complicate suppression of room effects. Because the frequency response and reverberance vary spatially, different points in the listening space affect sound very differently. Therefore, room equalization is essential for successful audio (see "Room Equalization"). Rooms with little reverberance and a flat frequency response, known as "dead" rooms, are preferable for VEs since they do not interfere with the virtual scene. Dead rooms have a trade-off since they require significantly more sound input to sound natural, which tends to yield a "brighter" sound from loudspeakers.

Acoustic Treatments

There are two types of acoustic treatments: absorptive and diffusive. Absorptive treatments diminish reverberance by absorbing acoustic energy over a range of frequencies. No single absorber type functions well over the entire frequency range. Therefore, when selecting absorbers, it is important to select a set that ensures coverage of the entire audible frequency range. Diffusors, on the other hand, absorb very little sound, spreading incoming energy in all directions, weakening reflections.

Effective room treatments utilize both diffusion and absorption. Current best practices place them asymmetrically, with diffusors spatially opposing absorbers and vice versa. In other words, diffusors and absorbers alternate and are spaced such that diffusors face absorbers on opposing walls. This arrangement ensures that each wave front is diffused and absorbed consecutively, allowing absorbers to work together while preventing intense early reflections. Placing absorbers opposite one another creates the possibility of waves fluttering back and forth between them, with slow decay; asymmetric installation works most effectively. It is not generally necessary to cover the walls from floor to ceiling; rather, treatment panels can be vertically centered about the average listening position.

Some manufacturers (for example, StudioPanel and Auralex) offer installation advice or design software that can help plan the layout pattern in oddly shaped rooms. Note that the principles of asymmetric layout and absorption over the entire audio range will be highly effective for most VEs.

Floors and ceilings present some special problems. Ceilings should be treated in a manner similar to the walls if possible. In spaces with tiled ceiling, replacing a portion of the tiles with Nubby acoustic tiles is fairly effective. Usually heavy floor treatment is not feasible in VEs; however, carpeting with thick rubber underlayment is effective and is certainly a great improvement over such hard surface materials as concrete or hardwood. Any large, hard surfaces, such as doors, pillars, and cabinetry, should also undergo acoustic treatment.

Loudspeaker Delivery Algorithms

Rendering Techniques

When designing an audio setup, weighing the pros and cons of each trade-off, it is helpful to have a basic understanding of rendering algorithms, their assumptions, and requirements.

Amplitude

Amplitude based schemes are the simplest, most common audio imaging methods. These algorithms leverage the principle of localization based on IID (see "Amplitude: IID Localization"). Increasing loudness of particular loudspeakers while diminishing that of corresponding loudspeakers, the algorithm alters the perceived angle of the source image. By maintaining a constant power output over all angles, the algorithm moves the source image with no changes in loudness. That is, although amplitudes of particular loudspeakers change, the total power incident at the ear is constant.

Amplitude schemes assume that all loudspeakers are effectively equidistant from the listening position, so they yield equal intensity at the listening position and their wave fronts arrive simultaneously. If the loudspeakers cannot be placed equidistantly from the listening position, amplitude and delay adjustments can compensate for small differences (see Rumsey, 2001).

Amplitude based schemes create virtual sources strictly on the loudspeaker boundary; they cannot produce a perceived image closer to or farther from the listener than the loudspeakers. Amplitude schemes are sensitive to listener location. If the listener is too close to a loudspeaker, precedence effects dominate localization.

Amplitude techniques suffer from "sweet spot" problems, meaning the effect falters outside a small, central area. Room equalization techniques can help widen the sweet spot to an acceptable size. Finally, amplitude techniques also lack an elevation model, though naive attempts offer reasonable results by using a large number of closely spaced loudspeakers.

Multichannel, 5.1, 7.1, and 10.2 Systems

Multichannel formats are conventionally referred to by two numbers separated by a period or "point" (for example, 5.1, 8.1, and 10.2). The number before the point refers to the number of loudspeakers, while the second number refers to the number of subwoofers in the system. This nomenclature does not specify the locations of the loudspeakers, though common usage has affiliated some names with particular layouts. For example, "5.1" usually refers to the setup with three frontal loudspeakers and two rear (surround) loudspeakers.

This 5.1 format is often misunderstood due to the name "surround sound." This term leads many to incorrectly assume that the 5.1 format allows for 360° virtual source placement. Rather, source placement suffers from large "holes" to the sides and rear, where the loudspeakers are too far apart for stable imaging. The three frontal loudspeakers provide fairly precise and stable source placement, while the rear two loudspeakers are intended for ambient effects, like reverberance or background sounds, to give a sense of the spatial environment. As such, this setup is suitable for environments where the participants will face only forward and surround imaging is not a priority.

The 10.2 format aims to address these shortcomings by adding loudspeakers to the sides and rear as well as two dipole loudspeakers (for diffuse field) and two height channels, which emulate early ceiling reflections in the virtual space (the most important cue affecting perception of the virtual acoustic space). As a result, 10.2 is ideally suited to theater environments with the added benefits of true surround imaging and excellent spatial effects. Interactive rendering for 10.2 is an ongoing area of research.

Delay

Delay based spatialization algorithms, sometimes referred to as delay imaging, leverage precedence (see "Precedence: ITD Localization"). By adjusting amplitudes and delay times for an array of loudspeakers, these algorithms alter perceived source locations. Delay methods are less common than the amplitude schemes, although they are often used in sound reinforcement applications. For large venues delay imaging may be preferable because of its reduced susceptibility to precedence artifacts, such as audience members on the left or right of the venue perceiving sound from only the nearest loudspeaker, rather than a spatialized image. Some hardware, such as front of house mixers, offers delay imaging. At the time of this writing, software implementations are not widely available, though a few research labs have experimented with this technique. As computational audio becomes more widespread, delay imaging may become more common, expanding the palette available to virtual environments.

Ambisonics

Ambisonics is a popular technique known for its mathematical elegance, flexibility, and extensibility, supporting arbitrary loudspeaker setups and an elevation model. However, critics complain that it yields a "phasey" sound and that the mathematical model is invalid since it assumes a point-source listener, which ignores the fact that the head has two ears. On the other hand, proponents of Ambisonics argue one must take a few minutes to learn how to listen to it for the maximal effect, at which point the "phasey" sound disappears. Some have drawn an analogy to stereoscopic visual images, which require some practice to view, but once learned, the effect is very convincing. Ambisonic spatialization can be applied as a post-process despite the common misconception that Ambisonics work only through special recording techniques. Higher order Ambisonics offers solutions for elevation, though increasing complexity audio reproduction system. The Web site www.ambisonic.net is an excellent source for further reading on Ambisonics techniques as well as for specific implementation details, such as loudspeaker arrangements and software packages.

Wave Field Synthesis (WFS)

WFS aims to reproduce a sonic wave field by using numerous loudspeakers (tens to hundreds). The technique is elegant and effective, though difficult to implement. The chief advantage of WFS is that it passes the "pointing test." That is, listeners will perceive the same location of a virtual sound irrespective of their location in the listening area. Unlike other systems where precedence can lead to incorrect localization, WFS causes listeners to the left of a virtual source to hear it on their right and vice versa. For example, given a virtual source placed in the middle of a theater, the entire audience would point toward the center location when asked to localize the source, rather than pointing to the same loudspeaker.

WFS carries moderate to large hardware cost and requires many computers and a great deal of calibration. The company IOSONO offers prepackaged systems and installations, ideal for theater environments. Critics of WFS complain about a phasey sound and that while the virtual sources pass the pointing test, the sources always seem to emanate from the loudspeaker boundary rather than a location in free space. Finally, the latency in WFS systems may be too high for certain applications.

EQUIPMENT CONSIDERATIONS

Loudspeakers

The market offers an expansive range of loudspeakers. Sorting through numerous variables and trade-offs can be daunting. Unfortunately the wide variances in listening spaces, VE setups, and budgets prevent a silver-bullet solution. Nonetheless, a few basic principles, covered in the following sections, serve as a good starting point for the selection of loudspeakers.

There are three loudspeaker types of primary interest for virtual environments: direct radiators, dipoles, and loudspeaker arrays. Direct radiators are meant to face the listener, with optimal performance on axis, much like a spotlight. These loudspeakers are readily localized since their position is audibly clear.

Dipoles, which radiate in a figure-eight pattern, are ideal for enveloping, nondirectional sound. They are normally arranged to radiate their energy in the directions perpendicular to that of the listener location so that all sound reaching the listener is reflected and diffuse.

Loudspeaker arrays are comprised of a set of radiators associated with a common channel. The individual radiators are often decorrelated, which creates a vague spatial impression over a large area. These arrays are effective for sounds that are not precisely located, such as rear background ambience. Conversely, correlated loudspeaker arrays used for "beam forming" allow control over the array's spatial radiation pattern. Each of these types has advantages and disadvantages for immersive audio. Audio setups may incorporate more than one type of loudspeaker, depending on goals and requirements (see Holman, 1999).

Each loudspeaker type uses a driver to produce pressure waves. In the ideal case, a single-driver loudspeaker would yield optimal imaging, since all frequencies would emanate from the same point. However, the broad bandwidth and high dynamic range of sound cannot be reproduced by a single-driver solution. Therefore, drivers of different sizes handle segments of the frequency range. The varying precision of localization with respect to frequency is at odds with multiple drivers at different locations. Subwoofers offer a means to distribute low frequency energy about the room, which allows satellite loudspeakers to employ smaller drivers in a compact enclosure, acting more like the ideal single-driver device. These are called multiway loudspeakers, often written as 2-way or 3-way, and so forth, where the number refers to the number of drivers used.

Finally, coaxial loudspeakers align their drivers about a central axis to create a point-source unit. Often these drivers are unhoused, requiring in-wall installation, though several manufacturers (for example, Tannoy, Bag End, and EMES) market coaxial studio monitors.

Frequency Response

Frequency response refers to the magnitude of output for each frequency in the input range. The ideal frequency response would be a flat curve from 20 Hz to 20 kHz, meaning that input frequencies with equal energy have equal energy in the output.

No loudspeaker extant has the ideal frequency response. When evaluating response curves, seek those as close to the ideal as possible, with smooth variations throughout the loudspeaker's intended listening range. In full-range loudspeakers, the listening range is 20 Hz to 20 kHz. In loudspeakers intended for use with a subwoofer, the response decays steeply toward the low frequencies. Therefore, the evaluation range for such loudspeakers extends down to the crossover point at which the subwoofer predominates. In other words, steep decay in the bass roll-off is not an indication of poor performance. Instead, evaluation of these curves must consider the subwoofer response as well (see "Crossover/Bass Management").

Manufacturers of high quality loudspeakers (for example, Genelec, Mackie, and JBL) often offer frequency response curves upon request, as well as in brochures and on their Web sites, in order to demonstrate the quality of their products. In products for which these data are unavailable upon request (for example, most computer and low end home stereo loudspeakers), performance is generally too poor for use in virtual environments.

Directivity

Loudspeakers' frequency responses vary with listening angle. Their low frequencies tend to radiate more broadly than their higher frequencies, which can be highly directional. Flatness and smooth transitions over the range of listening angles are the key criteria in assessing a loudspeaker's directional performance. In a direct radiator, high directivity is desirable for accurate localization (for example, the frontal direction). Directivity should vary as little as possible with respect to frequency to avoid coloration effects (Holman, 1999).

Some manufacturers publish a directivity index (DI), which measures in dB the spatial radiation pattern over the frequency range. Increasing DI indicates higher directivity where every 3 dB halves the radiation angles. For example, 0 dB implies an omnidirectional (spherical) radiation pattern, while 3 dB indicates a hemispheric pattern, 6 dB spans a quarter sphere, and so on (see Holman, 1999, for more details).

Ideally the curve of DI versus frequency should be as flat as possible. Any variations should be smooth since sharp changes can cause detrimental coloration in the output. Research suggests that a DI of roughly 8 dB in the mid frequencies is ideal (Holman, 1999; Rumsey, 2001).

Headroom and Dynamic Range

Headroom, given in dB, refers to the amplitude available between the operating level of a device and the level at which clipping distortion occurs. The *dynamic range* of a loudspeaker indicates the SPL range the loudspeaker can produce without distortion. Specifically, dynamic range is a value given in dB that indicates the ratio of the loudspeaker's maximum SPL to its minimum output, or *noise floor.* In loudspeakers of sufficient quality for VEs, the noise floor must be below audibility at the listening position.

Dynamic range deserves close attention when selecting loudspeakers. Loudspeakers should support a peak SPL of at least 103 dB at the listening position to allow sufficient headroom for equalization (Holman, 1999).

Crossover/Bass Management

Full-range loudspeakers have an even frequency response over the audible range 20 Hz to 20 kHz. Full-range loudspeakers are very expensive, large, and heavy. Because the auditory system does not localize very low frequency sounds very precisely, subwoofers offer a practical approach to full-range reproduction since limiting spectral range allows the satellite loudspeakers to be relatively small and inexpensive. In virtual environments wherein there may be several loudspeakers (even hundreds in some cases), it makes little sense to replicate low frequency capability for each loudspeaker.

Instead, bass management hardware filters low frequency signal content, routing it to the subwoofer(s). This arrangement effectively extends the spectral range of the satellites, making feasible the use of numerous loudspeakers for spatial audio. Successful implementation of a subwoofer-satellite system requires a *crossover* matching the capabilities of the transducers. The crossover bass manages frequencies below a specified cutoff point. As the satellite loudspeakers' frequency response decay in the low end, the subwoofer can take over. This transition must be smooth to avoid audible artifacts. Several manufacturers offer subwoofer/satellite systems with integrated bass management. Since bass energy can quickly consume the headroom of a subwoofer, overloading it, systems with a large number of satellite loudspeakers should distribute bass energy over multiple subwoofers.

Although the auditory system does not locate very low frequencies with precision, it can determine which side of the body the subwoofer is on. Therefore, for applications wherein spatial sources with significant low frequency content (for example, military vehicle sounds) play a significant role, place four subwoofers around the training area for spatial reproduction.

Near-Field Monitors

When listening to loudspeakers in a closed environment, there are two sources of sound: the direct sound from the loudspeakers and the reverberant sound in the room. A near-field monitor is a loudspeaker designed for close listening distances where the direct sound predominates, reducing perception of room acoustics. In practice counteracting room acoustics is complex, requiring more than short loudspeaker distances; however, the near-field approach can be very effective when combined with acoustic treatment (see "Room Acoustics") and are commonly used in VE setups.

Active and Passive Monitoring

Active loudspeakers contain an integrated amplifier, whereas passive loudspeakers are driven by an external amplifier. In either case, amplifier and transducer must be matched to one another. In the case of studio monitors, the designers take on the matching, tuning, and optimizing of the amplifiers for the specific characteristics of the transducers and crossovers. With passive loudspeakers, the burden of matching amplifiers is on the buyer.

Studio monitors often have other advantages as well. Many are meant to be used with a specific subwoofer and are matched accordingly. Features such as adjustable bass roll-off and volume knobs allow per-channel adjustments that are very convenient and flexible. Additionally studio monitors are meant for near-field use, with high directionality making them ideal for VEs. Generally studio monitors with matched subwoofers are the best option for VEs.

In some cases studio monitors are not appropriate. For example, in very large setups where the loudspeakers are distant from the listening position, much more powerful systems are in order. Other factors, such as mounting weight restrictions or other logistical concerns, may make decoupled amplifiers preferable. In situations such as live fire exercises where there is increased risk of repeated equipment destruction, decoupled amplifiers may relieve financial stress as only the transducers would require frequent replacement.

Pairing loudspeakers and amplifiers is a complex topic beyond the scope of the current discussion. But there are numerous online resources devoted to this topic. Perhaps the best resource is a knowledgeable representative at a large professional audio vendor (for example, B&H, GC Pro, Sweetwater Sound Inc., and so forth) or from the manufacturers themselves.

Finally, these two loudspeaker types have different wiring considerations. Because active loudspeakers have integrated amplifiers, they require separate power and signal cables. Passive loudspeakers instead require power to be sent along the signal lines, which can be problematic over long distances.

Setup and Calibration

The chosen rendering method will dictate the precise loudspeaker layout, but a few rules hold in general. Avoid wall cancellations and overly strong reflections by placing the loudspeakers far from walls. Dipoles, in particular, must be far from walls to create a diffuse field. Distance loudspeakers from ceilings and floors, which can cause acoustic loading that is detrimental to sound quality and can damage equipment.

Direct radiators offer optimal performance on axis (see "Directivity"). Since high frequencies are highly directional and readily localizable, loudspeakers are best placed with their tweeters at ear height, pointed toward the listening position. The loudspeakers should be placed equidistantly from the center of the listening area. In cases where equidistant placement is not possible for certain loudspeakers, hardware devices can compensate by delaying the signal of the closer loudspeakers such that the wave fronts from all loudspeakers arrive simultaneously at the listening position. Some automated equalization hardware will compensate for uneven placement (see "Room Equalization"). Many professional audio devices also provide adjustable delay for this purpose. Once placed, the loudspeakers require equalization and level alignment.

Room Equalization

Automating the equalization process is an active area of academic research and product development that has brought potential hardware solutions to the market with more likely to follow. Some devices aimed at the high end consumer market are suitable for virtual environments with compatible setups (for example, 5.1, 7.1, and 10.2). Such manufacturers as Audyssey, Denon, Creston, Marantz, NAD, Onkyo, and Phase Technology offer products in this category. Such professional audio manufacturers as Genelec and JBL offer self-calibrating systems integrated with active studio monitors.

For some VEs, such devices lack the necessary flexibility. For example, setups with a large number of loudspeakers are better served by manual equalization. Invaluable descriptions of the equalization process are available in Holman (1999) and Rumsey (2001).

Manual equalization is challenging, perhaps less a science than an art that relies on the tuner's ear and experience. Professional audio consulting services are available in most locales; though few specialize in multichannel audio, a competent consultant will be able to help novices to learn the fundamentals and achieve good quality equalization.

Monitor Level Alignment

Once equalized, monitor levels must be set uniformly using an SPL meter and a calibrated test signal. See Holman (1999) for a detailed description of this process. For safety, ensure the level on the playback device is *never* raised! (See "Safety").

Which level to select depends on the goals of the virtual environment; however, the SPL at the listening position should always be kept within safe limits (see "Safety") to avoid hearing damage or deafness. The combined SPL level from all loudspeakers should never exceed 120 dB, and exposure to levels above 100 dB should be brief.

By way of comparison, the standard for film is 83 dB SPL for pink noise at −20 dBF Srms (station remote manipulator system) (20 dB below full scale), yielding a maximum of 103 dB SPL. Dolby's surround mixing guidelines suggest 79 dB to 85 dB as target SPL values. Avoid the temptation to calibrate for a very high level unless it is necessary for the simulation. Most of the time, a level between 80 dB SPL and 95 dB SPL will suffice in VEs, which leaves headroom for equalization and keeps the level within safe limits.

Subwoofer Placement

Room acoustics are especially sensitive to subwoofer placement. The best way to find optimal placement is by experimentation with the equalization measurement setup in place to find the best response curve while feeding a pink-noise signal to the subwoofer (see "Room Equalization"). If the subwoofer lacks bass management circuitry, the pink-noise signal must be bandlimited to the subwoofer's maximum frequency. To avoid equipment and hearing damage, ensure that the subwoofer filters out frequencies below its lower threshold.

Small adjustments in subwoofer location can have a dramatic effect on room response. Patient, careful measurement is necessary to ensure optimal placement. A good starting point is slightly off-center with the driver between 6 and 20 inches from the front wall (consult manufacturer guidelines for specific distance requirements; placement too close to a wall can damage the driver). Then move the subwoofer a little to the left or right until it produces an optimal response at the listening position. Avoid corner placement, which can exaggerate bass response.

Because the loudspeakers and subwoofer can be different distances from the listening position, phase correction is vital. Mismatched phase will create a dip in the frequency response around the crossover point. Since each subwoofer affords different controls, the instruction manual is the best reference for how to correct for phase differences. Generally, this adjustment occurs after level adjustment (see "Subwoofer Level Alignment").

Subwoofer Level Alignment

Many subwoofers do not have a volume control, offering instead a sensitivity adjustment that is defined in terms of total SPL at a specified distance. With equalization measurement equipment in place, adjust the sensitivity or volume control so that at the listening position frequencies below the crossover point are at the same level as those above. Then proceed with phase adjustment. Note that subwoofer use requires bass management. If the chosen subwoofer does not have integrated bass management, install bass-management hardware in the signal path.

Headphones

With use of a dedicated amplifier, many headphones offer performance rivaling that of the best loudspeakers, yet at a significantly lower cost. Headphones offer the additional advantages that they avoid problems with room acoustics and are significantly easier to calibrate than a multichannel system. Open-ear headphones achieve excellent performance and are comfortable for long sessions, but do not isolate the listener from outside sounds. Closed headphones offer isolation, but can become hot and uncomfortable quickly. They also tend toward excessive bass due to pressure buildup in the closed space. Closed headphones, therefore, achieve high quality frequency response at higher financial cost than open-ear headphones. Finally, high end in-ear sets, such as those from Etymotic Research, Inc., offer a compromise yielding excellent performance and isolation with less discomfort than closed headphones. Most in-ear phones suffer from the "microphone effect" when the cable rubs against clothing or impacts objects, making them unsuitable for scenarios with much participant motion; however, the market has recently produced decent wireless headphones and earphones with reasonable performance. Be sure to audition such systems to ensure they meet the application demands.

Head-Related Transfer Functions

Spatial reproduction can be very effective over headphone systems employing head-related transfer function (HRTF) processing. Processing the source signal against a given HRTF for each ear yields a pair of waveforms that, when played directly into the ears, yields a spatialized source image. Because each person has a unique anatomy, each has a unique HRTF.

The ideal application of HRTF processing involves measuring each user's unique HRTF for use during playback. The measuring process is sensitive, time consuming, and generally requires the use of an anechoic chamber. While listener-specific HRTF renderings remain the most effective, they are generally inaccessible. However, much research has focused on generic HRTFs effective for all listeners. Most generalized HRTFs suffer from difficulties with frontal imaging, while rear and side imaging can be effective.

The results can be convincing. But since each ear has its own HRTF, efficacy varies per listener. However, with a good generalized HRTF, users can quickly adapt to the system. Because both ITD and IID cues are included for each frequency, HRTFs can provide highly accurate localization. HRTFs also avoid many of the pitfalls of other panning schemes. For example, there is no problem with precedence as the user walks around using an HRTF system. High quality headphones are ideal for HRTF processing.

There are two obstacles to using headphones in VEs. The first is that in many scenarios encumbering participants with additional equipment is unacceptable. Second, head rotation can break the spatial effect since a static source will appear to rotate along with the listener's head, which is contrary to normal experience. To leverage HRTF processing, VEs require a head-tracking system to correct for head rotations.

Several game-oriented sound cards offer headphone spatialization via HRTF processing with varied success. The analog output on even the best cards is generally too noisy (see "Hardware Selection") for VE use, so it is best to avoid game cards or to select cards that offer HRTF processed audio via digital output. Though Creative Labs has been the dominant manufacturer of game audio cards in recent years, such companies as Dolby and Nvidia are bringing new products to market that may offer new possibilities for VEs.

Some software packages with HRTF processing support several types of audio hardware. For example, FMOD runs on a variety of consoles and PC cards, as well as professional audio devices that ensure low noise output.

Recently "surround" and 5.1 headphones have come to market. These are in two classes, those targeted toward gamers and more high end earphones. The cheaper segment can be effective for gaming, but lacks the performance needed for a convincing virtual image. Even the higher end headphones suffer from the same problems as generic HRTFs and 5.1 systems, specifically difficulties with side and rear imaging. If possible, try out headphones in this category to aid evaluation.

AuSIM's GoldSeries products offer high quality spatial audio solutions for multiple listeners and a large number of virtual sources. They are available with integrated head-tracking hardware. Such high end solutions are prized for their nuanced sound and highly accurate localization The AuSIM products and their ancestors (for example, Convolvotron and Acoustetron) have a highly regarded position in headphone based virtual audio.

Individualized HRTFs through custom-fitted in-ear phones and a reference amplifier offer the highest quality sound. While such highly detailed reproduction is rarely necessary in a VE where sound is one of several stimuli, it is worth noting here as a point for comparison.

Headphone Amplification

Headphones of sufficient quality for use in VEs generally require a dedicated amplifier. Headphone amplifiers on the market range in price from around $50 to several thousand dollars. For VEs, a high quality, low noise amplifier with reasonably flat frequency response (around $200 to $600) is the base requirement and will suffice for most applications. VEs using high end headphones will benefit from a higher quality amplifier (in the range from $600 to $1,000). Scenarios in which reproduction with nuanced detail is crucial will need an even more sophisticated amplifier and excellent headphones (see "Vendors and Manufacturers").

Finally, for applications using HRTF processing via digital output, high quality headphone amplifiers with integrated digital-to-audio converters are a cost-effective option. Such manufacturers as Benchmark, HeadRoom, Grace Design, Grado, and STAX offer products in this area. Ironically, most professional audio (proaudio) headphone amps have inferior performance since they generally are studio task oriented, geared toward such functions as signal distribution and talk-back rather than toward critical listening, making them unsuitable for VEs.

To calibrate headphones simply apply the method described for loudspeakers (see "Monitor Level Alignment"), but with the microphones placed where the ears would be. Note that headphone amplification must remain fixed after calibration. Because of the possibility of hearing damage due to erroneously loud output, employ safety measures that ensure output level never exceeds a prescribed maximum (for example, a brick-wall limiter) (see "Safety"). Additionally, a policy of setting the volume to zero before each use, then gradually raising the volume to the calibrated level guarantees that no accidental audio bursts harm participants during scenario setup. If possible, listeners should not don their earphones until all devices and simulation software have been booted and initialized.

SAFETY

Powerful audio equipment is extremely dangerous. To protect the hearing of trainees and workers, engineer safety procedures and enforce them rigorously. A few simple precautions will protect people and equipment.

The threshold of pain is around 120 dB SPL, with immediate hearing damage or hearing loss around 145 dB SPL. Calibrate all loudspeakers to a maximum combined level below 116 dB SPL at the listening position. Require hearing protection during setup and calibration, and when testing new audio equipment or software drivers.

Install a brick-wall limiter in the signal path to each channel. These devices attenuate signals above a specified maximum level ensuring inappropriate signal levels do not reach the loudspeakers. Some devices (for example, dbx ZonePRO processors) provide limiters and can be networked to a universal volume/mute control, an excellent precaution. Always mute the system and turn the volume down before and after each run. Increase the volume gradually at the start of each session.

The most common and most dangerous problem in a multiloudspeaker system is the propagation of a single small error through all loudspeakers. A small pop, replicated 10 or more times becomes extremely loud. To protect against this common hazard, install a sound-pressure monitor in the listening space that cuts the power and signal to all loudspeakers if the measured sound reaches an unsafe instantaneous threshold (for example, a loud click) or exceeds a value integrated over time (for example, feedback).

Operators should consider custom earplugs with flat frequency response. This inexpensive precaution affords attenuated listening without undesirable coloration or filtering.

COMPUTING AUDIO

Platforms and Application Programming Interfaces

There are many platforms and application programming interfaces (APIs) for computing audio. In the context of VEs, CRE_TRON from AuSIM is perhaps the best known. The CRE_TRON API controls AuSIM's HRTF based audio engine, AuSIM3D, which offers high quality audio via headphones. AuSIM also offers direct integration with head-tracking hardware, useful for VEs intending to use headphones and HRTFs.

Some APIs, such as OpenAL, FMOD, and DirectSound, offer high level controls (for example, spatialized audio, filters, and environmental reverberance). These implementations generally assume standard loudspeaker arrangements common in video game setups. Yet VEs commonly utilize different setups with larger numbers of output channels and nonstandard loudspeaker layouts to achieve high quality reproduction. These VEs will require specialized audio platforms that offer spatialization over arbitrary setups. These systems support arbitrary loudspeaker setups through such algorithms as VBAP (Vector Base Amplitude Panning; Pulkki, 1997), Ambisonics, or SPCAP (speaker-placement correction amplitude panning; Sadek & Kyriakakis, 2004). Some of these systems offer an API based on a standardized interface, such as OpenAL (for example, ARIA [Sadek, 2004]), allowing them to be "dropped in" to existing systems.

VEs with very demanding requirements or complex software may need to develop an in-house audio engine on top of low level platforms such as ASIO, CoreAudio or PortAudio (Greenebaum, 2004). Finally, companies such as VRSonic that specialize in audio for VEs offer tools for content production, as well as services for setup and design.

Hardware Selection

The market offers a wide range of audio hardware devices with rich feature sets. A few key aspects of hardware selection are critical for VEs, namely, bit depth, sampling rate, and latency in addition to such general performance considerations as signal-to-noise ratio (SNR) and quality of digital-analog converters (DACs). For example, in the common case of an installation with many loudspeakers at high amplification, the signal-to-noise ratio is critical. A bad SNR inhibits the dynamic range of the system. Consider a training scenario with occasional gunfire; this scene requires a huge dynamic range. A high quality, well-isolated audio system may produce 80 dB of dynamic range, while a medium-grade system yields about 50 dB SNR. The 30 dB of additional dynamic range yields reproduction far superior and, in fact, necessary for the training scenario.

Consumer or video game hardware cards generally include the DACs directly on the card, which yields poor noise performance. For example, the electrical noise from hard disks, graphics cards, and so forth, contaminate the analog output in a clearly audible manner. These manufacturers list impressive SNR performance for their DACs, but these measurements are often conducted in isolation, ignoring the contaminating effects of an operating computer system. Small-scale testing before investment is the best way to ensure good noise performance. Users can test the noise performance with free software tools, such as the Right-Mark Audio Analyzer.

Due to the large amount of electrical system noise on a running computer, choose hardware with DACs on a separate interface or breakout box rather than attached to the system bus directly. Many of these interfaces connect to the bus with a PCI (peripheral component interconnect) or PCIe (peripheral component interconnect express) card, which is perfectly acceptable because the DACs' location in the external interface can isolate them from bus noise.

Many of these interfaces connect via a universal serial bus (USB) or FireWire rather than through a PCI card. Note, however, that a poorly designed breakout box may not protect against system noise; a well designed PCI card may shield against system noise more effectively. Because FireWire has higher priority than the USB, FireWire breakout boxes generally suffer less noise and fewer dropouts than USB hardware.

Many manufacturers (for example, MOTU, RME, Digidesign, and PresSonus) offer high quality external interfaces with isolation from system noise. Hardware with optical connections avoid electrical noise transmission by sending a digital signal over a nonconductive medium to an external digital-to-analog converter. This is the most effective way to combat bus noise.

Bit Depth

To capture the dynamic range of human hearing requires 24 bits, so 24 bit DACs are necessary; avoid 16 bit DACs. Internal processing (filtering, mixing, and so forth) requires higher bit depth for accurate computations. Most manufacturers of high quality hardware utilize a high bit depth processing chain. Be certain to look for this if using the device for any internal computations (for example, mixing, filtering, limiting, and gain).

Finally, note that the quality of the DACs is important. Low quality 24 bit DACs may have as few as 18 effective bits, with the remaining bits essentially noise. Seek as much information as possible about the DACs used in hardware under consideration. Such analysis tools as RightMark can help in this evaluation. Reputable manufacturers (for example, RME, MOTU, and so forth) generally have reasonable DAC performance.

Sample Rate

Hardware interfaces often have an adjustable sampling rate. In general, 48 kHz is ideal for most VEs. Some hardware offers sampling rates of 96 kHz or even 192 kHz. Debate over the use of these high resolution formats continues. However, while 48 kHz encompasses the entire audible frequency range in theory, practical complications suggest that high resolution formats will be prevalent in the future. For example, clock jitter and bit rounding create audible artifacts in frequencies near the Nyquist limit of the sampling rate. Some have also argued that higher sampling rates can offer lower latency, as well as improved internal processing during filtering.

Finally, some DACs that operate at higher clock rates (for example, 192 kHz) offer improved SNR performance when run at lower clock rates (for example, 48 kHz). Most VEs will not need the higher clock rates, though there is no harm in using hardware that supports them. However, if the higher sampling rate is not needed, set the hardware to 48 kHz to avoid the performance cost of processing the larger number of samples.

Buffer Length and Latency

The buffer length on the audio hardware affects both the audio latency and system performance. Latency refers to the time in between the time a sound sample enters a buffer and the time when it is heard. The sample must wait until the previous buffer is processed, making a direct correlation between buffer length and latency. Because the buffer processing speed is bound to the clock rate of the DAC, buffer length is directly related to real time. Each buffer has a certain processing overhead. Shorter buffers yield lower latency, but require more CPU time, while longer buffers consume less CPU, but cause greater latency. Tactile applications invoking a sampled sound (such as firearm triggers) require low latency sounds to avoid feeling sluggish or "gummy." High quality hardware devices offer latencies ranging from under 1 ms (millisecond) to 100 ms or more, allowing room for adjustment when trading latency against CPU performance.

ENVIRONMENTAL EFFECTS

Since each space has a unique acoustic character, emulating the acoustic characteristics of the virtual world solidifies the effect of the VE by blurring the line between the physical and the virtual. Game systems such as Creative Labs' Environmental Audio Extensions or FMOD offer filters and reverbs, modeling acoustic spaces and occlusions. These effects are generally not physically accurate, but are tuned to sound plausible and are quite effective in a video game setting.

However, as mentioned earlier (see "Platforms and Application Programming Interfaces") the spatialization algorithms in these systems require the type of setup used in a gaming environment and cannot be extended to the high end set-ups employed in VEs.

When physically accurate reverberance is required, VEs can leverage sophisticated acoustic modeling software to generate reverbs or use commercially available reverbs from measured data. Alternatively, VEs can use a system such as FMOD that offers digital signal processing functionality leveraging direct access to output channel to implement their own spatialization using an algorithm such as VBAP, Ambisonics, or SPCAP (see "Rendering Techniques" and "Platforms and Application Programming Interfaces").

First-order reflections (early reverberance) are the most important psychoacoustic cues regarding the surrounding space. Accurate reproduction of early reverberance materializes the virtual space, improving localization and immersion. When evaluating environmental effects solutions, give the highest priority to reproduction of accurate early reflections.

TRADE-OFFS

Audio computation platforms and hardware offer many trade-offs between performance, implementation complexity, equipment cost, and feature sets. Trade-offs include certain factors that are not represented in technical specifications, but nonetheless greatly affect development. For example, poor-quality hardware drivers are detrimental to system stability. Given a software malfunction, a good driver will exit gracefully, while a poor driver will crash the computer. Check the rate at which manufacturers offer updates for their drivers as an indicator of such bugs.

Latency and CPU performance are in direct opposition due to the increased overhead of processing the larger number of buffers. The situation is complicated further by driver implementations; lesser hardware interfaces tend toward worse performance at a given latency. At times, this sacrifice is worth the cost savings, whereas at other times it only makes sense to select to faster, more expensive hardware.

Similarly, game cards offer desirable features such as environmental effects and occlusion. A VE may choose these features at the expense of sound quality, setup flexibility, and system stability. Conversely, VEs can utilize reverbs based on sophisticated models or measured data at the cost of higher implementation complexity and higher computational expense.

These trade-offs extend into setup and calibration as well. Self-calibrating systems can save much time, at greater equipment cost, while manual calibration can achieve optimal quality with significant time investment. The possible trade-offs are too many to list and vary per VE. Each design must account for the specific needs and goals of the VE when determining which trades to make. Careful attention to these details during the design phase goes a long way toward a smooth, successful implementation.

VENDORS AND MANUFACTURERS

Following is a list of Web sites and vendors specifically mentioned in this text. Holman (1999, pp. 255–266) offers a more inclusive appendix of manufacturers and resources from measurement equipment to outboard equipment and multi-channel meters.

Acoustic Treatments
StudioPanel: www.studio-panel.com
Auralex: www.auralex.com

Automated Equalization
Audyssey: www.audyssey.com
Denon: www.denon.com

Headphones and Headphone Systems
HeadRoom: www.headphone.com
AKG: www.akg.com
Etymotic: www.etymotic.com
Grado: www.gradolabs.com
Sennheiser: www.sennheiserusa.com
Shure: www.shure.com
AuSIM: www.ausim3d.com

Loudspeaker Manufacturers
Genelec: www.genelec.com
JBL: www.jbl.com
Mackie: www.mackie.com
ADAM: www.adam-audio.com
Tannoy: www.tannoy-speakers.com

Professional Audio Vendors
B&H: www.bhphotovideo.com
GCPro: www.gcpro.com
Sweetwater: www.sweetwater.com

ACKNOWLEDGMENT OF SPONSORSHIP

The project or effort described here has been sponsored by the U.S. Army Research, Development, and Engineering Command (RDECOM). Statements and opinions expressed do not necessarily reflect the position or the policy of the United States Government, and no official endorsement should be inferred.

REFERENCES

Begault, D. (1994). *3D sound for virtual reality and multimedia.* Moffett Field, CA: Ames Research Center.

Blauert, J. (1997). *Spatial hearing: The psychophysics of human sound localization.* Cambridge, MA: MIT Press.

Cook, P. (Ed.). (2001). *Music, cognition, and computerized sound: An introduction to psychoacoustics.* Cambridge, MA: MIT Press.

Cook, P. (2002). *Real sound synthesis for interactive applications.* Natick, MA: A K Peters.

Crocker, M. (Ed.). (1998). *Handbook of acoustics.* New York: Wiley.

Everest, F. (Ed.). (2001). *The master handbook of acoustics.* New York: McGraw-Hill.

Greenebaum, K. (2004). *Audio anecdotes: Tools, tips, and techniques for digital audio.* Natick, MA: A K Peters.

Haliday, D., Resnick, R., & Walker, J. (2007). *Fundamentals of physics extended* (4th ed). New York: John Wiley & Sons, Inc.

Holman, T. (1999). *5.1 channel surround sound: Up and running.* Oxford: Focal Press.

Lyons, R. (2004). *Understanding digital signal processing.* Upper Saddle River, NJ: Prentice Hall PIR.

Pulkki, V. (1997). Virtual sound source positioning using vector base amplitude panning. *Journal of the Audio Engineering Society.*

Rumsey, F. (2001). *Spatial audio.* Boston: Focal Press.

Sadek, R. (2004). A host-based real-time multichannel immersive sound playback and processing system. *Proceedings of the Audio Engineering Society 117th Convention.*

Sadek, R., & Kyriakakis, C. (2004). A novel multichannel panning method for standard and arbitrary loudspeaker configurations. *Proceedings of the Audio Engineering Society 117th Convention.*

Sherman, W., & Craig, A. (2002). *Understanding virtual reality.* Morgan Kaufman.

Watkinson, J. (2001). *Art of digital audio.* Oxford: Focal Press.

Chapter 5

MULTIMODAL DISPLAY SYSTEMS: HAPTIC, OLFACTORY, GUSTATORY, AND VESTIBULAR

Çağatay Başdoğan and R. Bowen Loftin

The Sensorama is the prototypical embodiment of a virtual environment (VE), conceived and implemented years before "VR" (or "virtual reality") became a common term. Whereas VR has been often characterized as "goggles and gloves," Heilig (1962) developed a truly multimodal display system that provided for stereoscopic vision, binaural audition, haptics (wind in the face; vibration or "jolts"), and olfaction. Figure 5.1 shows the patent drawing for the containers that served as the Sensorama's olfactory sources. Those containers, coupled with the system's fan, comprise what is likely the first example of an olfactory display that was integrated with other display modalities. In many respects his invention still stands alone in terms of the degree of integration of multimodal displays in a practical device that provided a compelling virtual experience for the user. In this chapter we examine nonvisual and nonauditory displays that have been used or have the potential to be used in virtual environments for training.

INTRODUCTION

Motivation and Scope

In most virtual environments the visual display is dominant, usually followed in importance by the auditory display. These display modalities are described elsewhere (see Welch and Davis, Volume 2, Section 1, Chapter 1; Henderson and Feiner, Volume 2, Section 1, Chapter 6; and Whitton and Brooks, Volume 2, Section 1, Chapter 12). There are circumstances, however, where other display "dimensions" are critical to the effective training of a user. In fact, there is evidence that, in some cases, vision may not be the dominant sense (Shams, Kamitani, & Shimojo, 2000). In this chapter we provide access to the dimensions of haptics, olfaction, gestation, and acceleration/orientation. The inclusion of these display modalities is motivated by the need to create a virtual environment that

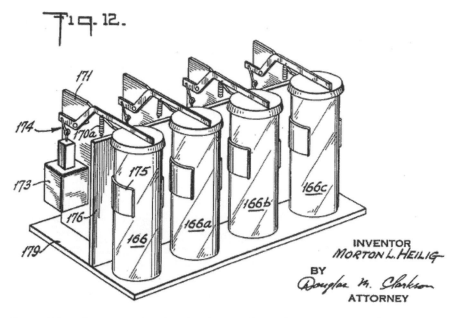

Figure 5.1.   The patent drawing for the containers that served as the Sensorama's olfactory sources is shown.

maps more fully onto the real world and to exploit some uniquely human reliance on senses other than vision and audition.

Loftin (2003) has considered the potential of multimodal displays to expand the human "bandwidth" for perceiving complex, multivariate data. In the training domain this may be even more important since we may wish to replicate the real world to the greatest extent possible. After all, humans routinely employ all of their senses simultaneously as they go about their normal tasks. Certainly, we can compensate when one or more senses are impaired (for example, the common cold can compromise the sense of smell), but such compensation may not be adequate for some training purposes. Also, the use of sensory modality as a substitute for another could lead to negative training or poor transfer from the training environment to the real environment.

Consider some of the common circumstances in which the nonvisual and non-auditory senses play important roles. A surgeon may depend on olfaction (the sense of smell) to detect that the bowel has been perforated (Krueger, 1995). Smells can be very important in producing the crucial contexts for some training environments, including the smell of fire, blood, cooking food, an animal presence, or vegetation. In some cases the presence of the correct smell could "make or break" the sense of realism (fidelity) that training requires.

In the technical descriptions, an effort has been made to build on what was provided in the *Handbook for Virtual Environments* (Stanney, 2002). Thus, we have typically included only updates on developments since 2001 for those technologies that were fully described in the *Handbook*. This approach applies primarily to the sections on haptic and vestibular displays. The *Handbook* contains a very short section on olfactory displays and nothing on gustatory displays. A recent and relatively comprehensive treatment of multimodal interfaces has been produced by Kortum (2008).

HAPTICS

Haptics Technology

Haptics is a highly interdisciplinary research area that aims to understand how humans and machines touch, explore, and manipulate objects in real, virtual, or teleoperated worlds. One of the most distinguishing features of touch from other sensory modalities is that it is a bilateral process. We can look and observe the objects using our eyes, but cannot change their state. However, when we explore an unknown object in our hand, we instinctually rotate it to change its state (Lederman & Klatzky, 1987). Haptic exploration not only gives an idea about the shape and surface properties of an object, but also provides information on its material properties, such as softness. Perception and manipulation through touch are both accomplished via tactile and kinesthetic channels. Various types of receptors located under one's skin are responsible for the tactile perception. These receptors can sense even very small variations in pressure, texture, temperature, surface details, and so on. Kinesthetic perception in the brain occurs through information supplied by the muscles, tendons, and receptors located in the joints. For example, while perception of textures or surface roughness is more of a tactile activity, feeling reaction forces when pushing an object involves kinesthetic system. Unfortunately, we know very little about how tactile and kinesthetic information is transmitted and processed by the brain.

Developing haptic devices that enable tactile and kinesthetic interactions with real and virtual objects has been challenging. Our haptic interactions with physical objects around us mainly involve the use of hands. The human hand has a complex anatomy and function, and developing interfaces that fully imitate its sensing and actuation capabilities is beyond our reach today. This challenge can be better appreciated if we consider that the human hand has 27 degrees of freedom, each finger can be actuated by more than one muscle group, and there are approximately 100 receptors in one centimeter square area of a finger pad. Several different haptic devices have been developed to enable touch interactions with objects in real, virtual, or teleoperated worlds (see the review of devices in Burdea, 1996). In general, the performance of a haptic device is highly coupled to its design. A high quality haptic device has a low apparent inertia, high stiffness, low friction, and minimal backlash. Actuator selection affects the range of dynamic forces that can be displayed using the interface. Moreover, high sensor resolution and force update rates are desired to achieve stable touch interactions. For example, the haptic loop must be updated at a rate close to one kilohertz to render rigid surfaces.

One way to categorize haptic devices is whether they are passive or active. For example, a keyboard, a mouse, and a trackball can be considered as passive devices since they supply input only (unidirectional). On the other hand, a force-reflecting robotic arm can be programmed to display forces to the user based on his or her inputs (bidirectional).

A second way that haptic devices can be categorized is based on whether they are grounded or ungrounded. For example, a joystick has a fixed base and is considered as a grounded haptic device. On the other hand, exoskeleton-type haptic devices are attached to the user's arm (and move around with it) and are considered ungrounded. Today, most of the devices in this category are bulky, heavy, and not very user friendly.

A third way to categorize haptic devices is based on whether they are net-force or tactile displays. The idea behind the net-force displays, such as the PHANTOM device (Massie & Salisbury, 1994), is to reduce the complex haptic interactions of a human hand with its environment to a single point. On the other hand, a net-force/torque display provides limited information about the complex distribution of forces that are perceived when, for example, a textured surface is stroked with one's fingertip. The tactile devices are developed to display distributed forces to a user. For example, an array of individually actuated pins (tactile pin array) has been used to perturb the skin at the user's fingertip.

Finally, one could also distinguish between impedance control, where the user's input motion (acceleration, velocity, and position) is measured and an output force is returned (as in a PHANTOM haptic device) versus admittance control, where the input forces exerted by user are measured and motion is fed back to the user, as in Haptic Master sold by Fokker Control Systems (http://www.fcs-cs.com/robotics). Impedance devices are simpler to design and are most common, while admittance devices are generally used for applications requiring high forces in a large workspace (Salisbury, Conti, & Barbagli, 2004).

Training Applications

In this chapter, we focus only on applications of active haptic devices in training of human operators since covering all applications of haptic devices would be a very exhaustive task. The early application of active haptic devices dates back to the 1950s. Force-reflecting devices were used to convey contact forces to a human operator during remote manipulation of radioactive substances at Argonne National Laboratory. The number of applications increased drastically in the 1990s since the appearance of commercial devices that enable touch interactions with virtual objects. Also, the concept of *haptic rendering* has emerged (Salisbury, Brock, Massie, Swarup, & Zilles, 1995; Srinivasan & Başdoğan, 1997). Displaying forces to a user through a haptic device such that he or she can touch, feel, and manipulate objects in virtual environments is known as haptic rendering (see the recent review in Başdoğan, Laycock, Day, Patoglu, & Gillespie, 2008). Analogous to graphical rendering, haptic rendering is concerned with the techniques and processes associated with generating and displaying haptic stimuli to the human user. A haptic rendering algorithm is typically made of two parts: (a) collision detection and (b) collision response. As the user holds and manipulates the end effector of the haptic device, the new position and orientation of the haptic probe are acquired, and collisions between the virtual model of the probe and virtual objects in the scene are detected. If a collision is detected, the interaction forces are computed using preprogrammed rules for collision response. The forces are then conveyed to the user through the haptic device to provide him or her with the haptic representation of the 3D object and its surface details.

With the development of desktop hapatic devices and commercial rendering libraries, the field has shown a significant expansion during the last decade. New applications have emerged in fields, including medicine (surgical simulation, telemedicine, haptic user interfaces for blind persons, and rehabilitation for patients with neurological disorders), dental medicine, art and entertainment (3D painting, character animation, digital sculpting, and virtual museums), computer-aided product design (free-form modeling, assembly and disassembly, including insertion and removal of parts), scientific visualization (geophysical data analysis, molecular simulation, and flow visualization), and robotics (path planning and telemanipulation).

In the following discussion of applications, we focus on the use of haptics in training of the human operator. For example, there is a need to improve the ability of humans to direct remote manipulation tasks; the improved performance can be achieved through simulation based training in virtual environments.

One of the applications of this concept is in space exploration. For example, today, the interaction between a human operator located on earth and a rover located on the remote planet is provided through a set of edited text commands only. However, this approach restricts the complexity of transmitted commands and likewise reduces the quantity and quality of data return. In addition, these commands do not always make the best set since they are not extensively tested before being transmitted to the rover. For example, if the task involves handling and manipulation of objects (for example, collecting rock samples) a rover faces several uncertainties when executing it (for example, whether the sample is at a reachable distance, how to hold the sample, and so forth). Planning, scheduling, and synchronization of rover tasks that involve autonomous manipulation of objects will be even more challenging in the future when multiple rovers are used concurrently for planetary exploration and they have to work cooperatively.

The National Aeronautics and Space Administration's (NASA's) Jet Propulsion Laboratory (JPL) has developed a multimodal virtual reality system for training a rover operator to plan robotic manipulation tasks effectively (Başdoğan & Bergman, 2001). This system utilizes dual haptic arms and a semi-immersive visualization system and is designed to train and prepare a rover operator for executing complex haptic manipulation tasks (see Figure 5.2). The training simulations involve a scenario where the operator commands a planetary rover while it collects rock samples. The observations and experiences gained from these simulations are used to help identify situations and issues the rover is likely to encounter when it performs the same tasks autonomously on the surface of Mars. In this regard, mapping the activities of a human operator to the activities of a robotic system—transforming inputs from the haptic arms into control signals for the robotic system—is a challenging research problem (Griffin, 2003).

Similar to the efforts at JPL, the Lyndon B. Johnson Space Center (JSC) at Houston trains spacecraft crew members for extravehicular activities (EVAs). EVA tasks, such as setting up an instrument, assembly, maintenance, or carrying out repairs, are inherently risky. One approach to minimizing risks is to train crew members in a multimodal virtual environment on earth, before they do it in space (Loftin & Kenney, 1995). A virtual model of the Hubble Space Telescope (HST) was constructed to train members of the NASA HST flight team on maintenance and repair procedures. Another approach is to use humanoid robots commanded through a telepresence interface to perform these tasks.

Robonaut, developed at JSC, is an anthropomorphic, astronaut-sized robot configured with two arms, two five-fingered hands, a head, and a torso (Ambrose et al., 2000). The earlier telepresence interface of the Robonaut system utilized the CyberGlove haptic system (Immersion Corporation) to guide the articulated movements of the Robonaut arm without force feedback to the human operator. Later, CyberGlove was replaced with dual force feedback joysticks to improve the grasping abilities of the operator (O'Malley & Ambrose, 2003).

Another popular application of haptics is in surgical training. From the start of medicine to the modern standardized surgical training programs, the training paradigm for surgeons has not changed substantially. Surgical training has been based traditionally on the "apprenticeship" model, in which the novice surgeon is trained with small groups of peers and superiors, over time, in the course of patient care. However, this training model has been placed under inspection, and its efficiency is being questioned by experts, physicians, and the public. According to the report "To Err Is Human" prepared by the National Academy of Science, Institute of Medicine in 1999, the human cost of medical errors is

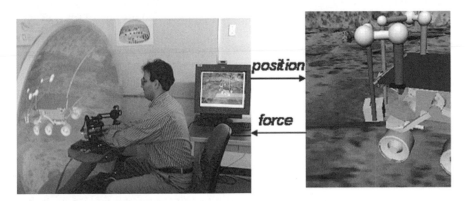

Figure 5.2.   This is a view of JPL's multimodal virtual reality system used for training with a fleet of rovers.

high, and more people die from medical mistakes each year than from highway accidents, breast cancer, or AIDS combined.

Minimally invasive surgery (MIS) is a revolutionary surgery technique in immediate need of improved training methods. MIS has been used in a range of procedures since the early 1960s (for example, if the surgery is done in the abdominal area, it is called laparoscopic surgery). This technology uses a small video camera and a few customized instruments to perform surgery. The camera and instruments are inserted into the surgery area through small skin incisions or natural orifices that enable the surgeon to explore the internal cavity without the need of making large openings. Major advantages of this type of surgery to the patient are short hospital stay, timely return to work, and less pain and scarring after the surgery.

Although MIS has several advantages over traditional open surgery, surgeons are handicapped by the limitations of the technology. For example, haptic cues are substantially reduced since the surgeon has to interact with internal organs by means of surgical instruments attached to long thin tubes. While the importance of training in MIS has been well acknowledged, there is no consensus on the best or most effective method to do this training. Box trainers, for instance, are an inanimate model equipped with real surgical instruments, endoscopic cameras, and plastic tissue models. These trainers provide an environment similar to that of real surgery settings. However, simulated surgical procedures are usually poor imitations of the actual ones. Currently, animal training is considered the most realistic training model available. This model is dynamic and approaches real operative conditions. Animal tissues, although not always of the same consistency as human tissues, do respond in a similar way to the forces applied to them. The use of animals for training purposes, however, is expensive and controversial. Moreover, the trainee's performance cannot be measured quantitatively.

Simulation based training using virtual reality techniques (see Figure 5.3) has been suggested as an alternative to the traditional training in MIS. Surgical simulators developed for this purpose enable the trainee to touch, feel, and manipulate virtual tissues and organs through the haptic devices, while displaying high quality images of tool-tissue interactions on a computer monitor as in real surgery (see the review in Başdoğan, Sedef, Harders, & Wesarg, 2007).

In addition to displaying forces arising from tool-tissue interaction during the simulation of surgical procedures, haptic devices can be also used for playing back prerecorded haptic stimuli. For example, a physician relies heavily on haptic cues when guiding a needle into epidural space. The appreciation of forces at each layer is important for the proper guidance of the needle. Dang, Annaswamy, and Srinivasan (2001) experimented with two modes of haptic guidance. In the first, the simulator displays a virtual guiding needle on the screen that moves along the same path and with the same speed as an expert in a prerecorded trial. If the user's needle position exactly matches that of the guiding virtual needle, the user feels the same forces that the expert felt. In the event of a mismatch, the virtual instructor applies a force to pull the trainee back to the prerecorded trajectory. In the second mode, or tunnel guidance, we disregard the

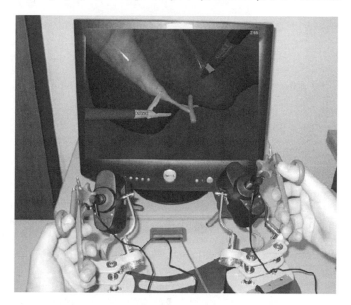

Figure 5.3. This is a view of simulation based training using virtual reality techniques.

time dependency of the recorded data such that users perform the task at their own speed. The needle's movement is limited to the prerecorded trajectory, allowing users to concentrate solely on the forces encountered at each layer along the needle's insertion path.

Another application of haptics in medicine is in the area of rehabilitation. Since the nervous system is highly adaptive and open to reprogramming, a haptic arm can be used to teach it how to control movements. For example, a force feedback robotic arm and artificial force fields have been used to train and improve the motor performance of patients with chronic impairment after stroke (Krebs & Hogan, 2006). Patients were asked to perform goal-directed, planar-reaching tasks that emphasized shoulder and elbow movements under the force guidance of the robotic arm. Clinical results with well over 300 stroke patients, both inpatients and outpatients, proved that movement therapy has a measurable and significant impact on recovery following brain injury.

There are also applications of haptic technology in military training. At Massachusetts Institute of Technology (MIT), under a large interdisciplinary program called Virtual Environments Technology for Training (VETT) funded by the Office of Naval Research, software and hardware technologies were developed to augment the perceptual and cognitive skills of the U.S. Navy students in training. For example, a virtual model of an electronics test console was developed to teach students basic electricity and electronics. Haptic interactions with toggle buttons, multimeter probes, and switches on the console were simulated (Davidson, 1996). In another study, experiments were designed to investigate whether haptic feedback improves their ability to control the direction of a surface ship while they navigate the ship in a complex virtual environment where there are other ships and harbor hazards such as bridges. The main goal of this study was to teach U.S. Navy students basic concepts of vector algebra and dynamical systems. The results of this study showed that subjects have learned the influence of ship inertia and water currents on its heading better under the guidance of force feedback (see Durlach et al., 1999).

Artificial Force Fields for Training and Task Guidance

One of the benefits of active haptic devices in training for telemanipulation tasks is that they can be programmed to guide or restrict the movements of the user by introducing *artificial force fields*. Artificial force fields, also known as *virtual fixtures,* have been shown to improve user performance and learning in telemanipulation tasks in real world and training tasks simulated in virtual environments (Rosenberg, 1993; Payandeh & Stanisic, 2002; Bettini, Lang, Okamura, & Hager, 2002; Bukusoglu, Başdoğan, Kiraz, & Kurt, 2006). The term virtual fixture refers to a software implemented haptic guidance tool that helps the user perform a task by limiting his or her movements to restricted regions and/or influencing its movement along a desired path (Rosenberg, 1993). The virtual fixtures can be thought of as a ruler or a stencil (Abbott & Okamura, 2003). By the help of a ruler or stencil, a person can draw lines and shapes faster and more precisely than the ones drawn by freehand. Similar to the passive stencil, an active haptic device can be programmed to apply forces to the user in a virtual environment to train him or her for executing a task more efficiently and precisely. Obviously, this concept is not only useful for training, but also for actual execution of the task in the real world.

In comparison to real physical constraints, the type and the number of virtual constraints that can be programmed are unlimited. Artificial force fields offer an excellent balance between automated operation and direct human control. They can be programmed to help the operator carry out a structured task faster. For example, studies on telemanipulation systems show that user performance on a given task can increase as much as 70 percent with the introduction of virtual fixtures (Rosenberg, 1993).

Some other applications of virtual fixtures include robotic-assisted surgery and optical manipulation (Abbott & Okamura, 2003; Başdoğan, Kiraz, Bukusoglu, Varol, & Doganay, 2007). For example, Başdoğan and his colleagues showed that displaying guidance forces through a haptic device improves the task learning and performance of the operator significantly in telemanipulation of microparticles via optical tweezers. The task was to construct a coupled microsphere resonator made of four microspheres by individually steering and binding three spheres to an anchor sphere. One group was trained and used a system giving only visual feedback; the other group trained with and used a system providing both visual and haptic feedback. An artificial force field was used to help subjects position the particles precisely and to make the binding process easier. The summation of guidance forces (an artificial force field) and the estimated drag force was displayed to the subjects in the second group through a haptic interface. After the training, the performance of both groups was tested in the physical setup. Experiments showed that guidance under haptic feedback resulted in almost two-fold improvements in the average path error and average speed.

Challenges

Aerospace, maritime, military, nuclear energy, and other high risk professions have been using simulators for training difficult and demanding tasks for the last 50 years. By integrating force feedback devices into simulators, some of these industries have augmented the perceptual, cognitive, and motor control skills of the human operators and reduced errors significantly. The flight simulators equipped with force feedback joysticks provide a convincing example for the importance of simulation technology and the significant role that haptics play in training. Just as flight simulators are used to train pilots nowadays, it is, for example, anticipated that surgical simulators will be used to train physicians in the near future. The role of haptic feedback in this application is also unquestionable. Moreover, several studies in the past have shown the significance of haptics in teleoperation tasks in real and virtual worlds. For example, artificial force fields not only enable us to train the human operator in virtual environments, but also help him or her execute the teleoperated task better and faster in the real world.

Significant progress has been made in academia and industry in haptics, but there are still many research questions waiting to be answered. While it is difficult, and outside the scope of this chapter, to answer all these questions, we highlight some of the outstanding research challenges that require further attention: one of the constant challenges in integrating haptics into virtual environments is the need for a variety of haptic devices with the requisite degrees of freedom, range, resolution, and frequency bandwidth, both in terms of forces and displacements. Also, the price of next generation haptic devices must be significantly lower in order to be purchased by all computer users. In this regard, it is worth mentioning the Falcon haptic device, which was recently introduced by Novint Technologies and costs less than $200. It is hard to imagine that a single universal device can be used for all applications since the requirements of each application are different. For example, the motions and forces involved in laparoscopic surgical operations are small. Ideally, the haptic device used for laparoscopic training must have a fine resolution and 6 to 7 degrees of freedom. On the other hand, a haptic device designed for rehabilitation applications may have a lower resolution, but require a larger workspace.

Another area of hardware design that requires further investigation is multifingered haptic devices and tactile displays. It has been demonstrated that when we gather information about the shape and size of an object through touch, our fingers and hand move in an optimal manner. Moreover, robotics studies show that at least three fingers are necessary for stable grasp. On the other hand, there are only a few multifingered haptic devices that are commercially available today. For example, CyberGrasp from Immersion Corporation is an exoskeleton having individual wires pulling each finger to prevent its penetration into a virtual object during the simulation of grasping. Designing and building multifingered haptic devices becomes increasingly more difficult as the degrees of freedom of the device increases. Hardware for displaying distributed forces on the skin also remains a challenging problem. Very crude tactile displays for VEs are now available in the market; many of them are vibrotactile displays. The tactile devices developed in research laboratories are mostly in the form of an array of pins actuated individually. Packaging an array of actuators that does not break or hinder an active user is highly challenging, and new technologies must be explored to make significant progress in this area (see the review in Biggs & Srinivasan, 2002).

There are also several challenges that remain to be solved in the area of haptic rendering. Computational cost of rendering virtual objects grows drastically with the geometric complexity of the scene, type of haptic interactions, and the material properties of the objects (for example, soft versus rigid). The simulation of haptic interactions between a point probe and a rigid virtual object has been achieved (that is, 3 degrees of freedom haptic rendering), and many of the point based rendering algorithms have been already incorporated into commercial software products, but the simulation of object-object interactions is still an active area of research (see the review of 6 degrees of freedom haptic rendering techniques in Otaduy & Lin, 2008). While point based interaction approaches are sufficient for the exploration of object surfaces, more advanced rendering techniques are necessary for simulating *tool-object* interactions. For example, in medical simulation, side collisions occur frequently between simulated surgical instruments and deformable organs, and 3 degrees of freedom haptic rendering techniques cannot accurately handle this situation (see the details in Başdoğan, De, Kim, Muniyandi, & Srinivasan, 2004). In fact, simulating the nonlinear dynamics of physical contact between an organ and a surgical instrument, as well as surrounding tissues, is very challenging, and there will be a continued demand for efficient algorithms, especially when the haptic display needs to be synchronized with the display of visual, auditory, and other modalities. In this regard, one of the missing components is the lack of detailed human-factors studies. Even if we assume that the hardware and software components of visual, haptic, and auditory displays will improve one day to provide richer stimulation for our sensory channels, the perception of the information is still going to be performed by the user. Hence, a better understanding and measurement of human perceptual and cognitive abilities is important for more effective training and better training transfer.

OLFACTORY DISPLAYS

Today few virtual environments employ olfactory displays. Nonetheless, olfaction is an important sense and has been shown to stimulate both emotional (Corbin, 1982) and recall (Chu & Downes, 2000; Degel, Piper, & Koester, 2001) responses. Most of us have had the experience of detecting a specific smell that "took us back" to a place or an event. In addition, olfaction can have both directional and nondirectional capabilities. From a training perspective there are certainly virtual environment application areas (medical, combat, electronic fault detection, and so forth) that have a demonstrable need for an olfactory "dimension."

Technology

Work on olfactory displays is fairly recent. A good body of literature on olfaction is extant (see, for example, Ohloff, 1994). Barfield and Danas (1996) established the "baseline" for this display technology in their paper. Another excellent compilation is Joseph Kaye's (2001) MIT master's thesis "Symbolic Olfactory Display." These two resources gather what was known prior to 2000 about olfaction and about technologies that, in principle, can support olfactory displays. A more recent review is that of Gutierrez-Osuna (2004). Myron W. Krueger (1995) specifically worked on the issue of mixing odorants to achieve specific scents in the context of medical simulation.

The Sensorama (Heilig, 1962) included a fan and a container that enclosed an odor-producing chemical and a device to open the container at a time that corresponded to visual images congruent with the odor produced by the container's contents. This system is likely the earliest example of an olfactory display integrated with other display devices.

Heilig's (1962) approach to producing smells on demand has not been significantly improved upon in the intervening years. At issue is the ability to (1) produce a specific smell when needed, (2) deliver the smell to the nose(s) of the user(s), and (3) dissipate the smell when it is no longer required. Each of these three elements presents serious technical challenges. Producing a specific smell is, in many cases, beyond current technical capabilities. Some smells are associated with chemicals or chemical reactions and may be producible on demand (see, for example, Krueger, 1995). Rakow and Suslick (2000) have developd technology to detect odors and have proposed the creation of a "scent camera," but their company, ChemSensing, Inc., has not yet marketed such a device. In 2000 a Korean company, E-One, proposed developing such a device as well (see http://transcripts.cnn.com/TRANSCRIPTS/0005/04/nr.00.html), but, again, nothing has reached the market. Delivery mechanisms are another area of concern. Just as in Heilig's (1962) approach, most devices depend on a fan to deliver the scent to the user or users. The Institute for Creative Technologies at the University of Southern California has developed a neck-worn system that places the source close to the user's nose (see http://ict.usc.edu/projects/sensory_environments_evaluation/). A good summary of past and current commercially available olfactory displays has been compiled by Washburn and Jones (2004). It is noteworthy that many commercial enterprises established to develop and market olfactory displays have not survived. An additional review is included in Davide, Holmberg, and Lundström (2001).

Training Applications

Although their potential has been recognized, few have attempted to incorporate olfactory displays in training applications. One of the first was developed at the Southwest Research Institute (Cater, 1994)—a virtual environment for training firefighters that provided both olfactory stimulation as well as thermal, visual, and auditory displays. Researchers in the U.S. Army have investigated the use of olfactory displays to provide the smell of blood, cordite, and other scents of the battlefield (Washburn, Jones, Satya, Bowers, & Cortes, 2003). In spite of these efforts, no virtual environment training applications have been deployed (as of this writing) that incorporate an olfactory display.

Challenges

Challenges abound as noted earlier. The most difficult is probably in the area of producing, on demand, a specific smell that fits the context of the training application. The solution to the problem will be a mixture of both science and art. The challenge of delivering the smell to the user(s) and dissipating it, while complex, is fairly straightforward and will likely have a variety of solutions depending on the training application's objectives and its physical relationship to the user(s). In spite of these issues, it must be recognized that there are human variables that will be beyond the control of the application and its users/operators. These variables include transitory (for example, the common cold) and permanent inability, on the part of the user, to actually detect a delivered scent.

GUSTATORY DISPLAYS

Technology

While gustatory (taste) displays have been discussed in the literature, no system has yet emerged that can be evaluated. Beidler (1971) provides a compendium of knowledge of the basis for the sense of taste in his handbook. Much more recently Maynes-Aminzade (2005) offered a light-hearted suggestion for "edible user interfaces" at CHI 2005. Food science does provide a basis for the development of gustatory displays. For example, handbooks (see, for example, Deibler & Delwiche, 2003) provide access to the literature of "taste" from a variety of perspectives. Thus, it can be said that we do know a great deal about how the sense of taste "works" and how to produce, chemically, some specific tastes. Just as in olfaction, however, translating this knowledge into a practical application will be quite difficult.

Challenges

Again, just as in the case of olfaction, there are the usual challenges of producing a specific taste on demand, delivering the taste sensation to the user(s), and then eliminating the taste as required. Beyond these problems we have the additional issues of the strong relationship between taste and smell (Ohloff & Thomas, 1971) and of large human variability in the abilities to discern a specific taste and, collectively, agree on a characterization of that taste.

VESTIBULAR DISPLAYS

Vestibular displays provide the senses of acceleration and orientation to the user. Obviously (see the illustration in Figure 5.4 of an early flight simulator, *circa* 1910), these "displays" are often mechanical in nature and provide a straightforward means of subjecting the user to the movements (accelerations) and orientations necessary for effective training. This recognition, over a hundred years ago, led to a robust industry dedicated to motion based platforms on which users are placed. Such platforms are found in many high performance flight simulators that routinely train pilots to operate aircraft and spacecraft (see, for example, Rolfe & Staples, 1988). Flight simulators certainly represent one "class" of virtual environments used for training (Brooks, 1999), but there are others that should be mentioned. Submarine simulators (for example, that are operated by the U.S. Navy at Pearl Harbor, Hawaii) typically incorporate motion bases for orientation. During a steep dive or an emergency surfacing operation, these simulators provide the users with the direct experience of trying to stay at or get to their stations in spite of a steeply sloping deck.

Technology

The technology of vestibular displays as represented by motion based platforms was reviewed thoroughly in Stanney (2002) and that source remains current as of this writing. Two specific points will be made here, however. The first is that low cost, "personal" motion based platforms are available and may be integrated with a virtual environment designed for training (see, for example,

Figure 5.4.   This is a picture of an early (1910) flight simulator.

Sterling, Magee, & Wallace, 2000). This integration is very simple, assuming that the necessary control software is available for a specific motion base. A second and rather interesting technique is to directly stimulate the human vestibular system. Cress and his colleagues have demonstrated that electrodes can be used to create the sensation of acceleration in a subject (Cress et al., 1997). Obviously, this technology may not find widespread acceptance and has not been studied in a large population to determine its degree of safety.

Training Applications

Given the literature references made above, we will not try to exhaustively address vestibular displays as a part of virtual environments for training in a global sense. Rather, here we will consider only the typical virtual environments (goggles and gloves) that have been developed for training purposes. The system described by Sterling et al. (2000) is, perhaps, the best example. In this case, the authors examined a "low cost" helicopter landing simulator using a small motion base, minimum controls, and a head-mounted display in comparison to a high cost, large-scale helicopter simulator. The results of their research suggest that the low cost system's effectiveness in training was comparable to that of the high end system.

Challenges

With the availability of low cost motion based platforms, the ability to integrate these into virtual environments designed for training is at hand. What is lacking is the requirement to do so. One possible explanation for this lack of applications is the dominance of the visual sense. For example, ship bridge simulators almost never incorporate motion based platforms. Yet, as anyone who has used such a simulator can attest, it is easy to get seasick if the visual displays provide scenes that incorporate only visual motion.

SUMMARY

Multimodal displays are an essential component of virtual environments used for training. Such displays offer the potential to provide sensory channels that are essential for some training applications. If virtual environments were limited strictly to visual and auditory displays, a significant fraction of the human sensory spectrum would be ignored. In some cases this could lead to less effective training or even to negative training.

This chapter addresses displays for the haptic, olfactory, gustatory, and vestibular sensory channels. Haptic displays, while limited, do offer significant technical maturity in some applications and have been demonstrated to add effectiveness to some training applications. Olfactory and gustatory displays are largely not available and have not yet been incorporated into fielded virtual environments for training. Vestibular displays are widely used in many virtual environments designed for training in aircraft and spacecraft piloting. The use of lower cost versions of these displays is now possible, and it is anticipated that they will find their way into more widely deployed applications. In all cases, significant challenges remain before these display modalities will become as common on visual and auditory displays, yet the need to deliver highly effective training demands that these technologies be available.

REFERENCES

Abbott, J. J., & Okamura, A. M. (2003). Virtual fixture architectures for telemanipulation. *Proceedings of the 2003 IEEE International Conference on Robotics & Automation* (Vol. 2, pp. 2798–2805). New York: Institute of Electrical and Electronics Engineers.

Aleotti, J., Caselli, S., & Reggiani, M. (2005). Evaluation of virtual fixtures for a robot programming by demonstration interface. *IEEE Transactions on Systems, Man, and Cybernetics—Part A: Systems and Humans, 35*(4), 536–545.

Ambrose, R. O., Aldridge, H., Askew, R. S., Burridge, R. R., Bluethmann, W., Diftler, M., Lovchik, C., Magruder, D., & Rehnmark, F. (2000). Robonaut: NASA's space humanoid. *IEEE Intelligent Systems & Their Applications, 15*(4), 57–62.

Barfield, W., & Danas, E. (1996). Comments on the use of olfactory displays for virtual environments. *Presence, 5*(1), 109–121.

Başdoğan, C., & Bergman, L. (2001, February). *Multi-modal shared virtual environments for robust remote manipulation with collaborative rovers.* Paper presented at the USC Workshop on Touch in Virtual Environments, Los Angeles, CA.

Başdoğan, C., De, S., Kim, J., Muniyandi, M., & Srinivasan, M. A., (2004). Haptics in minimally invasive surgical simulation and training. *IEEE Computer Graphics and Applications, 24*(2), 56–64.

Başdoğan, C., Kiraz, A., Bukusoglu, I., Varol, A., & Doganay, S. (2007). Haptic guidance for improved task performance in steering microparticles with optical tweezers. *Optics Express, 15*(18), 11616–11621.

Başdoğan, C., Laycock, S. D., Day, A. M., Patoglu, V., & Gillespie, R. B. (2008). 3-DoF haptic rendering. In M. C. Lin & M. Otaduy (Eds.), *Haptic rendering* (pp. 311–331). Wellesley, MA: A K Peters.

Başdoğan, C., Sedef, M., Harders, M., & Wesarg, S. (2007). Virtual reality supported simulators for training in minimally invasive surgery. *IEEE Computer Graphics and Applications, 27*(2), 54–66.

Beidler, L. M. (Ed.). (1971). *Handbook of sensory physiology. Volume IV: Chemical senses. Part 1: Olfaction.* Berlin: Springer-Verlag.

Bettini, A., Lang, S., Okamura, A., & Hager, G. (2002). Vision assisted control for manipulation using virtual fixtures: Experiments at macro and micro scales. *Proceedings of the IEEE International Conference on Robotics and Automation* (Vol. 2, pp. 3354–3361). Piscataway, NJ: Institute of Electrical and Electronics Engineers.

Biggs, S. J., & Srinivasan, M. (2002). Haptics interfaces. In K. Stanney (Ed.), *Handbook of virtual environments: Design, implementation, and applications* (pp. 93–116). Mahwah, NJ: Lawrence Erlbaum.

Brooks, F. P., Jr. (1999). What's real about virtual reality. *Computer Graphics and Applications, 19*(6), 16–27.

Bukusoglu, I., Başdoğan, C., Kiraz, A., & Kurt, A. (2006). Haptic manipulation of microspheres with optical tweezers. *Proceedings of the 14th IEEE Symposium on Haptic Interfaces for Virtual Environments and Teleoperator Systems* (pp. 361–365). Washington, DC: IEEE Computer Society.

Burdea, G. (1996). *Force and touch feedback for virtual reality.* New York: John Wiley & Sons.

Cater, J. P. (1994). Approximating the senses. Smell/taste: Odors in virtual reality. *Proceedings of the IEEE International Conference on Systems, Man and Cybernetics* (Vol. 2, p. 1781). New York: IEEE Computer Society.

Chu, S., & Downes, J. J. (2000). Odor-evoked autobiographical memories: Psychological investigations of Proustian phenomena. *Chemical Sensors, 25,* 111–116.

Corbin, A. (1982). Le Miasme et la jonquille: L'odorat et l'imaginaire social. XVIIIh-XIXm siècles. Paris: Librairie Chapitre.

Cress, J. D., Hettinger, L. J., Cunningham, J. A., Riccio, G. E., McMillan, G. R., & Haas, M. W. (1997). An introduction of a direct vestibular display into a virtual environment. *Proceedings of the 1997 Virtual Reality Annual International Symposium* (pp. 80–86). Washington, DC: IEEE Computer Society.

Dang, T., Annaswamy, T. M., & Srinivasan, M. A. (2001). Development and evaluation of an epidural injection simulator with force feedback for medical training. In J. D. Westwood (Ed.), *Proceedings of Medicine Meets Virtual Reality* (pp. 97–102). Washington, DC: IOS Press.

Davide, F., Holmberg, M., & Lundström, I. (2001). Virtual olfactory interfaces: Electronic noses and olfactory displays. In G. Riva & F. Davide (Eds.), *Communications through virtual technology: Identity community and technology in the internet age* (pp. 193–220). Amsterdam: IOS Press.

Davidson, S. W. (1996). A haptic process architecture using the PHANToM as an I/O device in a virtual electronics trainer. In J. K. Salisbury & M. A. Srinivasan (Eds.), *Proceedings of the First PHANToM Users Group Workshop* (Tech. Rep. No. AI-TR1596; pp. 35–38). Cambridge, MA: Massachusetts Institute of Technology. Available from http://www.sensabledental.com/documents/ documents/PUG1996.pdf

Degel, J., Piper, D., & Koester, E. P. (2001). Implicit learning and implicit memory for odors: The influence of odor identification and retention time. *Chemical Senses, 26,* 267–280.

Deibler, K. D., & Delwiche, J. (Eds.). (2003). *Handbook of flavor characterization: Sensory, chemical, and physiological techniques (Food Science and Technology).* Paris: Lavoisier Publishing.

Durlach, N. I., Srinivasan, M. A., van Wiegand, T. E., Delhorne, L., Sachtler, W. L., Cagatay Basdogan, C., et al. (1999). *Virtual environment technology for training (VETT).* Cambridge, MA: Massachusetts Institute of Technology. Available from http://www.rle.mit.edu/media/pr142/23_VETT.pdf

Griffin, W. B. (2003). *Shared control for dexterous telemanipulation with haptic feedback.* Unpublished doctoral dissertation, Stanford University, Palo Alto.

Gutierrez-Osuna, R. (2004). Olfactory interaction. In W. S. Bainbride (Ed.), *Berkshire encyclopedia of human-computer interaction* (pp. 507–511). Great Barrington, MA: Berkshire Publishing.

Heilig, M. L. (1962). United States Patent US3050870.

Kaye, J. (2001). *Symbolic olfactory display.* Unpublished master's thesis, Massachusetts Institute of Technology, Cambridge. Available from http://alumni.media.mit.edu /~jofish/thesis/symbolic_olfactory_display.html

Kortum, P. (Ed.). (2008). CHI beyond the GUI: Design for haptic, speech, olfactory, and other non traditional interfaces. Burlington, MA: Morgan Kaufmann (Elsevier).

Krebs, H. I., & Hogan, N. (2006). Therapeutic robotics: A technology push. *Proceedings of the IEEE, 94*(9), 1727–1738.

Krueger, M. W. (1995). Olfactory stimuli in virtual reality for medical applications. In K. Morgan, R. M. Satava, H. B. Sieburg, et al. (Eds.), *Interactive technology and the new paradigm for healthcare* (pp. 180–181). Amsterdam: IOS Press.

Lederman, S. J., & Klatzky, R. L. (1987). Hand movements: A window into haptic object recognition. *Cognitive Psychology, 19,* 342–368.

Loftin, R. B. (2003). Multisensory perception: Beyond the visual in visualization. *Computers in Science and Engineering, 5*(4), 565–568.

Loftin, R. B., & Kenney, P. J. (1995). Training the Hubble Space Telescope flight team. *IEEE Computer Graphics and Applications, 15*(5), 31–37.

Massie, T. H., & Salisbury, J. K. (1994). The PHANToM haptic interface: A device for probing virtual objects. *Proceedings of the ASME Winter Annual Meeting, Symposium on Haptic Interfaces for Virtual Environment and Teleoperator Systems, 55*(1), 295–300.

Maynes-Aminzade, D. (2005). Edible bits: Seamless interfaces between people, data and food. *CHI2005 Extended Abstracts* (pp. 2207–2210). New York: ACM Press.

Ohloff, G. (1994). *Scent and fragrances.* Berlin: Springer-Verlag.

Ohloff, G., & Thomas, A. (Eds.). (1971). *Gustation and olfaction.* New York: Academic Press.

O'Malley, M., & Ambrose, R. (2003). Haptic feedback applications for robonaut. *Industrial Robot, 30*(6), 531–542.

Otaduy, M. A., & Lin, M. C. (2008). Introduction to haptic rendering algorithms. In M. C. Lin & M. Otaduy (Eds.), *Haptic rendering* (pp. 159–176). Wellesley, MA: A K Peters.

Payandeh, S., & Stanisic, Z. (2002). On application of virtual fixtures as an aid for telemanipulation and training. *Proceedings of 10th IEEE International Symposium on Haptic Interfaces for Virtual Environment and Teleoperator Systems* (pp. 18–23). Washington, DC: IEEE Computer Society.

Rakow, N. A., & Suslick, K. S. (2000). A colorimetric sensor array for odour visualization. *Nature, 406,* 710–1784.

Rolfe, J. M., & Staples, K. J. (Eds.). (1988). *Flight simulation.* Cambridge, MA: Cambridge University Press.

Rosenberg, L. B. (1993). Virtual fixtures: Perceptual tools for telerobotic manipulation. *Proceedings of IEEE Annual Virtual Reality International Symposium* (pp. 76–82). Piscataway, NJ: IEEE Computer Society.

Salisbury, K., Brock, D., Massie, T., Swarup, N., & Zilles, C. (1995). Haptic rendering: Programming touch interaction with virtual objects. *Proceedings of the Symposium on Interactive 3D Graphics* (pp. 123–130). New York: ACM.

Salisbury, K., Conti, F., & Barbagli, F. (2004). Haptic rendering: Introductory concepts. *IEEE Computer Graphics and Applications, 24*(2), 24–32.

Shams, L., Kamitani, Y., & Shimojo, S. (2000). What you see is what you hear. *Nature, 408,* 788.

Srinivasan, M. A., & Başdoğan, C. (1997). Haptics in virtual environments: Taxonomy, research status, and challenges. *Computers and Graphics, 21*(4), 393–404.

Stanney, K. M. (2002). *Handbook of virtual environments: Design, implementation, and applications.* Mahway, NJ: Lawrence Erlbaum.

Sterling, G. C., Magee, L. E., & Wallace, P. (2000, March). *Virtual reality training—A consideration for Australian helicopter training needs?* Paper presented at the Sim-TecT 2000 Conference, Sydney, Australia.

Washburn, D. A., & Jones, L. M. (2004). Could olfacatory displays improve data visualization? *Computing in Science and Engineering, 6*(6), 80–83.

Washburn, D. A., Jones, L. M., Satya, R. V., Bowers, C. A., & Cortes, A. (2003). Olfactory use in virtual environment training. *Modeling and Simulation, 2*(3), 19–25.

Chapter 6

MIXED AND AUGMENTED REALITY FOR TRAINING

Steven Henderson and Steven Feiner

Augmented reality (AR) extends the capabilities and training benefits of virtual reality (VR) by integrating virtual content with a user's natural view of the environment, combining real and virtual objects interactively and aligning them with each other (Azuma et al., 2001). This is accomplished by using displays that can overlay virtual objects in the real world and registering the virtual and real worlds through the use of tracking. While some of these technologies are the same as or similar to those used in VR (Welch and Davis, Volume 2, Section 1, Chapter 1; Bolas and McDowall, Volume 2, Section 1, Chapter 2; and Towles, Johnson, and Fuchs, Volume 2, Section 1, Chapter 3), there are important differences, which we review later in this chapter. Figure 6.1 shows an experimental AR maintenance training system that uses a stereo head-worn display with a pair of attached cameras whose imagery is digitally combined with computer graphics.

AR can support training by complementing essential physical world characteristics with powerful virtual training constructs. AR thus preserves the natural context, realism, and multisensory interaction of a task, while adding such virtual enablers as overlaid instructions, feedback, and cuing, as well as representations of additional physical objects.

It is useful to position AR within the larger VR context of this text. Milgram, Takemura, Utsumi, and Kishino (1994) present a reality-virtuality continuum for classifying AR and VR applications. The *Reality-Virtuality* continuum (Figure 6.2) spans fully real environments at one end and fully virtual environments at the other. *Mixed reality* (MR) applications exist along this continuum, with AR systems deriving a majority of their content from the real environment and *augmented virtuality* systems including a majority of their content from the virtual environment. Following common usage, we will use the term AR for the entire range of MR systems.

Figure 6.1.   Experimental AR Maintenance Training System

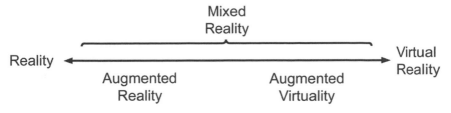

Figure 6.2.   The Reality-Virtuality Continuum (Milgram et al., 1994)

CAPABILITIES AND BENEFITS OF AR FOR TRAINING

Preservation of Task Context and Environment

By displaying virtual content directly on the real world environment, AR allows users to focus on the particular task or procedure being trained. This preserves the task's *context,* which is desirable for several reasons (Tang, Owen, Biocca, & Mou, 2003). First, maintaining context helps the trainee synthesize supporting information and make decisions within a constant, spatially accurate mental model. This reduces cognitive load and facilitates training transfer. Second, overlaying virtual versions of content normally presented in separate documentation can greatly reduce head and eye movement. This decreases work load, potentially improving health, efficiency, and endurance. Third, because the trainee operates in the task's natural context, AR can provide helpful cuing information, such as labels, arrows, and other artifacts to aid in physically negotiating a training scenario. This can reduce the transition time required to move among spatially extended subtasks, potentially shortening overall training time. Finally, feedback is provided in real time and within the natural view of a particular task. According to Vreuls and Obermayer (1985), this is a desirable characteristic for training feedback and performance diagnosis.

In addition to preserving context, AR also preserves the physical *environment* of a training scenario. This might involve using the complete native environment (for example, using AR at the actual job site) or a subset of the environment (for example, using AR to train aircraft engine repair in a classroom). Preservation of the natural environment provides important internal and external stimuli that might be difficult or expensive to replicate. This promotes realism, which can increase the confidence and knowledge transfer of trainees.

Dual Use Systems for Task Training and Execution

AR can operate across a wide continuum of virtual to real content, while preserving a common software and hardware architecture. This makes possible "dual-use" systems supporting training and execution of a task, depending on when, where, and what virtual content is displayed. This could allow a single AR system to support training and serve as a job aid for task execution. For example, a system might initially present training material using mostly virtual content. This could be advantageous at early stages of learning when it is important not to overwhelm a student and impractical to expose him or her to the complete physical task environment. As the student gains knowledge and experience, more of the physical world might be phased into the training. The system could ultimately transition to become a full-time job aid, while supporting continuation or remedial training in the future. These types of systems have proven to significantly increase competency in certain types of tasks (Boud, Haniff, Baber, & Steiner, 1999). Moreover, such systems can naturally promote user acceptance. If users are trained with an AR system, they will come to view the system as a supplement to the particular task or procedure (Young, Stedman, & Cook, 1999).

Hidden Objects and Information

AR can display objects that are normally hidden from a user's view. This includes objects hidden by design (for example, internal structures and mechanical subcomponents), objects hidden by visual occlusion (for example, landmarks obstructed by other buildings in a dense city), and objects hidden by the limits of human perception (for example, molecular structures). Since hidden objects might be vital, if not central, to a trainee's understanding of a particular task or procedure, AR can employ virtual objects to display or otherwise accentuate hidden real ones. This can involve using cutaway views (Figure 6.3) that fully replace portions of the real world with three-dimensional (3-D) models, semi-transparent overlays, pointers, or other techniques.

Figure 6.3.   Example Cutaway View Using Augmented Reality (Courtesy of Andrei State, University of North Carolina)

In addition to displaying hidden physical objects, AR can also display otherwise invisible information, such as parts labels, superimposed instructions, visual cues, and training feedback.

Mobility

Because AR training systems augment a user's natural view of the environment, the majority of these systems are potentially mobile. This can increase application portability and accessibility and reduce costs by minimizing the need for specialized or fixed facilities. However, mobility brings about a unique set of challenges, such as wide-area tracking, wearability, and power constraints.

AR RESEARCH AND APPLICATIONS FOR TRAINING

Foundations

The origins of AR date back to the early days of computer graphics research. From the late 1960s to the early 1970s, Ivan Sutherland and his students, working at Harvard University and the University of Utah, developed the first position- and orientation-tracked see-through head-worn display (HWD) for viewing computer-generated objects (Sutherland, 1968), along with the first AR interaction techniques (Vickers, 1972). In the 1970s and 1980s, a small number of researchers studied AR at such institutions as the United States Air Force Armstrong Research Lab, the National Aeronautics and Space Administration Ames Research Center, and The University of North Carolina at Chapel Hill.

In the early 1990s, Caudell and Mizell (1992) coined the term "augmented reality," introducing the idea of using AR to replace the large boards, paper templates, and manual documentation used in constructing wire harnesses for aircraft. This work resulted in several fielded experimental systems (Mizell, 2001). Bajura, Fuchs, and Ohbuchi (1992) developed a system that allowed a user equipped with an HWD to view live ultrasound imagery directly on a patient. Feiner, MacIntyre, and Seligmann (1993) demonstrated how AR could be used to aid in servicing a laser printer. Their system, shown in Figure 6.4, interactively generated 3-D maintenance instructions using a rule based component that tracked the position and orientation of the user and selected objects in the environment; it featured a tracked, optical see-though HWD that overlaid the instructions on the user's natural view of the task.

Over the past decade, researchers have explored the benefits of using AR for training in a number of application areas, which we review in the remainder of this section.

Industrial Training Applications

Augmented Reality for Development, Production, and Servicing (ARVIKA) was one of the largest AR research projects targeting the industrial domain. This collaborative effort, funded by the German Ministry of Education and Research

Figure 6.4.   Servicing a Laser Printer Using Augmented Reality (Feiner et al., 1993)

from 1999 to 2003, developed AR applications in the automotive, aerospace, power processing, and machine tool production sectors (Friedrich, 2002). Advanced Augmented Reality Technologies for Industrial Service Applications (ARTESAS) was a descendant of ARVIKA, focusing on automotive and aerospace maintenance. ARTESAS produced several prototype applications (Figure 6.5), which are featured in a compelling video demonstration (ARTESAS, 2007).

The AMIRE (authoring mixed reality) project explored using an AR training system to acquaint workers with an oil refinery (Hartmann, Zauner, & Haller, 2004). A tablet personal computer (PC) presented repair instructions, navigation information, and component labeling on video captured from the computer's video camera. Tracking was provided by an optical tracking system that used markers to identify checkpoints throughout the refinery.

Boulanger (2004) demonstrated an AR application for training repair of a telecommunication switch, in which trainees are guided by a remote tutor. The tutor watches real time video of the trainee's field of view and guides the trainee using

Figure 6.5. Conducting Maintenance Using the ARTESAS Prototype (ARTESAS, 2007)

virtual arrows overlaid on an HWD and two-way voice communication. Optically tracked markers are associated with 3-D models of the telecommunication switch and its main subcomponents (Figure 6.6). This allows the trainee and the tutor to manipulate the models to query and demonstrate repair procedures.

Academic Education

Researchers have also demonstrated AR training systems for academic subjects. Sheldon and Hedley (2002) designed a system to help teach undergraduates about Earth-Sun relationships. Students manipulate a 3-D model of the Earth with an optically tracked marker that allows them to change their viewing perspective and visualize learning objectives. Kaufmann and Schmalstieg (2002) addressed mathematics education in a system that allows students to collaboratively create and modify 3-D geometric models. A powerful layering concept gives control over each individual's view and enables the instructor to tailor the learning experiences and diagnose the progress of individual students.

Figure 6.6.   Telecommunications Equipment Servicing Using Augmented Reality (Courtesy of Pierre Boulanger, The Department of Computing Science at the University of Alberta, The School of Information Technology and Engineering, University of Ottawa, Ontario, Canada)

Medicine

Because of the dangers involved in some medical procedures, training is often performed with simulators. For example, Sielhorst, Obst, Burgkart, Riener, and Navab (2004) describe an obstetric training system that overlays graphics on anatomically correct mannequins. AR can also assist patients. For example, Luo, Kenyon, Kline, Waldinger, and Kamper (2005) demonstrated a system that teaches stroke victims to perform grasp-and-release exercises as part of finger extension rehabilitation. An HWD presents the patient with 3-D virtual objects to grasp, and an assistive orthosis, controlled by a therapist, provides dynamic assistance and tangible feedback as the patient grasps the target object.

Military and Aerospace

The military and aerospace domains are especially amenable to AR training applications. Livingston et al. (2002) introduced the Battlefield Augmented Reality System (BARS), a wearable situational awareness aid for warfighters that also doubled as a training aid. Brown, Stripling, and Coyne (2006) extended this work, conducting a user study that explored the use of BARS for training tactics. FlatWorld (Pair, Neumann, Piepol, & Swartout, 2003) used AR to augment Hollywood-inspired modular "flats" (movie set props) to create compelling environments for military training (Towles, Johnson, and Fuchs, Volume 2, Section 1, Chapter 3). Macchiarella and Vincenzi (2004) explored how AR can be used to teach aircraft design principles to mechanics and pilots. Further examples are described by Regenbrecht, Baratoff, and Wilke (2005).

Teleoperation

Milgram, Zhai, Drascic, and Grodski (1993) investigated AR for teleoperation. Their Augmented Reality through Graphic Overlays on Stereovideo project helps human operators visualize and control a remote robot's view of the environment. The same AR cues and information used in visualization are applied to communicate spatially accurate commands to the robot. Lawson, Pretlove, Wheeler, and Parker (2002) created a telerobotic AR system to aid in surveying and measuring remote environments, such as sewer pipes.

GENERAL STRUCTURE OF AR TRAINING SYSTEMS

Like VR in general, AR uses a wide range of different technologies, although with certain key differences. To help characterize the structure of AR training systems, we rely on a generalized design hierarchy, proposed by Bimber and Raskar (2005), shown in Figure 6.7.

The *base level* of this model includes hardware and software for tracking real world objects, displaying information to the user, and rendering computer-generated content. Most AR research efforts to date address this level. The *intermediate level*, implemented mostly in software, interacts with the user, presents and arranges content, and provides authoring tools. This level has not received enough emphasis in the past and contains many open research issues (Rekimoto, 1995). The *application level*, implemented entirely in software, consists of the overarching AR application and serves as the primary interface to the user. The *user level* represents the end user and is included to emphasize the human role.

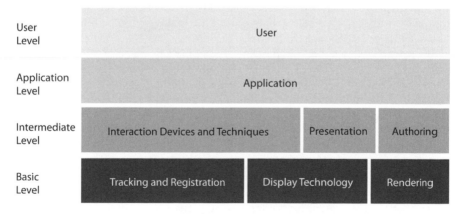

Figure 6.7.   Generalized AR Design Hierarchy; Adapted from Bimber & Raskar (2005)

Display

AR display technologies perform the task of merging virtual and real world environments. They fall into four general categories: head worn, handheld, stationary, and projective. Other chapters provide more general coverage of head-worn displays (Bolas and McDowall, Volume 2, Section 1, Chapter 2) and projective displays (Towles, Johnson, and Fuchs, Volume 2, Section 1, Chapter 3). In this section, we briefly examine displays in the context of AR.

Head-worn displays are worn on the user's head and present imagery to one eye (*monocular*) or both eyes (*biocular* if the images seen by both eyes are the same, *binocular* if the images form a stereo pair). HWDs (and other AR display technologies) are further categorized according to how they combine views of the real and virtual worlds. *Optical see-through displays* provide a direct view of the real world (mediated only by optical elements) and overlay virtual content on top of this view. The real and virtual worlds are merged using optical *combiners,* such as half-silvered mirrors or prisms. *Video see-through displays* use cameras to capture real world imagery, combine the real and virtual content digitally, and present it on the same displays.

Optical see-through displays have the advantage of presenting the real world at its full spatial resolution, with no temporal lag, full stereoscopy, and no mismatch between *vergence* (the angle between the lines of sight from each eye to a given real world object) and *accommodation* (the distance at which the eyes must focus to perceive that object). However, luminance is lost because of the reflectivity of the combiner, and many designs include filtration to avoid overwhelming the relatively dim displays used for the virtual world. The lag-free view of the real world also emphasizes the lag that occurs in presenting the virtual world. Commercially available optical see-through displays cannot selectively suppress the view of any part of the real world, so bright real world objects can be seen through virtual objects that are in front of them, even when the virtual objects are supposed to be opaque. One experimental system has overcome this obstacle by introducing a liquid-crystal array and additional optics in the optical path to the real world, allowing selectable areas of the real world to be blocked (Kiyokawa, Billinghurst, Campbell, & Woods, 2003).

In contrast, video see-through displays have the advantage of allowing essentially arbitrary processing of both the real and virtual worlds, making it possible to render virtual objects that fully obscure real ones. However, the real world is rendered at the resolution of the camera and display. Furthermore, because all imagery is typically presented on one display at a fixed perceived distance, both the real and virtual imagery typically suffer from vergence-accommodation mismatch, although this can be minimized if the system is used for content viewed at a preselected distance. When the camera is not effectively coincident with the user's eye, parallax error results, causing the image of the real world to differ geometrically from what the user would see directly. This can be addressed by careful optical design, for example, using mirrors to fold the optical path to the camera (State, Keller, & Fuchs, 2005). Finally, limited field of view and resolution in video see-through systems can make navigating large environments difficult.

Two sets of factors dominate the selection of HWDs. The first set is a function of electronic and optical properties, including display resolution, color capability, field of view, transmissivity, and stereoscopy. The second set is a function of the size, weight, and appearance of these devices. Unfortunately, optimizing one set of factors typically comes at the expense of the other. Current commercial stereoscopic HWDs are significantly larger and heavier than a pair of standard eyeglasses, the proverbial gold standard for mainstream acceptance. However, the potential market created by consumer handheld entertainment devices is making lightweight HWDs of resolution comparable to desktop displays commercially feasible.

Handheld video see-through displays (Rekimoto, 1997) couple a display screen and integrated camera; examples include mobile phones, media players, portable game machines, tablet PCs, and Ultra-Mobile PCs. While the small physical field of view of many of these devices (often mismatched with a wider camera field of view) and the need for handheld operation make them poorly suited for many AR training applications, they can play auxiliary roles as input devices or special viewing devices (Goose, Güven, Zhang, Sudarsky, & Navab, 2004).

Stationary displays mounted in the user's environment can be larger and heavier than head-worn or handheld displays, making them well suited for through-the-window applications in vehicles or other situations in which the display can be placed between the user and the augmented environment. For example, Olwal, Lindfors, Gustafsson, Kjellberg, and Mattsson (2005) describe a system that overlays operational data on the user's view of a milling machine.

Projective displays project virtual content directly onto the real world (Bimber & Raskar, 2005). The advantages of this approach include the ability to view an augmented environment without wearing a display or computer. Bright projectors combined with relatively reflective task surfaces can make this a good approach for some indoor domains, especially when multiple users need to experience the same augmented environment. However, many of these systems assume that all virtual material is intended to lie on the projected surface, limiting the kind of geometry that can be presented. Stereo projection is possible, in conjunction with special eyewear or the use of optical combiners in the environment, often in conjunction with head tracking. While many projective systems use stationary projectors, head-worn projective displays (Hua, Gao, Brown, Biocca, & Rolland, 2002) use lightweight head-worn projectors whose stereo imagery is reflected in the direction of the user from specially treated retroreflective surfaces in the environment. This allows multiple users to view individually tracked imagery on the same surfaces.

Tracking and Registration

Three considerations dominate the selection and integration of AR tracking technologies: registration, mobility, and frame of reference. *Registration* refers to the need to properly locate and align virtual objects with their real world counterparts and is one of the most important concerns in creating effective AR systems (Bimber & Raskar, 2005). Registration errors typically result from five sources: distortion in the display, imperfections in the virtual 3-D model, mechanical misalignments, incorrect display settings, and tracking errors. Since AR includes both real and virtual material, inaccurate tracking is much easier to detect.

The second tracking consideration is *mobility*. Training often involves large operating areas with varied lighting, magnetic, and structural conditions. This can rule out electromagnetic systems and approaches that tether users to their surroundings.

An application's *frame of reference* represents the third important AR tracking consideration. Some applications require tracking the user relative to the earth or some other large fixed coordinate system; other applications entail tracking the user relative to specific and often movable objects.

Based on these considerations, AR applications often use a subset of the tracking technologies covered in Welch and Davis, Volume 2, Section 1, Chapter 1, which we briefly review here with an emphasis on AR: optical, inertial, global navigation satellite systems, and hybrid.

Optical tracking systems detect light directly emitted from light-emitting diodes or other sources, or reflected from passive targets. They include *marker based tracking systems,* such as ARToolKit (Kato & Billinghurst, 1999) and ARTag (Fiala, 2005), which use video cameras to detect fiducial markers (predetermined black and white or colored patterns as depicted in Figure 6.8) positioned at known locations in the environment. Because cameras, hardware, and

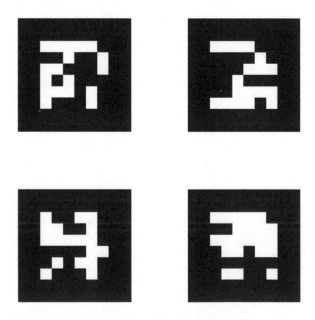

Figure 6.8.   Example Optical Tracking Marker (Fiala, 2005)

software needed to process digital video streams have become commodity items, these systems are inexpensive, provide a high level of accuracy, and work well in mobile environments. When the user views the real world through the same cameras used for tracking, this can also lessen the effects of lens distortion on registration. Since marker based tracking requires that markers be placed in the environment in advance and remain sufficiently visible, researchers have been trying, with encouraging results, to replace markers with natural environmental features, making possible *markerless tracking* (Bleser, Pastarmov, & Stricker, 2005; Comport, Marchand, Pressigout, & Chaumette, 2006).

While many tracking technologies in use for both VR and AR establish a global coordinate system within which the user's head is tracked, optical marker tracking is often used to track a small number of specific targets relative to the head or display. This is rarely satisfactory for HWD based VR, in which the position and orientation of the head must always be known for the virtual world to look right; however, in AR, the surrounding real world will always appear correct without tracking, and, in many applications, virtual material may need to be registered only with specific tracked objects. Consequently, AR applications of this sort can be implemented with optical marker tracking alone, using the same cameras with which the user views the world in a video see-through display.

Inertial tracking systems use accelerometers or gyroscopes, are compact and relatively inexpensive, and are not susceptible to variations in lighting. These characteristics support mobile orientation tracking configurations that work equally well indoors and outdoors. However, since these systems drift significantly over relatively short periods of time, they are typically configured as part of hybrid systems that provide ground truth through some other technology. For example, the earth's magnetic and gravitational fields may be used for orientation (noting inaccuracies caused by magnetically reactive environments), and global navigation satellite systems may be used for position.

Global navigation satellite system (GNSS) receivers determine their positions by computing their distances to satellites at known locations, based on signals that the satellites broadcast. The best known GNSS is the U.S. Global Positioning System. While the accuracy of regular GNSS receivers is measured in meters, some rely on additional differential error correction signals, broadcast from local base stations or satellites, which can provide as good as centimeter-level accuracy in the case of real time kinematic systems. Feiner, MacIntyre, Höllerer, and Webster (1997) used GNSS in their Touring Machine, the first outdoor mobile AR system, which displayed information about buildings on their campus. Other techniques for estimating position include triangulation based on signal strength from known short-range terrestrial sources, such as mobile phone towers or wireless network access points.

Hybrid tracking systems employ multiple complementary technologies and fuse their data to form a single estimate for location and/or orientation. For example, State, Hirota, Chen, Garrett, and Livingston (1996) used electromagnetic tracking and marker based vision tracking. High update inertial trackers have been combined with low update natural feature vision tracking (You, Neumann,

& Azuma, 1999) and marker based vision tracking (Foxlin & Naimark, 2003), making possible a higher update rate and uninterrupted tracking when natural features or markers are momentarily obscured.

Graphics Rendering

Graphics rendering refers to the low level computation required to generate virtual content (McDowell, Guerrero, McCue, and Hollister, Volume 2, Section 1, Chapter 8). This process is typically handled by commodity computer graphics cards and is normally transparent to a particular application. Since the real world is either not rendered (for optical see-through displays) or is captured by cameras (for video see-through displays), rendering requirements can be significantly lower for AR than for VR. However, rendering requirements can still present significant challenges for applications with demanding virtual content, especially for wearable systems.

Interaction Devices and Techniques

While many of the interaction devices and techniques used for VR are also used for AR, we focus on those that are particularly designed to address the coexistence of real and virtual objects. As in VR and 3-D user interfaces (UIs) in general, a dominating set has yet to emerge, as it has for 2-D UIs. However, some interesting approaches include the following:

Wand based selection. Vickers (1972) introduced the use of a handheld wand whose position-tracked tip was used in conjunction with a head-tracked HWD to define a vector from the user's eye into the environment to select real or virtual objects.

Magic lenses. Bier, Stone, Pier, Buxton, and DeRose (1993) developed "magic lens" filters that perform operations, such as magnification, selection, and information filtering, on screen regions in 2-D UIs. Looser, Billinghurst, and Cockburn (2004) adapted this metaphor, using an optically tracked paddle to display and control a 3-D magic lens through which objects can be viewed in AR (Figure 6.9).

Tangible AR. Building on the notion of tangible UIs (Ishii & Ullmer, 1997) that use everyday objects, tracked objects (for example, markers) can be associated with augmented content. For example, tracked tiles (Poupyrev et al., 2002) can manipulate linked content, such as video clips. The tiles take on one of two roles: *operation tiles* trigger actions based on proximity to other tiles, and *data tiles* are used as data containers. Slay, Thomas, and Vernik (2002) explored having a user hold multiple markers in his or her hand and use them as switches to "toggle" virtual content. The markers could also be used together to form basic gestures for selecting and tracking virtual objects.

Visible interaction volumes. Visualizing the volumes within which users can interact may help them better accomplish their tasks. For example, Olwal, Benko, and Feiner (2002) developed statistical geometric tools for identifying objects for multimodal selection by speech and gesture (Figure 6.10). Statistics, such as

Figure 6.9.   Magic Lens Interaction Technique (Looser et al., 2004)

distance to center and dwell time, are sampled relative to virtual volumes attached to the user's body (for example, a cone that follows a user's tracked hand when pointing) and combined with speech commands to determine the user's intentions.

Bare hand tracking. Lee and Höllerer (2007) use markerless optical tracking of a user's hand to allow selection and manipulation of three-dimensional models

Figure 6.10.   Using Visible Interaction Volumes for Augmented Reality User Interaction (Olwal et al., 2002)

with simple hand gestures. This supports tangible interaction without the need for specialized equipment or preparation of the tracking environment.

Presentation

The presentation layer uses primitives from the graphics rendering process to create, arrange, and animate higher level objects that form virtual content. Scene graph application programming interfaces provide abstractions for creating, organizing, and moving virtualized content and can serve as useful tools in the presentation layer. They are typically found in AR authoring and application development tools and game engines (discussed in the "Authoring" and "Application Design" sections of this chapter).

One of the continued challenges facing AR applications is the integration of virtual labels (and other annotations) into a presentation scheme. This seemingly trivial task becomes extremely complicated given the large number of labels potentially required in some AR training applications. For each label, the application must dynamically determine label position, size, transparency, and priority vis-à-vis occlusions of other objects in the 3-D scene (Bell, Feiner, & Höllerer, 2001).

Authoring

Authoring refers to the need for robust, generalized software tools for designing AR applications. Examples include work by Grimm et al. (2002), Güven and Feiner (2003), and Zauner, Haller, Brandl, and Hartman (2003). Haringer and Regenbrecht (2002) and Knopfle, Weidenhausen, Chauvigne, and Stock (2005) have created tools applicable to designing training applications. These tools offer several advantages, the most compelling being their support for users to modify applications with minimal need for programmer assistance. This allows aftermarket modification of an application and is particularly useful in training domains where scenarios can continually evolve.

Application Design

Application design concerns development of the overall software that integrates all major AR functions. Game engines (Hart, Wansbury, and Pike, Volume 3, Section 1, Chapter 14) offer an appealing foundation for the development of high quality, visually appealing AR applications by providing software libraries that support the functionality found in sophisticated computer games, including 3-D graphics and audio rendering, geometric modeling, physical simulation (including collision detection), and overlaid 2-D UIs. Game engines used in recent AR applications include Valve Source (2006) and Delta3D (Darken, McDowell, & Johnson, 2005). However, it is important to note that commercial game engines often have limited documentation and may make assumptions about the game genre (for example, the camera is the player's eye in a "first-person shooter" and moves with the simulated physics of the player's head). Goblin XNA (Oda, Lister, White, & Feiner, 2008) extends the XNA game development environment to address AR applications by adding support for live video, tracking (including the association of tracking markers with portions of the scene graph), and rendering of representations of real objects into the depth buffer to occlude virtual objects that pass behind them.

User Level Design Concepts

One set of considerations for the user level of the design hierarchy follows *classic principles and theories* found in human-computer interaction research. These include guidelines for design (Nielsen & Molich, 1992; Norman, 1990), theories (Bødker, 1991; Card, Moran, & Newell, 1983; Rosson & Carrol, 2001; Shneiderman & Plaisant, 2005), and 3-D UI design principles, such as those framed by Bowman, Kruijff, LaViola, and Poupyrev (2005).

A second set of considerations focuses on *wearability*. Because many AR systems are mobile, their design must support operation in a variety of settings without encumbering the user. Designers must package supporting equipment, such as displays, trackers, computers, and other devices in a way that does not endanger the user and is also easy to carry.

A third set of considerations deals with *acceptability* of AR technologies by the user. In addition to the considerations mentioned above, acceptability is also driven by visual appeal and complex social factors, such as the tendency to resist change. One approach to achieving acceptance incorporates the end user into the early stages of the design process (Mackay, Ratzer, & Janecek, 2000).

CONCLUSIONS

Combining virtual content with the user's natural view of the physical environment supports the creation of effective training environments that promote natural context, realism, and multisensory interaction. Moreover, AR can make possible useful systems that, after supporting training, gradually transition into ubiquitous tools that aid in day-to-day task completion. However, for AR training to become a commercial reality, several significant challenges must be addressed. The technologies that perform the core function of mixing real and virtual objects must become more powerful and less obtrusive. Large, heavy, high resolution displays and cameras must evolve into small, lightweight devices that are as ubiquitous and unassuming as eyeglasses. Computer systems must also shrink in size, while increasing in power. Finally, tracking technologies must become more accurate and robust and less dependent on specialized preparation of the environment.

Several recent technological advances are currently converging to hasten the realization of AR's potential for training. The cameras built into portable devices are becoming capable of increasingly accurate tracking. New displays, particularly handheld and head-worn displays driven by the consumer entertainment industry, will make AR systems smaller, less intrusive, and more mobile. Powerful game engines and commodity graphics devices are allowing creation and delivery of compelling virtual content for stationary and mobile users. These factors will continue to increase the capability and applicability of AR for training.

REFERENCES

ARTESAS. (2007). *ARTESAS—Advanced augmented reality technologies for industrial service applications.* Retrieved June 2007, from http://www.artesas.de

Azuma, R., Baillot, Y., Behringer, R., Feiner, S., Julier, S., & MacIntyre, B. (2001). Recent advances in augmented reality. *IEEE Computer Graphics and Applications, 21*(6), 34–47.

Bajura, M., Fuchs, H., & Ohbuchi, R. (1992). Merging virtual objects with the real world: Seeing ultrasound imagery within the patient. *SIGGRAPH Computer Graphics 26*(2), 203–210.

Bell, B., Feiner, S., & Höllerer, T. (2001). View management for virtual and augmented reality. *Proceedings of the ACM Symposium on User Interface Software and Technology* (pp. 101–110), New York: ACM.

Bier, E., Stone, M., Pier, K., Buxton, W., & DeRose, T. (1993). Toolglass and magic lenses: The see-through interface. *Proceedings of the International Conference on Computer Graphics and Interactive Techniques* (pp. 73–80). New York: ACM.

Bimber, O., & Raskar, R. (2005). *Spatial augmented reality: Merging real and virtual worlds.* Wellesley, MA: A K Peters.

Bleser, G., Pastarmov, Y., & Stricker, D. (2005). Real-time 3D camera tracking for industrial augmented reality applications. *Proceedings of the 13th International Conference in Central Europe on Computer Graphics, Visualization and Computer Vision* (pp. 47–54). Pilsen, Czech Republic: University of West Bohemia.

Bødker, S. (1991). *Through the interface: A human activity approach to user interface design.* Mahwah, NJ: Lawerence Erlbaum Associates.

Boud, A. C., Haniff, D. J., Baber, C., & Steiner, S. J. (1999). Virtual reality and augmented reality as a training tool for assembly tasks. *Proceedings of the IEEE International Conference on Information Visualization* (pp. 32–36). Los Alamitos, CA: IEEE Computer Society.

Boulanger, P. (2004). Application of augmented reality to industrial tele-training. *Proceedings of the Canadian Conference on Computer and Robot Vision* (pp. 320–328). Los Alamitos, CA: IEEE Computer Society.

Bowman, D., Kruijff, E., LaViola, J., & Poupyrev, I. (2005). *3D User Interfaces: Theory and Practice.* Boston: Addison-Wesley.

Brown, D. G., Stripling, R., & Coyne, J. T. (2006). Augmented reality for urban skills training. *Proceedings of IEEE Virtual Reality* (pp. 249–252). Washington, DC: IEEE Computer Society.

Card, S., Moran, T., & Newell, A. (1983). *The psychology of human-computer interaction.* Hillsdale, NJ: Lawrence Erlbaum.

Caudell, T., & Mizell, D. (1992). Augmented reality: An application of heads-up display technology to manual manufacturing processes. *Proceedings of the 25th Hawaii International Conference on System Sciences, 2,* 659–669.

Comport, A., Marchand, E., Pressigout, M., & Chaumette, F. (2006). Real-time markerless tracking for augmented reality: The virtual visual servoing framework. *IEEE Transactions on Visualization and Computer Graphics, 12*(4), 615–628.

Darken, R., McDowell, P., & Johnson, E. (2005). The Delta3D open source game engine. *IEEE Computer Graphics and Applications, 25*(3), 10–12.

Feiner, S., MacIntyre, B., Höllerer, T., & Webster, T. (1997). A touring machine: Prototyping 3D mobile augmented reality systems for exploring the urban environment. *Proceedings of the 1st International Symposium on Wearable Computers* (pp. 74–81). Washington, DC: IEEE Computer Society.

Feiner, S., MacIntyre, B., & Seligmann, D. (1993). Knowledge-based augmented reality. *Communications of the ACM, 36*(7), 53–62.

Fiala, M. L. (2005). ARTag, a fiducial marker system using digital techniques. *Proceedings of the IEEE Conference on Computer Vision and Pattern Recognition, 2*, 590–596.

Foxlin, E., & Naimark, L. (2003). *VIS*-Tracker: A wearable vision-inertial self-tracker. *Proceedings of IEEE Virtual Reality* (pp. 199–206). Los Alamitos, CA: IEEE Computer Society.

Friedrich, W. (2002). ARVIKA—Augmented reality for development, production and service. *Proceedings of the 1st International Symposium on Mixed and Augmented Reality* (pp. 3–4). Washington, DC: IEEE Computer Society.

Goose, S., Güven, S., Zhang, X., Sudarsky, S., & Navab, N. (2004). PARIS: Fusing vision-based location tracking with standards-based 3D visualization and speech interaction on a PDA. *Proceedings of the 10th International Conference on Distributed Multimedia Systems* (pp. 75–80). Skokie, IL: Knowledge Systems Institute.

Grimm, P., Haller, M., Paelke, V., Reinhold, S., Reimann, C., & Zauner, R. (2002). AMIRE—Authoring mixed reality. *Proceedings of the 1st IEEE International Workshop on Augmented Reality Toolkit.* Piscataway, NJ: IEEE Computer Society.

Güven, S., & Feiner, S. (2003). Authoring 3D hypermedia for wearable augmented and virtual reality. *Proceedings of the IEEE International Symposium on Wearable Computers* (pp. 118–126). Los Alamitos, CA: IEEE Computer Society.

Haringer, M., & Regenbrecht, H. T. (2002). A pragmatic approach to augmented reality authoring. *Proceedings of the International Symposium on Mixed and Augmented Reality* (pp. 237–245). Washington, DC: IEEE Computer Society.

Hartmann, W., Zauner, J., & Haller, M. (2004). A mixed reality based training application for an oil refinery. *Proceedings of the 2nd International Conference on Pervasive Computing* (pp. 324–327). New York: ACM.

Hua, H., Gao, C., Brown, L., Biocca, F., & Rolland, J. P. (2002). Design of an ultralight head-mounted projective display (HMPD) and its applications in augmented collaborative environments. *Proceedings of SPIE, 4660*, 492–497.

Ishii, H., & Ullmer, B. (1997). Tangible bits: Towards seamless interfaces between people, bits and atoms. *Proceedings of the SIGCHI Conference on Human Factors in Computing Systems* (pp. 234–241). New York: ACM.

Kato, H., & Billinghurst, M. (1999). Marker tracking and HMD calibration for a video-based augmented reality conferencing system. *Proceedings of the IEEE and ACM International Workshop on Augmented Reality* (pp. 85–94). Washington, DC: IEEE Computer Society.

Kaufmann, H., & Schmalstieg, D. (2002). Mathematics and geometry education with collaborative augmented reality. *Computers & Graphics, 27*(3), 339–345.

Kiyokawa, K., Billinghurst, M., Campbell, B., & Woods, E. (2003). An occlusion-capable optical see-through head mounted display for supporting co-located collaboration. *Proceedings of the IEEE and ACM International Symposium on Mixed and Augmented Reality* (pp. 133–141). Washington, DC: IEEE Computer Society.

Knopfle, C., Weidenhausen, J., Chauvigne, L., & Stock, I. (2005). Template based authoring for AR based service scenarios. *Proceedings of IEEE Virtual Reality* (pp. 249–252). Washington, DC: IEEE Computer Society.

Lawson, S. W., Pretlove, J. R. G., Wheeler, A. C., & Parker, G. A. (2002). Augmented reality as a tool to aid the telerobotic exploration and characterization of remote environments. *Presence: Teleoperators and Virtual Environments, 11*(4), 352–367.

Lee, T. & Höllerer, T (2007). Handy AR: Markerless inspection of augmented reality objects using fingertip tracking. *Proceedings of the IEEE International Symposium on Wearable Computers* (pp. 1–8). Los Alamitos, CA: IEEE Computer Society.

Livingston, M. A., Rosenblum, L., Julier, S., Brown, D., Baillot, Y., Swan, J., Gabbard, J. L., & Hix, D. (2002). An augmented reality system for military operations in urban terrain. *Proceedings of the Interservice/Industry Training, Simulation and Education Conference* (pp. 868–875). Arlington, VA: National Training Systems Association.

Looser, J., Billinghurst, M., & Cockburn, A. (2004). Through the looking glass: The use of lenses as an interface tool for Augmented Reality interfaces. *Proceedings of the International Conference on Computer Graphics and Interactive Techniques in Australasia and South East Asia.* (pp. 204–211). New York: ACM.

Luo, X., Kenyon, R. V., Kline, T., Waldinger, H. C., & Kamper, D. G. (2005). An augmented reality training environment for post-stroke finger extension rehabilitation. *Proceedings of the International Conference on Rehabilitation Robotics* (pp. 329–332). Los Alamitos , CA: IEEE Computer Society.

Macchiarella, N. D., & Vincenzi, D. A. (2004). Augmented reality in a learning paradigm for flight aerospace maintenance training. *Proceedings of the Digital Avionics Systems Conference, 1,* 5.1.1–5.1.9

Mackay, W., Ratzer, A., & Janecek, P. (2000). Video artifacts for design: Bridging the gap between abstraction and detail. *Proceedings of the Conference on Designing Interactive Systems* (pp. 72–82). New York: ACM.

Milgram, P., Takemura, H., Utsumi, A., & Kishino, F. (1994). Augmented reality: A class of displays on the reality-virtuality continuum. *Proceedings of Telemanipulator and Telepresence Technologies* (pp. 282–292). New York: ACM.

Milgram, P., Zhai, S., Drascic, D., & Grodski, J. (1993). Applications of augmented reality for human-robot communication. *Proceedings of the IEEE/RSJ International Conference on Intelligent Robots and Systems, 3,* 1467–1472.

Mizell, D. (2001). Boeing's wire bundle assembly project. In W. Barfield & T. Caudell (Eds.), *Fundamentals of wearable computers and augmented reality* (pp. 447–467). Mahwah, NJ: Lawrence Erlbaum.

Nielsen, J., & Molich, R. (1992). Heuristic evaluation of user interfaces. *Proceedings of the ACM Conference on Human Factors in Computing Systems* (pp. 249–256). New York: ACM.

Norman, D. (1990). *The design of everyday things.* New York: Doubleday.

Oda, O., Lister, L., White, S., & Feiner, S. (2008). Developing an augmented reality racing game. *Proceedings of the International Conference on Intelligent Technologies for Interactive Entertainment,* Brussels, ICST.

Olwal, A., Benko, H., & Feiner, S. (2002). SenseShapes: Using statistical geometry for object selection in a multimodal augmented reality system. *Proceedings of the International Symposium in Mixed and Augmented Reality* (pp. 300–301). Washington, DC: IEEE Computer Society.

Olwal, A., Lindfors, C., Gustafsson, J., Kjellberg, T., & Mattsson, L. (2005). ASTOR: An autostereoscopic optical see-through augmented reality system. *Proceedings of the IEEE and ACM International Symposium on Mixed and Augmented Reality* (pp. 24–27). Washington, DC: IEEE Computer Society.

Pair, J., Neumann, U., Piepol, D., & Swartout, B. (2003). FlatWorld: Combining Hollywood set-design techniques with VR. *IEEE Computer Graphics and Applications, 23* (1), 12–15.

Poupyrev, I., Tan, D. S., Billinghurst, M., Kato, H. A., Regenbrecht, H. A., & Tetsutani, N. A. (2002). Developing a generic augmented-reality interface. *Computer, 35*(3), 44–50.

Regenbrecht, H., Baratoff, G., & Wilke, W. (2005). Augmented reality projects in the automotive and aerospace industries. *IEEE Computer Graphics and Applications, 25* (6), 48–56.

Rekimoto, J. (1997). NaviCam—A magnifying glass approach to augmented reality. *Presence: Teleoperators and Virtual Environments, 6*(4), 399–412.

Rosson, M., & Carrol, J. (2001). *Usability engineering: Scenario-based development of human computer interaction.* Redwood City, CA: Morgan Kaufmann Publishers.

Sheldon, B. E., & Hedley, N. R. (2002). Using augmented reality for teaching earth-sun relationships to undergraduate geography students. *Proceedings of the IEEE International Workshop on Augmented Reality Toolkit.* Piscataway, NJ: IEEE Computer Society.

Shneiderman, B., & Plaisant, C. (2005). *Designing the user interface.* Reading, MA: Addison-Wesley.

Sielhorst, T., Obst, T., Burgkart, R., Riener, R., & Navab, N. (2004). An augmented reality delivery simulator for medical training. *International Workshop on Augmented Environments for Medical Imaging—MICCAI Satellite Workshop.* Available from http://ami2004.loria.fr/

Slay, H., Thomas, B., & Vernik, R. (2002). Tangible user interaction using augmented reality. *Proceedings of the Australasian Conference on User Interfaces* (pp. 13–20). Los Alamitos, CA: IEEE Computer Society.

State, A., Hirota, G., Chen, D. T., Garrett, W. F., & Livingston, M. A. (1996). Superior augmented reality registration by integrating landmark tracking and magnetic tracking. *Proceedings of the Annual Conference on Computer Graphics and Interactive Techniques* (pp. 429–438). New York: ACM.

State, A., Keller, K., & Fuchs, H. (2005). Simulation-based design and rapid prototyping of a parallax-free, orthoscopic video see-through head-mounted display. *Proceedings of the 4th International Symposium on Mixed and Augmented Reality* (pp. 28–31). Los Alamitos, CA

Sutherland, I. E. (1968). A head-mounted three dimensional display. *Proceedings of the AFIPS Fall Joint Computer Conference, 33,* 757–764. Washington, DC: Thompson Books.

Tang, A., Owen, C., Biocca, F., & Mou, W. (2003). Comparative effectiveness of augmented reality in object assembly. *Proceedings of the SIGCHI Conference on Human Factors in Computing Systems* (pp. 73–80). New York: ACM.

Valve Source. (2006). Valve source engine software development kit. Retrieved July 2006, from http://developer.valvesoftware.com

Vickers, D. L. (1972). *Sorcerer's apprentice: Head-mounted display and wand.* Unpublished doctoral dissertation, University of Utah, Salt Lake City.

Vreuls, D., & Obermayer, R. W. (1985). Human-system performance measurement in training simulators. *Human Factors, 27*(3), 241–250.

XNA. (2008). Retrieved February 2008, from http://www.xna.com/

You, S., Neumann, U., & Azuma, R. (1999). Hybrid inertial and vision tracking for augmented reality registration. *Proceedings of IEEE Virtual Reality* (pp. 260–267). Washington, DC: IEEE Computer Society.

Young, A. L., Stedman, A. W., & Cook, C. A. (1999). The potential of augmented reality technology for training support systems. *Proceedings of the International Conference on Human Interfaces in Control Rooms, Cockpits and Command Centres* (pp. 242–246). London: IEEE Computer Society.

Zauner, J., Haller, M., Brandl, A., & Hartman, W. (2003). Authoring of a mixed reality assembly instructor for hierarchical structures. *Proceedings of the IEEE and ACM International Symposium on Mixed and Augmented Reality* (pp. 237–246). Washington, DC: IEEE Computer Society.

Part II: Topics for Component Integration

Chapter 7

DESIGNING USER INTERFACES FOR TRAINING DISMOUNTED INFANTRY

James Templeman, Linda Sibert,
Robert Page, and Patricia Denbrook

It is challenging to create a three-dimensional (3-D) user interface for a simulation system to train dismounted infantry tactics, techniques, and procedures for close quarters battle (CQB). CQB is a complex skill that fully involves a person in the 3-D environment. Trainees must be able to move and act in a coordinated manner in order to practice the skills they will use in the field. Vehicle simulators need to provide only out-the-window viewing and a physical mock-up of the vehicle's actual controls (for example, steering wheel and gearshift). For a dismounted infantry simulator, however, the trainee's body is the "vehicle" operating directly in the virtual world. Developing such a complex user interface requires a detailed understanding of the task, knowledge of input and output device characteristics, and a design strategy that takes into account the fundamentals of human perception and action.

A user interface is the medium through which communication between the user and the computer takes place (Bowman, Kruijff, LaViola, & Poupyrev, 2005). It provides the *user's experience* with the simulation. Hinckley, Jacob, and Ware (2004) conclude that interaction design must consider both the motor control (input) and feedback (output) and how they interact with one another as an integrated whole. They cite Gibson's (1986) ecological approach to human perception, which says that the organism, the environment, and the tasks the organism performs are inseparable and should not be studied in isolation. Gibson coined the term *active perception,* in which perception and action are tightly linked. This fundamental coupling of perception and action in a motor/sensory feedback loop is what makes the design of a user interface for training dismounted infantry so hard. The design space is extremely large because of the vast number of possible interactions between different motor control techniques and sensory feedback methods.

A 3-D user interface for training dismounted infantry should allow the trainee to execute tasks similar to how they are performed in the real world, with close to the same feedback. Having the 3-D virtual world change *naturally* in response to the trainee's actions gives the trainee the impression of dealing directly with the virtual world. It provides the correct motor/sensory feedback loop that not only enables skill development, but also makes natural decision making possible. According to Hutchins (1996), human cognition is always affected by the complex world in which it is situated. Realistic interaction provides the cues needed to elicit and train tactical decision making.

This chapter presents a list of the properties of natural human action for creating 3-D user interfaces for training. The list can also serve as criteria for usability analyses and more formal evaluations. The chapter also discusses how we applied the properties in the design of two user interfaces developed under the Virtual Technologies and Environments program, funded by the Office of Naval Research, and with support from the Naval Research Laboratory.

BACKGROUND

Close Quarters Battle

The U.S. Marine Corps manual *Military Operations on Urban Terrain* (Marine Corps Institute, 1997) describes the duties of a four- to six-person search party conducting building clearing operations. The team is split into a search team and cover team: the search team methodically clears each room, hallway, and stairway in the building while the cover team maintains local security. The team operations diagramed in the manual are highly formalized and require skilled coordinated movements that are executed in a complex environment in which threats can come from any direction (the 360°/180° battle space—360° around, 90° above, and 90° below). The goal is to successfully engage all enemy threats, while avoiding injury and death.

Each team member moves in concert with other team members, walking smoothly to create a stable shooting platform while searching for target indicators that must be engaged the moment they are encountered. As team members move, they primarily keep their rifles pointed just below their line of sight so that when a target appears, they can immediately snap up their rifles to target the threat. By maintaining the alignment of the head, eyes, and rifle, they essentially move the entire upper body as a single rigid unit (similar to how a gun turret moves on a tank).

Essential Elements of Close Quarters Battle

The actions of CQB can be summarized as the coordination of looking, moving, and shooting. Looking to direct the person's view and weapons handling must be seamlessly integrated with the movement required to uncover and respond to threats. Kelly McCann (personal communication, 2001), a former U.S. Marine and subject matter expert in CQB, outlined the basic requirements: (a) It is vital to *coordinate looking with moving.* Since it can be deadly to neglect the corner of a room, riflemen should never move faster than their abilities to incrementally cover danger areas. (b) It is important to *coordinate shooting (moving from a ready into an aim stance, aiming, and pulling the trigger) with looking and moving.* Team members must be ready to shoot at all times, but must never shoot faster than their abilities to hit the target. (c) Team members must *coordinate their movements.* Team members must pace themselves to move as a unit as they clear the building and provide cover for one another. Team members orient themselves to cover all sectors of responsibility, with some providing vertical and rear security.

DESIGN STRATEGIES

A user interface is composed of interaction techniques, which link what the user does (input) to what is displayed (output/feedback). As such, interaction techniques provide the motor/sensory feedback loop necessary for active perception in the 3-D simulation.

Realistic simulation systems, such as those used to train CQB, have user interfaces that differ from other 3-D user interfaces in that the user relates to the virtual world through the user's avatar, the representation of the user's body that moves and interacts in the virtual world. Therefore, an additional aspect to the input mapping must be taken into account. Input design must consider not only the physical actions that comprise the interaction techniques, but also how those actions translate into the behavior of the user's avatar (the *effect* of those actions). In the case of a system to train CQB, the physical actions are what the user does to look, move, and shoot, and the effect is how the avatar reflects those actions.

Feedback (output) is the second half of the interaction technique equation. Feedback stimulates the senses and includes visual, auditory, and haptic displays. All channels are important, but visual feedback is dominant in most simulation systems, including those for dismounted infantry training, and will be the focus here.

Avatars

The user's avatar is driven by the user's actions in real time. Avatars differ in how much of the avatar's body is articulated and the level of control the user has over the avatar's behavior. Unlike avatars in many first-person shooter games that use canned animation sequences to portray the user's actions (for example, walking and running), our avatars are highly articulated (including head, torso, and legs), and the user drives the motion of the avatar directly. For example, the user's avatar turns to look by the same amount and in the same direction as the user's head turns. Avatars can be viewed in first or third person. In first person, the user "sees" out of the avatars eyes and the avatar is fully drawn so users can see their arms, legs, and feet. In third person, the user views the full avatar from a distance. In our system, the user interacts with the virtual world in first person; third person is used only for demonstration purposes.

Input: Properties of Natural Action

Designing interaction techniques to support dismounted infantry training is challenging. To guide the development process, we studied how experts perform real world tasks and developed a framework that lists the salient properties of natural physical action (Templeman & Sibert, 2006). In the real world, people perform actions by moving their limb segments to accomplish tasks. The set of actions that can be achieved is the result of constraints inherent in the structure of the human body that result from "[the] bony arrangement, net muscle activity, segmental organization of the body, scale or size, [and] motor integration (such as the need to provide postural support)" (Enoka, 2002, p. xix). Actions can be simple (for example, relaxing the grip on an object) or complex, involving several body segments to produce a coordinated effect (for example, running to strike a tennis ball). Likewise, users perform interaction techniques to accomplish tasks in the virtual environment. The properties of natural action guided our selection of physical actions for the interaction techniques that affect the behavior of the user's avatar. The list of properties applies to both realistic 3-D user interfaces, as well as more abstract ones. The difference is in the degree of similarity to the real world actions. The properties of natural action with an example of where each applies in the real world follow:

Body segments: For walking or running, the body leans forward and the legs move to propel the body over the ground.

Effort: For a given gait of locomotion, effort increases with speed due to "the increases in heart rate, ventilation rate, and the rate of oxygen consumption" (Enoka, 2002, p. 192).

Coordination: People have the ability to coordinate several actions at once. A tennis player can run up to and strike a ball in one unified motion. The effect can be achieved only by running and swinging the racket in concert. There are limits to coordination insofar as performing one action constrains other actions. Some limitations derive from the body's physical construction; it is difficult for a person to look backward while walking straight ahead. The most obvious form of constraint is that actions requiring the dedicated use of a body segment cannot be performed at the same time as an action involving that same segment. In other instances, the way an action is performed may be altered to afford concurrent operation. For example, two hands are used to hold a rifle; turning a doorknob requires a free hand and so disrupts the way the rifle can be held.

Degrees of freedom and range of motion: The head can be turned and tilted forward, back, and side to side over a limited range by exerting the muscles of the neck. To rotate the head farther, the body must turn, either by twisting the spine or rotating the pelvis while twisting the legs. Turning even farther requires turning the entire body, easily accomplished by stepping in place.

Rate and accuracy: It takes longer to aim and shoot with precision than to aim coarsely. Rate and accuracy are analyzed in terms of the speed/accuracy trade-off.

Open- or closed-loop control: If an action can be performed using only internal sensory feedback and without any external cues (for example, visual or auditory), the action is said to be open loop. People can look at a nearby object, close their eyes, and walk to it with fairly good accuracy under open-loop control (Philbeck, Loomis, & Beall, 1997). The opposite is closed-loop control in which a person relies on external feedback to adjust the action as it is performed, as when catching a ball.

All six properties, defined above, apply to the input actions that comprise the interaction techniques. The last three apply to the effect of those actions on the avatar. For the avatar to move correctly, the input must convey sufficient *degrees of freedom* (DOF) and *range of motion* to specify realistic behavior. A classic example is using a 3 DOF inertial tracker, which tracks only the orientation of the user's head. The 3 DOF of orientation are captured, but the head's 3 DOF of translation are lost. As a result, the avatar's head motion can be displayed only approximately; more importantly, no visual feedback is available to convey motion parallax. The *rate* and *accuracy* with which the avatar walks and runs through the virtual world affects the user's sense of timing and scale. Many games allow unrealistically fast movement at sustained speeds. It would be impossible to obtain correct timing estimates to plan a mission. *Open- and closed-loop control* are important because they relate how the interaction technique input actions guide the avatar's behavior. Open-loop control is the most demanding, but also the most important property. If an action in the real world can be achieved with open-loop control using only internal sensory feedback (without external cues), the interaction technique should also permit it.

Feedback: Visual Display Characteristics

In the real world, people live in a full-surround, high resolution, full-contrast world. No current, cost-effective display provides this level of visual fidelity. Therefore, it is important to know the limitations of display technologies to understand their affect on performance and training. An excellent discussion of visual display characteristics and depth cues for 3-D applications is found in Hinckley et al. (2004).

Both field of regard (FOR) and field of view (FOV) are critical for understanding realistic simulation systems. FOR is the amount of visual display space surrounding the user that is accessible by turning the head and body. FOV is the maximum visual angle that can be seen without turning the head. Dismounted infantry urban combat takes place in a 360°/180° battle space. The warfighter must rapidly respond to threats coming from any direction. The display must provide the full 360°/180° FOR, or the interaction techniques must compensate for the lack of one (a simple example is providing a button to rotate the virtual world about the user). In terms of FOV, less than 120° horizontal by 120° vertical FOV per eye affects how realistically the user can perform a visual search task: a narrow *horizontal* FOV is like wearing blinders, forcing the user to turn the head to take in a full view; a narrow *vertical* FOV makes it difficult to follow a path or pick up threats from above or below (Allen, 1989). The display's spatial resolution, contrast, and update rate are also important design considerations. They will determine whether users are able to see target indicators and distinguish friend from foe at the same range and with the same precision as in the real world.

USER INTERFACES TO TRAIN DISMOUNTED INFANTRY

To teach CQB, the interaction techniques comprising the user interface should give trainees close to the same ability to look, move, and shoot as they have in the real world. Skills and actions, such as walking through a door and aiming a rifle, should demand approximately the same timing and exposure to threats. Likewise, the avatar's behavior should closely resemble real world performance, moving at a similar pace and precision. In terms of sensory feedback, the trainee should be able to access the full environment.

We present, as examples, two interfaces we developed that seek to match the properties of natural action. *Gaiter* is an immersive, *body-driven interface* in which the user's body, rifle, and head-mounted display are fully tracked using a 6 DOF optical motion capture system. With Gaiter, the user walks in place to move through the virtual world and is able to freely turn in place. A head-mounted display provides access to a full FOR to "immerse" the user in the virtual environment, although the FOV is limited to 36° vertical by 48° horizontal per eye. A harness is used to center the user because people tend to drift forward when they walk in place. An instrumented rifle prop registers shots fired. Body driven refers to the fact that the user's major body segments are tracked, and the 6 DOF position of each segment directly controls the user's avatar at the same level of articulation. Gaiter is a general purpose interface because the interaction techniques allow close to the full range of actions people have in the real world, and it is considered high end because it employs expensive, large footprint hardware. *Pointman,* on the other hand, is a partially *device-driven,* low cost interface specialized for CQB training. (A good general discussion of system cost is found in Knerr, 2006.) Although head and foot motion are captured using head tracking and sliding foot pedals (rudder pedals for helicopter simulation games) making it partially body driven, locomotion is directed using a conventional dual joystick gamepad. The mappings of the joysticks are uniquely tailored to provide control over tactical infantry movement, unlike the mappings of the controllers used for conventional first-person shooter games. With Pointman, users are able to specify the direction of movement independent of the direction of the heading of the upper body. This independence allows the users to control how their avatars look, move, and shoot, with capabilities and constraints close to those people have in the real world.

Gaiter

The Gaiter user interface is a high end, fully immersive system in which the user's full body motion drives a fully articulated avatar (Templeman, Denbrook, & Sibert, 1999). The interaction techniques were designed to closely match the properties of natural action. A head-mounted display was chosen because it gives full access to the environment (an unlimited FOR), albeit at a lower resolution and with a reduced FOV than in the real world. An early prototype is shown in Figure 7.1.

Figure 7.1.   Gaiter: Note the Centering Harness, Tracking Cameras, and Tracking Markers on the Head-Mounted Display, Rifle Prop, and Body Segments

Whenever possible, the interaction techniques were designed to match the corresponding natural action one-to-one. A one-to-one mapping of body motion requires 6 DOF tracking. The orientation and translational components of the tracked motion are passed directly to the virtual simulation to specify the orientation and translation of the avatar's corresponding body segments. We use a one-to-one mapping to convey the motion of the head, arms, upper body posture, and the rifle prop. Weapons handling (moving between stances, reloading, and so forth) and shooting are a good example of a one-to-one interaction technique. Because we fully track the rifle prop, the user is able to see a virtual representation of the rifle as it would be seen directly. The user can aim and fire using a proper shooting posture, visual sight alignment, and body indexing (consistently holding the rifle stock in the same place against the shoulder and along the side of the cheek, known as a cheek weld). The user shoulders the rifle prop and establishes a cheek weld, looks "through" the virtual depiction of the rifle sights to acquire sight alignment and a sight picture, and pulls the trigger. The location of the hit is determined from the position of the rifle in the virtual world. In this way, the correct perceptual/action skills are used to locate the target, put the rifle on the target, and keep the rifle on the target while the shot is fired. Because the head-mounted display shows the imagery on a single focal plane, the skill of focusing the eyes on the front sight is not trained. We blur the image of the rear sight to add realism, but the degree of blurring is fixed and does not depend on the user's depth of focus. Flaws remain in the latency of the view presentation and in the precise visual alignment of the user's eyes, rifle sights, and target, which further refinement would improve.

One-to-one interaction techniques, such as handling a rifle, are a direct match with the properties of natural action. The rifle handling technique uses the same *body segments* as real world shooting. Since the rifle prop is fully tracked in 6 DOF, there are sufficient *degrees of freedom* to accurately depict shooting in the virtual world. *Effort* is comparable because the rifle prop weighs about the same as an actual rifle and has similar inertia. *Rate* of firing and *accuracy* are maintained if the visual aspects involved with shooting are correct. Finally, with practice, marksmen can obtain close to the *open-loop control* they achieve in the real world.

Not all interaction techniques can be designed as one-to-one mappings. Locomotion is a case in point. Users need a way to move over long distances in the virtual world while remaining within the tracked area of the motion capture system. The Gaiter locomotion technique is a gesture based technique that was designed to convey the essence of natural walking. We based our design on *motor substitution,* which suggests that by substituting a closely matched gesture for a natural action, the user can more easily employ familiar skills and strategies and more likely accomplish the task in a realistic manner (Templeman & Sibert, 2006).

An analysis of the properties of natural action for walking and running in the real world helped us match in-place stepping to natural locomotion. Additional refinement could improve the technique, but most people who have tried the system indicate that Gaiter gives them the sense of actually walking and running through the virtual world.

Body segments: Motor substitution recommends that the interaction techniques use the same or close to the same body segments, and thus the same motor control subsystems, to allow similar affordances and constraints. A leg based approach that uses stepping in place and actual turning of the body gives a good approximation of real world locomotion. Actual turning provides kinesthetic and vestibular feedback, which Chance, Gaunet, Beall, and Loomis (1998) showed are needed for people to orient themselves accurately in the environment.

Effort: In-place walking and running require significant effort, albeit less than natural walking and running. Through informal use, we have found that leaning into the harness while running in place makes it feel more like actual running.

Coordination: It is important that the locomotion control action interact with other actions (such as weapons handling) in a realistic manner to give the users close to the same ability and level of constraint to coordinate actions as they have in the real world. With Gaiter, body segments are employed as they are in the real world (legs for locomotion and hands for manipulating the rifle) and, as with real walking, stepping in place with natural turning operates in a body-centric coordinate system that allows reflexive action.

Degrees of freedom and range of motion: Gaiter applies 6 DOF tracking to the major body segments, the head-mounted display, and the rifle to provide full control over aiming.

Rate and accuracy: Gaiter is tuned to match real world walking and running speeds and to preserve the metrics between physical and virtual space. The horizontal extension of the user's knee and rate of in-place steps are mapped into the stride length and cadence of the avatar's virtual steps. The system is tuned to match the velocity associated with the transition between walking and running. With walking, one support foot is always on the ground. With running, both feet are momentarily off the ground at the same time. The resulting virtual motion ties optic flow (Gibson, 1986) to leg movement to make the interaction technique feel more like a simulation of walking rather than indirect control over locomotion.

Open- or closed-loop control: With practice, a user can calibrate to Gaiter and achieve open-loop control, which is consistent with the findings of Richardson and Waller (2007), who showed that practice corrects the underestimation of distance in virtual environments. Because the user can easily access the full environment with the head-mounted display, closed-loop control with vision is always available.

The distinguishing feature of the Gaiter locomotion technique is how it combines control actions based on motor substitution with a body-driven avatar that reflects the user's posture and movement. The user can naturally align other parts of the body, such as head, shoulders, arms, and torso, with the movement of the user's knees and feet. Users can intermix a wide range of one-to-one movements, such as turning, crouching, and bending, to look around objects in the virtual. The ability to turn naturally (one-to-one) is central to Gaiter. A user can reflexively turn toward or away from a sight or sound.

Pointman

Pointman is a compact, low cost interface that gives users the ability to execute realistic tactical infantry movements. The military has a growing interest in using games for training because they can support a large number of player/trainees and are portable and relatively inexpensive. However, console based gamepads, as currently used for first-person shooter games, encourage unrealistic tactics by promoting strafing motions: moving obliquely with respect to the viewing direction (Templeman, Sibert, Page, & Denbrook, 2007). Pointman encourages correct tactical movement in a desktop simulator. The Pointman user interface consists of a conventional dual joystick gamepad for locomotion and weapons handling, sliding foot pedals to specify displacement, head tracking for viewing and aiming, and a desktop or head-mounted display. Pointman is shown in Figure 7.2.

We studied the details of tactical movement for CQB to isolate its fundamental properties. When performing CQB in urban terrain, tactical infantry movement involves keeping the rifle aligned with the view while scanning for threats. In the words of the U.S. Marine Corps manual on rifle marksmanship, "[Cover] the field of view with the aiming eye and muzzle of the weapon. Wherever the eyes move, the muzzle should move (eyes, muzzle, target)" (Marine Corps Combat Development Command, 2001, p. 73). Figure 7.3, adapted from the Marine

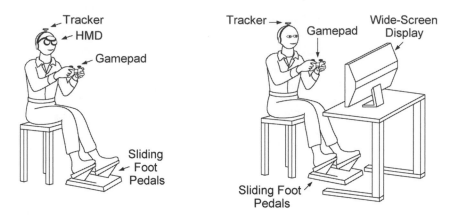

Figure 7.2.   Two Configurations of Pointman, Each with Head Tracking and Foot Pedals

Corps manual on urban operations (Marine Corps Institute, 1997), illustrates the tactical movement for visually clearing the area around a corner or through an open doorway (called "pie-ing"). A person turns the upper body as a rigid unit to point the rifle just past the corner of the doorway, while moving down the hallway. The objective is to incrementally see into the area just beyond the corner, while minimizing exposure to potential threats.

Tactical movement, therefore, involves maintaining a ready posture with the head, the upper body, and the rifle aligned and turned as a unit independent of the direction of movement. The fact of this alignment of the body in real world CQB provides a legitimate basis for reducing the degrees of freedom needed to specify the orientation of the avatar's upper body. It is useful to adopt terms used in both vehicular and human navigation literature (Beall & Loomis, 1996) to formalize the discussion. We define three components of motion in the horizontal

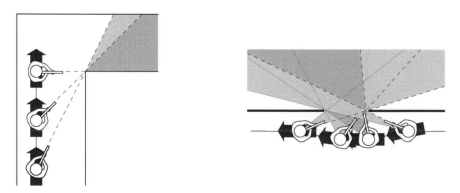

Figure 7.3.   Left: Turreting the Upper Body toward the Corner while Maintaining a Straight Course, the Tactically Correct Way to Clear a Corner; Right: Pie-ing Past an Open Doorway

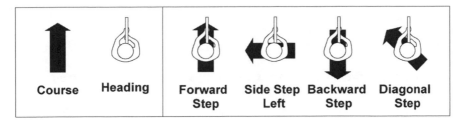

Figure 7.4.   Illustration of basic terms: here the direction of aim indicates the heading. The angle between the course and the heading determines the kind of step being taken.

plane: heading, course, and displacement. Upper body refers to the aligned head, upper body, and rifle.

Heading: angular direction the upper body faces.

Course: angular direction in which the pelvis translates.

Displacement: distance the pelvis translates.

In Figure 7.4, heading is shown as a top-down view of a person in a tactical ready posture. Course is the arrow pointing in the direction of translation. The angle between course and heading determines the kind of step taken.

The following classes of motion were derived from studying how course and heading vary as people walk and run in the real world (Figure 7.5).

Steering motion: Course and heading remain coaligned as a person moves along a path. Steering can be used to move toward a target or follow along a path. It is the most common type of pedestrian motion.

Oblique motion: Heading remains in a fixed direction as course varies. Oblique motion is used by marching bands.

Canted motion: Course and heading are maintained at a fixed angle offset. Steering motion is a subclass of canted motion. Notice that moving along a

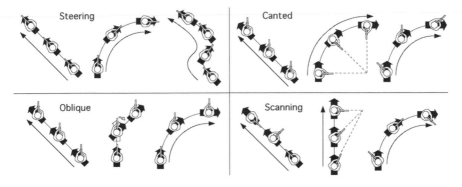

Figure 7.5.   Examples of Steering, Canted, Oblique, and Scanning Motion

straight path with course and heading pointing in the same direction qualifies as both canted and oblique motion, so the classes partially overlap.

Scanning motion: Heading is free to turn separately from the course. Scanning motion can be used to search from side to side while moving along a path or to direct the heading toward a target. Scanning while traversing a curved path is the only case in which the heading and course vary independently.

The properties of natural action were applied more abstractly in the design of Pointman than for Gaiter. The goal was the same: users must be able to control looking, moving, and shooting (the basic actions of CQB), with close to the same capability and limitation people have in the real world. What is different is that the set of potential input actions was not constrained to closely match their real world counterparts, which opens up the design space manifold. The guidelines for direct manipulation interfaces (such as the desktop interface) are helpful in evaluating possible designs. The fundamental goal of direct manipulation is to tie the control actions into the user's preexisting skills, abilities, and expectations (Jacob, Leggett, Myers, & Pausch, 1993). A "good" abstract interface, therefore, should exploit the user's intuition, take advantage of people's ability to coordinate actions, reduce the cognitive burden by limiting the number of artificial commands the user must remember, and provide sufficient information to support realistic avatar behavior in the virtual world.

The user interface for Pointman includes a locomotion technique to specify course and heading, a method to input the amount of displacement, weapons handling functions, and view and aim control. The user controls course and heading through the joysticks on a conventional dual-joystick gamepad. Joysticks are commonly programmed to provide rate control over turning and displacement, but with Pointman, both joysticks are directional controls. The preferred technique for specifying direction is to push the joystick against the circular outer rim in the initial direction and slide it along the rim to make adjustments. This action is easier than turning the joystick without support, and it results in a smoother, more precise motion. The left joystick is used to direct the course, and the right the heading. When both joysticks are used together, course and heading are specified independently, enabling the user to execute scanning motion to direct the avatar's actions in a tactically correct manner. There are two classes of motion that use just one joystick: steering motion (when the course and heading are coaligned as in walking along a path) is controlled using just the right joystick; oblique motion (when the view is fixed forward) is controlled with the left, the same as with the conventional joystick mapping. People are good at turning a specific number of degrees under open-loop control, for example, a 90° turn to the right, and Pointman supports that as well. In this case, the user pushes the joystick 90° from the neutral centered position in the direction of the turn. The maximum turning rate is limited to the maximum rate a person can actually turn the body. For displacement, length of stride and speed are controlled using sliding foot pedals, which mimic people's foot motion when they walk or run. Weapons handling is accomplished through button presses on the gamepad. One button is the trigger, and another cycles through the tactical rifle stances:

tactical, alert, and ready carry. Viewing and aiming control are provided by a 3 or 6 DOF tracker attached to the head. A full FOR is available using either a desktop or head-mounted display, but access is less direct than with Gaiter (or in the real world) because the user is seated and not able to turn the body.

Head tracking is used to control the yaw (turning about the vertical axis) and the pitch (tilting up and down) movement of the user's view and aim. Turning the avatar's heading is primarily accomplished using the right joystick, but the yaw derived from head tracking information is added to turn the view an additional amount (limited by how far the user's head can be turned without turning the body). If the tracker provides 6 DOF that includes translation, the user can lean in, out, and side to side, further increasing the realism. Moving the view up, down, and side to side is direct and natural with a head-mounted display. It is more complicated with a desktop monitor. As the user yaws the head, the avatar's head turns relative to the avatar's body by the same amount and in the same direction (one-to-one), the same as with the head-mounted display. For pitch, however, there is a limitation to how far the user can tilt the head back while still comfortably viewing the screen. Therefore, we amplify the actual tilting of the head by a linear scale factor that depends on the vertical dimensions of the display, so that the user does not have to pitch the head straight up or down for the avatar to look directly up or down in the virtual world.

Both desktop and head-mounted displays suffer from a limited FOV as compared with viewing in the real world, although it is less expensive to provide a wide FOV with a desktop display than with today's head-mounted displays using larger or multiple screens. Resolution is also important and varies by the display; the higher the resolution, the better users can detect targets and discriminate whether they are friend or foe.

An analysis of the final design shows how Pointman achieves the properties of natural action and allows users to "pie" corners, scan upon entering a room, and perform tactically correct team stairwell clears using a partially device-driven control.

Body segments: Even though Pointman uses the thumbs rather than the legs for turning the body and directing the course, users are still able to directly sense their alignment through the position of the joysticks. Other control actions use the same body segments as in the real world. Pitching the view and sighting the rifle are controlled with head movement. The movement of the feet on the sliding foot pedals controls stepwise displacement.

Effort: Because the head is tracked, adjusting the view is accomplished by moving the head as it is in the real world, taking a similar amount of effort. In the same way, using the foot pedals gives a sense of the distance traveled and the difference in effort needed to step at different rates.

Coordination: Several control actions must be coordinated to enable looking, moving, and shooting. Because they are all independent actions controlled with different parts of the body, they can be easily performed concurrently. The course and heading joysticks specify the direction of translation and the upper body's orientation. They are coordinated with the sliding foot pedals to specify displacement and move the avatar through the virtual world. The user controls view direction with the joysticks and by making fine adjustments with the head. Therefore, the direction of aim for shooting is linked to the direction of view, which corresponds to what experts do in the real world: The head, upper body, and rifle are rotated as a unit to face the target. Expert shooters also pitch their torso forward or back to aim up or down, which is available if Pointman is configured with 6 DOF head tracking.

Degrees of freedom and range of motion: Both head tracking and the foot pedals provide body-driven control over the avatar's movement. If the user's head is tracked in 6 DOF, the avatar's head pose is a direct one-to-one match. If the tracker provides only the 3 DOF in orientation, realism decreases; however, a direct link still exists between the user and the avatar because the avatar's head orientation appears similar to that of the user.

Rate and accuracy: Foot pedals allow the user to directly control the extent of each step and rate of movement, giving a sense of distance covered. As with real walking and running, the user is able to control the cadence of the avatar through reciprocating leg movements.

Open- or closed-loop control: The user can achieve open-loop control over movement by continuously sensing the relative positions of the joysticks and the direction of the head. Tactical movement often occurs in low or no light conditions, making it important to be able to direct one's movement without vision.

SUMMARY

Developing a user interface to train CQB poses challenges to provide interaction techniques that afford the essential capabilities needed to execute tactics, techniques, and procedures. We seek to transform the user's actions into the actions of the avatar in a way that allows the user to perform the requisite tasks in a tactically correct manner; otherwise, the exercise is merely a game. The properties of natural action, which were developed by analyzing how experts perform tasks in the real world, have proven useful in guiding the design and development of interaction techniques for training dismounted infantry. We studied the tactics, techniques, and procedures of CQB and determined that the fundamental actions are looking, moving, and shooting. A further analysis revealed that tactical movement relies heavily on the ability to look while moving along a path, with the head, upper body, and rifle moving as a single rigid unit. These insights led to the design of Gaiter, a body-driven interface, and Pointman, a system that combines a device-driven interface with body-driven control.

The properties of natural action are also useful in analyzing other dismounted infantry training simulators. For example, a system that uses a joystick mounted on a rifle prop for locomotion, such as the one we built for experimental purposes similar to Atlantis Cyberspace, Inc.'s Immersive Group Simulator or Quantum3D's ExpeditionDI, overloads the users' hands, adding control over course and speed to the actions of weapons handling and shooting. If a surround screen or head-mounted display is used, which allows the user to turn naturally, directing steering motion is easily performed by pushing the joystick forward to move in the direction the rifle is pointed and turning the upper body. However, it is tricky to turn to search for threats without disrupting the course. The user must compensate for turning the body (to redirect the heading) by counterturning with the joystick to maintain a straight course. This control structure makes scanning motion more difficult and encourages spiraling in toward the target (strafing), as occurs with conventional game controls.

The user interface is the key component in developing an effective simulator for training dismounted infantry. The goal is to develop interfaces that give trainees the ability to move and coordinate actions in the virtual world as they do in the real world. The benefit is in providing a safe, accessible, and cost-effective addition to live training.

REFERENCES

Allen, R. C. (1989). *The effect of restricted field of view on locomotion tasks, head movements, and motion sickness.* Unpublished doctoral dissertation, University of Central Florida, Orlando.

Beall, A. C., & Loomis, J. M. (1996). Visual control of steering without course information. *Perception, 25,* 481–494.

Bowman, D. A., Kruijff, E., LaViola, J. J., Jr., & Poupyrev, I. (2005). *3D user interfaces theory and practice.* New York: Addison-Wesley.

Chance, S. S., Gaunet, F., Beall, A. C., & Loomis, J. M. (1998). Locomotion mode affects the updating of objects encountered during travel: The contribution of vestibular and proprioceptive inputs to path integration. *Presence, 7,* 168–178.

Enoka, R. M. (2002). *Neuromechanics of human movement.* Champaign, IL: Human Kinetics.

Gibson, J. J. (1986). *The ecological approach to visual perception.* Hillsdale, NJ: Lawrence Erlbaum.

Hinckley, K., Jacob, R. J. K., & Ware, C. (2004). Input/output devices and interaction techniques. In A. B. Tucker (Ed), *The computer science handbook* (2nd ed., pp. 20.1–20.32). Boca Raton, FL: Chapman and Hall/CRC Press.

Hutchins, E. (1996). *Cognition in the wild.* Cambridge, MA: The MIT Press.

Jacob, R. J. K., Leggett, J. J., Myers, B. A., & Pausch, R. (1993). Interaction styles and input/output devices. *Behaviour and Information Technology, 12,* 69–79.

Knerr, B. W. (2006). Current issues in the use of virtual simulations for dismounted soldier training. *Proceedings of the NATO Human Factors and Medicine Panel Workshop: Virtual Media for Military Applications* (RTO Proceedings No. NATO RTO-MP-HFM-136, pp. 21.1–21.12). Neuilly-sur-Seine, France: Research and Technology Organization.

Marine Corps Combat Development Command. (2001). *Rifle marksmanship* (Marine Corps Reference Publication No. MCRP 3-01A). Albany, GA: Marine Corps Logistics Base.

Marine Corps Institute. (1997). *Military operations on urban terrain* (Marine Corps Institute Rep. No. MCI 03.66b). Washington, DC: Marine Barracks.

Philbeck, J. W., Loomis, J. M., & Beall A. C. (1997). Visually perceived location is an invariant in the control of action. *Perception & Psychophysics, 59,* 601–612.

Richardson, A. R., & Waller, D. (2007). Interaction with an immersive virtual environment corrects user's distance estimates. *Human Factors, 49,* 507–517.

Templeman, J. N., Denbrook, P. S., & Sibert, L. E. (1999). Virtual locomotion: Walking in place through virtual environments. *Presence, 8,* 598–617.

Templeman, J. N., & Sibert, L. E. (2006). Immersive simulation of coordinated motion in virtual environments. In G. Allen (Ed.), *Applied spatial cognition: From research to cognitive technology* (pp. 339–372). Mahwah, NJ: Lawrence Erlbaum.

Templeman, J. N., Sibert, L. E., Page, R. C., & Denbrook, P .S. (2007). Pointman—A device-based control for realistic tactical movement. *Proceedings of 3DUI* (pp. 163–166). Piscataway, NJ: Institute of Electrical and Electronics Engineers, Inc.

Chapter 8

RENDERING AND COMPUTING REQUIREMENTS

Perry McDowell, Michael Guerrero,
Danny McCue, and Brad Hollister

Large, distributed, multiparticipant training simulations require significant computing resources to run the appropriate simulation application at each user station, to enable interactive inputs and displays for the user, and to enable network communication among the participating computers. This chapter will briefly look at the major categories of computations for simulations and then take an in-depth look at the hardware of a typical personal computer (PC) based trainee station: central processing unit (CPU), memory and mass storage, graphics processing unit (GPU), and networking.

This chapter discusses the theory and nomenclature in the current state of the art of processing for interactive three-dimensional (3-D) and virtual environment based training systems and games. The goal is to give the reader the basic knowledge and vocabulary to discuss system processing and networking requirements with the programmers and engineers who will be designing and building the system. Although we attempt to define terms throughout the chapter, it is written with the expectation that the reader is fairly well versed with computer technology. Terms in *italics* are good keywords for searches of article databases, digital libraries, and online search engines.

OVERVIEW OF PROCESSING REQUIREMENTS FOR VIRTUAL ENVIRONMENTS

Virtual environments (VEs) are highly complicated computing applications and as such require some of the most computationally advanced systems. While other applications, such as a simulation of fluid flow around a body or a password-cracking application, may require faster computations, VEs are more complicated due to the range of computationally advanced requirements most have in multiple areas, such as rendering, simulation, physics, networking, and input and output from and to multiple devices.

Consider a simple VE for a ground-combat simulation trainer with the user in a head-mounted display, using an instrumented weapon, and leading a squad of

soldiers in similar VEs against a simulated enemy. The computational requirements for this straightforward VE are extremely complex. To be interactive the
scene must be rendered at more than 30 times per second for the display for each
eye in order to prevent jerky movements that will reduce the realism of the environment, make smooth control of interactions difficult, and increase the probability that the user will experience simulator sickness.

The tracking system must calculate the position and orientation of both the
weapon and the user's head, and this must be done with a minimum of latency
to avoid the same problems as not rendering quickly enough. The leader's system
must be networked with the systems of his squad members, again with a minimum of latency to prevent misrepresenting his team's locations in the world.

The system's artificial intelligence must compute the actions of the simulated
enemy in real time; unless the desired behaviors are modeled well and significant
computing power is available so that the behavior state is updated rapidly, the
synthetic enemy will not act realistically, causing the training to be ineffective.

The system must calculate all the physical interactions occurring in the world.
These include collision detection, determining whether the user and all the other
moving objects in the world have collided with any of the objects in the world,
and if objects do collide, determining the response of the colliding objects to
the collision. The last step is rendering a new scene that reflects the changes
caused by the collision.

The processing requirements for simulations are highly dependent on the number of real and simulated entities (people and moving objects, such as tanks), the
number of participants in the simulation, the fidelity of the simulated behaviors
and collisions, and the fidelity of the programs that generate data for visual displays and displays to other senses, such as audio. The hardware available to build
VE systems today owes much to the PC games market. The gamers' desire for
ever-higher levels of fidelity in all elements of games has driven the capabilities
of PCs, and particularly of graphics cards, in ways that enormously benefit the
training system designer.

PC BASED STATIONS FOR TRAINING

From the 1960s through the early 1990s the computer based simulation industry was dominated by vendors who provided proprietary hardware and software
solutions for rendering interactive 3-D imagery. Only in the past 10 to 15 years
have general purpose PCs displaced the proprietary hardware and provided
government agencies and the private sector with lower cost and more flexible
ways of meeting their training hardware requirements. The new paradigm is
building interactive 3-D and VE based training systems using commercial off-
the-shelf PCs. Even if one vender provides an entire simulator system, it is likely
to be composed of custom software running on commercial PCs instead of on
custom hardware. The rest of this chapter is focused on PC based systems for
simulation since, although still available, single-vendor, turn-key custom solutions are no longer the norm, and no one vendor dominates the marketplace, as
companies such as Silicon Graphics, Inc., did in the 1980s and 1990s.

Basic PC Architecture

Figure 8.1 shows a high level view of the architecture of a PC and its major parts. The *central processing unit* is the computing heart of the system, and it is located on the *motherboard.* The motherboard is the primary printed circuit board in the system and, in addition to the CPU, contains the data pathways, called *busses,* that connect the system components. In addition to the CPU, other major elements of the PC are the main *memory,* internal and external *mass storage,* and *peripheral processors* providing computational acceleration for targeted tasks, such as graphics and simulating physical reactions. Although peripheral processors can be mounted on the motherboard, the more powerful ones, for instance, high end graphics cards, plug into a fast bus on the motherboard.

Types of peripheral processors include graphics accelerator cards, which themselves contain *graphics processing units,* physics accelerator cards containing physics-processing-units, sound generation cards, and network interface cards. Of these, this chapter will cover only graphics cards. Physics cards are still rather rare; sound cards have little programmability and, in general, vary little except for those designed for very particular tasks such as Web servers or studio recording. Networking cards are essentially commodity products today, and we will discuss networking only with regards to some of the different methods a designer can choose for a large distributed simulation system.

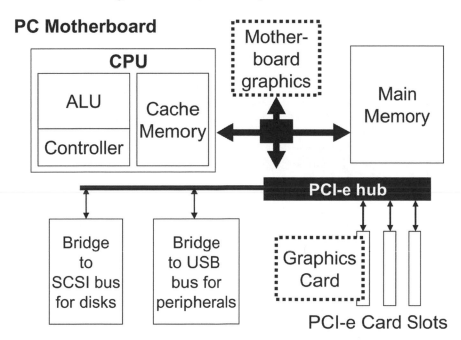

Figure 8.1.   Simplified block diagram of a PC motherboard. Graphics processing may be integrated on the motherboard or provided on a card plugged into a PCI-e bus slot.

Single and Multi-PC Systems

The hardware system running the application may consist of a stand-alone PC, such as is used for most single player games, or multiple PCs networked together. The latter case has many variations. In some systems the networked PCs all perform similar tasks, for instance, in a networked multiplayer game where each player's computer runs the same simulation (game) and the results and game state are shared over the network. In this situation, the hardware requirements are generally consistent across the networked computers.

A second multi-PC configuration is when a number of PCs, called a *cluster,* operate in parallel on a single task, with each PC performing a portion of the computation. An example is a cluster used for image generation where each PC renders a subset of each new frame. *Parallel execution* of subsets of the problem reduces the time required to complete the overall task. Computational load for a large simulation can also be shared by using different computers in a cluster to perform different tasks. In this case one (or multiple) PC might perform only image generation, while others perform input handling, artificial intelligence, or physics calculations. In all these multi-PC configurations, however, the individual machines' configurations are very similar, if not identical, to those used by PC gaming enthusiasts. Multiprocessor systems are discussed again in more detail in the "Multiprocessing" section of this chapter.

PC Busses

Data moves from one functional unit of the PC to another by way of busses, a set of parallel electrical conductors. A motherboard may have busses dedicated to communication between chips, for example, the main memory to the CPU bus, as well as busses that peripheral processor cards plug into. From the CPU's perspective, all other devices in the system—whether a graphics card, main memory, or an internal disk drive—are treated as addresses written to or read from via the motherboard's system of busses.

System performance is affected by the rate at which a bus can transfer data, and the data transfer rate is determined by how wide the bus is (how many bits can be transferred each clock tick) and the speed of the clock controlling data transfer. The bus between the CPU and the graphics card is particularly important as all data to be displayed travels across it. Most PC motherboards today use the peripheral-component-interconnect-express (*PCI-e*) bus. For maximum performance, particularly for graphics performance, system designers must ensure a match between the bus interface on the motherboard for expansion cards and the bus interface of any such card.

CPU Architecture and Performance

The design of the CPU, called the CPU *architecture,* includes several functional units: *cache* memory, *arithmetic and logic unit* (ALU), and a *control* unit (see Figure 8.1). A cache is memory that is on the CPU chip and that the controller can access faster than any other memory. Cache memory is, however, more expensive to manufacture than regular main memory. A CPU may contain one or more ALUs, the components that actually perform the computing operations. Program instructions and data are fetched from main memory and stored in cache. When a program executes, the control unit reads the instructions one at a time and generates the signals that make the ALU perform the action specified in the instruction. The *instruction set* of a processor is the list of all the operations that the CPU can perform. Examples are add, multiply, and read data.

Like almost all digital circuits, components of the CPU are designed with *synchronous logic,* which means that the timing of the sequence of operations executed in all components is controlled by a global clock signal, one operation per clock tick. Many operations in the instruction set take more than a single clock cycle to execute, and the design of the ALU determines exactly how many clock cycles it takes to perform a particular operation on a specific CPU.

CPU Speed

One specification touted as differentiating CPUs is their clock speed. If a CPU has a specification of a clock speed of 1.5 gigahertz (GHz), it means that the synchronizing clock ticks 1.5 billion times per second. The basic unit for clocks is hertz, which means cycles or oscillations per second. Because different processor models have different instruction sets, a faster clock speed does not always mean faster program execution: Unless they are the same model of CPU with identical instruction sets, a processor with a clock speed of 3.4 GHz will not necessarily process faster than a 1.5 GHz CPU.

The market has seen a steady rise in the performance of CPUs as manufacturing improvements have reduced the size of transistors and increased clock rates. Experts are saying that this path to improved performance is near its theoretical limit (Mistry et al., 2007). While exotic technologies, such as molecular or quantum computing, may replace today's silicon based computing someday (Tay, 2008), these are unlikely to be widely available during the useful life of this volume. The most prominent method of increasing computation speed using the traditional silicon based CPUs is multiprocessing.

Multiprocessing

Multiprocessing is simply using multiple processors to attack whatever problem is being solved. Multiprocessing can take many forms, and they are generally differentiated by where the processors are located in relation to each other: on the same chip, on the same motherboard, or in separate chassis.

Multiple processors on the same chip are called *multicore processors.* Examples include Intel's Quad Xeon or AMD's Phenom processors, each of which has four processors on a single CPU. These processors share both the main memory on the motherboard and the cache memory on the processor. When multiple CPUs are mounted on the same motherboard (each likely to be a multicore chip), each has its own cache memory, but they share the main memory. In computing clusters, or *loosely coupled* computing, the CPUs are generally located on different motherboards in different computers. The computers in the cluster are connected by a high speed network, such as gigabit Ethernet.

Multiprocessor systems with the CPUs on the same chip or on the same motherboard generally perform better and use less energy than clusters of PCs. However, clusters can be more economical, since the computers in the cluster do not need to be as powerful (and thus expensive) as a machine with the same capacity all on one motherboard. Clusters also scale better: as problem size increases, computers can be added to the cluster, increasing its computing power. Single motherboard multiprocessors generally must be replaced by another top-of-the-line machine when the problem becomes beyond its ability. Alternately, more computers of similar capacity can be added to form a cluster.

Writing software that exploits the power of multiprocessing will be challenging for current and new programmers. As Chas. Boyd, a member of the Direct3D team at Microsoft Corporation writes,

> Customers will . . . benefit only if software becomes capable of scaling across all those new cores. . . . For the next decade, the limiting factor in software performance will be the ability of software developers to restructure code to scale at a rate that keeps up with the rate of core-count growth.
>
> (Boyd, 2008, p. 32)

Here is an example of how increasing the number of processors to four (a common quad core CPU) and modifying the code will yield improvements in performance for a racing game. Just as now, the visuals will be produced using the systems GPU, but all the other computing requirements of the application will be split among the various processors. The user input and the networking might be processed on one processor, while the artificial intelligence guiding the other cars would be performed on another. The performance of the user's car is simulated in great detail on the third processor, and the physics of everything else in the game, which does not require as much realism, is processed on the final processor. Of course, programmers might find that there are better results by performing some of the calculations on the GPU, but finding the optimal performance balance will be the scope of research in the next decade or so.

Memory and Mass Storage

The processor's memory system also affects the performance of a computer. There are three major types of data storage: cache memory on the CPU chip, (main) memory on the motherboard, and mass storage (typically magnetic disk drives) that is either local to the system (internal or external to the chassis) or networked. Respectively, these three types of storage range from smallest to largest, from fastest access time to longest, and from most expensive to least expensive per bit stored. The main elements in evaluating memory's effect upon performance are the speed and the size of a system's memory.

Memory: Type and Size

Memory speed is most strongly affected by its type. Today's PCs most often use two forms of memory, dynamic random access memory (DRAM) and static random access memory (SRAM). The circuits in DRAM are simple and can be packed more densely than those of SRAM. However, the electrical charge that holds the data in DRAM must periodically be refreshed. This makes the supporting circuitry more complex. As of this writing, the highest performance systems use double-data-rate DRAM, which can be both read and written in a single clock cycle. The same characteristic of SRAM circuitry that makes it not require refreshing makes it faster. SRAM consumes more chip area for each bit of memory, and hence it is more expensive than DRAM. The cache memory is typically SRAM, and the main memory typically DRAM.

Memory size is also important for performance. The cache, which can be accessed by the CPU without leaving the chip, is relatively small. In early 2008, the largest cache on commonly available CPUs was 16 megabytes (MB) on the Intel Xeon 7000 processors. When the dataset to be stored is larger than the cache size, the data are stored in the main memory, which is accessed across a bus on the motherboard. Likewise, if the dataset to be stored is larger than the main memory, some of the data must be moved to the much slower to access hard drive. In early 2008, manufacturers commonly produced commercial computers with 2 to 4 gigabytes (GB) of main memory, with up to 8 GB available in advanced gaming machines.

Operating Systems and Maximum Main Memory Size

While the general rule "more is better" definitely applies to memory, one caution regarding memory size is required: the size of the *address space* that is supported by the operating system used puts a hard limit on the size of memory that can be used in the system. Operating systems today have either a 32 bit or 64 bit address space (and are called 32 bit or 64 bit operating systems). This means that there are 2^{32} (4.3×10^9) or 2^{64} (1.7×10^{19}) unique memory locations in the systems, respectively. While a 32 bit operating system can address a 4 GB memory, some of the addresses are reserved for memory on the graphics card as well as certain other hardware resources. Only 3 GB (+/−0.5 GB) of main memory are available for user programs. This limitation can be avoided by using a 64 bit operating system;[1] both Windows XP and Vista as well as Linux come in both 32 bit and 64 bit versions. The downside of 64 bit operating systems is that backward compatibility is limited because many applications written for 32 bit operating systems cannot run on a 64 bit operating system.

Mass Storage

Mass storage, most often magnetic disk drives, is currently the dominant provider of persistent information in computer systems. This dominance will soon

---

[1] 64 bit operating system can access 2^{64} memory addresses, or approximately 1.7×10^{10} gigabytes of information; this is anticipated to be sufficient for the foreseeable future.

be challenged by flash memory storage devices that have faster access times than magnetic disks. Mass storage is needed to hold programs and data that are loaded into main memory at run time to be used by one or more of the CPU, the GPU, and the physics processor. Datasets for VEs can be large and may contain such items as the geometry of animated models, interior environments, and exterior environments, such as terrain. Storage size and data access time are the primary metrics of mass storage systems.

GRAPHICS PROCESSING

Until the late 1990s graphics processing for interactive applications was accomplished using dedicated and often custom processing and display systems called *graphics accelerators.* These accelerators were almost exclusively implemented as a fixed-function rendering pipeline: transformation of the vertices that define the objects in the scene, determining which objects, or parts of objects, are visible from the current viewpoint, shading each pixel in the visible objects according to the lights in the scene, and writing the data to the display buffer. Early graphics cards for PCs, constrained by size in a time when the most powerful and flexible graphics accelerators were the size of a small refrigerator, had similar fixed pipelines. Acceleration for texture mapping was introduced to PCs on peripheral processor cards designed to accelerate rendering for PC based games. (See Whitton and Wendt, Appendix A, Volume 2, Section 1 Perspective for a brief introduction to texture mapping.) This advance that made visual scenes much richer and more realistic was the beginning of high quality, interactive graphics on PCs.

Graphics Processing Units

A new type of graphics accelerator began appearing in the early 1990s; its main feature is the GPU. Due to the high number of transistors that can be put on chips today, the single chip GPU is able to contain the many separate processors needed to efficiently implement the graphics rendering pipeline.

The GPU chip generally is mounted on a graphics card that is plugged into the motherboard and is interfaced to the CPU over a high speed bus that is often, for performance reasons, dedicated to this single purpose. Graphics cards contain the GPU chip, control units, and somewhere between 256 MB and 1 GB of memory. Graphics cards also include *video output* circuitry that converts the data of the rendered frames into signals in video graphics array or digital visual interface format to drive monitors, head-worn displays, and projectors. Most modern GPUs use so much power that they generate enough heat to require that they come with a dedicated fan.

Alternatively, a GPU chip can be mounted on the motherboard. In this configuration the GPU, rather than having dedicated memory, shares the main system memory with the CPU. Access to the main memory is slower than access to a dedicated memory, so the performance of GPUs mounted on the motherboard is lower than those on plug-in cards. In addition, GPUs for laptops typically are a generation (or two) behind desktop products, particularly with respect to the shader model they support (see the next section).

Programming the GPU

Succeeding generations of graphics chips and cards have had higher transistor counts, more processors, faster clock speeds, more memory, and higher graphics performance. The most significant change over the last 10 years has been the advent of user-programmable processing elements in the GPU. While the average training application programmer will never program the GPU, this capability gives rendering-software developers tremendous flexibility and, ultimately, control over the "look" of computer-generated scenes. The custom programs that execute on the programmable elements are called shaders, and almost all modern graphics hardware supports some level of shaders.

Shader Models

The different levels of shaders are designated with different shader model numbers; the higher the model number, the more portions of the graphics pipeline are user programmable and the more specialized rendering effects are possible. Table 8.1 shows the shader model supported by popular graphics cards and notes which processors are user programmable in that shader model. Figure 8.2 is a block diagram of a modern GPU. In the highest performance systems today the vertex shader, geometry shader, and pixel shader stages are all user programmable.

Early shader models had hard programming limitations, such as a maximum of 128 instructions and no floating point arithmetic. These restrictions are largely eliminated in more recent shader models, though GPUs are still not general purpose computing resources. Examples of operations that can be performed on the different shading processors follow:

- Vertex shader—Create model of terrain from a flat tessellated plane: As each vertex in the model is accessed, add to its height an offset corresponding to the height of the desired terrain at that point.

Table 8.1. Shader Models Supported by Graphics Cards

Graphics Card	Shader Model Supported
ATI Radeon HD 3870 X2	4.1
NVIDIA GeForce 8800	4.0
ATI Radeon X1900	3.0
NVIDIA GeForce 8800	3.0
ATI Radeon 9800 Pro	2.0
NVIDIA GeForce 8800	2.0
ATI Radeon 8500	1.1/1.4
NVIDIA GeForce 8800	1.1/1.3

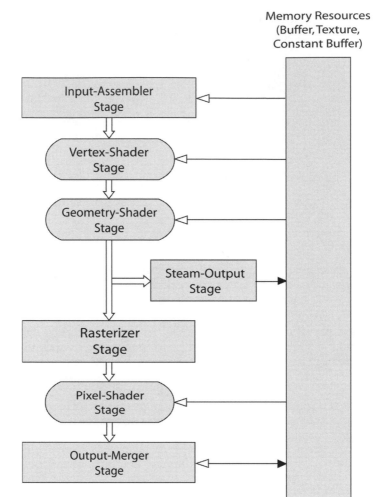

Figure 8.2.   Block Diagram of a Modern Graphics Processing Unit

- Geometry shader—*Amplify* datasets: As point primitives arrive at the geometry shader create a quad (quadrilateral primitive) centered on the original point. Similarly, to *deamplify,* collapse a quad into a point primitive located at the center of the quad.
- Pixel shader—Customize the appearance of any pixel on the screen: Program effects, such as night vision, depth-of-field, and motion, blur and apply them only to selected pixels.

As graphics processors evolve, shaders are becoming more deeply ingrained in real time rendering methodologies and the software that supports them. For instance, the DirectX 10 and OpenGL ES 2.0 application programming interfaces have completely abandoned the fixed function pipeline in favor of the program-mable one where vertex and pixel shaders are required for rendering. Shaders give rendering programmers the power to modify data as it moves through the graphics pipeline and to program any visual effect they can imagine. The inflex-ibility of the fixed function rendering pipeline is gone. Since programmable shad-ers are such a recent capability, developers are unlikely to have come close to fully exploring the possibilities enabled by them. Readers desiring a deeper understanding of shaders should see Engel (2003, 2004).

Workload Balance

In the days of the fixed pipeline, it was the responsibility of the hardware designers to ensure that the pipelined processing stages ran with approximately the same throughput rate so that overall performance was maximized—no stage sat idle waiting for the previous one to complete its computations; the processing load was balanced across the stages. While the GPU hardware is designed to be balanced when executing vendor-written software, user written programs can lead to inefficiencies if the load is not balanced across the shader stages.

A simple observation makes clear the need to pay attention to what processing is done in each stage: the vertex shader runs once per frame for every vertex of every object in the scene, perhaps 300,000 vertices. The pixel shader runs once for every pixel in every frame, 1,310,720 times for a 1,280 × 1,024 frame—about 1 million more times for each frame than does the vertex shader! As a general rule, only operations that *must* be executed in the pixel shader should be per-formed there. Any operation that can be reasonably moved upstream into the ver-tex shader (and subsequently have its output values interpolated to be inputs to the pixel shader) will provide significant performance savings.

Knowing how to best distribute application workload can be determined through the use of performance profiling. At the most coarse-grained level, time is divided between what is spent on the CPU with that spent on the GPU. A thorough discussion of performance profiling strategies is beyond the scope of this chapter, but suffice it to say that this is a crucial part of understanding how to optimize graphics performance. There are many tools available to aid in this process, such as Intel's Vtune, AMD's CodeAnalyst, GPU Perfstudio, and NVI-DIA's PerfKit.

General Purpose Computing on GPUs

Because the mathematical operations needed for graphics are similar to the operations needed for many types of scientific computing, it was natural that pro-grammers began using the programmable shading stages for nongraphics com-puting. This is so prevalent that is it called general-purpose GPU (GPGPU) computing. Fluid simulations, computer vision, and rigid body physics are exam-ples of nongraphics algorithms that can be accelerated by programming them on the GPU.

As GPGPU programming has become more commonplace, programming tools to help the coder write his or her code (as opposed to analyze it, as the tools in the preceding paragraph do) have become more common. Already, the largest makers of GPUs, NVIDIA and AMD, have created interfaces to help the programmers do this. NVIDIA's CUDA (Compute Unified Device Architecture) and AMD's CAL are designed to "abstract computation as large batch operations that involve many invocations of a kernel function operating in parallel" (Fatahalian & Houston, 2008). For more information about how one of these interfaces, CUDA, does this, see Nickolls, Buck, Garland, and Skadron (2008).

Practical Considerations

Choosing a Graphics Accelerator

A general rule-of-thumb with graphics processors is to always buy the fastest, most capable card available for development work. The cost differential is likely to be small and by the time the finished system is deployed, what was earlier top-of-the-line functionality will be available at an affordable price. Designers must, however, be cautious when the development is to be done on a desktop machine and the deployment vehicle is to be a laptop. That situation requires careful analysis of current and expected future performance of laptop graphics before the development platform is chosen.

Not all PCs are built with a large enough power supply to support the highest-performance graphics cards. Users configuring their own systems should look carefully at the power requirements of the overall system. Adequate power should not be an issue for users purchasing a preconfigured system from a reputable dealer.

Matching Shader Models across VE System Components

The game engines (see McDowell, Volume 2, Section 1, Chapter 10) that are the core software of many simulations and scenario based training systems are typically written to support a particular shader model. Mismatches between the shader models supported by the software and hardware always result in unused potential in either the hardware or software and images that include only the effects available in the lower model number. Buying a card that supports a higher level model will get you all of the features available from the game engine's current software release and enable you to enjoy the new features when the software is later updated to support the higher level model.

When More Than One Graphics Card Is Necessary

In some cases one graphics card is not enough, for instance, when the dataset is so large that the time to render a new frame is unacceptably long or when the application requires more than two video outputs. In the first case the output frame can be subdivided and each section assigned to a separate graphics card and then the partial images recombined for display. In the second case, for instance, a *display wall* consisting of an array of projectors, a separate card may be needed for every projector. The outputs of the multiple cards must be synchronized so that updates to the final image from each card all occur at the same time. Without synchronization, the overall composite image (created from the several sources) may appear unstable. As of this writing, NVIDIA and ATI offer SLI and CrossFire products, respectively, for splitting rendering across multiple graphics cards. Cards that offer *frame lock* or *gen lock* capability can be synchronized for multiprojector applications. These features are often available on cards designed for professional video applications.

Additionally, programmers are beginning to explore the possibilities multiple graphics cards provide for computations other than graphics. For example, the architecture of programmable graphics cards lends itself to any sort of computation where a great deal of parallelism is desired, such as physics, AI, or others. In these systems, one graphics card is used for normal graphics processing, while another is used for whatever other calculations the application programmers decide to send. This trend is likely to continue, since NVIDIA recently purchased Ageia, a maker of physics cards, and many industry insiders believe this is part of NVIDIA's efforts to expand the uses of its cards outside graphics.

NETWORKING

Networking has emerged as a cornerstone of virtual environments today. Although new single-user games are still being written, increasingly game worlds are becoming virtual places where multiple users interact. In the commercial arena, this has led to such massively multiplayer online games (MMOGs) as *World of Warcraft* and *EverQuest* and such online environments as *Second Life.* People often find the sense of kinship and camaraderie they experience while playing multiplayer games on the Internet more important than the gameplay itself. In fact, the popularity of *Second Life* makes that point clearly, since it is not a game; it does not have points or scores; it does not have winners or losers. Similarly, even though simulators for single-user training are developed, the focus is moving to training teams. Networked simulations allow teams to train together in the same virtual world and permit trainers or subject matter experts to participate as opposing forces in ways that computer-controlled characters cannot.

The networking requirements for games and simulations vary little. Application requirements drive the choice of networking technology. In a large virtual world such as *Second Life,* it is most important to support large numbers of simultaneous users in the same online environment, and it is acceptable to have longer latency—longer between updates reflecting the movement and actions of others in the scene. However, in training simulations, very low latency is required since it is unacceptable for a player to, for instance, fire at an enemy who is visible on the screen in one place, but whose actual location is somewhere else. This chapter will cover the advantages of limitations of three networking standards in common use: the distributed interactive simulation (DIS) architecture and the high level architecture (HLA), both created by the U.S. military, and the client/server paradigm commonly used in the game industry (as well as many other commercial applications).

The DIS architecture was originally created by Bolt, Beranek, and Newman in the late 1980s for the U.S. Army's *simulated network* (SIMNET) program. The idea was to allow hundreds of entities to take part in the same simulated exercise communicating via the relatively limited bandwidth that was available at the time. In the early 1990s, several other groups began using the DIS networking protocol in SIMNET as the networking component of their own simulations, and it became obvious that this protocol should be formalized. DIS was officially made IEEE (Institute of Electrical and Electronics Engineers) standard 1278 in 1993, and the IEEE has authorized several modifications to it over the years.

DIS works by sending protocol data units (PDUs) over the network using either the transmission control protocol or user datagram protocol network transport protocol. There are PDUs to represent each kind of data that must be shared in order for all participants to have enough understanding of the state of the entire simulation to be able to fully participate in it. For example, one of the most common PDUs is the *entity state* PDU, which passes the state (location, velocity, amount of damage, fuel, and so forth) of an entity to the other entities in the simulation. As the entity changes its state (for example, changes velocity), it sends out an entity state PDU to notify others in the simulation of its new state.

One of the most important parts of the DIS architecture is the fact that each entity keeps track of only its own location and uses *dead reckoning* to update the location of the other entities in the world for each frame between receipt actual location data in entity state PDUs. Dead reckoning is a method of estimating an entity's new position by predicting location over time by extrapolating from the last known position and velocity. A consequence of dead reckoning is that an entity's position can appear to jump when the position determined by dead reckoning is different from and is replaced by the real position when the next state PDU is received.

Another networking protocol created by the U.S. military is the *high level architecture*. HLA emerged in the mid-1990s as a standard intended to allow interoperability between the military's many dissimilar simulations. The military simulators were built by different contractors for different services, which had different needs. It is not surprising that the simulators could not communicate with each other. HLA was designed to correct this problem.

HLA has a vernacular with which training system designers should have at least a passing acquaintance. To be an *HLA compliant simulation* (referred to as a *federate*), the simulation must use a specified interface to pass information to a *run-time interface* (RTI). An RTI is not designed to be part of the simulation, but rather is software that plugs into the simulation and uses a common template to pass information from one simulation to the others. Multiple simulations connected via RTIs using a common template are called a *federation*. For each federation, there must be a *federation object model* that contains all the data objects, interactions, and attributes that will be passed among simulations.

RTIs are not part of the simulation, but rather they are additional software. Several vendors sell RTIs. Ideally, any RTI should be able to serve as the connector for a particular simulation and accurately communicate with an RTI of a different vendor acting for a different simulation. In reality it is not that easy: some vendors have augmented their RTIs to perform other tasks and to pass information other than that required by the HLA specification. This can cause interoperability problems.

There is debate about which protocol, DIS or HLA, is better. Most U.S. simulations are required by a Department of Defense directive to use HLA for communication. However, many other nations' militaries, not required to use HLA, choose to use DIS for their simulations. In reality, each has advantages and disadvantages, and the developer needs to perform due diligence in choosing a protocol for a large-scale simulation.

The other method of networking is the one that most multiplayer computer games use, a client-server architecture. The server, generally a very powerful computer with an extremely high speed network connection, holds the game "truth." The players' computers are referred to as the *clients,* and they connect to the *server,* which passes them information on the global state of the game. As a player performs actions (for example, move, shoot, or crouch), the client sends messages to the server, and the server in turn sends messages to the other players' clients to update them on the first player's actions.

How these messages are sent has quite a bit of effect upon the numbers of players that can interact in the same world. For example, in MMOGs, where there can be several thousand people on the same server at one time, quite often messages about player A's actions are sent only to those players near player A. This is an acceptable solution since those players a great distance from player A in the virtual world (and cannot see him or her) do not need to know about his or her actions. However, if too many players congregate in a small area of the virtual world, it can seriously degrade network performance and, hence, the rate at which state updates are received by each player.

CONCLUSION

Because PCs have surpassed vendor-produced custom solutions for simulations, virtual environments, and games, trainers who want to use any of these technologies need to be versant in the PC technology that will play such a major part of their training applications. The biggest change in the last 15 years has been the advent of the GPU, especially the opening of the pipeline to application programmers, and the parallelization of processors in both CPUs and GPUs. What the final product of these two changes will be is not yet known. As Kurt Akeley, member of the founding Silicon Graphics team who did pioneering work on OpenGL and is now at Microsoft Research, asks,

> What we're talking about isn't just whether we can use graphics processors to do general-purpose computing, but in the bigger sense, how will general-purpose computing be done? How will graphics processing and other technologies that have

evolved influence the way computing is done in general? That's a big issue that the world's going to be working on for the next five to ten years.

(Duff, 2008)

REFERENCES

Boyd, C. (2008). Data-parallel computing. *ACM Queue, 6*(2), 30–39.

Duff, T. (2008). A conversation with Kurt Akeley and Pat Hanrahan. *ACM Queue, 6*(2), 11–17.

Engel, W. F. (2003). *ShaderX2—shader programming tips and tricks with DirectX9.0.* Plano, TX: Wordware Publishing, Inc.

Engel, W. F. (2004). *Programming vertex and pixel shaders.* Boston: Charles River Media.

Fatahalian, K., & Houston, M. (2008). GPUs: A closer look. *ACM Queue, 6*(2), http://doi.acm.org/10.1145/1365490.1365498

Mistry, K., Allen, C., Auth, C., Beattie, B., Bergstrom, D., Bost, M, et al. (2007). A 45nm logic technology with high-k+metal gate transistors, strained silicon, 9 Cu interconnect layers, 193nm dry patterning, and 100% Pb-free packaging. *IEEE International Electron Devices Meeting—IEDM 2007* (pp. 247–250).

Nickolls, J., Buck, I., Garland, M., & Skadron, K. (2008). Scalable parallel programming with CUDA. *ACM Queue, 6*(2), 40–53.

Tay, E. (2008). The death of the silicon computer chip. *IT news* [Electronic version]. Retrieved April 23, 2008, from http://www.itnews.com.au/News/72838,the-death-of-the-silicon-computer-chip.aspx

Chapter 9

BEHAVIOR GENERATION IN SEMI-AUTOMATED FORCES

Mikel Petty

Virtual environment training simulations often include simulated entities (such as tanks, aircraft, or individual humans) that are generated and controlled by computer software systems rather than individual humans for each entity. Those systems, which are known as semi-automated forces (SAF) because the software is monitored and controlled by a human operator, play an important role in virtual environment simulations. The purposes of SAF systems, the main behavior generation approaches used in them, examples of important semi-automated forces systems and their applications, and open SAF research problems are described in this chapter.

After beginning with a motivating scenario to suggest their importance, this introductory section places SAF systems in the context of virtual environment simulations and describes some specific purposes and applications for SAF systems.

AN INFORMAL MOTIVATION

Consider the following scene. Four U.S. Army soldiers sit at the controls of a training simulator. The simulator, which is about the size of a garden shed, appears from the outside to be a connected set of computers, monitors, and large green fiberglass enclosures. From the inside, the simulator is a simplified but believably realistic recreation of the interior of an M1A1 Abrams, the U.S. Army's main battle tank. The four soldiers are the M1A1's crew. They manipulate the simulator's controls as they would in an actual tank, driving their tank through a simulated battlefield that they can see through the view ports of their tank. Computer generated images for each of the view ports show the battlefield as it would be seen from that point.

A second crew is at the controls of another M1A1 simulator. In the real world that simulator may be adjacent to the first, or it may be hundreds of miles away, but the two are connected by a computer network. In the simulated battlefield the second tank is following the first, about 30 meters behind.

As the two M1A1s move slowly forward, the commander of the lead M1A1 warily surveys the terrain from his vantage point in the cupola atop the turret, searching for the enemy vehicles that are likely to be nearby. As his tank crests a ridge, he spots a column of enemy tanks emerging from behind a tree line some 2,000 meters away. The enemy tanks are generated in the battlefield by another simulator node, attached to the M1A1 simulator via the network. However, they are not controlled by human crews; rather, computer software is generating their behavior, as well as that of many other vehicles in the simulated battlefield.

The commander of the lead tank radios the commander of the second M1A1, who cannot yet see the enemy tanks, and warns him of the threat. Then, over the simulator's intercom, he orders the driver to turn the M1A1 to face its frontal armor toward the enemy tanks and to stop so as to provide the gunner an easier firing problem. The commander's feeling of urgency is easily heard in his voice as he tells the gunner where the enemy tanks are, which one to engage first, and what ammunition to use. As quickly as his skills allow, the gunner rotates the M1A1's turret and elevates the main gun to align the aiming reticule with the first target. In quick succession he thumbs the laser range-finder button and squeezes the main gun trigger; the M1A1 simulator's sound system produces the sound of the main gun firing and the first enemy tank bursts into flames.

While the gunner executes his shot, the second M1A1 comes over the ridge and the commander of the lead M1A1 orders the second crew to engage the second enemy tank. The commander observes that the rest of the enemy tanks have responded to the incoming fire by reversing direction and taking cover behind the tree line. After the second M1A1 destroys another enemy tank, there are no targets visible. Several seconds pass while the commander assesses the situation. His apprehension growing, he orders both M1A1s to move back behind the ridge crest. But the decision comes a moment too late.

Before either M1A1 can complete the maneuver, enemy tanks have emerged from behind both ends of the tree line. One of the enemy tanks sights the lead M1A1, turns toward it, and quickly stops. Its turret swings around and the enemy tank fires. The sound system of the M1A1 simulator produces an unpleasantly loud crashing sound, and the screens of the simulator go black; the lead M1A1 has been destroyed by the enemy tank. Because this is simulation, the commander of the lead tank is not dead, but he is nonetheless dismayed and pounds his controls in frustration.

The scene just described has two crucial elements. First, the simulation succeeds in creating an environment with enough intensity and urgency to draw the soldiers into the simulated world. Second, it includes autonomous entities that oppose the simulation users, attempting to thwart and destroy them. To a large extent, both the simulation's intensity and its usefulness as a training system depend on the sophistication and realism of the behavior of the autonomous entities. How that behavior is generated is the subject of this chapter.

Distributed Simulation

Virtual environments, especially those that include SAF systems of the type discussed here, are typically constructed using a simulation technology known as *distributed simulation*. (SAF systems may also be used in other nondistributed systems.) In a distributed simulation, large simulation systems are assembled from a set of independent simulation nodes communicating via a network. Crewed simulators of the type described earlier and SAF systems may be nodes linked in a distributed simulation. Distributed simulation adds implementation complexity to the nodes, but it has benefits, including *scalability* (larger scenarios can be accommodated by adding more nodes to the network), *specialization* (simulation nodes optimized for a specific purpose can be combined to produce a complete simulation), and *geographic distribution* (the nodes need not all be at the same location).

In a distributed simulation the networked nodes report the attributes (for example, location) and actions (for example, firing a weapon) of interest regarding their simulated entities by exchanging network messages. A network protocol defines the format of the messages, the conditions under which specific messages should be sent, and the proper processing for a received message. Several standard distributed simulation network protocols exist, including distributed interactive simulation (Institute for Electrical and Electronics Engineers, 1995), high level architecture (Dahmann, Kuhl, & Weatherly, 1998), and Test and Training Enabling Architecture (TENA) (U.S. Department of Defense, 2002).

SAF Purpose and Advantages in Training

In a military training application, the virtual environment system is intended to provide a simulated battlefield in which training scenarios are executed. In such a battlefield, the trainees need an opposing force against which to train. One method of providing opponents is to have two groups of trainees in simulators fight each other. This method is sometimes used, and the trainees may enjoy the competitive aspects of the arrangement, but it increases the number of simulators needed at a training site and requires that to train any given military unit a second unit be available to provide the opposition. It also can mean that the trainees are faced with opponents who employ the same tactical doctrine as they do, which is not likely to be the case in combat.

A second method is to use human instructors who are trained to behave according to the desired enemy doctrine. This method does not reduce the need for simulators and is manpower intensive. Nevertheless, it is sometimes used, especially in live simulation (such as the dedicated opposing force at the U.S. Army's National Training Center located at Fort Irwin, California).

The third method is to use a simulation node that generates and controls multiple simulation entities using software, possibly supported by a human operator. Such nodes are known as semi-automated forces or computer generated force (CGF) systems. SAF systems can lower the cost of a virtual environment training system by reducing the number of crewed simulators and the number of humans required to operate the system for a given scenario size and by generating large numbers of computer-controlled entities. A SAF system can be programmed to behave according to the tactical doctrine of any desired opposing force and so eliminate the need to train and retrain human operators to use tactics appropriate to different enemies. In addition to providing opponents, SAF systems can also generate friendly forces, allowing a group of trainees to practice cooperation with a larger friendly force. Because a SAF system can be easier to control by a single person than an opposing force made up of many human operators, it may give the training instructor greater control over the training experience.

SAF SYSTEM CHARACTERISTICS

This section first outlines some of the common characteristics of SAF systems. It then focuses on methods for generating and validating SAF behavior.

Components and Capabilities

Certain characteristics are common to all existing SAF systems and are essentially inherent in the context in which those systems are used. Several important ones are discussed in the following:

Network connection and protocol. When SAF systems are part of a distributed simulation, they need a network connection and interface software to send and receive network messages in compliance with the network protocol standard.

Battlefield phenomenology models. The SAF-controlled entities exist in a battlefield that is a simulated subset of the real world, so the physical events and phenomena on the battlefield must be modeled within the SAF system. For example, if a SAF-controlled vehicle is moving, its acceleration, deceleration, turn rates, and maneuverability on different terrain types must be modeled. Combat interactions need to be modeled in accordance with the physics of weapon and armor performance characteristics.

Support for multiple entities. SAF systems are typically able to simulate multiple entities simultaneously. The SAF system's software architecture must provide a means to allocate processing time so that all of its controlled entities have their actions and behavior generated frequently enough to keep pace with the overall simulation.

Autonomous behavior generation. SAF systems use behavior generation algorithms to react autonomously to the simulation situation or to carry out orders given by an operator. This characteristic of SAF systems is the primary topic of this chapter and will be discussed in more detail later.

Operator interface. In addition to the autonomous behavior, most SAF systems provide an operator interface that allows a human operator to control the SAF entities. Figure 9.1 shows an example of a typical SAF system operator interface, from the One Semi-Automated Forces (OneSAF) system (to be discussed later). The operator may provide high level plans that are executed in detail by the SAF system, initiate and control behavior in situations that are beyond the SAF system's capabilities, or override autonomously generated behavior. SAF system interfaces typically provide a map display of the battlefield that shows the

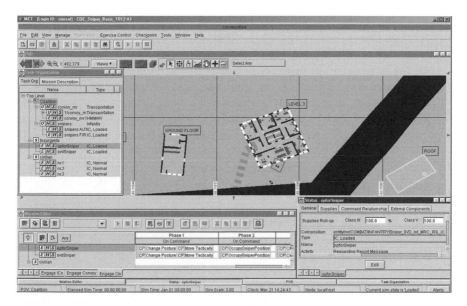

Figure 9.1.   Example SAF Operator Interface (OneSAF)

battlefield terrain and the simulated entities on it, together with a human command interface.

Behavior Generation

The actions of SAF-controlled entities within the virtual environment have two aspects, physics and behavior. The physics aspect was mentioned earlier. The movements and interactions of SAF-controlled entities are under the control of the physical models in the SAF system, which produce a level of physical realism appropriate to SAF applications.

The second aspect is behavior. Here the question is not how the SAF-controlled entities execute their actions, but what actions they execute. SAF entities are often representing either humans or vehicles with human crews and, as such, must act in ways that not only comply with the laws of physics, but make sense in terms of human behavior and tactical doctrine. Generating realistic behavior has been challenging due to the relative complexity of human behavior and the long-standing difficulty of encoding it in an algorithmic form suitable for computer execution. Generating behavior by simply having humans fully control the SAF entities via an operator interface is not satisfactory, as the goal of the SAF system is to make the behavior generation as autonomous as possible. Autonomous behavior generation for SAF entities requires that the patterns and rules of behavior be encoded in the algorithms of the SAF system.

The types of algorithms used in SAF systems for behavior generation can, broadly speaking, be grouped into two categories, here termed *cognitive modeling* and *behavior emulation*. Cognitive modeling approaches to behavior generation in SAF systems begin with the assumption that generating realistic human behavior is best done by modeling human cognition, or at least those portions of it pertinent to the behavior. Cognitive modelers assert that, to varying degrees, the computation that occurs within their systems is, in fact, modeling human cognition. Several broad cognitive modeling frameworks and architectures, each based on a particular theoretical model of cognition and intended to support a wide range of human behavior generation, have been developed and have seen use in multiple applications. Noteworthy general cognitive modeling examples include ACT-R (adaptive control of thought–rational) (Anderson & Lebiere, 1998), EPIC (executive process/interactive control) (Meyer & Kieras, 1997), SOAR (Laird, Newell, & Rosenbloom, 1987), and COGNET (cognition as a network of tasks) (Zachary, Ryder, Weiland, & Ross, 1992). More specialized aspects of SAF behavior have also been implemented using cognitive models, such as tactical air combat (Nielsen, Smoot, Martinez, & Dennison, 2001) and commander decision making (Sokolowski, 2003).

As with cognitive modeling, behavior emulation approaches to SAF behavior generation are also intended to produce realistic human behavior. However, in contrast to cognitive modeling, in behavior emulation there is no claim or intent that the algorithms used to produce behavior model human cognition. The goal of behavior emulation is solely to generate usefully realistic behavior for the SAF entities, without regard to whether the algorithmic processes used to generate the behavior correspond in any way to human cognitive processes.

Although considerable progress has been made in cognitive modeling, behavior emulation is currently more common than cognitive modeling in production SAF systems. Reasons for this include the reuse of legacy behavior emulation approaches to reduce development costs and the comparatively high computational expense of some cognitive modeling methods in real time SAF systems. Because of its prevalence in SAF systems, behavior emulation will be the focus here.

The most widely used approach to behavior generation in production SAF systems has been *finite state machines* (FSMs). The FSM approach falls into the behavior emulation category, as FSMs do not appear to be and are not claimed to be models of human cognition. (The FSM approach makes use of ideas from formal automata theory, but behavior generation FSMs do not have all of the mathematical properties of theoretical finite state automata.)

Over the last two decades variations of FSMs have been used to generate human behavior in a number of SAF and non-SAF systems (Maruichi, Uchiki, & Tokoro, 1987; Petty, Moshell, & Hughes, 1988; Smith & Petty, 1992; Calder, Smith, Courtemanche, Mar, & Ceranowicz, 1993; Aronson, 1994; Ahmad, Cremer, Kearney, Willemsen, & Hansen, 1994; Moore, Gieb, & Reich, 1995; Ourston, Blanchard, Chandler, Loh, & Marshall, 1995). The repeated use of FSMs suggests their intuitive appeal and effectiveness.

The common idea among FSM implementations is that a simulation entity's behavior is decomposed into a finite set of behavior patterns, or states, with identifiable and discrete conditions for transitioning between the states. An entity's controlling FSM is always assumed to be in one of its states. Associated with each state is an implementation of that state's behavior pattern in the underlying programming language, for example, a C function or a Java method. While the FSM is in a state, the entity's behavior is generated by executing that state's associated implementation; thus the current state of the FSM determines what behavior is being generated for the entity. Conditions that depend on events or attributes in the simulation are associated with transitions from one state to another in the FSM. When a transition condition is true, the FSM changes state, thereby changing the entity's behavior. In addition to complex predicates, the transition conditions may also be null, allowing a transition to occur as soon as the first state has executed, or simple time delays, to produce realistically timed changes in behavior.

Figure 9.2 is an example FSM taken from an early research SAF system (Smith & Petty, 1992), which is examined here to illustrate the technique. It controls the behavior of an infantry fireteam in the process of using an antitank guided missile. When the fireteam is given permission to fire such missiles (perhaps via the operator interface or by some other FSM), the FSM is started. The FSM's start state, di_open_file_atgm, automatically transitions after .25 seconds to the di_await_atgm_target state, where target acquisition and selection are performed. That state repeats every second until a suitable target is found. When this occurs, di_await_atgm_target first it starts another FSM, **face_target,** which causes the

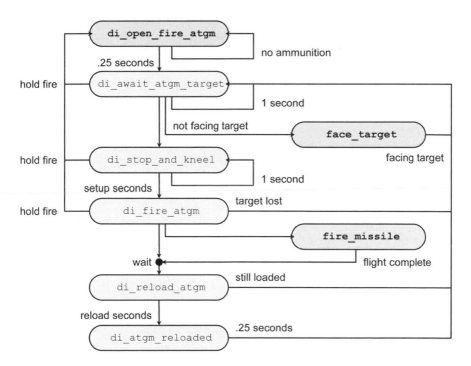

Figure 9.2.   Example SAF Finite State Machine

fireteam to face the intended target. It then transitions to the di_stop_and_kneel state, which brings the fireteam to a halt (it may have been moving while watching for a target) and then transitions to the next state, di_fire_atgm, after a delay corresponding to the missile setup time. Assuming the target is still visible, that state launches a missile by starting another FSM, **fire_missile,** which generates the missile launch flash, controls the missile in flight, and handles the missile's impact at the end of the flight. The di_fire_atgm state waits for the **fire_missile** FSM to report that the missile flight is finished, whereupon the di_reload_atgm state is started. That state reloads the fireteam's antitank missile (if sufficient munitions are available), and after a realistic time delay transitions to the di_a-wait_atgm_target state for another cycle.

The behavior described as being performed by a state is generated by the programming language code associated with the state. The FSM mechanism serves to partition a complex multistep behavior into simpler parts, to associate programming language code with each part, and to control the execution of that code and thus generate the behavior.

Behavior Realism Requirements

For the benefits of a SAF system to be realized, the SAF entities must behave in a usefully realistic manner. In general, interacting with a SAF will produce positive training only if the behavior generated for the SAF entities is physically realistic, behaviorally realistic, and doctrinally consistent. The training benefit of the virtual environment is reduced or lost if its physical realism does not adequately conform to trainees' experiences in the real world. Vehicles should operate according to their performance characteristics, and terrain must be considered when determining whether two entities have a line of sight to each other. Current SAF systems are generally sufficiently physically realistic.

Behavioral realism is more difficult. SAF-controlled entities must react to a given situation in a manner similar to the (real) entities that are being simulated. Because the simulated entities are often controlled by humans, the SAF behavior must appear to be similar to, and thus as intelligent as, human behavior in each situation. Fortunately for SAF developers, the context of their use often makes the SAF system's intelligent behavior requirement less difficult than the general artificial intelligence problem. For example, in a training simulation emphasizing vehicle combat, the repertoire of behaviors of a tank crew is much smaller than that of general human behavior, so intelligent behavior by a SAF-controlled tank is easier to generate than general intelligent behavior. Even so, generating intelligent behavior is still challenging, especially in a real time simulation that precludes the use of powerful but slow-executing artificial intelligence techniques.

SAF behavior must be doctrinally consistent in the sense that the actions of the SAF-controlled entities should be consistent with doctrine of the entities the SAF is simulating. For example, SAF entities purportedly part of the armed forces of a particular nation should maneuver and perform according to that nation's tactical doctrine. This goes beyond simple believability; a goal of military training systems is to allow trainees to practice against opponents that use the tactics of the expected adversary. With the increasing prevalence of irregular and asymmetric opponents with no fixed tactical doctrine, the meaning of doctrinal consistency is more difficult to define, but it remains important to present trainees with SAF opponents that exhibit behavior like that they will encounter in actual operations.

Behavior Validation

Simulation *validation* is the process of determining whether or not the results produced by a model are consistent with the actual phenomenon or process being simulated (Balci, 1998). Validation of SAF systems must include validation of the behavior generated for the SAF-controlled entities. Validating a model of human behavior is inherently problematic, as human behavior is complex and subtle, variable in almost all situations, and generally understandable only in the context of a time sequence of actions. Nevertheless, efforts have been made to develop methods to validate SAF behavior (Petty, 1995).

Models of specific aspects of SAF behavior sometimes prove amenable to quantitative or statistical validation methods; examples include operational decision making (Sokolowski, 2003) and reconnaissance route planning (Van Brackle, Petty, Gouge, & Hull, 1993). However, validating the full repertoire of SAF behavior often depends on observation of the generated behavior by subject matter experts who make qualitative assessments of the behavior based on their experience and expertise, a process termed *face validation.* Face validation can be unstructured, with experts simply observing the SAF behavior in a typical scenario, or highly structured, with multiple preplanned scenario vignettes designed to stimulate the SAF system in specific ways and elicit expected behaviors in response.

A special form of face validation applied to SAF behavior validation is the Turing test. First proposed as a test of intelligence for computer systems (Turing, 1950), for SAF validation the Turing test is often formulated this way: *Can observers of entities in a simulated battlefield reliably determine whether any given entity is controlled by humans or by a SAF system?* The Turing test, in both its original and SAF forms, is purely operational in that it deliberately ignores the question of how the SAF behavior is generated; it is interested only in the quality of the generated behavior. Many SAF developers believe that the Turing test is a useful SAF validation method (Wise, Miller, & Ceranowicz, 1991; Petty, 1994). Others argue that the Turing test cannot be relied upon as the sole means of evaluating a human behavior generation model, giving examples that demonstrate that, while it can be useful, it is neither necessary nor sufficient to ensure the validity of SAF behavior on its own (Petty, 1994).

EXAMPLE SAF SYSTEMS

This section describes two existing SAF systems, chosen because of their wide usage, their importance in military training applications, and the extensive effort and resources devoted to their development. There are many other SAF systems of various types in addition to these.

ModSAF

At one time ModSAF (Modular Semi-Automated Forces) was arguably the most important SAF system. During its period of use it was widely distributed, supported a diverse range of production and research applications, and was extensively modified and enhanced (Ceranowicz, 1994). ModSAF was the intellectual descendant of earlier SAF systems, and many ideas developed for ModSAF persist in newer SAF systems (including OneSAF, to be discussed later).

ModSAF could generate many different entity types, including fixed and rotary wing aircraft, tanks, infantry fighting vehicles, other vehicles, and groups of dismounted infantry, as well as platoon-, company-, and battalion-sized units. ModSAF included an operator interface component allowing a human operator to direct the entities, and a simulation component that simulated the individual entities, military units, and environmental processes. The latter performed both physical simulation (for example, vehicle dynamics and weapons effects) and behavioral simulation (for example, route planning and mission execution). ModSAF was a real time, time-stepped simulation with a variable update rate that depended on the computational load (Ceranowicz, 1994).

ModSAF was designed to have a modular software architecture. ModSAF modules were intended to constitute a repository of useful capabilities that could be used in different ways in different SAF systems and could be easily replaced by developers of new ways to provide SAF functionality. ModSAF included a variety of entity simulation modules in several categories (dynamics models, turret models, weapons models, sensor models, and damage models), which could be combined for a new entity via parameter file specifications. If a new entity type could not be assembled from the existing modules, new ones could be developed.

ModSAF relied on a human operator for two functions: to set up preplanned missions for ModSAF entities and units and to provide supervisory control of the behavior of the simulated entities during simulation runs. The operator performed those functions using a map of the virtual battlefield that showed the terrain and the entities (similar to Figure 9.1) and allowed the operator to create movement routes, military control measures, and battle positions. The operator could create preplanned missions for ModSAF entities that were divided into a number of phases; for each phase the operator defined the tasks a unit was to perform and the criteria for a transition to the next phase. The operator could also give commands for immediate execution by entities and units. Such intervention might have been necessary when ModSAF's automated behavior was not handling a situation correctly or when a scenario called for a specific event that must be arranged by the operator (Ceranowicz, Coffin, Smith, Gonzalez, & Ladd, 1994).

The basic building block of the ModSAF behavior generation mechanism was the *task,* which was a single nondecomposable behavior performed by an entity or unit (Calder et al., 1993). Tasks were implemented within ModSAF as finite state machines. A ModSAF FSM represented a task as a set of states that each encoded a component action of the task, a set of transition conditions that determined and caused transitions between the states, and a set of inputs and outputs for the task. Fairly complex behaviors were implemented as ModSAF FSMs; some interesting examples included near-term movement control (Smith, 1994) and finding cover and concealment (Longtin, 1994).

OneSAF

OneSAF is the U.S. Army's newest constructive battlefield simulation and SAF system. (Here the term "OneSAF" is used for brevity; it refers to the One-SAF Objective System.) It is the result of an extensive development effort, including extended preparatory experimentation with models and implementation techniques using an enhanced version of ModSAF known as the OneSAF Testbed. OneSAF is intended to replace a number of legacy entity based simulations, to serve a range of applications including analysis of alternatives, doctrine development, system design, logistics analysis, team and individual training, and mission rehearsal, and to be interoperable in live, virtual, and constructive simulation environments (Parsons, 2007). OneSAF's capabilities incorporate the best features of previous SAF systems (Henderson & Rodriquez, 2002) and include such advanced features as aspects of the contemporary operating environments (Parsons, Surdu, & Jordan, 2005), multiresolution terrain databases with high resolution buildings, and command and control systems interoperability (Parsons, 2007). OneSAF has been developed using modern software engineering practices and has a product line architecture that allows the software components of One-SAF to be reusable in different configurations for different applications (Courtemanche & Wittman, 2002).

The behavior generation mechanism in OneSAF combines tested concepts that have appeared multiple times in various forms in SAF research (primitive and composite behaviors) with the latest modeling approaches (agent based modeling) (Henderson & Rodriquez, 2002). As with ModSAF, behavior generation in OneSAF is behavior emulation, rather than cognitive modeling. The basic level of behavior representation in OneSAF is *primitive behaviors,* which are units of "doctrinal functionality" (Parsons, 2007), such as behaviors executable by One-SAF actors (in OneSAF *actor* is a generic term for entity or unit). Primitive behaviors typically consider perceptions about the simulated world and invoke actions in that world (Henderson & Rodriquez, 2002). They are denoted as primitive because they are implemented directly as programming language code and not further decomposed into sub-behaviors. They are not necessarily primitive in terms of behavioral complexity; they may be relatively simple (for example, UseWeapon) or relatively complex (for example, RequestAndCoordinateFireSupport). The OneSAF primitive behaviors constitute a repertoire of behaviors available for execution by OneSAF entities and units and for assembly into composite behaviors (defined later; Tran, Karr, & Knospe, 2004).

Composite behaviors are behaviors formed by combining other behaviors and may comprise both primitive behaviors and other composite behaviors. Composite behaviors can be assembled hierarchically, with lower level behaviors composed into higher level behaviors, and those behaviors in turn composed into still higher level behaviors. The behavior levels may correspond to military echelon levels (platoon, company, and battalion). OneSAF includes a behavior composition tool that provides a graphical editing environment in which behaviors can be composed. Using this tool, primitive behaviors and composite behaviors can be assembled into sequential and parallel execution threads controlled by branches and loops that may test predicates (conditions) in the state of the executing actor or the simulation (Tran, Karr, & Knospe, 2004). To provide familiarity, the behavior composition tool's graphical notation has both a visual appearance and a semantic content similar to the flowcharting notation widely used in program design since the 1960s (Henderson & Rodriquez, 2002). When a composite behavior is executed, the behaviors that make up the composite behavior are executed in the order defined by the connections and logic in the composite behavior's flowchart.

RESEARCH DIRECTIONS

An early examination of the state of the art of SAF systems identified 10 areas in which further research was needed (Fishwick, Petty, & Mullally, 1991). Four of those areas have been resolved, at least to the extent that they are no longer issues in SAF development. Two others have proven to be not as important in SAF systems as formerly thought. Four remain open; they are the following:

Behavior representation language. A long-standing goal has been a language (textual or graphical) in which SAF behaviors could be expressed in a form usable by subject matter experts, as opposed to software developers. Although there have been several initiatives in this direction, there is a fundamental difficulty: any language powerful enough to express the full range of desired behaviors seems to become as complex as a programming language, thus making it inaccessible to nonprogrammers. The OneSAF behavior composition process and tools are attempting to address this.

Automated planning. Planning for SAF entities still depends, ultimately, on the SAF operator. Here planning means organizing the high level activities of the overall SAF force, such as an operation plan for a brigade, not controlling the low level actions of individual SAF entities. SAF systems are currently much better at the latter than the former. SAF researchers and developers continue to strive for greater autonomy of SAF entities through automated planning.

Autonomous agent modeling. Autonomous agents in general interact with the environment and behave under the control of internal plans and algorithms; SAF entities certainly share these characteristics. Ideas from autonomous agent research have seen an increasing application in SAF development, and in OneSAF.

Validation. As described earlier, validation of SAF behavior is an important issue and remains an open research area. Broadly applicable quantitative methods are needed to take SAF validation beyond variations of face validation.

Two new areas of important research have emerged since the earlier list:

Scalability. Increases in the computational power of computer workstations that run SAF systems have resulted in concomitant increases in the number of SAF entities that can be generated by a typical workstation, but the increase in entities has not been proportional to the increase in computational power. This is primarily because the expectations of SAF users for increased fidelity in SAF physical models and increased sophistication in SAF behaviors have grown, consuming much of the increased computation power (Franceschini, Petty, Schricker, Franceschini, & McCulley, 1999). Generating a single SAF entity today requires considerably more computational power than it once did. Consequently, there is a continuing need to find ways to generate larger numbers of SAF entities using standard workstations. Moreover, there is a parallel desire to allow operators to control a larger number of entities; this depends on both improvements in operator interface design and on increased levels of automated planning, as mentioned earlier.

Asymmetric entities and tactics. SAF systems have traditionally been focused on generating behavior that accurately reproduced the tactical doctrine of the expected military foe. In contrast to the Cold War era, current real world adversaries increasingly do not have a fixed and formal tactical doctrine, instead behaving in ways described as asymmetric, and exhibiting continuous adaptation to friendly tactics. Implementing such behavior in SAF systems will be even more challenging than fixed doctrinal behavior. There are some asymmetric entities and tactics in OneSAF (Parsons, Surdu, & Jordan, 2005), but research is needed.

CONCLUDING COMMENTS

Semi-automated forces systems are an essential component of virtual environment training systems, generating both opposing and friendly entities that populate the virtual world and provide important training stimuli. Much progress has been made in their implementation, and excellent examples exist. However, SAF systems, in general, and the generation of autonomous behavior, in particular, are likely to be the subject of research for some time. Increased entity generation capacity, improved behavioral realism, broader behavior repertoires, and expanded use of cognitive modeling for behavior generation are all areas where additional work would be useful.

Although this chapter has focused on training applications, SAF systems can also be used nontraining purposes; for example, they may provide both friendly and opposing forces in an analysis application requiring many runs of a scenario to support statistical analysis, an application poorly suited for human control of simulation entities via crewed simulators.

REFERENCES

Ahmad, O., Cremer, J., Kearney, J., Willemsen, P., & Hansen, S. (1994). Hierarchical, concurrent state machines for behavior modeling and scenario control. *Proceedings of the Fifth Annual Conference on AI, Simulation, and Planning in High Autonomy Systems* (pp. 36–42). Los Alamitos, CA: IEEE Computer Society.

Anderson, J. R., & Lebiere, C. (1998). *The atomic components of thought.* Mahwah, NJ: Erlbaum.

Aronson, J. (1994). The SimCore tactics representation and simulation language. *Proceedings of the Fourth Conference on Computer Generated Forces and Behavioral Representation* (pp. 187–193). Orlando, FL: UCF–Institute for Simulation and Training.

Balci, O. (1998). Verification, validation, and testing. In J. Banks (Ed.), *Handbook of simulation: Principles, methodology, advances, applications, and practice* (pp. 335–393). New York: Wiley.

Calder, R. B., Smith, J. E., Courtemanche, A. J., Mar, J. M. F., & Ceranowicz, A. Z. (1993). ModSAF behavior simulation and control. *Proceedings of the Third Conference on Computer Generated Forces and Behavioral Representation* (pp. 347–356). Orlando, FL: UCF–Institute for Simulation and Training.

Ceranowicz, A. (1994, May 4–6). ModSAF capabilities. *Proceedings of the Fourth Conference on Computer Generated Forces and Behavioral Representation* (pp. 3–8). Orlando, FL: UCF–Institute for Simulation and Training.

Ceranowicz, A., Coffin, D., Smith, J., Gonzalez, R., & Ladd, C. (1994, May 4–6). Operator control of behavior in ModSAF. *Proceedings of the Fourth Conference on Computer Generated Forces and Behavioral Representation* (pp. 9–16). Orlando, FL: UCF–Institute for Simulation and Training.

Courtemanche, A. J., & Wittman, R. L. (2002). OneSAF: A product line approach for a next-generation CGF. *Proceedings of the Eleventh Conference on Computer-Generated Forces and Behavior Representation* (pp. 349–361). Orlando, FL: UCF–Institute for Simulation and Training.

Dahmann, J. S., Kuhl, F., & Weatherly, R. (1998). Standards for simulation: As simple as possible but not simpler: The high level architecture for simulation. *Simulation, 71*(6), 378–387.

Fishwick, P. A., Petty, M. D., & Mullally, D. E. (1991). Key research directions in behavioral representation for Computer Generated Forces. *Proceedings of the 2nd Behavioral Representation and Computer Generated Forces Symposium* (pp. E1–E14). Orlando, FL: UCF–Institute for Simulation and Training.

Franceschini, R. W., Petty, M. D., Schricker, S. A., Franceschini, D. J., & McCulley, G. (1999). Measuring and improving CGF performance. *Proceedings of the Eighth Conference on Computer Generated Forces and Behavioral Representation* (pp. 9–15). Orlando, FL: UCF–Institute for Simulation and Training.

Henderson, C., & Rodriquez, A. (2002). Modeling in OneSAF. *Proceedings of the Eleventh Conference on Computer Generated Forces and Behavioral Representation* (pp. 337–347). Orlando, FL: UCF–Institute for Simulation and Training.

Institute for Electrical and Electronics Engineers (1995). *IEEE Standard for Distributed Interactive Simulation—Application Protocols (Standard 1278.1-1995).* Piscataway, NJ: Author.

Laird, J. E., Newell, A., & Rosenbloom, P. S. (1987). SOAR: An architecture for general intelligence. *Artificial Intelligence, 33,* 1–64.

Longtin, M. J. (1994). Cover and concealment in ModSAF. *Proceedings of the Fourth Conference on Computer Generated Forces and Behavioral Representation* (pp. 239–247). Orlando, FL: UCF–Institute for Simulation and Training.

Maruichi, T., Uchiki, T., & Tokoro, M. (1987). Behavioral simulation based on knowledge objects. *Proceedings of the European Conference on Object Oriented Programming* (pp. 213–222). London: Springer-Verlag.

Meyer, D. E., & Kieras, D. E. (1997). A computational theory of executive control processes and human multiple-task performance: Part 1. Basic Mechanisms. *Psychological Review, 104,* 3–65.

Moore, M. B., Gieb, C., & Reich, B. D. (1995). Planning for reactive behaviors in hide and seek. *Proceedings of the Fifth Conference on Computer Generated Forces and Behavioral Representation* (pp. 345–352). Orlando, FL: UCF–Institute for Simulation and Training.

Nielsen, P., Smoot, D., Martinez, R., & Dennison, J. D. (2001). Participation of TacAir-Soar in roadrunner and coyote exercises at Air Force Research Lab, Mesa, AZ. *Proceedings of the Ninth Conference on Computer Generated Forces and Behavioral Representation* (173–180). Orlando, FL: UCF–Institute for Simulation and Training.

Ourston, D., Blanchard, D., Chandler, E., Loh, E., & Marshall, H. (1995). From CIS to Software. *Proceedings of the Fifth Conference on Computer Generated Forces and Behavioral Representation* (pp. 275–285). Orlando, FL: UCF–Institute for Simulation and Training.

Parsons, D. (2007, May). *One Semi-Automated Forces (OneSAF).* Paper presented at the DoD Modeling and Simulation Conference. Retrieved December 13, 2007, from www.onesaf.net

Parsons, D., Surdu, J., & Jordan, B. (2005, June). *OneSAF: A next generation simulation modeling the contemporary operating environment.* Paper presented at the 2005 European Simulation Interoperability Workshop, Toulouse, France.

Petty, M. D. (1994). The Turing test as an evaluation criterion for Computer Generated Forces. *Proceedings of the Fourth Conference on Computer Generated Forces and Behavioral Representation* (pp. 107–116). Orlando, FL: UCF–Institute for Simulation and Training.

Petty, M. D. (1995, December). *Case studies in verification, validation, and accreditation for computer generated forces.* Paper presented at the ITEA Modeling & Simulation: Today and Tomorrow Workshop, Las Cruces, NM.

Petty, M. D., Moshell, J. M., & Hughes, C. E. (1988). Tactical simulation in an object-oriented animated graphics environment. *Simuletter, 19*(2), 31–46.

Smith, J. (1994). Near-term movement control in ModSAF. *Proceedings of the Fourth Conference on Computer Generated Forces and Behavioral Representation* (pp. 249–260). Orlando, FL: UCF—Institute for Simulation and Training.

Smith, S. H., and Petty, M. D. (1992). Controlling autonomous behavior in real-time simulation. *Proceedings of the Southeastern Simulation Conference 1992* (pp. 27–40). Pensacola, FL: Society for Computer Simulation.

Sokolowski, J. A. (2003). Enhanced decision modeling using multiagent system simulation. *Simulation, 79*(4), 232–242.

Tran, O., Karr, C., & Knospe, D. (2004, August). *Behavior modeling. OneSAF Users Conference,* Orlando, FL. Retrieved December 13, 2007, from www.onesaf.net

Turing, A. M. (1950). Computing machinery and intelligence. *Mind, 59*(236), 433–460.

U.S. Department of Defense. (2002, November 4). *TENA—The Test and Training Enabling Architecture: Architecture reference document.* Foundation Initiative 2010 (Version 2002, Review ed.). Retrieved April 25, 2008, from https://www.tena-sda.org/display/intro/Documentation

Van Brackle, D. R., Petty, M. D., Gouge, C. D., & Hull, R. D. (1993). Terrain reasoning for reconnaissance planning in polygonal terrain. *Proceedings of the Third Conference on Computer Generated Forces and Behavioral Representation* (pp. 285–305). Orlando, FL: UCF–Institute for Simulation and Training.

Wise, B. P., Miller, D., & Ceranowicz, A. Z. (1991). A framework for evaluating Computer Generated Forces. *Proceedings of the 2nd Behavioral Representation and Computer Generated Forces Symposium* (pp. H1–H7). Orlando, FL: UCF–Institute for Simulation and Training.

Zachary, W., Ryder, J., Weiland, M., & Ross, L. (1992). Intelligent human-computer interaction in real time, multi-tasking process control and monitoring systems. In M. Helander & M. Nagamachi (Eds.), *Human factors in design for manufacturability* (pp. 377–402). New York: Taylor and Francis.

Chapter 10

GAMES AND GAMING TECHNOLOGY FOR TRAINING

Perry McDowell

This chapter looks at games and gaming technologies and how they are being used for training. However, why include a chapter about this in a handbook on virtual environments for training? Doing so implies that, at a minimum, games are a form of virtual environment, and they are being used for training or people are using gaming technology to build virtual environments. While both of these are true, the truth is that recent advances in gaming, virtual environments (VEs), and training technologies are blurring the line between what is a game, a VE, or a training device. This loss of differentiation is good and provides each community with new opportunities to expand, but it can make it difficult to keep up.

The coming together of these various disciplines is a very recent occurrence. In Stanney (2002), published just six years before this tome, not one of the 56 chapters contained the word "game" in the title. The closest chapter title to games is "Entertainment Applications of Virtual Environments," the final chapter before the conclusion. The Serious Games Summit, a workshop for those building games whose primary goal is something other than entertainment, prior to the Game Developers Conference, began only in 2004. Likewise, in 2003, the Interservice/Industry Training, Simulation & Education Conference, the largest military training conference in the world, had three papers or tutorials with "game" in the title. In 2006, there were approximately 30, including special sessions and a "serious game" contest to determine the best training game.

Although recent, this cross-pollination occurs in many areas and extends in many directions besides writings and conferences. For example, Nintendo's Wii remote is undoubtedly a piece of gaming hardware, but it is a clear descendant of the wand used in the earliest CAVE created by Carolina Cruz-Neira (Cruz-Neira, Sandin, DeFanti, Kenyon, & Hart, 1992), which, equally undoubtedly, is a VE. Likewise, many virtual environments are now using game engines, originally designed to create games, as the underlying software driving many parts of the virtual environment (Hashimoto, Ishida, & Sato, 2005). Additionally, in the past, when trainees were placed in an environment similar to that of their jobs, the vast majority of training applications were huge simulators, generally mimicking aircraft, tanks, or ships. Now, these large simulations are being replaced with, or more often, augmented by smaller, game-like systems. Also, the training community is expanding the number and types of tasks that can be trained using some combination of game and VE technology.

The most important point for the reader to take away from this chapter is this: games and gaming technologies can be exceptionally valuable tools for an educator or trainer to use, but they remain only that: tools. While some may claim that they will replace trainers (Prensky, 2000), most do not see this. Instead, games will become part of the whole training experience, included in curricula as just another method for trainers to help their students learn, such as readings, quizzes, lectures, and one-on-one tutoring. As Jenkins (2007) states, "Our goals are never to displace the teacher but rather to provide teachers with new resources for doing what they do best."

One key element in figuring out how and when to use these tools in a curriculum is the cognitive task analysis. A cognitive task analysis takes an in-depth look at a task and attempts to break it down into distinct subtasks and examines what is required for each. These can become quite long; for example, even the simple task of making toast looks complicated when broken down into subtasks and capabilities. These would include knowing how to adjust the toaster's settings, choosing the correct setting for the desired crispness, being able to the see the bread and the toaster, understanding what lever to push down to start the toasting, and having the physical strength/dexterity to manipulate the lever. Although this chapter will not go into cognitive task analyses in depth, to learn more, see Kirwan and Ainsworth (1992).

One note: although training and education are not the same things, games have the ability to do both. Space limitations prevent this chapter from going into the significant depth required to delineate the two; therefore, throughout this chapter both training and education will be combined together in the term "training."

METHODS TO CREATE TRAINING GAMES

There are several methods to create training games, but this chapter will cover the three that are the most common in the author's opinion: using commercial games, partnering with a game company to produce a game, and building (or having a game company build) a game from scratch for a particular training need.

Commercial Games

The simplest method to use gaming technology for training is to have students play a commercial off-the-shelf (COTS) game to learn. COTS games have proven very effective at teaching a wide variety of tasks. For example, many armies use *Steel Beasts,* originally released as a commercial game simulating tank warfare, to practice skills required to fight their modern tanks and other mechanized vehicles (eSim Games, 2007). Similarly, many teachers use Sid Meier's *Civilization* series to teach their classes history (Squire, 2004). In these cases, COTS games can be very effective as learning aids. *Steel Beasts* won the 2006 Serious Games Challenge Award (eSim Games, 2007), while Squire (2004) shows that *Civilization* improved students' knowledge of history.

Generally, the most important reason someone uses a COTS game for training rather than developing a game is the cost. Building a top-of-the-line commercial game from scratch can be a significant and costly undertaking; Halo 2, completed in 2004, credited over 190 people and had a budget over $40 million, and the budgets of the top games continue to rise exponentially (Reimer, 2005). Rather than paying that cost, the company bears the cost, and the trainers just buy copies of the game for their trainees. So long as the game, as it was built, can train, it can be used. For example, in discussing the Australian Army's use of *Steel Beasts* for tank training, an Australian Department of Defense spokesperson says in Braue (2007), "The key for defense is getting value for money, while meeting the training need." If an existing game can produce learning in the student faster than the other available methods, it makes sense to use the game.

However, using COTS games is not without risks and problems. Games produced to sell commercially are designed to do just that: sell commercially. When deciding whether to sacrifice realism to improve gameplay, user enjoyment, and therefore sales, it is an easy decision for the game designer: sales wins every time. Additionally, often the game must be significantly simpler than reality to make gameplay even possible; for example, if it took *Steel Beasts'* players as long to learn to control an M1A1 Abrams tank effectively as it does to teach a soldier to do so in reality (12–18 months), no one would bother to play the game.

Similarly, while the *Civilization* games have been used in many classrooms, there are many who feel that they provide students with a poor, misleading, or one-sided educational experience. Whelchel (2007) contains a laundry list of the problems, two of which are listed here. The first is that the game applies Western "ages" to non-Western cultures that did not experience them, giving a false delineation to non-European cultures. The second is that the game rewards players based upon their *Civilization*'s type of government, and "a capitalist democratic republic garners the most benefits, leading players to adopt an Amero-centric perception of the relative worth of political systems." These problems, among others, may cause someone playing the game to get an incorrect or biased view of world history.

This does not mean that COTS games cannot be a valuable asset to teachers and trainers, especially those who are constrained by budget. Even though *Steel Beasts* greatly simplifies the requirements for driving and fighting a tank, it can be assumed that trained soldiers can already do that, or at least will receive that training via other methods. Therefore, the fact that the game abstracts away the difficulty of those tasks is immaterial, and it can be used to train soldiers in how to employ their tank as part of a larger troop. Likewise, the inadequacies listed above for *Civilization* might be serious shortcomings in a graduate level course on comparative political systems. However, they are so far beyond the scope of a high school world history class that the game can be used effectively in that setting to demonstrate political decision making.

The key to effective implementation of a COTS game is to perform a thorough evaluation of the game and determine which tasks, if any, it can be used to train. Ideally, this will be a complete cognitive task analysis of the entire task, with a mapping between the required subtasks and those that the game trains. However, at a minimum it should consist of a trainer, with subject matter expert help if necessary, examining the overall task and the game and then making a determination of which subtasks the game trains.

It is crucial to do this because it is highly unlikely that a commercial game, made without any input from the trainer, will completely and perfectly train all parts of the overall task. Therefore, the training curriculum will have to be modified to remove redundant training covered by the game and, more importantly, ensure that tasks *not* trained in the game are addressed somewhere else in the curriculum. Returning to *Steel Beasts* with a somewhat fanciful example, it would be ineffective to make a soldier's training consist entirely of that game. After his training, he might have a good concept of how to maneuver a platoon of tanks against an enemy, but when he sits in the driver's seat of a tank, he would not have any idea of how to start it.

One other problem with COTS games as trainers is that there has to be an existing COTS game in the first place. For example, if a math teacher wants a game to teach calculus, he or she is unlikely to find a COTS game that would be effective; there just is not a market for the game to be developed in the first place. Likewise, the U.S. Navy is unlikely to find a COTS game to teach deck seaman to handle lines during mooring because such a commercial game would be unlikely to sell. Even though calculus, line handling, and a myriad of other tasks still need to be taught and would benefit from a game based approach, there will never be COTS games educators can use to teach them.

Partner with a Commercial Game Company

An option somewhere between using a COTS game and building one from scratch to train a particular application is to create a symbiotic relationship with a commercial game company to build a game. This arrangement, which we will call partnering, is where each group brings different resources to the collaboration and each group gets to use the resulting game, but it is a slightly different arrangement than merely contracting with a commercial company. In a simple contracting arrangement, which will be discussed later, a contract specifies exactly what kind of game the trainers want the game company to produce. The game company builds the game, the trainers use it to train, and the game company does nothing else with it. In a partnership, both groups want to use the final product: the trainers to teach, the game company to sell commercially. Normally the trainers provide the subject matter experts and access to equipment and locations in the game, the company provides the game production experts, and they split the cost of game production. The trainers get to use the game without any additional licensing costs, and the game company gets the profits from selling the game commercially.

When it works correctly, this can be a very beneficial relationship for both parties. The trainers get a game designed specifically for their training needs for less than the cost of contracting it out to a company. The company gets the help of subject matter experts for free, it does not have to bear the entire cost of development, and it can use the fact that the game is being used for training in marketing.

However, there are two major downsides to creating a trainer this way. The first is similar to a problem with COTS games: the task must be one that has a chance of being a commercially successful game. Because ground combat games are so popular, game companies line up for the chance to work with the U.S. Army or U.S. Marine Corps to produce a trainer for ground troops that they could resell. Likewise, flight simulators often sell well, so companies are willing to work with the U.S. Air Force to produce such a game. Unfortunately, many of the tasks required by the military, although crucial for combat success, are not likely to make games that are commercially viable. For example, logistics is critical to keep the military fighting, but *Logistic Technician,* a game where the player acts as a supply noncommissioned officer, is unlikely to be a commercial success. Therefore, even though the military needs to train supply soldiers and might want to create a game to train logisticians, it would be unlikely to find a partner.

The other problem with these relationships is that each partner requires a different outcome from the partnership. The trainer wants a training application, while the game company wants a commercial hit, and to each everything else (including the partner's desires) is secondary and considered less important. This dichotomy can lead to problems when decisions have two options, one better for training, the other better for gameplay and enjoyment. There are literally thousands of these decisions in every game development. Quite often these can be aggravated by a lack of communication or understanding between the groups. Trainers think that the obvious answer is the training-friendly option, while the gamers cannot conceive of making a decision to reduce the fun of the game. These differing goals often lead to games that are significantly better in one of these phases, but rarely produce a game that is both an exceptional training tool and a commercial success.

An example of this is the partnership between the U.S. Marine Corps and Destineer, a video game publisher, to create the *Close Combat: First to Fight* game, intended to be a drug reduction tool within the Corps. In the version intended for the Corps, the player would encounter a marine under the influence of drugs and have to deal with the consequences. The Marine Corps supplied funding and U.S. Marines to act as subject matter experts during the development of the game. However, it has not been used as a training tool by the Marine Corps due to problems with the techniques in the games. For example, to speak to someone in the game, the player must point his or her weapon at that person, which U.S. Marines are trained never to do unless they intend to shoot. Although a newer version is supposed to have fixed these problems, to date it has not been used as a trainer within the Marine Corps.

Build the Training Game from Scratch

Another option, and oftentimes the best in terms of the finished product meeting the training need, is to build a game from scratch. Other chapters in this volume will address how to do this in depth, so this chapter will be limited to describing some of the pros and cons of this to help determine whether this is appropriate. Additionally, this section will discuss some of the terms a trainer needs to understand in order to make this decision.

The biggest advantage of building a training game purposely for a given training need is having one, and only one, question when determining whether to include a feature: Will this feature improve the trainee's ability to learn the material? Unlike a COTS game, which likely gave no consideration to this, or a partnership, where this question had to be balanced with the commercial company's desire to turn a profit, every aspect of the design can be centered on how it makes the learner's experience better. With only one goal, designers can produce a significantly more focused product. Additionally, there is a significant reduction in the amount of discussion to determine whether a feature is bad for learning but good for commercial success, or vice versa, which leads to a faster production and a happier, more productive team.

The biggest disadvantage of building a training game from scratch is that the trainer must bear all expenses alone. As mentioned earlier, the top games can cost $40 million to produce, and clearly a local school board cannot approve such a budget item for a game to teach math better. Even the military, with some of the biggest training budgets, cannot afford such costs unless the game is expected to produce a larger savings elsewhere in the budget or a huge increase in performance. While training games do not need to match the high quality graphics, sound, and artificial intelligence of COTS titles in order to be effective, the high quality of COTS games is included when using a COTS game or partnering with a commercial game producer. If one or both of these other options is available, the trainer needs to decide whether the improvement derived from having a game specifically designed to meet his or her training need is worth the additional investment.

GAME ENGINES

One of the most prevalent ways that the virtual environment and training communities have borrowed from the game industry is in the field of software. The game industry has always been very competitive and as the cost of producing a game has risen into the tens of millions of dollars, the difference between a game that makes many times the initial investment and one that loses it is incredibly small. This has driven game engine builders to continually refine their engine to make it the fastest, the best looking, and the easiest to use. This competition has meant that each commercial game engine generally has had a life span of 2 to 3 years, so in the past 15 years there have been five to seven generations. Even by the impressive standards of the computer industry, few areas have achieved such a rapid growth. Each generation greatly surpassed the previous in performance, features, and ease of use, and this constant refinement has produced some remarkable software.

Of this software, the most prevalent are game engines, the underlying software that almost every game is built upon. As each game engine is different, sometimes radically, it is difficult to give a perfect description that precisely defines game engines that does not exclude many. A simple, if imprecise, definition is that a game engine does the tasks that are required to make the game work, but the game programmer would prefer not to do or think about while creating the game. In more exact terms, a game engine abstracts much of the lower level implementation away from the game programmer. For example, when a player shoots a weapon or drives a vehicle, the programmer knows this must be networked to the other players, but does not want to have to worry about making this happen at the transmission control protocol/Internet protocol layer. Rather, he or she would like to make a simple function call and let the game engine worry about turning that call into the message transferred to all the other players.

This is the case for almost all aspects of the game. In addition to networking, the core functionality of game engines generally includes a scene graph for rendering, physics (including collision detection and visibility determination), audio, memory management, threading, windowing, graphical user interfaces, and refereeing player interactions and determining the results. Additionally, most engines are now designed either to provide artificial intelligence automatically or to contain a framework to make it easy for the programmer to produce whatever the desired behavior. See http://www.devmaster.net/engines/engine_details.php?id=25 for a more detailed description of the components of the Unreal 3 game engine, one of the most popular game engines on the market.

Normally, each game engine is optimized for a specific genre of game, and often even specialized for a specific subgenre. For example, engines are customized not only for first-person shooter (FPS) games, role-playing games, or real time strategy games, but an engine for FPS games will likely be customized even further for an FPS game that is conducted mainly inside, or in a jungle environment, or a desert setting. This allows the engine programmers to make incredible optimizations for a specific type of game, so the result is that this game runs exceptionally well. However, it also limits the breadth of games that can be created using it.

However, game engines are no longer evaluated just by the quality of the games built atop them. Increasingly, an engine is judged by how easy it makes it for the game team to produce that product. Because of the strict time constraints in the game industry, a game that plays acceptably and is produced on time is often significantly more profitable than the perfect game that ships late and is plagued by delays and cost overruns. As mentioned earlier, the difference between success and failure can be very small, and games are canceled in mid-development for being late, as well as for being poorly done. Therefore, the engine's ability to improve the production flow (often called the pipeline) has become as important as its ability to produce impressive graphics.

A great example of this is the Unreal 3 engine, which Epic Games used to create the game of the year for 2006, *Gears of War*. One of the ways that the Unreal 3 engine improved the pipeline was adding a graphical programming tool Kismet that allowed nonprogrammers, such as level designers, to produce effects that previously could be created only by programmers. The level designer can produce the effect himself or herself, and it would exactly match his or her idea. If the effect is not computationally expensive, the script can be inserted directly into the game. If it is too computationally expensive to run in real time in scripting language, a programmer can once again program it in a faster language, generally C++, but now instead of having only the level designer's verbal description, he or she can see the exact effect the level designer desires. This makes it much easier for him or her to match it on the first try and makes production run much smoother. Currently, this capability is available only in a few of the most expensive game engines, but in the coming years it is likely to expand to a much wider range of engines.

NEEDED IMPROVEMENTS

While gaming technology offers great benefits for training systems now, there are several additional capabilities that need to be created before they reach their full potential. These include some improved technological capabilities, additional research into game based training, and some modifications to current methodologies and attitudes.

Needed Technological Advances

In order to fit games into curricula, one of the most important technical advances will be the ability for training games and learning management systems to communicate. A learning management system is an application, generally Web based, that leads the student through the curriculum, and it typically contains a syllabus, class assignments, links to readings, quizzes, the student's grades in the class, and other similar material. Common examples of learning management systems are Blackboard, Moodle, and Meridian. Learning management systems have become indispensable parts of distance learning classes for some time and are now being used by most on-site training classes also. Joining games and learning management systems is key to the future of game based training; more on this subject can be found in "Interfacing Interactive 3-D Simulations with Learning Systems" by Conkey and Smith (Volume 2, Section 2, Chapter 15).

Another technological improvement needed before game based training can reach its potential is the improvement of intelligent tutoring systems. As Dr. Jeff Wilkinson, Army Program Manager for the Institute of Creative Technologies, said during a session at the 2006 Serious Game Summit, "Experiential learning is not effective; guided experiential learning is effective." While learning can occur from students playing randomly with the only feedback being failing at the game, giving a player the ability to examine his or her mistakes and learn from them is a much quicker and better way to deliver information and train.

Unfortunately, this means that a trainer will have to review his or her game-play, either in real time or via a playback mechanism, and spend time to go over it with him or her. It would be more effective if there was a computer based system that did this initially instead of the trainer, with the trainee approaching the trainer only if the computer based remediation did not completely explain his or her deficiencies. This is what intelligent tutoring systems are designed to do. These tutoring systems are more than just simple lists of every mistake the player makes; instead, they are designed to analyze the mistakes and create a mental model of the player's knowledge.

The tutoring system then determines the best method of remediation to eliminate the gap between the player's current knowledge level and that required for successful completion of the training objective. The simplest method of remediation is to have the player reread texts covering his or her mistakes, but they can be significantly more complex. Hypertext documents, with links to allow the student to drill down further into concepts not completely understood, are slightly more advanced, while natural language systems designed to hold conversations just as a human tutor would are among the most complex. This tutoring does not have to occur after a training session; just as a human tutor often does, an intelligent tutor might coach the user during the game to help the student overcome an obstacle so he or she can reach other areas.

Finally, the improvement that might do the most to increase the number of games to be used as effective training aids is to get the tools to create them out of the hands of engineers and programmers and into the hands of trainers. Currently this means creating more advanced systems that do not require the same expertise to produce games. There is significant interest in creating simple tools, often called *scenario generators,* that would allow trainers to create training games without engineers. This would significantly reduce the cost and time to produce the training and allow scenarios to be easily modified by trainers as circumstances change. The Defense Advanced Research Projects Agency's *Real World* program is designed to create such tools. In the somewhat distant future, it would be ideal if a system could examine a trainee's record on the learning management system, determine what knowledge the trainee needed to complete to reach all required competencies, and then generate game scenario(s) that teach and evaluate him or her.

Needed Research

While lately there has been a great deal of research on using games for training, that research has largely centered on proving that games can provide training value. There needs to be significantly more research into a wide variety of subjects before games can truly reach their potential as training tools. Additionally, much of the published research has been discussions or examples where researchers used a game in training. O'Neil, Wainess, and Baker (2005) surveyed more than 4,000 articles published in the preceding 10 years, many of which were from fairly well respected journals, and found that only 19 were "empirical" studies. (Empirical was defined as having a control group and random assignment.) While there is much research *indicating* that games make effective training tools, there is very little *proving* it.

Additionally, the overall finding of their paper was that learning is dependent on the quality of instructional design and instructional strategies, not on the media. Learning games that are based on solid instructional methods (design and strategies) made effective learning tools, while games designed with weak or poor instructional methods normally did not. While this result should not be surprising, it creates several basic questions that need to be addressed by serious, empirical research, such as the following:

- What are the best instructional methods to employ in games?
- Do the best methods vary by the type of task being taught?
- What are the best types of games to train? Or, more properly, what is the best type of game to train a given task?
- Is this the same for all types of learners?
- If games train effectively, do they train efficiently, that is, better, faster, and cheaper than other training methods?
- If so, is this true in all cases, or for which domains is it not true?
- Games are likely to be only one part of curricula. When is the best time to use a game?
  a. At the beginning, because it will give context for why the material taught is important to the big picture even though the trainee does not have the knowledge/skills to do well?
  b. After some instruction, because trainees can practice what they have learned and reinforce it?
  c. After all the instruction, when they should be able to complete the entire task?
  d. Or throughout the course?
- Is there a checklist that can be created for building training games so that any subject matter expert can build a training game for his or her field, or is this an art form that requires specialized training?
- How much does fun play in the effectiveness of training games? (Pedants might ask "What is fun?" The answer to that question is too disputed to answer here. (For more information, see Koster, 2004, or Salen and Zimmerman, 2003.)
- Docs fun merely serve as a method to get a trainee to spend more time on a subject, or is it significant in the effectiveness of the training?
- Studies indicate that fun does not matter in short-term retention, but is that true for long-term retention of material?
- If using intelligent tutoring systems, is it better to point out errors during the game or after the trainee finishes?
- If so, is this the case for all tasks and learners?

- Are games better predictors of real world performance than current methods, such as tests and oral interviews?
- If so, for which tasks and game types does this hold true?
- Do differences exist in the effectiveness of game based training for people in different groups, such as gender, age, educational level, socioeconomic background, and gaming experience?
- Similarly, does this hold true if games are used as predictors of performance?

Needed Modifications to Methodologies and Attitudes

Many believe that games hold the possibility of improving almost any curriculum; however, whether they can reach that potential is based more on overcoming attitudinal and commercial barriers than technological ones. There are several of these barriers, but this chapter will cover only three: aversion to games by decision makers, the differences between game designers and educators, and the current commercial models of the gaming and simulation business.

The first of these is that certain people, especially those in positions of power or the current training establishment, dislike using games to train. Normally this is not based upon research indicating that games are ineffective at training, but rather something more visceral. At times, these can be addressed fairly simply, especially through education. For example, many teachers worry that using games for training is an attempt to replace them in the classrooms the way robots have replaced assembly-line workers. These fears can often be overcome by explaining to them that games are not going to replace them any more than television, movies, or the Internet did; in fact, they are merely another tool they can use to educate their students (Jenkins, 2007). Similarly, some people believe that training is very serious business, and games are considered frivolous. Most of these people have no objections to using computer based simulations for training, and they definitely would agree that training events should be engaging, but to use the common term for an engaging simulation, that is, "game," somehow implies to them that the trainees are partaking in child's play rather than in training. In this case, while education can work, often a simple name change can suffice. The U.S. Marine Corps, for example, uses tactical decision-making simulations, not games, to train marines; that most of these are largely indistinguishable from first-person shooter games is immaterial.

The second of these problems is the dichotomy between game designers and educators. While having educators more involved in the development of games has great potential for the expansion of their use in the classroom, it also has the possibility to destroy the value of games as teaching tools. One of the main reasons games are so effective in training is that they engage the learner. However, that is not always the case with games designed by educators, as many of the early computer learning games were. As Henry Jenkins, co-founder of the Massachusetts Institute of Technology (MIT) Comparative Media Studies Program, wrote, "Most existing edutainment products combine the entertainment value of a bad lecture with the educational value of a bad game" (Jenkins,

2002). Much of the blame for this must be placed upon the fact that these games were mainly designed by educators who were not trained in the art of making entertaining games. Giving educators the tools to build games without giving them the capability to build *engaging* games will create a multitude of games that are expensive failures because they became just another boring part of school.

The cure for this is to ensure that those creating the games understand both the educational side and the game design side, or at least respect their colleagues on the other side of the argument. Mark Oehlert, a researcher on game based training at the Defense Acquisition University, says,

> We need to work a lot harder on bringing instructional system design closer together with game design. Currently, they are two entirely different schools of thought, but we must do better in creating a hybrid. It's not technology that will slow serious games from reaching their potential; we've got plenty of technology. The question will be "How can we make powerful learning moments with these technologies?
>
> (McDowell, 2007)

The third is far more troublesome and may be the most serious obstacle to the widespread adaptation of training games: the business models of building training games. Currently, there is no good model of creating training games. The game industry is generally built around creating only a few games, with the hope that one or two will hit it big and generate millions of dollars of revenue. The licensing of most of the biggest game engines reflects this; they can cost upwards of $500,000 per game, not to mention that most of the code outside the engine and art assets are made for one game only. All these factors make it difficult to build many different games, but that is exactly what the training community needs since there are so many diverse training needs.

Additionally, another problem is that games are generally created, released, and then not maintained. As users update their computers and operating systems, the games companies do nothing to ensure that the older games will work on the new equipment. For commercial games, this normally is not an issue, but trainers would prefer to replace their games only when there is a change to the material, not because they upgraded computers. Similarly, if the material is changed, there is no way for the training command to change the game to reflect these changes without going back to the company, which might be unwilling to make the changes cheaply, if at all.

In order to drive these costs down, there needs to be a major shift in the business of making games. Potential solutions include open source products and increased reuse of the code, models, and art assets. There are many ideas on how to do this, but there is currently not much momentum to make the required changes.

CONCLUSION

The most important item in determining how to design a game based trainer is remembering that it is only one tool that the educator has to train the student and that the game must fit into the entire blended training solution. Similarly, it is critical for the trainers and subject matter experts to perform an analysis on the tasks to be trained to determine which can be trained using a game and how effectively the game trains these tasks. This ensures that any tasks not trained effectively in the game are covered in another part of the curriculum.

There are many ways to create games for training, and no one method is perfect in all cases. While COTS games are generally the cheapest option, in many cases there is not a COTS game available, or at least not one that trains the task well. Partnering with a games company can reduce costs, but it may be impossible to find a company willing to partner for a specific training need and, as always, it is difficult to build a single product with two goals in mind. While building a game from scratch ensures that it meets the training need, the costs can be prohibitive. The trainer who desires to use a game based solution as part of his or her training regimen needs to evaluate the training need, the trainees, and available resources in order to decide upon the best method to create the game.

Games have proven to be effective training tools, and they are likely to be used more in the future. It is up to the people who design and implement the games to build good games so as to ensure that the momentum games currently have in moving from the fringe to the mainstream continues.

REFERENCES

Braue, D. (2007). *Behind pretend enemy lines.* Retrieved December 8, 2007, from Army-Technology Web site, http://www.army-technology.com/features/feature1082/

Cruz-Neira, C., Sandin, D. J., DeFanti, T. A., Kenyon, R. V., & Hart, J. C. (1992). The CAVE: Audio visual experience automatic virtual environment. *Communications of the ACM, 35*(6), 65–72.

DevMaster.net. (2008). Retrieved July 30, 2008, from http://www.devmaster.net/engines/engine_details.php?id=25

eSim Games Press Release. (2007). Retrieved December 8, 2007, from eSim Games Web site, http://www.esimgames.com/press_releases.htm

Hashimoto, N., Ishida, Y., & Sato, M. (2005). Game-engine based virtual environments for immersive projection display systems. Proceedings of 2005 IPT & EGVE Workshop, R. Blach and E. Kjems (Eds.).

Jenkins, H. (2002). Game theory: How should we teach kids Newtonian physics? Simple. Play computer games. [Electronic version]. *MIT's Technology Review,* Retrieved December 23, 2007, from http://www.technologyreview.com/Energy/12784/

Jenkins, H. (2007, March). From serious games to serious gaming (part six): Common threads, Confessions of an aca-fan: The official weblog of Henry Jenkins. Retrieved April 18, 2008, from http://www.henryjenkins.org/2007/11/from_serious_games_to_serious_7.html

Kirwan, B., & Ainsworth, L. K. (Eds.). (1992). *A guide to task analysis.* London: Taylor and Francis, Ltd.

Koster, R. (2004). *A theory of fun. Phoenix.* Scottsdale, AZ: Paraglyph Press.

McDowell, P. L. (2007). Serious games: Why today? Where tomorrow? *M S and T,* Issue 2/2007, 26–30.

O'Neil, H. F., Wainess, R., & Baker, E. L. (2005). Classification of learning outcomes: Evidence from the computer games literature. *The Curriculum Journal, 16*(4), 455–474.

Prensky, M. (2000). *Digital game-based learning.* New York: McGraw-Hill.

Reimer, J. (2005). Cross-platform game development and the next generation of consoles, Ars technica, November 7, 2005 [Electronic version]. Retrieved April 18, 2008, from http://arstechnica.com/articles/paedia/hardware/crossplatform.ars/2

Salen, K., & Zimmerman, E. (2003). Rules of play: Game design fundamentals. Cambridge, MA: MIT Press.

Squire, K. D. (2004). Replaying history: Learning world history through playing Civilization® III. Doctoral dissertation, Indiana University.

Stanney, K. M. (Ed.). (2002). *Handbook of virtual environments: Design, implementation, and applications.* Mahway, NJ: Lawrence Erlbaum.

Whelchel, A. (2007). Using Civilization® simulation video games in the world history classroom. World History Connected, 4(2). Retrieved December 8, 2007, from http://historycooperative.press.uiuc.edu/journals/whc/4.2/whelchel.html

Chapter 11

VIRTUAL ENVIRONMENT SICKNESS AND IMPLICATIONS FOR TRAINING

Julie Drexler, Robert Kennedy, and Linda Malone

Due to the maturity and flexibility of virtual environment (VE) technology, which provides compellingly realistic visual images and allows users to be exposed to scenarios that would be dangerous or impractical in the real environment, VE systems can provide a safe and highly cost-effective alternative to real world training. Considerable evidence also suggests that VE technology can enhance task performance in a training environment (Kenyon & Afenya, 1995; Magee, 1995; Witmer, Bailey, & Knerr, 1996). However, while VEs may offer such advantages as low cost training, numerous studies on the effects of exposure to different VE systems indicate that motion sickness–like symptoms are often experienced during or after exposure to the simulated environment (Kennedy et al., 2003).

Simulators, which are a specific type of VE typically used to simulate a flying or driving environment, present two-dimensional, computer-generated images on a fixed-screen display (for example, cathode ray tube [CRT] and dome). The motion sickness–like symptoms associated with exposure to simulators, known as simulator sickness, have been a problem for over 40 years (Kennedy, Drexler, & Compton, 1997). In the first published report of simulator sickness, Miller and Goodson (1960) indicated that 78 percent of the flight students and instructors experienced some degree of sickness as a result of exposure to a military helicopter simulator. Since then, reports of simulator sickness have appeared in nearly all military simulators, including the U.S. Navy, Marine Corps, Army, Air Force (Crowley, 1987; Gower, Lilienthal, Kennedy, & Fowlkes, 1987; Kennedy, Lilienthal, Berbaum, Baltzley, & McCauley, 1989; Warner, Serfoss, Baruch, & Hubbard, 1993), and Coast Guard (Ungs, 1988), as well as automobile and tank simulators (Curry, Artz, Cathey, Grant, & Greenberg, 2002; Lampton, Kraemer, Kolasinski, & Knerr, 1995; Lerman et al., 1993).

Another specific type of VE system, a virtual reality (VR) device, employs a visually coupled device worn by the user to typically present three-dimensional, computer-generated images. Motion sickness–like symptoms have also been increasingly reported by a significant proportion of VR users, particularly those using helmet-mounted displays (HMDs; Hettinger, 2002; Kennedy, Jones, Lilien-thal, & Harm, 1994; Pausch, Crea, & Conway, 1992; Regan & Price, 1994). In order to distinguish between the symptoms from exposure to a VR system and simulator-induced symptoms, some authors have referred to the side effects of VR devices as virtual reality sickness or cybersickness (McCauley & Sharkey, 1992). Simulator sickness and cybersickness involve visually induced motion stimuli as opposed to traditional forms of motion-induced sickness that are caused by inertial motion. The symptoms that typically occur as a result of expo-sure to VEs include disorientation, nausea, dizziness, sweating, drowsiness, eye-strain, headache, loss of postural stability, and vomiting, although infrequent; the symptom severity can range from mild discomfort to debilitating illness (Drexler, Kennedy, & Compton, 2004; Kennedy, Fowlkes, & Lilienthal, 1993).

While simulator studies have shown that simulator sickness exhibits more oculomotor-related symptoms than conventional motion sickness, VR research indicates that cybersickness exhibits more disorientation-related symptoms (Ken-nedy, Dunlap, Jones, & Stanney, 1996; Kennedy, Lane, Lilienthal, Berbaum, & Hettinger, 1992). Moreover, investigations into the motion sickness–like symp-toms related to HMD based systems produce more severe levels of sickness and affect a greater number of users than simulators (Kennedy et al., 1996). In a sur-vey of simulator sickness in 10 different military flight simulators, approximately 10 to 60 percent of pilots reported some degree of sickness (Kennedy, Hettinger, & Lilienthal, 1990; Kennedy, Lilienthal, et al., 1989). In contrast, Kennedy, Jones, Stanney, Ritter, and Drexler (1996) found that the average level of sick-ness in their VR studies was not only significantly higher than those found in the flight simulators, but 85 to 95 percent of the participants reported experienc-ing symptoms.

FACTORS INFLUENCING SICKNESS IN VIRTUAL ENVIRONMENTS

Early military flight simulators, which first called attention to the sickness problem, had equipment limitations such as visual distortions, excessive transport delays, and flickering images that were considered to be the source of the discom-fort experienced by users (Drexler et al., 2004). Simulator sickness was, there-fore, initially thought to be due solely to the inadequacies of the equipment, so equipment improvements would eliminate the sickness problem (Kennedy, Jones, & Dunlap, 1996). However, as technological advances improved equip-ment fidelity and the visual scenes became more realistic, the incidence and severity of sickness actually increased (Kennedy et al., 2003; Kennedy & Lilien-thal, 1994; Kennedy et al., 1990).

Although the fundamental causes of motion sickness have not been completely identified, researchers have identified the following factors that influence the incidence and severity of VE sickness: characteristics of the individual user (for example, age, gender, exposure history, and current physiological state), expo-sure duration (that is, increased incidence and sickness severity are associated with increased duration), usage schedule (that is, repeated exposures generally reduce sickness severity), and various equipment features (Kennedy, Berbaum, Dunlap, & Smith, 1995; Kennedy et al., 1997; Kennedy & Fowlkes, 1992; Kolasinski, 1995; McCauley, 1984; Stanney, Kennedy, & Drexler, 1997). Obviously, the equipment creates the simulated environment and, of the major determiners of sickness, manipulation of VE equipment features provides the most direct, practical, and economical means to controlling sickness. Therefore, this chapter focuses primarily on the various system features that affect VE sickness.

Equipment Features

Specification of the equipment parameters that promote effective performance and realism, but avoid or minimize sickness, is critical for the design and use of VE systems (Drexler, 2006; Kennedy, Berbaum, & Smith, 1993). A number of design inadequacies or equipment limitations have been reported in the scientific literature as potential factors that contribute to sickness in VEs. In the following sections, the equipment features implicated as factors influencing sickness are presented and categorized according to the type of VE system in which they can be found. The common VE system features are presented first, followed by the features specific to HMD based systems (see Bolas and McDowall, Volume 2, Section 1, Chapter 2), and the features specific to projection based systems (see Towles, Johnson, and Fuchs, Volume 2, Section 1, Chapter 3). It is important to note that although see-through HMDs (designed for augmented reality applications) and desktop displays are VE systems, they are not included in this chapter, which is focused on more immersive based VE systems.

Common VE Equipment Features

Individuals largely rely on their visual senses during exposure to a VE system, and, as such, the visual display will provide the most salient and detailed information about the simulated environment (Durlach & Mavor, 1995; Wilson, 1997). The visual display not only provides "input" to the user, changes in the visual scene also represent the "output" of the user (Kennedy & Smith, 1996). However, VEs are very interactive and, as a result, the visual display systems engage "numerous oculomotor systems, and hence have the potential to produce motion sickness symptoms" (Ebenholtz, 1992, p. 303). The display characteristics that have been implicated as factors influencing sickness include the field of view, display resolution, viewing region, and temporal delays (refresh rate, update rate, and system latency).

Field of View and Display Resolution
Research has shown that wider fields of view (FOVs; that is, the horizontal and vertical angular dimensions of a visual display) provide better task performance (Bowman, Datey, Ryu, Farooq, & Vasnaik, 2002; Wilson, 1997). However, research on the effects of sickness related to FOV size indicate that, in general, wider FOV displays increase the incidence and intensity of sickness, particularly

symptoms of eyestrain, headache, and dizziness (DiZio & Lackner, 1992; Lawson, Graeber, Mead, & Muth, 2002; Lin, Duh, Parker, Abi-Rached, & Furness, 2002; Padmos & Milders, 1992; Pausch et al., 1992).

FOV is usually a trade-off with resolution (that is, image quality), but poor resolution can cause strain on the visual system as the user tries to focus on the simulated image, resulting in symptoms such as eyestrain and headache (Pausch et al., 1992). In wider FOV displays the available pixels are more spread out over the retinal area stimulated, which reduces display resolution (Bowman et al., 2002; Wilson, 1997). Accordingly, in simulators with computer-generated image display systems that have a fixed pixel capacity, high spatial resolution may be limited to a small FOV (Rinalducci, 1996). In contrast, narrower FOVs (that is, 40°–60° vertical by 60°–80° horizontal) with higher resolution can cause tunnel vision or increase disorientation effects (Bowman et al., 2002). Relatedly, Kennedy, Fowlkes, and Hettinger (1989) indicated that wide FOV displays can magnify the effects of any distortions in the visual display. Durlach and Mavor (1995) also noted that greater geometric image distortions occur in HMD displays with large FOVs because a greater degree of magnification is required to project the real world size image onto the small display screens.

Other research related to FOV size has suggested that the incidence of sickness is influenced by the amount of vection, the illusion of self-motion in the absence of physical movement (Hettinger, Berbaum, Kennedy, Dunlap, & Nolan, 1990; Hettinger & Riccio, 1992; Lawson et al., 2002) or flicker produced by the display. Several researchers have reported that displays with a wide FOV provide a more compelling sensation of vection as well as a better orientation within the simulated environment (Hettinger et al., 1990; Kennedy, Fowlkes, et al., 1989; Padmos & Milders, 1992; Pausch et al., 1992), but are also more likely to produce sickness symptoms (Hettinger, 2002; Hettinger & Riccio, 1992). Moreover, Durlach and Mavor (1995) reported that greater levels of motion sickness are produced when users make head movements in VE displays that induce vection. Sensitivity to flicker is greater in peripheral vision than in foveal (that is, central) vision (Boff & Lincoln, 1988b); thus, a wider FOV display will increase the likelihood that the user will perceive flicker because more of the peripheral vision will be stimulated (Pausch et al., 1992). Flicker is not only distracting to the VE user, it can also induce symptoms of motion sickness, particularly those related to the visual system (La Viola, 2000).

Viewing Region
The viewing region of a display is the area in which the system user is able to maintain an image of the simulated scene (Padmos & Milders, 1992). The design eye point, also referred to as the design eye, is the point located in the geometric center of the viewing region, the optimal position for the user to view the display (Pausch et al., 1992). Kennedy, Fowlkes, et al. (1989) explained that graphic displays such as those used in simulators only provide an accurate visual representation when they are viewed from the design eye (see also Kennedy, Berbaum, et al., 1987). Consequently, the visual image becomes increasingly distorted as

the eccentric distance from the design eye point increases (Padmos & Milders, 1992; Pausch et al., 1992), which can increase sickness (Kennedy, Fowlkes, et al., 1989).

Optical distortion can also occur in HMD based systems when there is a discrepancy between the interpupillary distance of the user (discussed in a later section) and the optical centers of the HMD display screens (Wilson, 1996; Mon-Williams, Wann, & Rushton, 1993). Moreover, optical distortions are generally likely with HMD based systems because the lenses are imperfect (Wilson, 1996). Prismatic distortions from the lenses could occur if the individual is not looking through the center of the lenses, such as when the headset is not properly adjusted or while the user looks around the visual environment (Wilson, 1996). Relatedly, a high degree of optical magnification is required to transfer the simulated scene on the small HMD display screens into a real world size image on the retina, and greater geometric image distortions occur as the degree of magnification increases because the display screens are positioned about an inch in front of the eyes (that is, a fixed close viewing distance), which can increase sickness (Durlach & Mavor, 1995).

Temporal Delays

VE systems are controlled by computers that must perform a large number of calculations in order to (1) generate the simulated visual imagery, (2) control the inertial or position tracking system, and (3) monitor and respond to the control inputs of the system user (Frank, Casali, & Wierwille, 1988). As the number of required calculations increases due to factors such as an increase in scene complexity, the temporal delay between a user's input to the system and subsequent changes in the system output, in terms of the visual display and motion-base, can also increase (Frank et al., 1988). Other factors that can affect computational and rendering speeds include wider FOV displays, higher image resolution, and visual scene changes that accommodate head movements (Durlach & Mavor, 1995). Moreover, Frank et al. (1988) asserted that separate computers with different update rates are often used for the visual and motion systems in simulators, which can exacerbate temporal delays and thereby make the visual-inertial delays asynchronous. While temporal delays can obviously affect the user's performance, temporal lags in VE systems also have the potential to contribute to sickness (Wilson, 1997). The factors that limit temporal resolution include display refresh rate, update rate, and system latency (Durlach & Mavor, 1995).

Refresh Rate.   Refresh rate, or frame rate, is defined as the frequency with which an image is generated on the display (that is, the time required to update the visual image on the screen; Blade & Padgett, 2002). The interactive nature of VEs requires high frame rates, although the specific frame rate required in any particular situation depends on the type of environment simulated (Durlach & Mavor, 1995). The refresh rate can affect the quality of the displayed images, but is also related to the perception of flicker (Durlach & Mavor, 1995; Wilson, 1996). Specifically, the refresh rate can interact with luminance (that is, the brightness or intensity of the light coming from the display) to produce flicker, which contributes to visual fatigue and sickness (Padmos & Milders, 1992; Pausch et al., 1992). For instance, higher luminance levels and higher contrast levels are known to increase flicker sensitivity while slower refresh rates can promote flicker in the visual display (Boff & Lincoln, 1988a). However, because of the interaction of refresh rate, luminance, and contrast, in order to suppress flicker the refresh rate must increase as luminance and contrast increase or vice versa (Pausch et al., 1992).

Durlach and Mavor (1995) asserted that the typical luminance level in HMD displays was sufficient to cause flicker for frame rates of 30 hertz (Hz) or less. Relatedly, La Viola (2000) suggested that perceived flicker could be eliminated in the fovea with a 30 Hz refresh rate, but a higher refresh rate was required to eliminate flicker in the periphery for large targets. Since sensitivity to flicker increases with larger FOVs, faster refresh rates (that is, 80 to 90 Hz) may also be required in FOVs larger than 70° in order to avoid flicker (Padmos & Milders, 1992). Therefore, May and Badcock (2002) suggested that with current display luminances, a frame rate of at least 120 Hz was required to avoid flicker (see also Bridgeman, 1995).

Update Rate.   Update rate, the rate or frequency with which a new image is generated and shown on the visual display, is typically measured in frames per second (fps; Padmos & Milders, 1992). The update rate is determined by the power of the computer hardware (that is, the computational speed) and is inversely related to the complexity of the visual scene (Dulach & Mavor, 1995; Pausch et al., 1992; Wilson, 1996). In other words, there is a trade-off between display update rate and visual scene complexity where faster update rates limit the level of visual complexity available (Wilson, 1997). For example, Wilson noted that a 30 fps update rate is a "comfortable" rate for the eye because it is similar to watching a video, but more detailed and complex applications can only support 10 to 20 fps.

A low update rate can cause the images in the visual display to shake and create contour distortions (Padmos & Milders, 1992), which can produce disorientation and other symptoms of motion sickness (May & Badcock, 2002). For example, Durlach and Mavor (1995) noted that update rates below 12 Hz can induce sickness. Therefore, the authors suggested that the minimum update rate for HMD systems is 12 fps in order for the display motion to be perceived as smooth and to provide some realism in the visual dynamics (see also Wilson, 1996). In computer-generated imagery (CGI) simulator displays (discussed in a later section), the maximum update frequency also depends on the complexity of the visual scene (that is, the number of polygons to be processed) as well as the total number of pixels that can be processed each second (that is, the pixel fill rate; Padmos & Milders, 1992). The authors noted that 30 Hz would be a sufficient update frequency for many simulator applications, but higher update frequencies would be required when faster angular speeds of displayed objects were used to avoid shaking images. However, Wilson (1996) indicated that update rate and system latency (discussed in the next section) are independent, so even with a fast update rate there may still be lags in the system that can cause disorientation.

System Latency. VEs are computer based systems, so computational limitations of the equipment can produce a temporal delay between operator input and subsequent changes to the visual display (Kennedy, Fowlkes, et al., 1989). In the scientific literature, various terms have been used for this type of delay including system lag/latency, system update rate, image delay, or transport delay. System latency is a combination of (1) the sampling time of the input controls, (2) the time to calculate a viewpoint change, and (3) the time between position change input from the host computer to the visual display system and rendering of the corresponding image (Padmos & Milders, 1992).

A large degree of system latency can affect the user's control of the simulated environment and can increase sickness (Padmos & Milders, 1992). Previous research in flight simulators has shown that when large system delays were present, pilots were unable to accurately predict the length of the delay, which caused them to base their current actions on a guess of the vehicle's position following their previous control input (Pausch et al., 1992). The authors reported that this technique, sometimes referred to as "guess and lead the system," usually failed and caused the pilot to overcompensate control of the vehicle, which produced oscillations. Consequently, abnormal accelerations caused by the operator-induced oscillations increased the potential for simulator sickness because very low frequency motion or visual distortions were produced as a result of the increased load on the computer (Kennedy, Berbaum, et al., 1995). Accordingly, system delays should be no more than 40 to 80 milliseconds (ms) in driving simulators and 100 to 150 ms in flight simulators (Padmos & Milders, 1992).

In HMD based systems, system lag or latency is defined as the amount of time required to send a signal from the position tracker (discussed in the next section) and subsequent presentation of the image on the display (Wilson, 1996)—in other words, the time between when an individual moves within the environment and when the movement is reflected in the visual scene. System lag in HMD based systems is composed of the position tracker delay, the delay in sending the position information to the computer, and the delay in processing the information and creating the image (Wilson, 1996).

System latencies of 100 ms or greater have been shown to induce sickness symptoms (Wilson, 1996). For example, DiZio and Lackner (1997) investigated the effects of system delay (that is, delay between head movements and updates to the visual scene) on motion sickness where system update delay (67, 100, 200, and 300 ms) and FOV (wide [126° × 72°] versus halving the linear dimension) were varied. The study found that significant motion sickness symptoms, including nausea, were induced in the shortest delay condition, and the severity of sickness increased monotonically with system delay. However, the results also showed that reducing the FOV reduced the effect of the update delay on sickness (that is, the severity of motion sickness was cut in half in the decreased FOV condition with a 200 ms system delay).

Features Specific to HMD Based Systems

The equipment features specific to HMD based systems that have been implicated as factors influencing sickness include the type of visual display, interpupillary distance, helmet weight, and position tracker.

Visual Display Type

HMDs typically contain two liquid crystal displays with magnifying optics positioned in front of each eye (Rinalducci, 1996). The displays are either binocular or biocular. Binocular displays present a slightly different image to each eye with some degree of overlap (about 60°) that provides stereoscopic depth information (that is, cues for the distance of objects) similar to viewing objects in the real world (Mon-Williams & Wann, 1998; Wann & Mon-Williams, 2002). Conversely, biocular displays present identical images to each eye so depth cues are not available (Mon-Williams & Wann, 1998).

Because humans have two eyes with some degree of spacing between them, a slightly different image is seen by both eyes when viewing an object under normal viewing conditions, which provides the ability to judge relative depth (that is, to see very small differences in depth; Rinalducci, 1996). Thus, when viewing a near object, our eyes turn inward together (that is, convergence) in order to see the object as a single entity and the curvature of the lens changes to focus the image on the retina (that is, accommodation; Ebenholtz, 2001; May & Badcock, 2002). Furthermore, accommodation and convergence are cross-linked so the eyes normally converge and accommodate for the same distance, and accommodation produces convergence and vice versa (Mon-Williams & Wann, 1998). In a stereoscopic HMD, the display is positioned only about an inch away from the eyes, but the images presented on the screens can show objects positioned at different optical distances (for example, 10 feet [ft], 100 ft, and so forth; Wilson, 1996). Accommodation is therefore fixed to the distance of the display in order to focus the displayed images, whereas the degree of convergence changes relative to the distance of the virtual objects being viewed (Rinalducci, 1996; Wann & Mon-Williams, 2002). Consequently, the normal accommodation-convergence relationship is disrupted because there is a mismatch between the amount of convergence and accommodation needed to view the display, resulting in symptoms such as eyestrain or headache (Ebenholtz, 1992; Kennedy, Berbaum, et al., 1987).

Several empirical studies have evaluated the effects of binocular and biocular system use on the visual system. Mon-Williams et al. (1993) examined the effects of using a binocular HMD on the visual system and found deficits in binocular vision after a relatively brief exposure (that is, 10 minutes). Participants also reported symptoms related to disturbances of the visual system including blurred vision, eyestrain, headache, difficulty focusing, and several participants also reported nausea. Rushton, Mon-Williams, and Wann (1994) hypothesized that the primary cause of the visual deficits found in the Mon-Williams et al. study was the conflict between the stereoscopic depth cues, image disparity, and focal depth (that is, the information that produced a conflict in accommodation and convergence). Therefore, they replicated the study using a biocular display and larger sample size. Biocular displays present the same image to each eye, so there is no dissociation between convergence and accommodation (Wilson, 1996). In contrast to the Mon-Williams et al. study, no significant changes in binocular visual performance were found for exposure periods of up to 30 minutes. Additionally, compared to the sickness found in the previous study, only a few participants reported mild symptoms of visual strain.

Mon-Williams and Wann (1998) later demonstrated that even during relatively short exposures (that is, 10 minutes) to a binocular HMD, a continual conflict between accommodation and convergence caused stress on the visual system. Study participants reported adverse visual symptoms (for example, eyestrain and headache) and measurable changes in visual functioning. Therefore, the authors concluded that the differences in effects on the visual system between binocular and biocular displays found in their previous studies were due to accommodation-convergence conflicts rather than the stereoscopic depth information provided in binocular displays. Based on their findings, the investigators also expressed concern that the changes in participants' visual functioning from exposure to the HMD could affect subsequent performance on visually demanding tasks such as driving. Thus, stereoscopic systems may support better task performance, but they also increase the likelihood for visual side effects compared to biocular displays because of the inherent conflict between accommodation and convergence (Wann & Mon-Williams, 2002; Wilson, 1996).

Interpupillary Distance

Some HMDs provide the ability to adjust the lateral distance between the eyepieces (that is, the display screens) in order to accommodate differences in the interpupillary distance (IPD) of the users, but others provide only a fixed distance between the optical centers of the display lenses (Mon-Williams et al., 1993). However, as mentioned previously, a discrepancy between the IPD and the optical centers of the display screens can create optical distortions in the visual imagery, which can produce stress on the visual system and increase sickness symptoms (Mon-Williams et al., 1993, 1995; Rushton et al., 1994; Wilson, 1996).

Helmet Weight

The weight of an HMD can vary from four ounces to more than five pounds (McCauley-Bell, 2002). However, changing the weight of the head alters the inertia of the head, which can be extremely provocative (Durlach & Mavor, 1995). Most HMDs are also coupled with a position tracking device that necessitates head movements in order to change the viewpoint of the simulated visual scene. DiZio and Lackner (1992) argued that the weight of an HMD creates sensorimotor rearrangements during head movements, which can increase sickness. They also noted that an HMD that weighs 2.5 pounds increases the effective weight of the head by at least 20 percent. Similarly, Durlach and Mavor (1995) pointed out that wearing an HMD that increased the weight of the head by

50 percent can, in general, increase a person's susceptibility to motion sickness during exposure to angular acceleration. For instance, DiZio and Lackner (1992) discussed the results of a study where participants were exposed to periodic angular accelerations and decelerations in a rotating chair. Motion sickness symptoms were more severe in participants wearing a weighted helmet during exposure than those with no load on their head.

Position Tracker

An important component of HMD based systems is the ability to detect and track the position and the orientation of the user's head in order to identify where the individual is looking within the environment and make appropriate changes to the simulated scene (Durlach & Mavor, 1995; Wilson, 1996). The majority of HMDs are directly coupled to the motion of the user's head using a position tracking system (Durlach & Mavor, 1995). A position tracker, consisting of sensors mounted to the HMD, first determines the position and orientation of the user's head and then transfers the information to the processing computer, which generates and renders an image that corresponds to a viewpoint change in the simulated scene based on the user's head movements (Biocca, 1992; Wilson, 1996). The accuracy of position information provided by a head tracker can vary, and as a result, can influence the incidence of sickness symptoms (La Viola, 2000). For instance, a study by Bolas (as cited in Wilson, 1996) indicated that nausea was a consequence of "poorly tracked systems, with slow response and noise in the tracking system" (p. 43). Additionally, the stability of the information provided by some tracking devices can produce jitter and, thus, distortion in the visual image that can induce sickness symptoms (La Viola, 2000).

Another temporal constraint of many VE systems is the lag associated with position tracking systems, which has been cited as the major factor contributing to update delays in HMD images (Durlach & Mavor, 1995). Delays between a tracker system acquiring position information and the viewpoint update on the screen can range from 10 to 250 ms for commonly used electromagnetic tracking systems (Draper, Viirre, Furness, & Gawron, 2001). Moreover, DiZio and Lackner (1992) asserted that temporal distortions in the visual display occur because "the visual displays and head tracking devices do not match human capabilities and graphics systems cannot keep up with rapid human movements" (p. 322). The latency of a position tracker is based on the time required to register the user's position or movement and send the information to the processor (Wilson, 1997). Once the signal is received by the processor, there is another delay in processing the position information and rendering the update in the visual scene (Wilson, 1997).

If position tracker delays are present, the user may perceive a difference in what is represented within the visual scene and what he or she is doing in the real world (that is, a mismatch between head motion and the visual display), which can affect task performance as well as induce sickness symptoms including nausea or dizziness (Allison, Harris, Jenkin, Jasiobedzka, & Zacher, 2001; Hettinger & Riccio, 1992). Moreover, position tracker delays can be especially nauseogenic in wide FOV displays because larger head movements are needed to acquire targets in the peripheral field (Durlach & Mavor, 1995). Durlach and Mavor maintained that tracker-to-host computer rates must be at least 30 Hz because delays between head motion and visual feedback less than 60 ms may induce sickness, and they argued that position trackers should not contribute more than 10 ms to overall system latency. A study by Draper et al. (2001), however, provided an exception to the general findings reported in the literature. In their experiment, two time delays (125 ms and 250 ms) were created using a delay buffer between the head tracker and the image processing computer. Their findings revealed that sickness symptoms were induced by exposure to the HMD system, but contrary to the investigators' hypothesis, there was no significant effect of time delay on sickness.

Features Specific to Projection Based Systems

The equipment features specific to projection based systems that have been implicated as factors influencing sickness include CGI displays, collimation, platform type, motion frequency, and temporal lag.

CGI Displays

Many simulators employ multiple CRT visual displays using computer-generated imagery (Kennedy, Fowlkes, et al., 1989). However, misalignment of the CGI optical channels can cause distortion in visual images because the design eye from which all CGI channels could be viewed simultaneously is eliminated (Kennedy, Berbaum, et al., 1987; Kennedy & Fowlkes, 1992). Therefore, the same optical distortions that occur when users move their heads outside of the design eye (see the previous discussion on viewing region) can be created and increase sickness. Additionally, if the focus of the CGI channels is different, different accommodative distances would be required to view a scene that was imaged at infinity (Kennedy, Berbaum, et al., 1987). The authors indicated that the consequence of these repeated changes in accommodation can be symptoms such as eyestrain or headache and noted that the incidence and severity of eyestrain was higher in simulators with CGI displays than in those with dome displays. Moreover, Kennedy, Berbaum, et al. (1987) argued that the number of CGI optical channels was generally proportional to the number of symptoms reported.

Collimation

Collimation relates to the parallel alignment of the light rays emitted by the visual display, which places the image at optical infinity (Padmos & Milders, 1992). Collimated images are typically used to increase realism in the simulated environment by creating an illusion of depth in two-dimensional images. In simulators, collimated images from more than one image channel (that is, display) are often seamlessly combined using concave mirrors (Padmos & Milders, 1992). Kennedy (1996) explained that an improperly collimated system can produce negative convergence and accommodation that can contribute to simulator sickness, especially symptoms associated with disturbances of the visual system (for example, eyestrain, headache, and so forth).

Platform Type

Simulator platforms are either fixed- or motion-base. In a fixed-base simulator, information regarding motion is provided solely by the visual display system, whereas motion-base simulators provide a subset of the inertial forces that would be present during real movement in the vehicle being simulated (DiZio & Lackner, 1992; Durlach & Mavor, 1995). Specifically, a motion-base simulator can provide motion cues compatible with initial but not sustained acceleration using two types of inertial cues: acceleration and tilt (Kennedy, Berbaum, et al., 1987). McCauley and Sharkey (1992) indicated that the hydraulic motion-base typically used on simulators provides six axes of movement with ±35° of angular displacement and two meters of linear displacement. Although motion-base systems are extremely expensive, they are used in specific applications (for example, flight simulators) to enhance the sense of motion provided by the visual display (Durlach & Mavor, 1995). However, visual movement through a simulated environment that is not accompanied by the normal inertial cues (that is, forces and accelerations) associated with movement through the real environment can induce sickness, particularly nausea (May & Badcock, 2002; McCauley & Sharkey, 1992). Consequently, the overall incidence of sickness is typically lower in simulators with a motion-base than those with a fixed-base (McCauley, 1984). Kennedy, Berbaum, et al. (1987) suggested that one reason for the lower incidence of sickness was due to differences in pilot head movements during exposure. The authors explained that in a motion-base simulator, pilots' head movements were similar to those in the actual vehicle, whereas the head movements in fixed-base simulators were often in conflict with the inertial stimulus, which increased the provocativeness of the simulation. There have, however, been a few reports that contradict the general findings of a difference in sickness incidence between fixed- and motion-base simulators (McCauley & Sharkey, 1992).

Motion Frequency

A strong relationship between sickness incidence and exposure to very low frequency whole-body vibration has been found in a variety of provocative motion environments including ships at sea, planes, automobiles, trains, and motion-base simulators (Guignard & McCauley, 1990). Research has indicated that the most nauseogenic frequency of motion is centered around 0.2 Hz; the lower limit for nauseogenic motion is frequencies below 0.1 Hz, and a decline in acceleration-induced sickness also occurs at frequencies above 0.2 Hz (Guignard & McCauley, 1990). It is generally agreed that sickness incidence in motion-base simulators depends on the frequency and acceleration characteristics of the motion produced by the platform (Kennedy et al., 1990). Specifically, the incidence and severity of sickness is usually greatest when the energy spectra from the motion-base is in the very low frequency range of 0.2 Hz (Kennedy et al.,

1990; Lawson et al., 2002; McCauley, 1984). Kennedy, Berbaum, et al. (1987) also reported that motion sickness is proportional to the acceleration in a system, so 0.2 Hz is more nauseogenic than 0.5 Hz. Moreover, an examination of the sickness rates in several motion based flight simulators indicated that the simulators that produced linear oscillations in the range of 0.2 Hz showed significantly higher incidence and severity of simulator sickness than motion-base simulators with low levels of energy in the 0.2 Hz region (Kennedy, Allgood, Van Hoy, & Lilienthal, 1987; Van Hoy, Allgood, Lilienthal, Kennedy, & Hooper, 1987).

Temporal Lag

Inaccuracies in motion cueing created by temporal delays between the control inputs of the simulator user and subsequent changes in the visual display, motion-base, or both have been implicated as a contributing factor to the incidence of simulator sickness (Kennedy & Fowlkes, 1992; Kennedy et al., 1990; McCauley, 1984). For example, Frank et al. (1988) evaluated visual-motion coupling delays and cuing order in a driving simulator using different combinations of transport delays (0, 170, or 340 ms) in either the visual system, motion system, or both. Their results showed that zero delay in either system was the most desirable condition, whereas delays in the visual or motion system increased participants' overall severity of sickness. However, visual delays affected sickness incidence more than motion system delays and when asynchronous delays occurred between the visual and motion systems, sickness was greater when the motion system led the visual system. In contrast, Padmos and Milders (1992) indicated that the visual imaging system should not have a time lag with respect to the inertial system. The general recommendation for reducing the potential for sickness due to cue asynchrony is to limit the delay between any two system cues to no more than 35 ms (Lilienthal, as cited in Pausch et al., 1992). Kennedy, Berbaum, et al. (1987) also recommended that lag in the motion-base should not exceed 83 to 125 ms, and there should be no more than 40 ms asynchrony between visual and inertial cues.

IMPLICATIONS OF VE SICKNESS ON TRAINING

State-of-the-art and compellingly realistic VE systems currently exist, but the pervasiveness of deleterious side effects associated with exposure has the potential to limit the utilization of VE systems, particularly as a training device. Specifically, if humans are unable to effectively function in the VE, training objectives may be compromised or could result in a negative transfer of the training effect, which has the potential to affect subsequent performance on the real world task (Canaras, Gentner, & Schopper, 1995; Lathan, Tracey, Sebrechts, Clawson, & Higgins, 2002). McCauley (1984) pointed out that sickness symptoms could distract users and/or decrease their motivation during a simulation based training exercise and ultimately compromise the effectiveness of the training protocol (see Hettinger et al., 1990; Kennedy et al., 1990). Users that experience symptoms during a simulation may also learn new behaviors (that is, coping mechanisms) such as minimizing head movements, using only the instruments (that is, not looking at the visual displays), or avoiding aggressive maneuvers in order to avoid or reduce sickness symptoms (Baltzley, Kennedy, Berbaum, Lilienthal, & Gower, 1989; Hettinger et al., 1990; Kennedy et al., 1990; Kennedy, Lilienthal, et al., 1989). However, while these behaviors may be appropriate for the simulated task, they may not be appropriate for performing the corresponding real world tasks (Lathan et al., 2002; Pausch et al., 1992). Moreover, any negative transfer of training to the real world device could cause users to lose confidence in the training they receive from the simulator, resulting in decreased simulator usage (McCauley, 1984; Pausch et al., 1992). Similarly, once a user experiences sickness, he or she may be reluctant to return to the VE for subsequent training or, alternatively, could disengage some of the system features (for example, the motion-base) to reduce the potential sickness (Crowley, 1987; McCauley, 1984). Individuals experiencing side effects may also be unwilling or unable to remain in the environment. Consequently, a proportion of those exposed may prematurely cease their interaction with the VE system prior to training completion. Furthermore, if the sickness problem is too severe and cannot be remedied, the device could be discarded, like the helicopter simulator reviewed in Miller and Goodson (1960). For the company that owns the VE system, both of these situations have economic implications associated with the purchase of equipment, either specific components or the entire system, which cannot be used.

The side effects of exposure to VE systems also have the potential to jeopardize the health and/or safety of users. One such threat is the persistence of symptoms (that is, aftereffects) for a prolonged period of time following termination of exposure to the system. Baltzley et al. (1989) investigated the time course of recovery from simulator sickness and found 75 percent of the pilots who experienced symptoms indicated the symptoms dissipated within one hour after simulator exposure. Of greater concern to user safety, however, was the authors' findings that indicated that 13 percent of all military pilots exposed to different simulators reported aftereffects that persisted more than four hours after exposure to the device; 8 percent experienced symptoms for six or more hours. Likewise, Stanney and Kennedy (1998) reported persistent aftereffects from exposure to an HMD based system; participants were still reporting significant levels of symptoms one hour after exposure to the device. Specifically, disorientation-type symptoms (for example, dizziness) were 95 times higher, gastrointestinal-related symptoms (for example, nausea) were 10 times higher, and visual disturbances (for example, eyestrain) were 7 times higher than pre-exposure levels. Unfortunately, the study was not designed to evaluate the time course of symptom recovery beyond the one hour post-exposure period. Extreme cases of prolonged VE aftereffects have also been reported. For example, Viirre and Ellisman (2003) reported that after a researcher used a desktop VE for 10 minutes, the user only experienced postural instability for a few minutes immediately after exposure; however, several hours later, there was an onset of vertigo and nausea that persisted for *four* days.

Additional threats to user safety occur when the side effects of VE exposure appear after the user has left the VE facility. One potential safety hazard is delayed effects; a user is symptom-free during or immediately following exposure to a VE, but symptom onset occurs during some period of time subsequent to stimulus exposure (Baltzley et al., 1989). For example, Miller and Goodson (1960) reported that while most of the individuals exposed to a helicopter simulator experienced sickness symptoms during the exposure, some users did not experience any symptoms until several hours after leaving the simulator. Of particular concern for users' safety was the authors' report of a flight instructor who was forced to stop his car and walk around in order to reduce the disorientation he was experiencing as a delayed effect of his earlier exposure to the simulator. Another threat to user safety is flashbacks, which occur when symptoms cease once exposure to a provocative stimulus is terminated, but symptom onset suddenly reoccurs later (Baltzley et al., 1989). McCauley (1984) cited a 1980 study by Kellogg et al. where pilots reported visual flashbacks that occurred 8 to 10 hours after exposure to a fixed-base flight simulator. Similarly, Stanney and Kennedy (1998) found that approximately 31 percent of the participants in their study reported flashbacks following VR exposure.

In response to reports of prolonged and delayed aftereffects, the military instituted mandatory grounding policies for post-simulator flights in order to guard against the negative aftereffects that can occur subsequent to training in a flight simulator (Crowley, 1987; Kennedy et al., 1992). A simulator sickness field manual, developed by the U.S. Department of Defense and distributed to all military simulator sites, stated that flight personnel should be grounded (that is, flights should not be scheduled) for at least 24 hours after simulator exposure or 12 hours after simulator sickness symptoms have subsided, whichever is longer (Naval Training Systems Center, 1989). Obviously, restrictions on the post-simulator activities of flight personnel can affect operational readiness, but the military also recognized the potential risk to pilots as well as to the expensive equipment under their control (Kennedy et al., 1990). Recently, the Department of the Navy (2004) issued an update to the NATOPS (Naval Air Training and Operating Procedures Standardization) General Flight and Operating Instructions that included policy and procedural guidelines on simulator sickness. In addition to warnings about the occurrence of prolonged and delayed aftereffects, the aviation safety instructions also mandated that (1) flight personnel experiencing simulator sickness abstain from flight duties on the day of simulator exposure and (2) flight personnel who have previously experienced simulator sickness cannot be scheduled for flight duty for at least 24 hours following exposure to a simulator.

Clearly, prolonged aftereffects, delayed effects, and flashbacks can present a significant threat to the afflicted user's activities for a considerable period of time following exposure. Kennedy and Stanney (1996) indicated that these types of long-term aftereffects occur in less than 10 percent of all flight simulator exposures. An overall incidence rate for HMD based systems has not been reported, although long-term aftereffects data from one study showed that 35 percent of participants reported symptoms more than four hours after exposure and

17 percent reported symptoms the following morning (Stanney, Kennedy, & Kingdon, 2002). Kennedy and Stanney (1996) also suggested that, compared to flight simulators, the advanced technology in VR displays will produce "an even more serious level of impairment" (p. 61). Nevertheless, long-term aftereffects create the potential for the legal liability of VE designers, manufacturers, and system owners if an accident occurs as a result of VE exposure. It has been suggested that disorientation-type aftereffects such as dizziness have the greatest potential for causing personal injury (Baltzley et al., 1989). Disorientation, drowsiness, fatigue, and nausea, which are frequently reported following exposure to VE systems, can also affect an individual's ability to safely perform routine tasks such as walking, riding a bicycle, or operating a motorized vehicle (Kennedy, Kennedy, & Bartlett, 2002). If an accident occurs after the user is released from the VE facility and the cause can be associated with the aftereffects of VE exposure, the manufacturer or company that owns the VE device could be found legally liable and, thus, be required to pay compensation for damages (Kennedy et al., 2002). At a minimum, the manufacturer or company could face costly and time consuming litigation in order to defend a product liability claim.

As VE technologies continue to develop, it is anticipated that VE systems will become less expensive and, thus, more widely accessible to diverse populations. The number of people who could experience adverse side effects will also increase resulting in a greater risk for product liability claims. Kennedy et al. (2002) therefore emphasized the need for manufacturers and owners of VE systems to take proactive steps in order to minimize their legal liability and outlined a seven-step system safety approach that could be used to assess the potential risks associated with the aftereffects of VE exposure to circumvent product liability issues.

REFERENCES

Allison, R. S., Harris, L. R., Jenkin, M., Jasiobedzka, U., & Zacher, J. E. (2001). Tolerance of temporal delay in virtual environments. *Proceedings of the IEEE Virtual Reality 2001 International Conference* (pp. 247–254). New York: IEEE.

Baltzley, D. R., Kennedy, R. S., Berbaum, K. S., Lilienthal, M. G., & Gower, D. W. (1989). The time course of postflight simulator sickness symptoms. *Aviation, Space, and Environmental Medicine, 60*(11), 1043–1048.

Biocca, F. (1992). Will simulator sickness slow down the diffusion of virtual environment technology? *Presence, 1*(3), 334–343.

Blade, R. A., & Padgett, M. (2002). Virtual environments standards and terminology. In K. M. Stanney (Ed.), *Handbook of virtual environments: Design, implementation, and applications* (pp. 15–27). Mahwah, NJ: Lawrence Erlbaum.

Boff, K. R., & Lincoln, J. E. (Eds.). (1988a). Flicker sensitivity: Effect of flicker frequency and luminance level. *Engineering data compendium: Human perception and performance, Vol. 1* (pp. 170–171). Wright-Patterson Air Force Base, OH: Aerospace Medical Research Laboratory.

Boff, K. R., & Lincoln, J. E. (Eds.). (1988b). Flicker sensitivity: Effect of target size. *Engineering data compendium: Human perception and performance, Vol. 1* (pp. 178–179). Wright-Patterson Air Force Base, OH: Aerospace Medical Research Laboratory.

Bowman, D. A., Datey, A., Ryu, Y. S., Farooq, U., & Vasnaik, O. (2002). Empirical comparison of human behavior and performance with different display devices for virtual environments. *Proceedings of the Human Factors and Ergonomics Society 46th Annual Meeting* (pp. 2134–2138). Santa Monica, CA: Human Factors and Ergonomics Society.

Bridgeman, B. (1995). Direction constancy in rapidly refreshed video displays. *Journal of Vestibular Research, 5*(6), 393–398.

Canaras, S. A., Gentner, F. C., Schopper, A. W. (1995, July). *Virtual reality (VR) training* (Final Rep. No. CSERIAC-RA-95-009). Wright Patterson Air Force Base, OH: Crew System Ergonomics Information Analysis Center.

Crowley, J. S. (1987). Simulator sickness: A problem for Army aviation. *Aviation, Space, and Environmental Medicine, 58*(4), 355–357.

Curry, R., Artz, B., Cathey, L., Grant, P., & Greenberg, J. (2002). Kennedy SSQ results: Fixed- vs. motion-base Ford simulators. *Proceedings of the Driving Simulation Conference "DSC2002"* (pp. 289–299).

Department of the Navy. (2004, March 1). *NATOPS General Flight and Operating Instructions (OPNAVINST 3710.7T), Section 8.3.2.17: Simulator sickness* (pp. 8–10). Washington, DC: Author.

DiZio, P., & Lackner, J. R. (1992). Spatial orientation, adaptation, and motion sickness in real and virtual environments. *Presence, 1*(3), 319–328.

DiZio, P., & Lackner, J. R. (1997). Circumventing side effects of immersive virtual environments. In M. J. Smith, G. Salvendy, & R. J. Koubek (Eds.), *Design of computing systems: Social and ergonomic considerations* (pp. 893–896). Amsterdam: Elsevier.

Draper, M. H., Viirre, E. S., Furness, T. A., & Gawron, V. J. (2001). Effects of image scale and system time delay on simulator sickness within head-coupled virtual environments. *Human Factors, 43*(1), 129–146.

Drexler, J. M. (2006). *Identification of system design features that affect sickness in virtual environments.* Unpublished doctoral dissertation, University of Central Florida, Orlando.

Drexler, J. M., Kennedy, R. S., & Compton, D. E. (2004, September). *Comparison of sickness profiles from simulator and virtual environment devices: Implications of engineering features.* Paper presented at the Driving Simulation Conference Europe "DSC 2004," Paris, France.

Durlach, N. I., & Mavor, A. S. (Eds.). (1995). *Virtual reality: Scientific and technological challenges.* Washington, DC: National Academy Press.

Ebenholtz, S. M. (1992). Motion sickness and oculomotor systems in virtual environments. *Presence, 1*(3), 302–305.

Ebenholtz, S. M. (2001). *Oculomotor systems and perception.* Cambridge, United Kingdom: Cambridge University Press.

Frank, L. H., Casali, J. H., & Wierwille, W. W. (1988). Effects on visual display and motion system delays on operator performance and uneasiness in a driving simulator. *Human Factors, 30*(2), 201–217.

Gower, D. W., Lilienthal, M. G., Kennedy, R. S., & Fowlkes, J. E. (1987, September). Simulator sickness in U.S. Army and Navy fixed- and rotary-wing flight simulators. In *Conference Proceedings of the AGARD Medical Panel Symposium on Motion Cues in Flight Simulation and Simulator Induced Sickness* (AGARD-CP-433; pp. 8.1–8.20). Neuilly-sur-Seine, France: Advisory Group for Aerospace Research and Development.

Guignard, J. C., & McCauley, M. E. (1990). The accelerative stimulus for motion sickness. In G. H. Crampton (Ed.), *Motion and space sickness* (pp. 123–152). Boca Raton, FL: CRC Press.

Hettinger, L. J. (2002). Illusory self-motion in virtual environments. In K. M. Stanney (Ed.), *Handbook of virtual environments: Design, implementation, and applications* (pp. 471–491). Mahwah, NJ: Lawrence Erlbaum.

Hettinger, L. J., Berbaum, K. S., Kennedy, R. S., Dunlap, W. P., & Nolan, M. D. (1990). Vection and simulator sickness. *Military Psychology, 2*(3), 171–181.

Hettinger, L. J., & Riccio, G. E. (1992). Visually induced motion sickness in virtual environments. *Presence, 1*(3), 306–310.

Kennedy, R. S. (1996). *Analysis of simulator sickness data* (Technical Rep., Contract No. N61339-91-D-0004). Orlando, FL: Naval Air Warfare Center, Training Systems Division.

Kennedy, R. S., Allgood, G. O., Van Hoy, B. W., & Lilienthal, M. G. (1987, June). Motion sickness symptoms and postural changes following flights in motion-based flight trainers. *Journal of Low Frequency Noise and Vibration, 6*(4), 147–154.

Kennedy, R. S., Berbaum, K. S., Dunlap, W. P., & Smith, M. G. (1995, October). *Correlating visual scene elements with simulator sickness incidence: Hardware and software development* (Phase II Final Rep., Contract No. N00019-92-C-0157). Washington, DC: Naval Air Systems Command.

Kennedy, R. S., Berbaum, K. S., Lilienthal, M. G., Dunlap, W. P., Mulligan, B. E., & Funaro, J. F. (1987). *Guidelines for alleviation of simulator sickness symptomatology* (Final Rep. No. NAVTRASYSCEN TR-87-007). Orlando, FL: Naval Training Systems Center.

Kennedy, R. S., Berbaum, K. S., & Smith, M. G. (1993). Methods for correlating visual scene elements with simulator sickness incidence. *Proceedings of the 37th Annual Meeting of the Human Factors Society* (pp. 1252–1256). Santa Monica, CA: Human Factors and Ergonomics Society.

Kennedy, R. S., Drexler, J. M., & Compton, D. E. (1997). Simulator sickness and other aftereffects: Implications for the design of driving simulators. *Proceedings of the Driving Simulation Conference (DSC'97;* pp. 115–123). Paris, France: ETNA.

Kennedy, R. S., Drexler, J. M., Compton, D. E., Stanney, K. M., Lanham, D. S., & Harm, D. L. (2003). Configural scoring of simulator sickness, cybersickness and space adaptation syndrome: Similarities and differences. In L. J. Hettinger & M. W. Haas (Eds.), *Virtual and adaptive environments: Applications, implications, and human performance* (pp. 247–278). Mahwah, NJ: Lawrence Erlbaum.

Kennedy, R. S., Dunlap, W. P., Jones, M. B., & Stanney, K. M. (1996). *Screening users of virtual reality systems for after-effects such as motion sickness and balance problems* (Final Rep. No. NSF1-96-4). Arlington, VA: National Science Foundation.

Kennedy, R. S., & Fowlkes, J. E. (1992). Simulator sickness is polygenic and polysymptomatic: Implications for research. *International Journal of Aviation Psychology, 2*(1), 23–38.

Kennedy, R. S., Fowlkes, J. E., & Hettinger, L. J. (1989). *Review of simulator sickness literature* (Technical Rep. No. NTSC TR89-024). Orlando, FL: Naval Training Systems Center.

Kennedy, R. S., Fowlkes, J. E., & Lilienthal, M. G. (1993). Postural and performance changes following exposures to flight simulators. *Aviation, Space, and Environmental Medicine, 64,* 912–920.

Kennedy, R. S., Hettinger, L. J., & Lilienthal, M. G. (1990). Simulator sickness. In G. H. Crampton (Ed.), *Motion and space sickness* (pp. 317–341). Boca Raton, FL: CRC Press.

Kennedy, R. S., Jones, M. B., & Dunlap, W. P. (1996). A predictive model of simulator sickness: Applications for virtual reality [Abstract]. *Aviation, Space, and Environmental Medicine, 67*(7), 672.

Kennedy, R. S., Jones, M. B., Lilienthal, M. G., & Harm, D. L. (1994). Profile analysis of after-effects experienced during exposure to several virtual reality environments. In *Conference Proceedings of the AGARD Medical Panel Symposium on Virtual Interface: Research & Applications* (AGARD-CP-541; pp. 2.1–2.9). Neuilly-sur-Seine, France: Advisory Group for Aerospace Research and Development.

Kennedy, R. S., Jones, M. B., Stanney, K. M., Ritter, A., & Drexler, J. M. (1996). *Human factors safety testing for virtual environment mission-operations training* (Final Rep. No. NASA1-96-2). Houston, TX: NASA Johnson Space Center.

Kennedy, R. S., Kennedy, K. E., & Bartlett, K. M. (2002). Virtual environments and product liability. In K. M. Stanney (Ed.), *Handbook of virtual environments: Design, implementation, and applications* (pp. 543–553). Mahwah, NJ: Lawrence Erlbaum.

Kennedy, R. S., Lane, N. E., Lilienthal, M. G., Berbaum, K. S., & Hettinger, L. J. (1992). Profile analysis of simulator sickness symptoms: Application to virtual environment systems. *Presence, 1*(3), 295–301.

Kennedy, R. S., & Lilienthal, M. G. (1994). Measurement and control of motion sickness aftereffects from immersion in virtual reality. *Proceedings of Virtual Reality and Medicine, The Cutting Edge* (pp. 111–119). New York: SIG-Advanced Applications, Inc.

Kennedy, R. S., Lilienthal, M. G., Berbaum, K. S., Baltzley, D. R., & McCauley, M. E. (1989). Simulator sickness in U.S. Navy flight simulators. *Aviation, Space, and Environmental Medicine, 60,* 10–16.

Kennedy, R. S., & Smith, M. G. (1996, November). *A smart system to control stimulation for visually induced motion sickness* (Phase II Final Report No. NAS9-19106). Houston, TX: NASA Lyndon B. Johnson Space Center.

Kennedy, R. S., & Stanney, K. M. (1996). Virtual reality systems and products liability. *The Journal of Medicine and Virtual Reality, 1*(2), 60–64.

Kenyon, R. V., & Afenya, M. B. (1995). Training in virtual and real environments. *Annals of Biomedical Engineering, 23,* 445–455.

Kolasinski, E. M. (1995, May). *Simulator sickness in virtual environments* (ARI Tech. Rep. No. 1027). Alexandria, VA: U.S. Army Research Institute for the Behavioral and Social Sciences.

Lampton, D. R., Kraemer, R. E., Kolasinski, E. M., & Knerr, B. W. (1995, October). *An investigation of simulator sickness in a tank driver trainer* (ARI Rep. No. 1684). Orlando, FL: U.S. Army Research Institute for the Behavioral and Social Sciences.

Lathan, C. E., Tracey, M. R., Sebrechts, M. M., Clawson, D. M., & Higgins, G. A. (2002). Using virtual environments as training simulators: Measuring transfer. In K. M. Stanney (Ed.), *Handbook of virtual environments: Design, implementation, and applications* (pp. 403–414). Mahwah, NJ: Lawrence Erlbaum.

La Viola, J. J., Jr. (2000). A discussion of cybersickness in virtual environments. *SIGCHI Bulletin, 32*(1), 47–56.

Lawson, B. D., Graeber, D. A., Mead, A. M., & Muth, E. R. (2002). Signs and symptoms of human syndromes associated with synthetic experiences. In K. M. Stanney (Ed.),

Handbook of virtual environments: Design, implementation, and applications (pp. 589–618). Mahwah, NJ: Lawrence Erlbaum.

Lerman, Y., Sadovsky, G., Goldberg, E., Kedem, R., Peritz, E., & Pines, A. (1993). Correlates of military tank simulator sickness. *Aviation, Space, and Environmental Medicine, 64*(7), 619–622.

Lin, J. J-W., Duh, H. B. L., Parker, D. E., Abi-Rached, H., & Furness, T. A. (2002). Effects of field of view on presence, enjoyment, memory, and simulator sickness in a virtual environment. *Proceedings of the IEEE Virtual Reality Conference 2002* (pp. 164–171). New York: IEEE.

Magee, L. E. (1995, March). *Virtual Reality Simulator (VRS) for training ship handling skills.* Paper presented at the NATO/OCTAN Research Study Group 16 "Advanced Technologies Applied to Training Design" Workshop: Virtual Environments Training's Future?, Portsmouth, England.

May, J. G., & Badcock, D. R. (2002). Vision and virtual environments. In K. M. Stanney (Ed.), *Handbook of virtual environments: Design, implementation, and applications* (pp. 29–63). Mahwah, NJ: Lawrence Erlbaum.

McCauley, M. E. (Ed.). (1984). *Simulator sickness: Proceedings of a workshop.* Washington, DC: National Academy Press.

McCauley, M. E., & Sharkey, T. J. (1992). Cybersickness: Perception of self-motion in virtual environments. *Presence, 1,* 311–318.

McCauley-Bell, P. R. (2002). Ergonomics in virtual environments. In K. M. Stanney (Ed.), *Handbook of virtual environments: Design, implementation, and applications* (pp. 807–826). Mahwah, NJ: Lawrence Erlbaum.

Miller, J. W., & Goodson, J. E. (1960). Motion sickness in a helicopter simulator. *Aerospace Medicine, 31*(3), 204–212.

Mon-Williams, M., & Wann, J. P. (1998). Binocular virtual reality displays: When problems do and don't occur. *Human Factors, 40*(1), 42–49.

Mon-Williams, M., Wann, J. P., & Rushton, S. (1993). Binocular vision in a virtual world: Visual deficits following the wearing of a head-mounted display. *Ophthalmic and Physiological Optics, 13,* 387–391.

Mon-Williams, M., Wann, J. P., & Rushton, S. (1995). Design factors in stereoscopic virtual-reality displays. *Journal of the SID, 3/4,* 207–210.

Naval Training Systems Center. (1989, October). *Simulator sickness field manual: MOD 4.* Orlando, FL: Author.

Padmos, P., & Milders, M. (1992). Quality criteria for simulator images: A literature review. *Human Factors, 34*(6), 727–748.

Pausch, R., Crea, T., & Conway, M. (1992). A literature survey for virtual environments: Military flight visual systems and simulator sickness. *Presence, 1*(3), 344–363.

Regan, E. C., & Price, K. R. (1994). The frequency of occurrence and severity of side-effects of immersion virtual reality. *Aviation, Space, and Environmental Medicine, 65,* 527–530.

Rinalducci, E. J. (1996). Characteristics of visual fidelity in the virtual environment. *Presence, 5*(3), 330–341.

Rushton, S., Mon-Williams, M., & Wann, J. P. (1994). Binocular vision in a bi-ocular world: New generation head-mounted displays avoid causing visual deficits. *Displays, 15*(4), 255–260.

Stanney, K. M., & Kennedy, R. S. (1998). Aftereffects from virtual environment exposure: How long do they last? *Proceedings of the Human Factors and Ergonomics Society*

42nd Annual Meeting (pp. 1476–1480). Santa Monica, CA: Human Factors and Ergonomics Society.

Stanney, K. M., Kennedy, R. S., & Drexler, J. M. (1997). Cybersickness is not simulator sickness. *Proceedings of the Human Factors and Ergonomics Society 41st Annual Meeting* (pp. 1138–1142). Santa Monica, CA: Human Factors and Ergonomics Society.

Stanney, K. M., Kennedy, R. S., & Kingdon, K. (2002). Virtual environment usage protocols. In K. M. Stanney (Ed.), *Handbook of virtual environments: Design, implementation, and applications* (pp. 721–730). Mahwah, NJ: Lawrence Erlbaum.

Ungs, T. J. (1988). Simulator induced syndrome in Coast Guard aviators. *Aviation, Space, and Environmental Medicine, 59*(3), 267–272.

Van Hoy, B. W., Allgood, G. O., Lilienthal, M. G., Kennedy, R. S., & Hooper, J. M. (1987). Inertial and control systems measurements of two motion-based flight simulators for evaluation of the incidence of simulator sickness. *Proceedings of the IMAGE IV Conference* (pp. 265–273). Phoenix, AZ: Image Society Incorporated.

Viirre, E., & Ellisman, M. (2003). Vertigo in virtual reality with haptics: Case report. *Cyberpsychology and Behavior, 6*(4), 429–431.

Wann, J. P., & Mon-Williams, M. (2002). Measurement of visual aftereffects following virtual environment exposure. In K. M. Stanney (Ed.), *Handbook of virtual environments: Design, implementation, and applications* (pp. 731–749). Mahwah, NJ: Lawrence Erlbaum.

Warner, H. D., Serfoss, G. L., Baruch, T. M., & Hubbard, D. C. (1993). *Flight simulator-induced sickness and visual displays evaluation* (Final Tech. Rep. No. AL/HR-TR-1993-0056). Brooks AFB: Armstrong Laboratory.

Wilson, J. R. (1996). Effects of participating in virtual environments: A review of current knowledge. *Safety Science, 23*(1), 39–51.

Wilson, J. R. (1997). Virtual environments and ergonomics: Needs and opportunities. *Ergonomics, 40*(10), 1057–1077.

Witmer, B. G., Bailey, J. H., & Knerr, B. W. (1996). Virtual spaces and real world places: Transfer of route knowledge. *International Journal of Human-Computer Studies, 45,* 413–428.

Chapter 12

EVALUATING VIRTUAL ENVIRONMENT COMPONENT TECHNOLOGIES

Mary Whitton and Fred Brooks

This chapter is about user studies designed to evaluate how the characteristics of the components of a virtual environment (VE) system affect the VE user's performance. As in this book section, *component* is defined broadly and encompasses hardware such as displays, software such as various rendering techniques, user interfaces that are part hardware and part software, and even complete VE systems.

We illustrate the diversity of the experimental design, metrics, and analysis techniques required to perform evaluations. We focus on participant tasks and metrics, what works and what does not work, and what we learned about doing evaluation. Some lessons follow directly from the studies; some are more general. The references provide details of the studies and review related literature.

This is not a primer on experimental design and statistics. For those new to user studies, we recommend Martin (2007) or Field and Hole (2003). Both are introductory and easy to read. Martin focuses on designing experiments, with an appendix on statistics; Field and Hole briefly cover experiment design and treat statistics in more detail. Berg (2006) comprehensively covers research methods in the social sciences, including such ethnographic techniques as observations and critical-incident interviews.

We treat, in turn, evaluations related to sensory-input fidelity, user interfaces, and system performance. We conclude with comments about the role of evaluation in system design. The studies described here mostly draw on work done from 1998 to 2007 by graduate students in the Effective Virtual Environments research group at The University of North Carolina (UNC) at Chapel Hill.

WHY EVALUATE COMPONENT TECHNOLOGIES?

Evaluating component technologies early in the design process results in better component selection, shorter development time, lower deployment costs, and more satisfied users and sponsor. To effectively isolate the performance of the component under test and to minimize potential confounds, it is useful to test the component embedded in a system with known performance characteristics. The test setting must, however, be able to stress the component at the performance levels required by the final system and application.

The earlier a problem is found, the less expensive—in both time and money—it is to fix. Consequently, evaluation—particularly usability evaluation—should not be a one-time event, but should be a series of evaluations performed during the design and development process. One does not want to find out in the field that users will not accept the display selected because it is not bright enough for the desert. Testing before final component selection leads to lower overall deployment costs since one avoids buying unneeded capability. If the impact of a component on user performance is evaluated beforehand, when budget constraints dictate the selection of a less capable component, designers know exactly what performance is being given up.

WHAT SHOULD BE EVALUATED AND HOW?

The task to be trained drives the level of performance required of the components, whether the component is the acuity required in the display or the behavioral fidelity of semi-automated entities. One type of evaluation compares performance achieved with other techniques for doing the same thing. The different techniques are the levels of the independent variable. An example is the study "Managing Avatar-Object Collisions" that compares the UNC-developed MAC-BETH (managing avatar conflict by a technique hybrid) method of managing avatar-object collisions to published rubber-band and constant offset methods (Burns, Razzaque, Whitton, & Brooks, 2007).

Another type of evaluation compares several levels of performance of a single component technology. An example is comparing performance in systems with different rendering *frame update rates* (Meehan, Insko, Whitton, & Brooks, 2002). We measured physiological response to our visual-cliff environment (hereafter called the *Pit*) at four frame update rates. First we had to develop a system that achieved the best update rate possible with then-available components. We then defined three additional levels of the independent variable by artificially reducing the frame update rate in the VE system. Once the independent variable levels were in place, we designed and executed a user study with dependent variables and measures appropriate to the component and task.

We have found two rounds of testing to be useful. First, we evaluate the component in a constrained environment that allows tight control of potential confounding factors. Second, we perform a more ecologically valid evaluation; that is, we design an evaluation task, setting, and scenario that approximate, to the extent possible in a university laboratory, a task, setting, and scenario in which the component will actually be used.

Component testing does not obviate testing the performance of completed systems and testing the efficacy of the final application. Evaluating the effect of end-to-end system latency on task performance is an example of the former; Volume 3, Section 2 of this handbook is devoted to training effectiveness and evaluation.

TESTBED ENVIRONMENT AND METRICS

Our work was facilitated by developing a testbed system. The *Pit* environment developed for Usoh et al. (1999) resulted in a VE system and a virtual scene that consistently evoked high emotional response in participants. Slater, Usoh, and Steed (1995), inspired by the work of Gibson and Walk (1960) that showed we fear falling at a young age, first did user studies in a virtual scene that required participants to walk along a high ledge; our *Pit* environment is a variation of theirs. Study participants explore a low stress virtual room while the door to the high stress room is closed; then the door to the *Pit* room opens and participants are asked to perform a simple task such as placing a beanbag on the chair that is visible in Figure 12.1. The task, included to increase participants' engagement with the virtual scene, always requires that the participant walk along the ledge (or walk out into space).

Although participants always have a task, our goal is to measure their response to the environment. Initially we used the Slater-Usoh-Steed questionnaire to measure participants' sense of presence in the virtual scene (Slater et al., 1995; Usoh et al., 1999). Later we adopted objective measures that are contemporaneous with the experience and correlate with presence. We, like others (Slater & Garau, 2007), no longer use post-experiment questionnaires as our primary measure of presence. Meehan's work (2001; Meehan et al., 2002) established the validity, reliability, and sensitivity of physiological measures as correlates of presence. Our most successful physiological metric has been delta heart rate: the difference between baseline heart rate in the low stress room and heart rate when the participant is standing on the ledge.

The *Pit* environment and the physiological measures have been used to study frame update rate (Meehan, 2001; Meehan et al., 2002), passive haptics (Insko, 2001), latency (Meehan, Razzaque, Whitton, & Brooks, 2003), and lighting fidelity (Zimmons, 2004).

EVALUATING SENSORY INPUT FIDELITY

Each of the studies reported here is concerned with the quality of the sensory input delivered by the system to the user, that is, as explained in Volume 2, Section 1 Perspective, concerned with the quality of the *immersion*. These studies all contribute to the understanding of the *fidelity requirements* for VE systems. (The relevance of fidelity for training effectiveness evaluation is the topic of Volume 3, Section 2.)

Evaluating the Impact of Field of View in Head-Mounted Displays

VE users wearing head-mounted displays (HMDs) often complain about the loss of peripheral vision due to narrow field of view (FOV). Almost all HMDs have a horizontal FOV of less than 60°, much less than the normal human FOV of about 200°. User performance degrades when the HMD FOV is less than about

Figure 12.1.   The *Pit* environment. (Top) The lab with wooden and foam passive haptics used to increase the strength of the illusion of the ledge. (Bottom) An overview of the virtual scene. Images courtesy of the Department of Computer Science, UNC–Chapel Hill.

50° (Piantanida, Boman, Larimer, Gille, &amp; Reed, 1992). Only an evaluation of performance with a wide FOV HMD could inform potential users and vendors of whether such HMDs, with FOV approaching 180°, improve user performance.

Tasks and Metrics

Arthur's (2000) participants performed tasks while using an HMD capable of FOVs of 176°, 112°, and 48° horizontal × 47° vertical (Arthur, 2000). All participants performed all tasks in all three HMD FOV conditions and, for control, in a commercial 48° × 36° FOV HMD (Virtual Research V8) and in a restricted real condition with a simple cowl restricting the participant's FOV to that of the V8.

Arthur's (2000) study had participants perform common tasks that included both egocentric and exocentric actions: visual search, walking through a virtual environment without running into walls, distance estimation, and spatial memory. The performance metric for the search and walking tasks was task time to completion; the metrics for distance estimation and spatial memory were distance and position error, respectively. To evaluate other aspects of usability, Arthur tested postural stability before and after HMD use, and participants completed the simulator sickness questionnaire (Kennedy, Lane, Berbaum, & Lilienthal, 1993) and the Witmer and Singer presence questionnaire (1998).

Findings

Arthur found that wider FOV led to shorter search times on the visual search task and shorter walking times for travel through a maze. There were no observable trends between FOV and values on the other measures—simulator sickness, postural stability, distance estimation, spatial memory, and presence. Participants using the relatively narrow FOV V8 HMD walked and searched faster than those using the widest FOV condition. Arthur speculated that this was due to better acuity and brightness in the V8.

Lessons Learned

1. Include an experimental condition that compares the tested component to a similar, familiar component. The wide FOV HMD is radically different from the commercial Virtual Research V8: It has six liquid-crystal display panels per eye, it weighs twice as much as the V8, and brightness and contrast vary across the display panels. The results for the V8 and restricted real conditions gave us confidence that the data we collected for wide FOV HMD users were reasonable.

2. Evaluating early prototype components may require additional specialized equipment. The FOV studies required not only access to a Defense Advanced Research Projects Agency–funded, Kaiser Electro-Optics–developed, experimental, wide FOV HMD, but also they required a large graphics system with 12 separate graphics pipelines and video outputs to drive the 12 display tiles in the HMD. The department's (then prototype) HiBall wide-area tracker (3rdTech, 2006) enabled Arthur to design the maze-walking task so that participants really walked in the lab.

Impact of Passive Haptics on Training Transfer

The most serious credibility problem we see with VEs is that one touches nothing while seeing apparently tangible objects. Insko's (2001) dissertation studied *passive haptics,* the registering of low fidelity physical mock-ups of virtual objects. In one study he examined the following question: For training done in a VE, do users learn better if passive haptics are added?

Conditions, Tasks, and Metrics

Insko's participants trained to navigate a maze by walking three times through a virtual model of the maze (see Figure 12.2 [top]). The display was a V8 HMD, the head tracker was UNC's HiBall, the locomotion technique was real walking, and virtual avatars of the participants' hands were registered to their real hands using a Polhemus tracker. Participants trained in one of two conditions: with passive haptics (see Figure 12.2 [bottom]) or without passive haptics but with visual and audio cues when their hands collided with the virtual maze walls. Participants were encouraged to use their hands to touch the maze as they walked through it. After training, the participants were blindfolded, taken to a real maze (identical to the passive haptics), and instructed to walk the maze. The metrics were task completion time and number of collisions with the walls. The experimenter logged unexpected or otherwise interesting events, including wrong turns.

Findings

Participants trained with passive haptics took significantly less time to walk the real maze and had significantly fewer collisions. Eleven of 15 who trained without passive haptics made the same wrong turn toward the end of the maze; only 2 of 15 who trained with passive haptics made the same error.

Lessons Learned

1. Log experimenter observations, both qualitative and quantitative. The logs can help explain outlier data points and support the exclusion of them from the statistical analysis. In the passive haptics study, observations caught the consistent, but unexpected, wrong-turn behavior.

   The observation that participants consistently tipped their heads to locate sound sources in three dimensions helped explain why our (unpublished) results comparing localization performance in two-dimensional (2-D) (Microsoft DirectSound) and 3-D (AuSIM Gold Series) sound-generation conditions differed from those reported in the literature. We found no significant performance differences attributable to the sound-rendering method for our participants who could freely walk about and move their heads. In previous studies, participants who were seated with their heads held stationary performed better on the localization task with the stimuli presented in 3-D sound (Wenzel, Wightman, & Foster, 1988).

2. Select the levels of the independent variable carefully, balancing the number of conditions and the number of research questions with the reality of study design complexity and number of participants required. For reasons of expediency, Insko did

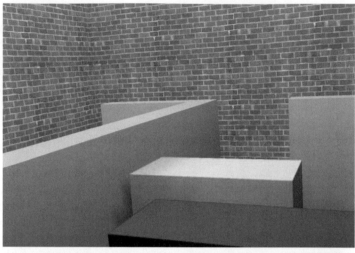

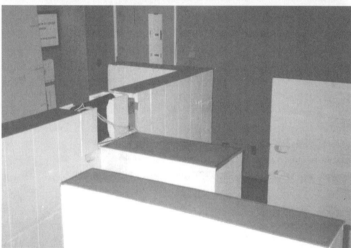

**Figure 12.2.   (Top) The virtual maze. (Bottom) The passive haptics maze. Partici-
pants trained in the virtual maze either with or without the passive haptics. After
training, the participants were blindfolded and then walked the real maze, set
up identically to the passive haptics. Images courtesy of the Department of Computer
Science, UNC–Chapel Hill.**

not include a condition exposing participants simultaneously to passive haptics and
the synthetic audio and visual cues. If he had, he could have examined the questions
of whether using all cues would result in even better real-maze performance than
with passive haptics alone and whether training with the audio tones, clearly absent
in the real world, would, in fact, mistrain and lead to poorer performance. This is
the perennial "training wheels" question for all simulation based training.

3. Require only one session with each participant if at all possible. It is often difficult to get volunteer or minimally compensated participants to return to the lab for the multiple sessions that training retention studies require. Expect to offer larger incentives for multisession studies and withhold most payment until after the final session.

Impact of Lighting Fidelity on Physiological Response

One intuitively expects that the more realistic the rendering of a virtual scene, the more VE users' responses to the scene and task performance will approach real world responses and performance. Zimmons (2004) tested this by evaluating physiological responses to two levels of lighting fidelity and two levels of texture fidelity in a 2 × 2 design. A fifth condition was an unrealistic model of the same scene.

Conditions, Tasks, and Metrics

Figure 12.3 shows three of Zimmons's conditions: low fidelity texture and ambient lighting, high fidelity textures with global illumination, and all the surfaces rendered with the same white-on-black grid texture. Zimmons's primary measure was delta heart rate, measured between the room with the normal floor and the room with the *Pit*. He administered the same series of questionnaires as Meehan (2001) and interviewed participants.

Findings
An ANOVA (analysis of variance) analysis over data from the five conditions revealed no significant differences and no trends in the delta heart rate measures. Even the scene rendered with a uniform grid texture evoked high levels of stress as indicated by a rise in heart rate. In interviews, over 60 percent of all participants mentioned feeling fearful.

Lessons Learned

1. Always run pilot studies. Besides bringing procedural problems to light, running a pilot study all the way from greeting participants through data analysis enables a statistical power analysis to determine if experiments are likely to differentiate among the conditions without an untenable number of subjects.

2. Null results do not mean the work is valueless, but never claim that lack of statistical significance of differences implies that the conditions are the same. There are two ways to emphasize the *practical* significance of any differences in measured values.

   a. Field and Hole (2003) suggest that authors always report *effect size* as part of their statistical results. Reporting effect size allows readers to judge for themselves if differences matter practically.

   b. Statistical techniques for *equivalence testing,* testing the hypothesis that sample populations do not differ, are available. An important application is in studies

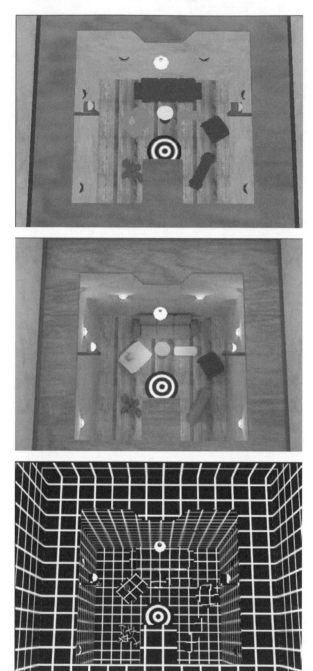

Figure 12.3.   The *Pit* environment displayed in three of Zimmons's rendering styles: (top) low quality lighting and low resolution textures; (middle) high quality lighting and high resolution textures; (bottom) rendered with a white-on-black grid texture applied to all objects. Images courtesy of the Department of Computer Science, UNC–Chapel Hill.

verifying the efficacy of generic compared to brand-name drugs. Wellek (2002) is a comprehensive study of equivalence testing written for statisticians.

Impact of Lighting Fidelity on Task Performance

Zimmons (2004) asked whether the style of lighting used in rendering abstract knot-like shapes affects performance in a visual search task. The conditions for this study were strictly controlled; even so, there were lessons for those planning training systems.

Conditions, Task, and Metrics

The task was to look at a rendering of a target knot-like figure and then, after the target disappeared, to locate the target figure from among a now-visible set of 15 similar knot-like figures or to indicate that the target knot was not in the search set. Figure 12.4 shows knots rendered in ambient lighting, local illumination, and global illumination, as well as the setup for the search task. Note that all of the knots in each search set were rendered with the same lighting style. To eliminate confounding factors, all knots were the same color, had the same surface material properties, and were rendered in gray scale. All pairwise combinations of the three target-knot lightings and three search-set lightings were tested. The measures were time to select and accuracy.

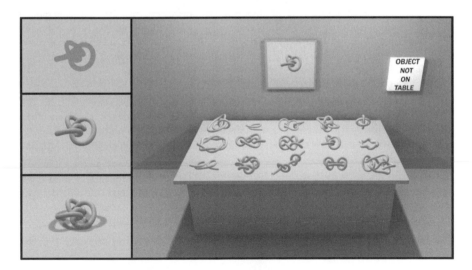

Figure 12.4.   (Left) Knots rendered in Zimmons's three lighting styles: (top) ambient lighting, (middle) local lighting, and (bottom) with shadows and interreflections. The large figure shows the search set with 15 knots. The target knot is displayed on the wall (as shown), but without the search set visible; then the target object disappears and the search set appears. Selection is made with a virtual laser pointer. Images courtesy of the Department of Computer Science, UNC–Chapel Hill.

Table 12.1.   Accuracy Scores for Different Conditions in the Knot Search Task

| | | Search Object Lighting Model (SOLM) | | |
		Global	Local	Ambient
Table Object	Global	80.3%	74.4%	48.6%
Lighting Model	Local	73.9%	77.3%	62.5%
(TOLM)	Ambient	54.5%	66.2%	70.3%

Findings

Table 12.1 shows accuracy scores for different combinations of target lighting and search-set lighting. The best scores are on the diagonal and are not always associated with the highest fidelity lighting! The more different the lighting between target and search set, the poorer the performance. We speculate that this is because the task is essentially a pattern-matching problem and the more dissimilar the rendering style between target and search set, the harder it was to recognize the underlying similarity between correctly matched knots.

Lessons Learned

1. Mitigate confounders by carefully considering all aspects of your stimuli and evaluation setup. Whereas the virtual environment for the visual search task was very simple—a room with a table and a picture frame—development of the stimulus models and images was complex and time consuming as lighting, brightness, and colors had to be matched. We unexpectedly added complexity to the data analysis of a locomotion study because the paths the participants walked were not all the same length. The consequence was that the data from the different segments could not be naively combined in repeated-measures analyses.

2. Useful knowledge can come from studies that are highly constrained and have little ecological validity. The knot study does not claim or show that the lighting approximation fidelity results can be generalized to other tasks, but it *provides a case that demonstrates that we must always ask the questions* of how much realism is needed.

3. While lower quality lighting approximations may be used during training to simplify the task for beginners, the final training condition should be as close as possible to those trainees will see in the field. Zimmons's (2004) data suggest that *consistency* of lighting style is more important for accurate identification of complex shapes than lighting *fidelity*.

EVALUATING USER INTERFACES

Sometimes a simple question can lead to a series of studies, as did our asking which locomotion technique is best for VE users. That simple question led to a long research thread of developing and comparatively evaluating locomotion interfaces. We report on two locomotion studies here.

Sometimes user studies are required during the development of a technique to give it principled rather than ad hoc foundations. One study of a user-interface component involved the development of a *psychometric function* to establish an experimentally determined value for a critical parameter.

Locomotion Technique Effect on Presence

Locomotion Conditions

Table 12.2 shows the five conditions we used for a series of locomotion studies. There are three viewing conditions (unrestricted, FOV restricted eyes, and HMD) and three locomotion conditions (real walking, walking in place, and flying with a gamepad/joystick). The five conditions are as follows:

- REAL—real walking and unmediated eyes,
- COWL—real walking and FOV restricted eyes,
- VEWALK—real walking and head-mounted display,
- WIP—walking in place and head-mounted display, and
- JS—joystick and head-mounted display.

The REAL condition gives us a standard against which to compare. The COWL condition was included so that we could isolate the effect of reduced FOV from the effects of HMD presentation of visual stimuli.

In our first locomotion study, reported next, there was no COWL condition and a push-button-flying interface was used in place of the joystick to better replicate a previous study.

Tasks and Metrics

A study of the impact of the locomotion technique on *presence* used the *Pit* environment (Usoh et al., 1999). The study replicated the work reported in Slater et al., 1995) using a similar virtual scene, task, metrics, and data analysis. We included the VEWALK condition in addition to the push-button-flying and WIP interfaces that were compared in the earlier study. The WIP interface, implemented with a neural network, was the same as used in the Slater, Usoh, and Steed study. Participants performed a task in the *Pit* environment and filled out

Locomotion Condition Visual Condition	Real Walking	Walking in Place	Gamepad/Joystick
Unrestricted	REAL	----	----
FOV restricted eyes	COWL	----	----
HMD	VEWALK	WIP	JS

Table 12.2. The Locomotion Conditions

the Slater-Usoh-Steed presence questionnaire and Kennedy's simulator sickness questionnaire (Kennedy et al., 1993).

Findings
Both VEWALK and WIP were significantly more presence inducing than push-button-flying. With no other factors in the model, VEWALK was more presence inducing than WIP. However, when oculomotor discomfort (a subscale of the simulator sickness questionnaire) was included, there was no difference between the VEWALK and WIP conditions. Oculomotor discomfort diminished presence for flying and WIP, but not for VEWALK.

Lessons Learned

1. Reuse, or minimally modify, experimental methods, measures, and analysis protocols from published works. The methods have already been vetted by publication reviewers, and it makes it easier to compare work across studies.
2. Pilot the task. Participants must be able to learn the interfaces and complete the task. Some participants were never able to successfully use the neural-network based WIP interface. Timing the task during piloting lets one estimate the length of experimental sessions and judge if participant fatigue is going to be an issue.

Locomotion Technique Effect on Training Transfer

Task, Secondary Task, and Metrics

We compared how well participants learned a task when trained in one of the five conditions. This study and task were designed to have some ecological validity with respect to training warfighters moving on foot and to require more complex movements than our previous studies. The task, moving from one side to the other of a virtual bombed-out building while avoiding gunfire, required participants to move quickly and stop precisely behind sheltering barriers (see Figure 12.5). Participants had to maneuver around sharp corners and avoid obstacles on the floor. (The low obstacles were outside the vertical field of view of the HMD when the participant was looking straight ahead.) To increase cognitive load, participants were also asked to count the occurrences of two audio events. In response to participant comments from the previous study, we developed an easier-to-use WIP interface for this study (Feasel, Whitton, & Wendt, 2008).

The performance metric was *exposure* to gunfire, measured in body-percentage seconds. Data from the head tracker were logged for time-trajectory analyses. The design was pre-test (REAL condition), training (in one of the five conditions), and post-test (REAL) to enable us to evaluate training transfer and the pattern of exposure scores across the training trials.

Findings
While data analysis is ongoing, early analysis of exposure data during the 12 training trials shows that training to competence with the WIP and JS

Figure 12.5.   Locomotion study environment. (Top) Virtual environment as seen in HMD. (Bottom) Physical environment with passive haptic approximations of objects in the virtual scene. The truck and shooters were purely virtual and were projected on the white wall visible in the top scene. The two visible barriers in the top image correspond to the two far barriers in the bottom image. The oval and the arrow approximate the HMD view direction. Images courtesy of the Department of Computer Science, UNC–Chapel Hill.

interfaces requires 5–10 minutes longer than training for the three conditions in which people really walk.

Lessons Learned

1. Train to competence in a setting with complexity comparable to the test scenario. Our training scene was, unfortunately, less cluttered than the test scenes and did not force the participants to maneuver through spaces as tight as those in the test scenes.

2. Do not underestimate the space, equipment, programming, modeling, logistical, and management resources required to design, implement, and execute studies with some ecological validity. Just the paper design of the four virtual scenes for this study took well over 80 hours. The layouts were constrained by analysis requirements, available building blocks for passive haptics, cable management issues, the need to switch from one physical (passive haptics) environment to another in three to four minutes, and the need that they be of comparable difficulty.

3. Pilot test to ensure that the experiment will discriminate among conditions. Our pilot test showed our task was too easy to yield discrimination. We added a distracter cognitive task, reasoning that if people were counting explosions and jets flying overhead, there would be fewer cognitive resources available for moving and hiding. If a relevant taxonomy of tasks is available, for example, Bloom's taxonomy of cognitive tasks, consult it when choosing tasks.

4. When possible, strive for within-subjects designs that expose all participants to all conditions. In the case of this locomotion study, participants could rate and rank the five interface techniques because they had experienced all five. In a subsequent study, the length of sessions dictated that each participant experience only one of the five conditions. That limited our ability to use participant comments to make sharp distinctions among the conditions.

5. Make use of a statistics consulting service if needed and available. Advice from such a service during study development helped ensure that we were able to answer our research questions with the study design and analysis we planned.

6. Do not expect all statistical analyses to be as simple as t-tests and ANOVAs. The experimental design may dictate more sophisticated techniques than those learned in a first statistics or experimental design course. In this study, the complexity unexpectedly rose when we found that the exposure data did not meet the normality criteria required for use of parametric techniques.

7. Ecological validity is hard to achieve. Real users should be involved in study design if at all possible, especially for testing training transfer studies.

8. Training transfer studies are difficult because they require a "real" condition. The laboratory environment imposes space and other limitations on that real condition. These limits often result in low ecological validity; the question arises as to how generalizable laboratory training transfer study results are to real world training.

9. Using military personnel as study participants may require review by the military human subjects protection organization. This includes Reserve Officers' Training Corps students; they are considered to be on active duty.

Managing Avatar-Object Collisions

Whereas one can develop interface techniques by trial and error, varying parameters until it "feels right," studies may be required to establish those parameters in a principled way. Burns (2007) used methods from psychophysics to establish the detection thresholds needed in his technique.

Some VE systems prevent unnatural interpenetrations of avatars and objects by stopping the avatar at the surface of the object. When this occurs for an avatar of a hand, the participant's real and virtual hands can move out of registration. Burns developed and evaluated an interface component technique, MACBETH, that moves the virtual and real hands back together imperceptibly (Burns, 2007; Burns et al., 2007).

Establishing Detection Thresholds

MACBETH manipulates the position and the velocity of the avatar hand relative to the position and the velocity of the participant's real hand. For the manipulation to be imperceptible, Burns had to determine at what levels people detect differences in real and avatar hand position and hand velocity. Detection thresholds are found by developing *psychometric functions*. Coren, Ward, and Enns (1999) include a very readable introduction to psychophysics, psychometric functions, and detection thresholds.

The basic method used to find a psychometric function is *staircase* presentation of stimuli. In an *up staircase,* the stimulus is first presented at a low value; if the subject does not perceive the stimulus, the level is raised step-by-step until it is perceived. *Down staircases* work similarly. There are various methods for managing the presentation of the stimulus after a *reversal*—when a participant goes from nonperception to perception (or vice versa) and for adaptively decreasing the size of the step to efficiently yield a more precise threshold.

Because thresholds are often different when approached from above and below, well designed studies interleave both up and down staircases. Psychophysical studies are often very time consuming; it may take an hour to reach the staircase-stopping condition, and there are typically multiple repetitions for each participant.

Comparing MACBETH to Other Techniques: Tasks, Environments, and Metrics

MACBETH was compared against two published techniques—rubber-band and incremental motion (Zachmann & Rettig, 2001). Burns designed two mazes as test cases. The task was to grab a ball from a start position and move it through a maze to an end position. The maze was only a bit wider than the ball, so collisions between the ball and maze walls were frequent. Metrics were time to completion and a series of pairwise forced-choice preference ratings. All permutations of pairs were tested to avoid order effects and enable comparison of the three techniques.

Findings

The study found that performance using MACBETH was better than or equally as good as performance with rubber-band or incremental motion. Participants preferred the MACBETH technique, finding it to be more natural than the others.

Lesson Learned

Devising an evaluation study often requires assumptions. Burns used a single up staircase method to determine the position-discrepancy detection threshold between the real hand and the avatar. Later, he used multiple, interleaved, adaptive staircases to determine the velocity-discrepancy detection threshold. Because the outputs of the two studies were not strictly comparable, Burns had to make some major, but plausible, assumptions in order to complete development of his technique. The lesson is the importance of reporting and justifying all assumptions. If the results seem implausible, revisit the assumptions.

EVALUATING SYSTEMS: PERFORMANCE AND EFFICACY

Evaluating the Effect of End-to-End System Latency

For HMD users, the fastest viewpoint-changing motion is head rotation. Hence, the most critical system response time is that between when head rotation begins and the display of an updated view. This *end-to-end latency* is an often-measured critical system parameter (Mine, 1993; Olano, Cohen, Mine, & Bishop, 1995). Task performance is shown to degrade with 80 ms (milliseconds) of latency (So & Griffin, 1995), and participants can perceive latency of as little as 10–12 ms (Ellis, Mania, Adelstein, & Hill, 2004).

Conditions, Tasks, and Metrics

As part of an exhibition at SIGGRAPH (Special Interest Group on Graphics and Interactive Techniques) 2002 we compared delta heart rate in participants experiencing our *Pit* environment with either 50 ms of average end-to-end latency or 90 ms average. We hypothesized that those experiencing low latency would have a stronger stress response than those in the high latency condition. We also administered the Slater-Usoh-Steed presence questionnaire.

Findings

The low latency system yielded a significantly higher delta heart rate between the two rooms. The Slater-Usoh-Steed presence questionnaire revealed no significant differences in reported presence: the physiological measure was more sensitive than the questionnaire.

Lessons Learned

1. Be pragmatic in the choice of experimental conditions. Although we could achieve 40 ms latency with our best hardware, we chose 50 ms as the low latency condition in case we had an equipment failure and had to continue with less-capable hardware.

A goal for the exhibition was that every participant have a very good VE experience, so we selected a high latency value, 90 ms, that is, 10 percent less than 100 ms, a generally accepted upper bound for interactive systems.

2. Develop and maintain a good working relationship with the group that oversees the ethical treatment of human subjects in research studies, called the Institutional Review Board in the United States. From earlier studies, the UNC Institutional Review Board was familiar with our work and the precautions we take to ensure participant safety. Although the locale was unusual, getting approval for this exhibition based study was straightforward.

Evaluating the Efficacy of a Collaboration System

The nanoManipulator Collaboratory is a system that extends the function of the nanoManipulator to enable distributed collaboration for visualization and analysis of scientific data (Sonnenwald, Whitton, & Maglaughlin, 2003). In a multifaceted study, we asked the following questions: Can science be done as effectively when scientists are noncollocated and using the Collaboratory system as when they are face-to-face using the nanoManipulator? What do the participants think of the system? Is the system likely to be adopted by the target users? Should development of tools for distributed scientific collaboration continue?

The nanoManipulator Collaboratory was developed in UNC's National Institutes of Health Center for Computer Integrated Manipulation and Microscopy under the direction of Diane H. Sonnenwald and Mary Whitton.

Participants, Conditions, Tasks, and Metrics

Twenty pairs of upper level undergraduate science majors performed two different laboratory tasks, on two different days, in two different experimental conditions: face-to-face and noncollocated. When noncollocated, they used the Collaboratory system. Half worked face-to-face first; half worked noncollocated first.

The laboratory task was to analyze data that had been gathered previously by working domain scientists. Each participant wrote a laboratory report for each session. Sessions were recorded (video and audio), and there was an experimenter/observer in the room at all times to note *critical incidents* (Hix and Hartson, 1993) (behaviors or events that might have affected outcome). Questionnaires and interviews followed each session. Grades on the laboratory reports provided quantitative data about the *quality of the science* done in each condition.

Participants' opinions, qualitative data, of the *usability of the system* were collected in questionnaires and in semistructured interviews. The interviews were transcribed and analyzed using open and axial coding (Berg, 2006). Participants' opinions of the *adoptability of the system* were gathered with a purpose-designed questionnaire based on the Rogers' diffusion of innovation theory (Rogers & Rogers, 2003).

Findings

There were no significant differences in either the scores on the lab reports completed in the two conditions or the scores on the adoptability questionnaire. When order of conditions for the two sessions was included in the model, the group that collaborated noncollocated first had significantly higher scores on the second task than the group that worked face-to-face first. At the time of the study, we had not yet become aware of equivalence testing (Wellek, 2002), and we had only the interview data to help us understand the results.

In the interviews the participants identified both positive and negative aspects of working face-to-face and working noncollocated. Some expressed a strong preference for working noncollocated, as it gave them their own space and sole use of the Collaboratory tool. Participants reported devising work-arounds for the perceived disadvantages of using the Collaboratory; they did not let perceived system deficiencies keep them from doing their tasks.

Lessons Learned

1. Study designs usually demand compromises. The quality of science would, ideally, be judged by long-term measures, such as number and quality of papers and grants that result. This study required short-term measures plausibly related to scientific quality.

   As conceived, study participants were to have been the system's target users— graduate research assistants, post-doctoral fellows, and working scientists. We quickly realized we were unlikely to find 40 of them willing to participate in an eight hour study. Our decision to use undergraduate students broadened the participant pool, but constrained the sophistication of the science lab tasks.

2. A full 2×2 design (adding the conditions where a group did both labs face-to-face and a group that did both labs noncollocated) would have been better for this study as we could have then eliminated any difference in difficulty of the two laboratory tasks as a factor in difference of scores between the first and second sessions. This would have, however, required twice as many pairs of participants and another six to eight months.

3. Developing new measurement tools and designing the statistical analysis are significant portions of the study design task and may require outside expertise. The center offering consulting on statistics will often also help with measurement tool development.

4. Multifaceted studies enable data *triangulation.* Triangulation, common in the social sciences, is the use of multiple research methodologies to study the same phenomena. The theory is that using multiple methodologies overcomes any biases inherent in the individual methods and, consequently, enables the researcher to draw conclusions from the aggregate data more confidently than from a single measure or method. In this study, the null statistical results were plausibly explained by the interview data that showed participants found positive and negative elements for both conditions and developed work-arounds. We were trying to find out if there were problems with scientific collaboratories that would suggest that development stop. Looking at the whole of our data, we are comfortable saying that we found no showstoppers, so development should continue.

5. Large, multifaceted studies are resource intensive—equipment and people. For this study two rooms, each with two computers, a force-feedback device, four cameras, two video recorders, two audio recorders, and wireless telephones, were tied up for eight months. Seven people shared the study execution and observation duties: on the order of 400 person hours to simply gather the data. The 40 participants were each paid $100. Including system development and the study, an average of four graduate students worked on the project each semester for four years, and three to five faculty members were involved over the life of the project.

THE ROLE OF EVALUATION IN SYSTEM DEVELOPMENT

Evaluation should not be an isolated event, but should, when possible, be part of every stage of component and system development. As requirements are seldom fully understood a priori by either the customer or the designer, an iterative design cycle—analyze, design, implement, and evaluate—is critical to achieve a usable product that meets expectations. Gabbard, Hix, and Swan (1999) address design and evaluation of VE systems from the perspective of *usability engineering*. A more recent discussion of the usability process model and how it integrates with development models can be found in Helms, Arthur, Hix, and Hartson (2006).

An important step in requirements analysis (Volume 1, Section 2) is translating those application requirements into system requirements. The particular requirements, then, are the starting benchmarks for component evaluation. In the iterative development cycle, those benchmarks may change

Gabbard et al. (1999) suggest that type of evaluation should change over the development cycle. A sequence of evaluations might include evaluation of a proposed design against expert guidelines, informal evaluation by a few target users or experts, formal usability evaluation by target users (formative studies), and, finally, formal comparison to alternate solutions (summative studies).

The investment required to evaluate iteratively can be substantial. The cost of not evaluating VE training systems—as individual components and as a system —can be not only a failed project, but also increased scepticism about the value of VE technology for training. Component evaluation is a precursor to formal experimental studies asking whether VE training systems do train, and if they do, are they also better than current training practice on such metrics as training better, faster, or cheaper. Application efficacy is the hardest evaluation of all, and the one most needed now to increase the use of VE in training systems.

ACKNOWLEDGMENTS

The authors gratefully acknowledge the major support for the work reported here from the Office of Naval Research (VIRTE Project). Additional support was provided by the NIH National Institute for Biomedical Imaging and Bioengineering, the NIH National Center for Research Resources, the Link Foundation, and SAIC, Inc. Equipment for the audio study was loaned to us by AuSIM Inc.

REFERENCES

Arthur, K. (2000). *Effects of field of view on performance with head-mounted displays* (Doctoral dissertation; CS Tech. Rep. No. TR00-019). Chapel Hill: The University of North Carolina at Chapel Hill, Department of Computer Science.

Berg, B. L. (2006). *Qualitative research methods for the social sciences* (6th ed.). Boston: Allyn and Bacon.

Burns, E. (2007). *MACBETH: Management of avatar conflict by employment of a technique hybrid* (Doctoral dissertation; CS Tech. Rep. No. TR07-002). Chapel Hill: The University of North Carolina at Chapel Hill, Department of Computer Science.

Burns, E., Razzaque, S., Whitton, M. C., & Brooks, F. P., Jr. (2007). MACBETH: Management of avatar conflict by employment of a technique hybrid. *International Journal of Virtual Reality, 6*(2), 11–20.

Coren, S., Ward, L. M., & Enns, J. T. (1999). *Sensation and perception* (5th ed.). Philadelphia: Harcourt Brace College Publishers.

Ellis, S. R., Mania, K., Adelstein, B. D., & Hill, M. I. (2004). Generalizability of latency detection in a variety of virtual environments. *Proceedings of the 48th Annual Meeting of the Human Factors and Ergonomics Society* (pp. 2083–2087). Santa Monica, CA: Human Factors and Ergonomics Society.

Feasel, J., Whitton, M. C., & Wendt, J. D. (2008). LLCM-WIP: Low-latency, continuous-motion walking-in-place. *Proceedings of IEEE Symposium on 3D User Interfaces 2008* (pp. 97–104). Reno, NV: IEEE.

Field, A., & Hole, G. (2003). *How to design and report experiments.* London: SAGE Publications.

Gabbard, J. L., Hix, D., & Swan, J. E. (1999). User-centered design and evaluation of virtual environments. *IEEE Computer Graphics and Applications, 19*(6), 51–59.

Gibson, E. J., & Walk, R. D. (1960). The visual cliff. *Scientific American, 202*(4), 64–71.

Helms, J. W., Arthur, J. D., Hix, D., & Hartson, H. R. (2006). A field study of the wheel: A usability engineering process model. *Journal of Systems and Software, 79*(6), 841–858.

Hix, D., & Hartson, H. R. (1993), *Developing user interfaces: Ensuring usability through product & process.* New York: John Wiley & Sons.

Insko, B. (2001). *Passive haptics significantly enhances virtual environments* (Doctoral dissertation; CS Tech. Rep. No. TR01-017). Chapel Hill: The University of North Carolina at Chapel Hill, Department of Computer Science.

Kennedy, R. S., Lane, N. E., Berbaum, K. S., & Lilienthal, M. G. (1993). A simulator sickness questionnaire (SSQ): A new method for quantifying simulator sickness. *International Journal of Aviation Psychology, 3*(3), 203–220.

Martin, D. W. (2007). *Doing psychology experiments* (7th ed.). Belmont, CA: Wadsworth Publishing.

Meehan, M. (2001). *Physiological reaction as an objective measure of presence in virtual environments* (Doctoral dissertation; CS Tech. Rep. No. TR01-018). Chapel Hill: The University of North Carolina at Chapel Hill, Department of Computer Science.

Meehan, M., Insko, B., Whitton, M., & Brooks, F. P., Jr. (2002). Physiological measures of presence in stressful virtual environments. *ACM Transactions on Graphics, 21*(3), 645–652.

Meehan, M., Razzaque, S., Whitton, M., & Brooks, F. (2003). Effects of latency on presence in stressful virtual environments. *Proceedings of IEEE Virtual Reality 2003* (pp. 141–148). Los Angeles: IEEE.

Mine, M. R. (1993). *Characterization of end-to-end delays in head-mounted display systems* (Tech. Rep. No. TR93-001). Chapel Hill: The University of North Carolina at Chapel Hill, Department of Computer Science.

Olano, M., Cohen, J., Mine, M., & Bishop, G. (1995). Combating rendering latency. *Proceedings of the ACM Symposium on Interactive 3D Graphics 1995* (pp. 19–24). Monterey, CA: ACM.

Piantanida, T. P., Boman, D., Larimer, J., Gille, J., & Reed, C. (1992). Studies of the field-of-view/resolution tradeoff in virtual reality. *Proceedings of Human Vision, Visual Processing and Digital Display III* (Vol. 1666, pp. 448–456). Bellingham, WA: SPIE.

Rogers, E. M., & Rogers, E. (2003). *Diffusion of innovations* (5th ed.). New York: The Free Press.

Slater, M., & Garau, M. (2007). The use of questionnaire data in presence studies: Do not seriously Likert. *Presence: Teleoperators & Virtual Environments, 16*(4), 447–456.

Slater, M., Usoh, M., & Steed, A. (1995). Taking steps: The influence of a walking technique on presence in virtual reality. *ACM Transactions on Computer-Human Interaction, 2*(3), 201–219.

So, R. H. Y., & Griffin, M. J. (1995). Effects of lags on human operator transfer functions with head-coupled systems. *Aviation, Space, and Environmental Medicine, 66*(6), 550–556.

Sonnenwald, D. H., Whitton, M., & Maglaughlin, K. (2003). Evaluating a scientific collaboratory: Results of a controlled experiment. *ACM Transactions on Computer Human Interaction, 10*(2), 151–176.

3rdTech. (2006). HiBall-3100™ Wide-Area, High-Precision Tracker and 3D Digitizer. Retrieved April 16, 2008, from http://3rdtech.com/HiBall.htm

Usoh, M., Arthur, K., Whitton, M. C., Bastos, R., Steed, A., Slater, M., & Brooks, F. P. (1999). Walking > walking-in-place > flying in virtual environments. *Proceedings of SIGGRAPH '99* (pp. 359–364). Los Angeles: ACM.

Wellek, S. (2002). *Testing statistical hypotheses of equivalence.* Boca Raton, FL: Chapman & Hall/CRC Press.

Wenzel, E. M., Wightman, F. L., & Foster, S. H. (1988). A virtual display system for conveying three-dimensional acoustic information. *Proceedings of the 32nd Annual Meeting of the Human Factors Society* (pp. 86–90). Santa Monica, CA: Human Factors Society.

Witmer, B. G. & Singer, M. J. (1998). Measuring presence in virtual environments: A presence questionnaire. *Presence: Teleoperators & Virtual Environments, 7*(3), 225–240.

Zachmann, G., & Rettig, A. (2001, July). *Natural and robust interaction in virtual assembly simulation.* Paper presented at the Eighth ISPE International Conference on Concurrent Engineering: Research and Applications (ISPE/CE 2001), Anaheim, CA.

Zimmons, P. (2004). *The influence of lighting quality on presence and task performance in virtual environments* (Doctoral dissertation; CS Tech. Rep. No. TR07-002). Chapel Hill: The University of North Carolina at Chapel Hill, Department of Computer Science.

SECTION 2
TRAINING SUPPORT TECHNOLOGIES

SECTION PERSPECTIVE
Jan Cannon-Bowers and Clint Bowers

Training support technologies, methods, and tools are those elements that can be added to virtual environments (VEe) to optimize their training value. As has been noted previously in this volume, simply creating a virtual representation of a task environment, no matter how faithful it is to the real world, provides only the context in which training can occur (Salas, Bowers, & Rhodenizer, 1998). Hence, it is imperative that a VE based training system incorporates features (derived from learning science) that will ensure that learning can (and does) occur. One way to organize the discussion of such methods and tools is to introduce the scenario based training approach. Scenario based training (SBT) refers to training that incorporates realistic scenarios as a basis to enable practice and feedback on crucial competencies (Oser, Cannon-Bowers, Salas, & Dwyer, 1999). According to Cannon-Bowers, Burns, Salas, and Pruitt (1998), the primary mechanism upon which learning occurs in SBT is through the scenario itself. Therefore, considerable care must be taken in developing scenarios and supporting elements (for example, performance measures) that directly support the targeted learning objectives.

Based on extensive experience in training U.S. Navy combat teams, Cannon-Bowers et al. (1998) proposed an overarching framework to describe the SBT process. We have modified this process slightly; the updated version can be seen in Figure SP2.1. According to Figure SP2.1, the SBT process begins with specification of the tasks that must be performed and translation of these into targeted learning objectives (that is, those knowledge, skills, abilities, and attitudes that are necessary for effective performance of the task. Once targeted learning objectives are specified, specific events can be scripted that provide trainees with the opportunity to learn the objectives and/or demonstrate mastery of them. These events are typically "tied together" through a scenario or story that provides a compelling and convincing backdrop.

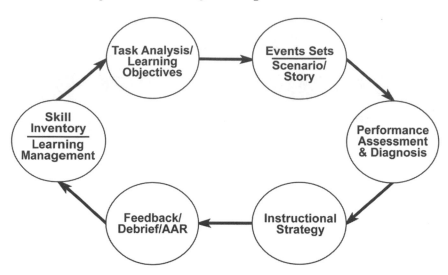

Figure SP2.1.   Scenario Based Training Process

Based on scenario/story events, specific instructional strategies can be selected. For example, for a particular learning objective it may be deemed best to scaffold performance before allowing the trainee to complete the task on his or her own. Scenario/story events also provide a basis upon which to develop specific, measurable performance assessment strategies. Such strategies may be built into the system (for example, automatically collected based on trainee responses), or they may exist as an external adjunct (for example, an instructor rating). Further, observed performance must be interpreted so that a diagnosis of the underlying causes of that performance is inferred. This is crucial to the specification of feedback and remediation strategies. It can also occur as an automated process (in the case of an intelligent tutoring system) or via the actions of a human instructor.

Once specified, feedback can be delivered on line (for example, as hints or cues to the learner during performance) or as a post-exercise debrief or after action review (AAR). At this point, any necessary remediation can be required of the trainee (for example, to review declarative or procedural knowledge in textbooks). The final step in the SBT cycle is to close the loop by recording the trainees' progress in a training episode so that it can drive specification of subsequent learning objectives. This step is crucial since it helps to ensure that training resources are expended efficiently by tailoring the presentation of learning objectives to the trainees' (or teams') particular needs. Modern training systems often feed into complex learning management systems for this reason.

The SBT process described here is meant to be a guide for training researchers and practitioners as they conceptualize the design of SBT systems. It also provides an organizing framework for couching a discussion of SBT. In fact, the chapters in Volume 2, Section 2 all fit fairly well into this conceptualization. The following sections provide more detail about the SBT process and describe how each chapter enriches our understanding of how to optimize it.

TASK ANALYSIS/LEARNING OBJECTIVES/COMPETENCIES

It has long been acknowledged that a detailed task analysis is a first essential step in developing a training system. Obviously, the targeted task must be well understood before training can be developed for it. For the most part, this would seem to be a fairly simple process, and job/task analysis methods have been in existence for many years (Annett & Stanton, 2006). However, in modern training systems, the task analysis process is complicated for several reasons. First of all, a growing emphasis has been witnessed in recent years on higher order skills, especially decision making and problem solving. This has led to a desire to better understand how experts perform in realistic environments, including specification of tacit or implicit knowledge (that is, that which is crucial to task performance, but not well articulated by the experts themselves; see Cianciolo, Matthew, Sternberg, & Wagner, 2006). Hence, new methods of eliciting knowledge have been developed in recent years to better describe the way that the task is best accomplished.

A second complicating factor in task analysis is that in many modern settings, the pace of change is extreme (particularly compared to environments in previous generations). This means that knowledge is not static; rather, it changes and evolves relatively quickly, requiring that training systems change quickly as well. Unfortunately, traditional task analysis methods were developed for systems with relatively static knowledge and do not adapt to changing conditions very well. To address this challenge, Chapter 18 (Shadrick and Lussier) describes a knowledge elicitation strategy that is designed to accommodate changing task requirements and conditions. This approach, which actually builds on the strengths of several traditional methods, may be useful in rapidly building scenarios, new concepts, and future conditions.

EVENTS/SCENARIO/STORY

Once the learning objectives have been established, they can then be used as input to the scenarios, forming the basis of the training exercise. Past researchers have conceptualized this process in terms of embedding *events* into scenarios that represent the learning objectives. An event, in this context, is any stimulus condition that is purposely scripted into a scenario in order to elicit a particular response. Scenario events have also been conceptualized as *triggers*—specific scenario conditions that will allow the trainee to practice the targeted learning objectives (Fowlkes, Dwyer, Oser, & Salas, 1998). Hence, the scenario events form the basis of trainee practice opportunities.

The scenario in scenario based training also serves another purpose, that is, to provide a context or narrative that ties events together. In this sense, the scenario or story also serves a motivational purpose in the sense that it engages the trainee in a realistic context. Recently, researchers have begun to theorize that narrative elements may actually enhance learning by helping guide trainees through the system (Ironside, 2006). Further, research into such concepts as immersion and presence seems to indicate that learning can be enhanced when trainees are psychologically engaged in the scenario. Stories and story based learning also help to ensure that the experiences trainees gain in training (as opposed to the real world) are authentic—that is, they are rich, faithful representations of the world that will enable the trainee to transfer his or her virtual experience into the operational environment.

In Chapter 19, Gordon describes the history of story based learning environments and how they have evolved over time. As technology advances, more complex, interactive media are being developed that allow for increasingly complex story based systems. Gordon describes development of a story based leadership training system and how this approach can be used to enhance learning.

PERFORMANCE MEASUREMENT/ASSESSMENT/DIAGNOSIS

Once scenario events are scripted and instructional strategies selected, the next step in the scenario based training development process is to specify the performance measures that will be implemented to assess trainee behavior. For the most part, measures of performance should flow out of the task analysis/cognitive task analysis that were conducted at the start of the process. This implies that as tasks are initially described, the conditions and standards of effective performance are also specified. At this time, it is often the case that measurement procedures or approaches are also selected. In the case of scenario based training these measures are often behavioral in nature (that is, they describe the specific behavioral response that is expected of the trainee).

On other occasions, measures are more cognitive, assessing the mental processes that trainees use in accomplishing tasks presented by the scenario. For example, Chapter 16 (Riley, Kaber, Sheik-Nainar, and Endsley) describes a technique for measuring situational awareness in trainees as a means to better understand whether trainees have a sufficient mental picture of scenario events and an awareness of crucial information in the environment. Likewise, Chapter 17 (Cain and Armstrong) provides a rationale for why it is important to understand and measure the cognitive workload presented by the scenario. In this case, the goal of measurement is to determine whether trainees are overloaded by the task demands, particularly as an indication of task difficulty. When it is determined that workload is excessive, measures can be taken to scale back or simplify task demands to better match the trainee's level of mastery and capability.

INSTRUCTIONAL STRATEGIES

Scenario based training environments provide a context in which learning can occur, but in and of themselves, they are not training systems without the addition of the elements displayed in Figure SP2.1. Of primary importance in this regard is the establishment of instructional strategies that optimize learning. In fact, there are many possible approaches to embedding instruction in scenario based training. For example, instructional decisions can be made regarding the difficulty of tasks presented to trainees, the form and timing of feedback (more will be said about this in a later section), the nature of hints and cues provided to trainees, the spacing of practice opportunities, and the like.

Chapter 20 (Lane and Johnson) describes how tenets from intelligent tutoring can be applied to more dynamic scenario based training situations. According to these authors, intelligent tutoring provides a framework for embedded instructional features—including measurement and feedback—into virtual learning environments. In fact, they argue that virtual environments may allow for additional opportunities, for example, by allowing pedagogical agents to become part of the story or narrative.

In another vein, Chapter 21 (Singer and Howey) describes an instructional approach to enhancing virtual environments by manipulating deviations from fidelity (that is, the actual task situation) as a means to improve learning. By using augmenting cues and adjuncting cues, provisions can be added to simulations that better support the learner by ensuring that necessary exposure to, and practice with, the stimuli can occur. For example, enhancing the salience of a stimulus in the environment through visual manipulation (for example, increased brightness) can help to direct the learner's attention so he or she appropriately confronts the stimulus.

FEEDBACK

As has been alluded to in previous sections, feedback is an essential element in scenario based training (Cannon-Bowers et al., 1998). As in all forms of training, feedback provides trainees with a detailed understanding of their own performance and how they need to correct behavior in order to enhance future performance. Much has been written about feedback in training, exploring such things as when and how often to give feedback, the format of feedback (for example, directive or reflective), the specificity of feedback, and who provides feedback (instructors or trainees themselves). This literature provides much useful guidance on how best to implement feedback mechanisms in training (Cannon-Bowers et al., 1998).

In Chapter 14 (Lampton, Martin, Meliza, and Goldberg), a framework for AARs is provided as a mechanism for providing feedback in scenario based training. These authors describe an approach that takes advantage of electronic data streams that can enhance the delivery of feedback. They also discuss several issues in implementing feedback (AARs) in virtual training systems.

LEARNING MANAGEMENT

The final step in a fully implemented scenario based training system is to record trainee performance and use that information to inform future scenario based training episodes. In operational environments this is too often accomplished informally, so that subsequent training sessions are suboptimized. Moreover, whereas more traditional distance learning content can be (relatively) easily tracked, performance in simulations and scenario based training is more complex. Hence, conventional learning management systems are not necessarily well suited to incorporate scenario based learning outcomes.

Chapter 15 (Conkey and Smith) is an attempt to bridge this gap by discussing how a learning management system (LMS) can be better connected to scenario based training. This involves a rethinking of concepts and practices that are typical in e-learning situations (for example, how performance is measured and recorded) and also of current learning management standards (for example, SCORM [Sharable Content Object Reference Model]). This type of thinking is essential in order for scenario based training to enter the "mainstream" as a viable training strategy. Conkey and Smith provide a good basis to begin this discussion.

SUMMARY/LESSONS LEARNED

As virtual technologies continue to develop, it is clear that they will be an increasingly popular vehicle in which to embed training. In order to optimize the transition to virtual training, it is essential that training researchers rely on the science of learning and performance as a basis to design effective training. While scenario based training has been the subject of scientifically based investigation only for about 20 years, much has been written and learned about how to optimize design. Chapter 13 (Stout, Bowers, and Nicholson) summarizes the extant literature in this area. In fact, these authors provide detailed guidelines for how best to design and implement scenario based training.

Based on the chapters in Volume 2, Section 2, along with other work in this series and beyond, it is fair to conclude that scenario based training has graduated from a new, untested technique to a relatively well-developed one. However, much needs to be done to fully realize the potential of this approach. Many of the chapters in Volume 2, Section 2 address future research needs. Our assessment is that further work needs to be done in several areas, most of which are related in some way to the issue of performance assessment. We say this because many of the issues that we believe are most pressing—dynamically measuring trainee performance, adapting feedback to trainee needs, implementing intelligent tutoring concepts, connecting training outcomes to LMSs, providing adaptive narratives, and establishing expert performance standards—are all related in one way or another to timely, accurate performance measurement. In modern virtual training systems, this is a multidisciplinary challenge since it involves human performance experts, as well as measurement experts, technologists, engineers, programmers, and learning scientists. We are optimistic that such research and development will occur, especially as new fields (for example, health care and law enforcement) begin to embrace scenario based training as a viable alternative.

REFERENCES

Annett, J., & Stanton, N. (2006). Task Analysis. *International Review of Industrial and Organizational Psychology* (Vol. 21, pp. 45–78). Hoboken, NJ: Wiley Publishing.

Cannon-Bowers, J., Burns, J., Salas, E., & Pruitt, J. (1998). *Advanced technology in scenario-based training. Making decisions under stress: Implications for individual and team training* (pp. 365–374). Washington, DC: American Psychological Association.

Cianciolo, A., Matthew, C., Sternberg, R., & Wagner, R. (2006). *Tacit knowledge, practical intelligence, and expertise. The Cambridge handbook of expertise and expert performance* (pp. 613–632). New York: Cambridge University Press.

Fowlkes, J., Dwyer, D., Oser, R., & Salas, E. (1998). Event-based approach to training (EBAT). *International Journal of Aviation Psychology, 8*(3), 209–221.

Ironside, P. (2006, August). Using narrative pedagogy: Learning and practicing interpretive thinking. *Journal of Advanced Nursing, 55*(4), 478–486.

Oser, R., Cannon-Bowers, J., Salas, E., & Dwyer, D. (1999). Enhancing human performance in technology-rich environments: Guidelines for scenario-based training. In E. Salas (Ed.), *Human/technology interaction in complex systems* (Vol. 9, pp. 175–202). Greenwich, CT: Elsevier Science/JAI Press.

Salas, E., Bowers, C., & Rhodenizer, L. (1998). It is not how much you have but how you use it: Toward a rational use of simulation to support aviation training. *International Journal of Aviation Psychology, 8*(3), 197–208.

Chapter 13

GUIDELINES FOR USING SIMULATIONS TO TRAIN HIGHER LEVEL COGNITIVE AND TEAMWORK SKILLS

Renée Stout, Clint Bowers, and Denise Nicholson

In recent years, a good deal of attention has been paid to employing virtual environments for training purposes, and the focus of this chapter is to provide guidance on doing so. The notion of virtual environments tends to conjure in the mind Hollywood examples of science fiction, such as the holodeck. It gives an impression of total immersion within the virtual environment with highly complex technology. The sense that this gives is that the environment is more "virtual" to the extent that real world stimuli are filtered out and presented by the technology, such as through the use of helmets, augmented visual displays, and haptic devices. On the other hand, using anything other than real world equipment or materials to perform real world tasks in real world environments constitutes a virtual, synthetic, or simulated environment—it is a simulation of the real world task environment. In this chapter, we consider the interface of a virtual environment to be just another medium for training and do not attempt to address how sophisticated this interface is. We instead focus on the training itself and that we are just using a virtual or simulated environment to accomplish the training. We use the term "simulation" versus "virtual environment" because we want to include synthetic or simulated environments at various points on the spectrum of being virtual, given that we believe that our guidelines apply across the spectrum. With this in mind, we now turn to providing an overview on the use of simulations for training before providing greater detail on the nature of our guidelines.

Using simulations to train complex, real world tasks is often perceived as a modern instructional technique, although it actually has a rich history. For example, as early as 2500 B.C., the Egyptians and Sumerians used figurines to depict different warring factions. The use of training simulations in the military also has a long historical precedence, with one of the most well-known uses being the first flight simulator, which was developed by Ed Link in 1936 and used to train U.S. Army airmail pilots.

Today, simulations are used in a variety of settings and for a variety of tasks, such as commercial and military aviation, space exploration, medicine, law enforcement, military combat operations, military and commercial equipment maintenance, military and commercial driving operations, and education. They have the ability to "replicate virtually any real world artifact" (Salas, Bowers, & Rhodenizer, 1998, p. 198), such as detailed terrain, equipment failures, adverse weather, and motion, as well as certain behaviors of virtual team members.

Indeed, within some environments, such as commercial aviation, simulation plays a fundamental role. For example, across the airline industry, whereas years ago all training was done in the aircraft, now it is commonplace for training to take place in the simulator, followed by an observational jump-seat ride, and then *no* actual hands-on training in the aircraft prior to the aviator's first revenue flight.

With the wide use of simulation in the field of practice there comes a concomitant widespread, yet erroneous, belief that simulation equals training (Salas, Milham, & Bowers, 2003). It is important to always keep in mind that simulations are just a *tool* that *can* be used for training (Salas et al., 1998). However, as such, they do have several advantages. For example, the following five advantages were listed by Hays (2006, p. 232):

1. Instructional simulations are available almost anytime when compared to using actual equipment that may be unavailable due to other commitments.

2. Simulations can be run faster than actual equipment because simulated exercises can be reset and rerun very quickly (for example, when training air traffic controllers, simulated aircraft or other simulated entities can be quickly added or removed from instructional scenarios).

3. Simulation scenarios are reproducible, so they can be used to teach lessons that require repetition.

4. Simulations can provide the learner with more trials in a given amount of time by eliminating tasks that are not central to the instructional objective. For example, if the objective is to train in-flight refueling, the simulation can omit takeoff or landing tasks.

5. Simulations can provide the learner with cause-and-effect feedback almost immediately, when it is most effective.

Hays (2006) also noted the advantage that simulations can provide trainees with a realistic preview of the operational environment and the jobs that they will perform. In addition, simulations can be used to train procedures that are too risky to do in the operational environment.

Moreover, empirical evidence has been found for the training benefit provided by simulations. For example, Hays and his colleagues (Jacobs, Prince, Hays, & Salas, 1990; Hays, Jacobs, Prince, & Salas, 1992) conducted a meta-analysis regarding using simulations for aircraft training. "In statistics, a meta-analysis combines the results of several studies that address a set of related research hypotheses" (Wikipedia, 2007a). They concluded that using simulations combined with aircraft training versus aircraft training alone was found to be favorable in more than 90 percent of the experiments reviewed.

Also, probably one of the most well-cited advantages of simulations is that they can provide cost savings. For example, a lifecycle cost analysis of a maintenance simulation revealed that training via the simulation was half as expensive as training on the real equipment (Cicchinelli, Harmon, Keller, & Kottenstette, 1980, as cited in Hays, 2006). The cost savings can be especially appreciated when low cost, such as personal computer (PC) based, simulations are used, which have also been found to provide training value (Baker, Prince, Shrestha, Oser, & Salas, 1993; Brannick, Prince, & Salas, 2005; Brannick, Prince, Salas, & Stout, 1995; Jentsch & Bowers, 1998; Stout, Salas, Merket, & Bowers, 1998).

Because of the widespread acceptance and use of simulations, especially in domains characterized by stress and dynamic task conditions, research has also been conducted regarding how to most effectively use simulations to train complex real world tasks and higher level cognitive and teamwork skills (these skills are explained below). However, unfortunately, the field of practice is replete with examples of training designers, developers, and implementers ignoring much of the guidance that has resulted from research. Perhaps one of the challenges facing these training personnel is that it is difficult to find in the literature a set of clear, easy to use guidelines for training higher level cognitive and teamwork skills. The current document attempts to compile such a set of guidelines. The guidelines are not empirically based, but were instead derived from suggestions in the literature, as well as based upon the current author's practical experience in the field.

It should be noted that the assumption the current authors make is that these guidelines will be used to train individuals and teams to perform in complex, dynamic situations. As described by Cannon-Bowers and Salas (1998, p. 19), these situations are characterized by the following conditions:

- Multiple information sources,
- Incomplete, conflicting information,
- Rapidly changing, evolving scenarios,
- Adverse physical conditions,
- Performance pressure,
- Time pressure,
- High work/information load,
- Auditory overload/interference, and
- Threat.

It is particularly under these types of conditions that higher level cognitive skills and teamwork skills are needed. Therefore, the guidelines in this chapter are focused on using simulations to develop these types of skills. Before proceeding to explain the organization of this chapter, it is worth a moment to explain what is meant by higher level cognitive skills versus psychomotor skills and to differentiate between teamwork skills and "task work" skills. Each will be addressed in turn.

Predominantly, three "domains" or areas of competencies have been discussed in the literature: cognitive, psychomotor, and affective. (The affective domain concerns attitudes and motivation and will not be addressed here.) Within the cognitive domain, Bloom, Engelhart, Furst, Hill, and Krahwohl (1956) derived a "taxonomy" or categorization of competencies from lowest level to highest level as follows: knowledge, comprehension, application, analysis, synthesis, and evaluation. An example of each of these follows:

1. Knowledge: able to list the major components of a diesel engine;
2. Comprehension: able to understand the meaning of nonliteral statements (for example, metaphor and irony);
3. Application: able to predict the angle of bank of the aircraft given a specific airspeed, tailwind, and turn ratio;
4. Analysis: able to distinguish facts from hypotheses;
5. Synthesis: able to propose ways to test a hypothesis;
6. Evaluation: able to indicate logical fallacies in arguments.

In contrast, a taxonomy for the psychomotor domain was developed by Simpson (1972) as follows from least complex to most complex: perception, set, guided response, mechanism, complex overt response, adaptation, and origination. An example of each of these follows:

1. Perception: able to recognize the problem in a failing air conditioner based on the sound it makes while running;
2. Set: able to position hands preparatory to typing;
3. Guided response: able to make appropriate hand signals to wave off aircraft as demonstrated;
4. Mechanism: able to start a fire with sticks;
5. Complex overt response: able to operate a particular weapons system;
6. Adaptation: able to pump car brakes to stop on ice (when not specifically taught);
7. Origination: able to create a more efficient method to disassemble a complex piece of machinery.

The specifics of these taxonomies are not important. Rather, the important point is that psychomotor tasks absolutely have a cognitive component (hence the "psycho" in "psychomotor"), but the focus is on doing a motor task. Cognitive skills go beyond just being able to carry out the motor portion of the task. They involve things that trainees must think about, such as assessing a situation, problem solving, decision making, and adaptability.

Regarding the difference between task work skills and teamwork skills, Cannon-Bowers, Tannenbaum, Salas, and Volpe (1995) and Smith-Jentsch, Johnston, and Payne (1998) made the following distinction. They explained that task work skills relate to the skills required to perform the job that are specific to the position (such as skills at interpreting a radar display) and are usually technical in nature (although they may include perceptual and cognitive components versus just motor components, such as the example given here). On the other hand, teamwork skills relate to skills required to coordinate activities with other team members to perform the mission.

Based upon the distinction between cognitive and psychomotor skills and then between task work and teamwork skills, the current chapter considers that training individual technical skills is different from training teamwork skills. It considers individual technical skills as containing both cognitive and psychomotor components. Conversely, training teamwork skills focuses on the team coordination requirements needed for performance. When discussing guidelines on using simulations to train teamwork skills, it therefore does not address training individual technical skills. Furthermore, when discussing guidelines on using simulations to train higher level cognitive skills, it focuses on developing such processes as situation assessment, problem solving, decision making, and adaptability versus lower level psychomotor or cognitive processes.

GUIDELINES FOR USING SIMULATIONS TO TRAIN HIGHER LEVEL COGNITIVE SKILLS THAT ARE NOT SPECIFIC TO TEAMWORK SKILLS (BUT ARE ALL RELEVANT TO TEAMWORK SKILLS)

Scenario and Training Environment

Embed triggers or events/opportunities for trainees to practice and receive feedback on critical tasks and competencies associated with learning objectives (Oser, Cannon-Bowers, Salas, & Dwyer, 1999; Stout et al., 1998).

- They allow trainees to demonstrate their proficiencies and deficiencies for the purpose of performance measurement, diagnosis, and feedback (Oser et al., 1999).
- Include a number of triggers for each learning objective that vary in difficulty and occur at different points in the scenario (Oser et al., 1999; Prince, Oser, Salas, & Woodruff, 1993).

Functional fidelity or "how the simulation works or provides the necessary information to support the task" (Hays, 2006, p. 245), including relevant context cues, trumps physical fidelity (Beaubien & Baker, 2004; Hays, 2006; Johnston, Poirier, & Smith-Jentsch, 1998; Ross, Phillips, Klein, & Cohn, 2005; Yusko & Goldstein, 1997) or "how the simulation looks; the physical characteristics of the simulation" (Hays, 2006, p. 245).

- Others have used the term psychological fidelity and indicate that it is more important than physical fidelity. For example, Beaubien and Baker (2004) defined psychological fidelity as "the degree to which the trainee perceives the simulation to be a believable surrogate for the trained task. Alternatively, it could be defined as the match between the trainee's performance in the simulator and the real world. For example, a PC based flight simulator could be defined as high in psychological fidelity if the trainees temporarily suspend disbelief and interact as much as they would in the real world" (p. 52). They further noted that, without the temporary suspension of disbelief, trainees are unlikely to behave as they would in the real world and that psychological fidelity can be maximized by developing scenarios that mimic the task demands of the real system.

- o A certain degree of physical or equipment fidelity is obviously needed to induce psychological fidelity, to incorporate relevant cognitive cues, and to enhance transfer of training (such as a noisy helicopter cockpit), but irrelevant physical details do not add to the training experience and may indeed detract from it (as discussed later in the chapter).

- o "Consider all matters that may be important to creating the illusion of reality. This includes wearing uniforms, gloves, and equipment" (Prince et al., 1993, p. 75) required in the real world. These should particularly be used if they cause constraints in the real world, such as weight restrictions of a pilot's helmet or survival gear (Prince et al., 1993).

- • Moreover, higher physical fidelity is not necessarily better—what is important is to accurately represent cognitive cues (Ross et al., 2005).

  - o "Although there is a tendency to believe that more fidelity is always better, the published research does not support this conclusion. Specifically, we were unable to identify any studies that found a direct correlation between the level of simulation fidelity and training related outcomes, such as learning, transfer, and safety. Like any other tool, the effectiveness of simulation technology depends on how it is used." (Beaubien & Baker, 2004, p. 55).

  - o Furthermore, Salas et al. (1998) cited four studies that found that simulations with greater scene detail and/or greater scene variety had little to no effect on trainee performance. They concluded that those funding the development of simulations must emphasize learning instead of technology.

  - o "The context must be authentic in relationship to how practitioners experience and act in real-life settings. Building a context to support authentic domain experience is not the same thing as simulating physical fidelity. Reproducing billowing smoke, elegantly drawn leaves on trees, or precise shadows is artistically rewarding, but irrelevant if those elements are not used in assessments or decisions typical of that situation. Meanwhile, failing to represent a tiny pile of freshly overturned dirt indicating that the nearby entrance of a cave has been disturbed can interfere with an authentic cognitive experience." (Ross et al., 2005, p. 22).

- • The level of fidelity that is required is based upon the learning objectives.

  - o For example, Hays (2006) provided the following example: "If a trainee is learning to fly a plane in a simulated cockpit, and the task is to fly at a specific altitude, then the simulated altimeter must be represented in enough detail that the learner can read the altitude. On the other hand, if the training task is only to locate the display next to the altitude indicator, then the simulation does not need to include a functioning altimeter" (p. 246).

Add features to increase the user's acceptance of the simulation and motivation to use it.

- • Have instructors espouse the simulation's usefulness (Hays, 2006).

  - o Trainees believed that training would be more useful (Cohen, 1990, as cited in Salas, Rhodenizer, & Bowers, 2000) and exerted more effort to transfer what they learned in training (Huczynski & Louis, 1980, as cited in Salas et al., 2000) when supervisors supported them attending the training.

o Performance was enhanced when supervisors participated in goal setting prior to training (Magjuka, Baldwin, & Loher, 2000, as cited in Salas et al., 2000).

• Use maps, charts, checklists, other documentation (for example, approach plates and NOTAMs—notice to airmen) and relevant peripherals (for example, headsets or headphones; a yoke or joystick; a simulated box for changing radio frequencies) just as they would be used in the real world (Prince et al., 1993; Stout et al., 1998).

Provide trainees with all of the background information that they would have in the real world prior to the start of the simulation (Yusko & Goldstein, 1997), and allow them adequate time to review this information.

Provide multiple and varied scenarios to help trainees generalize their competencies and adapt to novel situations, because training cannot possibly cover every existing and potential future situation (Ross et al., 2005).

• "Scenarios should allow participants to undergo different courses of action" (Salas et al., 2000, p. 508).

• "Scenarios should allow participants to perform the desired behaviors on multiple occasions" (Salas et al., 2000, p. 508).

• Avoid using only exemplar, clear scenarios; instead include many exceptions and variations (Ross et al., 2005).

• Incorporate into scenarios situations that have more than one right answer (Oser et al., 1999; Prince et al., 1993), especially avoiding one obvious right answer (Prince et al., 1993; Yusko & Goldstein, 1997).

o Also, incorporate scenarios "that have several specific and sensible avenues for a solution" (Swezey & Salas, 1992, p. 235) and require trainees to demonstrate the ability to perform tasks using different approaches (Swezey & Salas, 1992).

• Incorporate some scenarios that prohibit (with realistic causes) common ways of accomplishing the task to force trainees to find alternatives and elaborate their understanding of the task situation (Ross et al., 2005).

o Also, incorporate some scenarios that are designed to "go wrong" at certain points to allow trainees to confront and resolve anomalies (Swezey & Salas, 1992).

• In some scenarios, incorporate conflicting goals or rules, for example, an attacker using a civilian as a shield when given the rules of engagement of (1) do not injure innocent civilians and (2) defend yourself against an attacker (Ross et al., 2005).

o Incorporate into scenarios situations with information that is conflicting, ambiguous, incomplete, or incorrect (Oser et al., 1999), so that it emulates the degree of "chaos" found in the real world (Yusko & Goldstein, 1997).

Ensure that scenarios are sufficiently challenging, yet not too challenging (Hays, 2006; Prince et al., 1993).

• Scenarios should be "just beyond the trainee's current level of competence" (Kozlowski, 1998, p. 128).

• Increase complexity/challenge as trainees advance (Hays, 2006).

- "Experience using simulation for training . . . has demonstrated the value of providing easier simulations in the beginning, so that a single skill or two may be practiced before having to integrate all the skills into a dynamic situation" (Prince et al., 1993, p. 74).
  - Trainees are better able to adapt to simple conditions than to complex, dynamic ones (Swezey & Salas, 1992).
- Avoid artificially simplifying the simulation of the operational environment to, in turn, avoid giving the trainee an incorrect impression of the domain (Ross et al., 2005).
  Oversimplifying concepts, such as those in the medical domain, leads to the development of misconceptions and can impede further learning (Feltovich, Spiro, & Coulson, 1989, 1993).

Appropriately "chunk" or organize information so that it does not overwhelm the trainee and can be processed more effectively (Chase & Simon, 1973; Miller, 1956).

- Using a larger scenario, from which multiple "mini scenarios" or vignettes are drawn, can help; it can help to retain the full complexity of the real environment without oversimplifying concepts and without overwhelming the trainee (Ross et al., 2005).
- For novices and beginners, "basic knowledge should be utilized in focused problem sets within a small, but rich setting characteristic of the practice domain" (Ross et al., 2005).

Incorporate novelty, new information, surprises, and/or turns of events (Hays, 2006; Ross et al., 2005; Yusko & Goldstein, 1997).

- "Scenarios should introduce surprises during the execution of missions to provide practice in rapidly responding to the changed situation" (Ross et al., 2005, p. 57).
  - "For example, friendly units could become unable to perform (e.g., because they cannot reach their intended position, or because a weapon system breaks down); the enemy could move in a nontraditional way or bring a larger force than was reported by intelligence or reconnaissance; key roads could be too muddy to traverse or blocked by refugees demanding assistance; or, higher headquarters could deliver a new frag order based on an opportunistic target or other change in the situation" (Ross et al., 2005, p. 57).
- Baffling events and unmistakable anomalies can help trainees unlearn misconceptions (Ross et al., 2005).
- Add meaningful distractions, such as introducing an emergency when trainees are busy working on a required procedure—this forces them to assign priorities to tasks and to monitor their progress to ensure completion (Prince et al., 1993).
  - Eliminate meaningless distractions, such as errors in underlying simulation models (Hays, Stout, & Ryan-Jones, 2005).

Design the scenario such that effective trainees will do well and avoid no-win scenarios (Yusko & Goldstein, 1997). Similarly, do not include any tricks in scenarios (Prince et al., 1993).

Instructional Strategy

Avoid free play/discovery learning (Oser et al., 1999).

- Unsupported practice can leave opportunities to train and receive feedback on critical competencies to chance (Oser et al., 1999).
- Provide instructional support; without it, the training may not only be ineffective but may be detrimental to learning (Hays, 2006).
  - ○ The problems with discovery learning may center on difficulties that learners have in forming and testing hypotheses when this strategy is used (de Jong & van Joolingen, 1998, as cited in Hays, 2006).

Do not short-cut training time (Ross et al., 2005).

- "Insufficient time or inappropriate structure for exploring a domain may result in deficient or easily forgotten networks of concepts and principles that represent key phenomena and interrelationships in a domain" (Ross et al., 2005, p. 29).

Simulation exercises should be part of a larger instructional program (Hays, 2006; Prince et al., 1993).

- "Design scenarios as part of a total training program" (Prince et al., 1993, p. 74).
- Characteristics of the simulation are not as important as the design of the training program that uses the simulation (Caro, 1973, as cited in Hays, 2006).
- "High fidelity simulations can enhance the perceived realism of well designed training programmes, but cannot compensate for poorly designed ones" (Beaubein & Baker, 2004, p. 55).
- Providing information, followed by demonstration and then practice and feedback (via simulation) on required competencies is a recommended strategy (Prince et al., 1993; Serfaty, Entin, & Johnston, 1998).

Use whole- versus part-task trainers appropriately (Beaubein & Baker, 2004).

- Part-task trainers can take many forms, but all essentially segment a complex task into its main components (Beaubein & Baker, 2004).
- Use of part-task trainers is less costly and can help trainees develop lower level technical skills such that training on the highest level skills can be reserved for whole-task, full-mission simulations (Beaubein & Baker, 2004; Kirlik, Fisk, Walker, & Rothrock, 1998).
  - ○ Premature use of whole-task trainers may overwhelm trainees with environmental distractions, stress, and time pressure (Beaubein & Baker, 2004).
  - ○ On the other hand, "Part-task training must be supplemented with additional full-task training to provide the trainee with an opportunity to integrate part-task skills with cognitive activities required by the full-task context" (Kirlik et al., 1998, p. 111).
- When using part-task trainers, ensure that scenarios do not go beyond their reach (for example, if using a PC based flight simulator not capable of simulating equipment

malfunctions, do not include learning objectives on equipment-specific trouble-shooting; Prince et al., 1993).

Encourage mental simulation during the performance of some scenarios (Driskell & Johnston, 1998) to predict events and courses of action (Ross et al., 2005) (see also "Feedback" later in this chapter; the key is that mental simulation can be used during the performance of scenarios, during within-scenario feedback sessions, and during post-session debriefs).

- Help trainees to "stop and think" about their processes (Ross et al., 2005).
- "Trainees should be taught mental simulation as a way to improve skills and to evaluate and develop options for decisions that must be made in time-pressured environments" (Kozlowski, 1998, p. 129).

Help trainees to develop their "metacognitive" skills (that is, to be more aware of their own thinking processes and what they do and do not understand) (Salas et al., 2000).

- Junior first officers (that is, pilots) provided with metacognitive training were better at providing backup support (Jentsch, 1997, as cited in Salas et al., 2000).

Aim for "overlearning" (Driskell & Johnston, 1998; Schendel & Hagman, 1982; Hagman & Rose, 1983) for technical skills to free up attentional resources on higher level cognitive tasks.

- Overlearning is "a pedagogical concept according to which newly acquired skills should be practiced well beyond the point of initial mastery, leading to automaticity" (Wikipedia, 2007b).
  - "Pedagogical" is the same thing as a way of teaching or instructing.
  - "Automaticity" means that the task can be performed without conscious, effortful use of attentional resources (for example, one can chew gum and walk; one can drive a car and talk).
- Part-task trainers may be particularly suited to achieve overlearning (Beaubien & Baker, 2004; Kirlik et al., 1998).

Incorporate "scaffolding" into some scenarios (Beaubien & Baker, 2004).

- Various authors have defined this instructional practice in different ways, but most refer to decreasing instructional support as trainees advance. For this guideline, the current authors use scaffolding as described by Beaubien and Baker (2004) where instructors, facilitators, or role-players take over some of the simulated task requirements initially and, over time, gradually withdraw from the task.

Incorporate competition (Hays, 2006).

- Competition can be with a live opponent, against a computer-controlled opponent, or against a criterion score (Hays, 2006).

Performance Measurement/Assessment

Process measurement trumps outcome measurement (see "Feedback" later in the chapter for more details).

- "Develop performance diagnosis strategies and tools that will enable observers to identify deviations between observed and desired performance trends" (Oser et al., 1999, p. 199).

Have a measurement scheme delineated a priori (that is, in advance; Salas et al., 2000).

- Both processes and outcomes should be identified in advance (Salas et al., 2000).

Use multiple measures to obtain a more accurate representation of performance (Cannon-Bowers & Salas, 1997).

When possible, have a dedicated observer/rater (Smith-Jentsch, Zeisig, Acton, & McPherson, 1998).

Measure not only what trainees do, but also what they think about, and evaluate the degree of "goodness" of their thinking versus whether it is right/wrong (Ross et al., 2005).

Use tools to assist in capturing performance data (Cannon-Bowers, Burns, Salas, & Pruitt, 1998).

Feedback Delivery[1]

Have a feedback presentation scheme delineated a priori.

Process feedback trumps outcome feedback (or knowledge of results)—provide process feedback linked to outcomes (Oser et al., 1999; Ross et al., 2005; Salas et al., 2000; Smith-Jentsch, Johnston, et al., 1998; Yusko & Goldstein, 1997).

- In a nutshell, outcome measures answer whether the correct decision was made or correct action was taken (for example, did the bomb hit the target?), while process measures answer whether or not the decision was made correctly or actions were taken correctly (for example, what were the steps, communications, and so forth, that led to the bomb hitting or missing the target?).

  "Making the right decision does not mean the right process was used to arrive at the decision. Therefore, feedback concerning the team processes will be more diagnostic in determining where a team's weaknesses may be and more useful in helping the team to correct performance errors" (Salas et al., 2000, p. 495). (Note this quote is included here because the principle is relevant to individual performance as well.)

  Furthermore, aspects of the situation may be out of the trainees' control, so the right processes may be utilized yet success may not have been achieved (Yusko &

---

[1]The reader should also see Lampton, Martin, Meliza, and Goldberg (Volume 2, Section 2, Chapter 14) and Riley, Kaber, Sheik-Nainar, and Endsley (Volume 2, Section 2, Chapter 16) of the handbook for further guidance on feedback delivery and design and use of after action review (AAR) systems, respectively.

Goldstein, 1997). Providing negative feedback regarding the negative outcome would do little to change the situation.

- "Measurement of processes is critical for diagnosing specific deficiencies associated with how a given outcome was reached." (Oser et al., 1999, p. 186).

- Process measures are critical to providing feedback for purposes of training, and outcome measures are needed to identify which processes are more effective (Smith-Jentsch, Johnston, et al., 1998).

- Help trainees to accurately diagnose their limitations and reasons for poor performance and to develop self-assessment skills (Ross et al., 2005).

Train facilitators to provide effective feedback and coaching (Smith-Jentsch, Zeisig, et al., 1998; Yusko & Goldstein, 1997). (See also other types of training to provide to instructors under "Use of Instructors and Instructor Training" later in this chapter).

- "Coaching is a complex and difficult skill to master and also one of the most important... Although most people are not born great coaches, they can improve dramatically through systematic training and practice" (Yusko & Goldstein, 1997, p. 222).

- Active practice at giving feedback is necessary to impart skills at doing so (Smith-Jentsch, Zeisig, et al., 1998).

- Facilitators/coaches should do the following:

  o Create an open and trusting climate (Smith-Jentsch, Zeisig, et al., 1998; Yusko & Goldstein, 1997).

  o Show empathy, yet remain accurate and truthful (Yusko & Goldstein, 1997).

  o Encourage input from the trainees (Oser et al., 1999; Ross et al., 2005; Smith-Jentsch, Zeisig, et al., 1998).

  o Pause and make eye contact with trainees after asking for input (Smith-Jentsch, Zeisig, et al., 1998).

  o Reserve their input for times when trainees do not respond or to clarify issues or to elaborate upon them (Smith-Jentsch, Zeisig, et al., 1998).

  o Reinforce trainee participation in the feedback process (Oser et al., 1999; Ross et al., 2005; Smith-Jentsch, Zeisig, et al., 1998).

  o Focus on specific behavioral versus person-oriented feedback (with both positive and negative behavioral examples; Prince et al., 1993; Smith-Jentsch, Johnston, et al., 1998; Smith-Jentsch, Zeisig, et al., 1998; Swezey & Salas, 1992).

  o Follow up on behavioral examples provided by trainees by asking them how these affected or could have affected performance outcomes (Smith-Jentsch, Zeisig, et al., 1998).

  o Refrain from being judgmental (Yusko & Goldstein, 1997).

  o Emphasize that the feedback is just from their perspectives and not necessarily "objective reality" (Yusko & Goldstein, 1997).

A picture is worth a thousand words, so use video and/or audio playback (especially to capture communications) and display playback (Oser et al., 1999; Stout et al., 1998; Swezey & Salas, 1992).

- "Training technologies can show the trainees that they do not fully understand what is important by illustrating the consequences of focusing on the wrong part of the situation" (Ross et al., 2005, p. 47).

Use both during scenario feedback and AARs (Ross et al., 2005).

- Trainees benefit from feedback that is continual versus present only at the end of a session (Ross et al., 2005).

  Semistructured "time-outs" during the execution of some scenarios to encourage trainees to discuss their current interpretations of the situation, to mentally simulate how it will play out, and to predict the courses of action that would have the most desirable consequences would be beneficial. Likewise, post-session debriefs or after action reviews should encourage trainees to discuss their interpretations of the situation at various points in the scenario and how various courses of action either supported or failed to support the goals of the mission (Ross et al., 2005).

- System-initiated advice given during a computer based simulation helped individuals learn domain related concepts (Leutner, 1993).

- After observing simulated shipboard combat information center (CIC) exercises, Kirlik et al. (1998) concluded that post-scenario debriefing appeared to come too late for the trainee to benefit from the information.

Help trainees to understand when their knowledge structures are incomplete (Hays, 2006).

- Preconceptions should be made clear (Feltovich et al., 1993).

- Instructors should identify and prevent misconceptions early in training and guide trainees to correct their own misconceptions later in training (Kozlowski, 1998).

- Allow time during feedback to focus on disconfirming information to help trainees unlearn misconceptions (Ross et al., 2005).

- Allow trainees to "tell the story" and help them elaborate what is correct and unlearn what is not to help them unlearn misconceptions (Ross et al., 2005).

  o Use queries to explore the trainees' thinking (Ross et al., 2005).

- Model expert thinking by walking through the facts and correcting mistaken assumptions; "paint a picture" of the situation by walking through the facts and noting how decisions evolve and what their consequences are (Ross et al., 2005).

  o When behaviors are modeled by the instructors/facilitators, provide trainees with specific instructions of what to watch for (Jentsch, Bowers, & Salas, 2001).

    - Keep in mind that research has shown that negative (incorrect) behaviors are better recognized by trainees and behaviors are more recognized if consequences are shown (Jentsch et al., 2001).

    - Also, keep in mind that research has shown that trainees are better able to generalize modeled behavior to a transfer setting if they viewed both negative and positive behaviors than if they viewed just positive behaviors (Baldwin, 1992, as cited in Salas et al., 2000).

- When instructors are not available or when otherwise appropriate, use technologies to help learners compare their understanding and handling of the situation with that of experts (Ross et al., 2005).

Encourage mental simulations to reflect on one's performance in the scenario (Ross et al., 2005).

- Help trainees to identify what parameters of different scenarios have been changed and to identify what exceptions and variations occurred (and their impact on situation assessment and choice of courses of action) (Ross et al., 2005).
- Help trainees to reflect upon the situation and to revisit it from multiple viewpoints (Ross et al., 2005).
- Help trainees to self-examine their performances by asking and answering queries such as "what if . . . ?" or "how else can I . . . ?" (Ross et al., 2005).

Taper feedback as trainees progress (Ross et al., 2005).

- "The teacher's job is 'to hold the learners in their zone of proximal development by providing just enough help and guidance, but not too much" (Perkins, 1992, as cited in Ross et al., 2005, p. 30).
- "At the novice level, instructors or coaches or mentors are necessary to guide and direct the learning process, more so than at the later stages" (Ross et al, 2005, p. 54).

Use tools to organize the feedback session (Cannon-Bowers, Burns, et al., 1998).

Use of Instructors and Instructor Training

More is needed to train than just a thorough knowledge of the domain (Ross et al., 2005; Roth, 1998).

- "Job performance does not impute instructional competence" (Roth, 1998, p. 362).
- "At this time, the best facilitator is a person who knows the field *and* understands how to help people perceive situations and reflect at different stages of competency" (Ross et al., 2005, p. 26).
- A good instructor is the primary factor in creating an authentic training experience (Ross et al., 2005).

Provide training to instructors on the conduct of scenario exercises (Oser et al., 1999), in addition to providing training on providing feedback during or after the exercise, as discussed earlier in this chapter under "Feedback Delivery." This training should focus on helping them to do the following:

- Embed triggers or opportunities for the trainees to demonstrate key competencies (Oser et al., 1999).
- Observe and record key behaviors or rate performance with the performance measurement instruments (Oser et al., 1999; Prince et al., 1993).
- Monitor scenario progress relative to a plan (Oser et al., 1999).
- Adapt to unexpected situations and unexpected trainee responses in a realistic manner (Oser et al., 1999).

- Control the scenario such that these control functions are transparent to the trainees (Oser et al., 1999).
- Use the simulation equipment, including equipment that facilitates instructor control (Oser et al., 1999) (see also "scenario management plan" under "Logistical Issues" later in this chapter).
  - When training observers/raters, they should not only practice with extremes (that is, clearly good performance and clearly poor performance), but they should also practice with instances in between (Stout, Prince, Salas, & Brannick, 1995; Yusko & Goldstein, 1997).
    - Rater training should ensure that there are acceptable levels of agreement among raters (Stout et al., 1995; Yusko & Goldstein, 1997).
- Training should also be provided to role-players before they interact with the actual trainees (Yusko & Goldstein, 1997).
  - Training provided to role-players should include explaining that they should stay in their roles versus entering unrealistically into deliberations of the trainees (Prince et al., 1993).

Use only facilitators who are credible to the training audience (Prince et al., 1993) (for example, if the audience is surgeons, they are not likely to accept feedback on surgical decisions from a nurse).

Use apprentice level mentors versus true experts, because the latter has forgotten what tends to confuse trainees.

- This is because true experts have difficulty verbalizing or articulating what they know, because their knowledge has become very deeply ingrained (Ross et al., 2005).

Logistical Issues

Try out scenarios prior to implementation to test for problems (Oser et al., 1999) to ensure that they are sufficiently challenging, yet not too challenging or unnecessarily complex (Prince et al., 1993), and to establish realism (Johnston et al., 1998; Stout et al., 1998).

- Try out the scenarios with several different trainees who represent the training audience (Prince et al., 1993).
  - Before the pilot test, scenario designers should themselves try out the scenarios (Prince et al., 1993).
- Do not rely just on expert opinion regarding how challenging a scenario is—look at trainee performance during the pilot test (for example, the current authors worked with experts in the development of a scenario that they felt would be far too challenging for their trainees only to discover that it was indeed far too easy for the five trainees in the pilot test).
- Expect several iterations of the scenario before getting the "right" one to use with the training audience, because the construction of scenarios is not an exact science (Prince et al., 1993).

- Look for trainee actions that would take them off course of the scenario and find realistic ways to bring them back in (Stout et al., 1998).
  - "Controllers must be capable of modifying a scenario in real time in response to training audience decisions and performance . . . and . . . for ensuring continuity and realism" (Oser et al., 1999, p. 190).
  - "Use scenario control and management techniques that do not prevent the training audience from making decisions in a natural manner and that are transparent to the training audience" (Oser et al., 1999, p. 200).
- Look for common mistakes made by trainees to prepare facilitators or designated observers to capture them in their performance measurement and feedback schemes.

Allow adequate time to practice using the simulation prior to the first training session (Stout et al., 1998).

Identify all of the organizational resources that will be necessary for conducting the scenarios as early as possible (Prince et al., 1993).

- For example, if air traffic control (ATC) needs to be included in the scenario and there are no qualified individuals to play this role, some ATC messages can be prerecorded (Prince et al., 1993).

Prebrief simulation/scenario participants, including the trainees and facilitators (including role-players, controllers, and observers; Oser et al., 1999; Prince et al., 1993).

- Explain each of the following:
  - The purpose, focus, and objectives of the scenario (Oser et al., 1999);
  - The scenario schedule (Oser et al., 1999);
  - Rules for the scenario (Oser et al., 1999);
  - Scenario flow (Oser et al., 1999);
  - Participant responsibilities (Oser et al., 1999);
  - Any simulation-specific limitations that may impact performance (Oser et al., 1999; Stout et al., 1998).
    - When possible, incorporate simulation-specific limitations into the scenario (for example, for a flight simulator, minor simulator malfunctions can be placarded by "maintenance," just as they would in the real world (Prince et al., 1993).

"Develop and implement a 'scenario management plan' for control of the scenario" (Oser et al., 1999).

- "Identify the requirements for and roles of scenario control personnel for overall scenario management (e.g., senior controller, senior role-player, senior observer). The scenario management plan should include: a) clear procedures for beginning and ending the scenario, b) contingency plans to follow in case of unexpected events (e.g., communication problems, simulation problems), c) the flow of the scenario, and d) clear procedures for control of the scenario. During the scenario, progress needs to be monitored relative to the management plan" (Oser et al., 1999, p. 198).

- When the facilitator must time the introduction of a fault or provide a prompt, tie the timing to information that is easy for the facilitator to note, to maintain scenario consistency (Prince et al., 1993). For example, "if it is easier for the facilitator to see and keep track of the distance than the time, then his or her planned interventions should be based on distance measuring equipment rather than time" (p. 80).
  - An example prompt that may be needed was given by Prince et al. (1993): "For example, if it is not possible to land at the briefed airfield and an alternate must be selected, a crew may not recognize the need to make that decision in a predetermined reasonable amount of time. The facilitator, acting as controller, can then prompt them to state their intentions" (p. 80).
- Script the role of the facilitator to the extent possible to guard against casual redesign of the scenario (Prince et al., 1993).
  - Creation of subscenarios can help the facilitator from having to depart from the script when trainees take an unusual action that affects the rest of the scenario in an adverse way (Sherwin, 1981, as cited in Prince et al., 1993).

Allow adequate time for a thorough debrief (Smith-Jentsch et al., 1998).

GUIDELINES FOR USING SIMULATIONS THAT ARE SPECIFIC TO TRAINING TEAMWORK SKILLS (AND ARE NOT APPLICABLE TO TRAINING INDIVIDUAL HIGHER LEVEL COGNITIVE SKILLS, UNLESS OTHERWISE NOTED)

Scenario/Training Environment

Scenarios should involve all team members (Salas et al., 2000; Swezey & Salas, 1992) either by their actual participation or through the use of role-players (Prince et al., 1993).

When relevant, incorporate into scenarios situations where multiple organizations must coordinate for effective performance (Oser et al., 1999).

Allow time for team members to conduct a premission brief (such as a preflight brief) or to plan as they would in the real world (Prince et al., 1993).

Ensure that communications are conducted and channeled as they would be in the real world (Prince et al., 1993). (Note this guideline is potentially applicable to training individual higher level cognitive skills.)

- Include any background noise in the communication system that would be present in the real world (Lauber, 1981, as cited in Prince et al., 1993).
- Include realistic interruptions (for example, receipt of ATC messages; communications from other aircraft or agencies) (Prince et al., 1993).

Instructional Strategy

Teach team leaders to effectively prebrief the scenario (Tannenbaum, Smith-Jentsch, & Behson, 1998).

- "Team leaders do not necessarily possess the skills required for conducting effective briefings—for example, they tend to over-rely on one-way communications" (Tannenbaum et al., 1998, p. 264).

- "Teams do not naturally conduct effective briefings—for example, they tend to gravitate toward discussing outcomes and task work skills to the exclusion of teamwork skills" (Tannenbaum et al., 1998, p. 264).
  - Team leaders can be trained to conduct more effective briefings, such as how to probe more and to guide the team to consider teamwork behaviors (Tannenbaum et al., 1998).

Cross-train team members (Blickensderfer, Cannon-Bowers, & Salas, 1998; Cannon-Bowers, Salas, Blickensderfer, & Bowers, 1998; Salas et al., 2000; Swezey & Salas, 1992).

- Expose trainees to their team members' roles, responsibilities, and information needs (Salas et al., 2000).
- Train them on the tasks of other team members/how other members operate (Salas et al., 2000).
  - "Interdependencies among team members should be clarified" (Swezey & Salas, 1992, p. 227).
  - The team task analysis should drive what aspects of team member tasks should be focused upon in cross-training (Blickensderfer et al., 1998).
- Explain to trainees how their task performance is related to the overall goals of the team (Kozlowski, 1998).
- Use positional rotation to foster an understanding of other team members' positions (Blickensderfer et al., 1998; Cannon-Bowers, Salas, et al., 1998; Salas et al., 2000).
- Cross-training can help team members to anticipate each others' needs (Blickensderfer et al., 1998), which can potentially allow them to better monitor each others' performance and provide more effective backup support.

Help trainees to "stop and think" about their team processes during the execution of some scenarios (Ilgen, Hollenbeck, Johnson, & Jundt, 2005).

- Teach team leaders to articulate periodic situation updates, including problems with assessments, such as missing, unreliable, or conflicting evidence (Cohen, Freeman, & Thompson, 1998).
- "Team training should include techniques for training individuals to analyze their own errors, to sense when the team or individual team members are overloaded, and to adjust their behavior when overloads occur" (Swezey & Salas, 1992, p. 233).
- "Every team member should be able to recognize unexpected events and to describe actions which he or she would expect to take when an unexpected event interferes with, or changes, the team's purpose, structure, or dependency situation" (Swezey & Salas, 1992, p. 235).

Incorporate competition among different trainees/trainee teams.

Performance Measurement/Assessment

Have a team performance measurement scheme delineated a priori (that is, in advance) (Salas et al., 2000).

- "Team and individual process and outcome measures should be identified in advance" (Smith-Jentsch, Johnston, et al., 1998; Salas et al., 2000, p. 508).

- For example, Fowlkes, Lane, Salas, Franz, and Oser (1994) described a team performance measurement scheme that they and their colleagues at NAVAIR Orlando developed and applied to an aircrew coordination training (ACT) research and development program. This measurement scheme was named "TARGETs" for Targeted Acceptable Responses to Generated Events and Tasks. It followed the Synthetic Battlefield Authoring Tool (SBAT) approach and, working with subject matter experts, specific desirable behaviors were identified for each scenario that was developed. It focused not on right or wrong responses, but on what would be a *better* response for the crew to make based upon the situation at hand. When consensus could be obtained among the experts, the behavior was added as a metric. The behaviors were placed in checklist format such that observers could simply check whether or not the behavior was demonstrated. This methodology and measurement scheme has been applied with different types and levels of aviators, such as with undergraduate naval aviators (Stout, Salas, & Fowlkes, 1997) to multiservice distributed teams (Dwyer, Oser, Salas, & Fowlkes, 1999). Table 13.1 provides an example of using the SBAT with the TARGETs measurement scheme within the T-44 undergraduate naval aviation community. The last column provides examples of specific targeted behaviors of interest in the scenario, and the column that precedes it shows the trigger event that was embedded into the scenario to elicit the behavior of interest.

- As another example, Smith-Jentsch, Zeisig, et al. (1998) described a performance measurement and feedback scheme that they and their colleagues, also at NAVAIR Orlando, developed and applied to a research and development program for training shipboard CIC teams, called "TADMUS" for Tactical Decision Making under Stress. This measurement and feedback scheme was named "TDT" for team dimensional training. This approach focused on training raters to observe different "dimensions" of teamwork (that is, information exchange, communication, supporting behavior, and initiative/leadership) and specific instances of behaviors that occurred in the conduct of a scenario that could be linked to predefined behavioral examples of the particular dimension. For example, under the dimension of information exchange, a predefined behavioral example was "providing periodic situation updates that summarize the big picture." During the performance of a scenario, different specific behavioral examples of team members providing these status updates, or failing to do so when they should, would be collected. When practical, the approach used different observers for each dimension who then pulled their responses at the end of the scenario and helped the facilitator to organize the debrief around the four dimensions. This approach used a concept of "guided team self-correction" in which a facilitator or a team leader helps team members to provide their own behavioral examples first and encourages all team members to do so (see also more on teaching team self-correction under "Feedback" later in this chapter).

Use tools to assist in capturing team performance data (Cannon-Bowers, Burns, et al., 1998).

- For example, Cannon-Bowers, Burns, et al. (1998) and their colleagues used various tools to capture performance in the TADMUS research project, such as the Shipboard Mobile Aid for Training and Evaluation (ShipMATE). They described ShipMATE as a handheld computer that allowed observers to "1. Make written and spoken observations of trainee performance, 2. capture team communications and graphic displays

Table 13.1. Sample Use of SBAT with TARGETs Measurement Scheme

Task Analysis	Targeted Competency	Generic Behavioral Component	Training Objective	Scenario Trigger Event	Performance Measure (TARGETs)
Review of literature on teams and team training; attendance of a variety of ACT courses; review of T-44 training curriculum; detailed interviews with T-44 instructors	Communication	Acknowledge communication (for example, OK, roger)	Trainee shall acknowledge communications in a scenario event involving icing conditions	Ice buildup on the wings; passenger makes note of observation	Acknowledge passenger who observed ice buildup
	Situational Awareness	Identify problems or potential problems			Discuss implications of icing
		Verbalize a course of action	Trainee shall identify problems or potential problems in a simulation event involving icing conditions (same for verbalize course of action and demonstrate task awareness)		Ask air traffic control about icing
		Demonstrate awareness of task			Make new plan
					Consult flight handbook

Adapted from Stout et al. (1997). Enhancing teamwork in complex environments through team training. *Group Dynamics: Theory, Research, and Practice, 1*(2), 169–182.

of the scenario related to those observations, 3. track and preview significant events, and 4. make specific, event based observations with cuing from the system" (Cannon-Bower, Burns, et al., 1998, p. 371).

Feedback

Provide feedback to the team as a whole and to individual members of the team (Prince et al., 1993).

Encourage all team members to provide input during feedback sessions (Smith-Jentsch, Zeisig, et al., 1998).

- Ensure that input does not focus on one or only a few team members (Smith-Jentsch, Zeisig, et al., 1998).

Recap key events at the beginning of the feedback session (Smith-Jentsch, Zeisig, et al., 1998).

Summarize the feedback session at its conclusion (Frink, 1981, as cited in Prince et al., 1993). (Note this guideline and the preceding one are potentially applicable to training individual higher level cognitive skills.)

Teach team leaders to facilitate the feedback session (Smith-Jentsch, Zeisig, et al., 1998) for some scenarios. Leaders should do the following:

- Provide task-focused versus person-oriented feedback (Tannenbaum et al., 1998).
- Ask for examples of effective and ineffective behavior prior to stating their own observations (Salas et al., 2000; Smith-Jentsch, Zeisig, et al., 1998).
  - Ask team members for *specific* examples of effective and ineffective behaviors versus generalities (Salas et al., 2000; Smith-Jentsch, Zeisig, et al. 1998) (for example, "all team members used correct brevity codes" versus "our communications were good").
- Give self-critiques (Tannenbaum et al., 1998).
- Accept feedback from others (Tannenbaum et al., 1998; Smith-Jentsch, Zeisig, et al., 1998).
- Encourage participation from all team members (Oser et al., 1999; Ross et al., 2005; Smith-Jentsch, Zeisig, et al., 1998).
  - Reinforce this participation (Smith-Jentsch, Zeisig, et al., 1998).
- Make eye contact with all team members after asking for input (Smith-Jentsch, Zeisig, et al., 1998).
- Guide team members in providing constructive input (Smith-Jentsch, Zeisig, et al., 1998).
  - (Note all of these behaviors apply to facilitators as well, except for giving a self-critique.)

Teach team members self-correction skills (Blickensderfer, Cannon-Bowers, & Salas, 1994; Salas et al., 2000; Smith-Jentsch et al., 1998).

- Give the team members an opportunity to critique their own performance (Prince et al., 1993).
- Encourage all team members to participate in self-correction (Salas et al., 2000).
- When an instructor is not present, reviews should focus on the same types of questions used when instructors are present, such as adjustments that would be made to actions based on the outcomes of the scenario (Ross et al., 2005).
  - Encourage team members to include planning and strategizing in self-correction (Salas et al., 2000).

If trainees are failing at lower level procedural skills than the team training learning objectives intended to focus upon, "punt" and remediate these lower level skills (Kirlik et al., 1998).

- Incorporating real time automated system feedback on these types of skills during the conduct of team training exercises can free the instructor up for the higher level feedback (Kirlik et al., 1998).
  - It can also improve standardization, timeliness, and diagnostic precision of feedback, as well as reduce distractions caused by facilitator-trainee interactions, especially when performing time critical, dynamic tasks (Kirlik et al., 1998).

Use tools to organize the team feedback session (Cannon-Bowers, Burns, et al., 1998).

- For example, Cannon-Bowers, Burns, et al. (1998) indicated that one of the purposes of the ShipMATE tool, described earlier, was to aid shipboard instructors in preparing for and providing a debrief on team training scenarios.

Logistic Issues

Provide a prebrief telling the team that the focus of the training is on teamwork processes versus performance outcomes (Smith-Jentsch, Zeisig, et al., 1998).

Ensure that team members are proficient on their individual technical tasks before participating in a teamwork-oriented scenario (Kirlik et al., 1998; Kozlowski, 1998; Swezey & Salas, 1992).

- "Effective team training is founded on solid individual training . . . When individuals lack knowledge or competence in their own areas, they cannot focus their attention effectively on team processes or performance" (Kozlowski, 1998, p. 139).
- Technical skill is necessary but not sufficient when teams operate in high stress environments; stress exposure training is also needed (Driskell & Johnston, 1998).
- (Note guidance and feedback can be provided on individual technical skills during a teamwork-oriented scenario, but the focus should be on teamwork skills. The current authors observed costly training of multiple aircraft personnel conducting antisubmarine warfare exercises in which radar operators had not performed radar functions in quite awhile. As a result, much of the week's training was spent teaching them basic radar operations so that they could eventually meaningfully participate in the team exercise, wasting valuable training opportunities, as well as resources).

Allow adequate time for a thorough team debrief involving all team members (Smith-Jentsch, Zeisig, et al., 1998).

CONCLUSION

The guidelines proposed in this chapter follow the SBAT. There are many guidelines provided in this chapter, and the users of these guidelines can choose those that most suit their training needs. The most critical guideline to keep in mind, however, is that a thorough task or needs analysis must be conducted to develop effective learning objectives, and everything else that is done in the SBAT process must ensure that these learning objectives are met. Furthermore, if the simulations are not designed to support these learning objectives, the training delivered via these simulations will not be effective.[2]

REFERENCES

Baker, D. P., Prince, C., Shrestha, L., Oser, R., & Salas, E. (1993). Aviation computer games for crew resource management training. *The International Journal of Aviation Psychology, 3,* 143–156.

Baldwin, T. T. (1992). Effects of alternative modeling strategies on outcomes of interpersonal-skills training. *Journal of Applied Psychology, 77*(2), 147–154.

Beaubien, J. M., & Baker, D. P. (2004). The use of simulation for training teamwork skills in health care: How low can you go? *Quality and Safety in Health Care, 13* (Suppl. 1), i51–i56.

Blickensderfer, E., Cannon-Bowers, J. A., & Salas, E. (1998). Cross training and team performance. In J. A. Cannon-Bowers & E. Salas (Eds.), *Making decisions under stress: Implications for individual and team training* (pp. 299–311). Washington, DC: American Psychological Association.

Blickensderfer, E. L., Cannon-Bowers, J. A., & Salas, E. (1994). Feedback and team training: Team self-correction. *Proceedings of the 2nd Annual Mid-Atlantic Human Factors Conference* (pp. 81–85).

Bloom, B. S., Engelhart, M. D., Furst, E. J., Hill, W. H., & Krathwohl, D. R. (1956). *Taxonomy of educational objectives: Handbook I. Cognitive domain.* New York: David McKay.

Brannick, M. T., Prince, C., & Salas, E. (2005). Can PC-based systems enhance teamwork in the cockpit? *The International Journal of Aviation Psychology, 15*(2), 173–187.

Brannick, M. T., Prince, C., Salas, E., & Stout, R. (1995, April). *Assessing aircrew coordination skills in TH-57 pilots.* In C. Bowers & F. Jentsch (Chairs), Empirical research using PC-based flight simulations, Symposium conducted at the 8th International Symposium on Aviation Psychology, Columbus, OH.

Cannon-Bowers, J. A., Burns, J. J., Salas, E., & Pruitt, J. S. (1998). Advanced technology in scenario-based training. In J. A. Cannon-Bowers & E. Salas (Eds.), *Making*

[2]This project was supported by the Department of Navy, Office of Naval Research through the University of Central Florida under ONR Award No. N00014-07-1-0098. Any opinions, findings, and conclusions or recommendations expressed in this material are those of the author(s) and do not necessarily reflect the views of the Office of Naval Research or the University of Central Florida.

decisions under stress: Implications for individual and team training (pp. 365–374). Washington, DC: American Psychological Association.

Cannon-Bowers, J. A., & Salas, E. (1997). A framework for developing team performance measures in training. In M. T. Brannick, E. Salas, & C. Prince (Eds.), *Team performance assessment and measurement: Theory, methods and applications* (pp. 45–62). Mahwah, NJ: Lawrence Erlbaum.

Cannon-Bowers, J. A., & Salas, E. (1998). Individual and team decision making under stress: Theoretical underpinnings. In J. A. Cannon-Bowers & E. Salas (Eds.), *Making decisions under stress: Implications for individual and team training* (pp. 17–38). Washington, DC: American Psychological Association.

Cannon-Bowers, J. A., Salas, E., Blickensderfer, E. L., & Bowers, C. A. (1998). The impact of cross-training and workload on team functioning: A replication and extension of the initial findings. *Human Factors, 40,* 92–101.

Cannon-Bowers, J. A., Tannenbaum, S. I., Salas, E., & Volpe, C. E. (1995). Defining team competencies and establishing team training requirements. In R. Guzzo & E. Salas (Eds.), *Team effectiveness and decision making in organizations* (pp. 333–380). San Francisco: Jossey-Bass.

Caro, P. W. (1973). Aircraft simulators and pilot training. *Human Factors, 15*(3), 502–509.

Chase, W. G., & Simon, H. A. (1973). Perception in chess. *Cognitive Psychology, 4,* 55–81.

Cicchinelli, L. F., Harmon, K. R., Keller, R. A., & Kottenstette, J. P. (1980). *Relative cost and training effectiveness of the 6883 three-dimensional simulator and actual equipment* (Rep. No. AFHRL-TR-80-24). Brooks Air Force Base, TX: Air Force Human Resources Laboratory.

Cohen, D. J. (1990, November). What motivates trainees? *Training and Development Journal, 44*(11), 91–93.

Cohen, M. S., Freeman, J. T., & Thompson, B. (1998). Critical thinking skills in tactical decision making: A model and a training strategy. In J. A. Cannon-Bowers & E. Salas (Eds.), *Making decisions under stress: Implications for individual and team training* (pp. 155–189). Washington, DC: American Psychological Association.

de Jong, T., & van Joolingen, W. R. (1998). Scientific discovery learning with computer simulations of conceptual domains. *Review of Educational Research, 68*(2), 179–201.

Driskell, J. E., & Johnston, J. H. (1998). Stress exposure training. In J. A. Cannon-Bowers & E. Salas (Eds.), *Making decisions under stress: Implications for individual and team training* (pp. 191–217). Washington, DC: American Psychological Association.

Dwyer, D. J., Oser, R. L., Salas, E., & Fowlkes, J. E. (1999). Performance measurement in distributed environments: Initial results and implications for training. *Military Psychology, 11*(2), 189–215.

Feltovich, P. J., Spiro, R. J., & Coulson, R. L. (1989). The nature of conceptual understanding in biomedicine: The deep structure of complex ideas and the development of misconceptions. In D. A. Evans & V. L. Patel (Eds.), *Cognitive science in medicine: Biomedical modeling* (pp. 113–172). Cambridge, MA: The MIT Press.

Feltovich, P. J., Spiro, R. J., & Coulson, R. L. (1993). Learning, teaching, and testing for complex conceptual understanding. In N. Frederiksen, R. J. Mislevy, & I. I. Bejar (Eds.), *Test theory for a new generation of tests* (pp. 181–215). Hillsdale, NJ: Lawrence Erlbaum.

Fowlkes, J. E., Lane, N. E., Salas, E., Franz, T., & Oser, R. (1994). Improving the measurement of team performance: The TARGETs methodology. *Military Psychology, 6,* 47–61.

Frink, A. (1981). Performance evaluation and assessment. In J. K. Lauber & H. C. Foushee (Eds.), *Guidelines for the development of line-oriented flight training: Vol. 2. Proceedings of a NASA/industry workshop* (NASA Conference Publication No. 2184, pp. 122–126). Moffet Field, CA: NASA Ames Research Center.

Hagman, J. D., & Rose, A. M. (1983). Retention of military tasks: A review. *Human Factors, 25*(2), 199–213.

Hays, R. T. (2006). *The science of learning: A systems theory approach.* Boca Raton, FL: Brown Walker Press.

Hays, R. T., Jacobs, J. W., Prince, C., & Salas, E. (1992). Flight simulator training effectiveness: A meta-analysis. *Military Psychology, 4*(2), 63–74.

Hays, R. T., Stout, R. J., & Ryan-Jones, D. L. (2005). *Quality evaluation tool for computer- and web-delivered instruction* (Rep. No. NAWCTSD TR-2005-2). Orlando, FL: Naval Air Warfare Center Trainig Systems Division. (ADA 435 294).

Huczynski, A. A., & Louis, J. W. (1980). An empirical study into the learning transfer process in management training. *Journal of Management Studies, 17,* 227–240.

Ilgen, D. R., Hollenbeck, J. R., Johnson, M., & Jundt, D. (2005). Teams in organizations: From input-process-output models to IMOI models. *Annual Review of Psychology, 56,* 517–543.

Jacobs, J. W., Prince, C., Hays, R. T., & Salas, E. (1990). *A meta-analysis of flight simulator training research* (Tech. Rep. No. 89-006). Orlando, FL: Naval Training Systems Center.

Jentsch, F. G. M. (1997). *Metacognitive training for junior team members: Solving the copilot's catch 22.* Unpublished doctoral dissertation, University of Central Florida, Orlando.

Jentsch, F., & Bowers, C. (1998). Evidence for the validity of PC-based simulations in studying aircrew coordination. *The International Journal of Aviation Psychology, 8,* 243–260.

Jentsch, F., & Bowers, C., & Salas, E. (2001). What determines whether observers recognize targeted behaviors in modeling displays? *Human Factors, 43*(3), 496–507.

Johnston, J. H., Poirier, J., & Smith-Jentsch, K. A. (1998). Decision making under stress: Creating a research methodology. In J. A. Cannon-Bowers & E. Salas (Eds.), *Making decisions under stress: Implications for individual and team training* (pp. 39–59). Washington, DC: American Psychological Association.

Kirlik, A., Fisk, A. D., Walker, N., & Rothrock, L. (1998). Feedback augmentation and part-task practice in training dynamic decision-making skills. In J. A. Cannon-Bowers & E. Salas (Eds.), *Making decisions under stress: Implications for individual and team training* (pp. 91–113). Washington, DC: American Psychological Association.

Kozlowski, S. W. J. (1998). Training and developing adaptive teams: Theory, principles, and research. In J. A. Cannon-Bowers & E. Salas (Eds.), *Making decisions under stress: Implications for individual and team training* (pp. 115–153). Washington, DC: American Psychological Association.

Lauber, J. K., & Foushee, H. C. (Eds.). (1981). *Guidelines for the development of line-oriented flight training: Vol. 2. Proceedings of a NASA/industry workshop* (NASA Conference Publication No. 2184). Moffet Field, CA: NASA Ames Research Center.

Leutner, D. (1993). Guided discovery learning with computer-based simulation games: Effects of adaptive and non-adaptive instructional support. *Learning and Instruction, 3,* 113–132.

Magjuka, R. J., Baldwin, T. T., & Loher, B. T. (2000). The combined effects of three pre-training strategies on motivation and performance: An empirical exploration. *Journal of Managerial Issues, 6,* 282–296.

Miller, G. A., (1956). The magical number seven, plus or minus two: Some limits on our capacity for processing information. *Psychological Review, 63,* 81–97.

Oser, R. L., Cannon-Bowers, J. A., Salas, E., & Dwyer, D. J. (1999). Enhancing human performance in technology-rich environments: Guidelines for scenario-based training. In E. Salas (Ed.), *Human/technology interaction in complex systems* (Vol. 9, pp. 175–202). Stamford, CT: JAI Press.

Perkins, D. N. (1992). Technology meets constructivism: Do they make a marriage? In T. M. Duffy & D. H. Jonassen (Eds.), *Constructivism and the technology of instruction* (pp. 45–55). Mahwah, NJ: Lawrence Erlbaum.

Prince, C., Oser, R., Salas, E., & Woodruff, W. (1993). Increasing hits and reducing misses in CRM/LOS scenarios: Guidelines for simulator scenario development. *International Journal of Aviation Psychology, 3*(1), 69–82.

Ross, K. G., Phillips, J. K., Klein, G., & Cohn, J. (2005). *Creating expertise: A framework to guide technology-based training* (Final Tech. Rep., Contract No. M67854-04-C-8035). Orlando, FL: MARCORSYSCOM PMTRASYS.

Roth, J. T. (1998). Improving decision-making skills through on-the-job training: A roadmap for training shipboard trainers. In J. A. Cannon-Bowers & E. Salas (Eds.), *Making decisions under stress: Implications for individual and team training* (pp. 345–364). Washington, DC: American Psychological Association.

Salas, E., Bowers, C. A., & Rhodenizer, L. (1998). It is not how much you have but how you use it: Toward a rational use of simulation to support aviation training. *The International Journal of Aviation Psychology, 8* (3), 197–208.

Salas, E., Milham, L. M., & Bowers, C. A. (2003). Training evaluation in the military: Misconceptions, opportunities, and challenges. *Military Psychology, 15*(1), 3–16.

Salas, E., Rhodenizer, L., & Bowers, C. A. (2000). The design and delivery of crew resource management training: Exploiting available resources. *Human Factors, 42*(3), 490–511.

Schendel, J. D., & Hagman, J. D. (1982). On sustaining procedural skills over a prolonged retention interval. *Journal of Applied Psychology, 67*(5), 605–610.

Serfaty, D., Entin, E. E., & Johnston, J. H. (1998). Team coordination training. In J. A. Cannon-Bowers & E. Salas (Eds.), *Making decisions under stress: Implications for individual and team training* (pp. 221–245). Washington, DC: American Psychological Association.

Sherwin, P. (1981). Scenario design and development issues. In J. K. Lauber & H. C. Foushee (Eds.), *Guidelines for the development of line-oriented flight training: Vol. 2. Proceedings of a NASA/industry workshop* (NASA Conference Publication No. 2184, pp. 113–118). Moffet Field, CA: NASA Ames Research Center.

Simpson, E. J. (1972). The classification of educational objectives in the psychomotor domain. In *Contributions of behavioral science to instructional technology: 3. The psychomotor domain: A resource book for media specialists* (pp. 43–56). Washington, DC: Gryphon House.

Smith-Jentsch, K. A., Johnston, J. H., & Payne, S. C. (1998). Measuring team-related expertise in complex environments. In J. A. Cannon-Bowers & E. Salas (Eds.), *Making decisions under stress: Implications for individual and team training* (pp. 61–87). Washington, DC: American Psychological Association.

Smith-Jentsch, K. A., Zeisig, R. L., Acton, B., & McPherson, J. A. (1998). Team dimensional training: A strategy for guided team self-correction. In J. A. Cannon-Bowers & E. Salas (Eds.), *Making decisions under stress: Implications for individual and team training* (pp. 271–297). Washington, DC: American Psychological Association.

Stout, R. J., Prince, C., Salas, E., & Brannick, M. T. (1995, April). Beyond reliability: Using crew resource management (CRM) measurements for training. *Proceedings of the 10th International Symposium on Aviation Psychology.*

Stout, R. J., Salas, E., & Fowlkes, J. (1997). Enhancing teamwork in complex environments through team training. *Group Dynamics: Theory, Research, & Practice, 1,* 169–182.

Stout, R. J., Salas, E., Merket, D. C., & Bowers, C. A. (1998). Low-cost simulation and military aviation team training. *Proceedings of the American Institute of Aeronautics and Astronautics Modeling and Simulation Conference* (pp. 311–318).

Swezey, R. W., & Salas, E. (1992). Guidelines for use in team-training development. In R. W. Swezey & E. Salas (Eds.), *Teams: Their training and performance* (pp. 219–245). Norwood, NJ: Ablex Publishing Corporation.

Tannenbaum, S. I., Smith-Jentsch, K. A., & Behson, S. J. (1998). Training team leaders to facilitate team learning and performance. In J. A. Cannon-Bowers & E. Salas (Eds.), *Making decisions under stress: Implications for individual and team training* (pp. 247–270). Washington, DC: American Psychological Association.

Wikipedia. (2007a). *Definition of meta-analysis.* Retrieved January 16, 2007, from http://en.wikipedia.org/wiki/Meta_analysis

Wikipedia. (2007b). *Definition of overlearning.* Retrieved January 10, 2007, from http://en.wikipedia.org/wiki/Overlearning

Yusko, K. P. & Goldstein, H. W. (1997). Selecting and developing crisis leaders using competency-based simulations. *Journal of Contingencies and Crisis Management, 5* (4), 216–223.

Part III: Training Management

Chapter 14

AFTER ACTION REVIEW IN SIMULATION BASED TRAINING

Don Lampton, Glenn Martin,
Larry Meliza, and Stephen Goldberg

The after action review, or AAR, is a bedrock of modern military training for training teams, units, and organizations. The AAR is a method of providing feedback to units after operational missions or collective training exercises (U.S. Army Combined Arms Center, 1993). It is an interactive discussion, guided by a facilitator or trainer known as an AAR leader. During the AAR, unit members discuss what happened, why it happened, and how to improve or sustain performance in similar situations in the future. The AAR begins with a review of the unit's mission or goals. Establishing what happened should include exercise controllers, observers, and role-players, including the opposing force. However, the hallmark of the modern AAR technique is the active participation of the trainees.

The AAR is used extensively by the U.S. Army and the U.S. Marine Corps. Related procedures, varying in degree of formality, are used in naval and aviation training. While much of the work involved in developing and refining the AAR process was accomplished to support the training of military units, the AAR approach should be relevant to any organization that makes use of collective training methods (for example, police SWAT [special weapons and tactics] teams). The AAR has been applied to nonmilitary government applications (Rogers, 2004) and industry (Darling & Parry, 2001). A thorough history of the AAR process is presented by Morrison and Meliza (1999).

This chapter presents the potential training benefits of the use of simulation based AAR tools, as well as some of the technical challenges that may be faced when designing and implementing AAR systems. An overview is presented of the use of AARs in the field of practice of the army, as observed by the current authors and colleagues, based upon army doctrine. The focus of the chapter is the design, implementation, and use of an AAR system developed specifically for use with immersive virtual environment simulations for training small teams. The features and the specific training benefits that this AAR system can provide are described. Issues and challenges faced when designing and implementing this AAR system, and lessons that were learned in doing so, are discussed. Finally, guidance is provided for designing and implementing computer based AARs in general, which were derived from the specific lessons that were learned.

OVERVIEW OF THE AFTER ACTION REVIEW

The U.S. Army has documented the AAR doctrine extensively in formal training circulars and field manuals, including Training Circular No. 25-20, *A Leader's Guide to After-Action Reviews* (U.S. Army Combined Arms Center, 1993) and Field Manual No. 7-1, *Battle Focused Training* (Department of the Army, 2003). The AAR is considered a valid and valuable technique regardless of branch, echelon, or training task. It can be applied to both live and virtual training environments. In the live environment, the training participants use operational equipment on real world terrain to perform against an opposition force composed of a live opposition force, targets (live fire), or a combination of both. In virtual environments, the training participants use simulated equipment and weapons. Virtual training frequently uses semi-automated forces to populate the virtual environment with computer-generated friendly forces, enemy, neutrals, and civilians.

FEEDBACK IN THE AAR PROCESS

Holding (1989) pointed out that feedback is a critical component to all skill acquisition. Collective training exercises can provide intrinsic and extrinsic performance feedback (Brown, Nordyke, Gerlock, Begley, & Meliza, 1998).

Intrinsic feedback consists of the cues that exercise participants perceive about their own performance. For example, an infantry unit may call in artillery fire on a target. Intrinsic feedback would consist of the unit's observation that artillery rounds are impacting too far from the intended target. As a result of their perception of their performance, they would have the supporting artillery unit shift fires. Extrinsic feedback consists of information that the exercise participants do not ordinarily have available to them. It can provide insights into how to improve or sustain performance in the future.

Participants sometimes end an exercise with a limited perspective regarding what happened, based upon the information available to them and what they saw, heard, and otherwise sensed (intrinsic feedback). This limited perspective is referred to as "perceived truth." "Ground truth" is the term used to describe the actual situation that occurred. Trainees are often not able to perceive all that is going on around them, so perceived truth may frequently differ from ground truth. Events may be happening quickly and may be open to differing interpretations. Perceptions and memories of the occurrence, sequence, and timing of events can be greatly distorted leading to generation of causal relationships that are not based on the actual facts (Goldberg & Meliza, 1993).

Sometimes exercise participants recognize the impacts of their actions via intrinsic feedback, but at other times they are not aware of these impacts until they receive extrinsic feedback. Extrinsic feedback can be used to correct misperceptions and clarify events and effects. The AAR process may provide unit members with a view of collective (team, unit, or organizational) performance that was not apparent to, or viewable by, any one participant during an exercise (Meliza, 1999), including the trainers who were observing the exercise. The AAR uses a Socratic method in which a series of leading and open-ended questions are used by an AAR leader to help those in the training audience discover what happened and why.

A debrief or critique conducted by one or more observers of a training exercise is an alternative to the AAR (Scott & Fobes, 1982; Hoare, 1996). Historically, the critique preceded the AAR as the way of providing feedback by trainers. A person who had observed a training exercise lectured the trainees. A major difference between the AAR and the critique is that the critique provided the training participants with conclusions reached by the person giving the critique rather than facilitating the training participants to reach their own conclusions. Critiques could easily be construed as criticism because the opinions expressed were based on perceptions, judgments, and possibly misinterpretations of ground truth. Morrison and Meliza (1999) note that the critique often focused on errors committed and created a defensive atmosphere among the trainees.

In contrast to the critique method, in the modern AAR method the leader functions as a discussion facilitator. Training participants are expected to examine their performance through guided self-evaluation. They are encouraged to identify their problems and develop approaches to correct them. It has been suggested that use of the AAR feedback method results in units taking ownership of the diagnosis of problems and the corrective actions they identify (Scott & Fobes, 1982).

AAR FUNCTIONALITIES TO SUPPORT FEEDBACK

To be effective and efficient the AAR leader needs one or more starting points for the discussion and at least a general idea of where the discussion will head. The job of the AAR leader is made easier to the extent that he or she is already aware of the types of problems the unit has been experiencing. If all an AAR leader knows about a mission is that a unit sustained heavy casualties, the Socratic method will take a long time to identify the root causes of the problem. If the AAR leader knows that most of the casualties occurred within a few minutes of making contact with the enemy and that few friendly vehicles returned fire upon contact, then that leader is closer to identifying and understanding what happened and why.

In virtual simulations, AAR aids prepared from electronic data streams can document or illustrate aspects of performance that are close to the root causes of weaknesses and strengths. Developments in battlefield simulation technology have made it possible to provide AAR leaders with an electronic record describing unit or individual location, firing events, and communications over the course of an exercise. AAR software systems allow these data to be converted into a variety of AAR aids demonstrating critical aspects of unit performance (Meliza, 1999). These aids can be used during an AAR to describe or illustrate ground truth. For example, a graph showing the number of rounds fired by each vehicle in a platoon over time may make the point that only one of the vehicles in the platoon fired during the first five minutes of an engagement. To gain this information from the AAR process, a unit would have to slowly reconstruct the sequence of events based on the unit members' memories. AAR aids also offer the benefit of providing units with demonstrable ground truth when their recollections are at odds with what actually happened.

To the extent that AAR aids illustrate the root causes of exercise events, they expedite the AAR process. AAR aid generation capabilities that examine exercise data streams to check specific aspects of performance offer a means of helping AAR leaders and units diagnose strengths and weaknesses.

The most frequently used AAR aid is a sequential replay of exercise events. A replay, however, is not necessarily the most efficient or effective way of illustrating key aspects of performance. Long segments of the exercise may contain no individual events that are significant in isolation, and, therefore, AAR aids that summarize activity over a period of time can be more effective. A graphic showing shot lines (lines connecting shooter location to impact location) aggregated over a specific period of time can quickly show which potential targets were engaged and by whom during the period of interest.

A Recently Developed AAR Tool for Virtual Environments

In the 1999 to 2002 time frame, as part of an overall project to develop capabilities for simulation based training of dismounted combatants, the Dismounted Infantry Virtual AAR System (DIVAARS) was developed. The goal was to develop an AAR system that incorporated lessons learned from earlier AAR systems and was tailored to the unique requirements of small unit dismounted infantry training in a virtual environment. An emphasis was placed on being able to meet the special challenges of urban environments for military operations and training. The challenges are primarily visual in that buildings and other structures break up the visual field and limit the portion of the battlefield that can be observed by any one person (Lampton, Clark, & Knerr, 2003). This required an AAR system that could not only replay an exercise, but could also support the AAR goals of presenting exercise events and data in a manner that would facilitate trainee understanding of what happened, why it happened, and how to improve. DIVAARS recreates exactly what happened during the mission. During the replay the unit members can observe the location, posture, and actions of all the other members. DIVAARS can replay mission action exactly as viewed by any of the participants, providing the trainees with perspectives that would not be available with live training. These features not only support the trainees' explanation of why events happened, but also may help the unit members develop shared mental models of individual and unit tasks. Watching the replay may also strengthen group identification and cohesiveness. Finally, several DIVAARS features, such as depicting critical events in slow motion and from multiple perspectives, may enhance memory so those lessons learned are more likely to be employed in subsequent training and missions.

DIVAARS Features

Playback

A linear beginning-to-end playback is unlikely to be either the best or most efficient way to provide the trainees with an understanding of what happened during an exercise. The replay system includes such actions as pause, stop, play, step-forward, fast-forward, rewind, fast-reverse, and step-reverse. Variable playback speeds are available. In addition, the AAR leader has the capability to mark significant events during the exercise and jump directly to them during the AAR.

Viewing Modes

Viewing scenario events from different perspectives can support understanding what happened. Multiple viewing modes are available during both the exercise and the AAR. Ten preset views can be selected at any time prior to or during the exercise for immediate use. These can be used for perspectives or positions that the AAR leader thinks will be useful, such as the view from an enemy position. The variety of viewing modes provides added capabilities during the AAR process.

- Top-down view—A view of the database looking straight down from above. It can be moved left, right, up, down, and zoomed in or out. The AAR leader can also lock the view onto an entity, in which case it will stay centered directly above that entity as it moves through the database.

- Two-dimensional (2-D) view—This is the traditional plan view display. It is the same as the top-down view except that depth perspective is not shown.

- Entity view—By selecting any entity (including enemy or civilian), the AAR leader can see and display exactly what that entity sees. This includes the effects of head turning and posture changes.

- Fly Mode—The AAR leader can "fly" through the database using the mouse for control.

During the course of a replay the trainees will be able to see the mission from a number of perspectives. The top-down, 2-D, and fly views, views that are never available to trainees during the mission exercise, promote seeing the big picture and learning to see the battlefield. The entity view, seeing through the eyes of others, supports a number of training functions. Did the leaders see an action or problem, but fail to respond, or were they not looking in the right direction at all? Do squad members maintain 360° security and report promptly? What was the view from likely and actual enemy positions?

Movement Tracks

Movement tracks show, in a single view, the path an entity traveled during an exercise. Markers are displayed at fixed time intervals. Every fifth marker is a different shape than the four preceding it. The display of these markers can be turned on and off. The movement tracks provide a clear display of the path and speed of movement of each member of the unit. In addition, they provide indications of the unit formations and of the location and duration of halts in movement. Thus, the AAR leader may elect to skip or fast-forward through portions of the replay, knowing that the movement traces for those skipped segments will be observable when the replay is resumed.

Entity Identifier

A unique identifier is shown above the avatar (virtual representation) of each unit member. For example, 2SL is the identifier for the squad leader, second squad. The entity identifiers change size to be readable across all levels of zooming.

Viewing Floors of a Building

The AAR leader needs to be able to follow the action in military operations on urban terrain (MOUT) scenarios even when a unit enters a building. The AAR leader can select a building and then select a floor of that building to be displayed. Using this feature, the operator can view and display the avatars going through a building without the problem of upper floors being in the way.

Munition Visualizations

This feature helps to determine what objects are being shot by each entity and to identify patterns of unit fire. Bullet flight lines, artillery arcs, and missile paths are shown as appropriate for all weapon firings. Each visualization is the same color as the originating entity and gradually fades away after the shot.

Event Data Collection and Display

DIVAARS has the capability to track many events, including shots fired, kills by entities, movement, and posture changes. These data can be shown in a tabular format or graphical display. The AAR leader can use them as needed to make various teaching points. They can also be used to support subsequent data analysis for research and development applications. Critical incident events are automatically flagged, reducing workload on the AAR operator, and can be jumped to during playback. Examples of critical events are the first shot fired during a mission and fratricides. The ability to jump to marked events allows the AAR leader to quickly access a number of related events to support a discussion theme, such as quality of reporting, rather than dealing with incidents in the order they occur in a sequential replay. Security, use of resources, and mission tempo are examples of themes we have observed experienced AAR leaders address.

Ten different tables and graphs are available:

- Shots fired, by entity and unit;
- Kills, by entity and unit;
- Killer-victim table that shows who killed whom, with the option to show the angle of the killing shot (front, flank, or back) or the posture of the victim (standing, kneeling, or prone);

- Shots as a function of time, by entity, unit, and weapon;
- Kills as a function of time, by entity, unit, and weapon;
- Kills by distance from killer to victim, by entity, unit, and weapon;
- Rate of movement of each entity, and aggregated at fire team and squad levels;
- Percentage of time friendly units were stationary;
- Percentage of time friendly units were in different postures;
- Display of user-defined events.

DIVAARS Evaluation and Utilization

DIVAARS was developed as part of a comprehensive program to develop capabilities for dismounted combatant virtual training. It was evaluated within the context of the exercises conducted as part of the overall research program. Overall, DIVAARS was rated very highly by soldiers.

Table 14.1 contains soldier ratings of the system's capability to present information. The data represent soldiers' opinions drawn from a number of different projects. The conditions for each year differed in the composition of the teams of trainees, the individual AAR facilitators, the suites of virtual environment (VE) technologies used, and the mission scenarios.

These high ratings reflected favorably not only on the DIVAARS capabilities to support the goals of the AAR process, but also on the skill of the facilitators who lead the AARs. Although the terminology varied, all of the facilitators directed the AAR discussions to identify "improves" and "sustains." Improves addressed aspects of team performance that did no go well and how to do better the next time. Sustains identified and reinforced successful aspects of performance and provided positive notes to the AAR.

Since its development trials in 2001 and 2002, DIVAARS was used as the AAR tool in the Virtual Integrated MOUT Training System testing at Fort Campbell, Kentucky, in 2004 (Knerr & Lampton, 2005). It was used in tests of

Table 14.1.   Ratings of DIVAARS by Soldiers Participating in Dismounted Soldier Simulation Exercises

The AAR System Made Clear	Ratings	2001	2002	2004	2005
What happened	SA*	44%	82%	62%	68%
during a mission	A	56%	12%	31%	32%
	Total	100%	94%	93%	100%
Why things happened	SA	44%	76%	46%	62%
the way they did	A	39%	24%	35%	35%
during a mission	Total	83%	100%	81%	97%
How to do better	SA	28%	71%	54%	69%
in accomplishing	A	56%	24%	38%	23%
the mission	Total	84%	95%	92%	92%

*Note: SA = strongly agree; A = agree.

wearable-computer dismounted soldier training systems. DIVAARS was included in the suite of capabilities making up the U.S. Navy's Virtual Technologies and Environments (VIRTE) program.

Issues in After Action Review System Development

Design of Virtual AAR Systems

AAR systems are typically based on their planned use (for example, live versus virtual and/or domains such as military, medical, and so forth) and use varying technologies to fulfill their missions. Such systems range from straight analytical systems that produce only tables and graphs of performance to full reproduction virtual and live systems that use 3-D rendering or video recordings. Our focus is on the full virtual systems with a slight discussion of live and analytical systems.

Virtual AAR systems are either independent applications or dependent applications that use the simulation as a part of the AAR system. An independent AAR system records and plays back all data within it, handling all recording and all rendering. Alternatively, a dependent AAR system could record all data and retransmit them back to existing simulators for rendering (such as a stealth viewer, which renders the simulated environment).

Conceptually, every AAR system must run in a minimum of two phases. The first, the recording phase, is when all data are processed and stored. The data may be stored exactly as received, or they may be sampled at regular time intervals. The former has the advantage of storing exactly what was actually transmitted, while the latter simplifies later use of the data (although at the cost of storing more data as the samples would be recorded at a higher frequency than the transmitted data). In addition, an AAR system could include prerecording, preplayback, and post-playback phases to provide an AAR leader the ability to preplan the AAR and the ability to record notes on the exercise for later use.

For a system that stores actual data, data playback can bring some issues. The primary problem is that the data must be rerendered to fill in necessary gaps. For example, an application built on the distributed interactive simulation (Institute of Electrical and Electronics Engineers [IEEE] Computer Society, 1996), or DIS, protocol that stores the actual protocol data units (PDUs), or network packets, would be required to perform dead reckoning on the data in order to complete a playback rendering. Although this is initially straightforward, dead reckoning must be altered to handle varying speeds. DIS uses a "heartbeat" and a "time-out" value to handle simulators joining an exercise or leaving an exercise (including as a result of a system crash). Entity updates are typically sent every 5 seconds (the heartbeat), and entities for which no update has been received for 12 seconds are dropped (the time-out). For example, in "slow motion" replay mode an AAR system has to adjust the DIS heartbeat and time-out as another PDU may not "arrive" until a scale factor later (for example, replay at 0.25 speed would use a heartbeat of 20 seconds and a corresponding time-out time).

Similarly, dead reckoning must handle a "pause" function in the AAR system and stop updating entities.

Whether a system stores actual data or sampled data, playback still must address some important issues. These issues largely come from manipulating the data as the user plays back segments of the exercise. As the replay simulation time is altered, changes to the virtual environment must be addressed in appropriate fashion.

First, rewinding is a major issue during playback. If a system does not store samples of the position and orientation (that is, it is a nonsampling system), then velocity and acceleration parameters within the dead reckoning process must be negated to process correctly. In effect, the application must "rewind" the entities by simulating them in reverse. In addition, changes made to the virtual environment during the exercise in all virtual AAR systems must be "undone" as necessary. This can include relatively simple things, such as closing recently opened doors and removing textures of weapons effects from the sides of buildings. However, more complex changes must also be undone. If dynamic terrain is supported (for example, a hole blown into the side of a building in a breaching operation), then it must also be undone during a rewind operation (for example, the hole must be filled back in).

Second, jumping directly from one time to another, without "playing" the intervening events, must be handled. One major characteristic that makes an AAR system different from a replay system is the ability to jump through the data stream, show and discuss what is necessary, and then go on to a next exercise. To accomplish a jump through time, AAR systems must update each entity within the world without ignoring the effects of key events that occurred during that jumped time period. For example, while updating entities is a relatively straightforward process, such interactions as weapon fire and dynamic terrain changes still need to be performed and not skipped. It becomes necessary to build a file index that includes a notion of "important" data packets that get processed even during a jump operation.

It is important to note here the dependency on simulation time of these events. Simulators are often built that either lack a time concept (that is, do not place a timestamp on data at all) or ignore it (that is, do not fill in correct times). Whereas most simulators can simply process data once received, properly timestamped data are essential for AAR system playback. Without timestamps, the AAR system cannot know when a particular event should be processed relative to the events surrounding it. In a worst case scenario, the AAR system can place a timestamp on data as they are received before storing them.

Voice Communication

Voice and other fast streaming types of data warrant special attention in any AAR system that processes the data directly (whether virtual, live, or analytical). Such data are time sensitive and require the AAR system to keep pace both in recording and rendering.

During recording, the data must be retrieved from the communication mechanism (typically, the simulation network) quickly to avoid falling behind. Otherwise, the result is voice communication that does not synchronize properly with the simulation events. As the exercise continues, the discrepancy will grow and become more noticeable. However, addressing this issue alone is not enough.

During rendering at playback, the AAR system can have almost the opposite problem. As the voice data are retrieved from the recording, they must not only be read from the recording quickly enough (similar to reading from the network), but also rendered quickly enough. In an AAR system that is performing multiple tasks, keeping up with rendering can be a difficult issue. In addition, such an AAR system must monitor itself and realize when it has fallen behind.

To handle the recording and reading issue, a separate computational thread is often beneficial to provide the AAR system enough running time to accomplish handling all the data. For rendering, another separate thread is also beneficial so that the audio card can receive the data in time. A starved rendering system will come across as sounding as if it has a stuttering problem with small gaps between syllables. It is important to note that a rendering thread also must monitor itself to make sure it does not fall behind too much. Such latency will cause the voice communication to become offset from the simulation events (much like not reading from the network quickly enough). In this case, it is often better to drop some packets (and accept the slight audio glitch) to synchronize the voice data back with the simulation data.

An AAR Engine

Whether military or another domain, there are many capabilities needed in an AAR system. These include recording and playback of scenario data with full ability to pause, rewind, and jump to specific events. In addition, support for a graphical user interface and potentially other interfaces (such as an electronic whiteboard) could be included. On the other hand, there are also some features that may be specific for each domain. For example, a military AAR system would include visualization of weapon effects, but an AAR system for working with patients in cognitive rehabilitation might visually highlight all the key elements in the environment necessary for making coffee.

To address these issues, an engine for after action reviews could provide these capabilities, based on a fundamental architecture of common functionalities coupled with a plug-in architecture for specific domain features. In addition, the plug-in architecture allows users to add their own new capabilities to include in their AAR system. In order to allow the core functions and the plug-in modules to communicate, an event or messaging system would be required that allows all the components to communicate.

The System of Object Based Components for Review and Assessment of Training Environment Scenarios (SOCRATES) is one such engine (University of Central Florida, 2007). SOCRATES is not a new general-purpose AAR system, but rather it is an AAR engine. As such, it provides the common functionalities across all potential AAR systems into a single foundation for all training environment scenarios (much like a game engine provides the common needs of games). This architecture allows other modules to be loaded to essentially create a new after action review system. In addition to providing flexibility, the plug-in architecture also provides the capability not to load a feature. If a particular review system is being used on a less capable machine (such as a wearable computer of an embedded simulation), some features could be disabled.

DIVAARS is an example of an AAR system built upon the SOCRATES AAR engine. Each military-specific capability (such as viewing inside a building or shot visualization) is implemented as a plug-in. However, an AAR engine also allows the development of AAR systems in new domains that have not previously used the AAR process. For example, specialists in cognitive rehabilitation have recently been using modeling and simulation to increase cognitive ability in brain injury patients (Fidopiastis et al., 2005). As a part of this, they desire the ability to review each patient's performance whether in mock scenarios (such as a mock kitchen as a part of a rehabilitation clinic) or in virtual/augmented environments. An AAR system here would provide the ability to record and review a session with a patient in a cognitive rehabilitation setting.

DISTRIBUTED AARS

AAR systems have typically been designed to support multiple trainees at a single location. However, it is also necessary to conduct training, and AARs, within a distributed training environment with trainees at multiple physical sites (the extreme being each trainee at his or her own location). A distributed AAR system presents additional issues.

First, a distributed AAR system has to address interface issues. In an AAR leader based setting, there must be an auditory and visual component to the AAR. Each user must be able to communicate verbally across the distributed links. In addition, the rendering must occur at each user station. This requires the creation of a client AAR application that will receive commands and updates from the AAR leader's master station.

Typically, AAR sessions would occur in a group setting with the AAR leader standing in front of the trainees facilitating discussion. In a distributed setting, this is not the case, but elements of the face-to-face review need to be introduced. Some method allowing the AAR leader to highlight items and "point" to things would be required. A "telestrator" much like those used in sports broadcasts can be very useful in this setting (Martin & Cherng, 2007).

Beyond the interface, there are also communication issues between the master and client stations within the distributed AAR. Some communication protocol must be created for the master station to control the client stations (to allow the AAR leader to "play" the exercise, control the viewpoint, send out telestrator visuals, and so forth). SOCRATES uses an Extensible Markup Language (XML) based protocol to achieve this requirement. The XML is a generalization of the more known HyperText Markup Language used in the World Wide Web and allows generic data to be tagged qualitatively (its text based characteristic makes it easy to expand and act as a system-independent representation of data). Other systems have created their own binary protocol. Ultimately, a standardized protocol should be created that all AAR systems could implement and on which be based.

Communication schemes can also be an issue. In the simplest case, the master station receives all data in recording mode and then transmits simulation data to each client during playback. However, in some systems the network bandwidth available may be reduced, and it may be desirable to limit the network bandwidth required for the AAR. Alternatively, depending on the simulation data, it may actually be cheaper to transmit image data from the master station to the client stations rather than the simulation data itself.

Finally, depending on the network technologies used, there can also be storage issues in a distributed AAR system. If the network is severely limited, each embedded simulation may store its own data for AAR or limit transmission to a few nearby locations. In this case the "master" AAR station does not have all the data necessary to reproduce the exercise. A coordination of transmission of the data from client to client would be necessary to address who needs what data for rendering.

These last two issues (communication schemes and data storage) are currently the least understood technological research questions in distributed after action review. As research in embedded simulation and limited bandwidth networks progresses, many of these questions will be answered.

SUMMARY

Although it evolved from live training, the AAR process seems to fit exceptionally well with computer based simulation training. The AAR process and AAR aids have been tailored many times to fit different live and simulated training environments, missions, and unit equipment. The AAR process can work well with computer based simulations to quickly determine what happened during a simulation exercise and to support the discussion of why events occurred and how to do better. However, many challenges remain in implementing cost-effective new simulations based on game engine technologies, and identifying the most effective training strategies for their use.

Different approaches can be used to build AAR systems, each with its own issues. However, there are a number of core issues common to every AAR system, such as jumping to an event or time and synchronizing voice communications. An "AAR engine" to address these issues for a set of AAR systems can be an advantageous approach. This becomes more evident as distributed AAR sessions are considered and the handling of data across widely distributed nodes becomes an issue.

REFERENCES

Brown, B. R., Nordyke, J. W., Gerlock, D. L., Begley, I. J., & Meliza, L. L. (1998, May). *Training analysis and feedback aids (TAAF Aids) study for live training support* (Study

Report, Army Project Number 2O665803D730). Alexandria, VA: U.S. Army Research Institute for the Behavioral and Social Sciences.

Darling, M. J., & Parry, C. S. (2001). After action reviews: Linking reflection and planning in a learning practice. *Reflections, 3*(2), 64–72.

Department of the Army. (2003). *Battle-focused training* (Field manual No. 7-1). Washington, DC: Author.

Domeshek, E. A. (2004). *Phase II. Final report on an intelligent tutoring system for teaching battle command reasoning skills* (ARI Tech. Rep. No. 1143). Alexandria, VA: U.S. Army Research Institute for the Behavioral and Social Sciences.

Fidopiastis, C. M., Stapleton, C. B., Whiteside, J. D., Hughes, C. E., Fiore, S. M., Martin, G. A., Rolland, J. P., & Smith, E. M. (2005, September). *Human experience modeler: Context driven cognitive retraining and narrative threads.* Paper presented at the International Workshop on Virtual Rehabilitation, Catalina Island, CA.

Goldberg, S. L., & Meliza, L. L. (1993). Assessing unit performance in distributive interactive simulations: The Unit Performance Assessment System (UPAS). *Proceedings of NATO Defence Research Group Meeting, Panel 8: Defence Applications of Human and Bio-Medical Sciences. Training Strategies for Networked Simulation and Gaming* (Technical Proceedings No. AC/243(Panel 8)TN/5; pp. 173–182).

Hoare, R. (1996). From debrief to After Action Review (AAR). *Modern Simulation & Training, 6,* 13–17.

Holding, D. H. (Ed.). (1989). *Human skills* (2nd ed.). New York: John Wiley & Sons.

IEEE Computer Society. (1996). *IEEE standard for distributed interactive simulation—application protocols.* New York: Institute of Electrical and Electronics Engineers.

Knerr, B. W., & Lampton, D. R. (2005). *An assessment of the Virtual-Integrated MOUT Training System (V-IMTS)* (ARI Research Rep. No. 1163). Alexandria, VA: U.S. Army Research Institute for the Behavioral and Social Sciences.

Lampton, D. R., Clark, B. R., & Knerr, B. W. (2003). Urban combat: The ultimate extreme environment. *Journal of Performance in Extreme Environments, 7,* 57–62.

Martin, G. A., & Cherng, M. (2007). *After action review in game-based training* (Tech. Rep.). Orlando, FL: University of Central Florida, Institute for Simulation and Training.

Meliza, L. L. (1999). *A guide to standardizing after action review (AAR) aids* (ARI Research Product No. 99-01). Alexandria, VA: U.S. Army Research Institute for the Behavioral and Social Sciences.

Moreno, R. (2004). Decreasing cognitive load for novice students: Effects of explanatory versus corrective feedback in discovery-based multimedia. *Instructional Science 32,* 99–103.

Morrison, J. E., & Meliza, L. L. (1999). *Foundations of the after action review process* (ARI Special Rep. No. 42). Alexandria, VA: U.S. Army Research Institute for the Behavioral and Social Sciences.

Rogers, E. (2004). *Pausing for learning: Adapting the Army after action review process to the NASA project world* (NASA White Paper). Retrieved August 18, 2005, from http://smo.gsfc.nasa.gov/knowman/documents/whitepapers/Pausing_for_Learning.pdf

Scott, T. D., & Fobes, J. L. (1982). *After action review guidebook I. National Training Center* (ARI Research Product No. 83-11). Alexandria, VA: U.S. Army Research Institute for the Behavioral and Social Sciences.

University of Central Florida. (2007). *SOCRATES Overview.* Retrieved August 2, 2007, from http://www.irl.ist.ucf.edu/index.php?option=com_content&task=view&id=26&Itemid=81

U.S. Army Combined Arms Center. (1993). *A leader's guide to after-action reviews* (Training Circular No. 25-20). Fort Leavenworth, KS: Author.

Chapter 15

INTERFACING INTERACTIVE 3-D SIMULATIONS WITH LEARNING SYSTEMS

Curtis Conkey and Brent Smith

Training and education are a comprehensive process that does not simply consist of the transmission and learning of content. The next generation of instructional technologies will need to have the ability to track and assess individuals and teams at varying levels of proficiency while providing feedback and guidance so that errors in performance can be identified and corrected. Gaming and simulation have great potential to support adaptive learning by placing the learner in a real world environment and allowing the student to learn in context. The contextual experience enables learners to create their own constructs and apply them to unfamiliar situations. The push to adopt more engaging and immersive approaches for training and evaluating human performance in the context of Sharable Content Object Reference Model (SCORM)-managed learning environments relies on a complex partnering of technologies, standards, and specifications. The use of underlying technologies may simplify the assessment process and help standardize the manner in which a student is assessed, but foreseeable challenges must still be resolved.

INTERFACING SIMULATIONS WITH LEARNING SYSTEMS

Many organizations are engaged in transforming how they train. Many of these training programs are placing a strong emphasis on distance learning technologies, also known as e-learning. One challenge of these efforts is to produce e-learning content that is more than a mere replica of existing text based training. The technologies that enable e-learning continue to advance at a rapid pace. Computerized data management, advanced graphical presentation technologies, networked storage, and accessibility of information continue to influence how organizations capture, manage, and disseminate knowledge; transform that knowledge into learning opportunities; and deliver new learning opportunities to those who need them.

The next generation of instructional technologies will need to have the ability to track and dynamically assess individuals and teams at varying levels of proficiency in order to tailor learning content to individual needs while cost-effectively providing feedback and guidance so that errors in performance can be identified and corrected. These systems will bring together intelligent tutoring capabilities, distributed subject matter experts, in-depth learning management, and a diverse array of support tools across the continuum of learning experiences that a student will encounter in order to ensure a responsive, learner centric system.

The increased interest in interactive three-dimensional (3-D) simulations and game based training applications across the spectrum of education and training suggests their potential for becoming valuable extensions to traditional educational initiatives. These technologies represent the evolution of e-learning from existing page based through low level two-dimensional animated training to fully immersive, three-dimensional training, which places trainees virtually in the relative environment. Simulations and games have great potential to support a range of instructional strategies by placing learners into an environment where they can learn in context. However, simulations are only part of the mix of learning strategies that must be experienced by learners in order to create well-educated students. Blended learning environments will be a key component of future training capabilities. New technologies enable a managed learning environment to seamlessly integrate training management and delivery, to facilitate the exchange of information between disparate simulations and content, and to provide appropriate learner-centric training at the point of need. Current legacy training management systems and new emerging technology systems must be fully and seamlessly integrated to provide a single access and management point for all events and activities.

Assessment strategies within an enterprise learning organization should, in the future, include opportunities to continually monitor progress against a discrete set of metrics. Apart from traditional multiple-choice assessments, they should include the ability to dynamically access performance. Here simulations offer a unique capability to modify and insert new training resources into a learning strategy in order for learners to learn from their performances. As a student's level of proficiency increases, the learning strategy should conform to the evolving skill level of the student, and different feedback formats should provide immediate knowledge of performance thereby increasing the rate of acquisition and retention of learned behaviors. Various "use cases" for using simulations within a managed learning environment include the following:

- **Stand-alone training**—Pedagogy or contextual situations may require simulations that run without concurrent access to the Web or as an asynchronous educational intervention. However, centralized record keeping for student performance and the ability to centrally manage these applications is paramount.

- **Graduated student coaching**—Most pedagogical uses of simulations require learning systems that provide various levels of student feedback. This feedback is characterized in use cases in terms of show me (familiarization), let me (acquire and practice), and test me (validation), all of which require different levels of learner support.

- **Performance assessment**—Coaching and pedagogy for the "let me try" and "test me" use cases require the capability to track, store, evaluate, and report on a student's performance. This necessitates formal methodologies and data models for how we collect information from the instructional system and roll these events up into learning objectives that can be used as evidence of competency. In particular, these requirements are defined by critical tasks needed within the simulations and by performance measures defined for these critical tasks.

- **Concurrent assessment of multiple skills**—Instructional strategies require simulations that provide the ability for students to simultaneously demonstrate competency of many complex tasks. A single simulation session can provide feedback on multiple learning objectives.

- **Dynamic team interaction**—Team training is becoming increasingly common as tasks become interdisciplinary and require the interoperation of multiple skill sets. Simulation sessions can allow for controlled interoperational training among individuals while monitoring the achievement of learning objectives both individually and on a team level.

MANAGED LEARNING

The rise of computer based training (CBT) in the 1980s and the Internet in the 1990s raised the attractive possibility of practical reuse of training materials across multiple training programs. Long a dream for efficiency and cost-saving purposes, the advent of these technologies gave new urgency to the effort. These efforts would focus on the emerging distance learning training industry that was merging the capabilities of CBT and the Internet to produce a powerful new training capability that allowed for interactive, remote training.

Learning management systems (LMSs) became a key component of the emerging e-learning industry. An LMS is based on the concept of a centralized server delivering learning content to users over a network, thus enabling learning content to be widely distributed to anyone with a Web browser and access to the system. However, for this to be practical, standards efforts would be required that allowed for communication between the various noncompatible LMSs that were being developed. To facilitate these efforts the Advanced Distance Learning (ADL) Co-Laboratories were formed in 1997. A major success of the ADL effort has been the creation of the SCORM standard. Its primary goal is to enable the interoperation of LMSs and the reusability of the content in a Web based training environment.

Where content design and development are concerned, conformance to SCORM 2004 promotes reusable and interoperable learning resources across multiple learning management systems. Within the SCORM context, the term LMS implies a server based environment in which the intelligence resides for controlling the delivery of learning content to students. This involves gathering student profile information, delivering content to the learner, monitoring key interactions and performance within the content, and then determining what the student should next experience. At its simplest, SCORM 2004 is a model that references a set of interrelated technical specifications designed to meet high level requirements for Web based learning content. Within the SCORM context, content can be described, sequenced, tracked, and delivered in a standardized fashion. SCORM provides a common way to launch content and a common way for content to communicate with an LMS and exchange predefined data elements between an LMS and content during its execution. This enables a "learning objectives" approach to training by providing a means for interoperability between learning content, in the form of sharable content objects (SCOs). An SCO is a collection of assets developed to provide the instructional requirements of a learning objective. It is also the basic building block of the SCORM Content Aggregation Model (CAM). The CAM relates specifically to the assembling, labeling, and packaging of learning content into "content objects." SCORM requires the delivery of content objects that are sharable and reusable. It provides a tagging mechanism for discovery and access to content, but does not specify a repository structure for the content. This drives the requirement for the Content Object Repository Discovery and Registration/Resolution Architecture (CORDRA), a model for interconnecting repositories capable of learning content management, recovery, and reuse. The requirement for CORDRA comes from the obligation to create SCORM compliant content via Department of Defense Instruction 1322.20. It provides a tagging mechanism for discovery and access to content, but does not specify a repository structure for the content. CORDA meets that need.

In CORDA, each content object consists of a self-describing archive that bundles related learning resources with one or more Extensible Markup Language based manifest files. A learning resource is any representation of information that is used in this learning experience. In the SCORM environment, content objects do not determine, by themselves, how to traverse through a unit of instruction. Instead, the LMS processes "sequencing and navigation" rules using results from the content objects to determine the order in which a student will experience learning resources. In order to use interactive models, 3-D simulations, and games as learning resources, a method of integrating them into the SCORM paradigm is necessary. SCORM 2004, as it exists, does not fully address this need.

GAMES AND SIMULATION—DELIVERY AND DEPLOYMENT

The SCORM Run-Time Environment (RTE) specifies the launch of learning content, communications between content and an LMS, data transfer, and error handling. This RTE was developed for basic e-learning delivery methods from rudimentary page turners up to Flash animations. However, when the focus is shifted to interactive 3-D simulations, and/or games, the issues involved are significantly more complex. There are many types of simulations with varying levels of interactivity, immersion, and complexity. Games come in a multitude of genres and styles. They can be resident in a client browser or embedded into a separate system, which is a challenging issue when SCORM assumes Web based processes. Adding to the difficulty is the fact that often a simulation's resources require auxiliary processes and systems that must be initialized, configured, and available for a simulation based application to launch. For example, a personal computer simulation or game may require direct access to a machine's graphics subsystem in order to render an environment in real time and to the local file store (that is, hard drive) in order to store and quickly access needed resources. Web browsers and SCORM are not designed to handle this level of "system awareness." Further, SCORM also limits how an LMS is able to interact with an SCO and, consequently, a simulation.

Since the LMS in the SCORM architecture is required to operate in a Web based server/browser infrastructure, it has no inherent capabilities to directly launch or communicate with a native application session running on the client or other machine. One common approach to enable this capability is to use a Java applet or ActiveX component embedded in a HyperText Markup Language (HTML) Web page of the learning content to create and manage a message pipeline between the simulation and the LMS. In the SCORM environment, the LMS is responsible for establishing an application programming interface (API) for the content in the client browser to exchange data during each learning session. Communications from the content to the LMS are accomplished using ECMAScript, which can be used to "set" and "get" data values on the LMS server using the SCORM API provided by the LMS. The API defined by the SCORM is the standard Institute of Electrical and Electronics Engineers (IEEE) 1484.11.2-2003 API for content to runtime services communication. This API provides the basic capabilities needed to interface a simulation with an LMS. With appropriate development of a reciprocal API in a simulation or game it is possible to tether a simulation to a Web based, LMS direct training event and have active communications between the two. Figure 15.1 demonstrates this concept with a firefighter simulation that is tethered to an LMS.

One key benefit of e-learning technologies is the ability to deploy, update, and maintain training resources from a centralized server. Integrating LMS technologies with simulations expands this to include managing a simulation's resources from a centralized server. While SCORM provides a specification for packaging the content objects for delivery through an LMS, a simulation's resources may necessitate a large installation footprint that may need to be configured and available for a simulation based application to launch. Unlike traditional training applications, simulations and games can easily involve datasets running into the tens or hundreds of megabytes. With current technology, it is impractical to download this amount of data each time a user wants to run the simulation; until recently there have been few options to download, uncompress, install, cache, run, and update large applications from within the context of a Web browser. One option is to use "smart client" technologies, such as "Java Web Start" from Sun Microsystems, Inc., or "ClickOnce" from Microsoft Corporation. Smart client applications are similar to traditional applications in that they are installed locally on a user's machine and, as such, are able to make full use of local

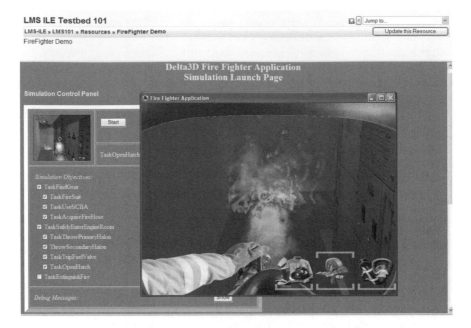

Figure 15.1.   LMS with Tethered Simulation

machine resources. However, smart client applications are also able to take advantage of the benefits of a traditional Web based application; they can be stored on a Web server and easily deployed to users' machines on demand; they can be updated by automatically downloading new or revised components, and they can communicate seamlessly with external Web services.

To the user, the experience is similar to launching a video from a Web page; however, when the simulation is launched, developers have the ability to download all of the required simulation code libraries, dependencies, and assets onto the client machine. The simulation can then be launched and run in a separate window, that is, "tethered" to the Web page, while communicating back to the launch page over a transmission control protocol/Internet protocol socket. On subsequent launches, the simulation launches immediately. If content developers decide to update the simulation by modifying code or changing assets, they may simply update the files on the LMS server, which will automatically compare files on the LMS with files located on the client machine and then download and install only the modified files on each user's machine. For reasons generally associated with increasing network security concerns, simulations will often require elevated permissions and cannot run within the standard Web interface. Additionally, network policies, such as firewalls, may not allow these types of applications to be run on the local machine/network. However, if the simulation application libraries are digitally signed, network administrators can set each machine up to allow or disallow a given application.

COMMUNICATIONS VIA SCORM

In SCORM, simulation content currently can be treated and processed (for example, described, sequenced, tracked, or delivered) like all other content. Within the SCORM paradigm, a course structure format (CSF) defines all of the course elements, the course structure, and all external references necessary to represent a course and its intended behavior. This CSF is intended to promote reuse of entire courses and encourage the reuse of course components by exposing all the details of each course element. The CSF describes a course using three groups of information. The first group, called global properties, is the data about the overall course. The second, called block, defines the structure of the course, and the third group, objectives, defines a separate structure for learning objectives with references to course elements within the assignment structure. SCORM presently provides a rules based "learning strategy" that enables sharable content objects (SCOs) to set the state of the global objectives. These records can store the learner's degree of mastery in the form of a score or a pass/fail state, or they may store the progress of the learner in terms of completion. However, SCORM's Computer Managed Instruction (CMI) data model and restriction on SCO-to-SCO communications limit the design of simulation content. SCORM uses the CMI data model to provide data for content and to capture result and tracking data used to control content delivery. The CMI model is weak in representing many attributes necessary for a simulation or game, including tracking results, learner attributes, assessment data, and content state.

Games and simulations typically have more complex requirements for data tracking and state management than what is currently possible within SCORM. In order for student performance to be tracked inside a simulation, the data communicated to the LMS must be confined to the data models and specifications that SCORM provides. A mechanism for assessment needs to be developed to allow student performance data to be extracted from a simulation and communicated to an LMS. Generally speaking, each SCO can contain a number of "objectives," and learner progress toward each objective can be tracked according to basic data values, such as completion status, success status, and score. While a simulation scenario may track many assessment variables internally, it needs to be able to combine these variables into data values that an LMS is able to understand.

One approach to solving this challenge is to aggregate the learner's actions into learning objectives and report them using the objectives data model. Sequencing rules can be created to map these to global variables so that these values can be used by sequencing rules for other SCOs. However, according to SCORM, these global variables can be written to only once; therefore, a global variable cannot be used to aggregate data over a set of lessons. Additionally, the existing sequencing rules can inspect only three aspects of a global variable: score, completion, and satisfaction. This limited set of data is generally not sufficient to support all the data types required for games or simulations. This is an area that requires further standards work, which we address later in the chapter.

ASSESSMENT OF SIMULATION BASED TRAINING

Currently, there is little consistency in how students are evaluated across different training environments, whether in the classroom, in the field, at home via e-learning, or in simulated training exercises. The problem is that assessment strategies and associated development tools have been nonstandard and closely coupled with the learning environment that they support. In other words, an assessment system developed for one learning domain can rarely be used or applied in other domains.

Existing assessment mechanisms can be loosely divided into two camps based on the type of learning environment in which they are used. Static assessment is generally associated with teaching methods where the content for a given unit of learning is the same; whether the content is comprised of lectures, text, pictures, or video, each student will experience the same material in more or less the same order. In these environments, assessment generally comes in the form of a written test with questions that the student answers in a linear fashion. The benefit of this form of learning is that this type of assessment can be highly structured and easily integrated into a curriculum.

In contrast, a *dynamic* learning environment generally refers to one in which the student interacts with the training material on some level, such as in games, simulations, or a live training exercise. In a dynamic learning environment, the training experience may be different each time the learner is engaged with it. The means of assessment in dynamic learning environments is varied. Learning pathways can no longer be defined in terms of highly structured, linear patterns and time frames. Rather, assessment must accommodate transitions between learning experiences and ultimately accommodate further training within other learning environments.

In order to overcome these limitations, training developers typically develop customized methods for assessing performance. In a game or simulation, there may be some internal scoring mechanism or, as in a live training situation, assessment may take the form of a subjective review by an observer/controller or an after action review. In most of these environments, if there is a scoring/assessment mechanism, it is most likely specific to a particular training system, is not meant to be used by external systems, and may not map directly to the overall learning objectives of a larger training curriculum. Games and simulations generally have no mechanism for interfacing to an LMS to record the data. Manual entry of performance into a student's educational history is not uncommon.

In recent years, there has been considerable interest (Darque, Morse, Smith, & Frank, 2006) in how to tie dynamic learning environments to other managed learning environments. The majority of this research is focused on assessment within a single training system and uses an approach that tracks a learner's response to critical events within that system. These events are tracked within a training system for use as evidence of whether or not a given learning objective has been satisfied.

However, there are several problems with coupling assessment logic to specific training systems. The biggest problem is the lack of standardization. Currently, there are no standard definitions or data formats for such concepts as "completion," "progress," "evidence," "assessment logic," and "results." Therefore, these components are often developed specific to each training system. This process of "reinventing the wheel" for each new training environment increases development times and discourages the development of mature, stable, reusable, and extensible components. It also inhibits the development of tools and utilities that could make it easier to create and modify assessment models.

In order to overcome existing assessment architecture limitations and to enable the standardized integration of simulations and games into learning environments, assessment functionality is being logically separated from learning content and learning management systems. As shown in Figure 15.2, a new software component called an "assessment engine" is tasked with listening to event data coming from the learning environment. The assessment engine processes these data according to a defined assessment model and broadcasts the results (that is, status, scores, and grades) to a training system (that is, LMS or AAR system). The assessment engine can be incorporated into a simulation or it may be an external module. Ideally it acts as middleware between the learning environment and the training system and, as such, frees them from having to

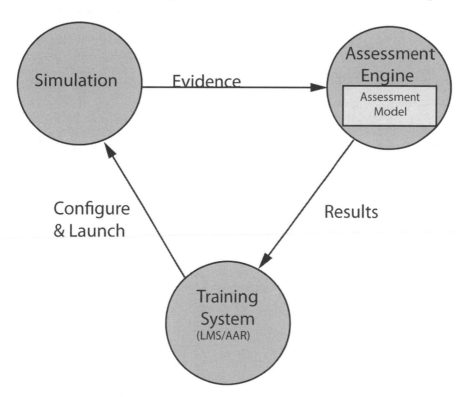

Figure 15.2.   Learner Assessment Data Model and Authoring Tools Assessment Engine

handle any assessment logic internally. This architecture also allows the assessment functionality to become more generic by allowing it to be used by any number of learning environments and/or training systems. In order to extract the assessment functionality into its own process, yet still work within a variety of system architectures, there needs to be a standardized set of data formats and messaging protocols to enable communication between the learning environment and the assessment engine, and the assessment engine and the training system (that is, evidence and results). These protocols, or APIs, serve as a contract among the three processes, allowing each component to run independently. This also makes it easier for an instructional component to be replaced by an entirely new instructional component if desired. For example, a game based simulation data log could be interchanged with an observer log taken from a live training exercise, as long as both logs generate similar event data as defined by the event data protocol.

BUILDING ASSESSMENTS INTO SIMULATION BASED LEARNING EXPERIENCES

For each simulation or game, the assessment process is broken into logical components. The first step in the assessment development process is to specify the constructs of each training objective that needs to be measured within each of these dynamic learning environments. Once performance measures are determined, they can be mapped to *events* within each environment. Events are raised as the user interacts with the learning environment. The events raised by each learning environment are designed to be relevant markers of events occurring during the training session.

In the case of a simulation, these events may be triggered by simple user actions, such as "student pushed button." Alternatively, the events may be defined on a higher level and encapsulate more complex concepts that capture the interaction between objects and other system components, such as "time" and "state" variables within the learning environment. The detail and complexity of what constitutes an event should be determined by instructional designers and simulation developers according to instructional needs and simulation or game architecture. A method of capturing and naming each event also needs to be developed in order to publish all events within each environment that are necessary to satisfy each task. The assessment engine listens to these events and uses them to track a learner's progress toward completion of defined tasks. An assessment data model is used to combine events and tasks in a hierarchal manner to form more complex tasks, which tasks ultimately culminate in one or more objectives. As a learner completes specific training objectives, the assessment component communicates this information to the training system.

The goals of the aforementioned assessment model are best met with a tiered development approach. The tiers can be conceptually divided into the learning environment tier, the data tier, and the assessment tier.

- The **learning environment tier** is the system and/or process where the actual training takes place. In the case of simulations, this tier will represent the student interacting with the simulation code. In the case of live or classroom training, this tier will represent all aspects of the physical training environment, including the students, the equipment, and the observer/controllers. At this level, the learning environment tier will be responsible for generating simple messages related to relevant events and system state. For simulations, these messages will be generated by the simulation code, and for live training the messages may be generated by other training equipment and/or the training observers (via an electronic form). The messages will notify the assessment engine when an assessment object changes state or raises an event, and they will either be sent directly to the assessment engine in real time or be stored in an intermediary data store. Once in the assessment engine, the messages will be validated against the data tier and processed according to the assessment tier.

- The **data tier** is defined as the data model and schemas that describe the assessment objects, events, tasks/objectives, and assessment logic for a given training environment. Each training objective will be defined based on the known list of messages (events) and state data that are published by the learning environment. The assessment model will define which events it is dependent on and any rules concerning the sequencing or timing of those events. It will also define progress measurement criteria, such as complete/not complete, percent complete, score, and so on.

- The **assessment tier** is defined as the layer that "listens" to training events from the learning environment tier and processes them according to rules defined in the data tier. This component also consists of formalizing the constructs of an event publishing system that listens for any events that are associated with training objectives within the learning environment. These events will need to be processed through an assessment model in order to track the state of each objective. It is important to note this architecture is a logical model and does not mandate where this assessment processing will take place or how information is communicated to other training systems. The assessment engine may be run within the context of a client application, a server application, or a Web service. It may even run within the same physical process as a simulation or other training system. However, even if the engine is physically running in the same process, it is still logically separated from the other components and can be updated and maintained separately.

The guiding principle here is that a training system needs to combine assessment variables into data values that other systems are able to understand. For example, SCORM 2004 provides standard specifications for assessment results and roll-up functions to aggregate assessment results. In order for a SCORM conformant LMS to track student performance during a dynamic learning experience, such as a simulation or game, the data communicated to the LMS must be confined to the data model that SCORM provides. However, as the assessment component processes events from the learning environment, there is the potential to collect other contextual information that can be used as evidence to support competency. From an instructional effectiveness point of view, the capture of this information could greatly increase the effectiveness of dynamic learning environments by allowing a more in-depth review of what a student has and has not mastered across multiple learning experiences. For instance, the ability to pass after action review data back to the LMS could greatly improve a remote teacher's ability to access a student's performance by allowing the teacher to actually play back the student's simulation exercise. With the broad ability to track events and student activity within simulation environments, an untapped means for assessment of performance is available for next generation training systems. The efforts behind competency based training seek to exploit these opportunities.

COMPETENCIES BASED LEARNING

The Standard for Reusable Competency Definitions is motivated in part by a growing international movement, led by the human resources community, to look at competency development through the bigger picture of expressing objectives and their relationships. At issue is how to express the fact that one objective (or competency) might be composed of several subobjectives and how to express ways in which data on subobjectives can be rolled up.

A competency based approach to assessment is considered by many as the bridge between traditional measures of student achievement and the future (Jones & Voorhess, 2002). However, there are numerous challenges associated with developing and assessing competency based learning initiatives. The definition of a competency for the purpose of this discussion is the combination of skills, abilities, and knowledge needed to perform a specific task. Figure 15.3 shows that for each individual student, skills and knowledge are acquired through learning experiences. Different combinations of skills and knowledge define the competencies that an individual may possess. Finally, different combinations of competencies are required to carry out different sets of tasks.

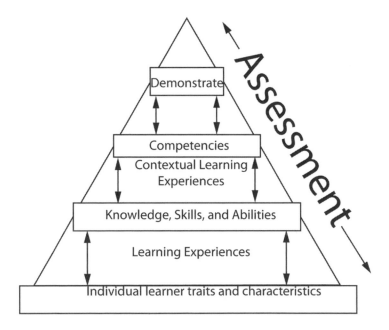

Figure 15.3.   Assessment Pyramid. Source: Department of Education

Current technology makes it possible to analyze the sequences of actions learners take as they work through a problem and compare these sequences of actions against models of knowledge and performance associated with different levels of expertise. Most assessments, however, provide snapshots of achievement at ticker points in time, but do not capture the progression of a learners' conceptual understanding (Learning Federation, 2003). This is where simulation and game based training can play a significant role. The ability to roll up events into training objectives via an assessment engine allows for the delivery of competency based learning.

EVOLVING STANDARDS FOR SIMULATION AND GAME BASED LEARNING

As indicated in the preceding discussion, many of the capabilities that the integration of simulation into LMS environments enables are only minimally enabled at this time due to minimal support from the existing SCORM standard. As this technology becomes more advanced and costs are reduced, we theorize that the training community will embrace games and simulations as simply another type of media that may be used to convey instruction. In the future, these technologies will interoperate with other learning technologies that have yet to be fully developed or implemented on a large scale. Advancement of standards will enable significant new capabilities for training environments.

Integration with personnel management systems and business processes will introduce new concepts, such as people, objects, assessment profiles, or developmental progression. Global learner profiles will play a large role in tracking a learner's progress across a wide range of training solutions. In the past, there has not been a consistent approach to the development of dynamic learning environments; none of the major courseware initiatives, such as reuse, interoperability, and sharing, have been addressed.

A primary goal of integrating simulations and games into the SCORM paradigm is to provide a generic, adaptable, and standardized mechanism for simulations to perform learner assessment. The term "learner assessment," in the context of this discussion, refers to the ability of the system to track a learner's progress through an interactive training environment and generate a set of performance metrics. These metrics (that is, scores, grades, and AARs) can be used to determine if the learner has satisfactorily met the defined learning objectives and to provide structured feedback and/or appropriate remediation to the student.

In order to meet these requirements, technology needs to be developed that allows in-depth assessments of student performance against a defined set of training objectives in order to identify student deficiencies and provide feedback to both students and instructors. The challenge, therefore, is to find an efficient way to do the following:

- Create a set of data models and protocols that can formally represent the complex interactions between the events raised within a simulated learning environment and the training objectives, task conditions, and standards defined within a given LMS.

These models must be able to account for the different relationships among the learner, other learners, and the environment where the training takes place.

• Provide standardized tools to create and/or modify assessment models so that trainers and instructors can design the way a student is evaluated inside each learning system.

• Develop an assessment specification that uses these models to track and assess student performance across multiple training environments.

• Define data warehousing structures to ensure that all of the activities that take place during a simulation are logged and available for review. From these data, patterns of routine cognitive activities can be discerned.

Recognizing the importance of these requirements, two IEEE standards committees have formed a collaborative study group to investigate the potential of formalizing a standard set of technical specifications to allow simulations and/or games to be launched and managed through SCORM-conformant content and learning management systems. The IEEE Learning Technology Standards Committee is chartered by the IEEE Computer Society Standards Activity Board to develop accredited technical standards, recommended practices, and guides for learning technology. Currently, three of the five components of SCORM (metadata, communications, and content aggregations) are based on Learning Technology Standards Committee standards, while a fourth (competency) is in progress.

Figure 15.4 shows key elements and interfaces that have emerged from the study group discussions. This diagram is coded. The stipple pattern is used to represent a dynamic learning environment that takes initial conditions and produces events during a learning experience. In the SCORM context, the learning

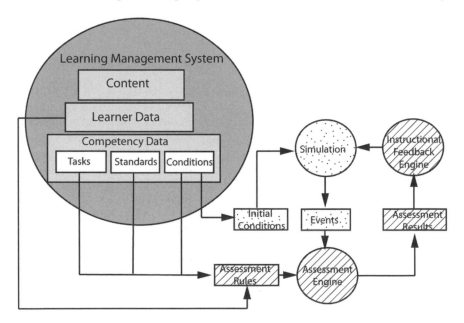

Figure 15.4.   Overview of LMS and Simulation Interfaces

management system (large shaded oval on the left) is responsible for managing three forms of data:

- Learner data, including learner identification and learner assessment records;
- Competency information, shown here in terms of tasks, conditions, and standards, but possibly including other forms, such as learning objectives; and
- Content, the traditional SCOs, typically HTML based data.

The assessment engine, in diagonal lines, takes streams of events generated by the simulation and generates assessment results by comparing these events to rule based models of assessment. While a simulation may track many assessment variables internally, it needs to be able to combine these variables into data values that an LMS is able to understand. This appears to be a common consideration across the study group and has been identified as an area that warrants further investigation for the development of potential standards. As shown in Figure 15.4, there is a mechanism to listen to events or messages from a simulation, process them, translate them into data that an LMS can understand, and communicate them to the SCORM data model either through the LMS or via Web services.

Together, these standards, technologies, and tools have the potential to make future training simulations even more accessible, adaptable, affordable, interoperable, and reusable. This objective is consistent with current trends to make training more dynamic and engaging, more accessible, more deployable, and less expensive. Although the required technologies exist and have been successfully demonstrated, the challenge is to formalize them together in an architecture that can be integrated and used across the spectrum of training strategies and media.

REFERENCES

Darque, B., Morse, K., Smith, B., & Frank, G. (2006). *Interfacing simulations with training content.* Paper presented at the NATO Modeling and Simulation Group Conference: Transforming Training and Experimentation through Modeling and Simulation.

Jones, E. A., & Voorhess, R. A. (2002). *Defining and assessing learning: Exploring competency-based initiatives (NCES 2002-159).* Washington, DC: U.S. Department of Education.

Learning Federation. (2003). *Learning modeling and assessment R&D for technology-enabled learning systems.* Washington, DC: The Learning Federation.

Chapter 16

ENHANCING SITUATION AWARENESS TRAINING IN VIRTUAL REALITY THROUGH MEASUREMENT AND FEEDBACK

Jennifer Riley, David Kaber,
Mohamed Sheik-Nainar, and Mica Endsley

Virtual reality (VR) technologies have become popular training mediums in both civilian and military domains (Liu, Tendick, Cleary, & Kaufmann, 2003 [surgical tasks]; Kaber, Wright, & Sheik-Nainar, 2006 [teleoperation]; Lampton, Bliss, & Morris, 2002 [dismounted infantry]). VR presents a dynamic and interactive means for engaging trainees while introducing instructional concepts. Simulations facilitate repetitive practice in prototypical situations that are more easily, quickly, and economically developed as compared to live rehearsals. Military personnel, for example, can be trained in VR on tactics, weapons use, or navigating unfamiliar terrain that might be encountered during future deployment. Advances in VR technology facilitate user training in rich visual scenes in distributed and multiplayer training opportunities. Such technologies are considered to be valuable instructional mediums for supporting skill development and increased knowledge transfer and retention (Ponder et al., 2003).

Though the use of simulated environments for training is attractive for several reasons, researchers suggest that technological advances alone do not necessarily result in skill transfer to reality. Salas and Cannon-Bowers (1997) stated that training technologies (such as virtual environments) must include elements that are relevant to core competencies of the domain in order to promote skill acquisition. For example, in the military, relevant competencies might include situation assessment, team coordination, planning, weapons skill, and leadership. Endsley and Robertson (2000) say that in addition to instructional elements, it is important to provide feedback on training in order to develop or fine-tune specific skills.

To really take advantage of VR and simulation technologies, it is important to incorporate measures to accompany instructional components in order to determine if trainees are meeting established standards for readiness. It is also useful to employ tools that can assess trainees' awareness of events and operational elements during training in order to understand why they exhibited certain behaviors and how they communicated their knowledge with team members. This type of tool would provide trainers with the information they need to make the training experience useful for building key cognitive skills associated with situation awareness (SA) and decision making. Today there are tools available to record training events in VR simulations that can be used to review the events with trainees afterwards, but trainers are hampered in being able to take full advantage of this capability. Trainers need additional tools to more fully capture the trainees' cognition during scenarios so that they can use this information to provide constructive feedback toward improving cognitive skill. This is particularly true for SA, which is a key component of expert cognitive performance.

SITUATION AWARENESS AND SITUATION AWARENESS SKILL DEVELOPMENT

Situation awareness is defined as "the perception of elements in the environment within a volume of time and space, the comprehension of their meaning and the projection of their status in the near future" (Endsley, 1988). The construct of SA has been demonstrated to be important to operational decision making and task performance in complex domains. For example, a soldier must develop an awareness of all mission relevant elements, including the location of teammates and their level of operational readiness, characteristics of the environment, status of devices, impact of weapons use, and potential actions of others in the environment. They, along with operators in similar dynamic environments (for example, law enforcement), need to be able to rapidly assess a situation, understand the effects on mission objectives, and precisely predict the likely outcome in their near future time and space. This information processing serves as a basis for dynamic decision making.

For teams, SA can be defined as the degree to which every team member possesses the SA required for his or her responsibilities (Endsley, 1995b). If any one person experiences an error in SA, it can potentially lead to failure for the team. Artman and Garbis (1998) said that a team can develop mental models of a situation that are partly shared and partly distributed between members. This extends the concept of team SA to include shared SA—instances in which two or more team members must share an understanding of informational elements to meet a common goal. Endsley, Bolte, and Jones (2003) point out that shared SA does not imply a need for complete sharing of all information requirements, but rather involves having the same understanding on the subset of information that is needed to meet overlapping goals for team roles.

Breakdowns in SA can be a result of failure to detect or properly interpret critical cues, memory errors, or missing information. Errors in team or shared SA are additionally impacted by problems with team processes (for example, inadequate or erroneous communications, lack of shared understanding or incompatible interpretations, diverging mental models, or failures to recognize deviations in

SA among team members). Endsley and Robertson (2000) identified a few target areas for improving the SA of pilots through training, which may also be applicable for improving SA in other domains. The authors discuss approaches, such as training for task management (for example, prioritization and dealing with interruptions), workload management and time sharing, contingency planning, training for comprehension and projection, and communications. They emphasize the need for structured feedback on SA, stating that it is critical to the learning process.

FEEDBACK IN TRAINING FOR SA ENHANCEMENT

For many years the military has used the after action review (AAR) to provide knowledge of results to training soldiers. An AAR is a structured assessment conducted after a mission or training activity that supports teams and leaders in discovering what happened during an event (Department of the Army, 1993). For virtual environment training exercises, Knerr, Lampton, Crowell, et al. (2002) have advocated the use of coaching and AAR by expert instructors. VR technology provides the capability for AARs, and one such tool used by the Army Research Institute (ARI) for the Behavioral and Social Sciences is the Dismounted Infantry Virtual After Action Review System (DIVAARS) (Knerr, Lampton, Martin, Washburn, & Cope, 2002). DIVAARS functions similar to a video recorder to capture a training exercise from different visual perspectives and includes the ability to tag events for later replay. In the present research effort, we developed a system to enhance training and augment the AAR through measurement and analysis on the trainees' SA. Specifically, SA measurement tools were developed to provide feedback on cognitive states and behaviors in conjunction with critical training event information.

To support SA feedback following VR training, SA measures should provide diagnostic results on trainees' knowledge of critical SA information, their ability to seek and integrate information effectively, and the quality of their situation assessment behaviors. Such measures must produce results that provide detailed insight into how well trainees actually achieve these aspects of SA. Salas and Cannon-Bowers (1997) stated that trainee performance measures and results can contribute inputs to the feedback process that are necessary for improving performance. The results of a robust SA measure can serve to define elements of the training environment and operational domain on which SA is being challenged and can provide support for diagnosing behaviors that lead to or degrade SA. Here we describe an SA assessment system that is designed to support SA skill development through SA-oriented training and feedback. The research was initially conducted to meet the needs of the ARI for a comprehensive computer based measure of SA that could be utilized to train dismounted infantry squads using advanced VR technology. It was extended to meet the needs of the Office of Naval Research Virtual Technologies and Environments program for training SA in Fire Support Teams (FiSTs).

DEVELOPING SA MEASURES FOR VR TRAINING

To identify candidate SA measures for VR training, we conducted a review of existing measures (Kaber, Riley, Lampton, & Endsley, 2005). We focused on the compatibility of the measures with the VR system and the degree to which the measures supported direct assessment of components in an infantry based model of SA (Endsley et al., 2000). We also considered the need for measures that would be minimally intrusive to trainee performance and the continuity of training scenarios.

Other researchers have conducted detailed reviews of SA measures in the past (see Endsley & Garland, 2000, for examples) that include information on implementation and equipment required for administration of the measures. In general, the types of measures include the following:

1. Direct, objective measures of SA, such as SAGAT (Situation Awareness Global Assessment Technique);
2. Direct, subjective measures of SA (either self- or observer rated);
3. Process measures that involve inferring SA from eye movements, verbal protocols, or team communications;
4. Behavior based methods that assess SA in terms of appropriateness of trainee actions to particular scenario events; and
5. Performance measures that infer SA from training situation outcomes.

We identified the general advantages and limitations of each measurement type. For example, direct subjective measures are easy to implement and provide a measure of individual SA. However, when rating one's perceived level of SA, a trainee often may not know what information he or she is not aware of and base SA ratings on limited knowledge of performance outcomes. Query methods are objective and less biased measures of SA, but they require a detailed analysis to construct and administer and may require assessments through freezes in the simulation. Considering the various strengths and weaknesses and the fact that different measures can provide different insights on trainee SA, we determined that a multiple measure approach would be most robust for use in VR training sessions. We also considered the need for SA measures that were not only validated, but that provided diagnostic information for training instruction.

Endsley et al. (2000) developed a model of SA specific to infantry operations. The model is based upon Endsley's (1995b) theory of SA, which presents the cognitive construct as a product of perception, comprehension, and projection of task states. The model depicts both cognitive and task factors that can impact SA. These include task factors, such as mission planning and preparation, system complexity, and operational pace; doctrinal factors, such as tactics, procedures, and rules of engagement; environmental factors, such as terrain and weather conditions; and individual factors, such as attention and memory limits, cognitive and spatial abilities, and effects of stress, fatigue, and overload. The model also includes aspects related to information sources (for example, digital systems, team members, or direct observation). It should be noted that while this model was developed specifically to depict SA in infantry operations, many of the elements are directly applicable to aspects of SA in the much broader military and civilian arena.

Using an established set of psychometric criteria (see Wickens, 1992, on criteria for measures of cognitive workload), we identified three candidate measures, which satisfied the specific requirements for unobtrusiveness and reliability in assessing SA and could be developed into an SA assessment system for training in VR. A direct query method (for example, SAGAT, Endsley, 1995a; 2000) allows for flexible and objective assessments of SA along all components of SA, as the queries can be tailored to the specific relevant aspects of SA that are incorporated in a training situation. For the present effort, we opted to develop real time SA probes, as these can be presented to trainees during task performance without requiring a freeze of the simulation, although they produce less information than SAGAT (for example, Jones & Endsley, 2000). In this case, verbal probes are developed to elicit operator responses to SA queries that are based on a detailed analysis of the SA requirements for the domain. The probes can come from an evaluator or be posed as naturally occurring questions from a commander or other team member in the training scenario, making them realistically imbedded in the training event. The trainee response to SA probes can be assessed for accuracy based upon actual situation data (ground truth), providing an objective assessment of the accuracy of trainee SA that can be used as feedback. For example, the trainee can be directly presented with evidence of any misperceptions, misinterpretations, or omitted but critical information so that he or she can make needed adjustments to cognitive models and attention patterns in the future.

In addition to the probe measure, we found that techniques involving expert observer ratings of SA can be implemented easily and allow for accurate assessments of whether behaviors or communications comply with SA acquisition and dissemination. Example measures include the Situation Awareness Behaviorally Anchored Rating Scale (SABARS; Strater, Endsley, Pleban, & Matthews, 2001) and team communication measures developed by Brannick, Prince, Prince, and Salas (1993) and Wright and Kaber (2003). SABARS is a post-trial rating made by an observer to evaluate the SA of trainees based upon a predefined set of physical behaviors, relevant to situation assessment, exhibited during an exercise. By basing the evaluation on predefined, SA relevant behaviors, SABARS avoids the problem of self-rating or of an observer trying to ascertain the trainee's state of knowledge. Rather, it measures whether relevant processes are being employed (situation assessment as opposed to SA itself). SABARS was developed specifically for platoon level operations and allowed observers to rate platoon leader behaviors on a scale from "very poor" to "very good." We developed a computer based implementation of SABARS that allows for multiple ratings of soldier behaviors during a single training trial.

As SA in military operations is heavily dependent on team communications, we included this aspect as a third and important measure for the system. Wright and Kaber (2003) developed a team communication and coordination measure for assessing overall team performance in complex systems control. The measurement technique involved counting and rating communications representative of critical team behaviors (dimensions of teamwork for the measure were previously identified by Brannick et al., 1993). The count and rating information was, in turn, used as the basis for a composite rating of team coordination. The measure is similar to SABARS, involving expert ratings of participant communication behaviors, but it also includes an objective measure of the frequency of specific key team communications. To implement a team communications measure focused on SA assessment, we adapted the team communications criteria used by the previous authors to reflect important aspects for SA in the specific domain and emphasized the process of achieving SA via acquisition and dissemination of situation data, within and outside of the core team (for example, asking questions and requesting situation reports). This technique requires monitoring the natural, unsolicited verbalizations of teams for specific information in communications and rating the quality of the statements. It provides useful diagnostic information associated with sharing critical SA information across the team.

THE SA ASSESSMENT SYSTEM

The Virtual Environment Situation Awareness Review System (VESARS) includes a suite of SA measures incorporating the three techniques described above and an application to review the training results. VESARS was developed to support two separate training domains—army infantry in urban environments and marine FiSTs. The initial design of VESARS for the infantry focused on SA measurement for a single trainee (for example, the squad leader) (Kaber et al., 2005; Kaber, Riley, Sheik-Nainar, et al., 2006). The modified design of VESARS, demonstrated for marine FiST, was created to facilitate SA measurement for a small team. The general underlying functionality of the applications is the same for individual and team SA measurement. However, the implementation of such measures, for individual or team assessment, is different.

SA PROBE DELIVERY

The SA probe delivery tool is used to administer SA probes to trainees during the training exercise. The tool supports an instructor in identifying relevant probes over the course of the training scenario, selecting and presenting probes, and recording trainee responses to probes. The system scores each probe as correct or incorrect by comparing the recorded trainee response with the ground truth of the simulation recorded by the administrator and stores the data for later access.

SA probes were developed using goal-directed (cognitive) task analysis (Endsley, 1993; Endsley et al., 2003). The goal-directed task analysis documents the important goals and decisions associated with a task or particular role, along with the resultant SA requirements needed to perform tasks. The SA requirements are dynamic information needs, rather than static procedural knowledge or rules that might be related to task steps. Defining the SA requirements for the target domain was a critical step in developing relevant SA probes for objective SA measurement. The probes presented to trainees map directly to the critical decisions that they must make in real situations.

Goal-directed task analysis (GDTA) is conducted through multiple interviews with subject matter experts (SMEs), along with observation of operations, and a review of domain specific literature. The SMEs are generally interviewed individually. The results of interviews are pooled to develop a goal hierarchy and, later, the completed analysis includes key decisions and SA needed for each goal. Preliminary goal hierarchies from the task analysis are analyzed by the same or different SMEs for refinement and validation. An example segment of the analysis for the position of Forward Air Controller in Marine FiST is presented in Figure 16.1.

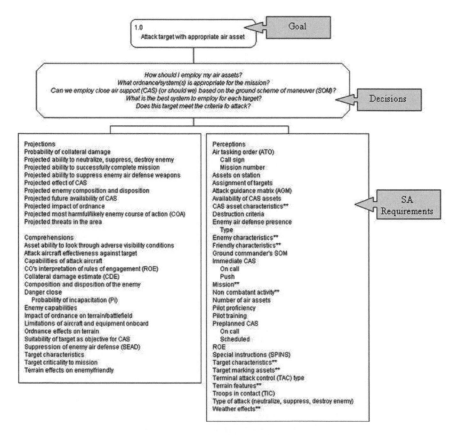

Figure 16.1. Graphical GDTA results include goals, decisions, and SA requirements.

The critical decisions identified in the goal-directed task analysis are used to generate a list of candidate SA probes. These probes are developed for each individual in a team and can be categorized in multiple ways: by level of SA, domain elements (for example, enemy, terrain, risk, and so forth), training objective, and phase of operation. The comprehensive list of SA probes for the domain is stored in a database that is accessed by VESARS. Table 16.1 presents example SA probes—at the three levels of SA (perception, comprehension, and projection) defined by Endsley (1995b)—developed for army infantry squads and marine FiSTs. To incorporate shared SA, the results of goal-directed task analysis for all team members are cross-analyzed to identify the shared goals and shared SA needs. In many cases, similar informational elements are needed for different purposes across team members. SA probes can be developed to determine if team members have the same understanding of these elements. VESARS identifies those probes used to assess shared SA and indicates the relevance of each probe to various team members. As some information requirements are relevant to all members of a team, some SA probes can be posed to any team member. However, some information requirements are applicable only to a limited set of team members. Such SA probes would be identified in VESARS as having relevance only to specific positions.

The VESARS interface for administering probes includes multiple features: (1) menus for viewing probes, (2) options for filtering and finding probes by category, and (3) a map of the virtual training exercise area. Once a probe is selected, it is put in a queue until it is delivered to one or more team members. There are options for recording the trainee response to the SA probe and the ground truth of the simulation, and options for saving the response data and/or posing the probe to another team member. Team members can be asked the same SA probe at nearly the same point in time. The scores are recorded so that instructors can determine which members of the team have the same understanding on specific shared SA items at that point in time in order to assess the quality of team SA (See Figure 16.2 for a graphic of the VESARS SA probe delivery tool.)

The SA probes and categorizations in VESARS are specific to a given domain based on the task analysis. Once SA requirements for a domain have been

Table 16.1.   Example SA Probes

Domain	Level of SA	Probe
Infantry squad	1	What is the civilian activity?
Infantry squad	2	Can you take cover?
Infantry squad	3	Will the enemy be able to detect your squad?
Marine Fire Support Team	1	Where is the target located?
Marine Fire Support Team	2	Do we need suppression of enemy air defenses?
Marine Fire Support Team	3	Will civilians be in danger if we engage the enemy?

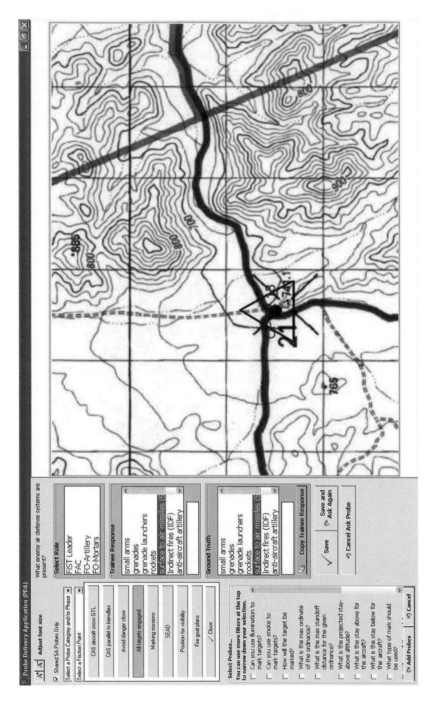

Figure 16.2. VESARS interface supports SA probe delivery and scoring.

elicited, the tool can be easily modified to reflect the new training domain. As an advantage, the VESARS developed for marine FiSTs can be utilized with any VR based training tool designed to train Fire Support Teams; it is not tied to a specific simulation or VR technology. We can also provide direct integration of VESARS with a specific simulation system by linking the SA probe delivery tool with the simulation (Kaber, Riley, Sheik-Nainar, Hyatt, & Reynolds, 2006). When integrated with a simulation tool, VESARS automatically presents appropriate SA probes to the trainer based upon trainee locations and simulated events.

THE SITUATION AWARENESS BEHAVIORAL MEASURE

The SA behavioral measure implemented in VESARS is used by an external observer to rate trainees with respect to physical behaviors consistent with good situation assessment in a given domain. This includes both team level behaviors and role-specific behaviors. At the team level, we identify the situation assessment behaviors that should be exhibited by members for acquiring and maintaining SA during an operation. These behaviors are often high level actions that should be observable across team roles for the majority of training scenarios to be experienced (see Figure 16.3). This measurement design allows a single observer to rate team level behaviors for multiple members at the same time. Evaluators can determine which team members excel at certain situation assessment behaviors and also identify those who may be struggling to acquire SA during training.

The behavioral rating scale also supports ratings for single individual trainees. In cases in which multiple raters are available, or training assessment is concerned with a particular role or individual, a rater can score a trainee on behaviors that are related to his or her role on the team. Rather than higher level team behaviors, in this case VESARS presents aspects of SA behavior important to acquiring and maintaining SA for a specific job. When multiple team members are rated individually, trainers can see which team members excel in their particular roles and which team members may hinder team SA because of individual SA errors.

In either team or individual SA assessment, VESARS presents to the evaluator the critical SA behaviors to observe. This particularly supports the less experienced evaluator, pointing out what to look for in evaluating situation assessment. Each behavior can be rated on a Likert scale including ratings from 1 ("poor") to 7 ("good") or "not observed." The not observed tag results in a rating of 0 and tracks situations in which an important SA behavior was expected, but not observed.

A particular utility of the VESARS behavioral rating system lies in being able to assess how the quality of a trainee's situation assessment behaviors change over time, as the ratings can be made throughout the training session and are recorded along the timeline. This avoids the post-trial memory recall problem associated with making an after action assessment of all behaviors and the overgeneralization that is common to such ratings. The VESARS behavioral ratings

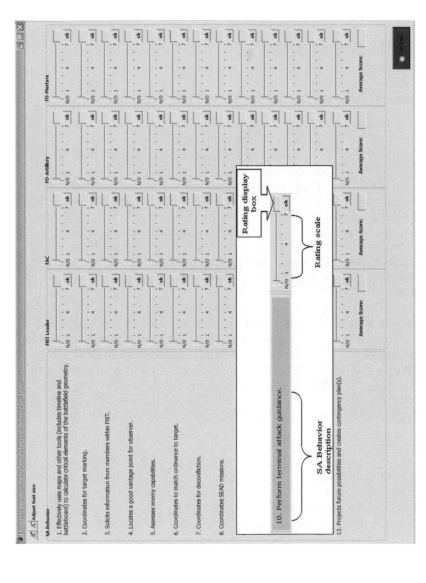

Figure 16.3. The VESARS team level SA behavior rating scale for marine FiSTs is presented (with magnified inset).

for each team member and each item on the rating tools are also averaged to provide a behavioral score for the role and for a particular situation assessment skill. The results are recorded at the end of a training trial into a data file for subsequent review.

THE SITUATION AWARENESS MEASUREMENT OF TEAM COMMUNICATIONS

To assess team communication with VESARS, training evaluators listen to the natural communications of the team members (either online or after action) and rate the quality of verbalizations for achieving SA. Various team communications can be categorized as relevant or irrelevant to expected SA communication items. Each item on the rating scale has been identified (with SMEs) as an important team communication for acquisition and dissemination of goal-related information. As trainee statements are rated, the tool tracks the frequency of "good" and "bad" SA communication for each item and each team member. At the end of a training trial, the rater has the opportunity to review the summary data for SA communications in order to provide an overall team communications rating. The overall rating ranges from 1—"hardly any skill in SA" to 5—"complete skill in SA." The SA communication data are stored for later review. VESARS provides descriptive phrases that serve as guidelines to the rater in order to assess the frequency and quality of SA-related team communication and rate them consistently from "1" to "5" (see Figure 16.4).

The team communications measure of SA primarily focuses on explicit communications between team members. There is a limited ability, however, to assess aspects of implicit communications using the behavioral rating tool (for example, observing team member actions or visual patterns). Even so, the behavioral tool mainly addresses nonverbal cues that are perceived as specialized (and explicit) codes (for example, signals, gestures, and postures), as is expected in the military environment.

Each of the tools as part of the VESARS can be presented on a desktop, laptop, or tablet PC (personal computer). The tablet PC implementation allows for movement in immersive virtual training setups and for raters to position themselves in close proximity to trainees. Figure 16.5 shows VESARS running on a tablet PC. Although it was developed for VR, VESARS can be easily used with desktop simulations or in live training environments.

THE SITUATION AWARENESS REVIEW AND FEEDBACK

The final component of VESARS provides for review and feedback on SA in the AAR. VESARS integrates and displays the data collected from the three measurement tools. The focus is on providing meaningful feedback to trainees on their SA, in terms of mission (SA) knowledge, situation assessment behaviors, and team SA communications. VESARS presents both summary data and detailed data from each measure through a series of interface tabs (see Figure 16.6).

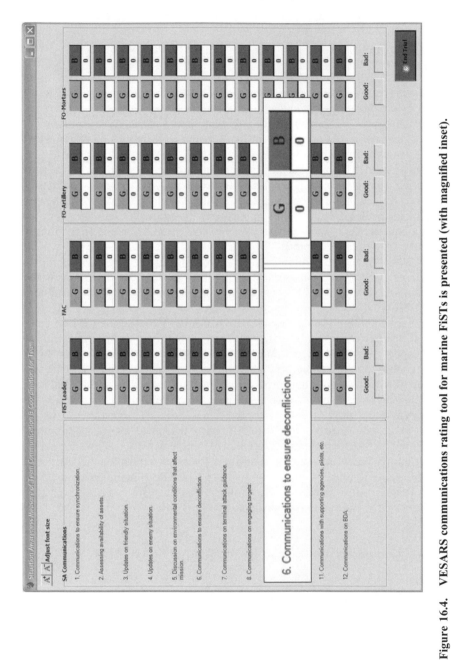

Figure 16.4. VESARS communications rating tool for marine FiSTs is presented (with magnified inset).

Figure 16.5. VESARS is implemented with a tablet PC for easy use in training simulations.

	SA Probes	SA Behaviors (Min rating = 0, Max rating = 7)	SA Communications
FiST	78%	3.1	64%
FiST Leader	81%	6.3	92%
FAC	82%	5.1	76%
FO-Artillery	66%	3.6	64%
FO-Mortars	76%	2.2	15%

SA Overview

Overview | SA Probes | SA Behaviors | SA Communications | Print...

- This table shows a summary of the trainee data.
- The first row shows the scores of the entire FiST on SA Probes (SA) probes, behaviors, and communications.
- The subsequent rows show the scores of each role within the FiST.

Figure 16.6. VESARS provides overview results for three measures.

VESARS provides key statistics on trainee SA toward improving the quality of AAR content. There are few other tools to support the AAR leader in presenting feedback on results to trainees following an exercise. Thus, the "take away" value for the trainees may hinge upon the ability of the AAR leader to identify critical behaviors and decision points during a scenario and relate trainee actual behaviors to needed skills and required competencies. This work can be particularly challenging in that AAR leaders may not be trained in SA theory, yet they may need to relate observed levels of SA to performance of combat skills. The VESARS provides this support for the AAR leader by helping him or her identify where losses in SA occur and what improvements are needed.

The "Overview" tab displays a summary of all SA data collected (see Figure 16.6). The SA probe scores are expressed as a percentage of correct responses to the SA probes. The behavioral scores are presented as the average situation assessment rating (from 0 ["not observed"] to 7 ["very good"]) for each team role. The summary of the communications data is presented as the percentage of "good" communications that occurred across the team. VESARS provides, at a high level, which member of a team experienced the greatest challenge in acquiring SA—a "red" circle around a score denotes the lowest score for each measure. VESARS provides access to detailed data on a particular measure for further analyses and training feedback by the AAR leader.

Beyond the overall summary of SA data, results from each SA measure can be reviewed in detail for each team member. The SA probes tab provides detailed results for each team member, including an overall score and accuracies in responding to probes targeting each level of SA (see Figure 16.7). The AAR leader can access detailed probe performance data on each member of the team and make comparisons with others. Data on individual probes, showing a table of all probes presented to the team, their responses, and the ground truth, can be accessed by each hyperlinked team member label.

In addition, VESARS can present shared SA data. The interface presents a count of probes on common knowledge, which were answered correctly by teammates. The trainer can see which team members were queried, which of the team members had the same SA, and whether the team understanding of the situation matched actual events. See Figure 16.8 for an example of shared SA results from the marine FiST domain.

Data on SA behaviors indicate how well the team or individual members performed, on average, in situation assessment. Results can be reviewed for specific behavioral items for a given team member role. Figure 16.9 presents a team view of situation assessment behaviors for the marine FiST. These data can be related to the SA probe results, providing information on which behaviors were performed and how this translated into inaccurate responses to SA probes. In addition, behavioral data presented over time can be linked to specific scenario events, providing insight into why SA may have been challenged at a particular point in time.

Similar data can be viewed on team communications. The trainer can view the percentage of good communications for the team or for individual team

	Overall SA	Level 1 SA (Perception)	Level 2 SA (Comprehension)	Level 3 SA (Projection)
FiST	78%	86%	77%	62%
FiST Leader	81%	79%	83%	82%
FAC	82%	95%	83%	50%
FO-Artillery	66%	76%	64%	55%
FO-Mortars	76%	84%	74%	63%

• SA Overview

Overview | SA Probes | SA Behaviors | SA Communications   Print...

• SA is the perception of the elements in the environment, the comprehension of their meaning in terms of task goals, and the projection of their status in the near future.
• This table shows a summary of trainee accuracy on SA probes. The first row shows the scores of the entire FiST on SA probes. The subsequent rows show the accuracy of each role within the FiST.
• Beside each role are scores on total SA, level 1 SA, level 2 SA, and level 3 SA. Level 1 SA refers to the perception of the elements in the environment, level 2 SA refers to the comprehension of the current situation, and level 3 SA refers to the projection of future status.

• Shared SA is the degree to which team members have a consistent picture of what is happening. Shared SA is evaluated by comparing the responses of the team members on SA probes that are common to two or more members.
• This table shows the accuracy of the FiST trainees on SA probes that they should have common knowledge on.

	Shared Probe Count
All teammates correct	7
1 teammate wrong	2
2 teammates wrong	0
3 teammates wrong	N/A
4 teammates wrong	N/A

Figure 16.7. SA probe data can be reviewed in detail.

members. The overall SA rating for team communications is also presented (see Figure 16.10). Results on communications can be graphically presented to trainees so that they quickly see which communications were performed well and which communication behaviors need to be modified to support team SA. These results can be related to SA probe results. Results indicating infrequent and inaccurate SA communications on certain items will also likely be associated with inaccurate responses to related SA probes. There may be instances in which the SA results from various measures conflict. For example, individuals may receive low overall SA scores based on their SA communication, but provide accurate responses to SA probes. In this example, the results would indicate team members who are skilled in acquiring individual SA, but lack the communication skills for supporting shared and team SA.

SUMMARY

As feedback is critical to learning, VESARS is expected to significantly enhance the benefit of simulation based training by assessing the SA of trainees and providing reviews of SA performance to enhance learning of critical behaviors and skills. The system couples validated objective and subjective measurement tools for comprehensive evaluation of SA. Much of the training value of VESARS lies in the method of targeting critical SA information needs for the domain being trained. The underlying SA analysis (for example, goal-directed

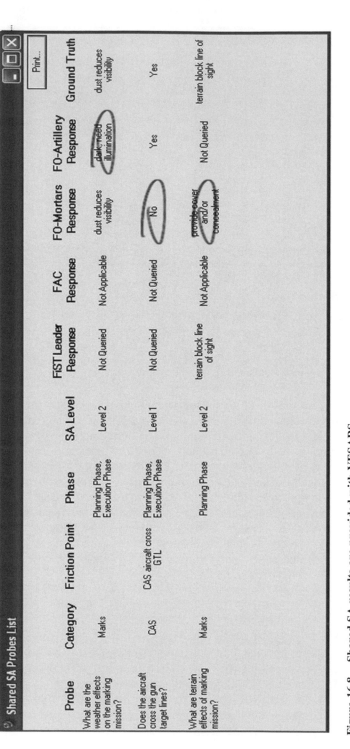

Figure 16.8. Shared SA results are provided with VESARS.

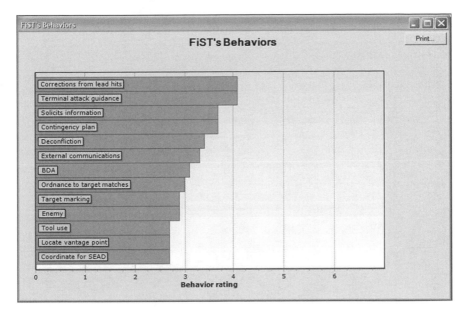

Figure 16.9.   VESARS behavioral data are presented in graphical form.

task analysis, assessment behaviors, and SA communications) serves to provide the instructional content that supports developing core competencies in a domain. This helps to enhance the training utility of sophisticated simulation tools. The SA analysis methods also provide insight into scenario events, activities, or missions that can be included in scenarios to tax SA, train specific situation assessment skills and communications, and ultimately enhance cognition and decision making in operations. The flexible and robust approach to SA measurement and analysis also makes it easy to provide structured feedback on the level of SA achieved during training situations. Beyond supporting structured feedback, VESARS could be used for assessing displays or training protocols. The SA scores of operators or trainees experiencing multiple display designs or training under alternate regimes can be compared to determine which design options will better support SA during operations or provide for more robust SA skill development. Multifaceted results would also denote the aspects of SA that are benefited.

Although current versions of VESARS are intended for SA assessment in military domains, the system is easily adaptable to new domains after conducting an analysis of SA requirements. As an advantage, the individual SA measures can be administered together or as separate components, depending upon the SA skills the trainer is interested in evaluating or further developing in trainees. Because VESARS can be loaded on separate machines (laptop, tablet, or desktop), it can also be used to assess SA of distributed training participants. Raters at different locations can view trainees in virtual environments. Each tool can collect and

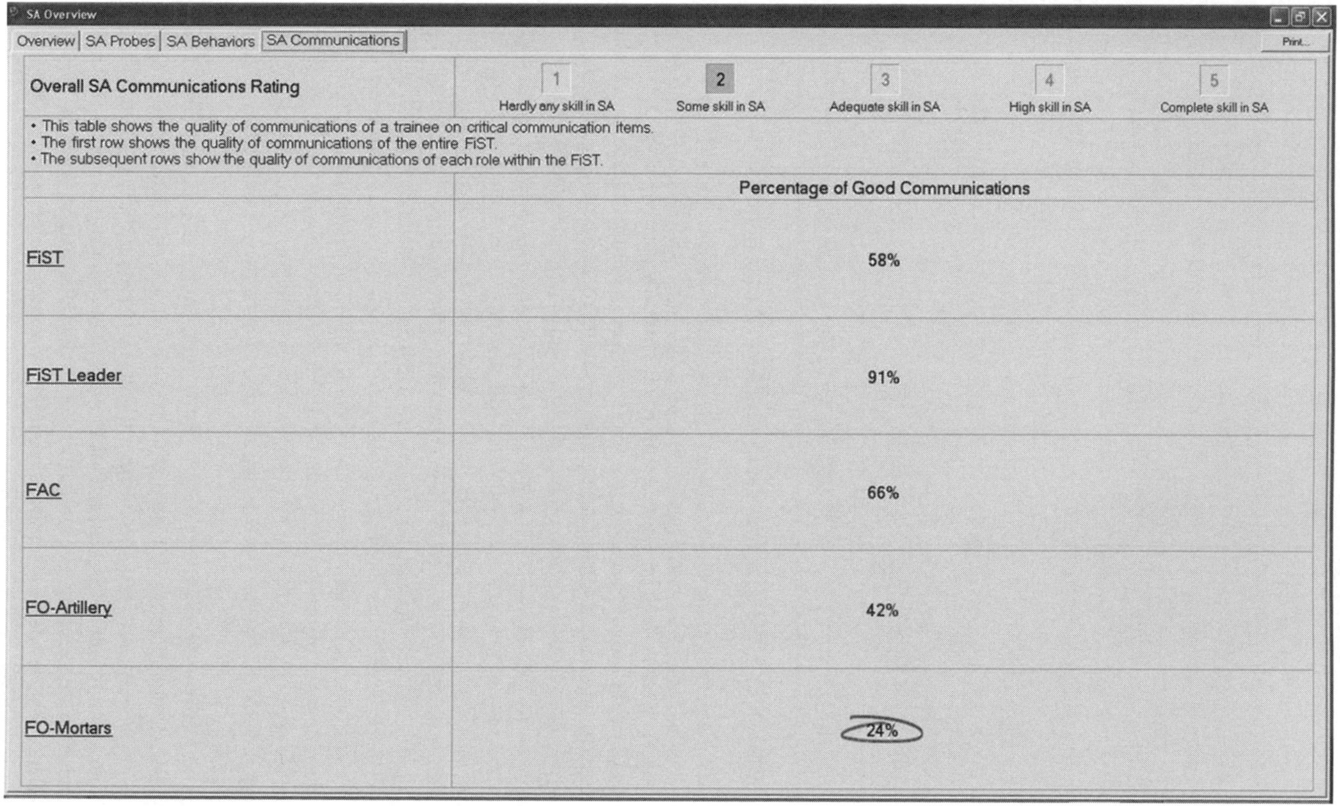

SA Overview

Overview | SA Probes | SA Behaviors | SA Communications

Overall SA Communications Rating

- This table shows the quality of communications of a trainee on critical communication items.
- The first row shows the quality of communications of the entire FIST.
- The subsequent rows show the quality of communications of each role within the FIST.

	1	2	3	4	5
	Hardly any skill in SA	Some skill in SA	Adequate skill in SA	High skill in SA	Complete skill in SA

Percentage of Good Communications

FIST	58%
FIST Leader	91%
FAC	66%
FO-Artillery	42%
FO-Mortars	24%

Figure 16.10. VESARS provides an overview of team communication results.

store SA results, which can be uploaded to a central system for distributed after action review and discussion.

Future research should be aimed at additional validation of VESARS. In previous research with VESARS for army infantry, the authors have demonstrated some sensitivity of the tool to scenario manipulations and individual differences among trainees (Kaber et al., 2005). This work was conducted with a very small participant sample, however, and, for certain measures, there were too few data collection points to completely validate the system. More robust validation requires access to a greater number of participant teams for longer periods of time and to training systems and situations that facilitate collection of other validated measures of SA (for example, SAGAT) along with VESARS measures, so that correlations between SA results could be assessed. The key is having the necessary control over training events in order to collect repeated measures for all responses across multiple scenarios and conditions to support the statistical analyses needed for robust validation.

ACKNOWLEDGMENTS

We thank subject matter experts at 29 Palms, California, and Camp LeJeune, North Carolina, for their contribution to task analysis for the marine FiST. We thank Mr. Dan Macchiarella and Lt. Col. John Hyatt for their contributions as SMEs and in reviewing SA measures and results. Justus Reynolds, Fleet Davis, Arathi Sethumadhavan, and Matthew DeKrey are acknowledged for hard work in task analysis and programming.

This effort was supported by a Small Business Innovative Research contract from the Office of the Secretary of Defense through the Army Research Institute and was further supported by the Office of Naval Research (ONR) Virtual Technologies and Environments Program grant. We are indebted to the project technical monitors, Don Lampton and Bruce Knerr of ARI and CDR Dylan Schmorrow of ONR. The views and conclusions presented in this chapter are those of the authors and do not necessarily reflect the views of the U.S. Army or the U.S. Navy.

REFERENCES

Artman, H., & Garbis, C. (1998). Situation awareness as distributed cognition. In T. Green, L. Bannon, C. Warren, & Initials Buckley (Eds.), *Cognition and cooperation. Proceedings of 9th Conference of Cognitive Ergonomics* (pp. 151–156). Limerick, Ireland.

Brannick, M. T., Prince, A., Prince, C., & Salas, E. (1993). The measurement of team process. *Human Factors, 37*(3), 641–651.

Department of the Army. (1993). *A leader's guide to after action review* (TC 25-20).

Endsley, M. R. (1988). Design and evaluation for situation awareness enhancement. *Proceedings of the Human Factors Society 32nd Annual Meeting* (Vol. 1, pp. 97–101). Santa Monica, CA: Human Factors Society.

Endsley, M. R. (1993). A survey of situation awareness requirements in air-to-air combat fighters. *International Journal of Aviation Psychology, 3*(2), 157–168.

Endsley, M. R. (1995a). Measurement of situation awareness in dynamic systems. *Human Factors, 37*(1), 65–84.

Endsley, M. R. (1995b). Toward a theory of situation awareness in dynamic systems. *Human Factors, 37*(1), 32–64.

Endsley, M. R. (2000). Direct measurement of situation awareness: Validity and use of SAGAT. In M. Endsley & D. Garland (Eds.), *Situation awareness analysis and measurement* (pp. 147–173). Mahwah, NJ: LEA.

Endsley, M. R., Bolte, B., & Jones, D. G. (2003). *Designing for situation awareness: An approach to human-centered design.* London: Taylor & Francis.

Endsley, M. R., & Garland, D. J. (2000). *Situation awareness analysis and measurement.* Mahwah, NJ: Lawrence Erlbaum.

Endsley, M. R., Holder, L. D., Leibrecht, B. C., Garland, D. J., Mattews, M. D., & Graham, S. E. (2000). *Modeling and measuring situation awareness in the infantry operational environment* (Research Rep. No. 1753). Alexandria, VA: U.S. Army Research Institute for Behavioral and Social Sciences.

Endsley, M. R., & Robertson, M. M. (2000). Training for situation awareness. In M. R. Endsley & D. J. Garland (Eds.), *Situation awareness analysis and measurement* (pp. 349–365). Mahwah, NJ: Lawrence Erlbaum.

Jones, D. G., & Endsley, M. R. (2000). Can real-time probes provide a valid measure of situation awareness? In D. B. Kaber & M. R. Endsley (Eds.), *Human performance, situation awareness and automation: User-centered design for the new millennium* (pp. 245–250). Atlanta, GA: SA Technologies.

Kaber, D. B., Riley, J. M., Lampton, D., & Endsley, M. R. (2005). Measuring situation awareness in a virtual urban environment for dismounted infantry training. *Proceedings of the 11th International Conference on Human-computer Interaction: Vol. 9. Advances in virtual environments technology: Musings on design, evaluation, and applications.* Las Vegas, NV: MIRA Digital Publishing.

Kaber, D. B., Riley, J. M., Sheik-Nainar, M. A., Hyatt, J. R., & Reynolds, J. P. (2006). Assessing infantry soldier situation awareness in virtual environment-based training of urban terrain operations. *Proceedings of the International Ergonomics Association 16th World Congress.* Maastricht, The Netherlands: Elsevier.

Kaber, D. B., Wright, M. C., & Sheik-Nainar, M. A. (2006). Investigation of multi-modal interface features for adaptive automation of a human-robot system. *International Journal of Human-Computer Studies, 64*(6), 527–540.

Knerr, B. W., Lampton, D. R., Crowell, H. P., Thomas, M. A., Comer, B. D., Grosse, J., et al. (2002). *Virtual environments for dismounted soldier simulation, training and mission rehearsal: Results of the FY 2001 culminating event* (Tech. Rep. No. 1129). Alexandria, VA: U.S. Army Research Institute for Behavioral and Social Sciences.

Knerr, B. W., Lampton, D. R., Martin, G. A., Washburn, D. A., & Cope, D. (2002). Developing an after action review system for virtual dismounted infantry simulations. *Proceedings of the 2002 Interservice/Industry Training Simulation and Education Conference.* Arlington, VA: National Training Systems Association.

Lampton, D. R., Bliss, J. P., & Morris, C. S. (2002). Human performance measurement in virtual environments. In K. M. Stanney (Ed.), *The handbook of virtual environments: Design, implementation and applications* (pp. 701–720). Mahwah, NJ: Lawrence Erlbaum.

Liu, A., Tendick, F., Cleary, K., & Kaufmann, C. (2003). A survey of surgical simulation: Applications, technology, and education. *Presence: Teleoperators and Virtual Environments, 12*(6), 599–614.

Ponder, M., Herbelin, B., Molet, T., Schertenlieb, S., Ulicny, B., Papagiannakis, G., et al. (2003, May). Immersive VR decision training: Telling interactive stories featuring advanced virtual human simulation technologies. *Proceedings of the 9th Eurographics Workshop on Virtual Environments*. Zurich, Switzerland: Eurographics Association.

Salas, E., & Cannon-Bowers, J. A. (1997). Methods, tools, and strategies for team training. In M. A. Quinones & A. Ehrenstein (Eds.), *Training for a rapidly changing workplace: Applications of psychological research* (pp. 249–279). Washington, DC: American Psychological Association.

Strater, L. D., Endsley, M. R., Pleban, R. J., & Matthews, M. D. (2001). *Measures of platoon leader situation awareness in virtual decision-making exercises* (Research Rep. No, 1770). Alexandria, VA: U.S. Army Research Institute for Behavioral and Social Sciences.

Wickens, C. D. (1992). *Engineering psychology and human performance* (2nd ed.). New York: Harper Collins.

Wright, M. C., & Kaber, D. B. (2003). Team coordination and strategies under automation. *Proceedings of the 47th Annual Meeting of the Human Factors and Ergonomics Society* (pp. 553–557). Santa Monica, CA: Human Factors and Ergonomics Society.

Chapter 17

ASSESSING COGNITIVE WORKLOAD IN VIRTUAL ENVIRONMENTS

Brad Cain and Joe Armstrong

This chapter discusses cognitive workload measurement within the context of virtual environments, describing some factors that affect workload and discussing some reasons for measuring workload in virtual environment applications. The chapter briefly discusses workload assessment techniques, including subjective ratings and performance based measures, noting a few in-depth workload measurement literature reviews.

INTRODUCTION

Complex work environments are typically associated with operators performing multiple tasks either simultaneously or in close succession to each other (Meyer & Kieras, 1997). Although execution of the individual tasks can often be described as a collection of procedural solutions, the interactions of concurrent tasks and the demands imposed on the operator create a chaotic system where task outcomes are very sensitive to the timing of events, the history and anticipated events, as well as the nature of the tasks involved. The need to understand and facilitate task flows within these complex environments to improve system performance has resulted in empirical investigations of the factors related to the cognitive aspects of task performance, with less emphasis placed on the physical workload demands. The complexity of these environments is further expanded through the inherent nonlinearity of the many interactions between the operator and a given system, as well as between multiple operators. Cognitive workload primarily focuses on determining the nature of the human information processing capacity (Reid & Nygren, 1988), including such issues as the number of cognitive resources that exist and the interactions that occur between them during task execution. The concept of cognitive workload is often considered to be an interim measure that is intended to provide insight into where increased task demands may lead to unacceptable system performance.

Implicit in the measurement of cognitive workload, hereafter simply referred to as workload, is the belief that as task difficulty or task demands increase, there is less residual capacity to deal with additional tasks; system performance usually decreases; response times and errors increase; control variability increases; fewer tasks are completed per unit time; and task performance strategies change (Huey & Wickens, 1993). In most cases, workload assessment focuses on high tempo periods, where errors of commission and omission are more prevalent; however, low tempo intervals are also important as a lack of operator engagement can reduce vigilance in situations where workload may be considered negligible despite a high level of effort required to maintain attention during monitoring for infrequent events. This has implications for designing operating procedures of virtual environments (VEs) that keep the operator suitably aroused and engaged with the task.

VEs were developed to provide a controlled experience for human operators to perform tasks similar to those performed in the real world. These artificial environments are abstractions of the real world with numerous compromises on fidelity of representation imposed by both technological limitations and cost. The usefulness of these devices lies in the cost-benefit trade-off that optimizes the benefits subject to the technological and cost constraints by implementing the essential features of the real world relevant to the application area in sufficient detail. VEs are used principally for engineering research and development and training, although mission rehearsal and tactics development are also likely candidates. Each application area has different objectives and requirements, but as they include a human in the loop to drive the performance of a simulated system, there is a need for a suitable representation of the environment and methods to assess the success of these representations.

In the context of assessing such human factors as workload during the systems design process, VEs are being used to provide input to all aspects of system design from requirements analysis, design, development, evaluation, and verification. At each phase of design, representations of a system can be assessed within a VE to ensure the system complexity does not exceed the operator's capacity to perform within acceptable workload limits, often at varying levels of fidelity depending upon the design phase. Testing of design concepts and procedures in VEs can identify excessive demands without formal workload measurement, but the assessment of intermediate states and estimates of residual capacity for operators to deal with emergencies or unanticipated events makes workload assessment a useful diagnostic tool. It is unclear, however, whether workload as measured in VEs necessarily translates into an equivalent demand as measured in the real world under similar circumstances.

For training, the objective is to provide a positive transfer of training that improves the operator's ability to perform in the real world with the real system. In this case, workload may be useful to assess the simulator's ability to convey adequately the necessary cues and information required while performing the required tasks, that is, as a metric of the degree of similarity of the essential features for training between the VE and the real world. Further, workload provides additional evidence for assessing competency that may not be adequately captured in pass/fail performance criteria. Seldom is it required or even desired to reproduce the real world exactly, as noted by Wickens (1992, p. 240). Workload measurement provides a quantitative measure of the subjective experience of performing some task in the VE that complements objective performance metrics to provide a more complete picture of the validity of the VE, as well as the operator's capability to perform selected tasks.

The range of possible VEs varies from desktop abstractions used for psychophysics experiments to fully immersive environments that support the conduct of full military exercises (Durlach & Mavor, 1995; Youngblut, Johnston, Nash, Wienclaw, & Will, 1996) provided the VE evokes responses similar to experiences in the real world (Magnusson, 2002; Nählinder, 2002). The level of realism associated with a given VE interacts with different levels of human performance, and the impact on workload is not always clear. It is important to assess how the differences between the VE and the real world affect cognitive processes through both subjective and objective performance measures of workload.

FACTORS AFFECTING WORKLOAD

There are numerous factors that can affect perceived workload, but they can be broadly classified into two categories: task factors and operator factors.

Differences between the real world and its VE representation have the potential to produce differences in the flow of information to the operator. While these differences may affect performance, it is not clear how those differences might affect workload, and differences between them may result in changes to the operator's approach to using the two systems. VE characteristics, such as lower fidelity visual representations, the lack of stressors and motivators, such as fatigue and survival, or the lack of proprioceptive cues may all serve to change the task demands for that system and thereby alter the operator's perceived workload. Workload and performance metrics must be selected to be sensitive to known differences to confidently predict real world expectations from VE results.

Perceptual Differences

Significant research and development have occurred within the realm of modeling and simulation to improve the supporting technologies that underlie. While many VE shortfalls have been identified over the past 10 years (Durlach & Mavor, 1995; Youngblut et al., 1996), VEs remain today, and technological advances have reduced the severity of many of these problems (Renkewitz & Alexander, 2007).

Typically, we acquire most of our information of dynamic, real world events visually. Synthetic environments have only recently been able to employ technologies that closely approximate the real world experience both in the richness of detail and the resolution of that representation. The degree to which a VE must approximate reality is highly dependent on the nature of the task, and differing VE applications will often have different visual display requirements. For example, the presentation of stereoscopic information and motion parallax to support the judgment of depth and distance may require a visual scene with only moderate resolution, while other tasks that involve fine visual acuity may require very high resolution but only biocular imagery. Other tasks, such as target identification, may require principally foveal displays, while others, such as target detection, may require a better presentation of peripheral information.

Shortfalls in the appropriate levels of fidelity in the key aspects of a VE may also affect performance, such as inadequate visual cueing that prevents helicopter hover maneuvers in closely coupled systems, such as deck landings or ground vehicle control in complex terrain, but the effect on cognitive workload is unclear. When there are conflicting cues in the environment as a consequence of technological limitations of the VE, the operator has to reconcile the relevant cues with the false cues. While degraded visual cues may lead to poorer performance in the VE than in the real world, it is unclear whether users will perceive that they have to work any harder to achieve that level of performance.

Audition and communication have typically received less attention in the VE literature than has vision. Interactions with virtual teammates, opponents, and bystanders should be natural. Computer speech production has improved to the point where it is intelligible and reasonably natural, but problems persist when dealing with virtual operators that require speech recognition and interpretation through natural language processing (Sanchez-Vives & Slater, 2005). While simple, constrained dialogue is feasible, broad lexicons, ambiguous meanings and real time simulation pose interpretation challenges for virtual agents. Implausible behaviors and decisions can occur as virtual agents violate underlying assumptions embedded in their rule bases. This in turn can lead to changes in performance and workload for the operator when interpreting entity behavior or increase the effort required compensating for the behavior of virtual teammates.

Unnatural constraints on how information has to be conveyed (restrictive vocabularies or manual text input) and loss of audible information (adversary detection or failure noises) mean that information has to be obtained in some less convenient means (for example, text messages or keyboard entry), leading to higher than expected workload. Further, studies of three-dimensional auditory cueing aid to visual search found that even small errors in the spatial location of the auditory presentation delayed visual detections, indicating that shortfalls in one information processing channel may result in greater workload in another channel if they present conflicting information.

Noise and vibration levels in VEs are generally lower than in the real world, resulting in less harmful experiences, although some simulators provide reduced levels for context. Despite providing some degree of realism, operators exposed to these sensations may experience less fatigue or clearer communications, lessening the perceived workload and improving performance over real world conditions.

Proprioceptive feedback and sensations of acceleration are typically limited in VEs due to the lack of or uncorrelated visual representations of body, limits in motion base displacements, and so forth. This leads to disparities among cues about body position, grasping, control manipulation, and movement within the

VE that the operator learns to compensate for or to ignore. Simulators often compensate with false acceleration cues because of physical constraints that can distract the user under certain conditions (for example, recentering of jacks during rapid helicopter control inputs can feel like the tail wheel striking the tail fan during a deck landing on a ship). Tactile feedback from simulator controls may lead to overcontrolling or lack of adequate control such that more effort is required to achieve the same level of performance, yet it may also lead to a loss of user acceptance, causing both lower performance and workload.

Cognitive Differences

Typically the VE is less complex than its real world equivalent: there are fewer sensory details to interpret, fewer distractions or alternatives to consider, and generally fewer methods to achieve one's goals. Scenarios are contrived, for good reasons, but this may lead to unrealistic conditions that the subject perceives as unlikely, causing lower trust or acceptance of the VE.

There are few consequences of failure in a VE, although competency testing and desire to perform adequately can be stressful. Knowledge that a VE is only a simulation may influence operator performance. Some maintain that it is the sense of presence or the perception of being in the synthetic environment that differentiates VEs from other synthetic environments or simulators. The journal *Presence* is largely devoted to this topic and the technological challenges facing the creation of presence, but even modest fidelity simulations can induce engagement, if not a sense of presence (Bowman & McMahan, 2007; Dekker & Delleman, 2007). Subjective workload provides a means of assessing operator acceptance to determine whether sufficient engagement has been achieved that, when coupled with objective measures of performance and subject matter expert opinion, provides a method to assess acceptance of the VE.

Behavior

Presenting a visual representation of teammates provides supporting cues to task performance, such as the ability to observe a teammate control inputs made or nonverbal signals. Tactile and haptic feedback from controls provides considerable information to the operator about the state of the local environment, particularly to subject matter experts. Conflicting feedback may cause ambiguity leading to confusion and extra reasoning. Without accurate representation of these behaviors and physical cues, the operator has to exert additional effort to collect relevant information by other means.

Operator State

Operators bring individual knowledge, skills, and abilities to the VE, sometimes collectively called traits that are relatively constant through an experience. Shortcomings in the VE ultimately affect the operator directly, often substantially moderating operator state during a VE experience. Simulator sickness can result from a mismatch between the visual and vestibular cues (Johnson, 2007; Kennedy, Lane, Bierbaum & Lilienthal, 1993) (see Drexler, Kennedy, and Malone, Volume 2, Section 1, Chapter 11), degrading the operator's ability to perform and leading to poorer performance or increased effort. Other unintended effects, such as the lack of representation of the operator's own body, can lead to disorientation and confusion.

Operator discomfort is a key factor that is seldom addressed in VE technology reviews. We know from military operations that adjusting close fitting helmets for personnel is an involved and critical process that is required to ensure that the helmet does not produce undue discomfort that will affect performance. Also, neck strain can occur when using night vision goggles, even with good designs under normal conditions. Unfortunately, VE helmet-mounted displays intended for general use seldom provide adequate adjustment to allow for individual differences, so discomfort and strain arise over time, distracting the operator from the primary task and affecting the perception of workload.

WORKLOAD MEASUREMENT METHODS

There are a number of reviews of workload in the open literature that discuss theoretical and applied issues that the reader may consult (for example, Cain, 2007; Castor, 2003; de Waard, 1996; Eggemeier, Wilson, Kramer, & Damos, 1991; Farmer & Brownson, 2003; Gopher & Braune, 1984; Gopher & Donchin, 1986). The following sections provide a brief look at some of the techniques that can be usefully applied in VEs. Physiological measures were not included here because of their specialized instrumentation requirements, but readers interested in these techniques may want to consult the relevant literature[1] (for example, Kramer, 1991; Kramer, Trejo, & Humphrey, 1996; Wilson et al., 2004; Wilson, 1998, 2001; Wilson & Eggemeier, 1991).

Subjective Ratings

Subjective workload measurements are the most commonly used techniques for gathering feedback from operators about the perceived demands of a task (Rubio, Diaz, Martin, & Puente, 2004; Tsang & Velazquez, 1996; Wickens, 1989; Xie & Salvendy, 2000). Subjective measures are relatively easy to administer and often have high face validity due to the active involvement of the operators in the evaluation process. They may also have good construct validity if there is a coherent theoretical framework that fits the operator's own perception of internal state while performing a task (Annett, 2002), but subjective assessments may not correspond to observed task performance. This is an important distinction as the perception of a situation, particularly a situation that induces

[1]See also the Association of Applied Psychophysiology and Biofeedback Web page: http://www.aapb.org, April 2008.

stress or requires substantial experience to understand subtle differences, can have a dramatic impact on the operator's perception of his or her ability to complete the assigned tasks (Annett, 2002; Hancock & Vasmatzidis, 1998).

There are several popular subjective workload metrics that attempt to be diagnostic of the task. The VACP (visual, auditory, cognitive, and psychomotor) method (Aldrich & McCracken, 1984; Aldrich, Szabo, & Bierbaum, 1989; McCracken & Aldrich, 1984) was perhaps the first multidimensional technique, and despite objections to inappropriate aggregation of ordinal data, VACP has been used extensively to reflect expert judgment in constructive simulations during system. The subjective workload assessment tool (Reid & Nygren, 1988; Reid, Shingledecker, & Eggemeier, 1981; Reid, Shingledecker, Nygren, & Eggemeier, 1981) is used to rate subjective experiences on three dimensions: time load, mental effort, and psychological stress. Conjoint scaling of the ordinal ratings creates interval ratings, a step not addressed by most subjective techniques. Hart and Staveland (1988) developed the National Aeronautics and Space Administration (NASA) Task Load Index (TLX) with six verbally anchored dimensions to represent individual differences of perceived contributions to workload. Castor (2003, p. 36) notes that five of the dimensions seem to cluster on a single factor that could be considered "workload," while the own performance dimension reflects a different aspect of task performance that is related to, but is separate from, the workload assessment. The DRAWS (Defence Research Agency Workload Scale) measurement technique (Farmer, Belyavin, et al., 1995; Farmer, Jordan, et al., 1995) asks subjects to rate task demands on three information processing dimensions: input, central, and output (an additional dimension, time pressure, was later added to these original three dimensions). The POP (Prediction of Operator Performance) model was developed as a predictive form of DRAWS; integrating subjective DRAWS ratings of individual task demands predicts the interference among concurrent tasks in constructive simulations. POP has been validated against human data from laboratory tasks, indicating that subjective techniques can have predictive validity in addition to construct and content validity if properly implemented.

Numerous comparison studies of these techniques have been published (Byers, Bittner, Hill, Zaklad, & Christ, 1988; Colle & Reid, 1998; Hart & Staveland, 1988; Hill et al., 1992; Nygren, 1991; Whitaker, Hohne, & Birkmire-Peters, 1997). Hart and Wickens (1990, p. 267) reported that of several subjective measures, NASA TLX correlated best with performance measures while displaying low intersubject variability and good user acceptance. While the use of multiple dimensions in some techniques may provide insight into task overload, it is still beyond their capability to explain or diagnose the theoretical reason for the cognitive overload (Annett, 2002; Damos, 1991; Jordan et al., 1996; Rubio et al., 2004).

Performance Based Measures

Since the primary reason for creating a VE is to create a convincing simulation of the real world, measurement of on-task performance is a natural approach to assessing system efficacy and operator demand. Performance measures of workload can be classified into two major types: primary and secondary task measures. In most VE investigations, the primary task will be of interest as it is usually an approximation of an in-service task. Wickens (1992, p. 392) notes that for primary task measures to be adequate for workload assessment, a number of conditions should be met: manipulation of the task must be sufficient to cause changes in task performance to infer remaining capacity; the demand of secondary tasks should not be the limiting factor, particularly if they use other modalities; other effects should not creep into the study (confounds such as learning or fatigue); and analysts must determine whether operator strategies affect performance and workload differentially, giving the appearance of dissociation between the two.

Secondary task measures are considered more diagnostic than primary task measures alone and are used to assess the remaining processing capacity while performing a primary task. The secondary task paradigm can be further classified into auxiliary task and loading task methodologies, but the intent of both is to increase operator load to the point where changes in effort or strategy are no longer able to compensate for changes in the demand manipulation of concurrent task execution without a corresponding change in performance.

Damos (1991, p. 114) suggests a number of considerations for selecting secondary tasks, noting that practice on individual tasks is not sufficient to ensure optimal dual task performance; the tasks must be also practiced together, an aspect related to the metacontroller's role in performance and workload measurement (Jex, 1988). While primary task measures are often based on an operational context, the contextual relevance or importance of secondary tasks varies. This can lead to subjects disregarding the secondary task so contextually relevant secondary tasks are preferred.

COMMENTS ON APPLICATION OF WORKLOAD ASSESSMENT

Wierwille and colleagues reported the results of a focused series of experiments stressing different aspects of mental demand on workload measurement methods (Casali & Wierwille, 1983, 1984; Wierwille & Connor, 1983; Wierwille, Rahimi, & Casali, 1985). The results indicated that various workload measurement techniques are differentially sensitive to the types of load manipulations. Less than half of the measurement techniques tested were appropriate in any given study, and fewer still had a monotonic relationship with the load manipulations. Wickens (1992), de Waard (1996), and Farmer and Brownson (2003), among others, provide critical reviews of workload measurement techniques, offering recommendations for human-in-the-loop simulation. O'Donnell & Eggemeier (1986) proposed several criteria to guide the selection of workload measurement techniques.

The dissociation between subjective and performance measures of workload is generally acknowledged, and there are numerous examples of it in the literature, although the causes are not well understood (de Waard, 1996; Farmer & Brownson, 2003; Farmer, Jordan, Belyavin, Birch, & Bunting, 1993; Vidulich &

Wickens, 1986; Yeh & Wickens, 1985). Dissociations can be observed as an insensitivity or a reversal of expected results by one of the measurement classes to task manipulations. Vidulich and Bortolussi (1988) observed that subjective measures tend to be sensitive to working memory demands and less so to response execution demands. Their hypothesis is that subjective workload is sensitive only to manipulations that are well represented consciously, so that varying demands in skill based tasks will not cause subjective ratings to change substantially. This suggests that subjective workload measures are well suited to assessing modern technologies that aid judgment or decision making, but are less suited for assessing physical or mechanical aspects of skill based tasks.

In summary, the literature covering the range of analytic techniques supporting the assessment of workload is extensive. Though there are many attributes associated with the concept of workload that further research, a sufficient body of knowledge exists to support practical applications of workload assessment tools and techniques. The following section provides a brief discussion on the practical application of workload assessment within a VE framework.

WORKLOAD ASSESSMENT VALIDITY

Most if not all workload methods have been developed and validated in a simulated environment where cues are presented to operators in some representation or abstraction of a real world equivalent task. Thus, regardless of what workload measurement devices are actually measuring, they probably measure it best in a synthetic environment. This suggests that there should be no special consideration required for applying workload measurement techniques in a VE. Adams (1997) notes that while measuring performance and workload in the field may not suffer from content validity, it does not validate the measurement method construct, and care must be taken to ensure a valid method is used.

Measurement of proficiency or transfer of training in a simulator calls into question the issue of content and construct validity. Simulators for training transfer and simulators for proficiency may be quite different, and a simulator that is good for transfer of training may not be good for proficiency testing and vice versa. Adams cites Weitzman that a score for instrument flying in a 1979, high fidelity flight simulator had a moderate correlation of 0.51 with the same measures in the real aircraft, raising doubts about the validity of both the measurement approach and the VE study. Studies such as this that incorporate workload metrics help to establish the technological requirements for valid VEs.

VEs typically provide a flexible framework from which to generate both subjective and objective measures of workload. This sets the stage, but does not guarantee that corresponding measurements can be made in operational settings to validate a VE. Some of the benefits that VEs afford include the following:

1. Flexibility of automated data collection capabilities integrated within the hardware and software infrastructure supporting the VE,

2. Ability to integrate a range of primary or secondary performance measures that would be impossible within operational equipment,

3. Ability to pause virtual scenarios at any time to obtain subjective measurements of workload on a momentary basis, and

4. Greater control over confounding nuisance variables that affect performance in an operational setting.

Advances in simulator technologies are also creating environments with a greater sense of presence such that the difference between simulated and real world performance is rapidly decreasing, thereby making the VE valuable as a preliminary design assessment tool. Research with VEs is helping to identify the essential elements and the degree of fidelity that is needed to provide a valid simulation. Workload assessment techniques may assist in determining the appropriateness of a VE for design or training. Yet, there are still a number of considerations that must be addressed when using VEs as part of an assessment tool for human performance measurement, especially in the context of metacognitive concepts such as workload. These considerations include the following:

1. How can the ecological validity of the laboratory conditions be established such that empirical results may be generalized to operational environments? There is currently no clear path to defining the characteristics of VEs required to ensure that measurements in a virtual world are extensible to the real world.

2. Will participants attribute sufficient realism to the VEs to treat the tasks within the environment in a realistic manner and experience workload comparable to that experienced in practice? For example, the very fact that a critical simulated event in a VE is not truly life threatening may change participant behaviors and perceptions, diminishing the level of stress and workload experienced.

3. VE studies may employ untrained or inexperienced participants to offset either the cost or difficulty of obtaining subject matter experts. Evidence suggests that expert performance may be substantially different from untrained participant performance, showing evidence of highly skilled automatized behavior that does not contribute to perceptions of subjective workload.

Validation of VEs is difficult, but without validation, there is little confidence that the results obtained with the VE are meaningful. Comparison of workload measurements from similar VE and real world tasks provides a critical component for the VE validation process.

CONCLUDING THOUGHTS

When selecting a workload measure, or a battery of measures, the analyst should consider the objective of the assessment. In the context of systems evaluation, then perhaps a univariate measure is sufficient. If a more diagnostic measurement is required, say to assess training proficiency, then multidimensional measures may be more appropriate or used in addition to a univariate measure. Primary and embedded secondary task measures relevant to the operational context are also recommended when evaluating workload in VEs, particularly during the course of a complex scenario where multiple measurement intervals may be required to form an understanding of the results.

Farmer and Brownson (2003) recommend that a battery of workload measures be selected for simulation based assessments and provide guidance on such a selection. This does not mean analysts should apply any or all measures from such a list, but that several should be considered for the insight they can provide. If a shotgun selection of methods is adopted, the analyst might well end up with a bewildering, contradictory set of results. A careful assessment of the task under study and its context is necessary to select an appropriate battery of workload measurement methods. This battery should include at least one objective measure and make use of quantitative subjective assessments (rather than simply subjective pass/fail ratings).

Regardless of the measures selected, the analyst should consider the human factors discussed in the various chapters of this handbook when drawing conclusions from workload analyses conducted in VEs, especially when comparing workload results between a VE and its real world counterpart. Considerable research remains to be conducted to better isolate the various factors in VEs that may contribute to differences in performance, changes in perception, and measurement of workload when compared to the real world. Improving our understanding of these factors will serve both to focus developers of VEs in selecting the most appropriate areas of technology to improve to better approximate the real world and to allow analysts using VEs as either training or testing environments to draw better, more accurate conclusions regarding human performance in these domains.

REFERENCES

Adams, S. R. (1997). *In-flight measurement of workload and situational awareness.* Paper presented at the TTCP UTP7 Human Factors in Aircraft Environments Workshop on the validation of measurements, models and theories, Naval Postgraduate School, Monterey, CA.

Aldrich, T. B., & McCracken, J. H. (1984). *A computer analysis to predict crew workload during LHX Scout-Attack Missions Vol. 1* (Technical Report No. MDA90333333-81-C-0504, ASI479-054-I-84(B)). Fort Rucker, Alabama: U.S. Army Research Institute Field Unit.

Aldrich, T. B., Szabo, S. M., & Bierbaum, C. R. (1989). The development and application of models to predict operator workload during system design. In G. R. McMillan, D. Beevis, E. Salas, M. H. Strub, R. Sutton & L. V. Breda (Eds.), *Applications of human performance models to system design* (Vol. 2, pp. 65–80). New York: Plenum Press.

Annett, J. (2002). Subjective rating scales: science or art? *Ergonomics, 45*(14), 966–987.

Bowman, D. A., & McMahan, R. P. (2007). Virtual reality: How much immersion is enough? [Electronic Version]. *Computer 40,* 257. Retrieved February 2008.

Byers, C. J., Bittner, A. C. J., Hill, S. G., Zaklad, A. L., & Christ, R. E. (1988). *Workload assessment of a remotely piloted vehicle (RPV) system.* Paper presented at the Human Factors Society's 32 Annual Meeting, Santa Monica, California.

Cain, B. (2007). *A review of the mental workload measurement literature* (No. RTO-TR-HFM-121-Part-II, AC/323(HFM-121)TP/62). Neuilly-Sur-Seine Cedex, France: North

Atlantic Treaty Organization, Research and Technology Organization, Human Factors and Medicine Panel.

Casali, J. G., & Wierwille, W. W. (1983). A comparison of rating scale, secondary-task, physiological and primary-task workload estimation techniques in a simulated flight task emphasizing communications load. *Human Factors, 25*(6), 623–641.

Casali, J. G., & Wierwille, W. W. (1984). On the measurement of pilot perceptual workload: a comparison of assessment techniques addressing sensitivity and intrusion issues. *Ergonomics, 27*(10), 1033–1050.

Castor, M. C. (2003). *Final Report for GARTEUR Flight Mechanics Action Group FM AG13: GARTEUR Handbook of mental workload measurement* (No. GARTEUR TP 45). Stockholm, SE: Group for Aeronautical Research and Technology in Europe.

Colle, H. A., & Reid, G. B. (1998). Context effects in subjective mental workload ratings. *Human Factors, 40*(4), 591–600.

Damos, D. L. (1991). Dual-task methodology: some common problems. In D. L. Damos (Ed.), *Multiple-task performance* (pp. 101–119). London: Taylor & Francis.

Dekker, E. D., & Delleman, N. (2007, July). *Presence.* Paper presented at the Virtual Environments for Intuitive Human-System Interaction.

de Waard, R. (1996). *The measurement of driver's mental workload.* Heran, The Netherlands: University of Groningen.

Durlach, N. I., & Mavor, A. S. (Eds.). (1995). *Virtual Reality. Scientific and technological challenges.* Washington, DC: National Academy Press.

Eggemeier, F. T., Wilson, G. F., Kramer, A. F., & Damos, D. L. (1991). Workload assessment in multi-task environments. In D. L. Damos (Ed.), *Multiple task performance* (pp. 207–216). London: Taylor & Francis, Ltd.

Farmer, E., & Brownson, A. (2003). *Review of workload measurement, analysis and interpretation methods:* European Organisation for the Safety of Air Navigation.

Farmer, E. W., Belyavin, A. J., Jordan, C. S., Bunting, A. J., Tattersall, A. J., & Jones, D. M. (1995). *Predictive workload assessment* (Final Rep. No. DRA/AS/MMI/CR95100/1). Farnborough, Hampshire, United Kingdom: Defence Research Agency.

Farmer, E. W., Jordan, C. S., Belyavin, A. J., Birch, C. L., & Bunting, A. J. (1993). *Prediction of dual-task performance by mental demand ratings* (No. DRA/AS/FS/CR93087/1). Farnborough, Hampshire, United Kingdom: Defence Research Agency.

Farmer, E. W., Jordan, C. S., Belyavin, A. J., Bunting, A. J., Tattersall, A. J., & Jones, D. M. (1995). *Dimensions of operator workload* (Final Rep. No. DRA/AS/MMI/CR95098/1). Farnborough, Hampshire, United Kingdom: Defence Research Agency.

Gopher, D., & Braune, R. (1984). On the psychophysics of workload: Why bother with subjective measures? *Human Factors, 26*(5), 519–532.

Gopher, D., & Donchin, E. (1986). Workload—An examination of the concept. In K. R. Boff, L. Kaufman, & J. P. Thomas (Eds.), *Handbook of Perception and Human Performance (Vol. 2): Cognitive Processes and Performance.* (pp. 41-41–41-49). John Wiley & Sons.

Hancock, P. A., & Vasmatzidis, I. (1998). Human occupational and performance limits under stress: The thermal environments as a prototypical example. *Ergonomics, 41* (8), 1169–1191.

Hart, S., & Wickens, C. D. (1990). Workload assessment and prediction. In H. R. Booher (Ed.), *MANPRINT: An approach to systems integration* (pp. 257–296). New York: van Nostrand Reinhold.

Hart, S. G., & Staveland, L. E. (1988). Development of NASA-TLX (Task Load Index): Results of empirical and theoretical research. In P. A. M. Hancock, N. (Ed.), *Human Mental Workload* (pp. 139–183). Amsterdam: North-Holland.

Hill, S. G., Iavecchia, H. P., Byers, J. C., Bittner, A. C., Zaklad, A. L., & Christ, R. E. (1992). Comparison of four subjective workload rating scales. *Human Factors, 34*(4), 429–439.

Huey, B. M., & Wickens, C. D. (1993). *Workload transition: Implications for individual and team performance.* Washington, DC: National Research Council, Commission on Behavioral and Social Sciences and Education, Committee on Human Factors, Panel on Workload Transition.

Jex, H. R. (1988). Measuring mental workload: Problems, progress, and promises. In P. A. Hancock & N. Meshkati (Eds.), *Human mental workload* (pp. 5–39). Amsterdam, NL: Elsevier Science Publishers B.V. (North-Holland).

Johnson, D. M. (2007, July). *Simulator sickness research summary.* Paper presented at the Virtual Environments for Intuitive Human-System Interaction, Neuilly-Sur-Seine Cedex, France.

Jordan, C. S., Farmer, E. W., Belyavin, A. J., Selcon, S. J., Bunting, A. J., Shanks, C. R., et al. (1996, September). *Empirical validation of the prediction of operator performance (POP) model.* Paper presented at the Human Factors and Ergonomics Society 40th Annual Meeting, Philadelphia, Pennsylvania.

Kennedy, R. S., Lane, N. E., Bierbaum, K. S., & Lilienthal, M. G. (1993). Simulator sickness questionnaire: an enhanced method for quantifying simulator sickness. *International Journal of Aviation Psychology, 3*(3), 203–220.

Kramer, A. F. (1991). Physiological metrics of mental workload: A review of recent progress. In D. L. Damos (Ed.), *Multiple task performance* (pp. 279–328). London: Taylor & Francis.

Kramer, A. F., Trejo, L. J., & Humphrey, D. G. (1996). Psychophysiological measures of workload: Potential applications to adaptively automated systems. In R. Parasuraman & M. Mouloua (Eds.), *Automation and human performance: Theory and applications* (pp. 137–162). Mahwah, NJ: Lawrence Erlbaum.

Magnusson, S. (2002). On the similarities and differences in psychophysiological reactions between simulated and real air-to-ground missions. *International Journal of Aviation Psychology, 12*(1), 3–18.

McCracken, J. H., & Aldrich, T. B. (1984). *Analyses of selected LHX mission functions: Implications for operator workload and system automation goals* (Technical Rep. No. MDA903-81-C-0504 ASI479-024-84). Fort Rucker, AL: U.S. Army Research Institute Aircrew Performance and Training.

Meyer, D. E., & Kieras, D. E. (1997). *Precis to a practical unified theory of cognition and action: Some lessons from EPIC computational models of human multiple-task performance.* (EPIC Tech. Rep. No. 8, TR-97/ONR-EPIC-8). Ann Arbor: University of Michigan, Psychology Department.

Nählinder, S. (2002, October). *Similarities in the way we react in a simulator and a real-world environment.* Paper presented at the SAWMAS First Swedish-American workshop on modeling and simulation.

Nygren, T. E. (1991). Psychometric properties of subjective workload measurement techniques: Implications for their use in the assessment of perceived mental workload. *Human Factors, 33*(1), 17–33.

O'Donnell, R. D., & Eggemeier, F. T. (1986). Workload assessment methodology. In K. R. Boff, L. Kaufman, & J. P. Thomas (Eds.), *Handbook of perception and human performance (Vol. 2): Cognitive processes and performance* (pp. 42-41–42-49). John Wiley & Sons.

Reid, G. B., & Nygren, T. E. (1988). The subjective workload assessment technique: A scaling procedure for measuring mental workload. In P. A. M. Hancock, N. (Ed.), *Human mental workload* (pp. 185–218). Amsterdam: Elsevier Science Publishers B.V. (North-Holland).

Reid, G. B., Shingledecker, C. A., & Eggemeier, F. T. (1981, June). *Application of conjoint measurement to workload scale development.* Paper presented at the Human Factors Society 25th Annual Meeting, Seattle, Washington.

Reid, G. B., Shingledecker, C. A., Nygren, T. E., & Eggemeier, F. T. (1981, October). *Development of multidimensional subjective measures of workload.* Paper presented at the Conference on Cybernetics and Society sponsored by IEEE Systems, Man and Cybernetics Society, Atlanta, Georgia.

Renkewitz, H., & Alexander, T. (2007, July). *Perceptual Issues of Augmented and Virtual Environments.* Paper presented at the Virtual Environments for Intuitive Human-System Interaction, Neuilly-Sur-Seine Cedex, France.

Rubio, S., Diaz, E., Martin, J., & Puente, J. M. (2004). Evaluation of subjective cognitive workload: A comparison of SWAT, NASA-TLX, and Workload Profile measures. *Applied Psychology, An International Review, 53*(1), 61–86.

Sanchez-Vives, M. V., & Slater, M. (2005). From presence to consciousness through virtual reality. *Nature Review Neuroscience, 6,* 332–339.

Tsang, P. S., & Velazquez, V. L. (1996). Diagnosticity and multidimensional subjective workload rating. *Ergonomics, 39*(3), 358–381.

Vidulich, M. A., & Bortolussi, M. R. (1988, October). *A dissociation of objective and subjective measures in assessing the impact of speech controls in advanced helicopters.* Paper presented at the Human Factors Society 32nd Annual Meeting, Santa Monica, California.

Vidulich, M. A., & Wickens, C. D. (1986). Causes of dissociation between subjective workload measures and performance. Caveats for the use of subjective assessments. *Applied Ergonomics, 17*(4), 291–296.

Whitaker, L. A., Hohne, J., & Birkmire-Peters, D. P. (1997, September). *Assessing cognitive workload metrics for evaluating telecommunication tasks.* Paper presented at the Human Factors and Ergonomics Society 41st Annual Meeting, Albuquerque, New Mexico.

Wickens, C. D. (1989). Models of multitask situations. In G. R. B. McMillan, D. Salas, E. Strub, M. H. Sutton, R. van Breda, L. (Eds.), *Applications of human performance models to system design* (Vol. 2, pp. 259–274). New York: Plenum Press.

Wickens, C. D. (1992). *Engineering psychology and human performance* (2nd ed.). New York: HarperCollins Publishers.

Wierwille, W. W., & Connor, S. A. (1983). Evaluation of 20 workload measures using a psychomotor task in a moving-base aircraft simulator. *Human Factors, 25*(1), 1–16.

Wierwille, W. W., Rahimi, M., & Casali, J. G. (1985). Evaluation of 16 measures of mental workload using a simulated flight task emphasizing mediational activity. *Human Factors, 27*(5), 489–502.

Wilson, G. C., et. al. (2004). *Operator functional state assessment* (No. RTO-TR-HFM-104, AC/323 (HFM-104) TP/48). Paris, France: North Atlantic Treaty Organisation (NATO), Research and Technology Organisation (RTO) BP 25, F-92201, Neuilly-sur-Seine Cedex, France.

Wilson, G. F. (1998). *The role of psychophysiology in future mental workload test and evaluation* (NATO Unclassified No. AC/243(panel-8)TP-17-SESS In. 98-02006). Dayton, OH: Armstrong Lab, Wright-Patterson AFB.

Wilson, G. F. (2001). An analysis of mental workload in pilots during flight using multiple psychophysiological measures. *International Journal of Aviation Psychology, 12*(1), 3–18.

Wilson, G. F., & Eggemeier, F. T. (1991). Psychophysiological assessment of workload in multi-task environments. In D. L. Damos (Ed.), *Multiple task performance* (pp. 329–360). London: Taylor & Francis.

Xie, B., & Salvendy, G. (2000). Review and reappraisal of modelling and predicting mental workload in single- and multi-task environments. *Work & Stress, 14*(1), 74–99.

Yeh, Y. Y., & Wickens, C. D. (1985, September/October). *The effect of varying task difficulty on subjective workload.* Paper presented at the Human Factors Society 29th Annual Meeting, Baltimore, Maryland.

Youngblut, C., Johnston, R. E., Nash, S. H., Wienclaw, R. A., & Will, C. A. (1996). *Review of virtual environment interface technology.* Alexandria, VA: Institute for Defense Analyses.

Part IV: Training Paradigms

Chapter 18

KNOWLEDGE ELICITATION: THE FLEX APPROACH

Scott Shadrick and James Lussier

The military training environment is transforming. No longer does the systems approach to training (for example, tasks, conditions, and standards; Branson et al., 1975) encompass all that must be trained. Traditional methods requiring lengthy systematic processes used in institutional training must give way to more rapid, but still sound, approaches that allow the military to keep pace with lessons learned in the theater of war. Training development methods rely on eliciting knowledge from experts. The knowledge elicitation process must be reexamined. Units in theater need to rapidly transfer their knowledge to units scheduled for deployment. The desire to quickly insert new technological developments into the current battlefield environment means that tactics, techniques, and procedures (TTPs) must be developed rapidly by taking advantage of limited numbers of experts. Addressing each of these involves the process of using knowledge elicitation techniques, the process of capturing domain knowledge underlying human performance, to support tactical scenario development for various virtual environments. This chapter provides an overview of knowledge elicitation for scenario development and presents a flexible approach to knowledge elicitation using simulation based vignettes.

KNOWLEDGE ELICITATION IN THE MILITARY TRAINING ENVIRONMENT

Domain knowledge and skill have been recognized as critical assets related to expert performance (Klein, 1992). Knowledge elicitation describes the process whereby an analyst captures that domain knowledge through systematic interaction with experts. Knowledge elicitation often relies on the direct observation of expert behaviors and other methods designed to capture existing internal cognitive processes. The outcomes of the elicitation effort can be decomposed to describe knowledge and cognitive processes that are linked to observable behaviors within the domain. While much research has been conducted on knowledge elicitation, the elicitation and integration of knowledge still remains one of the most time consuming, tedious, and essential tasks in designing systems (Chervinskaya & Wasserman, 2000).

Capturing expert knowledge supports three functions of training: (a) to improve and support human performance in decision-making tasks, (b) to design instruction to efficiently and effectively train individuals, and (c) to automate task functions that consist of human logic processes. The underlying goal of each of those functions is the development of a skill base for a specific domain that will augment performance through assistance, training, and automation. A fourth function is to support the effective analysis and synthesis of future requirements and events (that is, concept development) (Shadrick, Lussier, & Hinkle, 2005).

A number of efforts are under way to improve the quality of military training and, by extension, human performance. These efforts include (a) the development of new instructional models designed to accelerate the development of expertise, (b) the development of technologies to support the rapid identification of training needs and the development of training based on current and emerging issues, (c) the development of procedures for collecting robust stories, TTPs, and expertise in the form of tacit knowledge, and (d) the identification and development of training scenarios for virtual training environments. Each of those efforts involves capturing and codifying expert knowledge needed for the development of training using knowledge elicitation.

Knowledge elicitation methods are a key component of the information-gathering stage of task or cognitive task analysis. The methods attempt to provide a convenient way to accurately and easily allow experts to communicate their expertise. Despite the abundance of available elicitation techniques, capturing expert knowledge and understanding how the knowledge relates to problem solving capabilities remains an obstacle (Moody, Blanton, & Will, 1998/1999). Often, the elicitation of expert knowledge is vague or glossed over because it is largely ad hoc and nonscientific (Wright & Ayton, 1987). Klein, Calderwood, and MacGregor (1989) point out a tendency to emphasize explicit knowledge over implicit knowledge (also called tacit knowledge). Explicit knowledge is information that is easily accessed, expressed, stored, and applied. Implicit knowledge, on the other hand, is information that experts use repeatedly, but cannot be easily articulated. Experts, through years of practice, develop automatic habits. These unconscious chunks of knowledge usually go to the heart of what makes someone an expert. Knowledge elicitation methods that overemphasize explicit knowledge lead to "the mistaken conclusion that explicit knowledge is sufficient for performing a task well" (Klein et al., 1989, p. 463). For training development, elicitation techniques must be used to determine unique contributions of both implicit and explicit knowledge. Knowledge elicitation techniques can be used to more effectively and efficiently design, develop, evaluate, and update training products. Methods of knowledge elicitation support three needs in the military training environment: (a) institutional, (b) operational unit, and (c) concept development.

The institutional domain is comprised by the military's education system. It provides soldiers, marines, airmen, and sailors with the functional knowledge, skills, and abilities needed to perform. It primarily trains individuals to perform specified duties or tasks related to their positions. The institution provides initial military training, professional military education, and develops, teaches, and applies military doctrine. It provides support to operational unit training through exportable training support packages, mobile training teams, and combat training centers. Knowledge elicitation can be a key tool in enabling the institution to develop current training and doctrine, evaluate new TTPs, and update and refine institutional training to meet current demands.

Training and training development continues in the operational unit. Here, training focuses on collective training within a unit and associated individual and leader tasks. Operational training builds on the foundation provided by institutional training and introduces additional skills needed to support the unit's mission. During deployment, the operational unit is responsible for understanding emerging TTPs and developing materials to train the deployed force. That requires the use of knowledge elicitation techniques to understand expert performance and task requirements, and tools to support the rapid development of training products.

Concept development is used in the military to develop new systems and is concerned with future operational capabilities, training, and doctrine. It addresses how systems should be developed and how they will be employed. When the goal of knowledge elicitation is concept development, experts are required to generate best-guess estimates based on an anticipated set of new capabilities or TTPs. For example, as the army develops new unmanned aerial systems, there is a need to understand how to employ the new systems. While the participants in the knowledge elicitation exercise may be experts with existing systems, they are asked to predict how the new system will influence future operational conditions. Knowledge elicitation methods can be used to generalize current knowledge to future systems where detailed specifications are not yet known.

KNOWLEDGE ELICITATION IN TRAINING DEVELOPMENT

Before describing the role of knowledge elicitation in training and scenario development, it is necessary to provide a foundation for scenario based training and simulation. Scenario based training evolved from the problem based learning research. Problem based learning strategies have been implemented since the 1950s (Boud & Feletti, 1997). Savery (2006) describes problem based learning as an "instructional learner-centered approach that empowers learners to conduct research, integrate theory and practice, and apply knowledge and skills to develop a viable solution to a defined problem" (p. 12). As such, problem based learning focuses on authentic problems and scenarios (Savery & Duffy, 1995) to facilitate transfer of skills to real world contexts (Bransford, Brown, & Cocking, 2000).

Scenario based training applies the problem based learning model by specifically incorporating the use of context-rich situations. In scenario based training, training participants practice performing key tasks in realistic, live, virtual, or constructive virtual environments. Participants receive exposure to a variety of situations in which they can apply their knowledge to solve complex problems. The scenarios used for training must be developed to specifically trigger the desired performance to accomplish a particular training objective (Cannon-Bowers, Burns, Salas, & Pruitt, 1998; Stretton & Johnston, 1997).

Within the military training environment, scenario based training is used interchangeably with simulation based virtual environments and structured simulation based training, which typically use a training support package to facilitate training and practice. During the 1990s, the U.S. Army Research Institute conducted considerable research into the development of structured simulation based training. According to Campbell, Quinkert, and Burnside (2000), the structured training approach is

> characterized by its emphasis on deliberate purposeful building of training that takes advantage of simulation capabilities. The exercises provide for a focus on critical task in a planned sequence of performance that reinforces learning and builds on prior experience. The training is embedded in the context of tactically realistic scenarios, causing the unit [or individual] to be immersed in the tactical situation.
>
> (p. 4)

Scenario based training, simulation based or otherwise, relies on effective methods of task analysis, cognitive task analysis, team task analysis, and knowledge elicitation (Cannon-Bowers & Salas, 1997).

A Note Concerning the Use of Virtual Environments for Training

Lussier, Shadrick, and Prevou (2003) wrote that the maxim "train as you fight" has risen to such a level of familiarity in the U.S. Army that the maxim goes almost unquestioned. The idea is reflected in the belief that the best training methods rely on performing the task in a realistic environment. Yet, Salas, Bowers, and Rhodenizer (1998) wrote that the merging of the terms "simulation" and "training" and the widespread misconceptions concerning simulation have led to the overreliance on virtual environments and "the misuse of simulation to enhance learning of complex skills" (p. 197). Unfortunately, the ability to use simulations for specific training has not kept pace with the use of simulation for practice activities (compare Salas et al., 1998; Stewart, Dohme, & Nullmeyer, 2002). When new virtual simulators are acquired, they are treated as replications of the environment, and it is assumed that experience in the simulator will result in effective training. The higher the fidelity of the simulation, the stronger the assumption that training in the virtual environment will be effective and will transfer to the real environment. While simulation technology continues to evolve, the training technology has remained the same for decades (Salas et al., 1998).

To ensure quality training with simulation, the training must incorporate specific components based upon sound instructional principles (Black, 1996). The key components include the following: (a) identification of tasks, (b) presentation of enabling knowledge, (c) demonstration of how the task should be performed, (d) the opportunity for the trainee to perform the task, (e) provision for feedback to the trainee concerning task performance, and (f) the opportunity to practice the task to mastery under increasingly difficult, but realistic conditions (Black, 1996; Black & Quinkert, 1994; Holding, 1965). Lussier and Shadrick (2004) add additional requirements: an explicit description of elements that constitute correct performance of the task, performance measurement to assess whether the task is performed correctly, active and effective coaching, the opportunity for immediate repetition of poorly performed tasks, and a focus on tasks that are difficult, critical, or constitute areas of individual or collective weakness.

The challenge no longer lies in the capability of simulation to present a realistic virtual environment, but in the ability of trainers to ensure that the components of sound instruction previously mentioned are present (Lussier & Shadrick, 2004; Salas et al., 1998). Of the components of effective training listed in the preceding paragraph, tactical engagement simulations alone only truly enable the opportunity to perform and the opportunity to practice. Much additional exercise design work must be done to add the other components. That additional work requires training developers to understand task requirements, to identify appropriate tasks that need to be trained, to identify and/or develop TTPs, and to identify and/or develop appropriate scenarios by conducting a thorough cognitive task analysis and knowledge elicitation.

KNOWLEDGE ELICITATION TECHNIQUES

The selection of a knowledge elicitation method involves several considerations. Knowledge elicitation methods are typically divided into direct and indirect methods. Direct methods involve the researcher asking domain experts to describe how they perform their jobs. Examples include interviews, protocol analysis, simulation, and concept mapping. The effectiveness of direct methods depends on the experts' ability to articulate the information. Experts are usually able to easily verbalize declarative knowledge (explicit knowledge), such as descriptions of facts, things, methods, or procedures.

Indirect methods are more suitable when knowledge is not easily expressed by the expert. Tacit knowledge that has been learned implicitly through experience and overlearned automatic procedural knowledge can often be difficult for experts to describe. Indirect methods require the experts to describe their knowledge with the help of predefined structures, such as repertory grids, decision trees, card sorting, and laddering techniques.

Due to the complexity of most military domain areas and the difficulties associated with forecasting future capabilities and requirements, a combination of several methods is typically employed to collect information from knowledgeable experts. The next sections will briefly highlight popular methods of knowledge elicitation. The review is not intended to be exhaustive. The intent is to provide an overview of a few widely used methods that contributed to the development of a new method of elicitation focused on the elicitation of knowledge for use with scenario and concept development.

The Delphi Technique

The Delphi technique was developed to provide a method to elicit expert knowledge and develop group consensus (Dalkey, 1969). In Delphi approaches, experts do not interact directly with one another. The researcher gathers responses and provides them to other expert participants for review after which each expert submits a revised response. The process is repeated until consensus is established while avoiding groupthink bias. Difficulty arises in assessing the quality of the answer and, thus, whether groupthink existed in reaching consensus (Meyer & Booker, 1991). The Delphi method also requires significant time to implement.

Interviews

The interview method requires the researcher to ask experts questions in order to recall and describe the steps necessary to perform a task. In interviews, the researcher asks open-ended questions about the expert's reasoning in making decisions. The unstructured interview method allows the researcher to become familiar with jargon and gain an overview of the domain. The major disadvantage of unstructured interviews is that disorder can ensue if the expert speaks off topic or erroneously assumes that the researcher is knowledgeable in the domain (Hoffman, Shadbolt, Burton, & Klein, 1995). Structured interviews are preplanned to reduce the time required for the interview by focusing the expert on specific questions. Structured interviews require the researcher to have some knowledge of the domain. Semistructured interviews are often preferred since they allow the researcher to add questions to clarify points and to omit questions that become irrelevant as the interview unfolds. The technique promotes more continuity in the data than unstructured interviews. Continuity assists in the comparison and aggregation of responses from various experts. Semistructured interviews are more likely to produce data that are germane without the inefficiencies of collecting unnecessary data (Meyer & Booker, 1991).

Protocol Analysis

Protocol analysis requires the researcher to record the expert as the task is completed. That process often generates more valid knowledge than asking experts to verbally describe the steps required for the task (Wright & Ayton, 1987). The expert is required to "think aloud" while working through the problem or situation to identify knowledge elements and steps required for problem solving in the domain. Protocol analysis allows the expert to perform the task in a real world context while describing the cognitive activities. Protocol analysis is based on introspection and may interfere with the problem solving processes (Wright & Ayton, 1987). Thus, if the task has a substantial cognitive component, the think-aloud requirement may interfere with task performance. In retrospective protocol analysis, the expert is videotaped during task performance and interviewed after task performance to reduce cognitive interference.

OVERVIEW OF THE FLEX METHOD

While the previously described methods provide a number of advantages, a new method is needed to address the unique aspects associated with the development of new concepts and future conditions and scenarios. To address that need, the Flexible Method of Cognitive Task Analysis (FLEX) was developed (Shadrick et al., 2005). The FLEX method allows researchers to capture existing knowledge and facilitates the creation of new knowledge and concepts. The technique is similar to the information acceleration method used in the marketing domain to forecast consumers' responses to new products by providing early models to focus groups.

The FLEX method is an interview based problem solving approach that systematically develops and explores new concepts. The FLEX method grounds the experts' thinking in a concrete setting. Knowledge is captured by employing a vignette based scenario approach where experts are required to solve a complex problem by employing the resources and capabilities provided. Participants may interact with several variations of the scenario to explore the range of considerations. Similar to protocol analysis, participants are asked to verbalize their responses by thinking aloud. Each vetted response is provided to subsequent participants (for example, Delphi) to identify weaknesses, confirm strengths, and build upon the prior responses. This provides the participants with a way to evaluate, modify, and shape the scenario and expert response. It also allows the participants to develop additional, although related, scenarios and solutions. During the process, a semistructured interview is used to probe expert knowledge and gain a deeper understanding of expert reasoning. Responses from subsequent participants are fed back to the original participants for additional input. Finally, an interactive group discussion is used to allow for consensus building and validation. The following section summarizes the steps involved in developing FLEX scenarios and conducting a knowledge elicitation and concept development exercise (Shadrick et al., 2005).

Phase 1: Domain and Problem Identification

The domain and problem identification phase is used to define the domain area and identify problems of interest. The information is used to identify potential experts from a variety of relevant domains—particularly when technological advancements are expected to play a critical role in the scenario or concept development. Where future technologies are concerned, an environmental scan, backcast, and/or technological forecast should be conducted to assist in understanding the domain.

Phase 2: Initial Review and Analysis

The initial review and analysis phase is used to capture existing information about the domain and problem space. The phase is similar to what would be expected during traditional and cognitive task analysis. During this phase it is necessary to interview experts, document processes, and gather information about expert performance. In contrast to traditional task analysis, the goal is not to develop a complete list of tasks and duties for a given domain. The goal is to gain an understanding of domain expertise, task requirements, processes, and outcomes. During the review it is critical to identify areas where innovation may lead to improved performance and processes and to gain an understanding of current research and immediate technological innovation for the domain.

Phase 3: Refine Problem Space and Develop Initial Scenario

During the refine problem space and develop initial scenario phase, initial decisions about the knowledge elicitation scenario should be established. An initial group of domain experts is used to develop one or more scenarios with appropriate "branches." The branches should represent conditions where responses may vary depending on the context. The scenarios should be developed in an iterative fashion, allowing experts to develop a realistic situation capable of focusing the knowledge elicitation process on the areas of interest. At this stage, it is necessary only to establish the initial conditions for the knowledge elicitation process—it is not necessary to fully develop the situation.

Phase 4: Initial Knowledge Elicitation

During the initial knowledge elicitation phase, knowledge and concepts are elicited from experts from the relevant domain based on the scenario(s). The scenario serves as a starting point to focus the experts on a particular problem space. The elicitation process allows the experts to further refine the scenario by adding new information, challenging assumptions, anticipating unintended consequences, and predicting interventions. During the elicitation, experts are asked to discover new ways to solve problems associated with the scenario given hypothesized future capabilities. The elicitation focuses on both individuals and small groups (for example, dyads and triads) and combines experts from different specialty areas.

Phase 5: Data Reduction and Consensus Building

The data reduction phase allows a small group of experts, different from those in phase 4, to develop a consensus on the efficacy of the knowledge and concepts captured by aggregating data into common and meaningful responses. That information can be used to update the scenario to reflect the new knowledge or to create a new branch to highlight "what if" situations. The altering of the scenario allows the experts to "leave their fingerprints" on the scenario and allows for an iterative process for continuous improvement.

After revising the scenario it is necessary to reexamine the scenario with a new set of experts and provide the revised materials to former participants. This process provides a systematic way to evaluate the realism of the new information.

The goal of the iterative process is to develop a well-tested and documented solution for the purpose of developing new theories, principles, tools, techniques, and procedures.

Phase 6: Knowledge Representation and Concept Documentation

Knowledge representation provides a mechanism for documenting and displaying information in a usable format. In this context, knowledge refers to organized concepts, theories, principles, descriptions, and mental models of descriptive, procedural, and metacognitive information. The goal is to present the results of the knowledge elicitation process in a meaningful way. Knowledge can be represented using a variety of methods, including logic, semantic networks, production rules, frame based representations, decision trees, graphs, diagrams, charts, and tables.

APPLICATION OF THE FLEX METHOD

This section will provide two case studies documenting the use of the FLEX approach to elicit knowledge and develop appropriate scenarios.

Teams of Teams—The Homeland Security Example

Development of effective training for homeland security or natural disaster crises poses several unique problems. Developing an effective response to such events requires the coordinated efforts of multiple government agencies. For that reason, multiple groups of domain experts from diverse agencies must be involved in the analyses and training design processes (Landis, Fogli, & Goldberg, 1998). Another concern is that many experts may have only limited expertise. That is, experts may understand their own agencies' procedures. However, they may not have experienced them firsthand, and they may not understand how their agencies' procedures interact with those of other agencies. As a result, although they may have the necessary factual knowledge, they have not developed the proceduralized skills that are the hallmark of a true expert. Thus, there may be relatively few true experts. A key strength of FLEX lies in its ability to capture, create, and organize the knowledge of domain experts regarding events that have yet to actually occur when few experts are available.

The FLEX iterative process of knowledge elicitation, domain expert review, and rapid development was applied to develop prototype crisis response scenarios and training (Shadrick, Schaefer, & Beaubien, 2007). The process began with a review of documents provided by various army, state, county, and municipal government agencies. From those materials, an initial understanding of the various types of homeland security and natural disaster crises was developed, and effective crisis responses were identified. Next, FLEX interviews were conducted to validate the initial assumptions and to collect additional information for use in scenario development. The purpose of the interviews was to identify examples of historically effective and ineffective crisis response behaviors and to identify critical events for which the participants were ill prepared to respond. The interviewees included experts from eight military and civil-military, interagency partners. From the interviews, a series of high level scenarios was developed to conduct FLEX sessions.

The scenarios and training behaviors were subsequently reviewed by an additional set of experts and revised as necessary. The interviews also resulted in the development of a set of behavioral indicators that could be used to score performance during the training scenarios. The indicators serve as benchmarks of expert performance for a given scenario. During each successive round of expert interviews, the researchers were able to identify and resolve critical shortcomings in the proposed training content and format. After the third round of interviews, the experts did not identify additional changes, suggesting that the major issues had been resolved. This set of materials was then used to develop the final training program. In addition to the 10 training scenarios, the process also produced an expert mental model that could be used for crisis response.

Expert assessments of the training materials (including scenarios) were overwhelmingly positive, and the experts strongly supported the relevance of the materials (Shadrick et al., 2007). The content validity of the training was assessed by quantitative indices elicited from an independent sample of experts with crisis response experience. Results for the training items resulted in a content validity ratio of +1.0 with only 1 of 122 items receiving a negative value. Results for the conceptual grouping of information resulted in Cohen's kappa values of 0.78, percent agreement = 0.85. Subsequent implementation of the training scenarios resulted in significant performance improvement (Schaefer, Shadrick, Beaubien, & Crabb, 2008).

Future Requirements—Spinning Out Future Technologies to the Current Force

The U.S. Army is transforming to a lighter, highly mobile future force that can operate readily within joint, interagency, and multinational environments. This force is designed to be responsive, deployable, agile, versatile, lethal, survivable, and sustainable. Possession of these characteristics will enable future force units to see first, understand first, act first, and finish decisively. Future force units are designed to apply knowledge based capability to respond rapidly and decisively across the full spectrum of military operations through deployment with the Future Combat Systems.

As part of the development of the family of systems, the army has planned a series of spinouts or rapid transitions of future force technologies to the current force. The integration of future force technologies with current force systems that have been fielded for many years and were not designed for incorporating revolutionary new technologies will be a significant challenge. To meet this challenge TTPs must be provided with technology spinouts so that soldiers and leaders are not left to "figure out" how to integrate and employ each new technology provided. Thus, initial TTPs will need to be developed before the capabilities are actually produced.

As a result, traditional methods for developing TTPs may be inadequate. Traditional methods range from analysts and experts developing and presenting new concepts, to using large-scale simulation exercises in which groups of soldiers employ the capability, to user juries in which soldiers provide feedback on the developed capability. Each approach has its own strengths and drawbacks. Many researchers have noted the difficulties that experts have in realistically assessing the impact of future capabilities. Large-scale simulations are resource- and time-intensive endeavors that are difficult to control and replicate, thus lowering the validity of any findings. User juries require that the capability be well developed before the jury can occur. Therefore, there is a need to investigate TTP development methods to augment the methods above, methods that provide structured activities to measure, assess, and guide the TTP development process, yet are flexible enough to respond rapidly to a wide range of conceptual constructions.

To address the need described above, the FLEX method was applied with the goal of generating concepts for future operations that can be used to develop ideas about TTPs (for example, how a particular capability might best be used). Concept development sessions were used to present a depiction of a situation designed to start the participants thinking about how the army might function in the future. Each participant was shown a problem scenario relevant to an important army issue and asked to think through the specific situation. Then, a broader discussion was initiated to include considerations beyond the scenario presented in order to test the generality of the solutions devised for the specific scenario. A succession of participants confronting the same scenarios helped refine the concepts.

After several participants had completed the trial, responses and process observations were used to modify the scenario to allow it to become more realistic, more focused, and to incorporate participants' ideas for additional trials. This process of refinement and presentation was repeated until no new information was being generated. After final modifications were made, the scenario was presented to a small group in anticipation that additional information might be forthcoming from a group setting. The process was repeated until it reached the point of diminishing returns. After analysis of data from multiple participants, a composite response to the issue was produced. Further exploration may use new scenarios or a scaled world environment to systematically test the group solution.

The FLEX approach was able to stimulate participants and elicited unique, creative, and well-reasoned responses. There were, however, considerable individual differences. Some participants had difficulty critically evaluating the future concepts. Some participants appeared to be able to transition into looking at the situation from the viewpoint of how things might be in the future (2015–2020) quite readily. Others required considerable encouragement. Soldiers have a tendency to look at situations the way they have been trained (that is, mission, enemy, terrain, troops, time, and civilians), and they often tend to focus on a course-of-action analysis. In a concept development situation, it may require some training or encouragement to lead their thinking toward "how else could we do things, particularly if we had access to assets that don't even exist today?"

TTP SUMMARY FOR A RAID

Give each UAS a task and purpose. Direct two platoon UASs to recon objective early. Fly high to make the UAS harder to engage. Use the lead platoon UAS to conduct route recon, and hand off next platoon in order of march to recon, confirm, confirm/deny situation on objective. Hold trail platoon's and company commander's UASs in reserve in event either of the others gets shot down or goes down due to mechanical/technical errors. Keep the UAS as close to your ground forces as feasible without compromising mission requirements. Stay within direct fire range of your UASs so you can react to contact. Conserve UAS resources until you need them, such as on the objective. Use the UAS to support recon while moving to objective. Observe avenue of approach, escape routes, and enemy strongpoints. Use the commander's UAS for command and control. Alter flight patterns to improve survivability of the UAS, particularly in urban areas.

Mission

- Assign a specific task to each UAS.
- Keep the company UAS centrally located to help with command and control and serve as a reserve asset.
- Use the company UAS to observe dead space and confirm or deny enemy presence, obstacles, or other threats or impediments to movement.
- Divide the objective area into platoon sectors with each platoon responsible for specific reconnaissance and observation tasks.
- Specify launch and recovery triggers.
- Use the platoon UASs to support the cordon, being sure to cover ingress/egress routes and likely avenues of approach.
- Develop a movement and rotation plan that allows for continuous observation/coverage.

Enemy

- Fly from different directions, both near and far, to minimize the enemy's ability to detect the UAS and determine friendly intentions.
- Deploy the UAS to conduct recon of the builtup area just before you get to objective to reduce the enemy's reaction time.

Terrain and Weather

- Use the UAS to scan terrain and obstacles from different angles.
- In an urban terrain, use the UAS to do a detailed recon and to see inside buildings when possible.

Troops and Support Available

- Be sure to have backup observation platforms available to ensure security can be maintained if the UAS is destroyed.

- Use the UAS early in coordination with indirect fire assets to degrade enemy's ability to resist.

- Use the UAS to support soldiers who are clearing buildings; the UAS can see all exterior angles minus subsurface and can observe into the building interior.

Time Available

- For a short-term, mobile target, send a UAS out immediately to monitor the area and locate/track the target.

On the other hand, once they did start thinking futuristically, they were very creative and developed reasonable approaches to the problem.

Topolski, Leibrecht, Kiser, Kirkley, and Crabb (2008) used the FLEX method to develop TTPs for employing Class I unmanned aircraft systems (UASs) during a variety of simulation based exercises. The researchers were attempting to develop employment TTPs for the systems even before the systems were produced. Participants were provided background information on the area of operations and on the expected Class I UAS capabilities. In one exercise, participants were asked to employ the systems during a raid operation in urban terrain against an insurgent force. The sidebar provides sample TTPs developed using the process. The researchers assess the effectiveness of the FLEX method from the perspective of the researcher and participant. Both groups rated all aspects of the FLEX method highly.

SUMMARY

Potter, Roth, Woods, and Elm (2000, p. 321) wrote, "In performing cognitive task analysis, it is important to utilize a balanced suite of methods that enable both the demands of the domain and the knowledge and strategies of domain expertise to be captured in a way that enables a clear identification of opportunities for improved support." There is clearly a need for a systematic approach to eliciting information needed to more effectively develop scenarios and future concepts, processes, systems, and procedures. The method described here provides a flexible method for eliciting and creating scenarios, and concepts and information for investigating, creating, testing, and understanding future issues. The FLEX method also holds considerable promise when dealing with task domains that are expected to undergo rapid change, that involve distributed expertise, or that have not yet occurred. Future efforts will evaluate the actual efficacy and efficiencies realized implementing the FLEX method. Ongoing efforts, such as the U.S. Army Research Institute's project to develop training for large-scale interagency training and the development of TTPs for the Future Combat Systems, are using the method to further evaluate its effectiveness.

REFERENCES

Black, B. A., (1996). *How will simulation enhance training?* Unpublished manuscript [NATO RSG 26].

Black, B. A., & Quinkert, K. A. (1994). The current status and future trends for simulation-based training in armored forces from crew to battalion level. *Proceedings of the 35th NATO-DRG Symposium on Improving Military Performance through Ergonomics.* Mannheim, Germany. NATO AC/243-TP/6.

Boud, D., & Feletti, G. (1997). *The challenges of problem-based learning* (2nd ed.). London: Kogan Page.

Branson, R. K., Rayner, G. T., Cox, J. L., Furman, J. P., King, F. J., & Hannum, W. H. (1975). *Interservice procedures for instructional systems development* (Vols. 1–5, TRADOC Pam 350-30 NAVEDTRA 106A). Ft. Monroe, VA: U.S. Army Training and Doctrine Command.

Bransford, J. D., Brown, A. L., & Cocking, R. R. (Eds.). (2000). *How people learn: Brain, mind, experience, and school.* Washington, DC: National Academy Press.

Cannon-Bowers, J. A., & Salas, E. (1997). A framework for developing team performance measures in training. In M. T. Brannick, E. Salas, & C. Prince (Eds.), *Team performance assessment and measurement* (pp. 45–77). Hillsdale, NJ: Erlbaum.

Cannon-Bowers, J. A., Burns, J. J., Salas, E., & Pruitt, J. S. (1998). Advanced technology in decision-making training. In J. A. Cannon-Bowers & E. Salas (Eds.), *Making decisions under stress: Implications for individual and team training* (pp. 365–374). Washington, DC: APA Press.

Campbell, C. H., Quinkert, K. A., & Burnside B. L. (2000). *Training for performance: The structured training approach* (ARI Special Report 45). Alexandria, VA: U.S. Army Research Institute for the Behavioral and Social Sciences.

Chervinskaya, K. R., & Wasserman, E. L. (2000). Some methodological aspects of tacit knowledge elicitation. *Journal of Experimental & Theoretical Artificial Intelligence, 12,* 43–55.

Dalkey, N. C. (1969). *The Delphi Method: An experimental study of group opinion.* Santa Monica, CA: Rand Corporation.

Holding, D. H. (1965). *Principles of training.* Oxford, England: Pergamon.

Hoffman, R. R., Shadbolt, N. R., Burton, A. M., & Klein, G. A. (1995). Eliciting knowledge from experts: A methodological analysis. *Organizational Behavior and Human Decision Processes, 62,* 129–158.

Klein, G. (1992). Using knowledge engineering to preserve corporate memory. In R. R. Hoffman (Ed.), *The psychology of expertise: Cognitive research and empirical AI* (pp. 10–190). Mahwah, NJ: Lawrence Erlbaum.

Klein, G., Calderwood, R., & MacGregor, D. (1989). Critical decision method for eliciting knowledge. *IEEE Transactions on Systems, Man, & Cybernetics, 19*(3), 462–472.

Landis, R. S., Fogli, L., & Goldberg, E. (1998). Future-oriented job analysis: A description of the process and its organizational implications. *International Journal of Selection and Assessment, 6*(3), 192–197.

Lussier, J. W., & Shadrick, S. B. (2004, December). *How to train deployed soldiers: New advances in interactive multimedia instruction.* Paper presented at the Interservice/ Industry Training, Simulation, and Education Conference, Orlando, FL.

Lussier, J. W., Shadrick, S. B., & Prevou, M. I. (2003). *Think like a commander prototype: Instructor's guide to adaptive thinking* (ARI Research Product 2003-01). Alexandria, VA: U.S. Army Research Institute for the Behavioral and Social Sciences.

Meyer, M. A., & Booker, J. M. (1991). *Eliciting and analyzing expert judgment: A practical guide.* San Diego, CA: Academic Press.

Moody, J. W., Blanton, J. E., & Will, R. P. (1998/1999, Winter). Capturing expertise from experts: The need to match knowledge elicitation techniques with expert system types. *The Journal of Computer Information Systems,* Winter, 89–95.

Potter, S. S., Roth, E. M., Woods, D. D., & Elm, W. (2000). Bootstrapping multiple converging cognitive task analysis techniques for system design. In J. M. Schraagen, S. F. Chipman, & V. L. Shalin (Eds.). *Cognitive task analysis* (pp. 317–340). Mahwah, NJ: Lawrence Erlbaum.

Salas, E., Bowers, C. A., & Rhodenizer, L. (1998). It is not how much you have but how you use it: Toward a rational use of simulation to support aviation training. *International Journal of Aviation Psychology, 8*(3), 197–208.

Savery, J. R. (2006). Overview of problem-based learning: Definitions and distinctions. *The International Journal of Problem-Based Learning, 1*(1), 9–20.

Savery, J. R., & Duffy, T. M. (1995). Problem-based learning: An instructional model and its constructivist framework. In B. Wilson (Ed.), *Constructivist learning environments: Case studies in instructional design* (pp. 135–148). Englewood Cliffs, NJ: Educational Technology Publications.

Schaefer, P. S., Shadrick, S. B., Beaubien, J., & Crabb, B. T. (2008). *Training effectiveness assessment of Red Cape: Crisis Action Planning and Execution* (Research Rep. No. 1885). Arlington, VA: U.S. Army Research Institute for the Behavioral and Social Sciences.

Shadrick, S. B., Lussier, J. W., & Hinkle, R. (2005). *Concept development for future domains: A new method of knowledge elicitation* (Tech. Rep. No. 1167). Arlington, VA: U.S. Army Research Institute for the Behavioral and Social Sciences.

Shadrick, S. B., Schaefer, P. S., & Beaubien, J. (2007). *Development and content validation of crisis response training package Red Cape: Crisis Action Planning and Execution* (Research Rep. No. 1875). Arlington, VA: U.S. Army Research Institute for the Behavioral and Social Sciences.

Stewart, J. E., Dohme, J. A., & Nullmeyer, R. T. (2002). U.S. Army initial entry rotary-wing transfer of training research. *International Journal of Aviation Psychologist, 12* (4), 359–375.

Stretton, M. L., & Johnston, J. H. (1997). Scenario-based training: An architecture for intelligent event selection. *Proceedings of the 19th Annual Meeting of the Interservice/Industry Training Systems Conference* (pp. 108–117). Washington, DC: National Training Systems Association.

Topolski, R., Leibrecht, B. C., Kiser, R. D., Kirkley, J., & Crabb, B. T. (2008). *Flexible method for developing tactics, techniques, and procedures for future capabilities.* Arlington, VA: U.S. Army Research Institute for the Behavioral and Social Sciences.

Wright, G., & Ayton, P. (1987). Eliciting and modeling expert knowledge. *Decision Support Systems, 3,* 13–26.

Chapter 19

STORY BASED
LEARNING ENVIRONMENTS

Andrew Gordon

STORY BASED LEARNING ENVIRONMENTS

There is no substitute for experience in the acquisition of complex skills. The goal of virtual environment training is not to reduce the need for experience, but rather to provide experiences to trainees with less cost, risk, and time than would be required if these experiences were instead acquired on-the-job. Accordingly, the challenge in developing effective virtual environment training is designing experiences for trainees that support learning. In story based learning environments these experiences are designed to have distinctly narrative qualities: a set of characters, a temporal sequence of causally related events, a rich but relevant amount of descriptive detail, and a point. Typically the trainee participates as a character within this environment following a learning-by-doing pedagogical strategy, and the actions taken affect the outcomes of an emerging storyline. In the ideal case, the trainees in a story based learning environment walk away with a story to tell about their training experience—one that is not markedly different from the best stories that practitioners tell about their real world experiences.

The research history of story based learning environments over the last three decades has been driven by changes in technology, but defined by particular paradigms of instructional design. In the late 1980s the Learning Technology Center at Vanderbilt University was a center of research in story based learning environments, guided by the design principles of anchored instruction (Cognition and Technology Group at Vanderbilt, 1990). The university's Jasper Woodbury project used a hypertext-controlled video laser-disc player to present students with problems grounded in a fictional scenario, where completing the problems would enable the students to write their own ending to the story (Cognition and Technology Group at Vanderbilt, 1992). In the 1990s, Northwestern University's Institute for Learning Sciences led research on story based learning environments following a design philosophy known as goal based scenarios (Schank, Fano,

Bell, & Jona, 1993). These systems, typically constructed as software applications using desktop video to deliver story content, were constructed in diverse learning domains that included corporate tax advising, wetlands management, and counseling couples about sickle cell anemia. The late 1990s saw the commercialization of outcome-driven simulations (Cleave, 1997), a cost-effective design for goal based scenarios that was championed by Cognitive Arts, Inc., and others, deliverable as a Web application where story content was given as text with digital photographs of fictional situations. At the beginning of the twenty-first century, story based learning environments took advantage of advances in virtual reality and gaming technologies. This is best exemplified by the research projects of the Institute for Creative Technologies at the University of Southern California (Swartout et al., 2006; Gordon, 2004; Korris, 2004; Hill, Gordon, & Kim, 2004), which increasingly have followed the educational design principles of guided experiential learning (Clark, 2004).

Throughout this research history there has been a change in the nature of the story in story based learning environments. In the early anchored instruction prototypes the central story of the experience was a completely fictional narrative designed to appeal to the demographic of the target audience. In subsequent work on goal based scenarios, the central story of the experience was fictional, but it was delivered along with a collection of nonfiction stories that illustrated particular points or lessons relevant to events in the fictional storyline. These nonfiction stories consisted of short narratives of the real world experiences of skilled domain experts, often presented as desktop video clips as part of an automated tutoring component of the learning environment. Beginning with the commercialization of outcome-driven simulations in the late 1990s, these two types of stories (fiction and nonfiction) in story based learning environments became closely intertwined. In this work and in the story based learning environments that would follow, the collection and analysis of real world nonfiction stories became integral to the authoring of the fictional storyline and structuring of the user interaction. The stories in contemporary story based learning environments are defined by the real world nonfiction anecdotes that training developers collect from subject matter experts.

The evolving role of nonfiction stories in the development of story based learning environments brings a new perspective to this form of training application. In the past, these applications served as the delivery method for an explicit body of training content. Today, these applications function more as a complex form of communication, mediating between storytellers and the people who can best benefit from hearing these stories. Story based learning environments can be viewed as a form of digital storytelling, where the fictional storylines of learning environments are media that can preserve the underlying points of stories acquired through real world experience. Seen from this perspective, the main challenges for developers of story based learning environments concern the management of real world story content through the development pipeline. This includes the following key problems: How do developers collect stories of real world experiences that will serve as the basis for the training application? How should these stories be analyzed to identify their central points and relationship to training objectives? How can real world story content be fictionalized and utilized within the context of a virtual reality training application? In this chapter we discuss a number of best practices for each of these three development questions. As a context for this discussion, we begin by providing an example of a story based learning environment, the Institute for Creative Technologies (ICT) Leaders Project.

THE ICT LEADERS PROJECT: A STORY BASED LEARNING ENVIRONMENT

The ICT Leaders Project, a collaboration between the University of Southern California's Institute for Creative Technologies and Paramount Pictures, was a research effort aimed at allowing junior U.S. Army officers to practice making leadership decisions in the context of complex fictional scenarios realized in a virtual reality environment (Gordon, van Lent, van Velsen, Carpenter, & Jhala, 2004; Gordon, 2004; Iuppa & Borst, 2007). The trainee played the role of a U.S. Army captain commanding a company of soldiers on a peacekeeping mission in Afghanistan. The situation, which parallels the story developed for a live-action U.S. Army training film (Hill, Douglas, Gordon, Pighin, & van Velsen, 2003), involved providing security for a food distribution operation complicated by the presence of competing warlords. Rather than relying on scripted video, however, the ICT Leaders Project presented the story and fictional scenario in a virtual reality environment based on a commercial game engine, where cinematic scenes were interwoven among conversations with animated virtual soldiers and civilians in the environment.

The user experience in the ICT Leaders application was structured around a series of scripted cinematic scenes rendered in the virtual environment of the game engine. These scenes moved the storyline forward and presented challenging leadership problems where a decision had to be made by the user. These problems were always presented to the user by storyline characters, and the primary user interaction involved text based conversations with these characters. The user had the opportunity to raise questions and make comments concerning the problem, but in order to move the storyline forward the user needed to communicate a decision to the virtual character. The choice that the user made had a direct effect on how the storyline unfolded, where different choices caused the experience to follow different paths in a branching storyline structure. The application prototype included 11 decisions that make up the branch points of the storyline, and each of these decisions was motivated by a specific leadership point as evidenced by a nonfiction narrative of a leadership experience. These leadership stories were collected through directed interviews with experienced company commanders. Each story was subsequently analyzed to identify its central point, the lesson that challenges the expectations that novices have when adopting a leadership role.

The ICT Leaders Project used a commercial game engine, Epic Game's *Unreal Tournament 2003,* to create the virtual environment for the user experience. Using the standard "mod" editor that comes with this product, a new type of interactive application was developed that was very far removed from its original first-person shooter design. Custom terrain maps, character models, animations, sound effects, and props were created to produce an immersive virtual reality environment to serve as a backdrop for the fictional storyline. The storyline itself was authored with the help of a professional Hollywood scriptwriter, and professional voice actors were used to record the dialogue of the virtual characters. Cinematic scenes were designed with the assistance of a professional director to give the production a traditional cinematic style, particularly with respect to camera movement and cuts.

In the opening sequence of the application, the trainee takes on the role of Captain Young, who is to lead an infantry company in Afghanistan as a replacement for a previous captain removed due to a medical emergency. In the morning after his arrival, Captain Young meets with the first sergeant and executive officer to go over the security plan for a food distribution operation being conducted by a nongovernment relief organization. The executive officer assures the captain that everything is in order, but has a question regarding the leadership style that the captain will set for the company: Should soldiers in the company make their own decisions when problems arise, or should they consult the captain before taking initiative? This question ends the scripted scene, and the trainee is then allowed to discuss the issue with the executive officer using a text based dialogue interface. The trainee can ask questions and get further clarification from the executive officer by typing them into the system (for example, "How experienced are the junior officers in this company?"). Responses to these questions are selected using a text classification algorithm, built from a corpus of hand-annotated questions using machine learning technologies. The selected responses are then delivered to the trainee as recorded audio clips accompanied by character animations. Ultimately, the trainee must provide a decision with regard to the original question posed by the executive officer, either to let the soldiers take initiative or to request that they consult first with the captain. When either of these choices is entered into the text based dialogue interface, a branch in the storyline is selected and a new cinematic scene moves the trainee to the next decision point.

From the perspective of the research history of story based simulations, the ICT Leaders Project can be viewed as a type of outcome-driven simulation (Cleave, 1997) embedded in a virtual reality environment, where branches in the space of outcomes are selected using a text based dialogue interface. Aside from the work needed to support these extensions, the authoring of the ICT Leaders Project closely followed the approach established during the commercialization of this technology in the late 1990s, albeit with substantial influence from the Hollywood entertainment community (Iuppa, Weltman, & Gordon, 2004). As such, the methods used in the ICT Leaders Project address many of the concerns in the design of contemporary story based learning environments. In the remaining sections of this chapter, we discuss the three key issues of story collection, story analysis, and simulation design using this project to illustrate current directions in the evolution of these systems.

CAPTURING THE STORIES OF EXPERIENCE

The first-person nonfiction narratives that people share about their experiences are increasingly valued as an instrument for knowledge socialization—the sharing of knowledge through social mechanisms. Schank and Abelson (1995) argue that stories about one's experiences and the experiences of others are the fundamental constituents of human memory, knowledge, and social communication. Sternberg et al. (2000) argue that storytelling is particularly valuable as a means of communicating tacit knowledge. This enthusiasm for storytelling is echoed in the management sciences, where organizational storytelling is seen as a tool both for organizational analysis and organizational change (Boyce, 1996; McCormack & Milne, 2003; Snowden, 1999). Organizational stories are also increasingly used in the development of effective computer based knowledge management applications. Johnson, Birnbaum, Bareiss, and Hinrichs (2000) describe how story collection can be directly linked to work flow applications in order to provide story based performance support. This rising interest in the role of stories in organizations has paralleled the increased importance of stories in the development of story based training applications, creating synergies in the theory and practice of story management.

One of the central problems in the use of stories for knowledge management and training applications concerns the scalability of the methods used to collect them from the people who have interesting stories to tell. Today, the vast majority of stories that are used in organizational knowledge management and training applications are manually gathered through direct interviews with subject matter experts. The methods used to collect stories through interviews vary considerably; some more closely resemble cognitive task analysis techniques (Clark, Feldon, van Merrienboer, Yates, & Early, 2007), and others involve small group "story circle" meetings (Snowden, 2000).

For the ICT Leaders Project and others at the University of Southern California's Institute for Creative Technologies, an interview methodology evolved over a number of years that was particularly effective at gathering stories from U.S. Army soldiers (Gordon, 2005). Interviews were arranged for an average of 10 soldiers, 2 at a time, over sessions that lasted one hour each. These interviews were conducted in an extremely casual manner, where two or three members of the development team would talk with the 2 soldiers around a table, recorded using unobtrusive room microphones rather than individual or lavaliere microphones. The main goal of these interviews was to maximize the number of stories told by each pair of soldiers during the course of the hour-long session. The tactics were to trigger a memory of some real experience by asking leading questions related to the topic of the eventual training application and to set a conversational tone that would encourage soldiers to tell these stories. When soldiers began talking in abstractions and making generalizations, the tactic was to push them to get more specific and to describe an actual experience that illustrated the point of their generalizations—or contradicted them, as was often the case. When a soldier started telling a story of a real experience, the tactic was to encourage him or her to keep talking, mostly by avoiding the natural conversational tendencies to offer some commentary on his or her story or to respond with a related story from one's own experience. Often, a silent pause was enough to prompt him or her to continue with a story or to provide another example. A key aspect of these interviews was that they were always conducted with pairs of soldiers. When one soldier finished telling a story, the other would invariably be reminded of a story from his or her own experience. In the best cases, the interviewers could simply listen to the swapping of stories by the two soldiers, intervening only when the topics drifted away from training objectives.

For the ICT Leaders Project, these interview methods were employed to collect stories related to U.S. Army leadership skills. In the summer of 2002, interviews were conducted at the U.S. Military Academy at West Point with 10 U.S. Army captains, each having just completed service as a company commander and beginning a master's degree program in Behavioral Science in Leadership. Sixty-three stories of leadership were gathered using these story-collection interview methods, an average of just over 12 stories per hour.

Although effective for targeted research and development projects, interview methods such as this are not scalable solutions to the problem of organization-wide story collection. If story collections are to be widely used in the large-scale development of knowledge management and training applications, then the costs of collecting stories from subject matter experts and other members of organizations must be substantially reduced.

In the past few years, the phenomenal rise of Internet weblogging has created new opportunities for computer-supported story-management applications (for example, Owsley, Hammond, & Shamma, 2006). With the estimated number of weblogs exceeding 70 million in March 2007 (Technorati, 2007), there is a reasonable expectation that substantial numbers of people in any profession or large organization are already sharing their stories with the public at large. If storytelling in weblogs is at all similar in character to face-to-face storytelling among peers (Coopman & Meidlinger, 1998), then we would further expect that a significant portion of these stories are directly relevant to the training needs of organizations. A minimal-cost solution to the problem of creating story collections is to employ automated techniques for extracting first-person nonfiction narratives of people's experiences directly from these Internet weblogs. Gordon, Cao, and Swanson (2007) explored the use of contemporary natural language processing technologies to automatically extract stories from Internet weblogs, which they estimated accounted for 17 percent of all weblog text. They demonstrated that high precision (percentage of extracted text segments that were actually stories) was difficult to obtain using current techniques, with the best precision performance reaching 49.7 percent. Although significantly higher than the baseline of 17 percent, this level of performance is still below the level of inter-rater agreement achieved between two human judges, estimated at kappa = 0.68 (Gordon & Ganesan, 2005).

STORIES ON THE FRINGE OF EXPECTATION

In most science and engineering pursuits, first-person nonfiction stories are disparagingly referred to as "anecdotal evidence," a term meant to discredit the story as a suitable base for generalization. The argument here is that a single random incident may not be representative of the types of incidents that one would expect to encounter; only an appropriately large random sample of the experiences of practitioners can characterize the situations that new trainees are likely to encounter. In reality, stories may be the worst possible form of evidence if one were trying to learn something about the average case. People do not tell stories about the average case. The average case is boring. People tell stories about the things they find interesting, surprising, and unexpected. When one looks at a large number of stories from some domain of expertise, they do not sample the distribution of expected situations. Instead they each lay on a point along the edge of people's normal experiences, collectively defining the fringe of expectation. Gathering and analyzing the stories of the real world experiences of practitioners informs us not about the events that take place in the world, but rather about the expectations that these practitioners have about these events—and what they find surprising.

The concept of stories on the fringe of expectation is best illustrated when considering the fascinating stories that are told by night security guards of commercial office buildings. There was the time that a fire broke out in the trash chute. There was the time that an opossum crawled into the elevator shaft from the rooftop. There was the time the CEO of the company showed up in the middle of the night wearing pajamas. If these stories were representative of the lives of night security guards at commercial office buildings, then this might be one of the most exciting jobs on the planet. Sadly, the exact opposite is true. The representative experiences of night security guards are not the things that they tell stories about, to each other or anyone else. The stories that they do tell are the exceptions to the norm, the experiences that were markedly different from what they have come to expect in their routine practice. Gathering and analyzing these stories tells us more about the expectations of these professionals than the situations that are likely to occur overnight in commercial office buildings.

The position that stories are strongly related to expectations has been advanced within the fields of social and cognitive psychology. Bruner (1991) argued that the violation of expectations, which he referred to as canonicity and breach, is a defining characteristic of narrative as used by the mind to structure its sense of reality. Schank (1982) expanded on views held by Bartlett (1932) and observed that many features of human episodic memory can be explained if we view memories as organized by mental models and schemas that define our expectations of the world. Schank argued that people remember events when they are counter to their expectations and used these expectation violations as a basis for revising their mental models to more accurately reflect reality. Schank and Abelson (1995) later argued that natural human storytelling supported these learning processes, enabling groups of people to collectively learn from the surprising experiences of others. Although this perspective is controversial in the social sciences (Wyer, 1995), the concept of an expectation violation has proven useful in developing story based learning environments based on real world experiences.

To understand the importance of expectation violations in the development of training technology, consider the value of a good conceptual model to practitioners who must be adaptive in the execution of their skills. When they are in familiar environments and given familiar tasks, they can usually succeed by doing the same thing that has worked for them in the past. Where practitioners find themselves in situations that are only abstractly related to their experiences or training, they must adapt their normal behaviors. Here, a good causal understanding of the things in their environment—the people, organizations, politics, and systems—will aid them in developing successful plans by providing accurate expectations about the effects of their actions. When things happen as expected, plans are successful and tasks are accomplished. When things do not happen as expected (an expectation violation), then the natural human tendency is to identify where one's model of the world has failed. This tendency is the impetus for the formulation of rich episodic memories, the experiences that people think about over and over again in an effort to learn a better model of the way the world really works. Stories are the natural way that people share these experiences with others and serve as an effective means of using the collective experiences of others to help corroborate one's own experiences and collaboratively change the way that groups model their environment.

Collectively, the stories told by practitioners help identify where the models of novices and trainees are likely to be wrong or disputable and, as such, help identify the simulated situations that make the most effective use of training time. Developers of story based learning environments can capitalize on expectation violations to help embed pedagogically motivated decisions into their simulation. The identification of the expectation violation in a story supports the authoring of a decision situation, a fictional set of circumstances where a decision must be made where the best choice is dependent on whether or not the expectation or the expectation violation is believed.

This approach was used in the development of the ICT Leaders Project, where each of the stories that was collected from U.S. Army captains was analyzed to formulate the expectation violation and a fictional decision situation that hinged on the expectation. For example, one of these stories was from a captain who had commanded both combat infantry units, as well as noncombat service support units. He remembered tasking the service support soldiers to move the trailer section of a tractor-trailer rig over the course of a day when no tractor was available. The subordinate soldiers responded with excuses about why they would not be able to do the job, sought to find someone else to do the job for them, and questioned why it needed to be done the first place. The captain was struck by the difference in mindset when commanding combat infantry units that, given the same task, would simply get the job done and report back when it was completed. Why were the service support soldiers not like that? Why did they not behave with the same sense of purpose and initiative that was seen with the combat units?

This story informs us very little about the true difference between service support units and combat infantry units; this is merely anecdotal evidence that there might be some difference in mindset between these two groups. Instead, the utility of this story is that it identifies an expectation that is held by this captain about how subordinate soldiers should behave, one that was violated by this experience. In the ICT Leaders Project, a group of four researchers and training developers on the project came to the consensus about the expectation and expectation violation of this story as follows:

Expectation: Both combat and noncombat units realize the importance of their roles in the accomplishment of the larger mission and will perform accordingly.

Expectation violation: A sense of pride and importance must be developed in low performing noncombat units.

The next step in the analysis process is to use this formulation of the expectation violation to create a decision situation, one where the choice of what to do would be primarily determined by whether the expectation or its violation were believed to be true. Here the aim is to engineer a hypothetical situation where a decision has to be made, and where there are two options that are both viable, rational courses of action. In the ICT Leaders Project, the decision situation that was authored for this expectation violation was as follows:

Situation: A noncombat unit has been attached to the combat infantry company you command, and it is not performing well.

Choice rejected by the expectation: Wait for unit performance to improve as the soldiers realize their importance to the mission.

Choice supported by the expectation violation: Work with the soldiers in the unit to develop a sense of pride and importance.

In some cases it is possible to author a fictional decision situation that closely parallels some real decision that was made in the nonfiction story, but more often the decisions made in the real world do not have two or more well-balanced, viable, rational options from which to choose. Furthermore, authors of these situations need to guard against the presumption that one of the two options is the best choice or the right answer. Nor does the original story provide real support for one choice or another. Even if the events occurred exactly as they were described, they will rarely provide a strong justification for rejecting the expectations that are challenged. Instead, authors of these fictional decision situations should view them as ways of exploring the fringe of expectation, the fertile area that lies between the novice's mental models of the task domain and the experiences of practitioners. The right answers to these problems are not going to be determined through the analysis of a handful of stories, but rather through the varied practices of training doctrine development—a different challenge altogether.

THE FICTIONALIZATION OF LESSONS LEARNED

In the historical development of story based learning environments over the last three decades, the most evident changes are in the technologies used in their production. As mentioned in the first section of this chapter, early story based learning environments were produced using video laser-disc and computer hyper-media technologies in the late 1980s. This was followed by the appropriation of desktop video technologies in the early and mid-1990s, followed by Web applications in the late 1990s. Today, innovation in story based learning environments is largely connected to virtual reality and computer gaming technologies. While the early 2000s saw enormous enthusiasm for the integration of computer gaming technologies in the development of computer based training, the pairing of this technology with design paradigms in story based learning environments was not an obvious match. The design paradigm that was commercially viable at the time was that of the outcome-driven simulation (Cleave, 1997), a story based learning environment whose branching storyline structure lent itself particularly well to the hypermedia nature of Internet Web applications. In contrast, computer gaming technology is at its best when treated as a constructive simulation environment, where the situations encountered by trainees emerge through the careful tuning of initial situations and the simulation rules that govern the effects of actions. In short, the best simulation based training looked more like an airplane flight simulator, while the best story based learning environments looked more like a choose-your-own-adventure book (for example, Packard, 1979). It was not at all obvious how the two could be successfully paired.

The ICT Leaders Project might best be viewed as an early attempt to force these two technologies together into one training application. The approach taken by the development team was to author an outcome-driven simulation using the same methods that had been used for Web based training instantiations, where each of the fictional decision situations identified through the analysis of real world stories served as a branching point in a static branching storyline. Specifically, it was constructed as a tree with 11 branch points, each with two branches. The presentation of each decision situation and the consequences of selecting one of the two options were realized as scripted scenes, each using a consistent set of fictional characters and interrelated events. In authoring a rich fictional storyline for the ICT Leaders Project, the challenge was to instantiate each of the general descriptions of decision situations into a coherent narrative with dramatic impact (Iuppa et al., 2004).

Work on the fictional storyline for the ICT Leaders Project followed on the heels of the development of another media based training application based on the same corpus of interviews with U.S. Army captains, the Army Excellence in Leadership (AXL) project (Hill et al., 2003, 2004). In this work, the transcribed stories of leadership told in these interviews were used as source material for the development of the screenplay for a live-action training film, entitled *Power Hungry*. The 15 minute film depicts the fictional events occurring over the course of a day in the life of Captain Young. Captain Young is assigned to command an infantry company in Afghanistan during Operation Enduring Freedom, tasked with providing security for a food distribution operation conducted by a non-government relief organization. Conditions deteriorate as Captain Young divides his time between micromanaging his subordinates and meeting with local warlords, who eventually succeed in disrupting the operation through deception about their rivalries. The AXL research project at the University of Southern California's Institute for Creative Technologies later used this film and others like it to explore the development of distance learning technologies for case-method instruction (Hill et al., 2006). Much of the training value of this film comes from the discussions of the leadership style for Captain Young. The ICT Leaders Project based its fictional branching storyline in exactly the same scenario environment, seeking to capitalize on the richness of the fictional situation created in the *Power Hungry* film and to provide trainees with a means of playing the role of Captain Young in a learn-by-doing training application.

To instantiate the decision situation described in the previous section of this chapter (concerning noncombat units) the writers on the ICT Leaders Project cast the decision in the context of an argument between the first sergeant and the executive officer of the company. The storyline introduces a noncombat military unit to raise the issue, a small civil affairs unit that is attached to Captain Young's company to aid in their interaction with Afghanistan political leaders. They perform poorly at an assigned task, which is to oversee and manage a band of local militia forces that are partnering with the U.S. Army to ensure security for the food distribution operation. This concerns the first sergeant of Captain Young's company, and when he and the executive officer meet with Captain Young (a role-played by the trainee) he offers to give the civil affairs unit some coaching to improve its motivation. The executive officer disagrees, saying that it is likely that this motivational speech would hurt more than help and that the problems of the civil affairs unit are expected given the little time they have had to integrate with the rest of the company. The sergeant still does not agree and turns to Captain Young (the trainee) for a decision on what to do.

The great weakness of this style of story based learning environment, that is, an outcome-driven simulation, is that users are forced to select among a very small number of options in order to ensure that the consequences of these actions have both narrative coherence and lead directly to other decision situations. The trainee who is playing the role of Captain Young in the ICT Leaders Project must decide between two options in this decision situation, regardless of whether or not he or she has a more creative solution to the problem in mind. Perhaps the civil affairs unit should not be assigned the task of managing local militia in the first place. Perhaps the first sergeant should redirect his attention to improving the motivation of the local militia instead. Perhaps the executive officer should get involved directly and leave Captain Young alone to work on the bigger problems of the day. It is possible to provide an interface to the trainees that would allow them to make these types of creative choices (for example, Gordon, 2006), but it is harder to imagine predicting the effects of these choices given the current state of simulation technology. Harder still is the problem of keeping the storyline on track so that the effects of these creative actions ultimately lead the trainee to another pedagogically motivated decision situation.

In the present, the latter half of the first decade of 2000, current research in story based learning environments is closely aligned with research on technologies for interactive drama. The central question within the research area is how to ensure that a well-crafted story unfolds when the user plays the active role of a creative protagonist. Much of this work attempts to ensure that particular plot elements are included in the unfolding story regardless of the user's actions (Magerko, 2007; Riedl & Stern, 2006a; Mateas & Stern, 2003). Several researchers have noted the parallels between this concern and that of the developers of story based learning environments, who seek instead to ensure that trainees are presented with particular decision situations (Riedl & Stern, 2006b; Magerko, Stensrud, & Holt, 2006). Increasingly, these efforts are incorporating artificial intelligence planning and execution models to ensure story-like paths through state spaces that are far larger than could reasonably be authored by hand. However, the richness of the possible storylines is most limited by the believability of the behavior models used to control the actions of virtual human characters, which remains an incredibly difficult artificial intelligence research challenge (Swartout et al., 2006).

SUMMARY

At the beginning of this chapter, story based learning environments were characterized as a complex form of communication, mediating between real world experiences told as stories and the experiences of learners in virtual environments. Seen from this perspective, the main challenges for developers of story based learning environments concern the management of real world story content through the development pipeline. Three key processes in this pipeline were highlighted in this chapter, each representing areas where automation and innovation should be the focus of future research and development. First, stories of real world experiences are an invaluable means of communicating tacit knowledge, but the directed interview methods used today to collect stories from practitioners have problems of scalability. Second, stories of the experiences of practitioners can be analyzed to identify the expectations that they challenge and can be transformed into decisions to be made by learners in fictional situations. However, this style of analysis and transformation capitalizes on only one aspect of nonfiction stories related to learning, tightly constraining the way that these stories are incorporated into virtual learning environments. Third, the branching storyline techniques used to develop outcome-driven simulations in the 1990s transfer well to today's virtual reality environments, but new innovations in interactive drama are needed to allow learners in these environments to tackle problems in creative ways.

REFERENCES

Bartlett, F. C. (1932). *Remembering: An experimental and social study.* Cambridge, England: Cambridge University Press.

Boyce, M. (1996). Organizational story and storytelling: A critical review. *Journal of Organizational Change Management, 9*(5), 5–26.

Bruner, J. (1991). The narrative construction of reality. *Critical Inquiry, 18*(1), 1–21.

Clark, R. E. (2004). *Design document for a guided experiential learning course* (Final Rep., Contract No. DAAD 19-99-D-0046-0004). Los Angeles: University of Southern California, Institute for Creative Technology and the Rossier School of Education.

Clark, R. E., Feldon, D., van Merrienboer, J., Yates, K., & Early, S. (2007). Cognitive task analysis. In J. Spector, M. Merrill, J. van Merrienboer, & M. Driscoll (Eds.), *Handbook of research on educational communications and technology* (3rd ed., pp. 1801–1856). Mahwah, NJ: Lawrence Erlbaum.

Cleave, J. (1997). *A storyline-based approach to developing management role-playing simulations.* Unpublished Doctoral Dissertation, Northwestern University, Evanston, IL.

Cognition and Technology Group at Vanderbilt. (1992). The jasper experiment: An exploration of issues in learning and instructional design. *Educational Technology Research and Development, 40*(1), 65–80.

Cognition and Technology Group at Vanderbilt. (1990). Anchored instruction and its relationship to situated cognition. *Educational Researcher, 19,* 2–10.

Coopman, S., & Meidlinger, K. (1998). Interpersonal stories told by a Catholic Parish staff. *American Communication Journal, 1*(3).

Gordon, A. (2004, June). *Authoring branching storylines for training applications.* Paper presented at the Sixth International Conference of the Learning Sciences (ICLS-04), Santa Monica, CA.

Gordon, A. (2005). The fictionalization of lessons learned [Guest Editorial for Media Impact column]. *IEEE Multimedia 12*(4), 12–14.

Gordon, A. (2006, October). *Fourth frame forums: Interactive comics for collaborative learning.* Paper presented at the Fourteenth Annual ACM International Conference on Multimedia (MM 2006), Santa Barbara, CA.

Gordon, A., Cao, Q., & Swanson, R. (2007, October). *Automated story capture from internet weblogs.* Paper presented at the Fourth International Conference on Knowledge Capture (KCAP-07), Whistler, Canada.

Gordon, A., & Ganesan, K. (2005, October). *Automated story capture from conversational speech.* Paper presented at the Third International Conference on Knowledge Capture (KCAP-05), Banff, Canada.

Gordon, A., van Lent, M., van Velsen, M., Carpenter, M., & Jhala, A. (2004). Branching storylines in virtual reality environments for leadership development. *Proceedings of the Innovative Applications of Artificial Intelligence Conference* (IAAI-04; pp. 884–851). Menlo Park, CA: AAAI Press.

Hill, R., Douglas, J., Gordon, A., Pighin, F., & van Velsen, M. (2003). Guided conversations about leadership: Mentoring with movies and interactive characters. *Proceedings of the Fifteenth Innovative Applications of Artificial Intelligence Conference* (IAAI-03; pp. 101–108). Menlo Park, CA: AAAI Press.

Hill, R., Gordon, A., & Kim, J. (2004, December). *Learning the lessons of leadership experience: Tools for interactive case method analysis.* Paper presented at the 24th Army Science Conference, Orlando, FL.

Hill, R., Kim, J., Gordon, A., Traum, D., Gandhe, S., King, S., Lavis, S., Rocher, S., & Zbylut, M. (2006, November). *AXL.Net: Web-enabled case method instruction for accelerating tacit knowledge acquisition in leaders.* Paper presented at the 25th Army Science Conference, Orlando, FL.

Iuppa, N., & Borst, T. (2007). *Stories and simulations for serious games: Tales from the trenches.* Burlington, MA: Focal Press.

Iuppa, N., Weltman, G., & Gordon, A. (2004, August 10–13). *Bringing Hollywood story-telling techniques to branching storylines for training applications.* Paper presented at the Third International Conference for Narrative and Interactive Learning Environments, Edinburgh, Scotland.

Johnson, C., Birnbaum, L., Bareiss, R., & Hinrichs, T. (2000). War stories: Harnessing organizational memories to support task performance. *Intelligence 11*(1), 16–31.

Korris, J. (2004, December). *Full spectrum warrior: How the Institute for Creative Technologies built a cognitive training tool for the XBox.* Paper presented at the 24th Army Science Conference, Orlando, FL.

Magerko, B. (2007). Evaluating preemptive story direction in the interactive drama architecture. *Journal of Game Development, 2*(3).

Magerko, B., Stensrud, B., & Holt, L. (2006, December). *Bringing the schoolhouse inside the box—A tool for engaging, individualized training.* Paper presented at the 25th Army Science Conference, Orlando, FL.

Mateas, M., & Stern, A. (2003, March). *Facade: An experiment in building a fully-realized interactive drama.* Paper presented at the Game Developers Conference, Game Design track, San Jose, CA.

McCormack, C., & Milne, P. (2003). Stories create space for understanding organizational change. *Qualitative Research Journal 3*(2), 45–59.

Owsley, S., Hammond, K., & Shamma, D. (2006, June). *Computational support for compelling story telling.* Paper presented at the ACM SIGCHI International Conference on Advances in Computer Entertainment Technology, Hollywood, CA.

Packard, E. (1979). *The cave of time.* NY: Bantam Books.

Riedl, M., & Stern, A. (2006a, December). *Believable agents and intelligent story adaptation for interactive storytelling.* Paper presented at the 3rd International Conference on Technologies for Interactive Digital Storytelling and Entertainment, Darmstadt, Germany.

Riedl, M., & Stern, A. (2006b, May). *Believable agents and intelligent scenario direction for social and cultural leadership training.* Paper presented at the 15th Conference on Behavior Representation in Modeling and Simulation, Baltimore, Maryland.

Schank, R. (1982). *Dynamic memory: A theory of reminding and learning in computers and people.* New York: Cambridge University Press.

Schank, R., & Abelson, R. (1995). Knowledge and memory: The real story. In R. Wyer (Ed.), *Knowledge and memory: The real story* (pp. 1–85). Mahwah, NJ: Lawrence Erlbaum.

Schank, R., Fano, A., Bell, B., & Jona, M. (1993). The design of goal-based scenarios. *Journal of the Learning Sciences, 3*(4), 305–345.

Snowden, D. (1999). *Story telling for the capture and communication of tacit knowledge.* Unpublished doctoral dissertation, Indiana University, Bloomington, IN.

Snowden, D. (2000). The art and science of story or are you sitting uncomfortably?: Part 1. Gathering and harvesting the raw material. *Business Information Review, 17,* 147–156.

Sternberg, R., Forsythe, G., Hedlund, J., Horvath, J., Wagner, R., Williams, W., Snook, S., & Grigorenko, E. (2000). *Practical Intelligence in Everyday Life.* New York: Cambridge University Press.

Swartout, W., Gratch, J., Hill, R., Hovy, E., Marsella, S., Rickel, S., & Traum, D. (2006). Toward virtual humans. *AI Magazine, 27*(1), 96–108.

Technorati. (2007). *State of the Blogosphere /State of the Live Web.* Retrieved July 1, 2007, from http://www.sifry.com/stateoftheliveweb

Wyer, R. (Ed.). (1995). *Knowledge and memory: The real story.* Mahwah, NJ: Lawrence Erlbaum.

Chapter 20

INTELLIGENT TUTORING AND PEDAGOGICAL EXPERIENCE MANIPULATION IN VIRTUAL LEARNING ENVIRONMENTS

H. Chad Lane and Lewis Johnson

Modern virtual environments provide new and exciting opportunities for the learning of complex skills. Rapid progress in the commercial game industry, as well as in computer graphics, animation, and artificial intelligence research, has produced immersive environments capable of simulating experiences that can closely resemble reality. Educators and learning scientists have grasped these opportunities, motivated by the prospect of providing safe, authentic practice environments for real world skills not previously within the scope of computer-supported learning. Greater realism and more immersion seem to be in harmony with modern instructional design methodologies and theories of learning, such as situated learning (Brown, Collins, & Duguid, 1989):

> We argue that approaches such as cognitive apprenticeship that embed learning in activity and make deliberate use of the social and physical context are more in line with the understanding of learning and cognition that is emerging from research.
>
> (p. 32)

A tenet of situated cognition is that knowledge should be learned in its context of use, as well as within the culture of its practice. Computer based learning environments that seek to replace traditional paper based homework assignments tend to be based on the "culture of school" rather than the more real world cultural contexts discussed in the situated learning literature and thus rarely leverage the full capabilities of a computer to simulate these contexts. Virtual learning environments (VLEs), on the other hand, hold the potential to provide learners with greater authenticity and clearer connections to real world applications of skills they are acquiring.

However, there is a natural tension between the realism in VLEs and efficient, robust learning. For example, real world skills that may take months or years to apply (such as building a home) may not require faithful representation of time in a computer simulation (such as waiting two weeks for the delivery of materials). Relying exclusively on high fidelity and immersion therefore limits a VLE's ability to actually promote learning. Numerous studies have shown that learning is suboptimal, sometimes even hindered, when pure discovery and trial and error are used as the primary means for skill acquisition (Mayer, 2004; Kirschner, Sweller, & Clark, 2006). Guidance is therefore critical to avoid these pitfalls, especially for novices. Support can come from a variety of sources, of course, such as instructors, peers, carefully designed instructional materials, or even from within the learning environment itself. Our focus here is on the latter—that is, how we might scaffold learning automatically and from within a virtual learning environment. This chapter summarizes principles that have emerged from studies of human and computer tutors, as well as how artificial intelligence (AI) and intelligent tutoring system (ITS) technologies can be applied to the problem of providing guidance in immersive and virtual learning environments.

HUMAN AND COMPUTER TUTORING

Students working one-on-one with expert human tutors often score 2.0 standard deviations—roughly two grade levels—higher than students in a conventional classroom (Bloom, 1984). In contrast, the very best intelligent tutoring systems achieve learning gains of about 1.0 standard deviation (Anderson, Corbett, Koedinger, & Pelletier, 1995; VanLehn et al., 2005). The best computer-aided instructional systems—computer tutors that do not use AI techniques—produce learning gains of about 0.4 standard deviation (Niemiec & Walberg, 1987). Unfortunately, a precise answer to the question of why tutoring is more effective than other forms of instruction has remained elusive. Most hypotheses tend to focus either on the behaviors of the tutor—that learning occurs because of expert execution of tutoring tactics—or of the student—that learning occurs when the student makes deep contributions during a tutoring session. Each of these perspectives has implications for how intelligent tutors should behave in virtual environments, so in this section, we take a brief look at both of these hypotheses and the empirical evidence supporting them.

Why Is Tutoring Effective?

A popular claim for the effectiveness of tutoring is that human tutors are able to adapt and thus individualize instruction to fit the needs of the particular student being tutored. These adaptations can be made in response to a variety of student traits, including those involving the knowledge state of the student or the affective (emotional) state. For example, some expert human tutors implement mastery loops that involve the repeated assignment of problems that test a particular skill (or set of skills) until the student has confidently demonstrated competence (Bloom, 1984). Another tactic is to select or formulate problems in ways that will appeal to and motivate the student (Lepper, Woolverton, Mumme,

& Gurtner, 1993). Assigning an easier problem when a student's confidence is low is an example of a tutoring tactic in this category. Human tutors also implement different tactics based on student traits. For example, the policy of immediate feedback is a well-documented tactic applied by both human and computer tutors that increases learning efficiency (Merrill, Reiser, Ranney, & Trafton, 1992; Anderson et al., 1995), but may hinder students' self-assessment and self-correction skills (Schooler & Anderson, 1990). Immediate feedback is considered individualized in the sense that students' own specific sets of correct and incorrect actions determine what kind of feedback they receive—it is rare that two students will receive exactly the same tutorial interventions. Like problem selection, the content and timing of tutoring feedback can be based on the knowledge state of the student or on affective traits. Lepper et al. (1993) document a variety of lower level tutoring tactics intended to manage affect, such as maximizing success (through praise) and minimizing failure (via commiseration).

Some have argued that the best tutors balance the need for active participation of the student with the provision of guidance (Merrill et al., 1992). This means the student does as much of the work as possible, while the tutor provides just enough feedback to minimize frustration and confusion. Also, effective tutoring has been found to have less to do with didactic explanations by the tutor and more to do with the interaction between the tutor and the student. Chi, Siler, Jeong, Yamauchi, and Hausmann (2001) conclude that "students' substantive construction from interaction is important for learning, suggesting that an ITS ought to implement ways to elicit students' constructive responses" (p. 518). It is a common pattern in ITS research to first identify effective learning events and patterns in human tutoring, then attempt to emulate them in an ITS.

Intelligent Tutoring Systems

Given that research on intelligent tutoring is often inspired by empirical studies of human tutors, it is not surprising that computer tutors share many similarities with human tutors (Merrill et al., 1992). For example, when a student reaches an impasse, human and intelligent computer tutors both use similar approaches to help the student overcome the impasse: both monitor student reasoning and intervene to keep the student on a productive path. A major limitation for early generation tutoring systems was that they interacted with the learner primarily through graphical user interface gestures, such as menu selections, dragging and dropping, and so on. For example, in the Andes physics tutoring system (Van-Lehn et al., 2005), students draw force vectors on diagrams and enter equations into text fields. Andes provides immediate flag feedback by coloring correct actions green and incorrect actions red. Solicited help is available that allows the student to ask why an action is wrong or for advice on taking the next step. Andes implements model tracing, an algorithm originally appearing in the Cognitive Tutors from Carnegie Mellon University (Anderson et al., 1995). Model tracing tracks a learner step by step through a problem solving space, comparing the observed actions to those indicated by an expert model of the targeted skill and delivering feedback according to some pedagogical model or policy. Immediate feedback with solicited follow-up help is one such policy.

Human tutors have an advantage over computer tutors in that a much larger space of tutorial interventions is possible. For example, some important differences that distinguish human tutors arise from subtle cues from facial expressions, body language, conversational cues, or the simple use of dialogue (Fox, 1993). Given the 1 sigma "gap" between the effectiveness of expert human tutors and the best computer tutors, it is no surprise that a great deal of research in the last decade has gone into endowing computer tutors with more of the "features" of human tutors in the hope of narrowing the effect size difference. The use of interactive dialogue represents a major research focus over the last decade. Many such systems attempt to leverage the expressivity of natural language input and dialogue to remediate flawed conceptual knowledge (Graesser, VanLehn, Rosé, Jordan, & Harter, 2001), while others have used dialogue to encourage metacognitive and reflective thinking on problem solving (Core et al., 2006; Peters, Bratt, Clark, Pon-Barry, & Schultz, 2004; Katz, Allbritton, & Connelly, 2003). Just as dialogue opens up new avenues for tutorial intervention, so does research into pedagogical agents and virtual human instructors.

CONSIDERATIONS FOR INTELLIGENT TUTORING IN VIRTUAL ENVIRONMENTS

Rickel and Johnson (1997), who were among the first to propose the use of intelligent tutoring in virtual reality environments, point out that much stays the same: students will still reach impasses, demonstrate misconceptions, and will benefit from the guidance and help of a tutor. They highlight new methods of interactions afforded by VLEs:

- The tutor can inhabit the environment with the student, thus providing increased potential for "physical" collaboration.
- Similarly, an embodied tutor can communicate nonverbally, through gestures and facial expressions, for example.
- A virtual reality environment allows students to be tracked in new ways, such as by their visual attention and physical movements.

Thus, the scope of tutorial interactions is greatly increased in VLEs, in both directions: in performing tutorial interventions and in the bandwidth available for monitoring the learner. Researchers have explored the ways in which virtual environments differ from more traditional computer based learning environments that tend to be developed as substitutes for written homework. How well do traditional ITS approaches, such as those discussed in the previous section, map into tutoring in VLEs? What opportunities do VLEs make available that might enhance the effectiveness of an intelligent tutor? Here, we consider both directions: (1) how the advances from intelligent tutoring in traditional environments might be used to promote learning in VLEs and (2) whether more advanced immersive technologies might contribute to closing the 1 sigma gap between human and intelligent tutoring.

We limit our consideration to those VLEs specifically constructed for the learning of cognitive skills that also include an underlying simulation of some real world phenomena. We also restrict ourselves to those environments that seek a reasonably high level of fidelity and realism. Thus, included in the discussion are virtual worlds that permit exploration from a first-person perspective, simulations of complex equipment (that include an interface modeled directly on actual equipment), and simulations of natural phenomena, such as social, biological, or meteorological phenomena.

Expanding the Problem Space: Time and Movement

Many VLEs can also be classified as open learning environments. These are characterized by a greater amount of learner control and are generally considered to be more appropriate for learning in ill-structured domains (Jonassen, 1997). Because of the large problem space in many VLEs, solving the plan recognition problem (monitoring, understanding, assessing, and so forth) is often a significant challenge for ITSs. Here, we highlight two key challenges: tutoring in real time contexts and in environments that provide expanded freedom of student movement in a virtual space.

Tutoring in Real Time Environments

For problem solving tasks that are not time constrained (for example, solving algebra equations), computer based learning environments typically wait for the learner to act. This stands in contrast to many domains targeted by VLEs that require real time thinking, decision making, and acting. Ritter and Feurzeig (1988, p. 286) were among the earliest to wrestle with the problems of tutoring in a real time domain and highlight the following three major differences:

- The knowledge acquisition problem is more complicated since experts tend to "compile" their knowledge for efficient execution.
- Diagnosing errors is more complicated because time is typically not available to ask the student questions during practice.
- Assessing performance and conveying feedback is best done after task completion to avoid the risk of interrupting the learner (see Lampton, Martin, Meliza, and Goldberg, Volume 2, Section 2, Chapter 14).

The knowledge acquisition problem is not magnified only by constraints related to real time processing but also by the nature of ill-structured domains in general (Lynch, Ashley, Aleven, & Pinkwart, 2006), which are common domain targets of VLEs. Diagnosis of errors and assessment of performance are similarly not unique to real time domains, but are nonetheless more complicated because of time constraints during practice. Time-constrained problem solving often goes hand-in-hand with dynamic learning environments—that is, as time moves forward while the student deliberates, the state of the world may change in favorable or unfavorable ways. Here, we review several approaches to dealing with these challenges in terms of how ITSs have been implemented to support learning.

Ritter and Feurzeig (1988) describe TRIO (Trainer for Radar Intercept Officers), an ITS built to train F-14 interceptor pilots and radar operators to support the real time decision-making tasks involved with air defense and collaboration. The system presents the learner with radar displays and flight instruments that provide both needed information and the ability to take actions in the simulation. TRIO provides guidance in three ways:

- Before practice: demonstrations of expert performance,
- During practice: coaching support while the learner practices, and
- After practice: post-practice debriefing (after action review).

These interventions are driven by a rule based cognitive model of domain expertise (called the "TRIO articulate expert") that is capable of performing the intercept tasks the learner is acquiring. TRIO intervenes with a learner only if mission critical mistakes are being made (or about to be made) and leaves most feedback for the post-practice reflective period. This is a typical policy for ITSs operating in real time domains given the risks of competing for the working memory of a learner. The articulate expert focuses on finding the appropriate intermediate goals throughout execution of the task and uses these to help the student learn what went wrong and what should be done. The model is flexible enough to represent multiple solutions to a given problem.

Roberts, Pioch, and Ferguson (1998) adopted a similar approach in the development of TRANSoM (Training for Remote Sensing and Manipulation), an ITS for the training of pilots of underwater remotely operated vehicles (ROVs). Just as in TRIO, demonstrations, guided practice, and reflection also play key roles. Because of the real time nature of the task, TRANSoM also attempts to simultaneously avoid distracting the learner, while preventing session-killing errors from occurring. A key aspect to ROV operation is the maintenance of a mental model of the vehicle itself. This is a challenge given the limited inputs regarding the ROV's status (which is true in reality). To increase the chances of being nonintrusive, TRANSoM applies two techniques. First, all coaching support is delivered verbally so the visual modality is not in competition with the learner. Second, although unsolicited help is delivered in a manner similar to TRIO (when there is deviation from an expert solution path), students are also given the chance to ask for guidance when they feel they need it (that is, solicited help). Among other lessons learned, Roberts et al. (1998) suggest that the use of discourse cues, short utterances, and the simultaneous use of directive visual cues along with verbal feedback would increase the chances of a verbal feedback being effective in a VLE.

Tutoring in Open-Movement Environments

To promote the feelings of learner control and freedom, many VLEs, especially those that are game based, tend to allow free movement within a virtual world. This is consistent with the motivation for building open learning environments. It is typical in this category of VLEs to give the learner control of an avatar or vehicle to maneuver around in a virtual world. Usually done from a first-person perspective, it allows the learner to make such choices as what to explore, when, and for how long. The problem for an ITS in these environments is twofold. First, if the skill being practiced is directly related to the movements of the learner's avatar, it must be determined at what level of action the ITS should react. For example, does a turn in one direction represent an intention to move in that direction? Second, to what extent physical/motor skills transfer to the real word from virtual environments is an open question. Thus, most ITSs that permit free movement do so in order to maximize the learner's feeling of freedom and independence and less because it contributes to the acquisition of some underlying cognitive or physical skill.

Very few ITSs precisely track how learners maneuver in a virtual environment. Most systems observe only gross physical movements (from area to area) and interact when issues arise related to the events of the game in those physical areas. One exception is the Collaborative Warrior Tutoring system (Livak, Heffernan, & Moyer, 2004), an ITS that tracks physical movements in a three-dimensional (3-D), first-person shooter environment for the learning of tactical skills and military operations on urban terrain. Through the use of a cognitive model of room and building clearing skills that inspects the dynamically changing environment represented in the 3-D world, the ITS is able to assess the learner's movements (including buggy knowledge) and give hints and feedback on the fly. These interventions come as text overlaid on the view of the virtual world alongside communications between characters. The model of expert performance is also used to drive the behaviors of computer-controlled characters in the environment.

Most other ITSs that permit free movement in a virtual world do not track movements at this fine-grained level. For example, in the Tactical Language and Culture Training System (TLCTS) mission environment (Johnson, Vilhjalmsson, & Marsella, 2005), the learner is given game objectives and is free to move around an Iraqi village to achieve them. This requires visiting a variety of locations in the village (for example, the café) and interacting with locals in culturally appropriate ways through Arabic speech and gestures. This is similar to the approach taken in the narrative based learning environment Crystal Island (Mott & Lester, 2006). In this system, the learner plays the role of a scientist on an island where several of the inhabitants have become ill from an infectious disease. The learner must move around the island interviewing people, collecting evidence, and running tests. As in TLCTS, actual movements in the environment are important to the extent that they represent decisions—for example, if the learner walks toward a research station with a sample, it is reasonable to conclude he or she intends to test it for contamination.

Expanding the Space of Intelligent Tutoring Interactions

As discussed, VLEs that are open tend to provide a much larger problem solving space than more traditional computer based learning environments. Not only does this provide more freedom for the learner, but also for the ITS to perform a wider array of pedagogically motivated interactions. In this section we discuss two of these opportunities: through the use of pedagogical agents and via dynamic manipulation of the learning environment in ways that promote learning, sometimes called pedagogical experience manipulation.

Pedagogical Agents

Artificial intelligence research into the development of intelligent, communicative agents and virtual humans has led to interdisciplinary research on natural language processing, emotional modeling, gesture modeling, cultural modeling, and more (Cassell, Sullivan, Prevost, & Churchill, 2000; Swartout et al., 2006). Since people tend to treat human-like computer characters as they would humans (Reeves & Nass, 1996), there is potential for learners to "bond" more with intelligent tutors that express themselves through a human-like avatar. Previously in this chapter we discussed the 1 sigma gap between the best ITSs and expert human tutors and how dialogue based tutoring systems represent one attempt to bridge this gap. By endowing ITSs with features similar to those used by human tutors, the hypothesis is that this gap can be narrowed. For example, facial expressions might be used to express concern or approval, among other emotions, all of which are potentially useful as indirect feedback. Pedagogical agents tend to serve in one of two roles. The first is in the role of a coach or tutor with the goal of supporting learning through explicit guidance and feedback. The second is when the pedagogical agent assumes a role in an underlying narrative or story playing out in the virtual environment.

A wide range of pedagogical agents have been developed that play the role of tutor or coach (Clarebout, Elen, Johnson, & Shaw, 2002; Person & Graesser, 2002). Most provide hints and feedback to a learner during some problem solving task, provide explanations, communicate verbally and nonverbally, and seek to provide "just-in-time" support. Soar Training Expert for Virtual Environments, one of the earliest pedagogical agents, possessed all of the traditional capabilities of ITSs (delivered feedback, explanations, gave hints, and so forth), but also had the ability to lead the learner around the virtual environment, demonstrate tasks, guide attention (through gaze and pointing), and play the role of teammate (Rickel et al., 2002; Rickel & Johnson, 1997). Using animation, sound, and dialogue techniques, pedagogical agents can also attempt to manage the learner's affective state through encouragement and motivational techniques. For example, in the Multiple Intelligent Mentors Instructing Collaboratively system, an emotional instructional agent has been implemented that will express confusion, disapproval, excitement, encouragement, pleasure, and more (for example, Baylor & Kim, 2005).

In narrative based learning environments, pedagogical agents have the opportunity to be "part of the story" by assuming some role in the underlying narrative being played out in the environment. For example, in the Mission Rehearsal Exercise (MRE) system (Swartout et al., 2006), the learner, playing the role of a young lieutenant, is placed in a situation in which one of his platoon's Humvees has been in an accident with a civilian car. The sergeant in the scenario has the knowledge of how to resolve the crisis and will give guidance should the learner need it, such as pointing out the negative aspects to a particular order (for example, "Sir, our troops should not be split up."). A similar solution is used in TLCTS in endowing an accompanying sergeant with coaching ability, but making only solicited help available (Johnson et al., 2005). In recent versions of TLCTS, tutoring by the accompanying aide has been curtailed, as it was found that some learners got the false impression that only a limited number of choices were available, namely, those that the aide recommends. Instead, tutoring support is provided through the characters in the game, by their reactions to the learner, and at times by the leading questions that they ask of the learner. This approach is inspired by the tactics that good human role-players employ in role-playing exercises at training centers, such as the U.S. Army's National Training Center. Crystal Island also provides all of its tutoring support through the characters in the game (Mott & Lester, 2006), as well as affective support through empathetic characters (McQuiggan, Rowe, & Lester, 2008).

Empirical research on pedagogical agents is mixed in terms of how well they close the 1 sigma gap between computer and human tutors (Clarebout et al., 2002). Moreno, Mayer, and Lester (2000) found that the simple presence of an animated agent did not impact learning, but that speech (over text) led to improved retention and transfer in learning. The same study also showed that interactive dialogue was superior to more didactic utterances by the agent, which is consistent with studies of dialogue based ITSs that do not use pedagogical agents (Graesser et al., 2001). In research aimed at understanding how pedagogical agents can go beyond possessing only domain knowledge, Baylor & Kim (2005) found evidence that agents playing both a motivator and expert role simultaneously (which they refer to as a "mentor") outperformed agents in each of these roles alone in the ill-defined domain of instructional planning.

Wang et al. (2007) found that a key determiner of the effectiveness of a pedagogical agent is the extent to which the agent employs socially appropriate tactics that address learner "face," consistent with the politeness theory of Brown and Levinson (1987). Learners who interacted with a pedagogical agent that employed politeness tactics achieved greater learning gains than learners who interacted with an agent that did not employ such tactics, and the effect was greatest among learners who expressed a preference for tutorial feedback delivered in a polite, indirect way. Wang has since replicated these results with TLCTS, using politeness strategies delivered via text messages. These studies suggest that (a) the manner in which the agent interacts with the learner determines its impact on learning, (b) the effect varies with the individual characteristics of the learner, and (c) socially appropriate tactics can affect learning even without an animated persona.

Studies involving pedagogical agents generally show that learners prefer having a pedagogical agent to not having one, but more evidence needs to be collected to determine their actual value in promoting learning beyond what disembodied ITSs are able to do.

Pedagogical Experience Manipulation and Stealth Tutoring

A VLE's underlying simulation provides more subtle opportunities to promote learning beyond explicit guidance. In most VLEs, many forms of implicit feedback already exist that mirror feedback one can observe in real environments. For example, if a basketball is shot, implicit feedback comes from the visual evidence that the ball flies through the hoop or bounces off the rim. In a virtual environment, it may be that different events and behaviors may be more appropriate for learning at different times. It may be pedagogically beneficial to override a simulation such that it establishes ideal conditions for learning or produces implicit feedback that meets an individual learner's needs. In the basketball example, it may be better for the simulation to have the ball go in the hoop if the goal is to give the learner practice in playing in a tight game (assuming the basket would make the score closer). In this section, we briefly describe two such approaches: experience manipulation and stealth tutoring.

There are at least two strategies available for intelligent manipulation of a learner's experience in a VLE that can promote learning. The first is through the amplification or dampening of implicit feedback. For example, in simulations with virtual humans, it is possible to tweak their behaviors to achieve certain pedagogical objectives. For example, if a learner commits a cultural error, such as mentioning a taboo subject, it may be productive to have the character overreact to that error to support the learner's recognition of the mistake. If the implicit feedback is amplified in this way, the ITS would be supporting the metacognitive skill in the learner of recognizing that an error was made, which is a critical early step in acquisition of intercultural skills (Lane, 2007). Similarly, if a learner has repeatedly demonstrated knowledge of a given cultural rule, it may make sense to minimize time spent related to that already mastered material. This could be played out by virtual humans with shorter utterances and dampened visual reactions when applicable.

A second category of experience manipulation lies in the actual dynamic modification of the state of the simulation in ways that establish appropriate conditions for learning. Although modification of implicit feedback can be used in this way, there are other means. For example, in the Interactive Storytelling Architecture for Training (ISAT) system, the learner is guided through plot points that are selected based on an evolving learner model (Magerko, Stensrud, & Holt, 2006). The version of ISAT that runs in the domain of combat medic skills will manipulate the environment in ways that address the needs expressed by the learner model. For example, if a learner has difficulty identifying the proper order in which to treat multiple injured soldiers, ISAT is capable of adapting the injured soldiers' injuries and behaviors such that they test the specific weaknesses of the learner. In the combat medic domain, ISAT may adjust the damage an explosion inflicts on victims of an attack or tweak their behaviors resulting from sustained injuries—for example, rolling around on the ground or yelling. These examples of experience manipulation are intended to establish conditions for learning and allow the learner the chance to practice the right skills at the best times within a VLE.

Stealth tutoring, a specific kind of experience manipulation, focuses on methods of conveying tutor-like explicit guidance from within the VLE. Given that explicit help comes with the risk of learner dependence on it, there may be times when covert support may be preferable so that a learner is not aware help is being given. Crystal Island, and the underlying narrative and tutorial planning system U-Director, demonstrates stealth tutoring in a particularly elegant way (Mott & Lester, 2006). If the system detects that a learner is wandering around the island and failing to make progress, the underlying planning model will decide to direct the nurse character to share her opinion that some of the food on the island might be making people sick. This "hint" comes only after the detection of floundering and in an entirely plausible way (via a character who is concerned about the infectious disease). Of course, an accompanying risk of providing covert support is that, if detected by the learner, self-efficacy and confidence may subsequently suffer.

Narrative based learning environments make this kind of support possible. A similar method is used by the virtual human sergeant in the MRE when his initiative is set to "high"—he will more openly share his opinion regarding what needs to be done at any given time (Rickel et al., 2002; Swartout et al., 2006). Although these approaches both rely on virtual characters (and thus fit under the space of pedagogical agent interactions), other opportunities exist to give hints and guidance indirectly through the environment. Care must be taken, however, as with any pedagogical support approach, that the learner does not become dependent on this assistance.

CONCLUSIONS

In this chapter we described many of the issues facing designers of intelligent tutoring systems for virtual learning environments. Specific challenges arise from the nature of domains that VLEs make accessible, such as tutoring for real time skills and the problem of understanding student actions in open learning environments. Expertise is generally harder to capture and encode in such domains, when compared to domains that involve forms of symbol manipulation and that are less dynamic. Research into automatic approaches to acquiring domain knowledge in VLEs would support the longer-term integration of ITSs. We also described the role of pedagogical agents and how they can be used to promote learning in VLEs. Although current empirical evidence for the use of pedagogical agents remains unclear, they have been found to have many appealing properties for learners and to be beneficial in ways other than just promoting learning (for example, motivation). Pedagogical agents can also participate in an underlying narrative, and thus provide more opportunities for tutorial intervention. We described pedagogical experience manipulation in terms of how it can be used to adjust implicit feedback to promote a learner's recognition of success or failure and how it can be used to dynamically establish ideal conditions for learning. These new capabilities and new tactics may support "closing the gap" between expert human tutors and computer tutors, but significantly more empirical research is needed to find out.

Virtual learning environments with intelligent tutoring capabilities are beginning to be adopted on a widespread basis. For example, TLCTS learning environments are being used by tens of thousands of military service members (Johnson, 2007), and additional learning environments are being developed for nonmilitary use. Because these learning environments are instrumented and log all learner actions, they are an excellent source of data to assess the effectiveness of tutoring techniques in VLEs.

Several key questions remain unanswered in the literature regarding the use of ITSs in modern VLEs. For example, how distracting is explicit feedback? How do different modalities compare with respect to distraction? As far as pedagogical experience manipulation, what is the proper balance between narrative control and explicit tutorial control? What other kinds of guidance are possible through stealth techniques, such as difficulty management and task selection? When are explicit measures required and how do they compare when delivered via stealth approaches? What are the risks of stealth guidance and experience manipulation on learners with respect to confidence, self-efficacy, and help-seeking skills?

Modern VLEs make realistic practice in a computer based environment possible, and answers to these kinds of questions will have a great impact on how effective VLEs may become. There is no end in sight to the immersive potential for virtual environments—it is important to remember, as Rickel and Johnson (1997) pointed out, that learners will continue to exhibit misconceptions and hit impasses. In order to maximize the teaching power of modern VLEs, it will be important to continue to consider these empirical questions, understand the accompanying risks, and create technological advances that adhere to the principles of effective learning.

REFERENCES

Anderson, J. A., Corbett, A. T., Koedinger, K., & Pelletier, R. (1995). Cognitive Tutors: Lessons Learned. *Journal of the Learning Sciences, 4*(2), 167–207.

Baylor, A. L., & Kim, Y. (2005). Simulating instructional roles through pedagogical agents. *International Journal of Artificial Intelligence in Education, 15,* 95–115.

Bloom, B. S. (1984). The 2 sigma problem: The search for methods of group instruction as effective as one-to-one tutoring. *Educational Researcher, 13*(6), 4–16.

Brown, J. S., Collins, A., & Duguid, P. (1989). Situated cognition and the culture of learning. *Educational Researcher, 8*(1), 32–42.

Brown, P., & Levinson, S. C. (1987). *Politeness: Some universals in language use.* New York: Cambridge University Press.

Cassell, J., Sullivan, J., Prevost, S., & Churchill, E. (Eds.) (2000). *Embodied conversational agents.* Cambridge, MA: MIT Press.

Chi, M. T. H., Siler, S. A., Jeong, H., Yamauchi, T., & Hausmann, R. G. (2001). Learning from human tutoring. *Cognitive Science, 25*(4), 471–533.

Clarebout, G., Elen, J., Johnson, W. L., & Shaw, E. (2002). Animated pedagogical agents: An opportunity to be grasped? *Journal of Educational Multimedia and Hypermedia, 11*(3), 267–286.

Core, M. G., Traum, D., Lane, H. C., Swartout, W., Marsella, S., Gratch, J., & van Lent, M. (2006). Teaching negotiation skills through practice and reflection with virtual humans. In C. M. Overstreet & A. Martens (Eds.), *SIMULATION: Transactions of the Society for Modeling and Simulation International, 82*(11), 685–701.

Fox, B. A. (1993). *The human tutorial dialogue project.* Hillsdale, NJ: Lawrence Erlbaum.

Graesser, A. C., VanLehn, K., Rosé, C. P., Jordan, P. W., & Harter, D. (2001). Intelligent tutoring systems with conversational dialogue. *AI Magazine, 22*(4), 39–51.

Johnson, W. L. (2007). Serious use of a serious game for language learning. In R. Luckin et al. (Eds.), *Artificial intelligence in education* (pp. 67–74). Amsterdam: IOS Press.

Johnson, W. L., Vilhjalmsson, H., & Marsella, S. (2005). Serious games for language learning: How much game, how much AI? In C. K. Looi et al. (Eds.), *Artificial intelligence in education* (pp. 306–313). Amsterdam: IOS Press.

Jonassen, D. H. (1997). Instructional design models for well-structured and ill-structured problem solving learning. *Educational Technology Research and Development, 45*(1), 65–94.

Katz, S., Allbritton, D., & Connelly, J. (2003). Going beyond the problem given: How human tutors use post-solution discussions to support transfer. *International Journal of Artificial Intelligence in Education, 13,* 79–116.

Kirschner, P., Sweller, J., & Clark, R. E. (2006). Why minimally guided learning does not work: An analysis of the failure of discovery learning, problem-based learning, experiential learning and inquiry-based learning. *Educational Psychologist, 41*(2), 75–86.

Lane, H. C. (2007, July). *Metacognition and the development of intercultural competence.* Paper presented at the Workshop on Metacognition and Self-regulated Learning at the 13th International Artificial Intelligence in Education Conference, Marina del Rey, CA.

Lepper, M., Woolverton, M., Mumme, D. L., & Gurtner, J. L. (1993). Motivational techniques of expert human tutors: Lessons for the design of computer-based tutors. In S. P. Lajoie & S. J. Derry (Eds.), *Computers as cognitive tools* (pp. 75–105). Hillsdale, NJ: Lawrence Erlbaum.

Livak, T., Heffernan, N. T., & Moyer, D. (2004, May). *Using cognitive models for computer generated forces and human tutoring.* Paper presented at the 13th Annual Conference on Behavior Representation in Modeling and Simulation. Simulation Interoperability Standards Organization, Arlington, VA.

Lynch, C. F., Ashley, K., Aleven, V., & Pinkwart, N. (2006, June). *Defining "ill-defined" domains; A literature survey.* Paper presented at the Workshop on Intelligent Tutoring Systems for Ill-Defined Domains at Intelligent Tutoring Systems at the 8th International Conference on Intelligent Tutoring Systems, Jhongli, Taiwan.

Magerko, B., Stensrud, B., & Holt, L. S. (2006, December). *Bringing the schoolhouse inside the box—A tool for engaging, individualized training.* Paper presented at the 25th Army Science Conference, Orlando, FL.

Mayer, R. (2004). Should there be a three-strikes rule against pure discovery learning? The case for guided methods of instruction. *American Psychologist, 59*(1), 14–19.

McQuiggan, S., Rowe, J., & Lester, J. (2008). The effects of empathetic virtual characters on presence in narrative-centered learning environments. In *Proceedings of the 2008 SIGCHI Conference on Human Factors in Computer Systems* (pp. 1511–1520).

Merrill, D. C., Reiser, B. J., Ranney, M., & Trafton, J. G. (1992). Effective tutoring techniques: A comparison of human tutors and intelligent tutoring systems. *Journal of the Learning Sciences, 2*(3), 277–305.

Moreno, R., Mayer, R. E., & Lester, J. C. (2000). Life-like pedagogical agents in constructivist multimedia environments: Cognitive consequences of their interaction. In J. Bourdeau & R. Heller (Eds.), *Proceedings of the World Conference on Educational Multimedia, Hypermedia, and Telecommunications—ED-MEDIA 2000* (pp. 741–746). Charlottesville, VA: Association for the Advancement of Computers in Education.

Mott, B. W., & Lester, J. C. (2006). Narrative-centered tutorial planning for inquiry-based learning environments. *Proceedings of the 8th International Conference on Intelligent Tutoring Systems* (pp. 675–684). Berlin: Springer.

Niemiec, R., & Walberg, H. J. (1987). Comparative effects of computer-assisted instruction: A synthesis of reviews. *Journal of Educational Computing Research, 3,* 19–37.

Person, N., & Graesser, A. C. (2002). Pedagogical agents and tutors. In J. W. Guthrie (Ed.), *Encyclopedia of education* (pp. 1169–1172). New York: Macmillan.

Peters, S., Bratt, E. O., Clark, B., Pon-Barry, H., & Schultz, K. (2004). Intelligent Systems for Training Damage Control Assistants. In *Proceedings of the Interservice/Industry Training, Simulation, and Education Conference* (pages not available). Arlington, VA: National Training Systems Association.

Reeves, B., & Nass, C. (1996). *The media equation.* New York: Cambridge University Press.

Rickel, J., & Johnson, W. L. (1997). Intelligent tutoring in virtual reality: A preliminary report. In *Proceedings of the Eighth World Conference on Artificial Intelligence in Education* (pp. 294–301). Amersterdam: IOS Press.

Rickel, J., Marsella, S., Gratch, J., Hill, R., Traum, D., & Swartout, W. (2002, July/August). Toward a new generation of virtual humans for interactive experiences. *IEEE Intelligent Systems,* 32–38.

Ritter, F., & Feurzeig, W. (1988). Teaching real-time tactical thinking. In J. Psotka, L. D. Massey, & S. A. Mutter (Eds.), *Intelligent tutoring systems: Lessons learned* (pp. 285–302). Hillsdale, NJ: Lawrence Erlbaum.

Roberts, B., Pioch, N. J., & Ferguson, W. (1998). Verbal coaching during a real-time task. *In Proceedings of the Fourth International Conference on Intelligent Tutoring Systems* (pp. 344–353). Berlin: Springer.

Schooler, L. J., & Anderson, J. R. (1990). The disruptive potential of immediate feedback. *Proceedings of the Twelfth Annual Conference of the Cognitive Science Society* (pp. 702–708). Cambridge, MA.

Swartout, W., Gratch, J., Hill, R., Hovy, E., Marsella, S., & Rickel, J. (2006). Toward virtual humans. *AI Magazine, 27*(2), 96–108.

VanLehn, K., Lynch, C., Schulze, K., Shapiro, J. A., Taylor, L., Treacy, D., et. al. (2005). The Andes physics tutoring system: Five years of evaluations. In G. McCalla & C. K. Looi (Eds.), *Artificial intelligence in education* (pp. 678–685). Amsterdam: IOS Press.

Wang, N., Johnson, W. L., Mayer, R. E., Rizzo, P., Shaw, E., & Collins, H. (2007). The politeness effect: Pedagogical agents and learning outcomes. *International Journal of Human-Computer Studies, 66*(2), 98–112.

Chapter 21

ENHANCING VIRTUAL ENVIRONMENTS TO SUPPORT TRAINING

Mike Singer and Amanda Howey

The "enhancement" of virtual environments (VE) for training first requires a clear distinction between task fidelity and learning requirements, addressing alterations made to improve the efficiency and/or effectiveness of learning during discrete training episodes. This chapter reviews some of the research on the instructional enhancement of simulations for training, encompassing instructional features, dynamic graphics, and supportive instructional systems (unfortunately size limitations preclude a comprehensive literature review). The goal is to provide an organizing overview of the breadth and the depth of issues that have been investigated, to note some indications of current applications, and to point toward profitable future research. In short, this chapter will address what is currently known about the functions, features, and tools that work to enhance training during simulation based exercises.

In order to address important findings from simulation and virtual environments, a taxonomic framework is introduced that provides relational structure for the information and arguments presented. The basic framework is derived from a systems approach that encompasses training and leads to our reasoning about the constraints upon the enhancement of VE based training. The systems approach has a long history in training and many citations (for example, Hays & Singer, 1989). Briefly, a system has interrelated parts such that a change in one part causes a change in one or more of the other parts. Obviously this leads to subsystems and suprasystems that also have specific relationships. A training system has learners and information as inputs, costs and resources as limitations, and subsystem processes (which have characteristics and relationships, as discussed below) that address the transition to skilled performance, with proficient performers as output.

GOALS, STRATEGIES, TACTICS, AND FEATURES

We argue that for most directed learning approaches, there are generally four main components: goals, strategies, tactics, and features (Singer, Kring, &

Hamilton, 2006). These components refer to related subsystems in the training system as instructional features are applied through the use of tactics, which are employed as a part of a strategy for reaching an instructional goal guided by measurements that indicate the learners' past and current state and models that project the effective training. These different system components relate to one another in structured and supportive relationships (see Figure 21.1). By explicitly defining the concepts and describing their interrelationships, we can better understand previous empirical work in similar domains and apply that information to current techniques of interest, VE based training, and generalize prior research to new training domains of interest.

DEFINITIONS AND RELATIONSHIPS

Instructional Goals

Directed learning is the purposeful transfer of information, knowledge, skills, abilities, and/or attitudes from one source (for example, instructor, computer software, simulation, or other system) to an individual or group (Hays, 2001). Given this definition, the purpose of a directed learning program can be termed the *instructional goal.* This purpose has also been referred to as the instructional

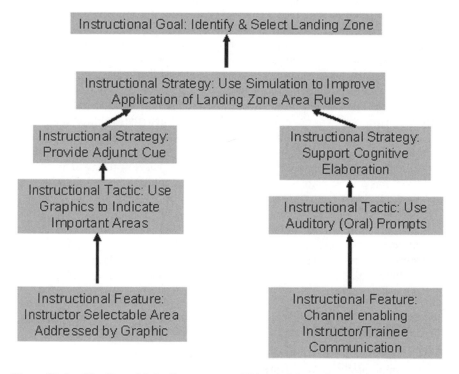

Figure 21.1.   The Four Main Components of Directed Learning Approaches

objective, outcome, or task. When relating the instructional goal to the supporting concepts, it often is better to consider the smallest coherent unit possible, usually labeled as a "task." Task is a difficult concept to define in an all-inclusive fashion, but generally is taken to refer to a unitary set or sequence of behaviors that enable a complete and meaningful job or mission function (for example, Miller & Swain, 1987). (For a more in-depth exposition, see Fleishman & Quaintance, 1984, or applicable chapters in the *Handbook of Human Factors and Ergonomics,* Salvendy, 1997.)

Training Strategies

Directed learning programs must have one or more (usually multiple) explicit approaches, or *instructional strategies*—a "plan, method, or series of activities aimed at obtaining a specific goal" (Jonassen & Grabowski, 1993, p. 20). As noted above, for each task to be learned, at least one strategy must be selected. Obviously, when reviewing a set of tasks as the instructional goal, it is usually more efficient to address all or as many tasks as possible with the same strategy. Some examples of strategies would include auditory presentation of a performance sequence, visual presentation of an information set and resultant solution, or supporting the dynamic interaction of trainee and equipment using simulation (or interacting with the real equipment).

Training Tactics

We can then support the strategies with "specific actions which are well-rehearsed and are used to enable the strategy" (Jonassen & Grabowski, 1993, p. 20). We refer to these as training or instructional tactics (Singer et al., 2006). Tactics are often based on or limited by available enhancements. For example, if one strategy is to explicitly drive cognitive elaborations during rule learning, one enabling tactic might be to employ auditory prompts (questions pertaining to rules used in task performance and leading to the desired cognitive elaborations) at appropriate points during a training session. If an instructor is present, has been trained in this tactic, and can use his or her voice to provide the prompt, this probably will work with a certain efficacy. In a VE used for training, especially if it is distributed geographically, one must have some artificial method (instructional feature) for providing or conveying the same auditory prompt. So these instructional tactics are maneuvers or manipulations that are employed within a strategy and can be used to change a learner's knowledge state, enabling the learner to reach the instructional goal. The application of these instructional tactics has to be controlled in some fashion, and the control itself might be considered an instructional feature. The control might be constant, selectable by the trainer, automated with trainer selectable conditions, under live control of an instructor, or under the control of an artificial intelligence program.

Training Enhancements or Instructional Features

In using tactics to support strategies and ultimately reach instructional goals, we argue that tactics require tools for support and implementation. These tools are the enhancements that have been traditionally identified as *instructional features* (Sticha, Singer, Blacksten, Morrison, & Cross, 1990; Ricard, Crosby, & Lambert, 1982). Instructional features thus refer to a wide variety of tools and/ or techniques that instructors can use to support and execute the instructional tactics and strategies. In this chapter, the term "instructional features" primarily refers to alterations of the simulation that change the operational fidelity of the simulation in some way for instructional effect (highlighting, blinking objects, intentional pauses, and so on).

FIDELITY

A short diversion has to be inserted at this point in order to clearly separate the "environment" from the "enhanced" pieces. Task requirements for performance provide the basic definition for the "what" and "how" that needs to be represented in a training simulation, the environment for task performance. This has been the focus of the learning psychologist (for example, Gagne, 1954) and human factors practioners (for example, Smode, 1971; Goldstein, 1987; Swezey & Llaneras, 1997) for many years. For example, if one is looking for a way to train soldiers to correctly identify and deactivate improvised explosive devices (IEDs), a task analysis will indicate the appropriate stimuli for identifying potential IEDs, as well as the environmental stimuli and functionality for deactivating the IED. The simulation must include several possible IEDs and associated situations in order to enable a variety of practice opportunities. The simulation must also allow the soldier to approach and deal with appropriate objects according to established protocol. Fidelity is the essence of the similarities, or the closeness of the simulation to its real world counterpart. Hays and Singer (1989) define two types of fidelity: physical and functional, although there are other ways to discuss fidelity in simulations. Physical fidelity addresses the "what" that is developed for a simulation, for example, the image of a trash pile and an IED. Functional fidelity defines the "how" in a simulation, including the state of the weapon (for example, loaded), capability for firing, damage caused to the target (for example, physics modeling), and sound of firing. Together the task specific physical and functional fidelity provide the initiating, guiding, and feedback stimuli that are absolutely necessary for task performance in the learning situation or simulation.

When we are interested in learning and transfer of training, high fidelity may not always be necessary or sufficient for this to occur. The trainer might have to compromise the fancy engineering and software tools that create an environment that is identical to the real world task for a more simplistic view that includes learning aids for the users (instructional features), as pointed out long ago by Smode (1971). This model of task fidelity, one of compromise and balance, is typically used to frame the instructional approaches that can be applied to reach instructional goals, as the most important deviations from fidelity are those that enhance the learning or retention of the skilled task performance.

INSTRUCTIONAL FEATURES AS ENHANCEMENTS

Conceptually, there are two ways to enhance a simulator in order to facilitate learning and transfer of training, both of which are based in deviations from fidelity. As Boldovici (1992) pointed out, the psychology of learning has always been focused on the arrangement and characteristics of stimuli in order to promote learning. In many normal task situations the relationships between the initiating, guiding, and feedback stimuli or cues can be probabilistic and difficult to learn. Even in the real environment, using a subset of the task cues or stimuli correctly may not guarantee correct performance. This can make key stimuli difficult to establish or learn as fundamental in the task performance situation. Therefore the meaningfulness or salience must be manipulated during training in some fashion, until the learner provides evidence through performance that the stimulus-response link has been satisfactorily established. Following from this logic, and from the logic of using deviations from fidelity to enhance learning, Boldovici proposed that adaptive training must alter stimuli in order to support the learner in recognizing and internalizing the salience of the initiating, guiding, and terminal or feedback stimuli of the task while learning actually occurs. In other words, the learner must understand the presence and use of the added or altered stimuli in order for it to be a helpful learning strategy.

Pure practice in the actual performance environment is the prototypical situation that simulation attempts to achieve. Anything that leads to deviations has changed the stimuli present in the simulated performance environment, through altering normal stimuli or adding stimuli not normally present in the performance environment. Boldovici (1992) addressed the former as augmenting or attenuating stimuli and the latter as supplementing (and fading) stimuli. These are most clearly defined as augmenting or adjuncting cues (from Boldovici, 1992).

Augmenting Cues

The augmentation approach centers on *changing* the characteristics of stimuli *that are normally present* in the task environment and may be used in learning to perform or improving performance on the task. One way to improve the detection and use of normal task stimuli is to enhance the potential salience of those stimuli in some fashion. One method of enhancement might be increasing some physical characteristic of the cue or stimulus—making it brighter, increasing auditory output, changing the dimensions, and so forth. Another method that can make the normal critical task stimuli more salient is to decrease the salience of surrounding or interfering cues. An example would be decreasing the brightness, reflectivity, saturation, or hue of surrounding objects to make the important stimulus "stand out" or be more perceptible to the trainee. Obviously, control over this class of cues is driven by selection of critical cues from the task analysis and insight into which cues are used to the greatest effect during task performance. The trainer must then determine which of the cues in the critical set to address, and when to alter them. The approach cannot stop at that point, but must then close the cycle of adaptive training by determining when and how to attenuate the alterations in the stimuli.

Adjuncting Cues

An alternative method for guiding or reinforcing learning performance is to add discriminative stimuli or cues to the simulation, referred to as adjunct cues. This is most clearly an instructional intervention, and with this approach there is an additional cognitive factor: the trainee must understand the purpose and the use of the additional stimuli. In terms of visual effects, an adjunct cue can be used to direct attention to the critical stimuli by pointing or marking the target stimuli in some way (for example, using an arrow to point at a location or placing a distinctive circle around a location). Coaching during an instructional session is also an adjunct cue, in that the visual (text or symbolic) or auditory information about the situation can also be inserted in the stimulus stream in an attempt to aid the learning process. In terms of auditory inputs, sounds can be used to orient the trainee to stimuli, or verbal coaching can be provided to guide the trainee. Other sensory domains can and have been used to add cueing to domains, such as haptics (for example, Hopp, Smith, Clegg, & Heggestad, 2005), temperature, olfactory (for example, Washburn & Jones, 2004), or multisensory inputs (for example, Jerome, 2006; Jerome, Witmer, & Mouloua, 2005; Albery, 2005). It should be clear that adjunct cues used in a training situation or simulation are no different from those used to aid performance of a task, as humans learn during every activity.

IMPLEMENTATION METHODS

By implementation we do not mean the technology of changing an environmental stimulus that is used in task performance within the simulation (augmentation) nor the technology for inserting extra stimuli (adjuncting) in the simulation. It should be apparent from the long history of simulation that has led to virtual environments that the technology is continually changing and improving (the age of some of our references should make this completely apparent). By implementation methods, we mean that consideration has to be given to the instructional control and use of any changes made to stimuli in the simulation.

The control and use of the different enhancements are the instructional tactics. Control refers to whether the enhancement can be controlled, by whom it can be controlled, and the parameters of that control. The simulation may have been implemented with enhancements that cannot be changed, for example, information stimuli that appear in a simulation when an operator is close enough. The feature may be restricted to the control of a trainer or may be implemented only during a review. The feature may be under the control of the trainee. The scope of implementation methods is immense, yet it is intimately connected to the instructional feature effectiveness.

Instructional Feature Control

Instructor Control Definitions and Example

Instructor control would allow the instructor to pace the course as necessary to ensure proper training. For example, the system may have automated evaluations determining when a trainee has fired a weapon at an impermissible target (for example, a nonthreatening civilian) and could notify the trainer, flag and time-stamp the action for after action review (AAR) use, or immediately intervene in several ways. Depending on how the trainee is performing, the instructor would be able to decide whether to turn the features on or off. One example of an instructor-controlled feature is coaching. The instructor, when appropriate, can give the trainees instructions and guide them through their tasks. In research looking at these kinds of interventions, interrogative coaching has been shown to be superior over no coaching interventions within short trials (for example, Singer et al., 2006).

System Control

This would range from programmed interventions through artificial intelligence–assisted interventions. An example is the mounted tactual cockpit display created by Gilson and Ventola (as cited in Lintern & Roscoe, 1980). The system provides adjunct information only when a trainee is off course or withdrawing, or it does not provide information when performance is correct. The Engagement Skills Trainer 2000 Simulator employs system-controlled cues when it determines a trainee has used incorrect fire. In that situation, the system stops the simulation and asks the trainee to "defend your action." Each time a shot is fired at an incorrect time, the system will stop the scenario and allow the trainee to explain to the trainer why the shot was fired. The trainer must then decide whether the trainee was successful in verbally defending his or her action before continuing with the scenario. At the most basic level *the system* always requires a trainer intervention when an error is committed.

Trainee Control

There are times when the trainee has control over the pace of the training. One example can be in computer based training courses. The trainee decides when enough material is covered on a page, and he or she is ready to move on to the next. This can be dangerous, as humans are typically overconfident in their reading comprehension of material (Matlin, 2005). Another example of trainee control is the ability to explore the simulator at his or her own discretion looking for areas of interest (as opposed to restricting him or her to one place or path) and the ability to pause the simulator or training. One example of a simulator with these features is being used by the U.S. Air Force to train network defensive operations using an intelligent tutoring system that allows trainees to explore the many areas and dimensions of the program and to pause the training when they need clarification or a break (Goan, 2006). This begs the question, should the trainee be able to obtain aid when desired—or turn off training (for example, "Mr. Clippy" from Microsoft Word) when intrusive? There is some research that shows that learners are not the best judges of their own learning and may not choose optimally when provided aid (Maki, Jonas, & Kallod, 1994).

Salience, Trust, and Reliability of the Instructional Features

In addition to type and control, there are three more important aspects to the cues we must consider: salience, trust, and reliability. When looking at the presence (or salience) of what we would call adjunct cues, Yeh and Wickens (2000) found detection-aiding cues to be effective, particularly with low salience targets. So when the trainee must learn to find hard-to-detect action prompts (such as a target), adding an adjunct cue (for example, in this example, a colored reticle) to that area on the target was found to be helpful. In addition, Yeh and Wickens were interested in trust and reliability of the cues. In one condition of their experiment they presented (adjunct) cues that were 100 percent accurate, and in another condition the (adjunct) cues were only 75 percent accurate. The benefits came with some costs, which were considered to be consistent with previous findings (Merlo & Wickens, 1999; Yeh, Wickens, & Seagull, 1999; Mosier, Skitka, Heers, & Burdick, 1998; Ockerman & Pritchett, 1998): when the cues were reliable and consistent, the trainees began to look only for those cues to act and failed to act when the events should have elicited a response (during testing). Once the cues were removed from the simulated environment the trainees might not know when to act given only the real world promptings.

Crutch Effects

When changing stimuli in a representative simulation, the trainer runs the risk of the learner incorporating the wrong stimulus mix for the learned responses. This can lead to nongeneralization/transfer to the work environment, or even unintentional discriminative learning that fosters nonperformance on the task. These are sometimes referred to as *crutch effects*. For example, Wheaton, Rose, Fingerman, Korotkin, and Holding (1976) suggested that it is potentially harmful to future performance to present the cues on every trial; rather, it is better to force the trainee to complete some tasks without the cueing.

An implicit characteristic of instructional tools is the time course of their application or use. The issues are when to apply and when to withdraw the enhancement. One option is to start with the adjunct or augmenting cues and then gradually remove them. Yeh and Wickens (2000) experimented with presenting cues sometimes when appropriate and other times when the cue should not have been present. When the cues became unreliable, the participants stopped using them, which had three primary effects: (1) reduced benefits of cueing, as participants did not rely on the adjunct cues, as shown in decreased performance on the task; (2) an increase in false alarms: participants blindly followed the adjunct cues as though they were always correct; and (3) decreased the attentional cost of cueing, as it helped with the problem of the participants using cues as crutches. On one hand, this approach is not effective for direct teaching of actions in the environment through the use of enhanced features; however, it does require the user to assess the accuracy of the cueing within the environment, which was not always observed. St. John, Smallman, and Manes (2005) also noticed this and discussed the issue of confirmation bias, or times when trainees blindly follow the cueing, regardless of the actual need for action as dictated by the environment or situation. Lintern and Roscoe (1980, p. 232) suggest that

> supplementary cues that provide more precise information can simplify the whole task considerably and allow the trainee to converge quickly on the correct control responses. Appropriate control behavior might be learned more rapidly under these conditions, and gradual withdrawal of the supplementary cues should then force the trainee to become increasingly dependent on the cues that are normally available without disrupting the newly learned control skills.

By doing so, the user generalizes to the natural cues in the environment and not the superficial cues that are added. Whether this could also support an increase in transfer is a research issue that has not been investigated, to our knowledge. However, it seems reasonable that having "transferred" within the training session could improve transfer to using actual equipment in the real world.

INSTRUCTIONAL FEATURES EXAMPLE APPLICATIONS

This section briefly reviews some recent enhancements for simulation based training, encompassing material that can be labeled instructional features, and supportive instructional systems. In our conceptual model, these are all tools that enable instructional tactics and support specific strategies. Graphics fit easily and obviously into the area of adjunct cues within simulations, typically presenting extra symbols or portraying motion using the simulated objects. Supportive instructional systems, encompassing (simulation-relevant) intelligent tutors, computer based instruction capabilities, and automated measurement systems also easily fall within the concept tools that support or enable instructional tactics as defined above. The focus is on establishing what is known about whether, when, and how to apply these widely varying tools to enhance training. Many current virtual environment simulations use instructional tactics and features, without addressing these factors as such or examining their individual instructional benefits.

Some new approaches, such as the application of augmented cognition technologies to intelligent tutoring systems (see Nicholson, Lackey, Arnold, & Scott, 2005), directly address the need for instructional research. The augmentation of intelligent tutoring systems (as discussed by Nicholson et al., 2005) proposes to use advanced methods of system control in the form of better student, expert, and tutor models combined with advanced measurement to change the difficulty of tasks (through augmenting the information required) or provide within-task coaching, or to provide after-task reviews (perhaps inserting adjunct cues). Presumably, the intelligent tutoring systems would employ instructional strategies, tactics, and features in supporting optimal learning for each trainee.

Other developing systems are incorporating tactics and instructional features in the belief that the application will enable effective learning and incentive for continued use (Ackerman, 2005). The U.S. Army's "Every Soldier a Sensor Simulation" uses within-experience feedback under automated control (visible information operation scores, as well as verbalizations during reports) and similar feedback during the automated review of the training experience. Since the simulation is built upon a game engine, increasing levels of difficulty provide advanced training and enthusiasm for continued play.

Ambush! (Diller, Roberts, & Willmuth, 2005) is a game based training system that includes voice communication among participants and observer/controller stations (with enhanced AAR support capabilities). This system is being used in conjunction with hands-on training for convoy operations, originally focusing on ambushes. The system is used to train both squads and platoons, and several groups can be run at once with different tasks and missions. The instructional tactics used in the simulation require halting the simulation for specialized or focused training (for example, medical aspects, leaders conducting interviews, and car searches) and then resuming the simulated mission after the focused training episode (which occurs outside the game, using physical mock-ups and interactions). The only noted instructional feature used is the relatively standard "freeze, save, and restart" of the ongoing situation, although the functionality is not labeled as such.

Another example of game based simulations is the Virtual Environment Cultural Training for Operational Readiness (VECTOR; Deaton, Sanatarelli, Barba, & McCollum, 2006). The major focus of the VECTOR effort was to investigate improvements in the intelligence and cultural validity of the nonplayer characters (NPCs) so that trainees could learn higher level adaptive, interactional skills. The immersive simulation allowed trainees to move around an urban area, interacting with a limited set of individuals from whom information could be acquired. The information acquisition required working within cultural constraints, gaining trust through interactions, and learning the social conventions of the culture in order to gain sufficient information to fulfill a mission. The most prominent instructional tactic is to deliver cultural information and guidance through the (automated) interpreter role while accompanying the trainee through the area. This is a coaching instructional feature, under the control of an automated system, providing corrective feedback for every wrong action. As the system was developed to investigate the technological aspects of intelligent NPCs, the effectiveness of the instructional tactic and supporting feature has not been evaluated. The system is being elaborated with increased authoring and trainer control over scenarios by the U.S. Army Research Institute (ARI) for the Behavioral and Social Sciences and will probably be evaluated during fielding in the near future.

Haptics can also be used in training to provide necessary task fidelity for the simulation, or haptic stimulation can be used as an instructional feature. One recent example of research into this area investigated the two different aspects of haptics: the provision of normal cues and metaphoric signals of normal task stimuli (Hafich, Fowlkes, & Lenihan, 2007). The application of haptics occurred through vibrating "tactors" attached to a vest, a leg, and arm bands. The "normal" stimulus was provided as an approximation of the normal cues from the environment, so all tactors on the front of the vest would vibrate to simulate an explosion from the front. A "metaphoric" haptic cue was more artificial, requiring decoding by the wearer; for example, an explosion might be conveyed by a pattern of vibrations of the tactor closest to the explosion. As might be expected, the naturalistic haptic cues were more correctly recognized in the tasks, but there were no performance changes found over the repeated trials (Hafich et al., 2007). The instructional tactic consisted of consistent application of the haptics throughout the learning trials. The metaphoric or symbolic haptics did not change performance or identification in comparison with no adjunct information provision, and the normal haptics stimuli were significantly better than either metaphoric or no information conditions. Hafich et al. point out that learning even the natural cues required several trials. From this we can infer that presenting even naturalistic cues that are low fidelity requires learning and that simplistic symbolic haptic information requires about the same learning before any effect might be found. Nevertheless, it seems that haptic cues can be used in complex task performance, although more research is needed on the effective application of those systems.

BiLat (Hill et al., 2006, p. 1) is "a game-based simulation that provides Soldiers a practice environment for conducting bilateral meetings and negotiations in a cultural context." In developing the game based simulation, the tasks were analyzed for learning objectives and developed interrelated story based scenarios. The simulation contains several different intelligent systems that support the interactions with the user and direct avatar behaviors during the meetings. One of the intelligent systems provides coaching during the meetings, as set by the instructor and providing a mix of situationally specific hints, corrections, or confirmations. This approach falls very directly into the adjunct provision (of hints or directions) and also can be tailored for reduced use based on the trainee's performance, thus potentially limiting or eliminating the crutch effect. The system uses the coaching system to implement a "reflective tutor" that provides feedback, conceptual questions, and "what if" questions during the training session or AAR. Finally, while not documented in their paper, a demonstration revealed that the game environment replicates a tactical operations center where preparation for the meetings is conducted by the trainee (accounting for most of the training). In this simulated center all usable information presentation systems are highlighted with light and higher definition graphics so that the trainee easily understands the sources to be used in preparing for the meetings. The BiLat game therefore provides an example of using instructional features to support the instructional tactic of guiding or scaffolding the users interactions in order to support learning objectives. Unfortunately, the simulation has not yet been evaluated for effectiveness (Hill et al., 2006), although it is being used in training at Fort Leavenworth, Kansas.

The authors are involved in an ongoing program conducted by the U.S. Army Research Development and Engineering Command referred to as Asymmetric Warfare Virtual Training Technology (Singer, Long, Stahl, & Kusumoto, 2008; Mayo, Singer, & Kusumoto, 2005). The program goal is to use distributed game technology to provide a generalized simulation for dismount soldier training and rehearsal, enabling large numbers of soldiers and automated forces to interact. The system was first developed to provide adequate fidelity for reasonable dismounted soldier operations requiring interaction and decision making and has record and replay capabilities for AAR. The simulated radio channels can be used for coaching by a trainer (although the trainee must link to that radio channel also).

Several new instructional features are being developed for the system, under contract to ARI, in order to conduct research into both instructional tactics and features. Foremost among these is implementation of a laser pointer, a colored vector or pointer controlled by a trainer that can be used for indicating objects and directions in the course of a training session. The laser pointer can also be used during AARs to call out important information. Several recording and replay enhancements are also being added: trainer control over trainee location so that distributed trainees can be brought to the appropriate virtual location and time for a replay interval; trainer control over distributed voice channels, enabling replay of the session sounds without interruption, lecture by the trainer, discussion by the trainees, and so forth; and the easy addition of timestamp controls (called bookmarks) by the trainer, enhancing trainer marking of training session key events. All of these features will be used in a program of research investigating learning gains from use and the effects of different employment tactics for the features.

CONCLUSION

This conceptual structure is an attempt to organize a somewhat unfocused area in order to apply what is known from past research, identify what is currently being used and researched, improve current applications, and provide a better structure for future research. We believe that by identifying and evaluating how instructional tactics are used to support instructional strategies, the instructional tactics can be more easily applied to different task domains. Identifying and evaluating how instructional features support those instructional tactics will also aid in their application to the increasingly ubiquitous game based simulations. One problem that such a structure may help address is the proliferation of instructional features without regard to how they affect instructional tactics or strategies. Just because one *can* add text information to a training simulation does not mean that the extra information actually improves the efficiency or effectiveness of that training. The problem is similar to adding features to automobiles; it seems like a good idea to add phones or in-vehicle computer systems (for example, global positioning system devices), but research shows that secondary tasks (dealing with the equipment) while driving decreases awareness and increases response times to emergencies (Ranney, Harbluk, & Ian Noy, 2005). We think that given our conceptual structure, this kind of research could be generalized to game based training.

REFERENCES

Ackerman, R. K. (2005, April). Army teaches soldiers new intelligence-gathering role [Electronic version]. *SIGNAL Magazine.* Retrieved July 10, 2007, from http://www.afcea.org/signal/articles/anmviewer.asp?a=731

Albery, W. B. (2005). Multisensory cueing for enhancing orientation information during flight. *Proceedings of the 1st International Conference on Augmented Cognition* (CD-ROM). Las Vegas, NV: Augmented Cognition International.

Boldovici, J. A. (1992). *Toward a theory of adaptive training* (Tech. Rep. No. 959). Alexandria, VA: U.S. Army Research Institute for the Behavioral and Social Sciences. (ADA 254903)

Deaton, J., Sanatarelli, T. P., Barba, C. A., & McCollum, C. (2006). *Virtual environment cultural training for operational readiness* (Tech. Rep. No. 1175). Alexandria, VA: U.S. Army Research Institute for the Behavioral and Social Sciences. (ADA 315125)

Diller, D. E., Roberts, B., & Willmuth, T. (2005). DARWARS Ambush!—A case study in the adoption and evolution of a game-based convoy trainer by the U. S. Army. *Proceedings of the 2005 Fall Simulation Interoperability Workshop,* Orlando, FL, September 2005.

Fleishman, E. A., & Quaintance, M. K. (1984). *Taxonomies of human performance: The description of human tasks.* Orlando, FL: Academic Press, Inc.

Gagne, R. M. (1954). Training devices and simulators: Some research issues. *American Psychologist, 9*(7), 95–107.

Goan, T. (2006). *A simulation-based, intelligent tutoring system for enhancing decision effectiveness in computer network defensive operations* (AFRL Tech. Rep. No. 20). Mesa, AZ: Air Force Research Laboratory. (ADA 325997)

Goldstein, I. L. (1987). The relationship of training goals and training systems. In G. Salvendy (Ed.), *Handbook of human factors* (pp. 963–975). New York: John Wiley & Sons.

Hafich, A., Fowlkes, J., & Lenihan, P. (2007). Use of haptic devices to provide contextual cues in a virtual environment for training. *Proceedings of the 28th Interservice/Industry Training Systems and Education Conference* (CD-ROM). Arlington, VA: National Training Systems Association.

Hays, R. T. (2001). *Theoretical foundation for advanced distributed learning research* (Rep. No. TR-2001-006). Orlando, FL: Naval Air Warfare Center Training Systems Division.

Hays, R. T., & Singer, M. J. (1989). *Simulation fidelity in training system design: Bridging the gap between reality and training.* New York: Springer-Verlag.

Hill, R. W., Belanich, J., Lane, H. C., Core, M., Dixon, M., Forbell, E., Kim, J., & Hart, J. (2006). Pedagogically structured game-based training: Development of the ELECT BiLAT simulation [Electronic version]. *Proceedings of the 25th Army Science Conference.* Retrieved April 5, 2007, from http://people.ict.usc.edu/~core/papers/2006-09-ASC06-ELECT-BiLAT-FINAL.pdf

Hopp, P. J., Smith, C. A. P., Clegg, B. A., & Heggestad, E. D. (2005). Interruption management: The use of attention-directing tactile cues. *Human Factors, 47*(1), 1–11.

Jerome, C. J. (2006). Orienting of visual-spatial attention with augmented reality: Effects of spatial and non-spatial multi-modal cues (Doctoral dissertation, University of Central Florida, 2006). *Dissertation Abstracts International, 67* (11), 6759. (UMI No. 3242442)

Jerome, C. J., Witmer, B. G., & Mouloua, M. (2005). Spatial orienting of attention using augmented reality. *Proceedings of the 1st International Conference on Augmented Cognition* (CD-ROM). Las Vegas, NV: Augmented Cognition International.

Jonassen, D. H., & Grabowski, B. L. (1993). *Handbook of individual differences, learning, & instruction.* Hillsdale, NJ: Lawrence Erlbaum.

Lintern, G., & Roscoe, S. N. (1980). Visual cue augmentation in contact flight simulation. In S. N. Roscoe (Ed.), *Aviation psychology* (pp. 227–238). Ames, IA: Iowa State Press.

Maki, R. H., Jonas, D., & Kallod, M. (1994). The relationship between comprehension and metacomprehension ability. *Psychonomic Bulletin & Review, 1,* 126–129.

Matlin, M. W. (2005). Memory strategies and metacognition. In *Cognition* (6th ed., pp. 171–206). New York: John Wiley & Sons.

Mayo, M., Singer, M. J., & Kusumoto, L. (2005, December). Massively multi-player (MMP) environments for asymmetric warfare. *Journal of Defense Modeling and Simulation.* Arlington, VA: National Training Systems Association.

Merlo, J. L., & Wickens, C. D. (1999). *Effect of reliability on cue effectiveness and display signaling* (Tech. Rep. No. 19990518 078, ADA363440). Urbana-Champaign, IL: U.S. Army Laboratory.

Miller, D. P., & Swain, A. D. (1987). Human error and human reliability. In G. Salvendy (Ed.), *Handbook of human factors and ergonomics* (pp. 219–250). New York: John Wiley & Sons, Inc.

Mosier, K., Skitka, L., Heers, S., & Burdick, M. (1998). Automation bias: Decision making and performance in high technology cockpits. *International Journal of Aviation Psychology, 8,* 47–63.

Nicholson, D., Lackey, S., Arnold, R., & Scott, K. (2005). Augmented cognition technologies applied to training: A roadmap for the future. *Proceedings of the 1st International Conference on Augmented Cognition* (CD-ROM). Las Vegas, NV: Augmented Cognition International.

Ockerman, J. J., & Pritchett, A. R. (1998). Preliminary investigation of wearable computers for task guidance in aircraft inspection. In G. Boy, C. Graeber, & J. M. Robert (Eds.), *HCI-Aero '98: International Conference on Human-Computer Interaction in Aeronautics.*

Ranney, T. A., Harbluk, J. L., & Ian Noy, Y. (2005). Effects of voice technology on test track driving performance: Implications for driver distraction. *Human Factors, 47,* 439–454.

Ricard, G. L., Crosby, T. N., & Lambert E. Y. (1982). Workshop on Instructional Features and Instructor/Operator Design for Training Systems. (NAVTRAEQUIPCIH341, ADA121770). Orlando FL: Naval Training Equipment Center.

Salvendy, G. (Ed.). (1997). *Handbook of human factors and ergonomics.* New York: John Wiley & Sons.

Singer, M. J., Kring, J. P., & Hamilton, R. M. (2006, July). *Instructional features for training in virtual environments* (Tech. Rep. No. 1184, ADA 455301). Arlington, VA: U.S. Army Research Institute for the Behavioral and Social Sciences.

Singer, M. J., Long, R., Stahl, J., & Kusumoto, L. (March, 2008). *Formative evaluation of a Massively Multi-Player Persistent Environment for Asymmetric Warfare Exercises* (Tech. Rep. 1227). Arlington, VA: U.S. Army Research Institute for the Behavioral and Social Sciences.

Smode, A. F. (1971). *Human factors inputs to the training device design process* (Rep. No. TR NAVTRAEQUIPCEN 69-C-0298-1). Orlando FL: Naval Training Equipment Center.

St. John, M., Smallman, H. S., & Manes, D. I. (2005). Assisted focus: Heuristic automation for guiding users' attention toward critical information. *Proceedings of the 1st International Conference on Augmented Cognition* (CD-ROM). Las Vegas, NV: Augmented Cognition International.

Sticha, P. J., Singer, M. J., Blacksten, H. R., Morrison, J. E., & Cross, K. D. (1990). *Research and methods for simulation design: State of the art* (Tech. Rep. No. 914). Alexandria, VA: U.S. Army Research Institute for the Behavioral and Social Sciences. (ADA 230 076)

Swezey, R. W., & Llaneras, R. E. (1997). Models in training and instruction. In G. Salvendy (Ed.), *Handbook of human factors* (pp. 514–577). New York: John Wiley & Sons.

Washburn, D. A., & Jones, L. M. (2004). Could olfactory displays improve data visualization. *Computing in Science and Engineering, 6*(6), 80–83.

Wheaton, G. R., Rose, A. M., Fingerman, P. W., Korotkin, A. L., & Holding, D. H. (1976). *Evaluation of the effectiveness of training devices: Literature review and preliminary model* (Research Memorandum 76-6, ADA076809). Alexandria VA: U.S. Army Research Institute for the Behavioral and Social Sciences.

Yeh, M., & Wickens, C. D. (2000). *Attention and trust biases in the design of augmented reality displays* (Tech. Rep. No. ARL-00-3/FED-LAB-00-1, ADA440368). Savoy, IL: Aviation Research Laboratory, University of Illinois at Ubana-Champaign.

Yeh, M., Wickens, C. D., & Seagull, F. J. (1999). Target cueing in visual search: The effects of conformality and display location on the allocation of visual attention. *Human Factors, 41*(4), 524–542.

ACRONYMS

AAR	after action review
AC	alternating current
ACM	Association of Computing Machinery
ACT	aircrew coordination training
ACT-R	adaptive control of thought–rational
ADL	Advanced Distance Learning
AHMD	advanced helmet mounted display
AI	artificial intelligence
ALU	arithmetic and logic unit
AMIRE	authoring mixed reality
AMLCD	active-matrix liquid crystal display
ANOVA	analysis of variance
API	application programming interface
AR	augmented reality
ARI	Army Research Institute
ARTESAS	Augmented Reality Technologies for Industrial Service Applications
ARVIKA	Augmented Reality for Development, Production, and Servicing
ATC	air traffic control
AV	augmented virtuality
AXL	Army Excellence in Leadership
BARS	Battlefield Augmented Reality System
CAD	computer-aided design
CAM	Content Aggregation Model
CAVE	cave automatic virtual environment
CBT	computer based training
CEO	chief executive officer
CGF	computer-generated force
CGI	computer-generated imagery
CIC	combat information center
CMI	Computer Managed Instruction
COGNET	cognition as a network of tasks
CORDRA	Content Object Repository Discovery and Registration/Resolution Architecture

COTS	commercial off-the-shelf
CPU	central processing unit
CQB	close quarters battle
CRT	cathode ray tube
CSF	course structure format
CUDA	Compute Unified Device Architecture
DAC	digital-analog converter
DC	direct current
DI	directivity index
D-ILA	direct image light amplifier
DIS	distributed interactive simulation
DIVAARS	Dismounted Infantry Virtual After Action Review System
DLP	digital light processing (trademark owned by Texas Instruments
DMAS	Digital Motion Analysis Suite
DMD	digital micromirror device
DOF	degrees of freedom
DRAM	dynamic random access memory
DRAWS	Defence Research Agency Workload Scale
DVI	digital visual interface
EPIC	executive process/interactive control
EVAs	extravehicular activities
FLCOS	ferroelectric/field sequential liquid crystal on silicon
FLEX	Flexible Method of Cognitive Task Analysis
FiST	Fire Support Team
FOR	field of regard
FOV	field of view
FPS	first-person shooter
FSMs	finite state machines
GDTA	goal-directed task analysis
GNSS	global navigation satellite system
GPGPU	general-purpose graphics processing unit
GPS	global positioning system
GPU	graphics processing unit
GUI	graphical user interface
HLA	high level architecture
HMD	head/helmet-mounted display
HRTF	head-related transfer function
HST	Hubble Space Telescope
HTML	HyperText Markup Language
HWD	head-worn display
ICT	Institute for Creative Technologies
IED	improvised explosive device
IEEE	Institute of Electrical and Electronics Engineers
IID	interaural intensity difference
IPD	interpupillary distance
ISAT	Interactive Storytelling Architecture for Training
ITD	interaural time difference

ITS	intelligent tutoring system
JPL	Jet Propulsion Laboratory
JSC	Lyndon B. Johnson Space Center
LCD	liquid crystal display
LCoS	liquid crystal on silicon
LEEP	large expanse extra perspective
LMS	learning management system
MIS	minimally invasive surgery
MIT	Massachusetts Institute of Technology
MMOG	massively multiplayer online games
ModSAF	Modular Semi-Automated Forces
MOUT	military operations on urban terrain
MR	mixed reality
MRE	Mission Rehearsal Exercise
NASA	National Aeronautics and Space Administration
NATOPS	Naval Air Training and Operating Procedures Standardization
NOTAMs	notice to airmen
NPCs	nonplayer characters
OLED	organic light-emitting diode/display
OneSAF	One Semi-Automated Forces
ONR	Office of Naval Research
OpenGL	open graphics library
PCI	peripheral component interconnect
PCIe	peripheral component interconnect express
PC	personal computer
PDU	protocol data unit
POP	Prediction of Operator Performance
R&D	research and development
RDECOM	Research, Development and Engineering Command
RGB	red, green, and blue
ROV	remotely operated vehicle
RTE	Run-Time Environment
RTI	run-time interface
SA	situation awareness
SABARS	Situation Awareness Behaviorally Anchored Rating Scale
SAF	semi-automated forces
SAGAT	Situation Awareness Global Assessment Technique
SBAT	Synthetic Battlefield Authoring Tool
SBT	scenario based training
SCORM	Sharable Content Object Reference Model
SCOs	sharable content objects
ShipMATE	Shipboard Mobile Aid for Training and Evaluation
SIGdial	Special Interest Group on Discourse and Dialogue
SIGGRAPH	Special Interest Group for Graphics and Intermixed Techniques
SIMNET	simulated network
SME	subject matter expert
SNR	signal-to-noise ratio

SOCRATES	System of Object Based Components for Review and Assessment of Training Environment Scenarios
SOLM	Search Object Lighting Model
SPL	sound-pressure level
SRAM	static random access memory
Srms	station remote manipulator system
SWAT	special weapons and tactics
SXRD	Silicon X-tal Reflective Display (trademark owned by Sony Corporation)
TADMUS	Tactical Decision Making under Stress
TARGETs	Targeted Acceptable Responses to Generated Events and Tasks
TDT	team dimensional training
TENA	Test and Training Enabling Architecture
TLCTS	Tactical Language and Culture Training System
TLX	NASA Task Load Index
TOLM	Table Object Lighting Model
TRANSoM	Training for Remote Sensing and Manipulation
TRIO	Trainer for Radar Intercept Officers
TTPs	tactics, techniques, and procedures
UAS	unmanned aircraft system
UCF	University of Central Florida
UIs	user interfaces
UNC	University of North Carolina
USB	universal serial board/bus
UWB	ultrawide band
VACP	visual, auditory, cognitive, and psychomotor
VBAP	Vector Base Amplitude Panning
VE	virtual environment
VECTOR	Virtual Environment Cultural Training for Operational Readiness
VESARS	Virtual Environment Situation Awareness Review System
VETT	Virtual Environments Technology for Training
VIRTE	Virtual Technologies and Environments
VR	virtual reality
WFS	wave field synthesis
XML	Extensible Markup Language

INDEX

ABOUT THE
EDITORS AND CONTRIBUTORS

THE EDITORS

DENISE NICHOLSON, Ph.D., is Director of Applied Cognition and Training in the Immersive Virtual Environments Laboaratory at the University of Central Florida's Institute for Simulation and Training. She holds joint appointments in UCF's Modeling and Simulation Graduate Program, Industrial Engineering and Management Department, and the College of Optics and Photonics. In recognition of her contributions to the field of Virtual Environments, Nicholson received the Innovation Award in Science and Technology from the Naval Air Warfare Center and has served as an appointed member of the international NATO Panel on "Advances of Virtual Environments for Human Systems Interaction." She joined UCF in 2005, with more than 18 years of government experience ranging from bench level research at the Air Force Research Lab to leadership as Deputy Director for Science and Technology at NAVAIR Training Systems Division.

DYLAN SCHMORROW, Ph.D., is an international leader in advancing virtual environment science and technology for training and education applications. He has received both the Human Factors and Ergonomics Society Leland S. Kollmorgen Spirit of Innovation Award for his contributions to the field of Augmented Cognition, and the Society of United States Naval Flight Surgeons Sonny Carter Memorial Award in recognition of his career improving the health, safety, and welfare of military operational forces. Schmorrow is a Commander in the U.S. Navy and has served at the Office of the Secretary of Defense, the Office of Naval Research, the Defense Advanced Research Projects Agency, the Naval Research Laboratory, the Naval Air Systems Command, and the Naval Postgraduate School. He is the only naval officer to have received the Navy's Top Scientist and Engineers Award.

JOSEPH COHN, Ph.D., is a Lieutenant Commander in the U.S. Navy, a full member of the Human Factors and Ergonomics Scoeity, the American Psychological Association, and the Aerospace Medical Association. Selected as the Potomac Institute for Policy Studies' 2006 Lewis and Clark Fellow, Cohn has more than 60 publications in scientific journals, edited books, and conference proceedings and has given numerous invited lectures and presentations.

THE CONTRIBUTORS

G. VINCENT AMICO, Ph.D., is one of the pioneers of simulation—with over 50 years of involvement in the industry. He is one of the principal agents behind the growth of the simulation industry, both in Central Florida and nationwide. He began his simulation career in 1948 as a project engineer in the flight trainers branch of the Special Devices Center, a facility now known as NAVAIR Orlando. During this time, he made significant contributions to simulation science. He was one of the first to use commercial digital computers for simulation, and in 1966, he chaired the first I/ITSEC Conference, the now well-established annual simulation, training, and education meeting. By the time he retired in 1981, he had held both the Director of Engineering and the Direct of Research positions within NAVAIR Orlando. Amico has been the recipient of many professional honors, including the I/ITSEC Lifetime Achievement Award, the Society for Computer Simulation Presidential Award, and an honorary Ph.D. in Modeling and Simulation from the University of Central Florida. The NCS created "The Vince Amico Scholarship" for deserving high school seniors interested in pursuing study in simulation, and in 2001, in recognition of his unselfish commitment to simulation technology and training, Orlando mayor Glenda Hood designated December 12, 2001, as "Vince Amico Day."

JOE ARMSTRONG is a Senior Consultant with CAE Professional Services in Ottawa, Canada, with a background in Cognitive Psychology, Human Factors Engineering, and computational modeling. He has a specific interest in the development and application of computational models of human behavior across a range of applications including R&D, acquisition support, and training.

ÇAĞATAY BAŞDOĞAN, Ph.D., is a faculty member at Koc University and conducts interdisciplinary research in the areas of haptics and virtual environments. Before joining Koc University, he worked at Nasa-JPL/Caltech, MIT, and Northwestern University Research Park. He has a Ph.D. degree in mechanical engineering from Southern Methodist University.

MARK BOLAS is an Associate Professor of Interactive Media in the University of Southern California's School of Cinematic Arts, an IEEE award recipient, and Director of Fakespace Labs. His work explores using HMDs and augmented reality to create virtual environments that engage perception and cognition, making visceral synthesized memories possible.

CLINT BOWERS is a Professor of Psychology and Digital Media at the University of Central Florida. His research interests include the use of technology for individual and team learning.

FRED BROOKS is Kenan Professor, UNC–Chapel Hill. He was Corporate Project Manager for the IBM System/360 hardware and software. He founded UNC's Computer Science Department. Books include *The Mythical Man-Month* and Blaauw and Brooks, *Computer Architecture: Concepts and Evolution.* Brooks received the National Medal of Technology and the Turing Award.

BRAD CAIN is a Defence Scientist and Professional Engineer at Defence Research and Development with a background in computational modeling for the Canadian Forces. His research interests include human behavior and performance modeling for application in simulation based acquisition and distributed training systems using virtual agents that incorporate human sciences knowledge.

JAN CANNON-BOWERS is a Senior Research Associate at the UCF's Institute for Simulation and Training and Director for Simulation Initiatives at the College of Medicine. Her research interests include the application of technology to the learning process. In particular, she has been active in developing synthetic learning environments for a variety of task environments.

CURTIS CONKEY, from NAWC-TSD-US Navy, is the Principle Investigator for the Learning Technologies Lab whose primary charter is to investigate emerging technologies for training. Curtis holds a Bachelor in Electronics Engineering, a master's degree in Computer Science, and is a Doctoral Student in Modeling and Simulation.

LARRY DAVIS, Ph.D., is a Research Associate at the Institute for Simulation and Training at the University of Central Florida. He is a member of the Applied Cognition and Training in Immersive Virtual Environments (ACTIVE) Laboratory where he is conducting research in interfaces and technology for use in virtual environments.

PATRICIA DENBROOK is a software developer and researcher in the fields of computer graphics, virtual reality, and advanced user interfaces. As a member of Naval Research Laboratory's Immersive Simulation Laboratory group, she is the software architect of the Gaiter and Pointman dismounted infantry simulation interfaces.

JULIE DREXLER is the Associate Director for Human-Systems Integration and Engineering Management in the ACTIVE Lab at UCF's Institute for Simulation and Training. She earned an M.S. in Human Engineering/Ergonomics and a Ph.D. in Industrial Engineering from the University of Central Florida. She has over 12 years of experience as a human factors research professional.

MICA ENDSLEY, Ph.D., is President of SA Technologies, a small business specializing in research, design, and training activities related to cognition and situation awareness. She has conducted research studies on a variety of issues related to situation awareness including, but not limited to, investigations of human error, and analyses of situation awareness requirements in numerous domains.

STEVEN FEINER, Ph.D., is a Professor of Computer Science at Columbia University, where he directs the Computer Graphics and User Interfaces Laboratory. He is co-author of *Computer Graphics: Principles and Practice* (Addison-Wesley) and currently serves as general co-chair for ACM Virtual Reality Software and Technology 2008.

HENRY FUCHS is Federico Gil Professor of Computer Science and Adjunct Professor of Biomedical Engineering at UNC–Chapel Hill. His interests include projector-camera systems, virtual environments, tele-presence, and medical applications. He is a member of the National Academy of Engineering and recipient of the 1992 ACM-SIGGRAPH Achievement Award.

STEPHEN GOLDBERG, Ph.D., is the Chief of the Orlando Research Unit of the U.S. Army Research Institute. He received a doctorate in Cognitive Psychology from the State University of New York at Buffalo. He supervises a research program focused on feedback processes and training in virtual simulations and games.

ANDREW GORDON is a Research Associate Professor of Computer Science at the Institute for Creative Technologies at the University of Southern California. He received his Ph.D. from Northwestern University in 1999. He is the author of the book *Strategy Representation: An Analysis of Planning Knowledge.*

MICHAEL GUERRERO is a senior engineer at Delta3D specializing in graphics technologies. He has contributed to commercial games on both the Nintendo DS and the PC and is now pushing the state of the art in simulation where he makes extensive use of vertex and pixel shaders to enhance the quality of Delta3D's applications.

Major **STEVEN HENDERSON** holds an M.S. in Systems Engineering from the University of Arizona and a B.S. in Computer Science from the United States Military Academy. He is currently pursuing a Ph.D. in Computer Science at Columbia University as part of the U.S. Army's Advanced Civil Schooling Program.

BRAD HOLLISTER holds a B.Sc. degree in Biochemistry and a M.Sc. degree in Computer Science from Clemson University. His interests span many fields. His professional endeavors are primarily associated with real time computer graphics. For most of his career, he has been employed in the simulation industry as a software engineer.

AMANDA HOWEY received the B.S. degree in psychology from Eckerd College and the M.S. degree in modeling and simulation, human systems track from the University of Central Florida. She is currently working toward the Ph.D. degree in applied experimental psychology and human factors psychology degree from the University of Central Florida.

LEWIS JOHNSON, Ph.D., is President and Chief Scientist of Alelo TLT LLC and formerly a Research Professor at the Information Sciences Institute of USC. His current research focuses on the adoption of interactive learning environments. He holds a B.A. in linguistics from Princeton University and a Ph.D. in computer science from Yale University.

TYLER JOHNSON is a Ph.D. student in the Department of Computer Science at the University of North Carolina at Chapel Hill. Since graduating from North Carolina State University in 2005, his doctoral work has focused on continuous calibration techniques for multiprojector displays.

DAVID KABER, Ph.D., is professor of industrial and systems engineering at North Carolina State University. He also directs the Ergonomics Laboratory and is an associate faculty in psychology. He received his Ph.D. from Texas Tech University in 1996 and has published research on presence and situation awareness in virtual environment simulations.

ROBERT KENNEDY, Ph.D., has been a Human Factors Psychologist for over 48 years and has conducted projects with numerous agencies including DoD, NASA, NSF, DOT, and NIH on training and adaptation, human performance, and motion/VE sickness. He is also an Adjunct Professor at the University of Central Florida.

DON LAMPTON is a Research Psychologist with the U.S. Army Research Institute (ARI) for the Behavioral and Social Sciences. He is the co-developer of the Virtual Environments Performance Assessment Battery (VEPAB), the Fully Immersive Team Training (FITT) system, and the Dismounted Infantry Virtual After Action Review System (DIVAARS).

H. CHAD LANE, Ph.D., is a Research Scientist at the USC Institute for Creative Technologies who specializes in artificial intelligence, intelligent tutoring systems, and cognitive modeling. His research focuses on learning in game based and immersive environments. He holds a Ph.D. in Computer Science from the University of Pittsburgh, earned in 2004.

R. BOWEN LOFTIN holds a B.S. (physics) from Texas A&M University (1970) and a Ph.D. (physics) from Rice University (1975). Bowen is Vice President and Chief Executive Officer of Texas A&M University at Galveston,

Professor of Maritime Systems Engineering, and Professor of Industrial and Systems Engineering at Texas A&M University.

JAMES LUSSIER, Ph.D., has worked for the U.S. Army Research Institute for the Behavioral and Social Sciences since 1984. He is the Chief of ARI-Fort Bragg Scientific Coordination Office supporting the U.S. Army Special Operations Command and ARI-Fort Knox Research Unit engaged in battle command and unit-focused training research.

LINDA MALONE is a Professor in Industrial Engineering. She is the co-author of a statistics text and has authored or co-authored over 75 refereed papers. She has been an associate editor of several journals. She is a Fellow of the American Statistical Association.

GLENN MARTIN is a Senior Research Scientist at the University of Central Florida's Institute for Simulation and Training where he leads the Interactive Realities Laboratory, pursuing research in multimodal, physically realistic, networked virtual environments and applications of virtual reality technology.

DANNY MCCUE realized his dream of developing commercial video games professionally after graduating with a Bachelor of Science in Computer Science and a minor in Education from the University of California at Santa Cruz. He now works at the MOVES Institute at the Naval Postgraduate School in Monterey, California.

IAN MCDOWALL has been involved in the development of stereo displays since the early 1990s. He is one of the founders of Fakespace Labs and has worked on the design and integration of many different stereo displays.

PERRY MCDOWELL is a Research Associate at the MOVES Institute and is the Executive Director for the Delta3D open source game engine developed there. A former naval officer, he has a B.S. in Naval Architecture from the U.S. Naval Academy and an MSCS from the Naval Postgraduate School. He currently teaches graphics and develops simulations for training, primarily military.

LARRY MELIZA earned his doctorate in psychology from the University of Arizona prior to joining the U.S. Army Research Institute. He has over 30 years of research and development experience in the measurement and design of collective training with a focus on feedback issues.

DENISE NICHOLSON, Ph.D., is the Director of the Applied Cognition and Training in Immersive Virtual Environments Laboratory at the University of Central Florida's Institute for Simulation and Training (IST). Her additional UCF appointments include the Modeling and Simulation Graduate Program, the Department of Industrial Engineering and Management Systems, and the College of Optics and Photonics/CREOL.

ROBERT PAGE has 20 years of experience as a Computer Scientist. Mr. Page is a member of the Immersive Simulation Section at the U.S. Naval Research Laboratory. He is the software architect responsible for designing Virtual Environments. Mr. Page received his M.S. in Computer Science from George Washington University.

MIKEL PETTY is Director of the University of Alabama in Huntsville's Center for Modeling, Simulation, and Analysis. He has worked in modeling and simulation research and development since 1990. He received a Ph.D. in Computer Science from the University of Central Florida in 1997.

JENNIFER RILEY, Ph.D., is a Senior Research Associate with SA Technologies. She received her doctoral degree from Mississippi State University in Engineering with an emphasis on human factors and cognitive engineering. Riley has conducted and published research on training for situation awareness and presence in virtual environments.

RAMY SADEK is a developer and researcher at the USC Institute for Creative Technologies. His research focuses on immersive audio rendering and high performance audio software architectures for virtual environments.

SCOTT SHADRICK, Ph.D., is a Team Leader and Senior Research Psychologist at the U.S. Army Research Institute's Fort Knox Research Unit. He has conducted research on the acceleration of adaptive performance, training complex cognitive skills, cognitive task analysis and knowledge elicitation techniques, performance assessment, and leader development.

MOHAMED SHEIK-NAINAR, Ph.D., is a Usability Research Scientist at Synaptics Inc. He received his doctoral degree in Industrial Engineering from North Carolina State University specializing in Ergonomics. He is currently conducting research on input methodologies, specifically touch interactions for mobile devices.

LINDA SIBERT has over 25 years of experience in the field of human-computer interaction, 19 at Naval Research Laboratory. Her recent work is in the design and evaluation of interfaces for virtual reality urban combat training systems. Ms. Sibert frequently reviews for journals and conferences and has numerous publications.

MIKE SINGER, Ph.D., is a research psychologist at the Army Research Institute for the Behavioral & Social Sciences. He received his Ph.D. in Cognitive Psychology from the University of Maryland in 1985 and has over 25 years of experience conducting training research, authoring over 75 reports, journal articles, papers, and chapters.

BRENT SMITH has served as Chief Technology Officer for Engineering & Computer Simulations since 1997. While at ECS, he has performed extensive research in the areas of collaborative distributed learning architectures, distributed simulations, and the use of commercial gaming technologies as educational tools for the U.S. military.

RENÉE STOUT received her Ph.D. in Human Factors Psychology from the University of Central Florida in 1994, has worked in the areas of training research, design, and development and human performance measurement for more than 20 years, and has more than 100 publications/professional conference presentations.

JAMES TEMPLEMAN is Professor of Psychology and Management at the University of Central Florida. He received the Distinguished Scientific Contribution Award from the Society for Industrial and Organizational Psychology and is a Fellow in the Society for Industrial and Organizational Psychology, the American Psychological Association, and the American Psychological Society.

HERMAN TOWLES is a Senior Research Engineer in the Department of Computer Science at the University of North Carolina at Chapel Hill. With over 30 years of graphics and video experience, he has been developing projective display systems and camera based calibration methodologies since joining UNC in 1998.

GREG WELCH is a Research Associate Professor of Computer Science at UNC–Chapel Hill. He works on motion tracking systems and telepresence. Prior to UNC he worked on the Voyager Spacecraft Project at NASA's Jet Propulsion Laboratory, and on airborne electronic countermeasures at Northrop-Grumman's Defense Systems Division.

JEREMY WENDT is a Research Assistant and Graduate Student at the University of North Carolina at Chapel Hill. His research has included modeling and rendering fluids, real time shadow generation, and virtual environments— focused primarily on locomotion interfaces. He works on a company-wide build and test system at NVIDIA.

MARY WHITTON is Research Associate Professor of Computer Science at the University of North Carolina at Chapel Hill. She develops and evaluates techniques to make virtual environments effective for applications such as training and rehabilitation. Ms. Whitton has an M.S. in Electrical Engineering from North Carolina State University.